D0087367

The Dilemmas of
Laissez-Faire Population
Policy in Capitalist Societies

The Dilemmas of Laissez-Faire Population Policy in Capitalist Societies

When the Invisible Hand Controls Reproduction

MARC LINDER

Contributions in Economics and Economic History,
Number 183

GREENWOOD PRESS
Westport, Connecticut • London

HB
883.5
.L55
1997

Library of Congress Cataloging-in-Publication Data

Linder, Marc.
    The dilemmas of laissez-faire population policy in capitalist
societies : when the invisible hand controls reproduction / Marc
Linder.
      p.   cm.—(Contributions in economics and economic history,
ISSN 0084–9235 ; no. 183)
    Includes bibliographical references and index.
    ISBN 0–313–30309–6 (alk. paper)
    1. Population policy. 2. Capitalism. 3. Free enterprise.
I. Title. II. Series.
HB883.5.L55   1997
363.9—DC20   96–32978

British Library Cataloguing in Publication Data is available.

Copyright © 1997 by Marc Linder

All rights reserved. No portion of this book may be
reproduced, by any process or technique, without the
express written consent of the publisher.

Library of Congress Catalog Card Number: 96–32978
ISBN: 0–313–30309–6
ISSN: 0084–9235

First published in 1997

Greenwood Press, 88 Post Road West, Westport, CT 06881
An imprint of Greenwood Publishing Group, Inc.

Printed in the United States of America

The paper used in this book complies with the
Permanent Paper Standard issued by the National
Information Standards Organization (Z39.48–1984).

10 9 8 7 6 5 4 3 2 1

LONGWOOD COLLEGE LIBRARY
FARMVILLE, VIRGINIA 23901

I was ever of opinion, that the honest man who married and brought up a large family, did more service than he who continued single and only talked of population.

Oliver Goldsmith, *The Vicar of Wakefield*, in
3 *The Works of Oliver Goldmsith* 7
(Peter Cunningham ed., 1908 [1766])

That the first want of man is his dinner, and the second his girl, were truths well known to every democrat and aristocrat, long before the great philosopher Malthus.... It has been equally well known that the second want is frequently so impetuous as to make men and women forget the first, and rush into rash marriages, leaving both the first and second wants, their own as well as those of their children and grand-children, to the chapter of accidents.

John Adams, "Letters to John Taylor," in
The Works of John Adams 6:445, 516
(Charles F. Adams ed., 1851 [1814])

LONGWOOD LIBRARY

1000286483

Contents

PART III
THE SOCIALIST RESPONSE

PART IV
PROCREATION, POVERTY, AND SOLIDARITY

Tables

Preface

> [N]o democratic population policy can meet with the approval of the mass of the people so long as each individual follows his own interests, is taught to serve himself and not others and is forced by the character of the environment...to act acquisitively and not co-operatively.... The individual *must not only feel but know* that he is working and living not for himself alone but the whole community.... He must know that his children will be *welcomed by the community as free contributions to the public good*.... It is absolutely unthinkable that a co-operative responsible attitude to the population problem can emerge in a competitive acquisitive society.[1]

The economic and sociopsychological microfoundations of the billions of the most decentralized conceivable decisions to engage in the acts requisite to the production of new labor power have never been adequately understood. From historical, economic, social, political, demographic, and legal perspectives this book studies the consequences for the labor markets of capitalist societies of their laissez-faire regime of human reproduction.

The focus here is on two interrelated questions. First: if labor is the absolute prerequisite for the surplus that capital must extract to keep expanding, how can individual capitalists and the capitalist mode of production in general rely for an adequate, let alone optimal, supply of workers on so happenstantial a process as the vectored outcome of billions of uncoordinated procreative whims? And second: to what extent does the production of children constitute an autonomous or at least an exacerbating cause of microlevel poverty for those producers? Although these questions may appear to be narrowly economistic, examination of the specific manner in which millions of individual procreators uncoordinatedly create a demographic schedule of generative replacement for exhausted labor power that inadvertently responds to or conflicts with systemic labor requirements is one way of shedding light on the social dynamics of capitalism.[2]

The central thesis of the book is that the planlessness of the reproduction of the biological basis of the workforce is no more (but also no less) a problem for capitalism than its spontaneous market processes. Capitalism's capacities for responding in a system-stabilizing manner to exogenous changes in the potentially working population are similar in scope and limits to its capacities for adjusting to other exogenous shifts in supply and demand. At least with regard to its normal, cyclically recurrent development—and abstracting from such system-transcending cataclysmic events as global environmental destruction—the system can accommodate such shifts, though often only by introducing other threats to stability. Capital, in other words, has its own built-in, albeit self-contradictory, mechanisms for dealing with what from the vantage point of abstract economic imperatives might appear to be suboptimal biological production of its human material.

That capitalist societies have in fact left the production and reproduction of their central commodity to anarchically operating noncommercial entities is clear. They have certainly not implemented the sarcastic proposal of the Saint-Simonian philosopher, Pierre Leroux, that the rich annually state their demand for poor people, who would then draw lots to see who would be permitted to have children. Indeed, only "[f]ew governments...have been able to...persuade a reluctant population to increase the size of its families." Even if it were the case, as one strand of feminist theory contends, that the implementation of state population policy "presupposes that women lose control of their 'means of production,' the uterus," the necessary implication today would be that the impossibility of concealing from women that the state was interfering with their autonomy would render such intervention infeasible. Moreover, such patriarchal interference with women's sexual autonomy and reproductive freedom as the state has historically imposed is not incompatible with a demographic laissez-faire regime: neither in the nineteenth century nor today, for example, are antiabortion initiatives designed to create an optimally filled labor supply for capitalist firms.[3]

Why capitalism has extended a noncommodity-producing laissez-faire regime to reproduction remains very much an open question. Some on the Left situate the chief impediment to a profit-making alternative in the nature of certain activities such as child care, which has failed to become a branch of capitalist industry because it presents "technical difficulties to the large-scale investment of capital." Both the lengthy gestation period and the many years of child-rearing constitute a prolonged production period unfavorable to profit maximization. The implausibility of mechanizing and automating the affective and labor-intensive parent-child relationship acts as a further obstacle to capitalization. Moreover, others emphasize, the instrumental relations and personal fungibility inherent in capitalist production are incompatible with the emotional attachments associated with the fostering of human development: "The most effective way to build an industrial economy based on private enterprise was to combine it with motivations that had nothing to do with the logic of the free market.... Human beings are not efficiently designed for a capitalist system of production."[4]

Axiomatic for the Right is that "a central purpose of human existence—perhaps *the* central purpose—is the reproduction of the species." Because
the family as "a universal institution...serves as the source, protector, and incubator
of...children...[a]ll other institutions...exist to support, preserve, or defend that
primary social form." The Right's specification of the relationship between that
institution and U.S. capitalism in particular is extraordinarily frank and revealing:

> A capitalist economic system is critically dependent on the successful
> functioning of the family. The nuclear family...provides the critical
> matrix for human reproduction while also serving as a highly mobile
> unit, able to follow the market signals that would raise their incomes
> while also increasing market efficiency. Moreover, the family con-
> tains...the necessary...incentives which make human beings behave in
> economically useful ways. As industrial capitalism cut persons off
> from the economic protections provided by kin and village, the family
> system made each male aware of his responsibilities to protect and pro-
> vide for his mate as she performed her maternal task. This arrangement
> generated economically and socially constructive anxiety....[5]

Whatever the causes of continued noncapitalist production of labor power,
that the capitalist mode of production, by relinquishing decision-making with respect to family size to individuals, also abandons direct control of the production
of its labor force is a functional concession to the ideology of individual liberty.
By abstaining from overt intervention at this particular locus of social reproduction,
the state cultivates and reinforces the image of the family as at least one reserve of
self-determination sheltering its inhabitants from the all too sharply perceived
domination and alienation of other institutionalized relationships. Here, the worker
can imagine, he or she reigns as supreme as his or her employer at the "hidden
abode of production": just as "No admittance except on business" marks off the
employer's dominion at the point of production, neither the state nor the employer
has any business interfering at the point of biological reproduction.[6]

Under the threat of mass disaffection from capitalism engendered by a
decade and a half of depression and mass destruction, some post-World War II
Western European states strove to deflect worker interest away from a class focus
in large part by constructing a comprehensive supraclass social welfare program.
By suggesting that the weak working class that had been the object of classical
social policy had become an outdated fiction, this strategy instead sought to project
the family across all classes and strata as the new object of social policy. The
comprehensive equalization of economic burdens among families would amount
to a fundamental reconstruction of the system of income distribution—not between
social classes or even income strata, but between child-poor and child-rich families.[7] That non-social-democratically structured capitalist societies such as the
United States, which, unintimidated by class conflict, never transcended rhetorical
concern with the family, have even disabled themselves from articulating in terms
of public policy the relationship between optimal family size for individual pro-

creators and optimal population size for society as a whole (let alone for capital) is the price that they pay for a peculiar anarcho-liberal form of legitimation.

Not only has capital refrained from penetrating family production of new labor power, but employers' structured indifference to that process entails an insistence on a labor-market and wage-formation system that disregards the fact that wages must finance the reproduction of labor power. Absent some form of collective corrective, these individual capitalist entities' studied neglect of the reality of the differential needs and demographic contributions of families of varying sizes might trigger societally indigestible disruption. The welfare state has therefore been interpreted as the use of state power to modify indirectly the reproduction of labor power by regulating the amount of money families have available for consumption and providing food, housing, education, and health services. Almost all state social policies, on this view, are designed to affect families' capacity to produce and raise children.[8]

Such indirect means of reproductive regulation, especially in a country with as underdeveloped a welfare state as the United States, may enable families to act less desperately and with greater microrationality without affording any impetus to procreational macrorationality. Relying on the employment- and income-related vicissitudes of the business cycle to shape those reproductive decisions may be a suboptimal method of regulation for some nonexistent pure capitalism, but it is of a piece with that system's overall irrational spontaneity. The consequences are manifest: macrosocietally unplanned reproduction creates disproportionalities in the form of maldistributed familial income insufficient to sustain an adequate standard of living for some parents and children. At the same time, the inevitable general or partial overproduction of labor into which reproduction eventuates, with a two-decade lag, must be financed by resources that could otherwise have supported further capital accumulation.

As capitalist societies have historically oscillated between perceived crises of overpopulation and underpopulation, the ruling regime of procreational laissez faire has impeded the formation of a process of solidarization even among fellow citizens of the same nation-state let alone among all human beings. Without any (democratically achieved or authoritarianly imposed) national consensus as to the desirable direction of demographic development or of the size of the next generation, each is reduced to acquiescing after the fact in everyone else's reproductive output. So long as there is a widely perceived fear of underpopulation, few would begrudge even the poor their large families; similarly, when overpopulation is seen as a threat to living standards or the environment, childlessness is hardly looked at askance. Conversely, however, when the ratio between the working population, which finances pay-as-you-go old-age pensions, and pensioners is deteriorating, payors who have also contributed future payors in the form of progeny may well view intentional nonreproducers as antisocial free riders; and, similarly, in the face of overpopulation, individual self-regarding decisions (or, even worse, reckless nondecisions) to procreate at levels that must exacerbate the population crisis may alienate conscientious nonreproducers or moderate reproducers, who are taxed to support such macrodemographically superfluous minor dependents. The question, however, is whether demographic crises as would generate such economic crises have in fact ever beset advanced capitalist societies or whether such cogenerational conflicts have ideological origins.

The contradiction between rationality and individual autonomy has characterized both capitalist and real-existing socialist societies. For the latter and any formations that succeed them, the dilemma consists in the improbability that any society that has failed to create members able to make reproductive decisions that are both personally and societally appropriate would bring forth state managers who could be trusted to make those decisions in locus parenti. A society that can educate such managers, however, would need neither them nor such surrogate decision-making.

In order to avoid misunderstandings and disappointments, it is equally important at the outset to stress what this book is not about. First, it does not concern itself at all with Third World population questions. One gauge of the enormous qualitative gap between population problems in advanced capitalist societies and impoverished ex-colonial countries is the fact that even such a devoted communitarian as Titmuss, whose trenchant socialist demographic critique furnished the epigraph to this preface, when advising a Third World government, struck a quasi-Malthusian tone. In light of the "far too menacing" population problem in Mauritius, where large families were "the biggest single cause of poverty," he recommended capping the family allowance benefit at three dependent children lest the program be criticized for "tacitly approv[ing] the procreation of large families."[9]

Second, although women necessarily bear the most immediate and crushing biological and physical burdens of procreation (and unnecessarily and nonbiologically that of child care), the book's self-consciously economist framework programmatically alludes, but precludes doing complete justice, to this gender difference of enormous historical and sociopsychological import.

And finally, the book touches only secondarily and comparatively on issues of race and single-mother families—as heroically astringent as this abstraction may be at a time when the latter alone account for more than one-third of those officially deemed poor in the United States.[10] By focusing, wherever data are available, on two-parent and two-earner—and, for the United States, white—families, which have the greatest chance of avoiding poverty, the book seeks to confront the thesis of child-related poverty with the hardest possible case.

Part I situates the discussion of the micro- and macroeconomic consequences of family size within the contemporary demographic debate. Chapter 1 introduces the income constraints associated with the working-class family life cycle and the prevailing economic theory of procreational motivation. Chapter 2 examines the contradictions inherent in the effort by the advanced capitalist state to articulate and implement a population policy. Part II analyzes the history of the theory and practice of invisible-hand Malthusianism. Chapter 3 discusses the origins and early development of invisible-hand demographic discourse among the classical English political economists, Smith, Malthus, Ricardo, and the Mills. This account is then embedded in contemporaneous public policy embodied in the British poor laws in chapter 4. Part III focuses on the working-class or socialist response to Malthusianism. The working-class neo-Malthusian movements in nineteenth-century Europe are presented in chapter 5. Marx's complex theory of surplus population is the subject of chapter 6. The most interesting intraproletarian debate on the issue of the micro- and macroeconomic consequences of large families, the so-called birth-strike controversy in Germany shortly before World War I, occupies chapter 7. Part IV brings the subject into the present and future. Chapter 8 offers a broad selection of empirical data on the relationship between poverty and family size according to number of children. Chapter 9 focuses on the most venerable and important state policy designed to combat poverty associated with the cost of supporting large families—family or children's allowances. Finally, chapter 10 reviews and evaluates current family policy debates with a view to the contribution they make toward enhancing overall social solidarity.

Gail Hollander, John Houghton, Andy Morriss, Larry Norton, Ingrid Nygaard, Geoffrey Palmer, Julius Sensat, and Larry Zacharias helped make procreation fathomable.

NOTES

1. Richard Titmuss & Kathleen Titmuss, *Parents Revolt* 120 (1985 [1942]).

2. Wally Seccombe, *A Millennium of Family Change: Feudalism to Capitalism in Northwestern Europe* 16 (1992).

3. Pierre Leroux, "De la Recherche des biens matériels, ou de l'individualisme et du socialisme: l'économie politique et l'évangile," *Revue sociale* 1 (3):66-79 at 69 (Feb. 1846); W. Frazer, *A History of English Public Health* 1834-1939, at 251 (1950) (quote); Anneliese Bergmann, "Geburtenrückgang—Gebärstreik: Zur Gebärstreikdebatte 1913 in Berlin," *Archiv für die Geschichte des Widerstandes und der Arbeit* 4:7-55 at 9 (1981) (quote).

4. Bruce Curtis, "Capital, the State and the Origins of the Working-Class Household," in *Hidden in the Household: Women's Domestic Labour Under Capitalism* 101-34 at 112 (Bonnie Fox ed., 1980) (quote); Diemut Bubeck, *Care, Gender, and Justice* 27-29 (1995); Emily Blumenfeld & Susan Mann, "Domestic Labour and the Reproduction of Labour Power: Towards an Analysis of Women, the Family and Class," in *Hidden in the Household* 267-307 at 296-97; Eric Hobsbawm, *The Age of Extremes: A History of the World*, 1914-1991, at 16, 414 (1996 [1994]) (quote).

5. Allan Carlson, *Family Questions: Reflections on the American Social Crisis* xvi (1989).

6. Karl Marx, 1 *Das Kapital*, in Karl Marx [&] Friedrich Engels, *Werke* 23:189 (1962 [1867]).

7. Gerhard Mackenroth, "Die Reform der Sozialpolitik durch einen deutschen Sozialplan," in *Schriften des Vereins für Sozialpolitik* (n.s.) 4:39-76 at 39-40, 52, 57-59 (1952).

8. Wally Seccombe, "Domestic Labour and the Working-Class Household," in *Hidden in the Household* 25-99 at 50; *idem*, "The Expanded Reproduction Cycle of Labour Power in Twentieth-Century Capitalism," in *ibid.* 217-66 at 232-33; Ian Gough, *The Political Economy of the Welfare State* 44-46 (1982 [1979]).

9. Richard Titmuss & Brian Abel-Smith, *Social Policies and Population Growth in Mauritius: Report to the Governor of Mauritius* 134-35 (1961). On his commutarianism, see, e.g., Richard Titmuss, *The Gift Relationship: From Human Blood to Social Policy* (1971 [1972]).

10. Of 36,880,000 persons estimated below the poverty line in 1992, 12,707,000 or 34.5 percent lived in families with a female householder, no spouse present, and with related children under 18. The inclusion of nonwhites outside of this type of family brings the total share of the poor accounted for by these two groups above one-half. U.S. Bureau of the Census, *Poverty in the United States: 1992*, tab. 5 at 10, 14 (Current Population Reports [CPR], P60-185, 1993). To be sure, the fact that "single-parent families are more likely to be poor...itself needs explaining. It is not an inevitable fact of nature." Stephanie Coontz, *The Way We Never Were: American Families and the Nostalgia Trap* 259 (1992).

PART I

SITUATING THE DEMOGRAPHIC DEBATE

The relations of production operate [with regard to the law of population] so that they do not have their starting point unmediatedly in the sexual glands; rather...the human being has a brain.... And this brain is the place where the sensorial or motor stimuli, which a mode of production exercises, are processed. The relations of production do not immediately determine for example the number of fertilizing coitions, but rather the effect of the relations of production on the relations of reproduction is mediated and quite complicated....

Fritz Brupbacher, *Kindersegen—und kein Ende?*
Ein Wort an denkende Arbeiter 3-4 (enlarged ed., 1909)

1

Laissez-Faire Puericulture

Poor people frequently assuage their own frustrations by seeking vicarious satisfaction through their children.... Child-raising seems, deceptively, to offer an area of control...in which adults have power to create human value according to their own, not their employers' direction.... Only the liberation of children from the burdens of being useful to adults can make child-bearing a free choice emanating from the desire to perpetuate human life, not oneself.[1]

The production of population and thus ultimately of the supply of labor is not undertaken "according to rational cost calculations."[2] How, then, can capitalism exist when its most essential prerequisite, labor power, is neither planned nor subject to the law of value—"since men are urged by their natural inclinations, and not by the state of the children-market, or by the desire for profit"—but produced by the nonprofit institution of the working-class family as it is influenced financially by the state and culturally by the bourgeoisie?[3] To what extent, for example, do household budgetary constraints as governed by the class distribution of assets and income compel individual-level reproduction conformity with the constraints of abstract economic rationality?

This chapter offers a first approach to answering these questions from an empirical and theoretical perspective. The opening section preliminarily[4] examines the extent to which the life cycle of the working-class family historically was and continues to be characterized by phases of impoverishment caused by the advent of children and the significantly increased expenditures they require, which are not matched by corresponding increases in income and may even be causally associated with a decline in family income as wives leave the paid labor force to become full-time mothers. The second section presents and engages the currently most fashionable microeconomic-demographic theory of reproductive behavior, the so-called new household economics, by confronting it with some of the social-psychological compulsions to procreate that make the reduction of childbearing to a species of self-production consumer durable implausible.

THE PROLETARIAN FAMILY LIFE CYCLE AND THE FAMILY WAGE

> The relation of parent to child is one of sacrifice. The interests of children and parents are antagonistic.... It may well be believed that, if procreation had not been put under the dominion of a great passion, it would have been caused to cease by the burden it entails.[5]

For the quarter-century Keynesian boom following World War II, some social policy theorists postulated the construction of a "fordist life cycle," which, through "a system of wage stabilization at historically high standards of living...eliminated the 'cycle of poverty'...traditionally associated with the working class life course." This system of mass production cum mass consumption, linked to an increasingly pervasive social wage that replaced income during periods of incapacitation, sickness, unemployment, and retirement, purportedly made it possible for some adult male industrial workers without college educations to avoid reproductively triggered cyclical impoverishment.[6] Yet as the end of the postwar reconstruction witnessed the "relative decline of the fordist life cycle,"[7] even among those who would reject the claim that poverty is still the proletarian condition in general, many agree that for those working-class families who make a reproductive contribution or sacrifice, a distinctly cyclical impoverishment arises from the discrepancy between consumption needs and income ("pauperism of consumption").[8]

The most intense squeeze on family income or consumption coincides with those phases when parents must support the greatest number of offspring simultaneously, relatively low-paid men's earnings have already passed their peak, and yet the wife-mother is least in a position to step out of her quasi-ascribed gendered role and to work for wages.[9] Even at the height of the relatively unselfconscious consumer mania of the mid-1950s, when the Committee for Research on Consumer Attitudes and Behavior sought to hitch the life cycle approach scientifically to family developmental stages to Fordist consumption patterns,[10] surveys confirmed not only that couples (whose heads were under the age of 45) with children had lower median incomes and liquid assets than their childless counterparts, but that more of them expressed dissatisfaction with their incomes and savings; not coincidentally, twice as many childless wives reported employment as did mothers.[11]

Such microdemographically exacerbated cyclical family impoverishment should not be surprising. After all, even on the most general theoretical level, Marx, who conceptualized the wage as sufficient to cover the costs of production of labor power—that is, the costs of workers' existence and procreation—assumed that this identity applied only to the class as a whole, not to the individual worker, "millions of whom do not receive enough to be able to exist and procreate...."[12] This divergence between individual and class living standards is rooted in the fact that the proletariat does not engage in reproduction and thus reproduce itself as a class but rather by means of millions of individual procreating units.[13] According to this model, then, a significant segment of the working class must, during some phases of the household's demographic and life cycle, fail to receive wages sufficient to buy the rudiments of the historically and societally prevailing level of subsistence.

Although such fertility-exacerbated class poverty undermines the viability and vitality of the next generation of workers through above-average and medically preventable mortality, it may also increase the supply of labor as wives and children of child-rich families are forced into the labor market to restore the balance between the value of (the father-husband's) labor power and subsistence that a competitive wage denies such large families. Perversely, the very attempt by individual proletarian families to eliminate the household budgetary deficit may undermine the position of the class as a whole by throwing huge numbers of lower-paid workers into an already overstocked market.[14] The connection between family size and poverty over the family cycle is modified in families operating family farms[15] since the father can more flexibly react to the per capita income squeeze by using his legally privileged access to his children's labor at an age that the state otherwise outlaws. Insofar as these accretions to the total societal labor supply are, as adults, unable to sustain themselves on the same farm, microeconomic rationality in this generation may reproduce itself as macroeconomic irrationality in the labor market in the next.[16]

Several late nineteenth- and early twentieth-century U.S. working-class surveys revealed the extent to which the proletarian husband-father's inability to earn a family wage on his own forced the wife and children to engage in wage labor to maintain the family's standard of living.[17] As early as 1875, Carroll Wright's study of 397 working-class families in Massachusetts revealed that only 36 percent of fathers were able to support their families alone whereas 64 percent were "assisted" by their wives or children. Although 56 percent of skilled workers managed to support their families alone, only 10 percent of the unskilled could do so. Whereas only 12 wives were employed, 325 children (including 177 aged 14 and under) worked. The earnings of these younger children accounted for 12 percent of total family income and 19 percent of income in families in which the husband-father was an unskilled laborer. The earnings of all children represented 24 percent of total family income, rising to 36 percent among the families of the unskilled. These results prompted Wright to conclude that "without children's assistance...the majority of families would be in poverty or debt."[18]

When Wright became U.S. Commissioner of Labor, he conducted much larger national and international surveys of working-class family budgets. In his annual report for 1890, Wright published cost-of-living data for 3,260 families of iron, steel, and coal workers in the United States and Europe. Again, astonishingly, only 36 wives were sources of family income. In contrast to the earlier and smaller state sample, however, in only 20 percent of the U.S. families with children did any children contribute income, ranging from 15 percent among coke workers to 31 percent among bituminous coal miners. Although the annual wages of the highest-paid husbands, bar iron workers, were more than twice as high as those of the lowest-paid, iron ore workers, almost identical proportions of their families with children included at least one who worked—16 percent and 17 percent respectively. These shares suggest that the mere fact that a lower-paid husband-father was the sole wage-earner did not necessarily mean that he earned a family wage; it may have meant that because the local industrial structure offered fewer opporunities for child labor, the per capita income of such families was especially low. Deviation from the male family-wage model was even greater in Europe, where children worked in 42 percent of all families with children.[19]

In his report for 1891, Wright published cost-of-living data for textile and glass workers in the United States and Europe, which disclosed an even greater reliance on child labor than the previous year's survey. Among the lowest-paid U.S. group, cotton factory workers, 16 percent of the wives in the United States and 22 percent of those in Europe were a source of family income. In the United States, children in 56 percent of the families with children contributed to family income compared to 49 percent in Europe. Among U.S. woollen workers, who were somewhat higher paid than cotton workers, the proportions were lower: 9 percent of wives worked and children in 34 percent of families with children contributed income. The corresponding figures in Europe, where woollen workers' wages were somewhat lower than those in cotton manufactures, were 19 percent and 54 percent respectively. Only the U.S. glass workers, whose wages were, respectively, 95 percent and 56 percent higher than those of cotton and woollen workers (and even 11 percent higher than those of bar iron workers), could be regarded as having approximated model family-wage earners. Only 2 percent of their wives contributed income, and in only 21 percent of the families with children did any of them work.[20]

Wright's two international surveys revealed the existence of family life cycles in the sense that they uncovered a monotonically increasing mean total family income and share of total income accounted for by children as the family's youngest child grew up. A reworking of Wright's data for the two years shows that mean total family income in the United States rose from $669 when the youngest child was under 5 years of age, to $769 when that child was 5 to 14 years old, and peaked at $834 when the youngest child was 15 or older. The share of family income accounted for by children during these three stages was 10, 23, and 27 percent respectively. The greater intensity of child labor in Europe expressed itself in correspondingly higher shares: 12, 31, and 46 percent of family income respectively.[21]

Wright's survey of more than 25,000 U.S. families in 1903 again underscored the tenuousness of the male family-wage model. It revealed that children in 23 percent of the families even with U.S.-born heads worked; in those with German- and Irish-born heads the proportion rose to 38 percent and 36 percent respectively. In addition, in 9 percent of all families the wives also contributed income.[22]

Some contemporaries and even historians have charged that a qualitative difference separated the role played by child labor in the strategies used by U.S.-born family heads and their immigrant counterparts to deal with the proletarian poverty cycle. Thus a Juvenile Court judge explained to a group of large Detroit employers in 1912 that "while American-born parents were glad to keep their children in school to sixteen," immigrants

> rear large families, and they begin, without exception almost, in poverty and rise through a gradually increasing line of prosperity to a point where the maximum number of children are of the working age...and then as the children marry...go down the poverty side again.... They...force them into work, and confiscate the entire wages...for the family support. They build largely on the commercial value of their children.[23]

In fact, however, Wright's 1903 survey disclosed that although 17 percent of the children of foreign-born heads worked compared with 13 percent of the children of U.S.-born heads, 45 percent of the former were in school in comparison with 43 percent of the latter.[24] Nevertheless, the data also revealed that most prominently among Irish families the fathers' low wages induced them to engage in a demographic labor-market strategy: high fertility, budgetary constraints, and child labor combined to enable these families to achieve total incomes comparable to those of native-born families despite the fathers' lower incomes.[25]

Wright's 1875 Massachusetts survey had also brought to light some evidence of the existence of a family cycle of work and income by correlating family size and sources of income. Among childless couples, wives accounted for 28 percent of total family income—a proportion far in excess of their contributions once they became mothers. Thus already the advent of the first child "keeps the mother at home" and her share declined to 3 percent; after the first child it became infinitesimal. Although the usefulness of the data is vitiated by a failure to indicate the age of the parents and whether family size had been completed, they nevertheless reveal that the children's contribution to total family income rose monotonically in parallel with the number of children: in families with 2, 3, 4, 5, and 6 children, the offspring's contribution to total family income amounted to 3, 23, 35, 42, and 50 percent respectively.[26]

Smaller-scale and less detailed studies of working-class budgets and standards of living in New York City at the beginning of the twentieth century confirmed the limited scope of the family-wage pattern. Among the 200 families in Louise More's 1907 survey, 47 percent of the wives and 37 percent of the children were employed; since 31 percent of the families also derived income from boarders or lodgers, the wives' and children's contributions were even greater. These three sources accounted for 9, 12 and 9 percent respectively of total family income.[27] These findings sufficed to refute the "popular impression, outside the working class,...that the entire income of the workingman's family is from the earnings of the head of the family." Instead, More found "comparatively few families of wage-earners...entirely dependent on the earnings of the head of the family." This structure may have prevailed "in families where there are several young children,...but...[a]s the children grow older and require less of her care at home, the mother takes in sewing or goes out washing, secures a janitor's place, cleans offices, and does whatever she can to increase the weekly income."[28] Similarly, only 47 percent of the 318 families investigated by Robert Chapin in 1909 were "able or willing to get along with what the father's wages bring in." Above-average working-class incomes, in particular, were "obtainable as a rule only by taking lodgers or by putting mother and children to work."[29] A survey of 11,000 families in industrial sections of Philadelphia in 1917-18 revealed that only 45 percent of families were supported by husbands alone.[30]

Studies of other late-nineteenth-century U.S. cities corroborate the low labor force participation rates of married women.[31] Among more than 7,000 women living with their husbands in industrial sections of Philadelphia at the end of World War I, only 14 percent were gainfully employed away from or at home.[32] Nationally, the decennial censuses revealed that the proportion of married women gainfully occupied by 1930 was still only 11.7 percent compared to 4.6 percent in 1890.[33] To be sure, this aggregate average concealed the enormous gap between white and black women. In 1920, for example, when only 6.3 percent of native white married women were engaged in gainful occupations, the share for black women was more than 5 times as high—32.5 percent.[34] Likewise, a study conducted by the U.S. Bureau of Labor Statistics in 1918 revealed that only 8.9 percent of white families had income from the wife's earning compared to 43.7 percent of "colored" families.[35]

Summarizing the available data on wages and standards of living on the eve of World War I, the economist Scott Nearing concluded "that it is financially impossible for an overwhelming majority of male wage-earners...to provide a fair standard of living for a family of three children, and further that a considerable proportion of these wage-earners do not receive a wage large enough to provide even a minimum standard of living...." Because wives and children supplemented these incomes, however, his conclusion did not mean that such a large share of families failed to secure a minimum or fair standard of living.[36] A decade later Paul Douglas still found that: "Families with two or more dependent children...find it difficult to subsist on prevailing wages and a large proportion of them are in actual need, the intensity of which increases as the number of dependent children increases."[37]

Coming in the midst of all these surveys demonstrating the limited reach of the family wage, its vindication by Samuel Gompers, the president of the American Federation of Labor (AFL), sheds more light on the multiple ideologies of the unions of the skilled than about the economic reality of working-class reproduction. Writing in the AFL's house organ in 1906, Gompers answered "absolutely, 'No,'" to his own question: "Should the Wife Help to Support the

Family?" Relying on "the holiness of motherhood" on the one hand and American exceptionalism on the other, he argued that even with regard to a mere laborer: "In our time, and at least in our country, generally speaking, there is no necessity for the wife contributing to the support of the family by working—that is...by wage labor. In our country...producing wealth in such prodigious proportions, the wife as wage-earner is a disadvantage economically considered, and socially is unnecessary."[38]

Where the AFL fled from the facts of life to patriarchal fantasy, poverty investigators retained a grip on reality. In view of the long tradition of French state demographic intervention, for example, it is not surprising that social observers in France early on remarked that a customary wage was insufficient to support a family with three young children.[39] A mid-nineteenth-century account of the household budgets of cotton workers in Mulhouse by Louis Reybaud, a former French legislator and author of numerous works on industry and the working class, presented one of the earliest narratives of the proletarian life cycle. Whereas the wage level sufficed to establish "equilibrium" for unmarried male workers without much effort, for married workers, the situation was complicated by the number and age of the children and the wife's working. Reybaud identified three distinct periods, each with its own physiognomy, in the life of the married worker. In the first, the most laborious but also the phase in which the worker was strongest, the household was full of young children who required supervision, were costly, and as yet yielded no return. Because pregnancy and lactation diminished the resources that the wife could contribute on her own account, the husband shouldered the financial burden almost alone. In the second period, when the children were between the ages of 8 and 15, the small sums that they contributed transformed them from burdens into resources. During these 12 to 15 years, the couple was at the height of their powers, experiencing easier circumstances and the possibility of saving some money. The third period, marked by the departure of the children and their financial contributions, was much less favorable. With their physical powers and wages in decline, the husband and wife could, if they had lacked the foresight to save during the good days for the bad, look forward only to public assistance or living with their children.[40]

Forty years later, a British poverty investigator undertaking one of the earliest detailed empirical studies of this cyclical deprivation impressively underscored the pattern sketched by Reybaud. In his turn-of-the-century privately funded large-scale survey of York, England, cocoa capitalist Seebohm Rowntree[41] diagrammed the representative worker's undulating movements into and out of poverty:

> The life of a labourer is marked by five alternating periods of want and comparative plenty. During early childhood...he will probably be in poverty; this will last until he, or some of his brothers or sisters, begin to earn money and thus augment their father's wage sufficiently to raise the family above the poverty line. Then follows the period during which he is earning money and living under his parents'

roof; for some of this period he will be earning more than is required for lodging, food, and clothes. This is his chance to save money. If he has saved enough to pay for furnishing a cottage, this period of comparative prosperity may continue after marriage until he has two or three children, when poverty will again overtake him. This period of poverty will last perhaps for ten years, *i.e.* until the first child is fourteen years old and begins to earn wages; but if there are more than three children it may last longer. While the children are earning, and before they leave home to marry, the man enjoys another period of prosperity—possibly, however, only to sink back again into poverty when his children have married and left him, and he himself is too old to work, for his income has never permitted his saving enough for him and his wife to live upon for more than a very short time.[42]

The snapshot of poverty that Rowntree developed for York captured only those workers who happened to be going through one of the poverty phases at the time of the survey. Later, when they passed out of this phase, however, others whom Rowntree had recorded as nonpoor would replace them. Thus the total proportion of laborer families suffering physical privation at some point in their life cycle considerably exceeded those below the poverty line at any given time. In particular, "every labourer who has as many as three children must pass through a time, probably lasting for about ten years, when...he and his family will be *underfed*."[43] In re-surveying York's working class almost four decades later, Rowntree confirmed the continued existence of three periods of economic stress in the course of the working-class life cycle. Specifically, he determined that about one-half of working-class children lived in poverty during the first four years of their lives and a similar proportion during old age; between the ages of 25 and 44, when most children were born to parents, the proportion of workers passing through periods of poverty was almost three-tenths. Rowntree's conclusion, however, that half of the working class spent part of their lives in poverty was fallacious since his snapshot did not permit him to discover whether those who were impoverished later in life were the same people who had been born into poverty or whether they were new recruits.[44]

During World War I, Rowntree remedied some of the defects of the frozen-in-time undercount by prevailing upon the Registrar-General to extract data from the 1911 census schedules for York on practically completed families—that is, those in which the mother was 40 to 45 years old. Although the data did not touch on income and poverty, Rowntree found that in only 16 percent of families were no dependent children living at home at the date of the census; 46 percent of families had three or more dependent children for 5 years or more and 36 percent for 10 or more years; 14 percent of families supported 5 or more children for at least 5 years.[45]

When the Registrar-General performed the same data extraction from the 1931 census, the declining birth rate was reflected in a somewhat diminished life cycle burden; nevertheless, 30 percent of all families still had 3 or more children for 5 or more years and 21 percent for at least 10 years, while 5 percent of families supported 5 or more children 5 or more years. Looked at from a slightly different perspective: in 1911, 72 percent of all children grew up in families having 3 or more dependent children for 5 years or more compared to 59 percent two decades later; the corresponding proportions for families supporting 3 or more children for 10 years or more were 59 percent and 46 percent respectively, and for those with 5 or more children for 5 or more years 38 percent and 15 percent respectively. Whereas in 1911, 21 percent of families supported at least 5 children simultaneously, by 1931 only 9 percent did; similarly, in 1911, 43 percent of children lived in families with at least 5 dependent children compared to 24 percent 20 years later.[46]

Rowntree's life cycle approach gained adherents among poverty investigators in the United States too. Statisticians for the U.S. Public Health Service, in the course of conducting an epidemiological study of pellagra among 4,000 families in South Carolina cotton-mill villages during World War I, confirmed the inevitability of proletarian poverty during certain phases of the life cycle. Among these near-subsistence-level workers, this period lasted 10 or 15 years—until the children themselves could begin working (at age 14) in the mills.[47] Later, Howard Bigelow popularized the use of the life cycle approach to the study of family consumption patterns. That Bigelow generalized this conceptualization of the proletarian condition was ironic in light of his individualizing and voluntaristic belief that "the family as the consuming unit is the supreme authority which by its purchases controls the course of production.... It is because there are whole groups of families that have not been able to adjust their personal affairs successfully to the changes in their environment that we are faced with many economic and social problems.... The place for most of us to attack them is in our own homes." Moreover, his cavalier assumption that as late as the 1950s the child-rich family could still "safely postpone its accumulation for old age, because if worst comes to worst it can fall back upon the combined earnings of several children for support" flowed from his conviction that "by improving our own manner of living, each of us...is doing something definitely to make the world a better place...." Nevertheless, Bigelow recognized that the child-rearing phases plunge subsistence-level families into poverty and reduce the living standards of others.[48]

In the 1970s, the economist A.B. Atkinson illustratively updated Rowntree's method using the example of a representative British worker whose wife gave birth to three children when he was 21, 24, and 29 years old respectively. Assuming that the worker's earnings placed him in the lowest income decile and that his wife began working part-time only when the youngest child reached 15, Atkinson determined that the family was in poverty until only the youngest child remained a financial charge; thus only from the man's early 40s until age 60 did the family's income exceed its needs.[49]

Ironically, such repeated findings of income cyclicity over the family's lifetime may contrast sharply with children's perceptions, which are skewed by their lack of the longer view. Thus in a report on a two-child, two-working-parent family in New York City whose $38,000 income leaves it "on the cusp of hard times and of making it," *The New York Times* recently quoted one of the children as foreseeing no improvement for her parents: "'[U]nless they hit the Lotto, this is how it's going to be the rest of their lives. And that's sad, to think that's it. This is as good as it's going to get.'" Presumably, however, once the younger, 13-year-old, child ceases to be a drag on her parents' finances, the husband and wife may well move on to a typical path in which their personal standard of living increases before retirement—unless it was the need to support children that induced the parents to work as hard as they did in the first place and the children's departure induces them to revert to the not yet atavistic model of the family wage in which the husband can fulfill his preference that his wife "'be at home.'"[50] As noted a century ago, what husbands who are ideologically wed to the family wage "object to is the wage-earning not the work of wives."[51] To the extent that the children fail to detect a causal connection between their own existence and what they perceive as their parents' financial plight, they may be unable to draw any consequences for their own procreative behavior.

In order to gauge the severity of the troughs of procreators' life cycles it is necessary to juxtapose it to that of nonreproducers. In the early 1960s Ann Smith Rice in her home economic dissertation undertook the most detailed national economic study of the life cycle of childless families in the United States based on unpublished data from the 1960 census of population and the contemporaneous Survey of Consumer Finances. Unfortunately, because the requisite nationwide data for constructing life histories of married couples had never been collected,[52] this study, too, was unable to provide a longitudinal study, and had to settle for merely describing the situation of childless families and parents in various phases of the life cycle at one point in time.[53]

Rice found that during the first two decades of marriage, the income of the childless was higher than that of parents because a larger proportion of wives—whose educational attainment exceeded not only mothers' but their own husbands' years of schooling—worked. During the first ten years of marriage, the modal childless couple's income lay between $8,000 and $10,000, whereas the greatest concentration of parents' incomes fell between $5,000 and $6,000. During this phase, the childless couples' median income was 6 percent higher; during the phase lasting from the 11th to the 23rd year of marriage, the gap rose to 9 percent. Only from the 24th year on did the parents' median income slightly exceed that of the childless. Whereas family income of the childless peaked during the second decade of marriage and declined during the third decade because a smaller share of wives worked, parents' income peaked during the third decade when at least one of their children became independent. During the first four years of marriage, 85 percent of childless wives contributed to the family's income and that contribution averaged 38 percent of the family's income; the corresponding proportions for mothers were 46 percent and 22 percent respectively. The proportion of childless wives contributing to family income then declined until after 20 years of marriage only 35 percent contributed; by that phase, 40 percent of mothers, largely finished raising children, were contributing.[54]

During all phases, however, the liquid assets of the childless were significantly higher. During the first four years of marriage, 25 percent of parents had no such assets compared to only 11 percent of the childless. The median liquid assets of the childless were five, four, and two times greater than those of the parents during the first, second, and third decade of marriage respectively.[55] It must be stressed that all the foregoing income and assets comparisons are understatements because the data are aggregate family averages and not per capita averages taking into account the procreators' larger families. The differential impact of reproductive contributions over the life cycle on the economic status of adults thus continues to impose itself.

More recent data from the Survey of Consumer Finances shed some additional light on procreationally differentiated lifetime wealth. In the 1980s, for example, the mean wealth of families without children (living at home) was twice as large as that of their counterparts with children. Similarly, of the richest 1 percent of households (with net worth of $1.7 million and $2.0 million in 1983 and 1989 respectively), 66 percent and 59 percent were married couples without children, whereas married couples with children accounted for 23 percent and 25 percent respectively. Although the relevance of this comparison is diluted by the lack of age-specific data, which could segregate out families whose heads were presumptively too old to have dependent children, it is nevertheless noteworthy that even among rich household heads 45 to 54 years old, one-half had no children living at home.[56]

The dismal conclusion from Rowntree's original turn-of-the-century survey—that the higgling of the labor market could not secure the needs of even the average working-class family—prompted Britain's new liberals to advocate a living family wage that was in part a charge on the "social surplus."[57] In the event, not all remedies went that far. One palliative for this type of cyclical deprivation associated with the phases of familial reproduction might entail intra- or interpersonal or intra- or interclass redistributional evening out of income peaks and valleys. Thus it might be possible through a compulsory insurance scheme to ward off this particular type of poverty. Workers in the aggregate could, for example, be forced to save enough during the relatively nonpoor phases of the life cycle to finance their class's reproduction. Nonproletarian classes could, however, also be compelled to subsidize proletarian procreation by means of general revenues from a progressive tax system. William Beveridge, a central figure in the construction of the British social security system, regarded this particular intervention, state-ordered child allowances, as "the greatest break with old tradition" among the innovations of the welfare state: "In addition to the recognised forms of distribution—wages and salaries, profits, rent, taxation...—there should be a new form: part of the national income should be assigned to those individual citizens who were undertaking the rearing of the citizens of the future, in order to make sure that they had the means for this task."[58]

Beveridge's baptism of a new category of national income falls within the social-democratic tradition of ascribing to the state sovereign power to distribute the social product autonomously of the constraints of capitalist production. A state-mediated system that coercively inserts a multidimensional measure into capitalist norms of compensation and income redistribution might constitute a conscious deviation from the bourgeois principle of abstract right and equality. This inchoate system of stipends graduated in accordance with family size was appropriately called the social wage because it took into consideration a criterion other than performance or productivity. Its more ardent advocates claimed for it the achievement of a "social revolution" insofar as it is based not on earning power but "the needs of the worker as citizen, husband and father."[59]

The question thus arises as to whether the identification, reported by the International Labour Office (ILO) in the mid-1920s, of the principle of "to each according to his needs" with the doctrine of the living wage was accurate, especially since the ILO noted that the latter was generally applied to a wage adequate to enable a male adult worker to maintain a family of average size—which varied from country to country.[60] Empirically, this supposition seems to have been premature; after all, even in the early post-World War II period, when, for example, Britain strongly supported family wages, and the typical father of two had to maintain dependent children only for 18 years of a working life that lasted as long as 50 years, enthusiasts conceded that the family and social wage still did not suffice to close the gap in living standards between a bachelor or childless couple and one-earner families passing, of necessity, through that formative stage.[61]

No more authoritative source on what qualifies as falling within the framework of "to each according to his needs" can be drawn on than Karl Marx himself. In sketching a possible transition to a postcapitalist society, Marx insisted that in the first stages, in which all the means of production are collectively owned, individual consumption would remain unequal because distribution would be regulated by the exchange of equivalents and some worker-producers would be contributing more labor than others. Equality before the law would therefore remain a bourgeois principle since legal equality is created by using labor as the equal measure for all workers, some of whom are physically or mentally superior to others:

> This equal right is *unequal* right for unequal labor. It recognizes no class differences because each is only a worker; but it tacitly recognizes workers' individual talent and hence capacity as natural privileges. *It is therefore a right of inequality, with respect to its content, like all right.* Right can by its nature consist only in the application of the same standard; but the unequal individuals...are measurable only by the same standard insofar as one brings them under the same point of view, captures them only from the one *certain* side, e.g. in the given case views them only *as workers* and sees nothing more in them, abstracts from all else.
>
> Further: One worker is married, the other not; one has more

children than the other etc. etc. Given equal amount of work performed and hence equal share in the societal consumption fund, the one thus in fact receives more than the other, the one is richer than the other, etc. In order to avoid all these abuses, right would have to be unequal instead of equal.[62]

Marx's conceptualization of the contradictions of a society in transition from capitalism to socialism can be restated as his reflections on the labor market's failure to value the production of the next generation's working class and the need to treat procreation as the production of a public good. Rather than being regarded, in Marx's terms, as a system of unequal right, reproductive subsidies can also be analyzed as a challenge to or a transcending of bourgeois right by virtue of their attack on the latter's rigid abstraction from human needs. Thus they become a hybrid system because they apply two measures—performance and number of children or, alternatively, material production and human reproduction—resulting in greater equalization of consumption. Alternatively, if the needs-based component is viewed instead as a measure of and compensation for the parents' contribution to the production of the next generation of workers, the system remains bourgeois but becomes less gendered. Even if, in other words, it were true that family allowances are in conflict with the capitalist principle that in an open market the same price must prevail for different units of the same commodity[63]—since the wage is an economic and juridical relationship rather than one of charity or controlled by a socialist theory of needs, a reproductively determined wage would lead to the repulsion from the labor market of fathers of large families[64]—it can plausibly be argued that a worker who produces many replacement proletarians for the capitalist class is selling a different commodity (his own labor power now and his children's later) than one who produces none—provided that they neither exceed the demand for such future workers nor become social charges.

THE MICROECONOMICS OF ALIENATED PRODUCTION
OF THE PRODUCERS

It is true that with every mouth God sends a pair of hands. But it is not true that with every mouth there comes a silver spoon....[65]

But it is not only money that is lacking, but also time. [T]he only scarce, non-augmentable good...is time. Above all children cost time, not money.[66]

A recent theoretical debate, based on conventional economic notions about supply, demand, and resource allocation, has led to speculation about capitalism, poverty, and children. Many socioeconomic realities fail to fit these conventional assumptions, and considerable empirical evidence underscores the irrationality of the microeconomic logic. The new microeconomic demography serves as an apologetics for capitalism and free markets insofar as people—and especially women—take on reproductive labor that has lower exchange value and higher opportunity costs because they continue to recognize a culturally enhanced use value of procreational production that shifts the ordinary pleasure-pain calculus and seems to lack any market proxies.

Market-knows-best economic demography, a procapitalist self-caricature of the shallowest variant of economic determinism, dares to tread where even Marx left gaps. Producers and sellers of commodities are indifferent to the specific, concrete character of their products, which are merely vehicles for the abstract and endless accumulation of capital or for realizing the income they require for their lives outside of production. In principle, the same tendency toward indifference inheres in the worker's relationship to the only commodity he or she has to sell—labor power. Although some workers rebel some of the time against this logic of capital and protest their alienation at the workplace, the contradiction between abstract and concrete labor cannot be expunged. Nevertheless, as the abstractification of labor reaches ever greater heights, capital, recognizing both a legitimation crisis and an impediment to the extraction of surplus value, seeks new methods of securing workers' attention at the workplace.[67]

At a time when management is besieged with alienated wage workers, economic demography insists on transferring the model of abstract economic rationality into the domestic sphere of the production of new labor power otherwise known as child-bearing and child-rearing. Whereas some feminists have criticized Marx for having failed to reflect on the value-theoretical consequences of capital's treatment of mothers' reproductive labor as worthless,[68] economic demography brutally closes the gap by dragging the creation of children into the sphere of commodity production. Importing the model of profit maximization from boardrooms into bedrooms, the new learning imposes a type of abstract individualism on the analysis of both working-class households' struggle for subsistence and bourgeois families' plans for the transmission of wealth that ignores the differential cultural constraints on the domestication of capitalist rationality.[69]

This one-dimensional microeconomic demography is blind to the fact that one of the unique characteristics of the self-producers/purchasers of children is that they are subject to intense social, economic, psychological, moral, and religious pressure to procreate: "Reproduction even more than sexuality is overlaid with attitudes the individual considers appropriate because he has been learning them ever since early childhood."[70] Although there is no gainsaying the advent in the twentieth century of various mechanisms to sustain high levels of consumption in general and of certain commodities in particular, they lack both the subtlety and the personhood-encompassing scope of the structure of norms constructing parenthood as a vital component of the human condition. No hidden persuader yet has dared to assert that its client's commodity "is central to individual identity and meaning in life." Those candid enough to concede that "the desire to reproduce is in part socially constructed," nevertheless assert that "at the most basic level transmission of one's genes...is an animal or species urge closely linked to the sex drive.... For many people 'breed'...is a central part of their life plan, and the most satisfying and meaningful experience they have."[71] And even critical Marxists do it, being "prepared to grant that there is a near-universal desire to procreate."[72]

Although no urge drives humans to perpetuate their species by acts quite so heroic as those of emperor penguins, who incubate eggs for weeks in exposed terrains in -60° Fahrenheit Antarctic winters, philosophical thinkers at least since Plato have attested to the extraordinary ends to which some of those humans will go to become immortal through the flesh who do not belong to the small minority that can achieve immortality through glorious deeds or creations of the spirit.[73] Vindicating a niche in the great genetic chain of being by way of "extending our selfhood into the future" has been styled a right every bit as fundamental as that to life itself.[74] Biological ur-drives this potent—"[w]e are genetically programmed to want and to value" children[75]—should not be in need of penal props; yet the sanctions attached to what are stigmatized as pathological, irresponsible, and pitiable deviations from this prescribed role have been applied with especial force against women.[76] As long ago as World War I, Leta Hollingsworth spelled out the "Social Devices for Impelling Women to Bear and Rear Children," which she found similar to those used to "get soldiers slain."[77]

By the same token, in certain societies at certain stages of development abstention from procreation has asserted itself sufficiently to make the more interesting question not why (abnormal) people do not have children, but why the majority continues to have children.[78] Demographic developments in Germany and Italy have in recent years sharply posed this question.[79] In these two countries, the total fertility rate, which at 2.11 births per woman would just replace the population under current mortality rates and assuming no net immigration,[80] fell from 2.48 and 2.55 in the first half of the 1960s to 1.28 in 1985 and 1.27 in the early 1990s respectively.[81] In Eastern Germany, where the wrenching conversion of a state-socialist into a capitalist economy prompted a decline in the birth rate by almost two-thirds from 1988 to 1993, the state appears dismayed by its citizens' economically rational "unprecedented birth strike," which is purportedly in part a reaction by women of the former German Democratic Republic to the unfamiliar need to reconcile children, consumption, and career.[82] In Brandenburg, for example, the government has offered 1,000 marks for the birth of each child in an effort to counteract capitalistically disoriented couples' reluctance "to have children because they are unsure whether they will be able to survive in the newly competitive society."[83]

Though extreme, such phenomena help explain why, with the end of the baby boom in the early 1960s, scholarly study of voluntarily childless adults began to view them as psychological nondeviants.[84] Studies have, for example, repeatedly shown that, despite the fact that parents state that they value children highly, "adults with children living at home report less happiness and less satisfaction with their marriages, friends, and leisure activities than adults not living with children." And despite the widespread assumption that parents value children especially for their companionship in old age, nonparents report the same or greater happiness than parents whose children have left home.[85]   On balance, then, the turn-of-the-century observation that a child was not "a good investment for the father of the family," who resembled a breeder whose animals absconded just when they were about to begin to return a yield apparently still remained subjectively plausible for some parents.[86]

Surveys also disclose that a major component of the desirability of parenthood is the instrumental use of children to achieve status and prestige. As contradistinguished from the interest in interacting with children in order to be part of an intriguing and stimulating qualitative growth process, the instrumental aspect emerges "because one does not want to go through life without becoming a parent, or because one would feel aimless or empty without a family, or because having children is a rite of passage in the attainment of adult status...a classic example being...people who loathe children but may have one or more simply to attain the status of being parents."[87]   Such pressures may be weakening in the face of heightened dedication to consumption and the work that supports it. Even in the United States, where the fall in fertility below the replacement rate—from 3.71 in the second half of the 1950s to 1.76 in 1985—has not reached European levels,[88] a feminist sociologist was prompted, in the context of the resultant structural antinatalism, to bemoan the fact that feminists' emphasis on the newly gained right and freedom not to reproduce had blinded them to the unintended consequences of demographic decline.[89]

The new economic-demographic approach is further encumbered by the fact that as households ceased to be centers of inanimate commodity production and ultimately became monoproducers, their one commodity is not children per se, who cannot legally be sold, but labor power. Since, however, it is impossible to foresee the demand for labor power (of any kind let alone of a particular kind) two decades in advance of its advent as a finished product in the labor market, whatever rationality attaches to the production-decision-making process must be tenuous at best. That rationality becomes even more attenuated on account of its surrogate character: parents make the decisions as to the creation of fresh labor power, yet ultimately the consequences of their misjudgments are borne individually by the children (and collectively albeit marginally by the class of labor power sellers) if labor market conditions turn out to be unfavorable.

The process of theoretical assimilation that the new economic demography underwent has assumed a mathematically sophisticated form since the 1960s. The starkness of the conversion is more poignant, however, in its unadorned, plain-language variant as set forth during a period when depopulation rather than overpopulation dominated the agenda. In the 1930s, for example, demographers assumed that children were primarily burdens exacerbating their "parents' discomfort and insecurity."[90]   Eager to ward off the demise of "Western civilization," Joseph Spengler, soon to become one of the world's leading demographic economists and historians, announced that:

> Children are economic commodities even as are books, dogs, or automobiles. The production of commodities...occasions pain to the producers. Men produce automobiles only when the price obtained for the automobiles offsets the pain of producing them. So with children. [M]illions of potential parents feel that the money value of children in an industrial civilization is *less* than the money cost of creating and rearing them. [A]n adequate price will induce the production of children even as it induces the production of automobiles.[91]

Despite the fact that those who procreate do so "because they feel that the joy and pleasure" of child-rearing exceeds the money cost, Spengler suggested that the state should pay "whatever wage is necessary to induce...couples to undertake the work" because "it is the state, and not parents, that benefits from the production of children."[92] Although some people may refrain from procreating because they lack the material resources to rear children, the assumption that money qua deus ex machina will automatically imbue financially strapped procreators with the experience, insight, tolerance, patience, sensitivity, interest, spontaneity, foresight, skill, maturity, emotional stability, and love that are required to promote the development of a socialized human being does not augur well for the longevity of Western civilization. Expressly commodifying children and reproduction and subjecting them exclusively to market direction would deprive them of the minimum exemption from the disruptive and destructive rigors of capital-logic that makes life under capitalism morally, emotionally, and culturally possible.[93] That economic demography, when it believes that the time has come to make the invisible hand visible, can find no higher source of legitimation than state necessity, is typical of a social formation that can no longer rely on "une véritable solidarité entre générations."[94]

Economic demographers must engage in considerable conceptual contortion to convert children into commodities. Economic theory assumes that consumers reveal preferences when they sacrifice leisure to work in order to produce or obtain the money to buy a commodity. The reproductive corollary that the self-produced supply of children must approximate the procreators' demand for children is, however, difficult to reconcile with experience:

> The problem with treating babies as a normal good is that they are produced by an activity that is not work, but is normally pleasurable, and...periodically...becomes intensely preferable to doing anything else. Consequently...it requires more work...to avoid conception than to produce babies. We cannot then assume that the number of babies produced simply fulfils demand for them.... As soon as we take the sex drive seriously, we must assume...that due to the "leisure preference" in coitus, the number of babies produced will be in excess of the number desired unless the costs of reliable birth control approach zero.[95]

Moreover, as British eugenicist-socialist Karl Pearson argued, unskilled laborers had little incentive to restrain their fertility since they would have to abstain from "one of the few pleasures which lie within their reach; a pleasure...which does not, like drinking, appear *immediately and directly* to reduce the weekly pittance."[96]

In spite of these obvious differences separating the production of labor from that of run-of-the-mill commodities, the Chicago School new household economics inaugurated by Gary Becker has undertaken a reconstruction of childbearing as the self-production of consumer durables.[97]   Children have, according to Becker, who has tried to generalize and develop Malthus's economic framework, become the only "major commodity" in which families, at least in the advanced capitalist world, have remained self-sufficient.[98] Even in Becker's view, this self-production is tempered by opportunity costs—especially as a result of wives' increasing earning power.[99] To the extent that richer parents share their wealth with their children, a rise in the effective price of children as income rises diminishes the demand for them.[100] This approach—which became plausible only in the wake of the "construction of the economically worthless child" as children ceased to be "the poor man's capital"[101]—replaced the nineteenth-century factory-worker model according to which "the family," viewing children as "producer durables," "acts like a firm supplying labor services. It has its own labor supply and can create more (with a considerable lag) through childbearing." A family, in deciding to increase its "stock of human capital for later stages in the life cycle," is consciously trading off the income the wife could be earning for the children's later contributions.[102] If the new economic-demographic learning, which at least has the merit of treating the domestic (intrafamily) autoproduction economy as a separate system from that of commodity production, is to be taken seriously even as analogy, a number of salient differences between children and traditional commodities must be attended to.

First, parents do not undertake such production for the same reason (profit) that guides individual firms' capital investment decisions. As "one of the few truly craftlike activities of modern life," parenting has become a "luxury...conducted despite, rather than because of, economic self-interest."[103] Here a pertinent analogy to noncapitalist (simple commodity producing) households suggests itself.   Just as the family farm/farm family produces commodities not in order to accumulate capital but merely in order to survive, it produces children who "become living insurance, from which one later expects back all the effort with interest."[104] Yet unlike the peasant landholder, who may not have been able to survive without spousal and child labor, the urban working-class male (and increasingly female as well) in welfare states who neither could nor needed to rely on offspring to finance his retirement, may be economically better off without children.   And whereas at one time parents might have begun procreating early and then struggled to keep their children at home as long as possible in order to make use of their labor or wages, such considerations cease to apply in a period when child labor laws virtually insure that children will largely represent a fiscal drain.[105]

Second, the production time or period[106] is very long for children in comparison to that of other commodities.   Today, in advanced capitalist countries—despite the efforts of some factions of capital to deregulate the employment of younger children[107]—it may take 16 to 30 years before a worker is finally prepared to enter the labor market. Despite these unique characteristics, the population or labor force theory of classical political economy assumed that human reproduction was regulated by the same laws that controlled the rest of production: ↑ demand → ↑ price (wages) → ↑ supply → ↓ price (wage).[108] Two centuries ago, when child labor was common, the process was accelerated, although even Thomas Malthus conceded that "the reduced cost of production [of labor] cannot, under sixteen or eighteen years, materially influence the supply of labour in the market."[109] A contemporary, Thomas De Quincey, underscored the aberrant character of the commodity labor power by delineating the impact of population on wages: if the rate of population change should "sustain the most abrupt change, it would take a score of years before that change could begin to tell upon the labour market."[110]

Another of Malthus's contemporaries, John McCulloch, author of England's "most successful" general economics treatise in the first half of the nineteenth century,[111] spelled out the supposed mechanism more explicitly: "When wages rise, a period of eighteen or twenty years must elapse before the influence of the increased stimulus given by the rise to the principle of population can be felt in the labour market." At the other extreme, according to McCulloch, a fall in wages occasioned by a diminution of the wage fund or an increase in population would not quickly bring about a decline in the supply of laborers through increased mortality unless they had "previously been subsisting on the smallest quantity of the cheapest species of food required to support mere animal existence." At the same time,

> the force of habit, and the ignorance of the people with respect to the circumstances which determine wages, would prevent any effectual check being given to the formation of matrimonial connexions, and the rate at which fresh labourers had previously been coming into the market, until the misery occasioned by the restricted demand...and the undiminished supply...had been generally and widely felt. [T]his...impossibility of speedily adjusting the supply of labour proportionally to variations in the rate of wages...gives to these variations their peculiar and extraordinary influence over the well-being of the labouring classes.[112]

Third, this long production period means that a rational self-producer must make long-term calculations that both dwarf in complexity those associated with other consumer durables and nondurables and that do not permit self-correction in midcourse because the unique commodity in question generally cannot be sold off, even at a loss, as, for example, might a house that becomes less utility-generating because the purchaser could not foresee that the neighborhood in which it is located would become less desirable after 10 or 20 years. The type of rational decision-making processes that purportedly prompts consumers to purchase toothpaste or even expensive automobiles is precluded if "[b]y the time a parent finishes discovering whether he really likes bringing up his first child, he has already had his last [and b]y the time it is clear what kind of world the children will live in—a question relevant to whether they should be brought into it—the children are grown...."[113]

Fourth, parents self-finance their output of offspring by means of installment payments that promote self-delusion concerning the ultimate costs. They do not, therefore, need any credit rating despite their failure to have made full disclosure to themselves regarding total cost over the lifetime of the transaction. Indeed, survey evidence suggests that parents "vastly underestimate" the amounts they spend on children even within the previous year. Whereas urban middle-class parents thought they were spending one-seventh of their income on their two children, estimates of actual direct costs averaged two-fifths of earned income.[114] Parents' underestimation of the opportunity costs of procreation in terms of foregone income, traditionally a function of the fact that the wife stops working or works less, must also be taken into account here.

Fifth, associated with this self-production is the further "fundamental distinction between children and commodities" that the cost of the former is a function of the family's income insofar as it is plausible to assume that a child "cannot be brought up at a much lower level of living than that of his parents."[115] Nevertheless, in some proletarian cultures inegalitarian consumption patterns can modify the parents' material deprivation. In early-twentieth-century England, for example: "Whatever it was that went to make the lower-working-class home 'cosy,' parents had first, often sole, rights in it.... To many people the idea of sharing food and possessions equitably with their children would have seemed preposterous...."[116] Sociopsychological pressures to procreate may be supraclass in character, yet they also assume specific class forms. Lee Rainwater's survey of working-class attitudes toward family planning in the 1950s in the United States is particularly revealing because it unearths or at least constructs patterns of passivity and fatalism that have subsequently been attributed to Aid to Families with Dependent Children (AFDC) recipients, who are perceived as the root of the large-family poverty problem.[117] Whereas the former group of relatively low-wage workers accepted their fate largely within a framework of unsubsidized income from employment, welfare mothers are the arch-Malthusian targets of demographic debate.[118]

The economic intermediaries that discriminate between solvent and insolvent demand for Audis and Bentleys cannot prevent parents who "cannot afford" a child from creating one. The freedom to self-create any number of children is, in contrast, so "sacrosanct" that it, "even in the face of financial difficulties, receives widespread moral (and, if necessary, tangible) encouragement.... In fact, by creating public support for the dominance of family 'values' over economic rationality, reproductive and social institutions are geared to *prevent* economic factors from inhibiting reproduction." Becker's analogy also collapses when confronted with the impossible imputation to parents of the legal right and social-psychological and moral ability to equalize the marginal utilities per dollar of consumption by reconfiguring their choices upon discovering that an incremental child-durable turned out to generate less utility than they had predicted.[119]

Consequently, the only obstacle standing between financially impecunious but fecund self-employed procreators and their self-made consumer durable is Malthus's pseudo-class-conscious admonition, echoed by John Stuart Mill,[120] that: "A labourer who marries without being able to support a family may in some respects be considered as an enemy to all his fellow-laborers."[121] In the absence of strict compliance with such counsel, however, Becker's hypothesis must deal with the following stylized set of assumptions. People who marry procreate unreflectively because having children is simply what married people do and children help cement the relationship.[122] In the face of such normative pressures, once people have decided to marry, they cease weighing procreational advantages and disadvantages[123]: "In that respect alone the idea of some utilitarian calculus is totally inappropriate for describing the cognition involved in having *some* children." Moreover, parents report that they believe that they have little or no control over the rising cost of children, not because the prices of the commodities and services that they buy for them have increased more rapidly than the rate of inflation, but because culturally coerced behavioral standards require them to extend the scope of such acquisitions and to move to ever higher levels of quality.[124] Indeed, given the facts that children are very expensive[125] and that parents are often unaware of how expensive they are or will be, it becomes plausible that "[i]f economic factors were decisive, no one in modern society would have any children."[126] And even where economic costs and benefits do influence fertility decisions, "they do so because couples believe and accept that it is important" to consider them.[127] Thus outside of a specific socio-historical and class-oriented ideology mandating continuous "inflation of child costs geared to the unlimited demands of a symbolic system of prestige and deference,"[128] such linkages cannot be adequately understood.

The new household economics also fails to engage the insight that because some level of procreation is socially prescribed, "the extent to which the level of resources may influence the level of childbearing is culturally restricted just as the concern for resources itself is influenced by social norms."[129] Thus if parents would produce and consume the same number of children regardless of their income, that is, if the number of children is the independent variable and parents accommodate their standard of living to that number;[130] and if, finally, the total cost imposed by a child (including college education) may quantitatively approach that of a house mortgage—must children not be viewed as very bizarre commodities? Even a lower-income husband-wife family (with annual income below $32,000) is estimated to spend $92,000 on a child through age 17, while a higher-income family (with income above $52,000) spends almost twice that amount.[131] After all, few consumers would take out three or four mortgages within a few years of one another. Yet the average two-parent family in the early 1980s could expect to devote almost one-quarter of its income to supporting a single child through college—a share that rose to two-fifths for two, and two-thirds for four children. The sums involved would have been sufficient, if they had instead been invested at the then prevailing historically high interest rates, to have permitted the parents to retire at age 47.[132] In addition, contrary to Becker's conceptualization of fertility decisions, procreators are in social reality not free to make any combinations of, or trade-offs between, numbers of children and money spent per child because class- and income-specific social conventions culturally constrict the range of choice. Thus, as a friendly critic remarked, "not even Becker...considers himself free to choose either two children who go to university or four children who stop their education after high school."[133] In other words, to the extent that each social stratum's standard of living is controlled by its "folkways," individual members cannot arbitrarily violate these societally given consumption standards without risking significant loss of social standing.[134]

The conceptualization of fertility decisions within the framework of homo œconomicus is also significantly complicated by the fact that in many millions of instances birth is still not only not the product of a decision but counter-intentional.[135] Some demographers' and sociologists' disbelief that "people in industrial society...have children...because they do not know how to avoid having children"[136] is misplaced. As the U.S. Congress found in 1970: "The problems of excess fertility for the poor result to a large extent from the inaccessibility of family planning information and services."[137] That scholarly skepticism is certainly wrong with regard to contraception; and although many who fail to contracept may know of the existence of abortion, they may not possess the requisite social knowledge or money to have one.[138] As the U.S. Surgeon General noted in connection with the finding that 57 percent of all births in the United States were unplanned or unwanted, overpriced long-term contraceptives deprive poor women of several of the most effective ways of avoiding pregnancies.[139]

Despite the broad evidence that individual, let alone class, socioeconomic rationality has not always reigned supreme over working-class procreativity, some social scientists, eager to refute "the functionalist assumptions of modernization theorists" and "trickle-down" arguments that the working class imitates the fertility patterns of the bourgeoisie with a lag, find it "important to stress the rationality and independence of working-class behavior."[140] And although Philippe Aries exempted workers without the prospect of social mobility, he depicted the West from the nineteenth century on as having subjected procreation to "the methods of rational and scientific organization, a sort of biological Taylorism."[141]

Contemporary surveys, however, cast considerable doubt on the absolute assertion that "[f]ertility does not just happen. The number of children born to a man and a woman reflects a family strategy. [P]eople have large families out of desire, not ignorance...."[142] U.S. survey data from the first half of the 1960s revealed that 17 percent of the births of all (married) respondents were characterized as unwanted compared to 36 percent among the near-poor and poor and 42 percent among the poor alone; among near-poor and poor blacks, the share reached 51 percent.[143]   Another survey from the same period revealed that especially lower-income couples had unwillingly arrived at a fourth child.[144] Later data showed that among ever-married black women 15 to 44 years old with incomes below the federal poverty threshold, the proportion of children born who were unwanted at birth was 43.8, 21.0, and 35.3 percent during the five years preceding 1973, 1982, and 1988 respectively. The corresponding figures for black women with incomes at 200 percent or higher of the poverty level were 18.0, 9.6, and 14.1 percent respectively—only marginally lower than the proportions among poor white women.[145] As demographers noted, because the poverty definition incorporates family size, "many couples would not have been classified as poor were it not for their having had unwanted children. Consequently, the results indicate the coincidence of poverty and unwanted births rather than a propensity of the 'poor' to have unwanted children."[146] Unplanned pregnancies—that is, births of children whom parents may in principle want but not at that juncture in the procreators' lives—warrant inclusion because they too can plunge the parents into irreversible poverty if they are as yet economically incapable of sustaining a family.[147]

Against the background of such procreational behavior, Judith Blake, from a quasi-Darwinian perspective, concluded that:

> Pro-natalist motives have helped societies survive thousands of years of want. The institutional context responsible for such motives is geared to combat the anti-natalist effect of poverty with desires that relentlessly override perceptions of current realities and demand the production of children in spite of everything. Regardless of child quality, or the toll it takes of individuals, this institutional complex concentrates on insuring the biological survival of the species.... We must recognize...that as yet we have no control over the social context of reproduction comparable to the control over consumer durables provided by the credit system.[148]

Precisely how the linkage between cyclical and secular economic developments and individual rational procreational decisions and that between the latter and macrodemographic and -economic growth are supposed to operate has never been adequately explicated. Thus, for example, the third British population census of 1821 asserted that: "The Manufacturing Population is naturally on the Increase; not only as every short period of prosperity and increased wages produces imprudent Marriages, but also because in many Manufactures, Children are able to maintain themselves at an early age, and so to entail little expense on their Parents, to the obvious encouragement of marriage,"[149] One possible interpretation of the population counters' story, then, is that workers were irrationally responding to short-term signs of prosperity by shortsightedly producing additional children, who might turn into good investments, contributing within a few years more income to the household than they cost, but who might also stop earning altogether at the next downturn.

By the same token, at least in the United States during the nineteenth and into the twentieth century, "the earnings of young children were of decisive importance in enabling laboring families to secure a property stake in the community"—or at least to survive. [150] Or, as the young Engels put it, "children are like trees, which superabundantly reimburse the expenditure spent on them...."[151] Unmentioned, to be sure, is the further possibility that the production and mass labor marketing of successive contingents of extraordinarily low-paid child-competitors might, Sisyphus-like, perversely reduce aggregate family income.[152] As George Bernard Shaw observed toward the end of the century:

> The commodity which the proletarian sells is one over the production
> of which he has practically no control. He is himself driven to produce
> it by an irresistible impulse...to multiply men so that their exchange
> value falls slowly and surely until it disappears altogether.... This is the
> condition of our English labourers to-day: they are no longer even dirt
> cheap: they are valueless, and can be had for nothing. The proof is the
> existence of the unemployed, who can find no purchaser.[153]

How then are workers supposed to be in a position to determine whether they will be able to support any (let alone how many) children during the next 22 years as well as to gauge future demand for their and their children's labor power if such long-term aggregate supply and demand conditions are unpredictable? "Even if the labourer possessed...an irrational passion for dispassionate calculation, the task of estimating his probable family income and even expenditure in the foreseeable future would tax the ingenuity of a trained economic forecaster, if only because of the irregularity of his prospective employment and earnings."[154]

NOTES

1. Linda Gordon, *Woman's Body, Woman's Right: A Social History of Birth Control in America* 404-405 (1981 [1974]).

2. Joseph Schumpeter, *Capitalism, Socialism and Democracy* 27 (1966 [1943]).

3. Francis Bowen, *American Political Economy* 142 (1969 [1870]) (quote); David Harvey, *The Limits to Capital* 163 (1989 [1982]).

4. Chapter 8 presents much more detailed and varied sets of data.

5. William Graham Sumner, *Folkways: A Study of the Sociological Importance of Usages, Manners, Customs, Mores, and Morals* 309-10 (1940 [1906]).

6. John Myles, "States, Labor Markets, and Life Cycles," in *Beyond the Marketplace: Rethinking Economy and Society* 271-98 at 273-75 (Roger Friedland & A. Robertson eds., 1990).

7. Franz Jánossy, *Das Ende der Wirtschaftswunder: Erscheinung und Wesen der wirtschaftlichen Entwicklung* (1966); Myles, "States, Labor Markets, and Life Cycles" at 277 (quote).

8. See, e.g., *Die Lage der Familien in der Bundesrepublik—Dritter Familien-bericht* 48-49 (Deutscher Bundestag, 8. Wahlperiode, Drucksache 8/3121, 1979). For evaluations of the family life cycle thesis, see Roy Rodgers, "The Family Life Cycle Concept: Past, Present, and Future," in *The Family Life Cycle in European Societies* 39-57 (Jean Cuisenier ed., 1977); Tamara Hareven, "Introduction: The Historical Study of the Life Course," in *Transitions: The Family and the Life Course in Historical Perspective* 1-16 (Tamara Hareven ed., 1978); Glen Elder, Jr., "Family History and the Life Course," in *Transitions* at 17-64. Mark Stern, "Poverty and the Life-Cycle, 1940-1960," *J. Social Hist.* 24 (3):521-40 at 522 (Spr. 1991), asserts on the basis of age-specific poverty rates that "[t]he life-cycle squeeze has disappeared," but offers no data on the number of children whom these adults support.

9. T. Marmor & Martin Rein, "Post-War European Experience with Cash Transfers: Pensions, Child Allowances, and Public Assistance," in The President's Commission on Income Maintenance Programs, *Technical Studies* 259-91 at 268 (n.d. [1969]); Walter Gove et al., "The Family Life Cycle: Internal Dynamics and Social Consequences," *Sociology and Social Research* 57 (2):182-95 (Jan. 1973); Valerie Oppenheimer, "The Life-Cycle Squeeze: The Interaction of Men's Occupational and Family Life Cycles," *Demography* 11 (2):227-45 (May 1974).

10. 2 *Consumer Behavior: The Life Cycle and Consumer Behavior* (Lincoln Clark ed. 1955).

11. John Lansing & James Morgan, "Consumer Finances over the Life Cycle," in *Consumer Behavior: The Life Cycle and Consumer Behavior* 2:36-51, tab. 3, 4, 6, 12, 14, at 37, 39-40, 46, 49. The data, from 1953 and 1954, were based on the Survey of Consumer Finances.

12. Karl Marx, "Lohnarbeit und Kapital," in Karl Marx [&] Friedrich Engels, *Werke* 6:397-423 at 406-407 (1959 [1849]).

13. Emily Blumenfeld & Susan Mann, "Domestic Labour and the Reproduction of Labour Power: Towards an Analysis of Women, the Family and Class," in *Hidden in the Household: Domestic Labour Under Capitalism* 267-307 at 287-88 (Bonnie Fox ed., 1980).

14. See Jack Wayne, "The Function of Social Welfare in a Capitalist Economy," in *Family, Economy and State: The Social Reproduction Process Under Capitalism* 56-84 (James Dickinson & Bob Russell eds., 1986); James Dickinson, "From Poor Law to Social Insurance: The Periodization of State Intervention in the Reproduction Process," in *ibid.*, 113-49 at 115-16.

15. Charles Loomis, "The Study of the Life Cycle of Families," *Rural Sociology* 1 (2):180-99 (June 1936).

16. Marc Linder, *Migrant Workers and Minimum Wages: Regulating the Exploitation of Agricultural Labor in the United States* 24-25, 61-62, 84-88 (1992).

17. Martha May, "Bread Before Roses: American Workingmen, Labor Unions and the Family Wage," in *Women, Work and Protest: A Century of US Women's Labor History* 1-21 (Ruth Milkman ed., 1985), offers a provocative analysis of the shift in the ideological content of the family wage by the Progressive Era without, however, reflecting on the reality-content of the slogan.

18. "Condition of Workingmen's Families," in [Massachusetts] Bureau of Statistics of Labor, *Sixth Annual Report* 189-450 at 357-58, tab. III-VII, X-XI at 360-65, 368-70, 384 (quote) (Pub. Doc. No. 31, Mar. 1875). The survey was "for its time a model of full reporting and careful analysis." George Stigler, "The Early History of Empirical Studies of Consumer Behavior," *J. Pol. Econ.* 62 (2):95-113 at 100 (Apr. 1954). See also Jeffrey Williamson, "Consumer Behavior in the Nineteenth Century: Carroll D. Wright's's

Massachusetts Workers in 1875," *Explorations in Entrepreneurial Hist.* (2d ser.) 4 (2):98-135 (Winter 1967); John Modell, "Patterns of Consumption, Acculturation, and Family Income Strategies in Late Nineteenth-Century America," in *Family and Population in Nineteenth-Century America* 206-40 at 207-208 (Tamara Hareven & Maris Vinovskis eds., 1978): John McClymer, "Late Nineteenth-Century American Working-Class Living Standards," *J. Interdisciplinary Hist.* 17 (2):379-98 (Aut. 1986).

19. Calculated according to [U.S.] Commissioner of Labor, *Sixth Annual Report, 1890: Cost of Production: Iron, Steel, Coal, Etc.*, tab. XXIII.A.-B. at 1356 (rev. ed. 1891). There is a discrepancy between the U.S. data in part A and B of this table; although the lower figures are used here, even according to the higher figures, only in 22 percent of all families with children were the latter at work.

20. Calculated according to [U.S.] Commissioner of Labor, *Seventh Annual Report, 1891: Cost of Production: The Textiles and Glass,* Vol. II, Part III: Cost of Living, tab. XXVI.A.-B. at 1706, tab. XXVII.A.-B. at 1716, tab. XXVIII.A-B. at 1726 (1892). The data for wives are presumably underestimates because they exclude the work performed by wives in producing the income that many families derived from boarders.

21. Michael Haines, "Industrial Work and the Family Life Cycle, 1889-1890," *Research in Econ. Hist.* 4:289-356, tab. A.4 at 330-35 (1979).

22. [U.S.] Commissioner of Labor, *Eighteenth Annual Report, 1903: Cost of Living and Retail Prices of Food*, tab. I.G.at 241, I.H. at 243, III.F. at 363 (1904).

23. Allan Nevins, *Ford: The Times, the Man, the Company* 519 (1954) (quoting from the minutes of the special meeting of the Employers' Association of Detroit which Detroit Juvenile Court Judge Henry Hulbert addressed on Jan. 16, 1912).

24. [U.S.] Commissioner of Labor, *Eighteenth Annual Report, 1903*, tab. I.H. at 242-43.

25. Modell, "Patterns of Consumption, Acculturation, and Family Income Strategies in Late Nineteenth-Century America" at 225-39.

26. "Condition of Workingmen's Families," 371, tab. XI at 370.

27. Louise More, *Wage-Earners' Budgets: A Study of Standards and Cost of Living in New York City* tab. V at 84-85 (1907).

28. *Ibid.* at 83.

29. Robert Chapin, *The Standard of Living Among Workingmen's Families in New York City* 55 (1909).

30. Susan Kingsbury, "Relation of Women to Industry," *Papers and Proceedings of the Fifteenth Annual Meeting of the Am. Sociological Society* 141-58, tab.I at 143 (1920).

31. For greater detail about the premier location of heavy industry, see S. Kleinberg, *The Shadow of the Mills: Working-Class Families in Pittsburgh, 1870-1907,* at 25, 144, 313 (1989). See also Karen Mason, Maris Vinovskis, & Tamara Hareven, "Women's Work and the Life Course in Essex County, Massachusetts, 1880," in *Transitions* at 187-216, tab. 6.1 at 197.

32. Gwendolyn Hughes, *Mothers in Industry: Wage-Earning by Mothers in Philadelphia* 25 (1925).

33. U.S. Bureau of Labor Statistics, *Handbook of Labor Statistics 1936 Edition* 1103 (Bull. No. 616, 1936).

34. U.S. Bureau of the Census, *Women in Gainful Occupations 1870 to 1920*, tab. 51 at 78 (Census Monographs IX, 1929) (by Joseph Hill). See generally, Lynn Weiner, *From Working Girl to Working Mother: The Female Labor Force in the United States, 1820-1980* (1985).

35. "Cost of Living in the United States—Family Incomes," *Monthly Labor Rev.* 9 (6):1693-1705, tab. 1 at 1695-96 (Dec. 1919).

36. Scott Nearing, *Financing the Wage-Earner's Family: A Survey of the Facts Bearing on Income and Expenditures in the Families of American Wage-Earners* 107-108 (1914).

37. Paul Douglas, "Some Objections to the Family Wage System Considered," *J. Pol. Econ.* 32 (6):690-706 at 695 (Dec. 1924).

38. Samuel Gompers, "Should the Wife Help to Support the Family?" *Am. Federationist* 13 (1):36 (Jan. 1906).

39. [Marie Joseph] de Gérando, *De la Bienfaisance publique* 1:58 (1839).

40. Louis Reybaud, *Le Coton: Son régime—ses problèmes, son influence en Europe* 115-16 (1982 [1863]).

41. See Asa Briggs, *Social Thought and Social Action: A Study of the Work of Seebohm Rowntree, 1871-1954* (1961); Gertrude Himmelfarb, *Poverty and Compassion: The Moral Imagination of the Late Victorians* 169-78 (1992 [1991]).

42. B. Seebohm Rowntree, *Poverty: A Study of Town Life* 136-37 (new ed., 1908 [1901]).

43. *Ibid.* at 137-38, 135.

44. B. Seebohm Rowntree, *Poverty and Progress: A Second Social Survey of York* 155-60 (1941). The two surveys were not linked and did not even use the same definition of poverty.

45. B. Seebohm Rowntree, *The Human Needs of Labour* 16-48, 146-47 (n.d. [1918]).

46. B. Seebohm Rowntree, *The Human Needs of Labour* 148-51 (1937).

47. Edgar Sydenstricker, Willford King, & Dorothy Wiehl, "The Income Cycle in the Life of the Wage-Earner," *Pub. Health Reports* 39 (34):2133-40 (Aug. 22, 1924). The study characterized as low economic status the period during which income fell below the mean for all families.

48. Howard Bigelow, *Family Finance: A Study in the Economics of Consumption* v-vi, 340, 322-41 (rev. ed., 1953 [1936]).

49. A.B. Atkinson, *The Economics of Inequality* 199-201 (1975).

50. Charisse Jones, "Family Struggles on Brink of Comfort," *N.Y. Times*, Feb.18, 1995, at 1, col. 3, at 9, col. 1, 4 (nat. ed.).

51. Ada Heather-Bigg, "The Wife's Contribution to Family Income," *Econ. J.* 4:51-58 at 55 (1894).

52. Paul Glick, *American Families* 71 (1957).

53. Ann Smith Rice, "An Economic Life Cycle of Childless Families" 35-36 (Ph. D. diss., Florida State University, 1964). Rice summarized her dissertation in Paulena Nickell, Ann Smith Rice, & Suzanne Tucker, *Management in Family Living* 22-25 (5th ed., 1976).

54. Rice, "An Economic Life Cycle of Childless Families," 43-45, tab. 12 at 59, tab. 16 at 69. Rice patched together census income data for 1959 and wives' contributions from the 1963 survey.

55. *Ibid.*, tab. 19 at 76.

56. John Weicher, "Changes in the Distribution of Wealth: Increasing Inequality?" *Fed. Reserve Bank of St. Louis Rev.* 77 (1):5-23, tab. 5 at 17, 19, tab. 8 at 20 (Jan.-Feb. 1995).

57. L.T. Hobhouse, *Liberalism* 82-109 (1964 [1911]).

58. Lord Beveridge, "Epilogue," in Eleanor Rathbone, *Family Allowances* 269-77 at 269, 270 (1947).

59. Wolfgang Müller & Christel Neusüß, "Die Sozialstaatsillusion und der Widerspruch von Lohnarbeit und Kapital," *Sozialistische Politik* 2 (6/7):4-67 at 9-13 (June 1970); Gertrude Williams, "The Myth of 'Fair' Wages," *Econ. J.* 66 (264):621-34 at 631, 633 (Dec. 1956) (quote).

60. International Labour Office, *Family Allowances: The Remuneration of Labour According to Need* 3-4 (Studies & Reports: Ser. D [Wages & Hours] No. 13, 1924).

61. Williams, "The Myth of 'Fair' Wages" at 632-34; J. M. Jackson, "Wages, Social Income, and the Family," *Manchester School of Econ. & Social Studies* 29 (1):95-106 at 95, 102 (Jan. 1961).

62. Karl Marx, "Randglossen zum Programm der deutschen Arbeiterpartei," in Karl Marx [&] Friedrich Engels, *Gesamtausgabe (MEGA)* 25:9-25 at 14-15 (1985) [1875]).

63. Eduard Heimann, "The Family Wage Controversy in Germany," *Econ. J.* 33 (132):509-15 at 509 (Dec. 1923).

64. Paul Leroy-Beaulieu, *Traité théorique et pratique d'économie politique* 2:568-69 (6th ed. 1914).

65. Lionel Robbins, "The Optimum Theory of Population," in *London Essays in Economics: In Honour of Edwin Cannan* 103-34 at 122 (T. Gregory & Hugh Dalton eds., 1927).

66. Günter Heismann, "Ein Volk unter Schock," *Die Woche*, July 28, 1994, at 12 (Lexis) (quoting Herwig Birg, a demographer).

67. Marc Linder, *Reification and the Consciousness of the Critics of Political Economy: Studies in the Development of Marx' Theory of Value* 317-26 (1975). For an exemplary account with regard to white collar workers, see Siegfried Kracauer, *Die Angestellten: Aus dem neuesten Deutschland* in *idem, Schriften* 1:205-304 (1971 [1929]).

68. Ludmilla Müller, "Kinderaufzucht im Kapitalismus—wertlose Arbeit; über die Folgen der Nichtbewertung der Arbeit der Mütter für das Bewußtsein der Frauen als Lohnarbeiterinnen," *Probleme des Klassenkampfs* 6 (1):13-65 at 20-24 (1976).

69. Wally Seccombe, "The Expanded Reproduction Cycle of Labour Power in Twentieth-Century Capitalism," in *Hidden in the Household* 217-66 at 262-63; *idem, A Millennium of Family Change: Feudalism to Capitalism in Northwestern Europe* 32 (1992).

70. Frederick Wyatt, "Clinical Notes on the Motives of Reproduction," *J. Social Issues* 23 (4):29-56 at 29 (1967).

71. John Robertson, *Children of Choice: Freedom and the New Reproductive Technologies* 24 (1994).

72. Seccombe, *A Millennium of Family Change* at 32.

73. Malcolm Browne, "Eggs on Feet and Far from Shelter, Male Penguins Do a Shuffle," *N.Y. Times*, Sept. 27, 1994, at B5, col. 1 (nat. ed.); Plato, *Symposion* 207d-209d.

74. Arthur Dyck, "Population Policies and Ethical Acceptability," in *The American Population Debate* 351-77 at 364, 368 (Daniel Callahan ed., 1971).

75. Partha Dasgupta, "The Population Problem," in *Population—The Complex Reality: A Report of the Population Summit of the World's Scientific Academies* 151-80 at 161 (Francis Graham-Smith ed., 1994).

76. J.E. Veevers, *Childless by Choice* 3-12 (1980).

77. Leta Hollingsworth, "Social Devices for Impelling Women to Bear and Rear Children," *Am. J. Sociology* 22 (1):19-29 (July 1916).

78. T.H. Marshall, "What the Public Thinks," in *idem* et al., *The Population Problem: The Experts and the Public* 1-63 (1938); Anna Silverman & Arnold Silverman, *The Case Against Having Children* (1971); Hans Jürgens, "Sind zwei Kinder schon zuviel?" in *Keine Kinder—Keine Zukunft? Zum Stand der Bevölkerungsforschung in Europa* 43-50 at 44 (Lutz Franke & Hans Jürgens eds., 1978).

79. Alan Cowell, "In an Affluent Europe, the Problem is Graying," *N.Y. Times*, Sept. 8, 1994, at A4, col.5 (nat. ed.).

80. The total fertility rate is a hypothetical projection of the average number of children that women entering their childbearing age in a given year will have during their lifetimes based on the actual age-specific reproduction of fertile women in that year. Because birth rates vary from year to year, the probabilities of childbearing change as each cohort of women passes through its fertile period. Consequently, the actual average number of children ever born to a cohort frequently deviates considerably from that projected by the total fertility rate. Larry Barnett, *Population Policy and the U.S. Constitution* 4-5 (1982).

81. Alexander Jung, "Kein Kinderspiel," *Die Woche*, Mar. 12, 1994, § Wirtschaft at 12 (Lexis).

82. Heismann, "Ein Volk unter Schock"; James Witte & Gert Wagner, "Declining Fertility in East Germany After Reunification: A Demographic Response to Socioeconomic Change," *Pop. & Dev. Rev.* 21 (2):387-97 (June 1995).

83. Stephen Kinzer, "$650 a Baby: Germany Pays to Stem Decline in Births," *N.Y. Times*, Nov. 25, 1994, at A3, col. 1 (nat. ed.). See also "Eine häßliche Geburtenprämie," *Süddeutsche Zeitung*, Aug. 4, 1994, at 4 (Lexis); "Ein Land verödet," *Die Woche*, Aug. 4, 1994, § Wirtschaft at 12 (Lexis).

84. J. E. Veevers, "Voluntary Childlessness: A Review of Issues and Evaluations," *Marriage & Family Rev.* 2 (2):1, 3-26 (1979). See also Elaine May, *Barren in the Promised Land: Childless Americans and the Pursuit of Happiness* (1995).

85. Sara McLanahan & Julia Adams, "The Effects of Children on Adults' Psychological Well-Being: 1957-1976," *Social Forces*, 68 (1):124-46 at 124-25 (Sept. 1989).

86. Robert Hertz, "Socialisme et Dépopulation," *Les Cahiers du socialiste*, No. 10, at 20-21 (1910).

87. Judith Blake & Jorge del Pinal, "The Childlessness Option: Recent American Views of Nonparenthood," in *Predicting Fertility: Demographic Studies of Birth Expectations* 235-64 at 238 (Gerry Hendershot & Paul Placek eds., 1978).

88. Dirk van de Kaa, "Europe's Second Demographic Transition," *Pop. Bull.* 42 (1):1-57 (Mar. 1987); United Nations Dept. of Int. Econ. & Social Affairs, *World Population Prospects 1988*, tab. 12 at 152, 154 (Pop. Studies No. 106, 1989); *idem, World Population Monitoring 1991: With Special Emphasis on Age Structure*, tab. 31 at 56 (Pop. Studies No. 126, 1992); U.S. Bureau of the Census, *Households, Families, and Children: A 30-Year Perspective*, fig. 5 at 9 (CPR P23-181, 1992) (written by Terry Lugalia); *idem, Statistical Abstract of the United States: 1994*, tab. 94 at 78 (1994) (the total fertility rate in the United States had by 1990 risen to just below the replacement rate).

89. Joan Huber, "Will U.S. Fertility Decline Toward Zero?" *Sociological Q.* 21:481-92 at 485-86 (Autumn 1980).

90. Lincoln Day & Alice Day, "Family Size in Industrialized Countries: An Inquiry into the Social-Cultural Determinants of Levels of Childbearing," *J. Marriage & the Family* 31 (2):242-51 at 246 (May 1969).

91. Joseph Spengler, "The Birth Rate—Potential Dynamite," *Pop. & Dev. Rev.* 17 (1):159-69 at 167 (Mar. 1991 [1932]).

92. *Ibid.* at 168.

93. Karl Polanyi, *The Great Transformation* 73 (1971 [1944]). For skepticism that couples adjust their fertility at all to monetary incentives, see Henk Heeren, "Pronatalist Population Policies in Some Western European Countries," *Pop. Research & Policy Rev.* 1:137-52 at 150 (1982).

94. Eveline Sullerot, "Rapport présenté, au nom du Conseil économique et social," in "La Situation démographique de la France et ses implications économiques et sociales: bilan et perspectives," in *Journal Officiel de la République Française* 1978, No. 15 791-860 at 860 (Aug. 10, 1978).

95. Wally Seccombe, *Weathering the Storm: Working-Class Families from the Industrial Revolution to the Fertility Decline* 191 (1993).

96. Karl Pearson, "The Moral Basis of Socialism," in *idem, The Ethic of Freethought* 301-29 at 321 (2d ed. 1901 [1887]).

97. For an overview, see Susan Cochrane, "Children as By-Products, Investment Goods and Consumer Goods: A Review of Some Micro-Economic Models of Fertility," *Pop. Studies* 29 (3):373-90 (Nov. 1975).

98. Gary Becker, "An Economic Analysis of Fertility," in *Demographic and Economic Change in Developed Countries* 209-31 at 216 (1960).

99. For calculations of the opportunity costs, see Ritchie Reed & Susan McIntosh, "Costs of Children," in U.S. Commission on Population Growth and the American Future, *Research Reports: Economic Aspects of Population Change* 2:333-50 at 341-44 (Elliott Morss & Ritchie Reed eds., 1972).

100. Gary Becker, *A Treatise on the Family* 96-102 (1981).

101. Viviana Zelizer, *Pricing the Priceless Child: The Changing Social Value of Children* 5 (1985) (quote); Theodore Schultz, "The Value of Children: An Economic Perspective," *J. Pol. Econ.* 81 (2) pt. II:S2-S13 at S5 (Mar.-Apr. 1973) (quote).

102. Haines, "Industrial Work and the Family Life Cycle, 1889-1890" at 296-97.

103. Nancy Folbre, "Of Patriarchy Born: The Political Economy of Fertility Decisions," *Feminist Studies* 9 (2):261-84 at 279 (Summer 1983).

104. Susan Mann, *Agrarian Capitalism in Theory and Practice* 131-35 (1990); Max Horkheimer, "Allgemeiner Teil," in *Studien über Autorität und Familie: Forschungsberichte aus dem Institut für Sozialforschung* 3, 63 (1936) (quote).

105. Charles Sellers, *The Market Revolution: Jacksonian America, 1815-1846,* at 11-12, 17, 240 (1991).

106. See Karl Marx, 2 *Das Kapital: Kritik der politischen Ökonomie*, in Karl Marx [and] Friedrich Engels, *Werke* 24:241-50 (1963 [1885]).

107. For example, the National Restaurant Association, whose members employ more than 9 million workers in the United States, have proposed fewer restrictions on their employment of 14-year-old school children. "Employers Seek to Ease Restrictions on Teen Work," *Labor Relations Reporter* 147:282-83 (Oct. 31, 1994).

108. Sydney Coontz, *Population Theories and the Economic Interpretation* 168 (1961).

109. T.R. Malthus, *Principles of Political Economy* 242 (1820).

110. Thomas De Quincey, *The Logic of Political Economy,* in *idem, Political Economy and Politics* 118-294 at 221 (David Masson ed., 1970 [1844]).

111. Joseph Schumpeter, *History of Economic Analysis* 477 (Elizabeth Schumpeter ed., 1972 [1954]).

112. John McCulloch, *The Principles of Political Economy* 332, 333 (5th ed. 1864).

113. David Friedman, *Laissez-Faire in Population: The Least Bad Solution* 5 (1972).

114. Thomas Espenshade, "The Value and Cost of Children," *Pop. Bull.* 32 (1): 43-44, tab. 17 at 28, tab. 24 at 43 (Apr. 1977). The corresponding figures for urban middle-income parents were about one-fifth and one-half. The survey data referred to Hawaiian Caucasians. In addition to self-delusion concerning monetary costs, parents can, after the fact, also "reinterpret" anticipated nonmonetary costs and benefits to reduce or eliminate disparities. Joseph Spengler, *Population and America's Future* 147 (1975).

115. Bernard Okun, *Trends in Birth Rates in the United States Since 1870*, at 177 (1958). Looked at from a different perspective: "The fact that the richer family requires a greater proportionate increase of income to maintain the standard of living of a childless couple is due chiefly to the greater proportion of that increase which the richer families spend on sundries and luxuries...." A. Henderson, "The Costs of Children. Parts II and III," *Pop. Studies* 4 (3):267-98 at 274 (Dec. 1950).

116. Robert Roberts, *The Classic Slum: Salford Life in the First Quarter of the Century* 74 (1983 [1971]).

117. Lee Rainwater, *And the Poor Have Children: Sex, Contraception, and Family Planning in the Working Class* (1960).

118. In the long course of that debate the terms of the discourse have remained remarkably constant although the groups to which the aberrant procreational labels are affixed change. For example, the German socialists' chief pre-World War I theoretician, Karl Kautsky, in an extraordinarily dull reprise of his quasi-Malthusian, non-Marxist work on population 30 years earlier, offered a particularly lurid description of contemporary lumpenproletarians, whom he compared to savages. Their completely indiscriminate sexual intercourse, however, was accompanied by a fertility that was limited neither by life circumstances, as with savages, nor by possessions, as with the higher classes. Moreover, the advent of additional children did not worsen their condition; on the contrary, a larger contingent of offspring actually promoted their livelihood—living on charity—by appealing to donors' pity. Karl Kautsky, *Vermehrung und Entwicklung in Natur und Gesellschaft* 180-81 (1910).

119. Judith Blake, "Are Babies Consumer Durables? A Critique of the Economic Theory of Reproductive Motivation," *Pop. Studies* 22 (1):5-25 at 16-17, 24 (Mar. 1968). Although Leibenstein's strictures on Becker's "as if" theorizing—"[p]eople do not 'buy' children"—are well taken, his most important argument is untenable. Installment self-financing may mask the cost, but it is nevertheless untrue that "one cannot see what is given up in order to obtain a child." As Leibenstein himself concedes, empirical studies show that budget constraints operate to prevent very low income groups from affording more children. Harvey Leibenstein, "An Interpretation of the Economic Theory of Fertility: Promising Path or Blind Alley?" *J. Econ. Lit.* 12:457-79 at 462, 469 (1974).

120. See below ch. 3.

121. Thomas Robert Malthus, *An Essay on the Principles of Population* (1st ed.), in *idem, On Population* 34 (Gertrude Himmelfarb ed., 1960 [1798]).

122. For evidence that married couples' fertility planning is not economically motivated, see James Cramer, "Births, Expected Family Size, and Poverty," in *Five Thousand American Families—Patterns of Economic Progress: Special Studies of the First Five Years of the Panel Study of Income Dynamics* 2:279-305 (James Morgan ed., 1974).

123. Julian Simon's pollyannish view that people everywhere implement Malthus's preventive checks in response to income restraints is more a rhetorical debating point than an empirically useful argument. Julian Simon, *The Ultimate Resource* 177-87

(1981). That he cites Rainwater, *And the Poor Get Children* for the proposition is, in light of the latter's unrelenting disclosure of the self-abandonment of the poor to their procreational fate, preposterous.

124. John Caldwell, "Mass Education as a Determinant of the Timing of Fertility Decline," *Pop. & Dev. Rev.* 6 (2):225-55 at 227-28 (June 1980); Samuel Preston, "Changing Values and Falling Birth Rates," in *Below-Replacement Fertility in Industrial Societies: Causes, Consequences, Policies* 176-95 at 186 (Kingsley Davis et al. eds., 1986); George Alter, "Theories of Fertility Decline: A Nonspecialist's Guide to the Current Debate," in *The European Experience of Declining Fertility, 1859-1970: The Quiet Revolution* 13-27 at 16 (John Gillis et al. eds., 1992). What flaws the orthodox microeconomic argument that the costs of children are exogenously given is its failure to incorporate the circumstance of overarching importance that as self-producers parents can initiate the process of production despite the fact that any credit intermediary would inform them that bankruptcy of the enterprise is the inexorable outcome.

125. *Town & Country* magazine claims that the total cost of raising a child to the age of 18 is $679,483 including such items as $10,000 for an automobile. "Costly Children" *N.Y. Times Magazine*, June 26, 1994, at 12.

126. Kingsley Davis, "Foreword," in Thomas Espenshade, *The Cost of Children in Urban United States* v-vi (1973). A curious explanation of the end of the post-World War II baby boom emphasizes that: "As affluence grew, the family possessions multiplied and keeping the children from destroying them became more time-consuming." John Caldwell, *Theory of Fertility Decline* 251 (1982).

127. Joan Busfield & Michael Paddon, *Thinking About Children: Sociology and Fertility in Post-War England* 134-36, 141, 250 (1977).

128. Judith Blake, "Income and Reproductive Motivation," *Pop. Studies* 21 (3):185-206 at 205-206 (Nov. 1967).

129. Busfield & Paddon, *Thinking About Children* at 41.

130. Ironically, this reproductive behavioral guideline corresponds to Catholic precept, which counsels believers to adjust living standards to requirements of a larger family rather than subordinating the latter to desires for ever higher levels of personal consumption. See Blake, "Income and Reproductive Motivation" at 194-99.

131. "Expenditures on a Child by Husband-Wife Families, 1992," Family Economics Rev. 6 (3):34-36 (1993). See also "Costly Children," *N.Y. Times Magazine*, June 26, 1994, at 12.

132. Lawrence Olson, *Costs of Children* 55-58 (1983). Even for the 1920s it was estimated that an average family devoted the equivalent of three to four years of the family's income raising one child. Louis Dublin & Alfred Lotka, *The Money Value of a Man* 22-40 (1930); *idem, ibid.* 44-58 (rev. ed. 1946).

133. James Duesenberry, "Comment," in *Demographic and Economic Change in Developed Countries* at 231-34 at 233.

134. Rudolf Heberle, "Social Factors in Birth Control," *Am. Sociological Rev.* 6 (6):794-805 at 801 (Dec. 1941).

135. Larry Bumpass & Charles Westoff, "Unwanted Births and U.S. Population Growth," *The American Population Debate* 266-73 at 267 (Daniel Callahan ed., 1971); The Commission on Population Growth and the American Future, *Population and the American Future* tab. 11.1 at 97 (1972).

136. John Simons, "Culture, Economy and Reproduction in Contemporary Europe," in *The State of Population Theory: Forward from Malthus* 256-78 at 257 (David Coleman & Roger Schofield eds. 1986).

137. H.R. Rep. No. 1472, 91st Cong., 2d Sess., reprinted in 1970 *U.S. Code Congressional & Administrative News* 5068, 5070.

138. For survey data on teenagers' knowledge of contraception and the much greater frequency with which poor teenagers have children, see Colin McMahon & Carol Jouzaitis, "Taboos Leave Many Teens Unprotected," *Chicago Tribune*, May 24, 1994, at 1 (Lexis); Rhonda Hillbery, "A Silver Lining?" *Minneapolis Star Tribune*, June 7, 1994, at 1A (Lexis).

139. Warren Leary, "Contraceptives Are Called Too Costly," *N.Y. Times*, Mar. 19, 1994, at 8, col. 4 (nat. ed.).

140. Michael Katz & Mark Stern, "History and the Limits of Population Policy," *Politics & Society* 10 (2):225-45 at 226 (1980).

141. Philippe Aries, "Two Successive Motivations for the Declining Birth Rate in the West," *Pop. & Dev. Rev.* 6 (4):645-50 at 646 (Dec. 1980).

142. Katz & Stern, "History and the Limits of Population Policy" at 226, 245.

143. Leslie Westoff and Charles Westoff, *From Now to Zero: Fertility, Contraception and Abortion in America* 301-302 (1971).

144. Ronald Freedman & Lolagene Coombs, "Economic Considerations in Family Growth Decisions," *Pop. Studies* 20 (2):197-222 at 205-206 (Nov. 1966).

145. Linda Williams & William Pratt, "Wanted and Unwanted Childbearing in the United States: 1973-88," in National Center for Health Statistics, *Advance Data*, No. 189, tab. 3 at 4 (Sept. 26, 1990). See also "Wanted and Unwanted Births Reported by Mothers 15-44 Years of Age: United States, 1973," National Center for Health Statistics, *Advance Data*, No. 9, tab. 1 at 5 (Aug. 10, 1977). "Wanted and Unwanted Births Reported by Mothers 15-44 Years of Age: United States, 1976," *idem*, *Advance Data*, No. 56, tab. 2 at 5 (Jan. 24, 1980).

146. Larry Bumpass & Charles Westoff, "The 'Perfect Contraceptive' Population," *Science* 169 (3951):1177-82 at 1179 (Sept. 18, 1970). Unwantedness rises monotonically with birth order; *ibid.* tab. 4 at 1179.

147. Reed & McIntosh, "Costs of Children" at 346. Even intentional procreation shortly after marriage is said to lead to reduced lifetime accumulation of assets insofar as parents who become subject to such money and time pressure are unable to "invest" more in their own education. Ronald Freedman & Lolagene Coombs, "Childspacing and Family Economic Position," *Am. Sociological Rev.* 31 (5):631-48 at 632 (Oct. 1966).

148. Blake, "Are Babies Consumer Durables?" at 25.

149. *Population: viz. Enumeration and Parish Registers; According to the Census of M.D.CCC.XXI*, at xxx (1822).

150. Stephen Thernstrom, "Is There Really a New Poor? in *Poverty: Views From the Left* 83, 90 (Jeremy Lardner & Irving Howe eds., 1970). See also Eileen Boris, *Home to Work: Motherhood and the Politics of Industrial Homework in the United States* 175 (1994). A study of the southern sharecropper in the United States revealed that he had four times as many children as farm owners because "[t]he more children he had, the bigger the crop he could grow, the greater the share for the landlord, and therefore the more likely a landlord would be to offer him employment." B. Gröger, "The Meaning of Land in a Southern Rural Community: Differences Between Blacks and Whites," in *Farm Work and Fieldwork: American Agriculture in Anthropological Perspective* 189, 199 (Michael Chibnik ed., 1987).

151. Friedrich Engels, "Umrisse zu einer Kritik der Nationalökonomie," in Karl Marx [&] Friedrich Engels, *Werke* 1:499, 519 (1964 [1844]). See the demographically much more cautious approach of the leader of the German Social Democratic Party: "The

peasant is delighted with every calf that his cow brings him, he counts with gusto the number of young ones that a sow produces for him..., but he is gloomy when his wife bestows upon him a new increment in addition to *the* number of offspring, whom he believes he can bring up without heavy cares—and that number can*not* be great...." August Bebel, *Die Frau und der Sozialismus* 136-37 (1973 [1879]).

152. This unintended consequence may still flow from the reproductive behavior of migrant farm workers in the United States. Linder, *Migrant Workers and Minimum Wages* at 54-55, 87-88, 252-54.

153. G. Bernard Shaw, "The Basis of Socialism," in *Fabian Essays in Socialism* 15-83, 33 (G.B. Shaw ed., n.d. [1889]).

154. A.W. Coats, "The Classical Economists and the Labourer," in *The Classical Economists and Economic Policy* 144-79, 165 (A.W. Coats ed., 1971 [1967]).

2

Is Capitalist Population Policy
Laissez Procréer?

> Let us clear from the ground the metaphysical or general
> principles upon which, from time to time, *laissez-faire* has been
> founded.... Nor is it true that self-interest generally *is* enlightened;
> more often individuals acting separately to promote their own ends are
> too ignorant or too weak to attain even these. Experience does *not*
> show that individuals, when they make up a social unit, are always less
> clear-sighted than when they act separately.... The time...has come
> when each country needs a considered national policy about what size
> of Population, whether larger or smaller than at present or the same, is
> most expedient. And having settled this policy, we must take steps to
> carry it into operation.[1]

If the aggregate supply of new labor is the vector of billions of self-regarding
micro-social-psychological decisions—if, that is, when "a woman conceives and
bears a child, it is safe to assume that the State is not overmuch in her mind"—what
guarantees that the result promotes macroeconomic optimality let alone the
accumulation of capital? Because the supply of labor at any given moment appears
fixed, "not by anything then happening, but by the habits and actions of millions
of disconnected households a generation back," whereas the demand for labor is
the aggregate of current individual demands by hundreds of thousands of
competing employers, "[d]iscrepancy between two things so distinct in immediate
origin is obviously possible."[2]

That a sharp conflict can also erupt between micro- and macroeconomic
rationality became a prominent theme, for example, in the French power-holders'
attempts to combat what they viewed as that country's fatally uncompetitive
underpopulation. In the explanation accompanying the filing of a bill to award
premiums or annuities to mothers of four or more children, Adolphe Messimy, a
former Minister of War, stated in 1912 that:

> Why, today, does one say it is disastrous to raise children? Because in the modern family and especially in the bourgeois family, when the father has paid for the education of the child for twenty years, the latter goes off and produces nothing for the family, which has raised him.
>
> But from the point of view of the country, it is far from being so. The child once grown up will produce and will constitute for the money expended in his education a magnificent investment.

Messimy then explained that even in a working-class family, it cost 4,000-5,000 francs to raise a child to the age of 13, at which point he became a demi-ouvrier; later the child as worker would receive wages of 1,500 to 2,000 francs annually for 40 to 50 years and obviously produce much more—otherwise no one would employ him—thus generating a return of 40 percent.[3] The problem was that economic self-interest was not calculated to promote this social or national dividend because the investors, the parents, bore the cost of producing the worker without any return. Such a divergence represents the canonical welfare-economics case for "interference with normal economic processes...to increase the dividend."[4] But has capital, disguised under the name of "society,"[5] in fact intervened into procreational decisions to this end? And if spontaneous demographic outcomes are not favorable, why has capital not intervened into this laissez-faire regime?

This chapter first explores whether it makes sense to speak of an optimum population in a capitalist society. It then introduces and ultimately disposes of the objection that patriarchal state interference with women's sexual autonomy and reproductive freedom (in the form of statutory bans on contraception and abortion) is inconsistent with the claim that capitalist population policy is laissez faire. Finally, it analyzes whether capital can articulate and implement a population policy designed to promote that optimum. The failure of capital and of the central state apparatus in the United States during the post-World War II period to agree on the definition of such an optimum let alone the need for establishing any population policy provides the illustrative material for the discussion.

IS THERE AN OPTIMUM POPULATION?

> From the *histoires raisonées* of Ricardo...it would be quite justifiable to infer that, once the world was populated at all, any increase in population was a disadvantage.... Even from an economic point of view, the advent of Eve was a misfortune![6]

What is the optimum population from capital's perspective? Many demographers and economists have, for the past century, expressed considerable skepticism as to whether the notion of an optimal population size has any practical value at all.[7] For William Beveridge, optimum density as the golden mean balancing precariously between over- and underpopulation "suffers from the two defects of being unknowable and never the same for two moments together." Gunnar Myrdal characterized the theory of optimum population as "a speculative figment of the mind without much connection with this world; it does not give any guiding rule for the practical and political judgment of reality."[8]

The complexity of economic consequences of alternative possibilities has meant that economists have failed to reach a consensus on the optimum rate of population change in the United States.[9] At the peak of the Pax Americana in the mid-1950s, Kingsley Davis, a Parsonian functionalist, knew that the optimum would strike a balance between the "very large numbers for...sheer military and industrial strength" and "fewer numbers for...maintaining a high level of living," but he was unable to sketch any criteria for framing such a determination.[10] Daniel Moynihan, even as the federal government for the first time expressed concern about overpopulation in the United States, asked: "'Is there an optimum population for the country? Who can say?'"[11] Even Julian Simon, an extreme market-knows-best pronatalist, concedes that "even in the very simplest case," the macroeconomic welfare impact of an additional child is not only "thoroughly messy and generally indeterminate" but is incapable of a strictly scientific evaluation. Conceding that the short-run impact must be negative because children consume without producing, all Simon can offer is the speculation that the long-term effect "may be positive" because the connection between population growth and productive and infrastructural scale economies is "tenuous."[12] Finally, the 18 U.S. congressmen who introduced a joint resolution in 1970 placing the federal government's imprimatur on zero population growth conceded that although "stabilizing population may be a terribly urgent priority...we do not know what constitutes an optimum population for this country."[13]

Although he was neither explicit nor clear on the point, Malthus must have presumed that Britain (and other countries) had already achieved an optimum level of population such that every additional person (or worker) would trigger diminishing returns.[14] The notion of optimum population in the sense of the highest possible per capita national income does in fact hinge on the hypothetical counterbalancing of two forces in tension with each other: the "law" of diminishing returns, which imagines that per capita output rises as population declines; and that of external economies, which posits that in a complex social division of labor, larger populations generate benefits that cannot be captured by the smaller populations favored by diminishing returns because a smaller than optimum labor force cannot make maximum use of the indivisibilities of some factors of production.[15] In an early formulation, for example, James Mill observed that: "There is a certain density of population which is convenient, both for social intercourse, and for that combination of powers by which the produce of labour is increased. When these advantages, however, are attained, there seems little reason to wish that population should proceed any further. If it does proceed further,...it lessens [the net revenue]...."[16]

Some economists, rejecting a Malthusian interpretation of the maximum demographic carrying capacity, agree that the phenomenon of optimality would have to relate to that population (at any given time) above and below which per capita income decreases.[17] Keynes implied this view in his debate with Beveridge in the 1920s on overpopulation (rather than optimum population) when he asked rhetorically: "Is not a country overpopulated when its standards are lower than they would be if its numbers were less? [T]he question of what numbers are desirable arises long before starvation sets in, and even before the level of life begins to fall."[18] As a macroeconomic analogy to the "law" of diminishing (and increasing) returns—which even as a microeconomic doctrine presupposes an unreal constancy of certain factors and variability of the remaining factor of production—the theory of optimum population as applied to a dynamic historical societal process is doomed to irrelevance.[19]

Because of the lack of any easy conversion between the individual and collective consequences of population change, the relationship between demography and economics is much less straightforward than is commonly recognized. The observation that, ceteris paribus, smaller families are economically less pressured than larger ones does not necessarily mean that the macro-societal analog is similarly structured. Under certain circumstances, reproductive free riders benefit only so long as most others continue to procreate sufficiently. Thus a person whose income derives from a business that depends on increases in population may individually benefit from sharply curtailing her own fertility but only so long as the rest of society continues to produce more children. Under certain circumstances, a total fertility strike would not only not reduce unemployment in the short run, but, by producing a smaller labor force and diminished demand, might even generate underpopulation-induced unemployment.[20]

Unsurprisingly, few if any analysts believe that anyone has discovered a method for determining what the optimum population is—especially since any per capita welfare optimum would also have to take into account the personal and class distribution of income and the level and distribution of the subjective costs of production including the disruptiveness of cyclical depressions and booms.[21] Indeterminacy of so many intertwined factors prompted one of the chief economic reporters to the U.S. Commission on Population Growth and the American Future to confess agnosticism "regarding an 'economically desirable' family size."[22] Moreover, in a period of intense internationalization, production for and trade with the world market make it possible to escape at least from the limitations of putative national under- or overpopulation. As Beveridge remarked in his debate with Keynes: "The first principle of population to-day is that, under conditions of economic specialisation and international trade, the population problem in any particular country cannot profitably be considered without reference to other countries. The problem in every country is a problem of the distribution of population of the world as a whole."[23] And, finally, the notion of an optimum is made even more complicated by the fact, recognized by orthodox economics as early as Marshall, that "deduction must be made for the growing difficulty of finding solitude and quiet and even fresh air...."[24]

From the narrower vantage point of capital, the notion of an optimum population would have to incorporate elements promoting the development of the forces of production such as the division of labor, cooperation, science, and the proliferation of numerous dense population centers of exchange and thus of optimal scale economies and consumer market size.[25] Indeed, it was on this linkage of increasing population with intensified markets and a deepening division of labor on the one hand and increasing returns on the other that the Ricardian socialist Thomas Hodgskin grounded his refutation of Malthus.[26] For capital in general, an optimum population would therefore have to be conceptualized differently. It would entail a population large enough to forge a labor force that during all phases of the industrial cycle suffices for capital's self-valorization demands without being so redundant that the income required to aliment the reserve armies becomes a drag on capital accumulation: "A demographic Laffer curve, discovered, let us imagine, sketched on a tablecloth in the Hoover Institution canteen, tells us that six-child families are bad for business and zero children bad for business, but somewhere in between is a fertility regime under which the economy can optimally thrive."[27]

When the capital-friendly U.S. domestic population control and zero population growth agenda began to take hold of public opinion in the late 1960s, it was, for reasons of political legitimation, tactically clever to emphasize that whereas the bulk of population growth was accounted for by the contracepting nonpoor, above-average fertility among the poor was not so much a population as a poverty problem.[28] Not all economic demographers, however, were discreet. Joseph Spengler, for example, in a commissioned report to the federal government's Commission on Population Growth and the American Future in 1972, revealed that "[f]ar more important at present than how many people is what kind of people." The segment of the population that stood most in need of demographic exorcising was the "born losers, dependent on the welfare system." This group's disappearance could be expedited by "drying up its sources...."[29] These mere objects of pity are functionally equivalent to Malthus's "unhappy persons," the children of large families which arrived too late for the mythical "original division of land," and who therefore "in the great lottery of life, have drawn a blank."[30]

This Malthusian reinvention of seventeenth-century English poor-law policy and anticipation of mid-1990s' right-wing welfare reform was embedded in a broad attack on labor-protective legislation.[31] Unlike their counterparts in the golden era, before the New Deal, today's "losers" find their access to employment "limited by the requirement that employers pay them, not in keeping with their productivity, but somewhat in line with the wages paid quite productive workers and the living standards shared by the latter."[32]

To the extent that capital can shift the cost of the maintenance of the reserve army on to others,[33] the sustainable optimum population may be enlarged. By the end of the Napoleonic wars, for example, the diminished demand for soldiers and sailors and the increased taxation absorbed by poor law relief meant that "it was by no means so obvious that the increasing numbers of the 'lower orders' was advantageous to the ruling classes."[34] Or as Malthus himself realized, restating the issue of optimum population within the framework of the wage-fund doctrine: "It is not easy to determine what is the price of labour most favourable to the progress of wealth."[35] Likewise, the Depression of the 1930s in the United States revealed the fiscal limits of the reserve army. After mentioning several unemployed people who continued to have children (including triplets), *Time* commented that the "urge to procreate...today provides relief administrators...with one of their toughest and most ticklish problems." Faced with 22 million people on the dole costing the states and federal government $180 million monthly and "producing a quarter of a million children a year...[r]elief administrators want to use scientific birth control to constrain that impoverished sixth of the population" that was accounting for one-third of the next generation. Concerted implementation of such state demographic policy was, however, stymied by "fear of the Roman Catholic Church."[36]

IS DEMOGRAPHIC LAISSEZ FAIRE COMPATIBLE WITH PATRIARCHAL STATE CONTROL OF WOMEN'S SEXUAL AUTONOMY AND REPRODUCTIVE FREEDOM?

> For more than three decades, population scientists have pursued, without much success, that Questing Beast, the psychological determinants of fertility. But like the mythical King Pellinore, we seem to find only the beasts' fewmets.[37]

Before discussing whether capital has a population policy, it is necessary to explore a logically prior question: Is the characterization of capitalism as a laissez-faire reproductive regime merely a time-bound artifact of the period, encompassing the final third of the twentieth century, since the U.S. Supreme Court's constitutionalization of the right to reproductive freedom? Is, then, the characterization of capitalist population policy as laissez faire inconsistent with the legal prohibitions on contraception and abortion in effect for 100 years or more beginning in the mid-nineteenth century? Such a claim hinges on the hidden empirical assumptions that such laws not only were designed as macroeconomic measures to control population, but that they actually significantly interfered with procreation. Finally, it would be necessary to prove that such laws conflicted with the purposes of capitalist population policy by dysfunctionally affecting the supply of wage labor; proponents of the claim would have to show that such laws exerted a negative impact on proletarian reproduction. It would be irrelevant to show merely that restrictions on birth control had an impact on nonworking-class population growth since specifically capitalist population policy is not primarily concerned with the reproduction of the bourgeoisie.

As U.S. fertility and birth rates, which at the outset of the nineteenth century far exceeded any ever registered in Europe, fell after midcentury below those of a number of European countries, some groups voiced concern that this decline was a result of "'prudence' on the part of the community, not as a State, which encourages population, but as individuals."[38] Indeed, even some legislative bodies commented on this trend in connection with penalizing the propagation of contraception and abortion. Such generalizations, however, are not pertinent in this context. For these complaints focused on the decline in fertility among "the native American" population and in particular on the fact that "the more wealthy and intelligent class of married persons limit the number of their children to one or two [through] induced abortions."[39] Contemporary opinion generally believed that middle- and upper-class Protestants were the chief users of abortion in the mid-nineteenth century. Consequently, when, toward the end of that century, abortion again became associated with the poor rather than the higher-income "native" population, it ceased to be "as demographically significant or as socially threatening to men in the policymaking positions...."[40]

The alleged pivotal piece of national anti-birth control legislation, the so-called Comstock Law of 1873 ("An Act for the Suppression of Trade in, and Circulation of, obscene Literature and Articles of immoral Use"), was not driven by any perceived need to interdict the working class's successful efforts to limit their numbers. The congressmen who explained the bill focused their attention on the popular "disgust" for and the need for suppressing the "abomination" of pornographic materials. Representative Merriam, who collaborated with Anthony Comstock in the latter's war on "this pestilential literature," was primarily concerned both that the "purity and beauty of womanhood has been no protection from the insults of this trade" and that nine-year-old children's minds were being polluted. Significantly, when, a half-century later, the birth-control movement agitated on behalf of repeal, one of its principal legislative history points was that not even Comstock himself had intended to penalize the dissemination of "normal birth control information"; rather, his goal had merely been "to free the young people...from contamination by those...trafficking extensively in smutty literature and inducements to sex perversion."[41]

Nor can the Comstock Law and similar state laws be meaningfully interpreted as throwbacks to seventeenth-century mercantilism's "almost fanatic zeal for an increase in population...."[42] Comstockery was not the product of a policy of state self-aggrandizement in a struggle for international competitive supremacy. Hobbes may have argued that the sovereign's duty with regard to "multitude," an aspect of a people's temporal good, was "to increase the people...by ordinances concerning copulation...," but Anthony Comstock did not.[43] Antiabortion laws had more to do with regulating and protecting the public from a medical profession that appeared to be a menace to health than with shaping untoward demographic developments.[44] Similarly, the criminalization of abortion in Britain at the beginning of the nineteenth century was a product, on the one hand, of a humanitarian movement to abolish the law on infanticide, and, on the other, of doctors' professionalization campaign to eliminate rival practitioners. And even if the legislation can also be interpreted as the "ruling classes...asserting their rights to police the reproductive actions of the lower orders" which led to a "decline in women's rights to limit their pregnancies," there is no evidence that it was designed as a specifically capitalist instrument of population control.[45]

It makes no more sense to cast the misogyny inherent in the World War I-era judicial decision (under a state criminal statute banning the dissemination of information about contraception) denying women "the right to copulate with a feeling of security that there will be no resulting conception" as repopulationist than the recent religiously driven "pro-life" movement in the United States.[46] This insight underlies the observation made by Crystal Eastman, a feminist and socialist, during World War I, that although "capitalism thrives on an over-supplied labor market...with our usual enormous immigration to be counted on as soon as the war is over, it is not likely that an organized economic opposition to birth control will develop."[47] Finally, even if Comstockery's intent had been repopulationist, it would have been an outright failure; for "despite Comstock, large families were becoming scarce among native-born Americans even before 1910...."[48]

That a laissez-faire regime of reproduction can coexist with antiabortion and anticontraception laws was made abundantly clear by the position adopted by Margaret Sanger, the leader of the birth control movement in the United States. Despite having been repeatedly prosecuted herself under such statutes, she nevertheless protested what she expressly called the country's laissez-faire population policy:

> We are a nation of business men and women. We believe in efficiency, accuracy, and sound economic policy. [I]t is high time that not only American science but American business as well should begin to analyze the cost to the community of the haphazard, traditional, happy-go-lucky methods in producing the Americans of to-morrow—the *laissez-faire* policy approved by those who forget that the Biblical injunction "be fruitful and multiply" was given to Noah immediately after the Flood, when...the entire population of the globe was eight.[49]

Feminist theoreticians have explored the complexity and contradictoriness of state "populationist (political-economic) and the sexist (patriarchal) dimensions of fertility control policies" in class- and race-divided societies, in which "'pronatalist' and 'antinatalist' policies coincide." Rosalind Petchesky, for example, recognizes that "the policy of imposing patriarchal controls over women's fertility and sexuality is difficult to balance with a policy of population control aimed at the poor or racial minorities. The state's promotion of fertility control measures in the service of populationist ends may unwittingly facilitate their use by the 'wrong' women (ruling-class wives and unmarried daughters), in the service of their sexual and reproductive freedom." State mediation of this conflict between population and sexual control is made even more complicated by the state's need to maintain its legitimacy by accommodating some non-ruling-class demands. As an example, Petchesky mentions the third quarter of the nineteenth century when the decline in birth rates and rise in abortion prompted efforts to discourage birth control among middle-class women and apply negative eugenics to the poor and foreign-born. But it is precisely here that even her critical approach becomes insufficient as Petchesky argues that the class and racial interests of compulsory sterilization as a populationist strategy are transparent: "A poor and unskilled mass of unemployed comprises not only a cheap labor reserve economically but also a potential source of social rebellion...."[50]

This insightful analysis nevertheless fails to explain how the state's visible demographic hand could ever fulfill this mediating role by calibrating and implementing the production of the optimal size of the reserve army at any given time let alone dynamically for 20 years ahead of time. To make the calculation it would, at a minimum, be necessary to know: (1) individual employers' fluctuating demand for such labor and the wages that would insure that the requisite amount of labor would be forthcoming; (2) the aggregate private and societal costs in terms of all the components of the social wage (including unemployment insurance and the non-employment-related welfare system); and (3) the quantitative point at which a functional reserve army of the unemployed is transformed into a gang of mutineers. To list these informational desiderata is to reveal the epistemo-logical—not to mention the practical—hopelessness of the undertaking by the state in a capitalist society constrained by the anarchy of competition among millions of employers and self-legitimational needs to satisfy certain popular expectations that would preclude the kind of mass procreational invasiveness that such proletarian population planning would presuppose. After all, even the mid-twentieth-century planned parenthood organizations that urged the formulation of national population planning shrank back from authoritarian models without explaining how the procreative acts of 100 to 200 million people could be democratically coordinated. It is precisely for these reasons that a laissez-faire regime is consistent with state interference with female sexuality, and that, as Linda Gordon has observed: "Despite the apparent dominance of population-control-eugenics advocates for much of the last century, in fact that group has accomplished very little."[51] The fact that the secular decline in the birth rate continued through and despite decades of patriarchal sex legislation further undermines the claim that such state intervention is incompatible with laissez-faire reproduction.[52]

These complexities have attended population policy at least since industrialization created a contradiction between bourgeois sexual prudery and fear of population. Because birth control would have destroyed the link between the relegation of women to motherhood and sex, the goals of population control and sexual control became "somewhat at odds." The response to Malthus's population theory was doubly divided between radical and liberal attitudes toward social control and between concern for sexual control and population control; consequently, Malthusianism and anti-Malthusianism bore a complicated relationship to each other.[53] Such ideological-legitimational reasons help explain why political actors as disparate as Jeremy Bentham and President Dwight Eisenhower have eschewed state intervention into procreational decisions as coercively inexpedient and wholly improper as a state function or responsibility.[54]

This overlay of demographic policies beholden to conflicting purposes emerged early in the work of James Mill, who is credited with having achieved the merger of political economy and Malthusianism—at least in its neo-Malthusian, that is, pro-birth control form. In his *Elements of Political Economy* Mill was constrained to concede that neither the rewards nor punishment that legislatures had at their disposal

> to alter the course of human actions...is very applicable to the purpose of counteracting the tendency in the human species to multiply. Suppose a law were proposed for annexing penalties to the father and mother of a child, the circumstances of whom were inadequate to its maintenance; it would not be easy to find a mode of punishing, which would be equal to the effect, without producing almost as much uneasiness in society as that which it would propose to remedy: neither would it be very possible to ascertain and define the state of circumstances which is, and that which is not, adequate to the maintenance of one, or two or any other number of children. To apply rewards to the case of not having any children, in such a manner as to operate usefully upon the principle of population, would be still more difficult.[55]

Mill was therefore reduced to propagating the popular sanction of intense approbation and disapprobation "to secure the great body of the people all the happiness which is capable of being derived from the matrimonial union, without the evils which a too rapid increase of their numbers involves."[56]

A century and a half later, the same constraints still restricted the demographic policy universe in polities based on mass legitimation—with the significant modification that advances in birth control technology and the widespread availability of cheap contraceptive devices had displaced the focus of debate to the proper demarcation of the private and public spheres separating the freedom to engage in and the prohibition of certain conduct. In societies pervaded by widely if not universally accepted state regulation of many kinds of individual behavior, "in the sphere of reproduction, complete individual initiative is generally favored even by those liberal intellectuals who...most favor economic and social planning. Social reformers who would not hesitate to force all owners of rental property to rent to anyone who can pay, or to force all workers in an industry to join a union, balk at any suggestion that couples be permitted to have only a certain number of offspring."[57]

DOES CAPITAL HAVE A POPULATION POLICY?

> [D]on't worry, he [the worker] will produce the boy himself, even if not exactly for the entrepreneur's sake! He does not, like other commodity providers of the market, even need to be stimulated by a "profit" to produce this article! He provides it for the sake of the thing itself, if the

thing will just work.[58]

How does capital react in the face of perceived over- or underpopulation? The United States has not witnessed underpopulation propaganda since President Theodore Roosevelt[59] galvanized "race suicide" plaints, accusing "the man or woman who...has a brain so shallow and selfish as to dislike having children [of being] in effect a criminal against the race...."[60] Roosevelt, who later regretted "the profound and lasting damage unwittingly done by Malthus,"[61] castigated those who wished to limit fertility so that the children could "'taste a few of the good things of life"'[62] or "preferred automobiles and lap-dogs and put vapid excitement above the performance of the highest duty...."[63]

These presidential polemics were not, however, prompted by scarcity in the labor market, which was already overflowing with precisely the immigrants whose massive advent, coupled with declining birth rates among the Anglo-Saxon stock, had purportedly brought about the phenomenon that the racialists, eugenicists, antifeminists, and antibirth controllers were lamenting.[64] "[U]nregulated immigration," as labor economist and historian John Commons observed in 1920, was "America's convenient reserve army of the unemployed," which made it unnecessary for employers even to think about planning their utilization of labor while restraining wages and augmenting the surplus for capital.[65] Nor has worldwide labor sourcing lost its functionality for U.S. capital. President Bush's Council of Economic Advisers, for example, reconfirmed in 1990 that: "When labor market mobility is insufficient to eliminate area- or industry-specific labor shortages, employers often turn to immigrants. Throughout U.S. history...immigrants traditionally have adapted well to the U.S. labor market and have contributed significantly to long-run U.S. economic growth." These quasi-exogenous demographic injections have in part, but only in part, been responsible for the fact that the labor market has been "remarkably efficient in adapting to economic change." Consequently, "[l]abor markets typically do not experience long-run imbalances...." Of special relevance here is that these benefits of "the natural workings of the market"[66] flow independently of the "natural workings" of procreation. This reasoning expressly underlay the Immigration Act of 1990, which was designed to meet labor shortages and contribute to the smooth operation of the labor market.[67]

If the United States has not experienced a labor shortage since the closing of the frontier, in Europe eugenicists complained on the eve of World War I that the proliferation of birth control "had destroyed the pressure which carried an English population as the great colonizing force into every quarter of the globe...." Consequently, the absence of "surplus population" meant that no longer would "a boom in the mining industry...be followed, as that of 1871 was, by a rise in the birthrate, but by an immigration of Polish or other foreign workers."[68] At a time when "the woollen and cotton manufacturing towns of England [we]re not reproducing themselves" because wages were "wholly inadequate to maintain" large working-class families, British eugenicists even found it "absurd...to still further reduce the economic value of the child by carrying on his or her school days till 16 years."[69]

European states, in contrast to the United States government, have periodically, in association with undulating industrial cycles and continental military and imperialist rivalries, initiated repopulation campaigns. France, where such campaigns appear to be perpetual, is arguably the best example of the failure of the visible hand of the capitalist state to control reproductive outcomes. From the aftermath of the disastrous Franco-Prussian War of 1871 and the world wars to de Gaulle's call for a doubling of the French population to 100 million, the French people have been impervious to the state's efforts to frustrate their voluntary infertility.[70]

Whereas France and Germany had approximately equal populations on the eve of the Franco-Prussian War of 1871, by World War I, Germans outnumbered the French by 60 percent. Between these once and future military antagonists: "Numbers appeared at the beginning of the twentieth century as a question of life or death...: these are conclusions quite different from that which Malthus's disciples claimed to elevate to an economic law."[71] The other major European powers also recorded much higher rates of increase than France. "Thus, as the First World War was declared, France was already on the eve of committing a national 'suicide' which she had been gradually preparing for more than a century."[72] Paul Leroy-Beaulieu, a leading French economist, worrying about the "relative sterility" that had already overtaken France but remained merely a distant possibility for France's rivals, railed against the feminist movement for having brought about a procreationally perilous "masculinization of the woman"; after all, a stationary economy itself would eventually become "effeminate."[73] In an age of mass armies: "Since numbers were the most easily measurable feature of armies, the decision of the French Assembly of 1872 to have an armed force as numerous as Germany's set going the competition in which each increase of peacetime effectives induced every potential enemy to follow suit, arguing in terms of balance of power politics." This French "rage for numbers"[74] led Messimy, the former War Minister, to introduce a bill in 1912 establishing premiums or an annuity for all mothers with four or more children.[75] Leroy-Beaulieu viewed France's demographic future with such alarm that, despite his reputation as one of the "laissez-faire ultras," he found Messimy's proposal insufficient; instead, he proposed reduced military obligations for the fathers and sons of normal (that is, three-child-or-more) families, reservation of state employment for members of such families, and, since the state budget was already overflowing with bounties for horses and hemp, non-means-tested state bounties for "la production des hommes"—third and higher-parity children.[76]

France's enactment, following World War I, of a repressive criminal statute strictly prohibiting the propagation of contraception and abortions failed to halt the decline of natality despite the fact that the well-developed neo-Malthusian movement had been crushed. The 400,000 abortions performed annually in addition to the widespread and ineradicable practice of coitus interruptus insured that by the 1930s France "was so demographically ill-equipped that there would be little hope of serious sustained resistance to any reasonably prepared and determined invader." As World War II began, France's birthrates were the world's lowest.[77]

At the beginning of the century, Darwinian eugenicists like the Fabian socialist Sidney Webb warned of the British race's "deterioration, if not...suicide" unless the state offered a financial "endowment of motherhood" to avoid "adverse selection."[78] During the Great Depression of the 1930s, when immiseration and widespread contraceptive use made population decline possible, "it [w]as sometimes said that...the final condemnation of capitalism is that under it people are induced to keep their families so small that they no longer replace themselves."[79] The post-World War II British Royal Commission on Population underscored the theme of underpopulation by observing that not even the atomic bomb had eliminated the military significance of numbers: "The radical change in the relative numbers of the French and German peoples...exerted a profoundly important influence on the European balance of power and on wider international affairs." It suggested that below-replacement level fertility in postwar Britain would not only undermine that country's international economic, military, and imperial roles, but as replicated elsewhere in Europe, became "merged in more fundamental issues of the maintenance and extension of Western values, ideas, and culture."[80]

As more recent discussion in France, the center of secular complaints of underpopulation, have made clear, however, state intervention to promote growth may be as legitimationally risky as population control programs. The emergence of widespread support for sexual and procreational autonomy even among nonradical women has made traditional state rhetoric and policy obsolete. The Conseil économique et social recognized, for example, that offering parents 15,000 francs for the birth of a third child might be the most efficacious means of achieving a demographic goal, but because it would be resented by many as a lure and demagogic, its political and social costs would exceed its demographic benefits.[81] Thus in 1970, French Defense Minister Michel Debré, "a leading Gaullist proponent of a population increase to maintain France as a major power" in the face of the country's continued importation of workers from Algeria and the Soviet Union's encouragement of larger families, was "hooted" when he told a convention of women sponsored by *Elle*, France's most popular women's magazine, that "they had a duty to increase the birth rate."[82]

Organized immigration renders underpopulation—that is, a tight labor market that forces employers to increase wages—relatively easy to remedy; indeed, the recruitment of adults whose unproductive youthful consumption years have been financed elsewhere frees up more income for productive investment. As President Nixon's Commission on Population Growth and the American Future, chaired by John D. Rockefeller III, patiently explained to "the business community," with whose opinion the Commission's preference for slower population growth was at variance:

> [T]he historical association of population growth with economic expansion...reflects in large part the fact that periods of rapid economic expansion attracted immigrants to our shores and thus quickened population growth.... Additions to population through immigration are far more stimulating to economic growth than are additions by natural increase...because while babies remain dependent for many years before beginning to contribute to output, many immigrants are of working age and thus become immediately productive.[83]

The primary obstacle to this strategy is political—labor-market oriented working-class opposition and more diffuse nativist-racist counterpropaganda. The silver lining for those concerned about the potential proletarian extinction is, as the neo-Malthusian Paul Ehrlich optimistically observed, that (in case the implementation of his alarmist analysis brought about underpopulation): "Fortunately, people can be produced in vast quantities by unskilled labor who enjoy their work."[84] At the other extreme, overpopulation has historically been amenable to reverse treatment—state-aided emigration. Although the ancient Greek states initiated this practice as far back as the eighth century B.C. and imperialist powers such as Britain continued it, neither the United States nor the advanced European countries are pursuing the possibility.[85]

By the same token, it is unclear that within wide biological limits population really matters to capital—especially in light of the delegitimating repercussions it could expect from any efforts to interfere with what the U.S. Supreme Court has elevated to constitutionally protected individualistic rights both to procreate and not to procreate. For more than a half-century, the Court has declared that reproductive freedom is "one of the basic civil rights of man." And although the Supreme Court initially framed the right as fundamental to "the perpetuation...the very existence and survival of the race," it later transformed the right into an emanation of privacy: "If the right of privacy means anything, it is the right of the *individual*...to be free from unwarranted government intrusion into matters so fundamentally affecting a person as the decision whether to beget a child."[86] The state may override such a right only by reference to one of its own "compelling" interests. In light of the apparently macroreproductive origins or at least implications of this judicially created right, it is noteworthy that a majority of the Supreme Court has asserted, albeit in dictum, that "a State may have legitimate demographic concerns about its rate of population growth. Such concerns are basic to the future of the State and in some circumstances could constitute a substantial reason for departure from a position of neutrality between abortion and childbirth."[87]

Moreover, the most liberal justices in recent decades, Justices Thurgood Marshall and William Brennan, together with the author of the opinion vindicating a constitutional right to abortion, Harry Blackmun, agreed in dissent that it was "conceivable that under some circumstances this might be an appropriate factor to be considered as part of a State's 'compelling' interest...."[88] Significantly, the most prominent American constitutional law scholar, the left-liberal Laurence Tribe, has conceded that collective choice might prevail over individual autonomy "in a period of concern with overpopulation. Government policies narrowly and nondiscriminatorily tailored to limit population growth need not be invalidated by" the aforementioned line of cases.[89] Speculative though such constitutional concessions may be, they must be considered seriously in conjunction with seemingly extreme and undemocratic proposals for implementing zero population growth. Although a compelling case for a universal maximum or minimum two-child policy might be theoretically imaginable, recent uproars over a mandatory reproductive ceiling in the People's Republic of China and quasi-compulsory procreation in Romania under the Ceausescus should serve as an object lesson to agents of capital in the advanced industrial societies that it should focus on other more important and less explosive struggles on its agenda.[90]

By the late 1960s, when Mollie Orshansky's family-size-linked poverty thresholds dominated empirical discourse on the poor in the United States, it had become impossible to ignore the number of children altogether.[91] When the Senate Subcommittee on Foreign Aid Expenditures of the Committee on Government Operations held hearings, entitled *Population Crisis*, in 1965 on the creation of offices of population problems within the Department of State and of Health, Education and Welfare (HEW), "it marked the first time that a committee has dared discuss...the once politically taboo subject of birth control."[92] The tentativeness and fragility of this turning point was symbolized by the fact that ex-President Eisenhower recanted his former opposition to governmental "corrective action in controlling population growth" in order to prevent "human degradation and starvation" and issued a traditionalist poor-law warning about "the repetitive production of children by unwed mothers, apparently lured by the resulting increase in income from welfare funds [which] provid[ed] financial incentive for increased production by the ignorant, feeble-minded or lazy." Eisenhower himself recoiled from the logical consequences of his new position when he acknowledged that legal sterilization as the ultimate effective measure "unquestionably would shock great segments of our citizenry."[93] The timid approach to population control that the Johnson administration implemented was lambasted by Senator Ernest Gruening, the chairman of the subcommittee and the prime congressional mover, who charged that HEW was "afraid" of dealing openly and effectively with population growth.[94]

Even the commission that President Johnson had appointed to study income maintenance programs, which oozed sympathy for the poor, assigned primary causation of poverty to the social-economic structure, and rejected the claim that the poor were to blame for their own circumstances, was constrained to concede that "the costs of supporting a large number of children can result in poverty for workers with even relatively high earnings."[95] Although the suggestion that the economic pressures of procreation burdened even nonpoor families served to detach the stigma of irresponsible overpopulation from a segregated caste of poor, the commission did state that "for many families poverty is a result of having more children—frequently unplanned children—than the parents can adequately support." Its advocacy of subsidized birth control for the poor, however, reinforced the Rockefeller population establishment's notion that as yet the state should not intervene to dampen enthusiasm for wanted children.[96]

The so-called rediscovery of poverty in the United States during the 1960s did, however, prompt a spate of neo-Malthusian admonitions. Thus President Johnson's Committee on Population and Family Planning, in suggesting that (without openly stating explaining why) the poor were the best candidates for birth control, warned that: "Excessive fertility can drive a family into poverty as well as reduce its chances of escaping it."[97] During the peak years of intense interest in the war against poverty and population control, demographers careened to the other extreme, virtually identifying poverty with high fertility. Merely because the Social Security Administration integrated family size into its new definition of poverty, Arthur Campbell, the federal government's chief of natality statistics, drew "attention to the fact that the fertility of the poor will always be high." He corroborated this claim by noting that the fertility rate among the poor was 50-60 percent higher than among the nonpoor in the first half of the 1960s; as a result, the dependency ratio—that is, the number of children under 18 years old for every 100 adults between the ages of 18 and 64—was twice as high. In 1966, for example, 100 poor adults had to provide for 130 children, whereas their nonpoor counterparts had responsibility for only 62. The disproportionate distribution of children was further underscored by the following data from 1964: of the children ever born to 35- to 44-year-old wives of household heads in the lowest family income class (under $2,000), only 15 percent lived in families with two children while 20 percent lived in families with seven or more children; the corresponding shares in the richest income class (over $10,000) were 29 percent and 2 percent.[98]

Perhaps the most sustained policy-driven analysis during this period of the relationship between child-rich families and poverty was undertaken by Harold Sheppard, a social scientist at the Upjohn Institute for Employment Research and staff consultant to the Senate Subcommittee on Employment, Manpower, and Poverty, which turned out more than a score of volumes of testimony and reports in the late 1960s on the War on Poverty. Taking exception to the prevalent view that because large family size was the result of poverty, raising family income was a prerequisite to limiting fertility, Sheppard called attention to the possibility that family size was itself a cause of poverty. Sheppard operated within the contemporary mainstream demographic-sociological conceptualization of urban-bound rural southern blacks as recapitulating "the modernization process" that had ushered in the so-called demographic transition in nineteenth-century Europe and that First World population controllers had begun to urge on the Third World.[99] Viewing the poor within the United States as "somewhat equivalent to the population of a poor nation as a whole," Sheppard argued that birth control was the common policy denominator:

> The increasing gap between most underdeveloped countries
> and the developed ones—a gap resulting in large part from the

differential rates of population growth—might well serve as a model in our attempts to understand how, *within* one country, some parts of the population in poverty fail to move out of poverty while the rest of the country continues to improve. The problem of poverty in such circumstances is not exactly a product of the machinations of "the power structure" or the "system," unless one wishes, of course, to believe that it is to the best interests of the wealthy and powerful that the poor continue to remain poor through a pattern of excessively high fertility rates.[100]

The unexplicated irony to the contrary notwithstanding, the question is not whether some measure of poverty is functional for capitalism, but rather the point at which the political unrest and the tax-financed alimentation of the unemployed become insupportable. Sheppard's program fit comfortably within the Rockefeller demography cartel's agenda, which targeted eliminating unwanted births. A contemporaneous estimate speculated that the "total economic benefit," which consisted of both the incremental annual income which the family would not have to spend to avoid being thrust down into the ranks of the poor by the advent of another child and the additional income that women who avoided pregnancy could earn, exceeded the total costs of the requisite subsidized family planning services by a factor of 26.[101] This analysis appeared to envision the costs as incurred by the public and the benefits as privately inuring to birth-controlling families. To the extent, however, that additional procreation triggers entry into the poor-law system, fertility reduction by eligible candidates for public payments constitutes a saving to the nonpoor including capital. More relevant to capital is the intended proletarianization of mothers, which adds to the labor supply now rather than in 18 to 30 years—that is, a time the labor-market needs of which are as yet unpredictable.

President Nixon inaugurated an unprecedented verbal revolution in U.S. state demographic policy in his special message to Congress on population growth on the eve of the lunar landing in 1969. Nixon not only enunciated the first express national fertility-reduction policy for 5 million poor women in the United States—"[u]nwanted or untimely childbearing is one of several forces...driving many families into poverty or keeping them in that condition"—but also raised the issue of the need for social institutions to plan to house, employ, educate, transport, and provide health care to the next 100 million people "in a humane and intelligent way." Realizing that it was not enough that "[p]erceptive businessmen project the demand for their products many years into the future by studying population trends," Nixon sought to identify the "special responsibility" of the federal government as aggregate capitalist "for defining these problems and stimulating thoughtful responses": "Perhaps the most dangerous element in the present situation is the fact that so few people are examining these questions from the viewpoint of the whole society."[102]

The ambiguities and halfheartedness of the Nixon administration's approach to demographic questions, however, transcended gender. That it remained incapable of tearing away from laissez faire became clear in its initial rhetorical support for and then withdrawal from state intervention to facilitate the deconcentration of the existing population in the United States in order to avoid both regional depopulation and overpopulation. In ultimately accepting the free-market dogma that the sum of individual entrepreneurial investment-locational decisions produces maximum aggregate efficiency, the national government insured that the United States continued to be the only advanced capitalist society to subordinate the illusion of workers' freedom of locational choice to the reality of freedom of corporate choice.[103]

Consistent with the view of political stalemate, the high point of this national family planning movement in the United States was the Family Planning Services and Population Research Act of 1970.[104] Taking as its starting point the claim that low-income families produced more the three children whom most couples in the United States wanted because they lacked access to family planning information and services, Congress failed to go beyond appropriating funds to be made available for voluntary family planning services.[105] This approach was congruent with the goal set forth by President Johnson's Committee on Population and Family Planning, which consisted in "achieving a society in which all parents can have the number of children they want when they want them."[106] Merely bringing fertility in line with procreators' apparent desires—a guideline that scarcely merits being called a population policy[107]—did not, however, meet long-term systemic needs as perceived by John D. Rockefeller III and interpreted by the academic demographers' cartel that his family financed. In 1967 Rockefeller had urged that the real problem was one of "mass motivation. In the long run, it will not be enough to make it possible for women to avoid having unwanted children. Even in a world of wanted children, population may grow too fast. The most effective way to encourage a trend toward smaller families is in...information and education...to build understanding of the problem."[108]

The debate over how expeditiously the Rockefeller program could be implemented became contentious. In particular the unorthodox husband-and-wife sociologist-demographers, Kingsley Davis and Judith Blake, were involved in a dispute with the Rockefeller-founded Population Council over family planning, which in their opinion was too timid and conservative an approach to achieve zero population growth. Already in 1952, when John D. Rockefeller III was organizing the birth-control-oriented Population Council, Davis's effort to conjure up an atmosphere of demographic crisis requiring commensurate action had been crushed.[109] In the 1960s, Davis and Blake's opponents in the demography establishment, whom Davis accused of failing to "break out of the tryanny of what is and think effectively of what can be," were in turn "horrified" by Davis's impetuosity, which they intimated would destroy the opportunity to develop the framework of values without which enduring change was ultimately impossible.[110] As Rockefeller's Commission on Population Growth phrased it: innovation discontinuous with "the fundamental values of American life...would be a Pyrrhic victory indeed."[111]

Davis had a long history of sowing sociodemographic controversy. During the Depression of the 1930s, when underpopulation seemed to be the greater danger, he had sketched a brave new world scenario as an objection to the introduction of effective reproductive subsidies. Assuming that a macro-demographic replacement rate required some families of five and six children, Davis argued that "tremendous sums" would be needed to elicit the requisite procreativity from people who were no longer motivated by the intrinsic emotional value of child-bearing and child-rearing. The initial consequence of such fiscal largesse would "[u]ndoubtedly, as many people fear," be the emergence among "families at the bottom of the social scale" of a literal neo-Roman proletariat who "would find this a delightfully easy method of earning a livelihood." Inexorably, however, this step would set in motion a process leading to state certification and standardization together with professionalization and functional specialization (into bearers and rearers) and ultimately the creation of "a new type of reproductive system compatible with our urban-industrial-mobile social organization." Thus the "logical end-result" of the family allowance system would be the replacement of the familial mode of reproduction by an "efficient" and "eugenic" system. Davis arrived at this conclusion because such pronatalism both shares ruling-class Malthusian suspicions that in every poor person lurks a greedy procreator and assumes that the sole purpose of family allowances is to secure replacement-rate reproduction. Davis therefore saw the regime as pinned between subsidies that are too small to trigger the right reproductive response and too large to preserve familial socialization patterns.[112]

Davis and Blake's common point of attack was mainstream population controllers' superficial focus on "moderniz[ing] demographic behavior...on the basis of greater rationality"[113] by eliminating unwanted births rather than on the more radical step of persuading people to want fewer children. Davis linked his accusation that the orthodox were semantically misleading the public about the reach of their proposals to a rejection of the efficacy of the demographic invisible hand. The political compromise that the pseudo-population planners had made with the ideological status quo traded away effectiveness for immediate acceptability. By labelling as rational whatever number of children parents literally planned to create (and seeking to deal only with the inadvertent excess), the quasi-official population movement "evade[d] the basic question of population policy, which is how to give societies the number of children they need." Devolving responsibility for national population planning on to individual families, who retained an unquestioned right to reproduce on any scale they deliberately chose, was tantamount to the abandonment of planning because there "is no reason to expect that the millions of decisions about family size made by couples in their own interest will automatically control population for the benefit of society. On the contrary...what is rational in the light of a couple's situation may be totally irrational from the standpoint of society's welfare."[114]

The root weakness, according to Davis, of the Rockefeller approach was its failure to smash the ideological icons of family and privacy and its lack of

candor in encouraging the public to believe that individually rational reproduction
sufficed "without the need for painful social changes": "By sanctifying the doctrine
that each woman should have the number of children she wants, and by assuming
that if she has only that number this will automatically curb population growth to
the necessary degree, the leaders of current policies escape the necessity of asking
why women desire so many children and how this desire can be influenced."
Having decided that one-half of the out-of-control procreators were disproportionately responsible for the inordinate desire for children in the United States,
Davis argued that appropriate changes in the social structure and economy would
have to precede any enduring transformation of fertility behavior.   The
"radicalism" that family planners could not imagine proposing did not extend to
abolishing the private appropriation of the societal surplus let alone the
introduction of a "Communist Utopia," but focused on family structure, sexual
mores, and above all the position of women.[115]

In addition to several straightforward reversals of governmental subsidies
for families such as child taxes and high fees for marriage licenses, Davis proposed
a "modification of the complementarity of the roles of men and women." In order
to put an end to men's quasi-monopoly on a participation in the wider world that
was based on women's (self-)assignment to housework and motherhood, "women
could be required to work outside the home, or compelled by circumstances to do
so." If given equal opportunities and pay, and "if social life were organized around
the place of work rather than around the home or neighborhood, many women
would develop interests that would compete with family interests."[116] For Davis,
the increase in female labor force participation rates was purely instrumental: it was
designed to reduce fertility. Although this ulterior motive might not necessarily
make it less effective, the obligatory proletarianization that Davis presciently
mentioned was indirect. By using its command over the economy, the state can use
its power to determine economic conditions including "how much individuals can
spend."[117]

Even as Davis was throwing down the gauntlet, the flow of married
women and mothers into paid employment was becoming effective in depressing
the total fertility rate below the replacement rate, without even requiring direct state
intervention: the inability of even small families to secure an adequate standard of
living based on only one wage-earner's income has, together with a transformation
in women's consciousness, driven female labor participation rates to a record high:
"A family lifestyle dependent on two incomes has become the norm in American
society."[118] As a soon-to-be Secretary of Labor disclosed in the mid-1970s: "How
are multiworker family members...'hooked'? A standard of living clearly beyond
the reach of the average wage earner is urged upon them not only by manufacturers
and retailers...but also by the government, which publicizes appealing standards of
living."[119]

The mid-1970s marked a watershed: dual-worker married couples
surpassed the "traditional" family in which only the husband is in the labor force
as the modal family pattern. If in 1940 almost seven families in ten were of the

traditional type and only one-tenth dual-earners, by the end of the 1980s, the latter were twice as common as the former.[120] From 1970 to 1990, the labor force participation rate of wives with children under six years doubled from 30 percent to 59 percent while that of childless wives increased only from 42 percent to 51 percent. During the brief period from 1976 to 1990, the participation rate of mothers who had given birth during the previous 12 months rose from 31 percent to 53 percent.[121] From 1970 to 1992, the proportion of married couples with children under six years of age working year-round full-time more than tripled—from 7 percent to 24 percent.[122] Alone from 1975 to 1988, the proportion of married couples with children under 18 years of age in which only the father was in the labor force fell from 53 percent to 33 percent, while that of dual-earner families rose from 43 percent to 63 percent.[123] By 1992, in 69 percent of married-couple families with children both parents worked; in 30 percent of them both worked full-time year-round.[124]

The differences among income groupings are instructive. From 1970 to 1986, for example, the proportion of (full-time year-round) one-worker married couples with children fell from 66 percent to 57 percent, while that of two-worker families rose continuously from 14 to 26 percent. Whereas the share of two-worker married couples with children within the highest income quintile and the middle three quintiles increased from 29 percent to 44 percent and from 13 percent to 26 percent respectively, in the lowest income quintile the share rose only from 5 percent to 7 percent. This differentiation is underscored from another perspective. From 1970 to 1986, the average number of full-time year-round workers among married couples with children in the lowest income quintile actually declined slightly from 0.63 to 0.61, whereas the corresponding increase in the average for the three middle quintiles and the highest quintile was 0.99 to 1.18 and 1.31 to 1.45 respectively. While earnings failed to keep pace with inflation for many families, the "rise in the number of workers per family appears to be the principal reason why incomes increased."[125]

Indeed, even this unprecedented entry of wives and mothers into paid employment has proved inadequate to sustain the standard of living, thus inducing millions to work at two or more jobs. Whereas in 1970, almost six times as many men as women were multiple job holders, by 1996 not only were they almost evenly divided, but women's rate of multiple job-holding marginally exceeded men's.[126] Mothers this busy making the difference "between welfare and getting by" apparently lack the time for heroic reproductive feats.[127]

Thus the "hunger" that even liberal economists sought to enlist to motivate AFDC mothers to work could also be brought to bear against working-class mothers. This same insight made headway in Britain in the 1970s. When, despite the existence of family allowances for more than three decades, the Royal Commission on the Distribution of Incomes and Wealth rediscovered the concentration of poverty in families with more three or more children, the first policy choice was to increase mothers' labor force participation. Capital, as Marx observed, has its own mechanisms for making itself relatively independent of biological increases in population.[128]

Davis's views soon acquired sufficient notoriety to attract an interview with *The New York Times*. He reiterated that the chief barrier to reduced fertility was not technological but motivational. In order to effectuate his goal of making large families undesirable or impossible, Davis repeated his proposal of financial incentives such as the elimination of income tax disadvantages for childless taxpayers or the introduction of a child tax. Paul Ehrlich went even further, proposing both child taxes and luxury taxes on cribs and diapers. Emblematic of the hopelessness of such a radical approach was the failure of even Senator Robert Packwood's 1970 bill prospectively to cap the number of income tax exemptions for dependent children at two. Senate Bill 3632, which was designed to place the federal government's imprimatur on smaller families, was a pendant to two other bills to create governmental responsibility for making contraceptive devices available to every man or woman regardless of economic circumstances by initiating "massive family planning" and to insure every woman the back-up opportunity to terminate unwanted pregnancies by removing legal restrictions on abortions nationwide. Although Packwood's target of zero population growth was ostensibly motivated by a desire to "waylay[] our environmental doom" caused by Americans' overconsumption, he stressed that his program would exert its most dramatic impact on poor blacks, whose rate of unwanted of pregnancies was more than twice as high as among nonpoor whites.[129]

A charge from Rockefeller's Commission on Population Growth to report on the relationship between the family and demographic change furnished Davis with his ultimate opportunity *pour épater le bourgeois*. Harking back to his heterodox views of 1937, Davis gleefully observed that fertility was so much higher than mortality because the family as an atavistic, "primitive" institution was "performing its replacement function too well. Advocacy of the kinds of changes that would dampen the family's reproductive efficiency was, however, "not appreciated." Such lack of gratitude did not deter him from sketching a "complete reform of the human family...the best of two worlds—the insect world and the human world"—in which professional female childbearers and specialized child rearers would liberate the rest of society from reproductive chores. If his suggestion that antinatalism could be effective only by campaigning for changes that would militate against family formation did not succeed in alienating Chairman Rockefeller, Davis's reminder that "[t]he institution of inheritance would not apply" in his radically reformed society presumably did.[130]

Blake's contribution was also irreconcilable with the Rockefeller program's short-term vision. She, too, started from the proposition that the overpopulation problem was rooted not in the failure to close the gap between actual births and wanted births, but in the family-size goals themselves. To reduce the number of desired births it was necessary to identify and neutralize the underlying institutionalized coercive familial pronatalism. Pronatalism was underwritten by the standardization of gender-specific reproductive and occupational roles, which propelled the vast majority into procreation. Coercion was manifest, for example, in school indoctrination and the threat of loneliness. The mere fact that people are socialized in families predisposes them to internalize familial norms and to look forward to performing parental roles themselves. Underestimation of the noneconomic utilities attached to childrearing such as the achievement of the quasi-prescribed social statuses of parents and especially of feminine creativity misled policy-makers. Such motivations accounted for the fact that a minuscule proportion of the population desired celibacy or childlessness. Rather than proposing new policies, Blake pleaded simply for lifting penalties on already existing antinatalist tendencies, the most potent of which she presciently identified in feminism. Antinatalism involved not only making children more expensive but also less rewarding. Since she believed that pricing children off the market was impractical in a wealthy society, Blake focused on altering the reward structure—enabling especially women to derive status and self-esteem from nonreproductive activities.[131]

Although Blake and Davis seemed to be articulating the same demographic objectives as the Rockefeller population establishment, which placed great emphasis on systematically laying the groundwork for winning the hearts and genitalia of the American people, their insistence on bluntness and precipitate transvaluation of family values and their refusal to abide by the July 4th shibboleths cast them in the role of outcasts. The stylistic gap between Davis and Blake on the one hand and the mainstream neo-Malthusians on the other is captured by the closing sentence of the report submitted by President Johnson's Committee on Population and Family Planning that Rockefeller co-chaired: "In working to avoid a population crisis, this nation will...help strengthen the voluntary exercise of a basic human right, the right of parents to have the number of children they want, when they want them." By the same token, the Nixon-Rockefeller Commission, in an admittedly confused and confusing exposition of the common denominator sheltering the views of all its members, did state that its overall perspective was consistent with the position that aimed at a national debate "to achieve the best collective decision about population issues...."[132]

Rufus Miles, Jr., the chairman of the board of trustees of the Population Reference Bureau, while echoing some of the same themes as Davis and Blake, came closer to capturing the essence of the Rockefeller approach. Recognizing that the free market and freedom of choice were not conferring demographic benefits on the United States, Miles concluded that either free choice would have to be abandoned or the minds of the reproductive free choosers would have to be reoriented. Since coercive regulation of family size was clearly counterproductive in a representative democracy whose overwhelming majority would oppose it, Miles was forced to opt for "the long, uphill route of encouraging the American people to modify their basic attitudes and behavior...." The chief motivational impediment to zero population growth was that "[u]nfortunately, couples do not seek their self-interest in economic terms alone"; because people in search of psychic rewards were willing to pay dearly to buy children, the chief task was "to persuade couples to act more in their own economic self-interest...." Arguably the most promising prospect for deconstructing those once socializationally indispensable but now intractable psychic rewards and converting them into economic rewards more easily accessible to macroeconomic management was to focus on those "[m]any parents—primarily mothers—[who] seek large families as a psychic defense against lack of interesting employment, lack of a sense of belonging to a satisfying social group, or lack of other forms of self-realization." Even more explicitly than Blake, Miles therefore made the enlargement of better paid employment opportunities for women the centerpiece of the initiative to reduce family size.[133]

  One of the reasons that the state in the United States did not make explicit its implicitly pronatalist population policy, even after the demise of the quarter-century post-World War II Keynesian boom, is that capital itself was unable to articulate its own unified or at least dominant policy. This fractioning was due in large part to the fact that the demand for the output of individual firms and industries would be affected in spectacularly different ways by population growth, stagnation, or decline. And although it appears plausible that capital would be less disunited with regard to proposals to limit the *faux frais* that are financed by state confiscation of accumulatable surplus, the groups of high-profile capitalists and managers that began in the 1960s to mobilize public opinion in favor of birth control in order to curtail population growth and reduce taxes have yet to achieve the material success they sought.[134] Thus it may be ideologically satisfying to imagine the Rockefeller population control initiative as effecting a change in the state's role in accordance with "the shifting interests and strategies of the dominant groups in society.... Members of the capitalist class, acting mainly through philanthropic organizations, articulate a strategy of population planning consistent with the needs of capitalist society." But the problem, both for individual capitals and even more so for social capital in general, as represented by the ideal aggregate capitalist, the state, is identifying those needs not only or so much in the present, but 20 years later when the results of the new population policy will make themselves felt in the labor market. Undocumented and unsupported allegations concerning "the current mode of capital accumulation [for which] there is no longer a necessity to reproduce a growing labor force" do not advance analysis—especially when they are immediately contradicted ("[c]onsistencies are not ironclad") by the concession that "growth in retail and service sectors is fueled by a large pool of unorganized women...."[135]

  The Nixon-Rockefeller Commission on Population Growth appeared to believe that it had devised a way to avoid legitimational entanglements. Because it wanted to moderate population growth, it could advertise that its "immediate goal" was merely "to modernize demographic behavior...: to encourage the American people to make population choices, both in the individual family and society at large, on the basis of greater rationality rather than tradition or custom, ignorance or chance." One "outmoded tradition" that the Commission designated "no longer appropriate" was "formal and informal pronatalist pressures." But especially when such traditional behavioral constraints were denounced as "coercive," the Commission's approach was bound to conflict with a newly refurbished ideology of family values that cut across the party-political spectrum.[136]

More particularly, the rise of a politically potent antiabortion movement may have made the Commission's strategy moot; it may also explain why ultimately Nixon himself rejected the Rockefeller Commission's acceptance of abortion as an instrument of population control.[137] If, as economist Victor Fuchs believes, optimum population size is only one of many population policy concerns and "one of the least important for the United States," then the Commission's game may not be worth the candle: "Many people are likely to regard the question of the method used to influence population size as far more important than that of size itself."[138] Given the perceived heavy-handedness of state intervention into a solidly protected sphere of privacy that would be required to achieve collective control over fertility, proponents have acted strategically in seeking to conjure up the atmosphere of demographic crisis that alone would justify action:

> If the means to influence fertility must fall within the range of policies exemplified by (1) mutually agreed upon coercive programs, (2) massive propaganda campaigns that convince parents that having more than two children somehow constitutes a nonpatriotic or at least socially irresponsible act, or (3) social reforms expressly designed to weaken the institution of the family, then, to be taken seriously, impending disaster must be invoked.[139]

The failure to make the prospect of such a disaster plausible to the masses both solidifies the claim as to the closure of the realpolitical demographic universe and rehabilitates Marx's view that given the spontaneous, immanent mechanisms that capital has at its disposal to deal with its labor requirements, capitalism can rely on the working class's proclivity to procreate for the constant reproduction of the working class as a constant condition for the reproduction of capital.[140] More interesting than a vindication of Marx, however, is the possibility that the capitalist class and the labor movement have come to agree with his assessment of the relative irrelevance of fertility. In the United States, capital has for many decades accommodated its changing labor requirements largely by means of uncontrolled, controlled, and even special occupationally tailored immigration.[141] Not underpopulation or, more accurately, a wage-tested general scarcity of labor, has driven population policy. Instead, debate has focused on the other chief variable, limiting the *faux frais* of accumulation in the form of modern poor law subsidies of the surplus surplus-value producers—that is to say, a nonfunctionally and increasingly dysfunctionally large reserve army of the unemployed.[142] This perspective emerged clearly in 1965 when Planned Parenthood's Commerce & Industry Committee, "a blue-chip group of 41 top businessmen" led by Sidney Swensrud, the former chairman of Gulf Oil Corporation, issued a report, made public by Lammot du Pont Copeland, the president of Du Pont, demonstrating large capital's intensifying interest in domestic birth control. As Swensrud told *Business Week*:

"[B]usinessmen are all too aware of the mounting costs of relief and welfare programs; they are major sources of the taxes needed to sustain these programs. Birth control is the key to reducing these costs through reducing the number of unwanted children born to the poor and poorly educated; this group...represents our most critical population problem."[143]

Two years later, the Deputy Assistant Secretary for Family Planning and Population in the Johnson administration was able to report to Congress that this new unit within HEW was "encouraged that declines in birth rate are registered in areas of the lowest educational attainment—the highest incidence of poverty...the largest number of children per family."[144]

The same period witnessed concerted efforts by other representatives of capital, including the Rockefeller interests, to press the same domestic agenda.[145] In Europe, in contrast, capital has periodically feared absolute scarcities of labor caused by low domestic fertility. But to the extent that labor and racial politics have induced European employers to supplement the importation of cheaper labor from the East and South with family allowance systems, there is little evidence that such subsidies have ever materially promoted domestic procreation.[146]

Labor unions, too, displayed demographic agnosticism. At the height of the clamor for population control under the Nixon administration, the United Automobile Workers, pressing for an Economic Bill of Rights providing for a useful job and a guaranteed annual income for all, told the Commission on Population Growth and the American Future that neither unlimited population growth nor stabilization had ever eliminated deprivation or unemployment: "The problem has always been...that we have never really properly planned for people in this country, either as job holders or as residents, regardless of what size the population was, is, or will be." And the AFL-CIO itself approached the neutral or agnostic position by rejecting both population growth and reduction as well as any policy that deviated from voluntarism.[147]

As fears of overpopulation career toward demands for remedies of underpopulation in sync with the intersection of phases of the industrial cycle and more secular changes, it becomes plausible that capital may be in no better position to articulate demographically rational projections for its own interests than are individual procreators. As Marshall, with a century's hindsight understood, neither individual capitals nor the aggregate capitalist may know what is demographically optimal for them or it in the present let alone the future. In Malthus's time, according to Marshall, "while the recruiting sergeants and employer of labour were calling for measures tending to increase the growth of population, more far-seeing men began to inquire whether the race could escape degradation if the numbers continued long to increase as they were then doing." Demographic agnosticism is even more impressively displayed by demographers' inability at the end of the twentieth century to decide whether the United States would be better off if population growth had ceased at the beginning of the century.[148]

Radical swings in demographic opinion have been common. Before

World War I, increases in population were widely held to promote prosperity, whereas the post-World War I period, even in the absence of "a fundamental change in the economic system," witnessed a widespread official perception that growing numbers were a burden.[149] During the 1930s, eugenicists warned that not only were the United States and other "civilized countries" failing to replace those dying, but that the "feeble-minded" were out-reproducing "educated people."[150] In 1955, near the zenith of the post-World War II baby boom (which was merely a resumption of birth rates antedating the historical low point reached during the Great Depression of the 1930s), *Time* declared that: "Only a few years ago a rate of population increase as high as the present one would have brought howls of impending calamity." Although the magazine conceded that the relationship between population and economic growth was little understood, "enough is known to discredit Malthus.... The lingering worry is whether [society] will have enough people to consume the goods." So little agreement obtained concerning the economic consequences of population change that at the same time Joseph Spengler, the leading demographic historian in the United States, cautioned that continued population growth would intensify economic problems, which in turn would trigger state intervention. During the height of the cold war he warned that "the stork would have managed to do what the followers of Marx had found themselves unable to do for all they tried—fasten fetters on mankind."[151]

Even more poignantly, the ruling West German Social Democratic Party, under attack in 1980 by the Christian Democrats for having failed to stem the decline in population, retorted that the net reproduction rate could not be influenced by state measures.[152] Moreover:

> We Social-Democrats do not want a population policy, we also do not need a population policy. We don't want to raise children in order to secure the defense capability of the Federal Republic. We also don't want to raise children in order to guarantee the contract between the generations in pensions insurance.... We also don't need a population policy in order to furnish the labor market with workers or to have sufficient consumers of produced mass goods.... Why actually should it be disadvantageous for the labor market if rationalization by means of micro processors no longer has to lead to intensified unemployment?[153]

This hands-off approach is congruent with another view prevalent in Germany and elsewhere according to which no population policy, no matter how indirect, can ever be justified in a democratic republic. The basis for such a rejection is rooted in the conviction that if the majority through its behavior demonstrates, for example, that it does not share the state's goal of maintaining demographic stability, it would be impossible democratically to legitimate the enforcement of the underlying set of values which the citizenry no longer regards as binding. Nor, it is argued, can the general welfare or common good serve as a justification because it, too, would have to derive from the same deeply rooted values.[154]   A potential flaw in this reasoning is its tacit assumption that the individuals whose billion-fold exercise of the right to procreational self-determination aggregates to a condition that the state characterizes as under-population or overpopulation are fully aware and approve of the consequences. If in fact they did understand and accept the manifold collective ramifications of their individualistic behavior, it seems implausible that they would have elected a government that radically disagrees with them on such a life-and-death question; but if such a situation actually came to pass, it might easily be granted that the state's dictatorial imposition of a four-child or a one-child policy cannot be justified.[155]   As Myrdal put it: "In a democracy a population policy is a contradictio in adjecto if, when a true understanding of the population trend is disseminated...the broad masses...do not react...in a positive way."[156]

      This need to build deep-rooted popular support for a policy that invades the sacred precincts of sexuality and family pervaded the Rockefeller domestic U.S. population program and in part explains that group's disagreement with what it perceived as Blake's and Davis's hopelessly premature and radically discontinuous proposals.   It is, for example, no longer politically possible to argue quasi-fascistically, as a noted statistician did in the 1920s, that in the demographic "conflict between the immediate interests of the individual and the more permanent interests of the State...[w]e may express our freedom as individuals only within the limitations that the continued existence of the State is assured."[157]

      Where, however, one generation of individualists does not comprehend the dire societal implications for itself or those to follow, then state efforts to educate (and debate) the citizenry and to implement ancillary policies to encourage or discourage childbearing and -raising would assume a different political-moral quality.   Such state intervention vis-à-vis individualists exercising their self-vindicated freedom to bestow any number of children on the world and to expect society to "accommodate the macrodemographic results of microdemographic decisions"[158] would nevertheless presuppose what no one has yet demon-strated—that any advanced capitalist country either is under- or overpopulated or faces any aggregate demographic crisis that requires urgent, immediate, collectivistic measures that cannot be comfortably assimilated to received notions of individualistic freedom.[159]

      As Rockefeller himself later noted of his Commission's recommenda-tions: "[W]e saw no threat to the business or to the welfare of the people...by the population continuing to decline, if it was done in an orderly fashion over a period of years." The failure of the Rockefeller program to convince the masses of any impending grave generalized population crisis in the United States, and the partial collapse of the population control movement into right-wing, racist-tinged antitax, antiwelfare groups may—together with a fertility rate that plunged below replacement level—explain why the movement has receded into oblivion.[160] Indeed, the simultaneous emergence of the antiabortion movement is profoundly ironic since not only does it lack a basis in population policy, but implementation of its program would presumably bring about an increase in population of precisely those racial-ethnic and class groupings that protested in the 1960s and 1970s that they were the targets of genocidal demographic conspiracies.

NOTES

1. John Maynard Keynes, "The End of Laissez-Faire," in *idem, Essays in Persuasion* 312-22 at 312, 319 (1963 [1926]).

2. Alexander Gray, *Family Endowment: A Critical Analysis* 107 (1927); W.H. Beveridge, *Unemployment: A Problem of Industry* (1909 and 1930) 4 (new ed. 1930 [1909]).

3. Annexe No. 1936, in *Annales de la Chambre des Députés: Documents parlementaires*, 83: Session ordinaire, Première partie, at 1256, 1258 (1912).

4. A.C. Pigou, *The Economics of Welfare* 172 (4th ed. 1962 [1920]).

5. Vegelahn v. Guntner, 44 N.E. 1077, 1081 (Mass. 1896) (Holmes, J., dissenting).

6. Lionel Robbins, "The Optimum Theory of Population," in *London Essays in Honour of Edwin Cannan* 103-34 at 108 (T. Gregory & Hugh Dalton ed., 1927).

7. See e.g., *ibid.* at 124; A.B. Wolfe, "On the Criterion of Optimum Population," *Am. J. Sociology* 39 (5):585-99 (Mar. 1934); Simon Kuznets, "Population Change and Aggregate Output," *Demographic and Economic Change in Developed Countries* 324-40 at 339 (1960); Mark Blaug, *Economic Theory in Retrospect* 75 (4th ed. 1985 [1962]). Most of the contributors to *Is There an Optimum Level of Population?* (S. Fred Singer ed. 1971) appeared to believe that there may be optima, but that they changed over time and along various axes.

8. Beveridge, *Unemployment* at 375-76; Gunnar Myrdal, *Population: A Problem for Democracy* 143-44 (1940). See also Harvey Leibenstein, *A Theory of Economic-Demographic Development* 188 (1954).

9. Frank Lorimer, "Issues of Population Policy," in *The Population Dilemma* 143-78 at 167-68 (Philip Hauser ed. 1965 [1963]).

10. Kingsley Davis, "'Ideal Size' for Our Population," *N.Y. Times Magazine*, May 1, 1955, § 4, at 12-37 at 37.

11. Jack Rosenthal, "Nixon Signs Bill Creating Commission on Population," *N.Y. Times*, Mar. 17, 1970, at 26, col. 3-6.

12. Julian Simon, *The Economics of Population Growth* 410, 418, 425, 476, 488-89 (1977).

13. *Cong. Rec.* 116:20332, 20335 (1970) (statement of Sen. Tydings). Congress did not even vote on S.J. Res. 214.

14. Maurice Dobb, *Papers on Capitalism, Development and Planning* 55-56 (1970 [1967]).

15. Myrdal, *Population* at 140; *Declaration of U.S. Policy of Population Stabilization by Voluntary Means, 1971: Hearings Before the Special Subcommittee on Human Resources of the Senate Committee on Labor and Public Welfare*, 92d Cong., 1st Sess. 276 (1972) (prepared statement by Alan Sweezy); Leibenstein, *A Theory of Economic-Demographic Development* at 174.

16. James Mill, *Elements of Political Economy* (3d ed. 1826), in *idem, Selected Economic Writings* 242 (Donald Winch ed. 1966).

17. Knut Wicksell, *Vorlesungen über Nationalökonomie auf Grundlage des Marginalprinzips: Theoretischer Teil* 1:49-50 (Margarethe Landfeldt tr., 1969 [1913]); Edwin Cannan, *Wealth: A Brief Explanation of the Causes of Economic Welfare* 67-71 (1914).

18. John Maynard Keynes, "Is Britain Overpopulated?" *New Republic* 36:247-248 at 248 (Oct. 31, 1923). During the Great Depression, Keynes ahistorically absolutized his position: "Unquestionably a stationary population does facilitate a rising standard of life...." J.M. Keynes, "Some Economic Consequences of a Declining Population," *Eugenics Rev.* 29 (1):13-17 (Apr. 1937).

19. Gerhard Mackenroth, *Bevölkerungsiehre: Theorie, Soziologie und Statistik der Bevölkerung* 322-24 (1953).

20. Robert Kuczynski, *Population Movements* 65-79 (1936).

21. Hugh Dalton, "The Theory of Population," *Economica* 8 (22):28-50 at 31 (Mar. 1928); James Mirrlees, "Population Policy and the Taxation of Family Size," *J. Pub. Econ.* 1:169-98 at 171 (1972).

22. Allen Kelley, "Demographic Changes and American Economic Development: Past, Present and Future," in U.S. Commission on Population Growth and the American Future, *Research Reports: Economic Aspects of Population Change* 2:9-44 at 15 (Elliott Morss & Ritchie Reed eds., 1972). See also Ansley Coale, "Population and Economic Development," in *The Population Dilemma* 46-69 at 59 (Philip Hauser ed., 1965 [1963]).

23. W.H. Beveridge, "Population and Unemployment," *Econ. J.* 33:447-75 at 468 (1923).

24. Alfred Marshall, *Principles of Economics* 267 (8th ed. 1969 [1890]).

25. Karl Marx, *Ökonomische Manuskripte 1857/58*, in Karl Marx [&] Friedrich Engels, *Gesamtausgabe (MEGA)*, II/1.2:496, 635, 637 (1981); Kuznets, "Population Change and Aggregate Output" at 326; Kelley, "Demographic Changes" at 15-18; Harvey Leibenstein, "The Impact of Population Growth on the American Economy," in Commission on Population Growth and the American Future, *Research Reports: Economic Aspects of Population Change* 2:49-65 at 56-58.

26. Élie Halévy, *Thomas Hodgskin* 58-62 (1956); Scott Gordon, "The London Economist and the High Tide of Laissez Faire," *J. Pol. Econ.* 63 (6):461 (Dec. 1955).

27. Geoffrey McNicoll, "Economic Growth with Below-Replacement Fertility," in *Below-Replacement Fertility in Industrial Societies: Causes, Consequences, Policies* 217-37 at 217 (Kingsley Davis et al. ed., 1986).

28. Rufus Miles, Jr., "Whose Baby Is the Population Problem?" *Pop. Bull.* 36 (1):1-36 at 18 (Apr. 1970).

29. Joseph Spengler, "Declining Population Growth: Economic Effects," in Commission on Population Growth and the American Future, *Research Reports: Economic Aspects of Population Change* 2:91-133 at 119-20.

30. Thomas Robert Malthus, *An Essay on the Principle of Population* (1st ed.), in *idem, On Population* 74 (Gertrude Himmelfarb ed., 1960 [1798]).

31. See below ch. 4 and 10.

32. Spengler, "Declining Population Growth" at 119-20. Just as Spengler expects the disappearance, if not of the "losers" themselves, then at least of their unemployment as soon as employers are liberated from the shackles of productivity-suppressing state intervention, Simon asserts that minimum wage laws are migrant farm workers' worst enemy. Julian Simon, "New Cure for the Jobs Shortage, " in *idem, Population Matters: People, Resources, Environment, and Immigration* 256-60 (1990 [1988]). For a critique of such views, see Marc Linder, *Migrant Workers and Minimum Wages: Regulating the*

Exploitation of Agricultural Labor in the United States (1992).

33. Marx, *Ökonomische Manuskripte 1857/58* at 497-98. Denying that the costs of the reserve army of the unemployed are a "class issue, in which the interest of the capitalist economic elite differs from that of the lower, or working, classes" proves too much because it transforms any specifically capitalist question into a supra-class issue whenever the tax system permits capital to impose part of the costs onto other classes. Irwin Garfinkel & Sara McLanahan, *Single Mothers and Their Children: A New American Dilemma* 88 n.1 (1986).

34. Mabel Buer, "The Historical Setting of the Malthusian Controversy," in *London Essays in Economics in Honour of Edwin Cannan* 137-53 at 147.

35. Thomas Robert Malthus, *An Essay on the Principle of Population* (6th ed.), in *The Works of Thomas Robert Malthus* 3:618 (E.A. Wrigley & David Souden eds., 1986 [1826]).

36. "Relief and Babies," *Time* 25 (14):30, 32 (Apr. 8, 1935).

37. Frederick Campbell, Brenda Townes, & Lee Beach, "Motivational Bases of Childbearing Decisions," in *The Childbearing Decision: Fertility Attitudes and Behavior* 145-59 (Greer Fox ed., 1982).

38. Ansley Coale & Melvin Zelnik, *New Estimates of Fertility and Population in the United States: A Study of Annual White Births from 1855 to 1960 and of Completeness of Enumeration in the Censuses from 1880 to 1960*, at 32-41 (1963); Horatio Storer, "On the Decrease of the Rate of Increase of Population Now Obtaining in Europe and America," *Am. J. Sci.*, 2d ser., 43 (128):141-55 at 146 (Mar. 1867 [1858]) (quote).

39. "Additional Report from the Select Committee to Whom was Referred S. B. No. 285," *The Journal of the Senate of the State of Ohio* 63:233 (1867) (Appendix).

40. James Mohr, *Abortion in America: The Origins and Evolution of National Policy, 1800-1900*, at 90-95, 240, 243 (1978).

41. Act of Mar. 3, 1873, ch. 258, 17 Stat. 598 (making it a misdemeanor to sell, give away, exhibit, or publish any obscene book or "any drug or medicine, or any article whatever, for the prevention of conception, or for causing unlawful abortion..."); *Cong. Globe*, 42d Cong., 3d Sess. 1525, 1437 (1873) (Sen. Conklin & Sen. Thurman); *Cong. Globe*, 42d Cong., 3d Sess. Appendix 168-69 (1873) (Merriam); Mary Dennett, *Birth Control Laws: Shall We Keep Them, Change Them or Abolish Them* 20, 19 (1926). On the general Christian moral campaign of which Comstockery was a part, see C. Thomas Dienes, *Law, Politics, and Birth Control* 20-48 (1972).

42. 2 Eli Heckscher, *Merkantilismen: Ett led i den ekonomiska politikens historia* 140 (1931).

43. Thomas Hobbes, *De corpore politico or the Elements of Law*, in 4 *The English Works of Thomas Hobbes* 214 (William Molesworth ed., 1841 [1640]).

44. Mohr, *Abortion in America* at 31-32. For a different but less well-researched and persuasive approach, see John Harper, "Be Fruitful and Multiply: Origins of Legal Restrictions on Planned Parenthood in Nineteenth-Century America," in *Women of America: A History* 245-69 (Carol Berkin & Mary Norton eds., 1979). A depopulationist abortion activist in the 1960s claimed, based on only two abortion decisions, that: "Obviously, the courts considered an expanding popoulation a primary objective of these statutes. [T]he United States needed factory workers to fill the volcanic demands after the Civil War, and agricultural hands to sow and reap the vast new frontiers in the West." Lawrence Lader, Abortion 88-89 (1966). Lader overlooks the fact that one decision antedated the Civil War by 15 years and the other was handed down six decades later. Moreover, both opinions are so heavily laden with religio-moral rhetoric that interpreting them in instrumental-industrial

rather than biblical terms is acontextual.

45. Angus McLaren, *Reproductive Rituals: The Perception of Fertility in England from the Sixteenth Century to the Nineteenth Century* 113-44 (1984) (quotations at 113 and 144).

46. People of New York v. Margaret Sanger 26, Margaret Sanger Papers, Smith College, quoted in James Reed, *From Private Vice to Public Virtue: The Birth Control Movement and American Society Since 1830*, at 107 (1978).

47. Crystal Eastman, "Birth Control in the Feminist Program," in *Crystal Eastman on Women and Revolution* 46-49 at 49 (Blanche Cook ed., 1978 [1918]).

48. Peter Fryer, *The Birth-Controllers* 200 (1965).

49. Margaret Sanger, "Is Race Suicide Possible?" *Collier's*, Aug. 15, 1925, at 25.

50. Rosalind Petchesky, *Abortion and Woman's Choice: The State, Sexuality, and Reproductive Freedom* 69, 16, 69, 71, 78, 88 (rev. ed. 1990 [1984]). See also Ruth Dixon-Mueller, *Population Policy and Women's Rights: Transforming Reproductive Choice* 33 (1993): "The women's movement...has been caught in a double bind on the birth control question, largely because the feminist concept of fertility control as an individual, autonomous act of empowerment has been eclipsed by the political concept of population control as a public policy imposed by governmental authorities or other ruling elites."

51. Linda Gordon, *Woman's Body, Woman's Right: A Social History of Birth Control in America* 346-47, 417 (quotation) (1981 [1974]). The claim that "birth control is...integral to the rational economic planning of capitalism" and "the consequent need to regulate the labor force requires population policies that directly control women" is totally bereft of documentation or substantiation. Mie Watanabe, "Reproduction and Capitalist Development: Uses of Birth Control and Abortion," in *Welfare in America: Controlling the "Dangerous Classes"* 119-37 at 134 (Betty Mandell ed., 1975).

52. Angus McLaren & Arlene McLaren, *The Bedroom and the State: The Changing Practices and Politics of Contraception and Abortion in Canada, 1880-1980*, at 9 (1986).

53. Gordon, *Woman's Body, Woman's Right* at 73-74.

54. Jeremy Bentham, *Manual of Political Economy*, in *Jeremy Bentham's Economic Writings* 1:221, 272 (W. Stark ed., 1952 [1793-95]); Dwight D. Eisenhower, *Public Papers of the Presidents of the United States*, ¶ 287, News Conference of Dec. 2, 1959, at 785, 787-88 (1959).

55. Mill, *Elements of Political Economy* at 238. On Mill, see E.P. Thompson, *The Making of the English Working Class* 776 (1963).

56. Mill, *Elements of Political Economy* at 238.

57. Kingsley Davis, "Population Policy: Will Current Programs Succeed?" *Science* 158:730-39 at 737 (Nov. 10, 1967). See also Frank Lorimer, "Issues of Population Policy," in *The Population Dilemma* at 143, 168. "Population policies generally treat human beings as *means*, whereas in a social policy context they are regarded as *ends*." Ann-Sofie Kälvemark, *More Children of Better Quality? Aspects on Swedish Population Policy in the 1930s* at 138 (1980).

58. Ferdinand Lassalle, *Herr Bastiat-Schulze von Delitzsch: Der ökonomische Julian oder Kapital und Arbeit*, in *idem, Gesammelte Reden und Schriften* 5:268 (Eduard Bernstein ed., 1919 [1864]). Lassalle was making a pun. Starting from the assumption that labor, like everything else sold in the market, is subject to one standard—the relationship of supply and demand as determined by the costs of production/procreation (Erzeungungskosten)—he asked how much it cost to produce/beget a worker and answered that the worker had to be paid enough to cover the usual necessaries.

59. But see Ben Wattenberg, *The Birth Dearth* (1987).

60. Letter from Theodore Roosevelt to Mrs. Van Vorst, Oct. 18, 1902, in Theodore Roosevelt, *Presidential Addresses and State Papers* 2:508-10 at 508-509 (n.d.). Roosevelt continued to press the theme of "the crime of race suicide" after he left office. Theodore Roosevelt, "Twisted Eugenics," in *idem, Literary Essays*, in *The Works of Theodore Roosevelt: National Edition* 12:197-207 at 202 (1926 [1914]).

61. Theodore Roosevelt, "Race Decadence," in *idem, Literary Essays*, in *The Works of Theodore Roosevelt: National Edition* 12:184-96 at 196 (1926 [1911]).

62. Theodore Roosevelt, "The Woman and the House,'' in *idem, American Problems*, in *The Works of Theodore Roosevelt: Memorial Edition* 17:225-33 at 231 (1925 [1905]).

63. Theodore Roosevelt, "A Premium on Race Suicide," *Outlook* 105:163-64 at 164 (Sept. 27, 1913).

64. Isaac Hourwich, *Immigration and Labor: The Economic Aspects of European Immigration to the United States* 221-27 (1912); Gordon, *Woman's Body, Woman's Right* at 136-58. Roosevelt himself, however, also accused the children of immigrants of "wilful sterility." Roosevelt, "Race Decadence" at 191.

65. John Commons, *Races and Immigrants in America* xxiv (new ed. 1967 [1920]) (quotation); Joseph Spengler, "Some Economics Aspects of Immigration into the United States," *Law & Contemporary Problems* 21: 236-55 at 243 (1956).

66. *Economic Report of the President* 164, 185, 160 (1990).

67. House Report No. 723(I), 101st Cong., 2d Sess., *reprinted in* 1990 *U.S. Code Congressional & Administrative News* 6710, 6721.

68. Virginia Abernethy, *Population Politics: The Choices That Shape Our Future* 218 (1993); Ethel Elderton, *Report on the English Birthrate*, Part I: *England, North of the Humber* 235 (1914) (quote). See also C. Carrington, *The British Overseas: Exloits of a Nation of Shopkeepers* 495-513 (1950).

69. Ethel Elderton et al., *On the Correlation of Fertility with Social Value: A Cooperative Study* 45 (Francis Galton Laboratory for National Eugenics, Eugenics Laboratory Memoirs 18, 1913).

70. Paul Vincent, "La Famille normale," *Population* 5 (2):251-69 (Apr.-June 1950); Richard Tomlinson, "The French Population Debate," *Public Interest* No. 76 at 111-20 (Summer 1984); André Armengaud, *Les Français et Malthus* 70-72 (1975); Dr. Rommel [Alfred Pernessin], *Frankreich gerichtet durch sich selbst* 194-205 (1886).

71. Annexe No. 1936, in *Annales de la Chambre des Députés: Documents parlementaires*, 83: Session ordinaire, Première partie, at 1256, 1257 (1912).

72. Colin Dyer, *Population and Society in Twentieth Century France* tab. 1 at 5, 28 (quotation) (1978).

73. Paul Leroy-Beaulieu, *La Question de la population* 285-86, 272-73, 291 (1913).

74. Alfred Vagts, *A History of Militarism: Civilian and Military* 217, 219 (rev. ed. 1967 [1939]).

75. *Annales de la Chambre des Députés*, 10me Législative, *Débats parlementaires*, Session ordinaire de 1912, vol. II (1912) (May 28, 1912, M. Messimy); Annexe No. 1936.

76. Joseph Schumpeter, *History of Economic Analysis* 841 (Elizabeth Schumpeter ed., 1972 [1954]) (quote); Leroy-Beaulieu, *La Question de la population* at 465-81 (quote at 478).

77. 1 Jean Freville, *La Misère et le nombre: L'Epouvantail malthusien* 14-15 (1956); Angus McLaren, *Sexuality and Social Order: The Debate over the Fertility of Women and Workers in France, 1770-1920*, at 1-2, 169-83 (1983); Dyer, *Population and Society in Twentieth Century France* at 78-79, 146-47 (quote at 78).

78. Sidney Webb, *The Decline in the Birth Rate* 17, 19 (Fabian Tract No. 131, 1907). See also Elderton, *Report on the English Birthrate* at 238.

79. A.M. Carr-Saunders, *World Population: Past Growth and Present Trends* 244, 250 (1937 [1936]).

80. [U.K.] Royal Commission on Population, *Report* 133-34, 103 (Cmd. 7695, 1949).

81. Eveline Sullerot, "Rapport présenté, au nom du Conseil économique et social," in "La Situation démographique de la France et ses implications économiques et sociales: bilan et perspectives," in *Journal Officiel de la République Française*, 1978. No. 15, 791-860 at 860 (Aug. 10, 1978).

82. Henry Giniger, "Women Assail French Policy on Births," *N.Y. Times*, Nov. 23, 1970, at 12, col. 1.

83. [U.S.] Commission on Population Growth and the American Future, *Population and the American Future* 41 (1972). On the origins of the commission, see *Establish a Commission on Population Growth and the American Future: Hearing Before the Senate Committee on Government Operations*, 91st Cong., 1st Sess. (1969).

84. Paul Ehrlich, *The Population Bomb* 176 (1969 [1968]).

85. Alfred Zimmern, *The Greek Commonwealth: Politics and Economics in Fifth-Century Athens* 255-59, 331-37 (n.d. [1911]). See also Plato, *Leges* 735e-736a, 740e-741a. On the completely different functions of ancient and modern emigration, see Karl Marx, "Forced Emigration," in Karl Marx [&] Frederick Engels, *Collected Works* 11: 528-34 at 530-31 (1979 [1853]).

86. Skinner v. Oklahoma, 316 U.S. 535, 536 (1942); Eisenstadt v. Baird, 405 U.S. 438, 453 (1972).

87. Maher v. Roe, 432 U.S. 464, 478 n.11 (1977).

88. *Ibid.* at 489 n.*.

89. Laurence Tribe, *American Constitutional Law* 1340 n.20 (2d ed. 1988 [1978]). See also *idem, Abortion: The Clash of Absolutes* 111 (1991).

90. See below ch. 3; Michael Teitelbaum, "International Experience with Fertility at or Near Replacement Level," in U.S. Commission on Population Growth and the American Future, *Research Reports: Demographic and Social Aspects of Population Growth* 1:645-58 at 655-57 (Charles Westoff & Robert Parke, Jr. eds., 1972).

91. See below ch. 8.

92. *Population Crisis: Hearings Before the Subcommittee on Foreign Aid Expenditures of the Senate Committee on Government Operations*, 89th Cong., 1st Sess. (1965); John Finney, "Eisenhower Backs Birth Curb Study," *N.Y. Times*, June 23, 1965, at 1, col. 4 (quote).

93. "Letter by Eisenhower on Birth Control," *N.Y. Times*, June 23, 1965, at 21, col. 2-4.

94. *Population Crisis: Hearings Before the Subcommittee on Foreign Aid Expenditures of the Senate Committee on Government Operations*, Pt. 4, 89th Cong., 2d Sess. 775-85 (1966).

95. The President's Commission on Income Maintenance Programs, *Poverty Amid Plenty: The American Paradox* 23, 25 (1969) (quotation at 25).

96. *Ibid.* at 28, 75 (quotation at 75).

97. President's Committee on Population and Family Planning, *Population and Family Planning: The Transition from Concern to Action* 15 (1968).

98. Arthur Campbell, "Family Planning and the Reduction of Poverty in the United States," in *Population Crisis: Hearings Before the Subcommittee on Foreign Aid Expenditures of the Senate Committee on Government Operations*, 90th Cong., 1st Sess. 181-95 at 182-83 (1967); U.S. Bureau of the Census, "Fertility of the Population: June 1964 and March 1962," tab. 6 at 18 (CPR, Ser. P-20, No. 147, 1966). Three decades later, as fertility fell below replacement level, the gap was somewhat compressed. In 1992, the number of children ever born to married women in the labor force in families with the highest incomes (over $75,000) was 1.7 compared to 2.2 and 2.4 children respectively in the lowest-income groups (less than $10,000 and from $10,000 to $20,000). U.S. Bureau of the Census, "Fertility of American Women: June 1992," tab. 3 at 11 (CPR, P20-470, 1993) (written by Amara Bachu).

99. Harold Sheppard, "Effects of Family Planning on Poverty in the United States," in U. S. Senate, Subcommittee on Employment, Manpower, and Poverty of the Committee on Labor and Public Welfare, *Examination of the War on Poverty: Staff and Consultant Reports* 3:715-35 at 717, 727 (90th Cong., 1st Sess., Committee Print, 1967); Adelaide Hill & Frederick Jaffe, "Negro Fertility and Family Size Preferences: Implications for Programming of Health and Social Services," in *The Negro American* 205-24 at 219-20 (Talcott Parsons & Kenneth Clark eds., 1970 [1967]); Philip Hauser, "Demographic Factors in the Integration of the Negro," in *ibid.* at 71-101 at 88-90.

100. Sheppard, "Effects of Family Planning on Poverty in the United States" at 723.

101. Campbell, "Family Planning and the Reduction of Poverty in the United States" at 190-91.

102. Richard Nixon, *Public Papers of the Presidents of the United States*, ¶ 271: "Special Message to the Congress on Problems of Population Growth," July 18, 1969, at 521, 524-29 (1969).

103. James Sundquist, *Dispersing Population: What America Can Learn from Europe* 1-36, 239-41, 256-58 (1975).

104. Martha Ward, Poor Women, *Powerful Men: America's Great Experiment in Family Planning* 67-69 (1986); Pub. L. No. 91-572, 84 Stat. 1504.

105. House Report No. 1472, 91st Cong., 2d Sess., *reprinted in U.S. Code Congressional & Administrative News* 5068, 5070.

106. President's Committee on Population and Family Planning, *Population and Family Planning* at 15.

107. Dienes, *Law, Politics, and Birth Control* at 293.

108. John D. Rockefeller III, "The Citizen's View of Public Programs for Family Limitation," in *Fertility and Family Planning: A World View* 493-98 at 496-97 (S. Behrman et al. eds., 1967). Garrett Hardin echoed Rockefeller's admonition by urging schools to help children resist social pressure and formulate alternative goals to marriage and parenting. Garrett Hardin, "Multiple Paths to Population Control," in *The American Population Debate* 259-66 at 265 (Daniel Callahan ed., 1971 [1970]).

109. Peter Collier & David Horowitz, *The Rockefellers: An American Dynasty* 286 (1977 [1976]).

110. Letter by Kingsley Davis to editor, *Science* 159:828-29 (Feb. 23, 1968) (quote); Phyllis Piotrow, *The World Population Crisis: The United States Response* 154 (1974 [1973]) (quote); letter by William McElroy et al. in *Science* 159:827 (Feb. 23, 1968). See also Bernard Berelson, "Beyond Family Planning," *Science* 163:533-43 (Feb. 7, 1969).

111. Commission on Population Growth and the American Future, *Population and the American Future* at 15.

112. Kingsley Davis, "Reproductive Institutions and the Pressure for Population," *Sociological Rev.* 29:289-306 at 304-305 (1937). For detailed discussion of family allowances, see below ch. 9-10.

113. Commission on Population Growth and the American Future, *Population and the American Future* at 15.

114. Davis, "Population Policy" at 738, 732, 737.

115. *Ibid.* at 733-34, 738.

116. *Ibid.* at 738. Davis's reference to an involuntary incorporation of women into the labor force conjures up Rosa Luxemburg's harangues against the wives of the bourgeoisie as "mere parasites of the surplus value that their husbands extract from the proletariat," who functioned solely as "instruments of natural procreation for the ruling classes." Rosa Luxemburg, "Frauenwahlrecht und Klassenkampf," in *idem, Gesammelte Werke* 3:159-65 at 162-63 (1973 [1912]). Davis's approach, however, was not only class-neutral, but presumably did not echo Luxemburg's claim that the modern proletarian woman was the first to become a human being by participating in struggle, cultural work, and history: "For the propertied bourgeois woman her house is the world. *For the proletarian woman the whole world is her house....*" Rosa Luxemburg, "Die Proletarierin," in *ibid.*, 3:410-13 at 411 (1914). Startlingly, the leading radical critics of the U.S. poor-law system advocate economic reforms that would "restor[e] lower-class occupational, familial, and communal patterns. Since men...would no longer find themselves unemployed or employed at wages insufficient to support women and children, they would be able to resume breadwinner roles." Frances Piven & Richard Cloward, *Regulating the Poor: The Functions of Public Welfare* 345 (1972 [1971]).

117. Davis, "Population Policy" at 738. Later, Davis found another urgent demand for married women on the labor market—replacing healthy retirees, who were, in his view, too busy, if not being born, then playing golf, to be dying promptly enough to cease burdening the economy. In an intriguing temporal extension or inversion of Malthusianism, Davis argued that once old-age pensions are impersonally financed by the commons rather than by named children, "there is no moral constraint on their [retirees'] economic demands." Despairing, however, of the political feasibility of putting an end to this tragic raid on the commons by lowering retirement payments, Davis proposed restocking the commons by inducing those over 65 not to stop working. Kingsley Davis, "Our Idle Retirees Drag Down the Economy," *N.Y. Times*, Oct. 18, 1988, at A31, col. 2. This strategy of increasing the supply of labor not biologically but by squeezing the reserves of the nonemployed has for some decades been a formal goal of state family policy in several European countries, which use their family benefits programs in part to induce mothers to enter the labor market. *Family Policy, Government and Families in Fourteen Countries*, 12-13, 32-34, 477-78 (Sheila Kamerman & Alfred Kahn eds., 1978).

118. John Herbers, "Income Gap Between Races Wide as in 1960, Study Finds," *N.Y. Times*, July 18, 1983, at A1, col. 2, A8, col. 2 (fertility rate); U.S. Women's Bureau, *Handbook on Women Workers: Trends and Issues* 10 (1994) (quote).

119. Sar Levitan, Garth Mangum, & Ray Marshall, *Human Resources and Labor Markets: Labor and Manpower in the American Economy* 34 (2d ed., 1976 [1972]). Marshall became Secretary of Labor in 1977.

120. Howard Hayghe, "Family Members in the Work Force," *Monthly Labor Rev.* 113 (3):14-19, chart 1 at 16 (Mar. 1990).

121. U.S. Bureau of the Census, *Households, Families, and Children: A 30-Year Perspective*, fig. 21-22 at 28-29 (CPR, P23-181, 1992) (written by Terry Lugalia).

122. Howard Hayghe & Suzanne Bianchi, "Married Mothers' Work Patterns: The Job-Family Compromise," *Monthly Labor Rev.* 117 (6):24-30, tab. 6 at 29 (June 1994).

123. Hayghe, "Family Members in the Work Force," tab. 3 at 17.

124. U.S. Bureau of the Census, *Poverty in the United States: 1992*, tab. 19 at 114-15 (CPR, P60-185, 1993); *idem*, *Households, Families, and Children*, fig. 33-34 at 42-43.

125. U.S. Congressional Budget Office, *Trends in Family Income: 1970-1986*, tab. A-11 to A-15 at 80-85, 58-61 (quote) (1988). Interestingly, however, the median adjusted income of two-worker married couples rose only marginally more than that of one-worker couples from 1970 to 1986—24 percent and 21 percent respectively. *Ibid.*, tab. A-16 and A-17 at 86-87.

126. Louis Uchitelle, "Moonlighting Plus: 3-Job Families on the Rise," *N.Y. Times*, Aug. 16, 1994, at A1, col. 1 (nat. ed.); John Stinson, Jr., "Multiple Jobholding Up Sharply in the 1980's," *Monthly Labor Rev.* 113 (7):3-10, tab. 1 at 4 (July 1990); *Employment and Earnings* 43 (1):tab. A-36 at 202 (Jan. 1996).

127. Peter Kilborn, "More Women Take Low-Wage Jobs Just So Their Families Can Get By," *N.Y. Times*, Mar. 13, 1994, § 1, at 11, col. 1 (nat. ed.).

128. "How Welfare Keeps Women from Working," *Business Week*, Apr. 7, 1973, at 51; "Low, Lower, Lowest," *Economist*, June 3, 1978, at 21-22; below ch. 6 (on Marx).

129. Robert Reinhold, "Family Planning Is Called Futile," *N.Y. Times*, Oct. 5, 1969, at 51, col. 1; Paul Ehrlich, *The Population Bomb* 137 (1970 [1968]); S. 3632, 91st Cong., 2d Sess. (1970); Robert Packwood, "Incentives for the Two-Child Family," *Trial* 6 (5):13, 16, (Aug.-Sept. 1970).

130. Kingsley Davis, "The American Family in Relation to Demographic Change," in Commission on Population Growth and the American Future, 1 *Research Reports: Demographic and Social Aspects of Population Growth* 235-65 at 239, 241, 263 (Charles Westoff & Robert Parke, Jr. eds., 1972).

131. Judith Blake, "Demographic Science and the Redirection of Population Policy," in *Public Health and Population Change: Current Research Issues* 41-69 (Mindel Sheps & Jeanne Ridley eds., 1965); *idem*, "Ideal Family Size Among White Americans: A Quarter of a Century's Evidence," *Demography* 3 (1):154-73 (1966); *idem*, "Population Policy for Americans: Is the Government Being Misled?" *Science* 164:522-29 (1969); *idem*, "Reproductive Motivation and Population Policy," *BioScience* 21 (5):215-20 (Mar. 1971). In contrast, John Noonan, Jr. & Cynthia Dunlap, "Unintended Consequences: Laws Indirectly Affecting Population Growth in the United States," in The Commission on Population Growth and the American Future, 6 *Research Reports: Aspects of Population Growth Policy* 111, 143-44 (Robert Parke, Jr. & Charles Westoff eds., 1972), argued that economic deprivations suffered by large poor families already constituted an antinatalist policy and merely lacked the powerful symbolism of an accompanying governmental message that they were designed to reduce population growth. Blake would presumably have interpreted this point as a vindication: precisely because economics alone cannot deter procreation, the spouse- and parent-centered psychological reward structure must be revamped.

132. President's Committee on Population and Family Planning, *Population and Family Planning: The Transition from Concern to Action* 43 (U.S. H.E.W., 1968); Commission on Population Growth and the American Future, *Population and the American Future* at 13. To be sure, this same position viewed the population problem "more as the sum of such individual problems than as a societal problem transcending the interests of

individuals...." *Ibid.*

133. Miles, "Whose Baby Is the Population Problem?" at 19, 21, 22, 25-27.

134. Stephen Enke, "Population Growth and Economic Growth," *Pub. Interest* No. 32 at 86-96 (Summer 1973); Stephen Viederman & Sharmon Sollitto, "Economic Groups: Business, Labor, Welfare," in *Population Policy and Ethics: The American Experience* 325-46 at 325-36 (Robert Veatch ed., 1977).

135. Thomas Shapiro, *Population Control Politics: Women, Sterilization, and Reproductive Choice* 18 , 180-81 (1985).

136. Commission Population Growth and the American Future, *Population and the American Future* at 15, 12; Judith Blake, "Coercive Pronatalism and American Population Policy," in Commission on Population Growth and the American Future, 6 *Research Reports: Aspects of Population Growth Policy* at 81-109. Against the background of this constellation of class forces, Peter Bachrach & Elihu Bergman, "Participation and Conflict in Making American Population Policy: A Critical Analysis," in Commission on Population Growth and the American Future, 6 *Research Reports: Aspects of Population Growth Policy* at 579-607 at 603-604, offer an insufficiently specified critique in asserting that "the exclusionary and upper-class nature of the population movement suggests...a desire to secure a future in which their privileged positions and life styles will be preserved."

137. Collier & Horowitz, *The Rockefellers* at 373-75.

138. Victor Fuchs, "Some Notes on the Optimum Size of Population, with Special Reference to Health," in *Is There an Optimum Level of Population?* 223, 224 (S. Fred Singer ed., 1971).

139. Paul Demeny, "Welfare Considerations in U.S. Population Policy," in Commission on Population Growth and the American Future, 6 *Research Reports: Aspects of Population Growth Policy* 153-72 at 171.

140. Karl Marx, 1 *Das Kapital: Kritik der politischen Ökonomie*, in Karl Marx [&] Friedrich Engels, *Werke* 23:598, 599 (1962 [1867]). Population movements, in an alternative formulation, may play a subordinate role in the materialist conception of history—an effect of the economic, territorial, and general cultural conditions. M. Beer "Zur Bevölkerungslehre," *Neue Zeit*, 25/I:567, 568 (1906-1907). Marx's view has frequently been attacked as revealing that population, reproduction, and the family were all black boxes to him. E.g., Richard Lewinsohn, "Die Stellung der deutschen Sozialdemokratie zur Bevölkerungsfrage," *Schmollers Jahrbuch für Gesetzgebung, Verwaltung und Volkswirtschaft im Deutschen Reiche* 46:191-203 (1922). Joan Huber, "Will U.S. Fertility Decline Toward Zero?" *Sociological Q.* 21:481-92 at 482 (Aut. 1980), argues that the theories of Marx, Durkheim, and Weber seem "outdated, like the 19th century theories of colonialism that implicitly assume that dark-skinned 'natives' would always be servants or slaves," because, having overlooked the consequences of the demographic transition, they "assumed that women's maternal status was a constant, not a variable."

141. Manuel Gottlieb, "The Theory of Optimum Population for a Closed Economy," *J. Pol. Econ.* 53 (4):289-316 at 298-99 (Dec. 1945).

142. Murray Bookchin, "Population Politics," *Rat*, Nov. 13-15, 1969 (quoted in J. Mayone Stycos, "Some Minority Opinions on Birth Control," in *Population Policy and Ethics* 169-96 at 190.

143. "Birth Control: Businessmen Back It," *Business Week*, May 15, 1965, at 34.

144. *Population Crisis: Hearings Before the Subcommittee on Foreign Aid Expenditures of the Senate Committee on Government Operations*, 90th Cong., 1st Sess. 52 (1967) (statement of Katherine Oettinger).

145. Lawrence Lader, *Breeding Ourselves to Death* (1971); Steve Weissman, "Why the Population Bomb Is a Rockefeller Baby," *Ramparts* 8 (11):42-47 (May 1970); Viederman & Sollitto, "Economic Groups" at 325-36.

146. See, e.g., Marios Nikolinakos, *Politische Ökonomie der Gastarbeiterfrage: Migration und Kapitalismus* (1973); D.V. Glass, *Population: Policies and Movement in Europe* 145 (1940).

147. The Commission on Population Growth and the American Future, *Statements at Public Hearings of the Commission on Population Growth and the American Future* 7:157-59 at 159, 157 (1972) (statement of John Yolton, UAW); H. Samuel, "Population and the American Future," *Am. Federationist* 79 (5):13-17 at 17 (May 1972).

148. E.P. Hutchinson, *The Population Debate: The Development of Conflicting Theories up to 1900*, at 1-2, 380 (1967); Marshall, *Principles* at 148; Paul Demeny, "Comment," *Pop. Index* 36 (4):459-65 at 463 (Oct.-Dec. 1970).

149. Kuczynski, *Population Movements* at 61-63. Hilde Wander, "Kinder als wirtschaftlicher Faktor?" in *Keine Kinder—Keine Zukunft? Zum Stand der Bevölkerungsforschung in Europa* 51-58 at 51 (Lutz Franke & Hans Jürgens eds., 1978), absolutizes the post-World War II experience in asserting that periods of declining births always trigger heated debates about the economic consequences whereas periods of rising fertility fail to spark such interest.

150. Paul Popenoe, "Can We Afford Children?" *Forum* 98 (6):315-18 at 315, 317 (Dec. 1937).

151. "Of People and Plenty," *Time* 65 (2):11 (Jan. 10, 1955); Joseph Spengler, "Population Threatens Prosperity," *Harv. Bus. Rev.* 34 (1):85-94 at 94 (Jan.-Feb. 1956).

152. *Verhandlungen des Deutschen Bundestages*, 8. Wahlperiode: *Stenographische Berichte* 114:16,436 (Mar. 6, 1980) (Brandt).

153. *Ibid.* at16,447-48 (Mar. 6, 1980) (Kuhlwein).

154. Jürgen Heinrichs, "Bedeutet Familienplanung ein Geburtenminus?" in *Keine Kinder—Keine Zukunft?* 83-90 at 86-87.

155. An extreme example of such a scenario was the proposal of a German doctor, who, finding mere Malthusian moral restraint insufficient, suggested threading and soldering boys' penises until they married. C. Weinhold, *Von der überwiegenden Reproduktion des Menschenkapitals gegen das Betriebskapital* 73-74 (1828).

156. Myrdal, *Population* at 121.

157. Louis Dublin, "The Fallacious Propaganda for Birth Control," *Atlantic Monthly* 137:186-94 at 191 (Feb.1926). Such an authoritarian-statist approach loses all feasibility when its racist-eugenicist roots are self-exposed: "There is always grave danger...of weakening the social organization by increasing the proportion of defective and dependent stock. For it is always the least desirable parents who are the last to curtail their fecundity." Louis Dublin, "Has America Too Many Children?" *Collier's,* Apr. 25, 1925, at 23.

158. Paul Demeny, "Pronatalist Policies in Low-Fertility Countries: Patterns, Performance, and Prospects," in *Below-Replacement Fertility in Industrial Societies: Causes, Consequences, Policies* 335-58 at 338 (Kingsley Davis et al. eds., 1986). See also Colin Clark, "New Light on Population," *Listener* 49 (1256):503-504 at 504 (Mar. 26, 1953): "No political leader..., no economist...has the slightest right to interfere with the birth of children.... It is parents who have the right to demand of Prime Ministers and economists that they should so organise the world that children should have enough to eat."

159. "There is nothing intrinsically worrisome about declining population growth or even declining population; West Germany...did rather well in the 1970's and 80's." Nicholas Eberstadt, "Marx and Mortality: A Mystery," *N.Y. Times*, Apr. 6, 1994, at A21, col. 1 (nat. ed.).

160. *World Population: A Global Perspective: Hearings Before the [House] Select Committee on Population*, 95th Cong., 2d Sess. 133 (1978) (testimony of John D. Rockefeller III); Demeny, "Welfare Considerations in U.S. Population Policy" at 171.

PART II

THE HISTORY OF INVISIBLE-HAND MALTHUSIANISM IN THEORY AND PRACTICE

The Age of Reason ended in the French Revolution. The Age of Stupidity began with Malthus.... Man is not a rational being—he is a being of passion and stupidity, who does quite the opposite of what his reason tells him to do. He therefore cannot be left free but must be coerced by government.

John Commons, *Institutional Economics:*
Its Place in Political Economy
1:244; 2:877 (1959 [1934])

3

The Invisible Hand Goes Demographic: Bourgeois Political Economy's New Trope

> Populousness, like opulence, will thrive best, if all is left to the *sponte acta* of individuals.... The apprehension of a deficiency of population for want of regular intercourse between the sexes in the way of marriage is altogether upon a par with an apprehension of the like result from a general disposition in mankind to starve themselves.[1]

Even if a societally or capital-logically optimal population size or rate of change could be theoretically quantified, what are the concrete individual and collective processes that would bring about optimality? If parental altruism can be relied on to internalize potential intragenerational externalities, and if "in a stable culture, it is not unreasonable to expect that family size norms embody reliable information about the economic conditions that will be faced by the next generation," then it becomes plausible that "reproductive rights are ceded to the family in almost all societies, even though population size has important collective consequences." But if even altruistic parents who consciously adjust fertility decisions with their offspring's future welfare in mind may find that "[b]ecause of the scope and speed of the social and economic changes... [they cannot] correctly anticipate the impact on the family of an additional child,"[2] how can they possibly anticipate the aggregated impact on society of all other procreators' fertility decisions? This conceptualization of parenthood choices is made even more complicated by the fact that "self-regarding and other-regarding motives are inextricably intermixed."[3]

If human beings engaged in copulation may not even be exercising conscious control over their output, then they can be said to be planning aggregate national (or international) population size even less than they plan national income or automobile production when they individually decide on a particular occupation or car. At the very least, by externalizing some of the costs of childrearing onto society at large and/or particular others, parents are presumed by orthodox economics to be procreating or engaged in conferring benefits on their children beyond the level that would be associated with full internalization of costs.[4] If society had democratically decided and planned to allocate resources for this higher level of fertility, then the dichotomization of the cost burden would arguably be moot. But as long as procreational decisions remain committed to the individual-private sphere and some significant part of the consequences is borne by those who did not participate in the decision-making process, micro-planning (or spontaneity for that matter) must result in macro-irrationalities.

This conclusion is warded off by economists for whom it is axiomatic that the antipaternalistic "central tenet of welfare economics—that people are the best judges of their own welfare"—both means that reproductive decisions are presumptively rational for the procreators and is paired with a disbelief that children are a source of external diseconomies in spite of overwhelming and obvious evidence that much of the cost of childrearing is borne collectively rather than individually.[5] Glen Cain, for example, sees in "the willingness to assume" the high costs of raising children "convincing evidence for the proposition that children provide them with a great deal of utility." He also regards externalities as "minor." With equal force it could be inferred that the huge number of abortions that women (and or couples) seek each year demonstrates how unwilling producers are to assume these costs. When the manifold and rising economic, political, legal, and moral impediments to abortion are taken into consideration, the voluntary character of reproduction appears in a much darker light. And if the putatively rational procreational decision-making process is understood to be honeycombed with the deep deposits of internalized coercive parentage norms, then it becomes unclear whether even individual reproducers—let alone society—can, as Cain believes, avoid the fate of laboratory rats who "end up with a revealed preference for a way of life that we...abhor."[6]

This market- and father-knows-best-propelled denial is also made possible by the subsumption of the children under the will and judgment of their procreators; instead of considering the possibility that children are themselves autonomous persons, orthodox economics automatically assumes that, if the parents deem the returns to be at least as large as the costs of childrearing, no independent judgment is permissible as to whether some children's standard of living and opportunities for self-development and societal contribution are optimal or whether redistribution is remedially required for this generation and/or a different demographic norm should be established for the next.

Against the background of these systemic constraints, it becomes a "gigantic, utterly unwarranted assumption that the sum of all these separate desires will always work out providentially to a practically manageable birth rate."[7] And even if procreators' decisions are rational for them individually, absolutely privileging all of their choices as to "the number of children they want...evades the basic question of population policy, which is how to give societies the number of children they need."[8] Conversely, although a smaller aggregate population may be beneficial to the economy as a whole or capital in general, this fact or possibility alone does not necessarily create "the appropriate motivation for any individual to limit his family size."[9] After all: "There is no evidence that any considerable number of married couples at the end of the 19th century decided to have smaller families because they thought that the country might be over-populated—any more than there is evidence that an argument of the converse kind enters into decisions of married couples today...."[10] Nor did Malthus or any of his followers ever demonstrate that humans orient their fertility toward the relationship between population and resources "even when they know about it (which is seldom)."[11] How, then, does the invisible hand ever get a grip on reproduction?

This chapter initiates the exploration of this question by examining the origins of demographic invisible-hand rhetoric in Adam Smith and its self-contradictory development in the fountainhead of economic demography, Malthus. For although Malthus presupposed the existence of a process of demographic self-equilibration, his lack of trust in the invisible hand's genital grip prompted him to contest the working class's autonomous control over its fertility and to favor state intervention to limit paupers' reproduction. Finally, the discussion turns to the surprising and little-studied advocacy of a state-interventionist course by that arch-liberal John Stuart Mill and how such discourse ultimately shaped the currently influential authoritarian social policy of such anti-invisible-handers as Garrett Hardin. The analysis reveals that whereas invisible-hand economic demography is incoherent as an account of how a societally optimal population could be achieved, the proposals of prominent advocates of a visible state hand are discontinuous with democratic norms.

Chapter 4 then resumes the discussion by embedding the new eco-demographic theory in the transformations that British poor law policy were undergoing in the late eighteenth and early nineteenth centuries. That significant aspects of that policy in part still guide the U.S. approach to controlling what is perceived as procreation-related poverty and sanctioning poverty-related population growth enhances the importance of studying this formative period.

THE ECO-DEMOGRAPHIC INVISIBLE HAND

> [H]ow often have we read in Malthusian benefactors of the species: 'The working people have their condition in their own hands; let them diminish the supply of labourers, and of course the demand and the remuneration will increase!' Yes, let *them* diminish the supply: but who are they? They are twenty-four millions of human individuals, scattered over a hundred and eighteen thousand square miles...; each unknown to his neighbor.... Smart Sally in our alley proves all-too fascinating to brisk Tom in yours: can Tom be called on to make pause, and calculate the demand for labour in the British Empire first? Nay, if Tom did renounce his highest blessedness of life, and struggle and conquer like a Saint Francis of Assisi, what would it profit him or us? Seven millions of the finest peasantry do not renounce, but proceed all

the more briskly; and with blue-visaged Hibernians instead of fair
Saxon Tomsons and Sallysons, the latter end of that country is worse
than the beginning. O wonderful Malthusian prophets! Millenniums
are undoubtedly coming, must come one way or the other: but will it be,
think you, by twenty millions of working people simultaneously
striking work in that department; passing, in universal trades-union, a
resolution not to beget any more till the labour-market become
satisfactory?[12]

Demography has answered the question as to what mechanism might
enable the invisible hand to guide human procreativity with what it views as an
unproblematic sociological extension to humans of the Darwinian principle of the
balance of nature.   Labeled "unconscious rationality"[13] or the Theory of
Demographic Regulation, it asserts abstractly that: "Every society tends to keep its
vital processes in a state of balance such that population will replenish losses from
death and grow to an extent deemed desirable by collective norms. These norms
are flexible and readjust rather promptly to changes in the ability of the economy
to support population." For technologically advanced societies, the theory states
more specifically that "high birthrates come to be perceived by the collectivity as
dysfunctional because they cause the size of the family to be larger than that
deemed desirable by the prevailing norms." Reproductive regulation therefore
becomes identified with both group and individual welfare. In contrast to the
Darwinian model, the theory of demographic regulation thus posits that the human
species "has a norm that implies, at any given time, what constitutes 'good' or
'desirable' population trends...." It is here that the invisible hand makes its
(invisible) appearance.   For the collective norms are said to function as
transformers of self-regarding individualistic notions into macrodemographic
outcomes: "These norms are not explicit opinions about desired population size....
Instead, they are opinions concerning what constitutes the ideal size of completed
family...an entity that may be translated directly into population growth and is
therefore a cultural value reflecting the 'demographic cultural policy' of the
society."[14]

Regardless of whether this theory of "demographic homeosta-
sis...operat[ing] beyond individual consciousness" is descriptively accurate, the
question here is whether a societal process so conceived generates optimal results
or whether the societal norm should be articulated openly as the collective-
ecological policy of society as a whole rather than unconsciously.[15] The utilitarian
defense of a laissez-faire procreative regime is ultimately based on circular
reasoning. While conceding that decisions to "buy" children may differ from and
be qualitatively more complex than those involving run-of-the-mill commodities,
invisible-handers believe that they would be even more difficult for the state. Thus
even if the state can collect and process infinitely more information much more
cheaply than individual parents, the problem that it seeks to solve is also
proportionately more complicated:

> Each parent need only decide on the costs and benefits to himself and his child of having the child. The effects of increased population on the welfare of the poor...or the climate of the earth and the effect of different age distributions...on the social structure...are almost irrelevant.... It is precisely this sort of division of labor, under which an unmanageably large problem is divided into a multitude of parts, each to be solved by the individual that the part affects, which makes the free market such an efficient mechanism for solving economic problems.[16]

This Smithian approach to reproduction, which overlooks the fact that the individual, despite her self-interest, is as little able to foresee future market conditions as the state,[17] misconceives the problem by illicitly assuming it away. The mere dispensation of individual procreators from a duty to incorporate other-regarding considerations into their decisions does not make the anarchic and dysfunctional societal consequences of their acts more manageable let alone solve them. There is no doubt that a collective decision-making process taking numerous macrosocietal factors into account is much more complex than an individual's self-regarding decision. The reason obviously is that a planned process is seeking to avoid or remedy the untoward ramifications created by billions of societally blind micro-decisions. The free-market approach to reproduction also misstates the nature of the decision made by the collectivity. Whereas individual procreators presumptively make their decisions based on personal financial and emotional capacities, the state would not need to offer individualized prescriptions of family size by reference to (potential) parents' unique psychological characteristics. All the state would have to do is establish a dynamic economic-demographic framework within which individual family sizes should fit.

This demographic application of the invisible-hand trope is a result of the discipline's traditional commitment to methodological individualism, which orients it especially toward psychological facts—decisions and attitudes—of individuals.[18] Indeed, doctrinal Malthusianism has been characterized as accounting on the national or global level for the attitude of the household that limits family size in order to improve its own standard of living without regard to the national repercussions. Although this political-epistemological position biases demographers against explanations in terms of collectivities such as capital, capitalism, or class, substantively they have been forced, as are all methodologically conscious individualists, to deal with the phenomenon of the unintended and unwanted societal by-products of countless individual actions. Since, as that arch-methodological individualist, Karl Popper, observed, Marx was the first to conceive of social theory as the theory of such repercussions,[19] it is unsurprising that the beneficial outcomes associated with the invisible hand emerged as a counterpole to Marxism's focus on systemic self-contradiction as a motor of societal development. As a French socialist anti-Malthusian observed in 1910:

> The theoreticians of capitalism maintain that social well-being should result mechanically from the free combinations of personal

interest; foresight and calculation were recommended to all the individuals, but forbidden to the collectivity. All social history of the 19th century is nothing but a series of direct denials given to this doctrine; depopulation consummated the fiasco. It has appeared that even the reproduction of the species, which seemed to depend only on instinct alone, depended, on the contrary, narrowly on social conditions whose commonality should have kept a close watch on the development.[20]

Adam Smith's immortal allusion to the invisible hand is tucked away in a chapter of *The Wealth of Nations* devoted to the uselessness or injuriousness of state restraints on imports of goods that can or cannot be bought more cheaply domestically.[21] Assuming that the profits of domestic trade were as great as those yielded by foreign trade, Smith argued that individuals would employ their capital at home because security was maximized and risk minimized. Since capital employed at home gave employment to a greater number of inhabitants of the home country, permitting individuals "to find out the most advantageous employment for whatever capital he can command...naturally, or rather necessarily leads him to prefer that employment which is most advantageous to the society." Under these circumstances, then, although a merchant, by engaging in the home trade, intended only his own gain, he was "in this, as in many other cases, led by an invisible hand to promote an end which was no part of his intention. Nor is it always the worse for society that it was no part of it. By pursuing his own interest he frequently promotes that of the society more effectually than when he really intends to promote it."[22] Smith's argument was coupled with the claim that capitalists are in a better position to advance both their own self-interest and the societal interest than an intervening state:

> What is the species of domestic industry...of which the produce is likely to be of the greatest value, every individual...can, in his local situation, judge much better than any statesman or lawgiver can do for him. The statesman, who should attempt to direct private people in what manner they ought to employ their capitals, would...assume an authority which could safely be trusted, not only to no single person, but to no council or senate whatever....[23]

Smith almost expressly applied the virtuous invisible-hand analysis to procreation. Earlier in *The Wealth of Nations*, before using this trope, Smith had noted that the "liberal reward of labour" not only widened the limits that "the scantiness of subsistence can set...to the further multiplication of the human species," but "that it necessarily does this as nearly as possible in the proportion which the demand for labour requires."

> If this demand is continually increasing, the reward of labour must necessarily encourage in such a manner the marriage and multiplication of labourers, as may enable them to supply that continually increasing

demand by a continually increasing population. If the reward should at any time be less than what was requisite for this purpose, the deficiency of hands would soon raise it; and if it any time should be more, their excessive multiplication would soon lower it to this necessary rate. The market would be so much under-stocked with labour in the one case, and so much over-stocked in the other, as would soon force back its price to that proper rate which the circumstances of the society required. It is in this manner that the demand for men, like that for any other commodity, necessarily regulates the production of men.... It is this demand which regulates and determines the state of propagation in all the different countries of the world.[24]

For Smith, then, both categorically and empirically wages "must be such as may enable [workers], one with another, to continue the race of journeymen and servants, according to the increasing, diminishing, or stationary demand of the society may happen to require." Noteworthy here is that Smith, like Marx a century later, was committed to a labor-force-centered theory of population change: nonproletarian demographic development was, for Malthusian reasons, of little practical or theoretical interest to him: "Every species of animals naturally multiplies in proportion to the means of their subsistence.... But in civilized society it is only among the inferior ranks of people that the scantiness of subsistence," or, in terms of primary income distribution, "poverty...is extremely unfavourable to the rearing of children."[25]

Equally significant, however, is that neither Smith nor his followers accounted for how the invisible hand calibrates wages and worker-replacements in a labor market that does not take family size into account. In other words, they failed to "explain by what force labourers of one generation are impelled to ask, and employers to concede, the rate of wages needed by the small minority of labourers who are at any one time responsible for the size of family needed to keep up the population of the next generation." Farthest-reaching of all Smith's arguments is the implication that human beings or at least laborers were no more than commodities themselves.[26]

Regardless of the truth-content of Smith's claims about the salubrious effects of the invisible hand on the production of commodities, what warrant did Smith have for asserting that the same mechanism applied to the macro-demographic outcome of billions of acts of sexual intercourse very few if any of which were motivated by the goal of perpetuating the human species let alone securing an optimal labor force for capital? After all: "People have children to please themselves, not to advantage the State...." Even if the successful trading-member of capitalist societies enlists his brethren's support by interesting their "self-love in his favour" and thus "by treaty, by barter, and by pur-chase...obtain[s]...the greater part of those mutual good offices" everyone requires, how did Smith imagine the demographic market where traders could bargain for the fertility that would translate into the societal population most beneficial to their individual economic interests?[27]

Even a cursory investigation into the relationship between individual procreation decisions and macrolevel demographic outcomes would have revealed insuperable obstacles for Smith's invisible hand. First, without a strong government presence the laissez-faire environment would lack the appropriate individual incentives and assurances, and second, the enforcement and information costs of providing these missing elements would, given the vast numbers of independent decision-makers involved, be enormous. In light of this generalized prisoners' dilemma involving billions of individual uncoordinated decisions, how could Smith have expected to assimilate children as public goods to the fungible commodity model? What evidence, moreover, have orthodox economists offered that, by matching their family size to their income, individual families quasi-automatically insure that aggregate population size will be optimized? Have they analytically transcended Smith's epistemologically naive conversion of the fallacy of composition into a tenet of social theory and policy—namely, that: "What is prudence in the conduct of every private family, can scarce be folly in that of a great kingdom"?[28]

MALTHUS AND THE VISIBLE HAND OF THE STATE

> Had Adeline read Malthus? I can't tell;
>   I wish she had: his book's the eleventh Commandment,
> Which says, 'Thou shalt not marry,' unless *well*:
>   This he (as far as I can understand) meant.
> 'Tis not my purpose on his views to dwell,
>   Nor canvass what 'so eminent a hand' meant;
> But certes it conducts to live ascetic,
>   Or turning marriage into arithmetic.[29]

Early nineteenth-century economics divided into two camps on the issue of proletarian misery: the optimists, who claimed that capitalist misery was a temporary phenomenon and that the condition of the working class would improve both absolutely and relatively; and the Malthusians, who asserted that misery was necessary and inevitable in the absence of a limitation of child production, which was the only solution of the social question.[30] Crucial to an understanding of Malthus's rigid position on state abstinence vis-à-vis the material fate of poor large families is the fact that it was an integral part of his view that inequality was an essential motor of progress: "If no man could hope to rise or fear to fall, in society, if industry did not bring with it its reward and idleness its punishment, the middle parts would not certainly be what they now are."[31] That the particular progress Malthus had in mind was the accumulation of capital he revealed in the appendix to the fifth edition of his *Essay on the Principle of Population*. In this crucial passage, published two decades after the first edition—itself "nothing but an anti-socialist pamphlet"[32]—Malthus let the cat out of the bag as to why contraceptive freedom could not be reconciled with the sociopsychological microfoundations of a system predicated on a production of surplus that was in principle limitless:

> I should always particularly reprobate any artificial and unnatural modes of checking population, both on account of their immorality and their tendency to remove a necessary stimulus to industry. If it were possible for each married couple to limit by wish the number of their children, there is certainly reason to fear that the indolence of the human race would be very greatly increased; and that neither the population of individual countries, nor of the whole earth, would ever reach its natural and proper extent.[33]

Such pure Malthusianism survives only among economists who believe that the individual systematic implementation of contraception, by eliminating the pressure of population, also removes "most of the stimulus to economic development."[34]

Malthus's rejection of contraception is of a piece with his opposition to old-age pensions for workers and their families. The suggestion by one of Malthus's chief foils, Condorcet, that such aid, financed from the workers' own savings as well as of those who die before retirement age, could help eliminate inequality, dependence, and misery, prompted Malthus's scathing rebuke that "if the idle and the negligent are placed upon the same footing with regard to...the future support of their wives and families, as the active and industrious, can we expect to see men exert that animated activity in bettering their condition which now forms the master spring of public prosperity?" Malthus regarded any kind of breach in the terroristic labor regime driven by fear of starvation as undermining the viability of capitalism. Rather than analyzing the prohibition of economic security in terms of the antagonistic class society it undergirded, Malthus opted for a biodemographic description akin to an ecological carrying capacity: "Were every man sure of a comfortable provision for a family,...and were the rising generation free from the 'killing frost' of misery, population must rapidly increase."[35]

Malthus's brutal frankness about the political-economic functionality of what appeared as a morally or religiously motivated prohibition of contraception undermines Kingsley Davis's epistemological critique of Malthus's population theory. Davis sees Malthus's "confusion of moral evaluation with scientific analysis [as] a weakness of his conceptual framework" as a consequence of which his theory was inadequate scientifically even during his own era.[36] Yet, as an ideological holding action—until contraceptive means became cheap, effective, and well-known—Malthus's proscription of birth control as antithetical to indolence control may in fact have revealed deep insight into the psychosocial underpinnings of class governance during the transition period before the behavioral requirements of capital had been internalized as second nature.

Capitalism has, to be sure, shown itself to be flexible enough to live with, if not to require, contraception. In the 1920s, for example, a group of British Liberals led by Keynes even gathered under the watchwords Capitalism and Contraception.[37] Exasperated by "the Capitalist leaders in the City and in Parliament" who were "incapable of distinguishing novel measures for safeguarding Capitalism from what they call Bolshevism," Keynes shocked some of those attending the Liberal Summer School at Cambridge in 1925[38] by asserting that birth control and contraceptives

> interlock with economic issues which cannot be evaded. Birth control touches...the liberties of women, and...the duty of the State to concern itself with the size of the population just as much as with the size of the army or the amount of the budget. The position of wage-earning women and the project of the Family Wage affect not only the status of women, the first in the performance of paid work, and the second in the performance of unpaid work, but also raise the whole question whether wages should be fixed by the forces of supply and demand in accordance with the orthodox theories of *laissez-faire*, or whether we should begin to limit the freedom of those forces by reference to what is "fair" and "reasonable"....[39]

One reason for capitalism's eventual turn toward a less rigid demographic approach is the fundamentally different basis of the industrial reserve army in the early nineteenth century and developed capitalism. In Malthus's time, the reserve army originated in the relatively slow rate of and thus insufficient capital accumulation; later, accelerated or overaccumulation of capital generated a surplus of workers.[40] Moreover, when the limits of extensive exploitation ("absolute surplus value" production) became visible as the length of the working day hit against a physiological ceiling and the employment of ever younger children against a biological floor, capital accumulation had to become primarily reoriented toward intensive exploitation ("relative surplus value" production). The requisite rise in productivity presupposed both an increase in the qualifications of the working class, achieved in part through longer years of education, and a further intensification of the labor process. Because neither of these prerequisites was reconcilable with massive reliance on child workers, such labor became tendentially obsolete. With the economic depreciation and ultimately the legal prohibition on the use of their labor power, children lost most of their revenue-generating value to their parents; concomitantly, they became more valuable to capital as future skilled workers—especially insofar as the burden of financing the acquisition of these skills could be imposed on the parents. Since parents could no longer, to use the model implicit in classical political economy's theory of population, regard their production of children "as a means of investing in 'capital goods' for the sake of a future return," that cost-shifting would have to—and did—bring smaller families in its wake.[41]

Modern capitalism is also more dependent on high rates of working-class consumer spending than in 1800, when Malthus justified the existence of a so-called third class of nonproducing strata by reference to the urgency of the realization (or effective demand) problem confronting capitalism. What Malthus did not foresee was the rise of a stratum of relatively well-paid, intentionally childless workers who were devoted to spending more on themselves than many working-class parents can spend on large families.[42] Malthus was nevertheless correct in emphasizing the importance of a critical mass of population: even if lavishly consuming workers could sustain effective demand, if they were too busy shopping to reproduce, the next generation would be severely drained as a source of surplus value.

Malthus mixed mundane economics and the social-psychology of status with idealized romantic love in explaining class-specific procreational proclivities. Assuming that only married humans indulged passion, Malthus divined that population growth had remained below its theoretical limits in part because "a foresight of the difficulties attending the rearing of a family acts as a preventive check...in some degree through all the ranks of society in England. [S]ome men, even in the highest rank...are prevented from marrying by the idea of the expenses that they must retrench...on the supposition of having a family." Considerations that might be trivial at this level took on "much greater weight...as we go lower." Thus a "man of liberal education, but with an income only just sufficient to enable him to associate in the rank of gentlemen," knew that the cost of raising children would thrust him down to the ranks of "moderate farmers and the lower class of tradesmen." Such a descent "at this round of the ladder, where education ends and ignorance begins," was not a "chimerical, but a real and essential evil," which induced such men to delay marriage. Where passion caused them to break through the customary restraints, a calculation underlay such actions; for "it would be hard indeed, if the gratification of so delightful a passion as virtuous love, did not, sometimes, more than counterbalance all its attendant evils."[43]

At the other end of the English social scale, Malthus identified an even greater scope for the field of operation of the preventive check:

> The labourer who earns eighteen pence a day and lives with some degree of comfort as a single man, will hesitate a little before he divides that pittance among four or five, which seems to be but just sufficient for one. [H]e must feel conscious, if he thinks at all, that should he have a large family, and any ill luck whatever, no degree of frugality, no possible exertion of his manual strength could preserve him from the heart rending sensation of seeing his children starve....[44]

That such low-paid workers, whose poverty concededly preceded and therefore was not caused by their large families, failed to listen to reason was, in Malthus's opinion, in no small part due to the poor-law system, which weakened the sense of independence that would otherwise also have operated to deter imprudent marriages.[45] Since many would never receive wages in excess of a "pittance," that is, since even the bachelor-proletariat was mired in poverty, and since the institution of marriage was quasi-natural for Malthus, it is misleading to characterize workers as having behaved irrationally in failing to conduct a cost-benefit analysis of each procreational act. It was not a matter of being "fatalistic, feckless, irresponsible, without a belief in the future...." Indeed, if Weberian *Zweckrationalität* means "consciously choos[ing] among known alternatives on the basis of their probable effect,"[46] then penurious laborers may well have been rational—given their Hobson's choice between the prospect of a life without familial relationships and of conferring on their children the same poverty to which generations of workers had become accustomed.

Rather than having "advocated a public effort to foster the embourgeoisement of the poor," Malthus in fact perceived and approved of a societal structure that preordained such poverty.[47] According to his version of the asocial contract ushering in the transition from Godwin's egalitarian utopia to capitalism, with the establishment of private property and marriage, "these two fundamental laws of society,"

> inequality of conditions must necessarily follow. Those who were born after the division of property, would come into a world already possessed. If their parents, from having too large a family, could not give them sufficient for their support, what are they to do in a world where every thing is appropriated?... The members of a family which was grown too large for the original division of land appropriated to it, could not then demand a part of the surplus produce of others, as a debt of justice. [F]rom the inevitable laws of our nature, some human beings must suffer from want. These are the unhappy persons who, in the great lottery of life, have drawn a blank.... All who were in want of food would...offer to work for a bare subsistence, and the rearing of families would be checked by sickness and misery.[48]

Although Malthus "always" assumed the efficacy of a process of demographic self-equilibration, his counterintuitively optimistic position derived from the structure of his theory of population, within which, "[s]trictly speaking, over-population was impossible...."[49] That Malthus, however, self-contradictorily did not trust the invisible hand's grip on the genitalia to promote some kind of optimum population, emerges from the fact that whereas on the one hand he opposed entrusting to individual workers or working-class families autonomous control to limit their fertility, on the other he urged state intervention to curtail pauper procreation.[50] In one of his boldest and harshest public policy inter-ventions—which gainsays all efforts by Keynes and others to cast Malthus's *Essay* as "profoundly in the English tradition of humane science [and] marked by...an immense disinterestedness and public spirit"[51]—Malthus urged power-holders "formally to disclaim the *right* of the poor to support." To that end he proposed that no child born within a marriage that took place more than a year after the enactment and no illegitimate child born two years thereafter "should ever be entitled to parish relief." Thereafter:

> if any man chose to marry, without a prospect of being able to support a family, he should have the most perfect liberty to do so. Though to marry in this case, is in my opinion clearly an immoral act, yet it is not one which society can justly take upon itself to prevent or punish; because the punishment provided for it by the laws of nature, falls

directly and most severely upon the individual who commits the act, and through him, only more remotely and feebly, on the society. When nature will govern and punish for us, it is a very miserable ambition to wish to snatch the rod from her hands, and draw upon ourselves the odium of executioner. To the punishment therefore of nature he should be left, the punishment of want.... He should be taught to know, that the laws of nature, which are the laws of God, had doomed him and his family to suffer for disobeying their repeated admonitions; that he had no claim of *right* on society for the smallest portion of food, beyond that which his labour would fairly purchase....

If this system were pursued...the only difficulty would be, to restrain the hand of benevolence from assisting those in distress in so indiscriminate a manner as to encourage indolence and want of foresight in others.

It may appear to be hard, that a mother and her child, who had been guilty of no particular crime themselves, should suffer for the ill conduct of the father; but this is one of the invariable laws of nature.... In the moral government of the world, it seems evidently necessary, that the sins of the fathers should be visited upon the children....[52]

This extreme biological-naturalistic turn Malthus appropriated from Joseph Townsend, an English clergyman, whom he failed to acknowledge until the second edition of the *Essay* in 1803.[53] In his *Dissertation on the Poor Laws*, which formed a watershed dividing Adam Smith's belief in progress from the Malthusian preoccupation with overpopulation,[54] Townsend had urged the state to refrain from seeking to improve upon the disciplinary powers of nature, by which he manifestly meant the class-bound assets endowment consequent upon the accumulation of capital:

The wisest legislator will never be able to devise a more equitable, a more effectual, or...a more suitable punishment, than hunger is for a disobedient servant. Hunger will tame the fiercest animals, it will teach...obedience and subjection, to the most brutish, the most obstinate, and the most perverse.... It seems to be a law of nature, that the poor should be to a certain degree improvident, that there may always be some to fulfil the most servile, the most sordid, and the most ignoble offices in the community. [T]hereby...the more delicate are not only relieved from drudgery, and freed from those occasional employments which would make them miserable, but are left at liberty...to pursue those callings which are suited to their various dispositions, and most useful to the state. As for the lowest of the poor, by custom they are reconciled to the meanest occupations, to the most laborious works, and to the most hazardous pursuits; whilst the hope of their reward makes them chearful in the midst of all their dangers and their toils. [W]hat is it but distress and poverty which can prevail upon the lower classes...to encounter all the horrors which await them...? ... There must be a degree of pressure, and that which is attended with the least violence will be the best. When hunger is either felt or feared, the desire of obtaining bread will quietly dispose the mind to undergo the greatest hardships....[55]

By infusing political economy with Townsend's naturalization of class conflict and his conversion of economic laws into a biotheodicy, Malthus, whom the economist Nassau Senior called "our most eminent living philosophical writer," enabled the ruling classes both to deny responsibility for the poverty of the new proletariat—by assigning the blame to the workers themselves—without undermining the legitimacy of their power and to inculcate in the poor "self-dependence without developing in them a dangerous independence."[56] Both Ricardo and Malthus grasped enough of the incentives for wage labor required and furnished by capital to cast significant doubt on Polanyi's extravagant claim that neither "understood the working of the capitalist system"; after Townsend had introduced nature in the form of scarcity and hunger as the great regulative in lieu of government or laws, Polanyi argued, political economy had recourse to naturalism to explain the misery of the masses.[57] It is, to the contrary, far more plausible that Ricardo's adaptation in his *Principles* of Malthus's tenets of population enhanced the value of political economy in the eyes of its "prosperous readers [who] saw the Malthusian theory employed to amend the deficiencies in the doctrine of Smith which had...limited Smith's usefulness to the middle class."[58]

Malthus himself made it clear that workingmen whose "impulses of passion" were out of control had only themselves to blame for their impoverishment. Anticipating culture-of-poverty theorists, Malthus emphasized the circumstances that made "the lower classes...unable or unwilling to reason from the past to the future, and ready to acquiesce, for the sake of present gratification, in a very low standard of comfort and respectability...." Among the prerequisites for imbuing workers with prudential habits he listed civil and political liberty. The former enabled people to plan for the future by assuring free scope to their industry by securing their property to them; the latter, in turn, enforced the former in part by "obliging the higher classes to respect them...." How disfranchised proletarians, whose only species of property, their highly perishable labor power, rarely permitted them to accumulate any other species, could ever acquire bourgeois habits, Malthus never explained.[59]

As if preparing the working class for compulsory relegation to Procreators Anonymous, Malthus insisted that:

> When the wages of labour are hardly sufficient to maintain two children, a man marries and has five or six.... He accuses the insufficiency of the price of labour to maintain a family.... He accuses the avarice of the rich, who suffer him to want what they can so well spare. He accuses the partial and unjust institutions of society, which have awarded him an inadequate share of the produce of the earth.... In searching for objects of accusation, he never adverts to the quarter from which his misfortunes originate. The last person that he would think of accusing is himself, on whom...the principal blame lies....[60]

The advice that Malthus offered the working class and the state poor-law policies that he sought to influence presupposed the forever-lastingness of capitalism: "The structure of society...will probably always remain unchanged. [I]t will always consist of a class of proprietors and a class of labourers...." Against this dehistoricized background, Malthus issued a warning to workers: "A market overstocked with labour, and an ample remuneration to each labourer, are objects perfectly incompatible with each other. In the annals of the world they never existed together." If, then, workers, whom Malthus identified with the poor, wished to avail themselves of the high wages that capitalism made possible, Malthus counseled, "we" would have to explain to "them" "that the withholding of the supplies of labour is the only possible way of really raising its price, and that they themselves, being the possessors of this commodity, have alone the power to do this."[61] It was this lockstep logic linking procreation, labor market, and poverty that set a reformist-ameliorist framework that would both enrage and attract labor unions and socialist parties into the twentieth century. Thus it was also in this narrower sense that Malthus's "extraordinary achievement [was] to have formulated the terms of discourse on the subject of poverty" well beyond his death.[62]

Malthus was very careful to argue that whatever advances labor might achieve would be secured only through individual procreative behavior in conformity with the eternal laws of population; collective action was doomed to failure.[63] Thus Malthus was, to be sure, willing to concede that, in light of the considerable amount of unnecessary labor:

> if the lower classes...could agree among themselves never to work more than six or seven hours in the day, the commodities essential to human happiness might still be produced in as great abundance as at present. But it is almost impossible to conceive that such an agreement could be adhered to. From the principle of population, some would necessarily be more in want than others. Those that had large families would naturally be desirous of exchanging two hours more of their labour for an ampler quantity of subsistence. How are they to be prevented from making this exchange? It would be a violation of the first and most sacred property that a man possesses, to attempt, by positive institutions, to interfere with his command over his own labour.[64]

Apart from the obvious issue as to why the principle of population is inconsistent with uniformly small families decided upon voluntarily, the answer to Malthus's question as to how to avoid a working class race for the bottom is equally obvious: family allowances. Such subsidies would make it unnecessary for workers to sell as much as possible of the only property they have to sell—their and their numerous children's labor power. Indeed, allowances might even arrest the "seemingly irrational" proletarian strategy of high fertility in order to produce more wage labor per household.[65]

Remarkably, Malthus grasped this logic and inconsistently even advocated its implementation as policy. With a view toward a more enlightened future, Malthus envisioned "such prudential habits among the poor as would prevent them from marrying when the actual price of labour, joined to what they might have saved in their single state, would not give them the prospect of being able to support a wife and five or six children without assistance."[66] But, Malthus conceded,

> even this degree of prudence might not always avail, as when a man marries he cannot tell what number of children he shall have, and many have more than six. [I]n this case I do not think that any evil would result from making a certain allowance to every child above this number; not with a view of rewarding a man for his large family, but merely of relieving him from a species of distress which it would be unreasonable in us to expect that he should calculate upon. And with this view, the relief should be merely such as to place him exactly in the same situation as if he had had six children.[67]

Even more implausibly, Malthus approved of a law that would bestow pensions on those with ten and twelve children on the ground that it "might relieve particular individuals from a very pressing and unlooked for distress, without operating in any respect as an encouragement to marriage."[68] This view is just one example of the kind of confused thinking that led George Stigler to conclude that Malthus "had one great weakness—he could not reason well. He could not construct a theory that was consistent with either itself or the facts of the world." Malthus was much less confused with regard to the taxing mechanism for a family allowance: he categorically rejected bachelor taxes. In view of the inadquacy of wages to support large families and the number of poverty-induced deaths, if many newborn were not "greatly thinned" by premature mortality, impossible demands would have to be made of the wage-fund. Consequently, those who remain unmarried do not reduce the actual population but merely premature mortality and therefore deserve no punishment.[69]

Whatever the inconsistencies in his reasoning, Malthus was even more wedded to the wondrous notion that even reproduction was controlled by an invisible hand that also swatted away would-be free riders. In order to achieve improvement, according to Malthus:

> It is not necessary of us to act from motives to which we are unaccustomed; to pursue a general good which we may not distinctly comprehend, or the effect of which may be weakened by distance and diffusion. The happiness of the whole is to be the happiness of individuals.... No co-operation is required.... He who performs his duty faithfully will reap the full fruits of it, whatever may be the number of others who fail. This duty is...merely that he is not to bring beings into the world for whom he cannot find the means of support.[70]

Here Malthus overlooked the free riders, who can develop an individualist strategy at the expense of the rest of their class comrades.[71] For poor-law administrators since Malthus may have counseled the working class that higher living standards are unattainable without limiting fertility: "Yet while an abstract 'working class' may suffer, any specific family may benefit. It must take the labor market as it finds it; in past centuries more children per family have usually meant more income per family." In fact, whereas macroeconomically an increase in population led, during the preindustrial period, characteristically to a decline in per capita income, the enormous productivity advances unleashed by the Industrial Revolution broke this link. Nevertheless, even later, once child labor was suppressed, "within any individual family matters were much as they had previously been for the society as a whole."[72]

Malthus's position resembled the argument advanced at the beginning of the twentieth century by some "birth-strike" advocates to the effect that regardless of the impact on the proletariat as a class, individual working-class parents could promote their own welfare by limiting family size.[73] Schumpeter's disqualification of Malthus applied to these individualistic birth-strikers as well. He asserted that "a surface observation...greatly facilitated" the survival of Malthus's "fundamentally untenable or worthless" doctrine:

> clearly, the most obvious reason for misery and squalor in the individual proletarian family was size. The inference that all would have been better off and happier if all had restricted the number of their children follows by means of the same fallacy that led people to infer from everyone's tendency to make the best of his situation that, if all are left to their own devices, a maximum of "happiness" must result for all.[74]

An extensively and minutely articulated cultural, institutional, psychological, and ideological context must be and has been created to sustain (working-class) parents' interest in quantitatively adequate levels of procreation. The reason that it is unfruitful to contrast individual motivations and macrosocietal outcomes and to be baffled by "supra-intentional causality" such as invisible hand tropes[75] is that:

> The point does not consist in the fact that inasmuch as everyone pursues his own private interest, the totality of private interests, that is the general interest is attained. The point is rather that the private interest itself is already a societally determined interest and can be achieved only within the conditions posited by society and with the means provided by it; hence it is bound to the reproduction of these conditions and means. It is the interest of private persons; but its content, as well as the form and means of its realization, is given by societal conditions independent of all.[76]

This programmatic mediation of a methodological individualism that reduces the explicability of social phenomena to individuals only and a methodological collectivism that assumes the existence of supra-individual entities with higher-order explanatory power may be illustrated by reference to the private production of wage laborers. Here it is crucial not to collapse methodological collectivism into models of unconscious rationality or invisible-hand-induced demographic homeostasis. Socioeconomic forces and mechanisms operating beyond the level of individual consciousness or choice can nevertheless bring about disequilibria and crises:[77]

> People do not have birth rates, they have children. Their willingness to bear and rear children—to expend their human and material resources in this manner—cannot be taken for granted. Rather, childbearing and child rearing take place in an organized context which strongly influences people to do one set of things—reproduce—and not to do other activities that would conflict or compete with reproduction.[78]

In other words, subtle and unthinking internalization and not-so-subtle imposition of norms may inculcate the attitudes and induce the behavior required to transform biological reproduction into material and ideological reproduction of the social order. Precisely because neither Malthusian nor utilitarian attempts to link fertility to economic factors attend sufficiently to the way people "give meaning to the situations in which they find themselves and base their actions on such meanings and interpretations," even some economic demographers have found them wanting.[79]

JOHN STUART MILL AND THE AUTHORITARIAN SIDE OF CLASSICAL LIBERALISM

> [I]n the absence of state intervention population will not assume the size consonant with whatever set of communal ends is generally subscribed to by the population. This lack of consonance is traceable primarily to the fact that in a completely free enterprise economy it is apparently impossible...to establish such a set of relationships among the individuals composing that economy as will assure to each reward or punishment in proportion to his contribution to, or subtraction from, the sum total of communal welfare.[80]

Despite his status as the fountainhead of modern political-economic liberalism, John Stuart Mill developed a coherent body of policy regarding state intervention into procreational decisions and conduct that would surprise, if not embarrass, his late-twentieth-century followers. Already as a 17-year-old, Mill was arrested for distributing Francis Place's *verbotene* pamphlets encouraging the working class to limit its reproduction through the use of contraceptive sponges.[81] As an economist, Mill early on expressed his admiration of Malthus's achievements on behalf of workers. In contrast to Adam Smith, who believed that in the stationary state—"towards which things must be at all times tending"—workers "must be pinched and in a condition of hardship," Malthus, paradoxical as it might seem, forged the insight that the laboring classes' condition was "susceptible of permanent improvement."[82] For the period of semibarbarism, when "it probably was not desirable that population should be restrained," Mill credited "the pressure of physical want" with having created the "stimulus...to the exertion of labour and ingenuity" necessary for the formation of industrial society. Contemporary Europe, however, no longer needed such privation "to make men...better workmen...." Nevertheless, he was contemptuous of do-gooders who sentimentally "ignore[d] totally the law of wages, or...dismiss[ed] it...as 'hard-hearted Malthusianism,' as if it were not a thousand times more hard-hearted to tell human beings that they may, than that they may not, call into existence swarms of creatures who are sure to be miserable, and most likely to be depraved...."[83]

In the chapter of *On Liberty* designed to illustrate the book's maxims—namely, that the individual is free to do anything that does not "concern the interests" of anyone else, and that society may intervene against actions that "are prejudicial to the interests of others"—Mill, revealing how much of Malthus inhered in neo-Malthusianism, dealt extensively with the state's obligation to control any person's power over others, including procreational freedom. However:

> This obligation is almost entirely disregarded in the case of the family relations.... It is in the case of children, that misapplied notions of liberty are a real obstacle to the fulfilment by the State of its duties. One would almost think that a man's children were supposed to be literally...a part of himself.... It remains unrecognized, that to bring a child into existence without a fair prospect of being able, not only to provide food for its body, but instruction and training for its mind, is a moral crime, both against the unfortunate offspring and against society.... [T]o bestow a life which may be either a curse or a blessing—unless the being on whom it is to be bestowed will have at least the ordinary chances of a desirable existence, is a crime against that being. And in a country either over-peopled, or threatened with being so, to produce children, beyond a very small number, with the effect of reducing the reward of labor by their competition, is a serious offence against all who live by the remuneration of their labor. [L]aws which...forbid marriage unless the parties can show that they have the means of supporting a family, do not exceed the legitimate powers of the State: and...they are not objectionable as violations of liberty.... Yet the current ideas of liberty...would repel the attempt to put any restraint upon his inclinations when the consequence of their indulgence is a life, or lives, of wretchedness and depravity to the offspring, with manifold evils to those sufficiently within reach to be in any way affected by their actions.[84]

The policy consequences of Mill's application of his principles of freedom to procreation were very restrictive because reproducers may have a prejudicial impact on others. Mill therefore denied that anyone had "a right to bring creatures into life, to be supported by other people…. If a man cannot support even himself unless others help him, those others are entitled to say that they do not also undertake the support of any offspring which it is physically possible for him to summon into the world."[85]

To suggest just how far liberalism has departed from Mill's vision, it suffices to look at a recent major economic-demographic study of the United States by a liberal economist whose "simple welfare rule of thumb" is: "If the social costs of an extra child are borne only by his parents and older siblings, the extra birth is the family's business and not society's."[86] Contemporary liberalism thus privileges biological paternalism; for when it assigns procreational decisions to the discretion of "the family," experience suggests that the decision-makers—if indeed any conscious decision to procreate lies behind the next birth—are not the totality of affected family members, but at most the parents. Yet society intervenes in all manner of ways after birth to increase the welfare of children—including the drastic step of removing children from the control of abusive parents.

Why has post-Millian liberalism become libertarian with regard to procreators' power to determine the size of their realm? The only plausible defense of state abstentionism is that the state is no better at predicting the future in general and the life of these individual children in particular than are the parents.[87] Although much speaks in favor of permitting human beings to enhance their autonomy by making as many decisions as possible affecting their lives and perhaps the lives of the children whom society authorizes them to shape, it is disingenuous to assert that a board or group of people using an actuarial base containing millions of life histories has no greater perspective than a single person with little or no overview of how successfully others have managed to support large families.[88]

Uninhibited by such doubts, Mill, out-Malthusing Malthus, expressed astonishment that some contemporaries saw "hardship in preventing paupers from breeding hereditary paupers in the workhouse itself." Mill's strictures on procreative freedom culminated in this astounding super-Malthusian antiliberal proposal: "It would be possible for the state to guarantee employment at ample wages to all who are born. But if it does this, it is bound in self-protection, and for the sake of every purpose for which government exists, to provide that no person shall be born without its consent."[89] Even Mill's employment of last resort had its limits. For although Mill did, to be sure, support state-mediated redistribution to aliment those children who have already been born to poor parents,

> it is another thing altogether, when those who have produced and accumulated are called upon to abstain from consuming until they have given food and clothing, not only to all those who now exist, but to all whom these or their descendants may think fit to call into existence…. The attempt would of course be made to exact labour in exchange for support. But… [w]hen the pay is not given for the sake of the work, but

the work found for the sake of the pay, inefficiency is a matter of certainty: to extract real work from day-labourers without the power of dismissal, is only practicable by the power of the lash.[90]

A straight line descends from Mill's framework—which can be traced back to French proposals that workers be adopted, as it were, by their employers, who would, together with the obligation of maintaining them, have the right to forbid them to marry—to biologist Garrett Hardin's neoauthoritarianism: "If the community has the responsibility of keeping children alive it must also have the power to decide when they may be procreated."[91] Advocacy of the anti-invisible-hand position in the United States has, during the last third of the twentieth century, been most prominently associated with Hardin's antidemocratic, overpopulationist version. In his immensely influential piece, "The Tragedy of the Commons," he admonishes the world to "exorcise the spirit of Adam Smith in the field of practical demography." Once it was discovered that the assumption that, guided by their own lights, "men will control their individual fecundity so as to produce the optimum population," was wrong, reexamination of the defensibility of "our individual freedoms" advanced to the head of the global political agenda.[92]

The tragedy of the commons is a subset of the type of irrationality associated with an invisible but broken hand. The latter, larger field encompasses individually rational actions producing a result that no one desires. The tragedy of the commons is narrower in that it would not include the depopulationist version. If, for example, individuals act rationally in limiting their fertility because they want to minimize the restrictions of child rearing, the unintended and undesirable decline in population would not constitute a commons ruined by overexploitation.[93]

Hardin's model can be better understood by studying his self-professed inspirational source, William Forster Lloyd, the Drummond professor of political economy at Christ Church, Oxford University, in the 1830s. The year before the New Poor Law was enacted, Lloyd published his *Two Lectures on the Checks to Population*, which makes the foundations of Hardin's approach transparent. Taking as his starting point the conventional Malthusian assumption of the impossibility that increases in food production would keep pace with natural population growth, Lloyd examined the contribution of the preventive checks to population to the inexorable restoration of equilibrium. Because "[s]ystems of equality, with a community of labor and goods," allegedly impeded the action of preventive checks, he began with these institutions.[94]

Lloyd justified his animus against equality by reference to private property in land, which served two purposes. Productively it gave individual owners an incentive to produce and to avoid wasteful destruction; demographically it allocated definite shares of produce large enough to provide for "the comfortable maintenance of a family." This method of determining the number of families to be supported by means of the prior division of land was superior to granting admission to the table to all who are born and then determining each person's (insufficient) share by the number of admissions. The beneficial consequences of private productive wealth justified inequality without which exertion would be dulled. The hierarchy of riches associated with inequality induced men to engage in the behavior that would enable them to rise in the world. Inequality could, however, become excessive in relation to its demographic function. Where too few appropriated too much property and "the class of mere labourers is great, the principle of population would...justify the appropriation of the field of employment, and a monopoly of labour." Since the latter monopoly was much more difficult to sustain than one of property, its equivalent was "the diffusion of a sufficient degree of property throughout...society."[95]

Such was the big picture sketched by Lloyd, familiarity with which, according to Hardin, might have spared Marx "his worst errors...."[96] In analyzing regimes of equality, Lloyd supposed the case of two people who labored jointly, agreeing to share the product as common property. By combining forces, they transformed their motivational structure, which in their prior Robinson Crusoe existence had been guided "by the magnitude of the personal consequences expected by each individual...." Now, in contrast, each obtained only half the gain of his additional exertions and bore only half the loss of his shirking. Once the number of partners became large, the personal consequences of the individual's work effort or wastage became so minuscule as to lose its purchase on his will.[97]

Lloyd's joint producers or joint commons users are gritting their teeth as they enter into relationships with others. At bottom they remain rugged individualists with no conception of the larger progressive sociocultural transformation wrought by the division of labor and cooperation. They continue to compare only the narrow advantages of joint production with some mythical natural state of loners into which they may retreat at the slightest perception of a quantitative advantage. Even after their plunge into sociability, they remain "fundamentally autonomous, self-serving, irresponsible creatures, as radically alienated from each other as they are from the grass on which they feed their cows." Consequently, Hardin is merely refuting a self-made caricature when he asserts that Lloyd offered the "definitive disproof of the Marxist imperative"—the communist "to each according to his needs," which, "where each person is free to judge his own needs, necessarily leads to tragedy in a world of scarcities."[98]

The demographic function of Lloyd's parable was simply to illustrate an action-consequence structure in which present and future are opposed to each other—in which actors must compare a present individual pain and a future collective benefit or a present individual pleasure and a future collective pain. In a large society, in which the individual's share of the future collective good or bad is evanescent, it is rational for the individual, even where he is fully aware of the collective consequences, to ignore them. Projecting this scheme onto the theory of population, Lloyd inserted marriage as the present pleasure and the financial burdens of reproduction as the future pain. Alluding, perhaps, to the old poor law system, Lloyd argued that if the collective paid for the children, everyone would choose the present pleasure, leading to the dreaded Malthusian denouement. Nevertheless, the ensuing overpopulation, far from being the fault of the imprudent people themselves, might be caused by "the constitution of society...."[99]

Ignoring the complex contradictory movements of the accumulation and profitability of capital, Lloyd posited that the only impediment to full employment was a lack of subsistence for the entire potential working population. But assuming that "those who have the food of the country at their disposal" have enough to support all, Lloyd asserted that employment then entitled each to "a proportional share of the general stock of subsistence." Thus if the labor of an unmarried man commands 1/10,000,000 of the food stock, as soon as he marries and produces children capable of immediate employment, their labor will command 2/10,000,001 of the stock. The total burden that reproduction imposes on him "consists in the difference between one out of ten million, and one out of ten million and one parts," which must remain individually "imperceptible." Consequently, the defective motivational structure that he had already identified "under a community of goods" reproduces itself even under capitalism: "there is a want of appropriation to each person of the consequences of his own conduct. All suffer through the act of one, and no encouragement to moral restraint is offered to individuals." Nor would the procreational micro-calculus change if Lloyd relaxed his assumption of full employment in favor of an equal chance of employment. For even if a potential father knew that employment was a game of musical chairs, he could rationally believe that the risk of unemployment was equally and randomly distributed among the childless and the child-rich: "Being himself exposed to it...from the increase of population resulting from the marriages of others, he will not anticipate any sensible increase of danger to himself, from the competition of his own children."[100]

In order to suggest the universality of the logic, Lloyd constructed two parallel cases. The first involved two societies: in one parents assumed the entire burden of child support, whereas in the other the children began maintaining themselves at an early age; the second case was characterized by enclosures and commons. The parallel consisted in the density—of the population in the one and of the stocking in the other. Both enclosed and common fields or pastures have a "point of saturation...beyond which no prudent man will add to his stock," but that point is different in the two. In the privately owned field, the owner would not knowingly stock beyond the saturation point because all that the additional cattle consumed would be deducted from what was available to the original stock. In the privately appropriated commons, however, since losses are shared, the individual appropriator would gain more than he lost. Lloyd then asserted that employment is also a common open to the born and unborn and thus "constantly stocked to the extreme point of saturation." Thus neither in the real world of the English working class nor in Lloyd's fictitious community of labor and goods—where the increase in resources still mandated prudent procreation, yet that obligation was insufficiently divided and appropriated—would the prudent alone reap the benefit or the imprudent alone "feel the evil consequences." And even in the best case, where new-born maintained themselves immediately, it would not be the case that "nobody else is the worse for their being brought into the world" since Lloyd assumed that beyond the saturation point diminishing returns had already set in.[101]

Finally, the same defective motivational structure prompted Lloyd to cast doubt on the plausibility of Malthus's hope that moral restraint would reduce the supply and raise the price of labor. Since "among laborers who have only the sale of their labour on which to depend for their maintenance...there is no individual benefit to be derived from abstinence," whereas the benefits of marriage were palpable, the outcome was clear. And even if workers did abstain, Lloyd could see no hindrance to the emergence of free riders, who would use the new higher wage level to raise a large family; the few material hardships that such a decision would entail vis-à-vis the childless would never suffice to recommend celibacy or even delay in beginning reproduction "since, among laborers, the natural age for marriage coincid[es] nearly with the time when their income is the greatest, and when...they are best able to endure privations...."[102]

Hardin has added but little to Lloyd's analysis. Adopting the analogy of the earth to a commons, Hardin insists that unimpeded access to a pasture inevitably induces each individual herdsman, as "a rational being," to let as many of his own cattle graze there as possible. Since he privately appropriates "all the proceeds from the sale of the additional animal," whereas the negative effects of overgrazing are shared by all herdsmen, eventually "[f]reedom in a commons brings ruin to all." Why Hardin has chosen to style the cattle farmers as market-maximizers subject to the inexorable compulsions of capital accumulation rather than as members of a·community which regards the products of nature as sources of concrete use values, which are not subordinated to limitless self-expansion, is unclear. Hardin's implicit capital-logic leads him to assert that cattlemen who owned rather than leased ranges would in fact have a profit-oriented incentive not to undermine the viability of the basis of their livelihood: "The tragedy of the commons as a food basket is averted by private property," which generates this beneficial result because the owner-entrepreneur is individually responsible in the sense that he is the immediate victim of his own bad decisions.[103]

Others have demonstrated, however, that just as a private owner of a resource may microrationally destroy a rain forest for short-term profits from ranching, conversely, some historical and contemporary collectively controlled commons have been well maintained for centuries. Hardin has failed to consider the possibility that the transition from more communal societies to capitalism undermined that function of social systems that had helped integrate individual members' understanding of their short-run personal advantage with the whole community's long-run benefit.[104]

The remaining question is why the working class in advanced capitalist societies, whose reproduction is free of capital-logical incentives, would reproductively foul the global commons. It is clear why the compulsions of a capitalist economy force firms to create externalities. Hardin merely assumes, however, presumably by modeling humans as capitalist maximizers, that individual potential procreators are as hopelessly caught up in larger forces as are individual capitals. But whereas laws of accumulation condemn firms to compete or disappear, and humans of all classes in advanced capitalist societies may be subject to various societal compulsions, there is no evidence that they are trapped by analogous reproductive laws. Consequently, they could achieve, through a process of mutual and self-education that is unavailable to competitive capitals, collective demographic decisions.

For Hardin, however, the tragedy of the demographic commons originates in the fact that the world does not function as Malthus imagined it: because of society's deep commitment to the welfare state, the vice of human overbreeding no longer brings "its own 'punishment' to the germ line...." Consequently, that state must ask: How shall it "deal with the family, the religion, the race, or the class...that adopts overbreeding as a policy to secure its own aggrandizement?"[105] Although Hardin fails to explain in what sense individual above-average procreation rises to the level of a policy let alone an act of self-aggrandizement rather than of ignorance or carelessness, he is certain that collective education is powerless to reform the conscience of those who accurately perceive their (microsocietal) self-interest. And because reliance on mere moral appeals would counterproductively lead to overbreeding by the asocial, he opts for "mutual coercion mutually agreed upon by the majority of the people affected." He concedes that "coercion is a dirty word to most liberals now, but...by saying it over and over without apology or embarrassment," it can become acceptable. If abandonment of the "freedom to breed" is urgently required, Hardin neglects to explain how a democracy can save the world in the absence of majoritarian support for mutual coercion, which for him represents "a spectrum, ranging from tax incentives to detention camps."[106]

Recognizing the authoritarian corner into which he had painted himself, Hardin has logically shifted to the establishment of a dictatorship of "[f]ortunate minorities [who] must act as the trustees of a civilization that is threatened by uninformed good intentions." To be sure, he is referring to Third World "over-breeding," which he sees as tempting Americans to share their food in a disastrous "'one mouth, one meal'" policy, to which he opposes an "allocation of rights based on territory...." In principle, however, having come this far, Hardin must be prepared to defend an analogous allocation of rights within a national territory as between the recalcitrant who "emulate the rabbits" and the trustees of the commons.[107]

An even more radical demographic approach that exactly tracks the tragedy of the commons surpasses Hardin's tolerance for authoritarianism. It was outlined by a congressman in 1854 during the debate over the Kansas-Nebraska bill. Mike Walsh, a Democrat from New York, availed himself of a common southern trope portraying the northern wage worker as a slave of the employing class (rather than of an individual owner), who, after having "added wealth, by his labor and his toil, to the community...is turned adrift without any, among all the different employers whom he has aided in enriching, to give him a mouthful of victuals or a night's lodging." The slave owner, in contrast, "has to" provide for his slave in sickness and old age. Walsh then characterized the difference between slavery and capitalism as

> simply this: If a dozen of us own a horse in common, we want to ride
> him as much as possible, and feed him as little as possible. [Laughter.]
> But if you or I own a horse exclusively, we will take good care to feed
> him well, and not drive him too much to endanger his health....[108]

The tragedy of the proletarian demographic commons could therefore be overcome by converting labor power from a regime of common exploitation and private ownership by the worker to exclusive private use and ownership by a single slave owner, whose firm would self-sufficiently produce its own labor inputs. But even if individual slave owners had the economic incentive to promote the volume of procreation that would result in an optimal microdevelopment of labor power, an invisible hand would still have been required to coordinate thousands of plantation-level decisions to generate an optimal macrodemographic outcome.[109] Such a state-slave society would be more coercive than even Hardin proposed.

The prominence of Hardin's demographic anti-laissez-faire stance must be understood in a broader context. Beginning in the 1950s, when First World social scientists and state officials charged with coordinating international economic relations constructed a case for the existence of overpopulation in the Third World, demography recognized as never before that microlevel procreational sovereignties did not necessarily generate a collective optimum. The emergence of below-replacement-level reproduction in Europe and North America from the 1960s forward reinforced this insight. But the resurgence of market-knows-best economic theories and policies in the 1980s resurrected invisible-hand demography.[110]

NOTES

1. Jeremy Bentham, *Method and Leading Features of an Institute of Political Economy*, in *Jeremy Bentham's Economic Writings* 3:305, 361-62 (W. Stark ed., 1954 [1801-1804]).

2. National Research Council, *Population Growth and Economic Development: Policy Questions* 81 (1986).

3. James Field, *Essays on Population* 278 (1931).

4. Joseph Spengler, *Population and America's Future* 158 (1975).

5. T. Paul Schultz, "An Economic Perspective on Population Growth," in *Rapid Population Growth: Consequences and Policy Implications* 148-74 at 165 (National Academy of Sciences, 1971) (quote); Joseph Spengler, "Population Problem: In Search of a Solution," *Science* 166:1234-38 at 1235 (Dec. 5, 1969); David Friedman, *Laissez-Faire in Population: The Least Bad Solution* 17-21 (1972).

6. Glen Cain, "Issues in the Economics of a Population Policy for the United States," *Am. Econ. Rev.* 61 (2):408-17 at 412, 415, 416 (May 1971). See also Paul Demeny, "Discussion," *Am. Econ. Rev.* 61 (2):421 (May 1971).

7. Antony Flew, "The Structure of Malthus' Population Theory," *Australasian J. Phil.* 35 (1):1-20 at 19 (May 1957).

8. Kingsley Davis, "Population Policy: Will Current Programs Succeed?" *Science* 158:730-39 at 738 (Nov. 10, 1967).

9. Harvey Leibenstein, *Economic Backwardness and Economic Growth: Studies in the Theory of Economic Development* 160 (1957).

10. [U.K.] Royal Commission on Population, *Report* ¶ 89 at 36 (Cmd. 7695, 1949).

11. Kingsley Davis, "The Theory of Change and Response in Modern Demographic History," *Pop. Index* 29 (4):345-66 at 351 (Oct. 1963).

12. Thomas Carlyle, *Chartism*, in *The Works of Thomas Carlyle in Thirty Volumes* 29:118, 200-201 (1899 [1839]).

13. E.A. Wrigley, "Fertility Strategy for the Individual and the Group," in *Historical Studies of Changing Fertility* 135-54 (Charles Tilly ed., 1978). Confusingly, Wrigley refers to the possibility of contrasting the unconscious rationality of individuals in traditional society with the conscious rationality of couples in industrial societies. *Ibid.* at 152. An invisible-hand mechanism converting individual-level rationality into macro-rationality would have to be operative even in the latter case.

14. Donald Bogue, *Principles of Demography* 51-52 (1968).

15. Ron Lesthaeghe, "On the Social Control of Human Reproduction," *Pop. & Dev. Rev.* 6 (4):527-48 at 528-29 (Dec. 1980) (quote); Paul Demeny, "Welfare Considerations in U.S. Population Policy," in U.S. Commission on Population Growth and the American Future, 6 *Research Reports: Aspects of Population Growth Policy* 153-72 at 157 (Robert Parke, Jr. & Charles Westoff eds., 1972).

16. Friedman, *Laissez-Faire in Population* at 6.

17. Carl Roesler, *Zur Kritik der Lehre vom Arbeitslohn: Ein volkswirthschaftlicher Versuch* 60 (1861).

18. R.M. Smith, "Transfer Incomes, Risk and Security: The Roles of the Family and the Collectivity in Recent Theories of Fertility Change," in *The State of Population Theory: Forward from Malthus* 188-211 at 189 (David Coleman & Roger Schofield eds., 1986).

19. Alfred Sauvy, "Le Malthusianisme anglo-saxon," *Population* 2 (2):221-42 at 221 (Apr.-June 1947); K. Popper, *The Open Society and Its Enemies* 2:93, 323 n.11 (1973 [1945]). See also Julius Sensat, "Methodological Individualism and Marxism," *Economics & Phil.* 4:189-219 (1988).

20. Robert Hertz, "Socialisme et Dépopulation," *Les Cahiers du socialiste*, No. 10, at 24 (1910).

21. Earlier Smith had described an even more perspicacious invisible hand:

> The rich only select from the heap what is most precious and agreeable. They consume little more than the poor; and in spite of their natural selfishness and rapacity, though they mean only their own conveniency, though the sole end which they propose from the labours of all the thousands whom they employ be the gratification of their own vain and insatiable desires, they divide with the poor the produce of all their improvements. They are led by an invisible hand to make nearly the same distribution of the necessaries of life which would have been made had the earth been divided into equal poritons among all its inhabitants; and thus, without intending it, without knowing it, advance the interest of the society, and afford means to the multiplication of the species.

Adam Smith, *The Theory of Moral Sentiments* 304 (1976 [1759]). On the background of the notion of an invisible hand, see D. Raphael, *Adam Smith* 71-73 (1985). In contradistinction to Smith's nonrationalist notion, Kant sketched an invisible hand not as a matter of knowledge but of *Vernunftglaube.* Immanuel Kant, *Idee zu einer allgemeinen Geschichte in weltbürgerlicher Absicht,* in Immanuel Kant, *Werke in Zwölf Bänden* 11:33-50 at 33-34 (1957 [1784]).

22. Adam Smith, *An Inquiry into the Nature and Causes of the Wealth of Nations* 421, 423 (Edwin Cannan ed., 1937 [1776]).

23. *Ibid.* at 423.

24. *Ibid.* at 79-80.

25. *Ibid.* at 80, 79.

26. Eleanor Rathbone, *The Disinherited Family: A Plea for the Endowment of the Family* 10-11 (1924) (quote); Gertrude Himmelfarb, "Introduction," in Thomas Malthus, *On Population* xxiii (Gertrude Himmelfarb ed. 1960). For a more nuanced view of the transitional character of Smith's theory of the market, see David McNally, *Against the Market: Political Economy, Market Socialism and the Marxist Critique* 43-61 (1993).

27. Alexander Gray, *Family Endowment: A Critical Analysis* 107 (1927); Smith, *Wealth of Nations* at 14-15.

28. Paul Demeny, "Population and the Invisible Hand," *Demography* 23 (4):473-87 at 476-77 (Nov. 1986); Smith, *Wealth of Nations* at 424 (quote).

29. Lord Byron, *Don Juan,* XV, 38 (1824).

30. Karl Kautsky, "Malthusianismus und Sozialismus," *Neue Zeit* 29/I:652-62 at 655 (1911).

31. Thomas Robert Malthus, *An Essay on the Principle of Population* (1st ed.), in *idem, On Population* at 133 (Gertrude Himmelfarb ed., 1960 [1798]). See generally Samuel Levin, "Malthus and the Idea of Progress," *J. Hist. Ideas,* 27(1): 92-108 (Jan.-Mar. 1966).

32. Edwin Cannan, "The Malthusian Anti-Socialist Argument," *Econ. Rev.* 2 (1):71-87 at 75 (Jan. 1892).

33. Thomas Robert Malthus, *An Essay on the Principle of Population,* in *The Works of Thomas Robert Malthus,* 3:607 (6th ed.; E.A. Wrigley & David Souden eds., 1986 [1826]).

34. Colin Clark, "Do Population and Freedom Go Together?" *Fortune* 52 (6):136-39, 203-208 at 139 (Dec. 1960).

35. Marie Jean Condorcet, *Esquisse d'un tableau historique des progrès de l'espirit humain* 261-62 (1966 [1795]); Malthus, *Essay* at 55, 56 (1st ed. 1798).

36. Kingsley Davis, "Malthus and the Theory of Population," in *The Language of Research: A Reader in the Methodology of Social Research* 540-53 at 553 (Morris Rosenberg ed., 1965 [1955]).

37. Rathbone, *The Disinherited Family* at 233.

38. John Maynard Keynes, "Am I a Liberal?" in *idem, Essays in Persuasion* 323, 327 (1963 [1931]) (quote); R.F. Harrod, *The Life of John Maynard Keynes* 426-28 (1972 [1951]).

39. Keynes, "Am I a Liberal?" at 333.

40. Henryk Grossmann, *Das Akkumulations- und Zusammenbruchsgesetz des kapitalistischen Systems (Zugleich eine Krisentheorie)* 381 (1929).

41. Jürgen Kuczynski, *Studien zur Geschichte der Lage des arbeitenden Kindes in Deutschland von 1700 bis zur Gegenwart,* in *idem, Die Geschichte der Lage der Arbeiter unter dem Kapitalismus* 19:87-120 (1968); Carol Brown, "Mothers, Fathers, and Children:

From Private to Public Patriarchy," in *Women and Revolution: A Discussion of the Unhappy Marriage of Marxism and Feminism* 239-67 (Lydia Sargent ed., 1981); Mark Blaug, *Economic Theory in Retrospect* 76 (4th ed., 1985 [1962]) (quote).

42. Marc Linder, *Der Anti-Samuelson: Kritik eines repräsentativen Lehrbuchs der bürgerlichen Ökonomie* 2:150-60 (1974); below ch. 10.

43. Malthus, *Essay* at 26-27 (1st ed. 1798).

44. *Ibid.* at 27.

45. *Ibid.* at 27-28. For such workers it would not have been the case that: "To bring a large number of children into the world...is to give that many hostages to fortune." James Bossard, *The Large Family System: An Original Study in the Sociology of Family Behavior* 106 (1956).

46. William Pedersen, *Malthus* 124, 187 (1979).

47. *Ibid.* at 124.

48. Malthus, *Essay* at 74 (1st ed. 1798).

49. Flew, "The Structure of Malthus' Population Theory" at 19; Mabel Buer, "The Historical Setting of the Malthusian Controversy," in *London Essays in Economics in Honour of Edwin Cannan* 137-53 at 138 (T. Gregory & Hugh Dalton eds., 1927).

50. As E. Penrose, *Population Theories and Their Application: With Special Reference to Japan* 28 (1935 [1934]), pointed out, Malthus implied that the purpose in postponing marriage was merely to secure a sufficiently high wage to create a self-supporting family—not to obtain the maximum income that would be consistent with later economists' notion of optimum population. Angus McLaren, *Birth Control in Nineteenth-Century England* 143 (1978), argues that early nineteenth-century theories of population were modeled on laissez-faire economics insofar as they accepted that demographic laws "could not be countered by institutional interference."

51. John Maynard Keynes, "Robert Malthus," in *idem, Essays in Biography* 81-124 at 101 (Geoffrey Keynes ed., 1963 [1933]). Yet Keynes also acknowledged that: "The work begun by Malthus and completed by Ricardo did...provide an immensely powerful intellectual foundation to justify the status quo...; and it was just recompense that they should have thrown up Karl Marx as their misbegotten progeny." J.M. Keynes, "The Commemoration of Thomas Robert Malthus," *Economic J.* 45 (178):230-34 at 230-31 (June 1935).

52. T.R. Malthus, *An Essay on the Principle of Population* 2:320-24, 327-30 (4th ed. 1807).

53. Thomas Malthus, *An Essay on the Principle of Population* (7th ed., 1872), in *idem, On Population* at 148 (Himmelfarb ed.).

54. Karl Polanyi, *The Great Transformation* 93, 111, 114-16 (1971 [1944]). The claim that the trope of fear of poverty as a spur to industry lay at the heart of Malthus's reconstruction of political economy overlooks Townsend's role. Emma Rothschild, "Social Security and Laissez Faire in Eighteenth-Century Political Economy," *Pop. & Dev. Rev.* 21(2):711-44 at 727 (Dec. 1995).

55. Joseph Townsend, *A Dissertation on the Poor Laws by a Well-Wisher to Mankind* 27, 35 (1971 [1786]).

56. Stefan Collini, Donald Winch, & John Burrow, *That Noble Science of Politics: A Study in Nineteenth-Century Intellectual History* 70 (1983); E. Santurri, "Theodicy and Social Policy in Malthus' Thought," *J. Hist. Ideas* 63 (2):315-30 (Apr.-June 1982); Nassau Senior, *Two Lectures on Population*, in *idem, Selected Writings on Economics* i (1966 [1829]) (quote); Thomas Sowell, "Malthus and the Utilitarians," *Canadian J. Econ. & Pol. Sci.* 28 (2):268-74 at 272 (May 1962); Reinhard Bendix, *Work and Authority in Industry* 78

(1974 [1956]) (quote).

57. Polanyi, *Great Transformation* at 114-15, 123. See also McNally, *Against the Market* at 220.

58. Harold Boner, *Hungry Generations: The Nineteenth-Century Case Against Malthusianism* 81 (1955). Boner's specific claim that Smith exempted labor from the operation of supply and demand is inaccurate since Smith, as noted above, did begin to apply supply and demand to the production of workers.

59. Thomas Robert Malthus, *Principles of Political Economy*, in *The Works of Thomas Robert Malthus* 5:184 (E.A. Wrigley & David Souden ed., 1986 [1820]). Nevertheless, a century later, the American dissident, Scott Nearing, portrayed Malthus as a democratic savior of the Western world from catastrophe, "telling the men at the margin whose families were either unregulated in size or else regulated only by subsistence, that they were free and equal to every other man and had a like right to 'rise.' The thought was new. 'How can I rise?' asked the laborer. 'Stop having children,' replied the economist." Scott Nearing, "'Race Suicide' vs. Overpopulation," *Popular Sci. Monthly* 78 (1):81-83 at 83 (Jan. 1911).

60. Malthus, *Essay* at 497 (7th ed.).

61. *Ibid.* at 593, 501, 500.

62. Gertrude Himmelfarb, *The Idea of Poverty: England in the Early Industrial Age* 126 (1985 [1983]). William Thornton, *Overpopulation and Its Remedy* 118-19, 269-70 (1971 [1846]), understated Malthus's reach in claiming that the theory could be reduced to the admonition not to marry before being able to afford to raise children.

63. Nevertheless, Malthus favored repeal of the antiunion Combination Laws on the laissez-faire ground that they "operated against the general principle of wages finding their natural level." However, since he also favored severe punishment of workers for intimidating "masters, or other men," and since nineteenth-century Anglo-American courts developed an extraordinarily capacious notion of unlawful intimidation by unions, it is unclear how significant Malthus's concession was. *Sixth Report from the Select Committee on Artizans and Machinery* 601 (House of Commons, 1824).

64. Malthus, *Essay* at 107 (1st ed.).

65. Karen Michaelson, "Introduction: Population Theory and the Political Economy of Population Processes," in *And the Poor Get Children: Radical Perspectives on Population Dynamics* 11-35 at 13 (Karen Michaelson ed., 1981).

66. Malthus, *Essay* at 585 (7th ed.). Franklin had held a similar view of marital deterrence a half-century earlier. Benjamin Franklin, "Observations concerning the Increase of Mankind, Peopling of Countries," in *The Papers of Benjamin Franklin* 4: 225-34 at 227-28 (Leonard Labaree ed., 1961 [1751]). See also David Hume, "On the Populousness of Ancient Nations," in *idem, Essays, Moral, Political, and Literary*, in *idem, Essays and Treatises on Several Subjects* 1:397-469 at 400 (new ed., 1800 [1752]).

67. Malthus, *Essay* at 585-86 (7th ed.).

68. *Ibid.*

69. George Stigler, "Sraffa's Ricardo," *Am. Econ. Rev.* 43(4) pt. 1:586, 591 (Sept. 1953); Malthus, *Essay* at 278 (7th ed.). See also *ibid.* at 554.

70. Malthus, *Essay* at 496 (7th ed.).

71. Even Samuel Hollander, "On Malthus's Population Principle and Social Reform," *Hist. Pol. Econ.* 18 (2):187-236 at 188, 231 n.40 (1986), who is at pains to show that Malthus is not a reactionary, concedes that Malthus neglected the "obvious problem" of free riders.

72. Stanley Lebergott, "Population Change and the Supply of Labor, " in *Demographic and Economic Change in Developed Countries* 377-414 at 383 (NBER, 1960) (quote); E. Wrigley, *Population and History* 191 (1969) (quote).

73. See below ch. 7.

74. Joseph Schumpeter, *History of Economic Analysis* 581-82 n.9 (Elizabeth Schumpeter ed., 1972 [1954]).

75. Jon Elster, *Making Sense of Marx* 22-25 (1985).

76. Karl Marx, *Grundrisse der Kritik der politischen Ökonomie* 74 (1953 [1857-58]).

77. *Cf.* Lesthaeghe. "On the Social Control of Human Reproduction" at 528-30.

78. Judith Blake, "Coercive Pronatalism and American Population Policy," in U.S. Commission on Population Growth and the American Future, 6 *Research Reports: Aspects of Population Growth Policy* 81, 86 (Robert Parke, Jr. & Charles Westoff eds., 1972).

79. Joan Busfield & Michael Paddon, *Thinking About Children: Sociology and Fertility in Post-War England* 250 (1977).

80. Joseph Spengler, *France Faces Depopulation: Postlude Edition*, 1936-1976, at 295 (1979 [1938]).

81. Norman Himes, "John Stuart Mill's Attitude Toward Neo-Malthusianism," *Econ. J.* (Econ. Hist., Ser. No. 4), Jan. 1929, at 457-84; William Langer, "The Origins of the Birth Control Movement in England in the Early Nineteenth Century," *J. Interdisciplinary Hist.* 5(4): 669-86 (Spring 1975).

82. John Stuart Mill, "The Claims of Labor," in *idem, Dissertations and Discussions: Political, Philosophical, and Historical* 2:260-96 at 264, 262 (1864 [1845]).

83. John Stuart Mill, *Principles of Political Economy* 358 (W. Ashley ed., 1926 [1848]).

84. John Stuart Mill, *On Liberty*, in *The Philosophy of John Stuart Mill* 294, 306-307, 310-11 (Marshall Cohen ed., 1961 [1859]).

85. John Stuart Mill, *Principles of Political Economy*, in *idem, Collected Works* 2:358 (1965 [1848]).

86. Peter Lindert, *Fertility and Scarcity in America* 3 (1978).

87. James Mirrlees, "Population Policy and the Taxation of Family Size," *J. Pub. Econ.* 1:169-98 at 197-98 (1972).

88. Friedman, *Laissez-Faire in Population* at 5.

89. Mill, *Principles of Political Economy*, in *idem, Collected Works* 2:358-59. Gertrude Himmelfarb, *On Liberty and Liberalism: The Case of John Stuart Mill* 119-22 (1974), in her discussion of "this very considerable departure from his principle of liberty," fails to present its scope and consistency

90. Mill, *Principles of Political Economy* at 363 (Ashley ed.).

91. Alban de Villeneuve-Bargemont, *Économie politique chrétienne, ou recherches sur la nature et les causes du paupérisme, en France et en Europe, et sur les moyens de le soulager et de le prévenir* 3:175-76 (1834); Garrett Hardin, "The Right to Breed," *N.Y. Times*, May 6, 1971, at 43, col. 5 at 6.

92. Garrett Hardin, "The Tragedy of the Commons," *Science* 162:1243-48 at 1244 (Dec. 13, 1968).

93. But see Paul Adams, "Children as Contributions in Kind: Social Security and Family Policy," *Social Work* 35 (6):492-98 at 492 (Nov. 1990).

94. W.F. Lloyd, *Two Lectures on the Checks to Population*, in William Forster Lloyd, *Lectures on Population, Value, Poor-Laws and Rent* i-ii, 15-17 (1968 [1833]). Hardin presents Lloyd as a disinterred *vir obscurus. Managing the Commons* 8 n. (Garrett

Hardin & John Baden eds., 1977). Yet 35 years earlier, Roy Harrod celebrated him as the originator of marginal utility analysis. *Encyclopaedia of the Social Sciences* 9:555 (1937 [1933]). See generally, Richard Romano, "William Forster Lloyd—a non-Ricardian?" *Hist. Pol. Econ.* 9 (3):412-41 (Fall 1977).

95. Lloyd, *Two Lectures on the Checks to Population* at 71-75. In a later set of lectures on the poor laws, Lloyd recurred to this theme by arguing that "[t]he true method of promoting moral restraint...with respect to marriage, and diminishing the pressure of population against subsistence, consists in elevating, and in giving security to, the condition of...a number of persons limited by reference to the number of families which the country is...competent to maintain in comfort...." W.F. Lloyd, *Two Lectures on Poor-Laws* 71 (1836), in Lloyd, *Lectures on Population.*

96. Garrett Hardin, *Living Within Limits: Ecology, Economics, and Population Taboos* 223 (1993). For the amusing claim that Lloyd foreshadowed Marx's theory of exploitation, see B.J. Gordon, "W.F. Lloyd: A Neglected Contribution," *Oxford Econ. Papers* 18 (1):64-70 (Mar. 1966).

97. Lloyd, *Two Lectures on the Checks to Population* at 18-19.

98. Arthur McEvoy, *The Fisherman's Problem: Ecology and the Law in the California Fisheries 1850-1980*, at 253 (1990 [1986]) (quote); Hardin, *Living Within Limits* at 216, 218 (quote).

99. Lloyd, *Two Lectures on the Checks to Population* at 19-23.

100. *Ibid.* at 26-29. In order to simplify his demographic point, Lloyd assumed that the workers' "power of labouring shall commence from the moment of birth" at which time it can provide the same proportion of the infant's necessities as the parent's labor power can of his. Amusingly, Lloyd saw only the following difference between his hypothesis and British industrial reality: "whereas the discoveries in manufactures seem to render it possible to turn to account the labour of children at an earlier age than formerly, and we may expect that with the progress of discovery it will be possible to turn it to account at a still earlier age, I now, for the convenience of argument, assume the progression to have advanced up to the very beginning of life." *Ibid.* at 24-25.

101. *Ibid.* at 30-33.

102. *Ibid.* 34-36.

103. Hardin, "The Tragedy of the Commons" at 1244, 1245 (quotes); Garrett Hardin, "An Operational Analysis of 'Responsibility,'" in *Managing the Commons* at 66-75.

104. Daniel Fife, "Killing the Goose," in *Managing the Commons* 76-81 (1971); Colin W. Clark, "The Economics of Overexploitation," in *ibid.* at 82-95 (1974); Michael Taylor, *Anarchy and Cooperation* 8-9 (1976); Michael Taylor, *The Possibility of Cooperation* 26-28 (1987); McEvoy, *Fisherman's Problem* at 12.

105. Hardin, "Tragedy of the Commons" at 1246. Hardin's collaborator, John Braden, creatively adapted his sociobiological approach: the fact that as between two noninterbreeding populations that occupy the same ecological niche the faster breeder will displace the slower may not be completely transferrable to interbreeding human beings, but it sufficed to prompt Braden to express grave concern over a breeding war allegedly propagated by Black Power advocates in the United States—at precisely the time when suspicion was rife that the state-sponsored birth control and population control initiatives were designed to curtail the growth or perhaps even the stock of poor blacks. John Braden, "Population, Ethnicity, and Public Goods: The Logic of Interest-Group Strategy," in *Managing the Commons* at 252-60 at 253, 255.

106. Hardin, "The Tragedy of the Commons" at 1247-48; Garrett Hardin, *Exploring New Ethics for Survival: The Voyage of the Spaceship Beagle* 199 (1972). Just how far Hardin is prepared to go in this antidemocratic direction emerges from one of his "lifeboat ethics" scenarios. Garrett Hardin, "Living on a Lifeboat," in *Manging the Commons* 261-79 at 277 (1974).

107. Garrett Hardin, "The Survival of Nations and Civilization," *Science* 172 (3990):1297 (June 25, 1971).

108. *Cong. Globe*, 33d Cong., 1st Sess. 1224 (1854).

109. In fact, slave owners did not exercise such control. Robert Fogel, *Without Consent or Contract: The Rise and Fall of American Slavery* 114-53 (1991 [1989]).

110. Demeny, "Population and the Invisible Hand."

4

Do Poor Laws Make Poor People?

> [T]he more you degrade the workers...the more you throw them back...on the one pleasure...left to them—the gratification of their instinct for producing fresh supplies of men. You will applaud this instinct as divine until at last the excessive supply becomes a nuisance: there comes a plague of men; and you suddenly discover that the instinct is diabolic, and set up a cry of "over population."[1]

The evolution of invisible-hand demographic discourse in classical British political economy, analyzed in the previous chapter, will be embedded here in the contemporaneous public policy debates over the shaping of the poor laws. The gravamen of Malthusianism's late eighteenth- and early nineteenth-century contribution was its attack on the changing socioeconomic function of this legislation: just at the time when local administrators "were distributing relief with a reckless extravagance, Malthus endowed the economists with arguments...to pass a wholesale condemnation upon the system of poor relief" for encouraging the poor to procreate faster than subsistence could be increased. Yet despite the fact that its "harsh attitude...towards the proletariat recommended Malthusianism to the middle class," the new economic-demographic learning did not officially assert itself until the enactment of the New Poor Law in 1834, which denied relief to the able-bodied unless they entered into workhouses. Underlying this historical lag was the momentous impact of the French Revolution: "the governing classes in general...were obsessed by the fear that an agrarian revolution might occur in England.... In their opinion the poor rate was an insurance against unrest; and they were prepared to pay an enormous premium to safeguard themselves against this terrible danger."[2]

The more human face of the turn-of-the-century poor law resulted from a new social division of labor which transferred some of its most repressive functions to other agents. Until the eighteenth century, the poor laws were, in the words of Sidney and Beatrice Webb, "designed not so much to relieve 'the poor'...as to restrain the demands of the manual workers from setting a higher price on their labour...and, by savage punishments, to discipline the whole propertyless class to the continuous and regular service, in agriculture and manufactures, of those who were becoming their masters." In the course of the Industrial Revolution, however, this "task of holding down the common people to their divinely appointed duty of continuous work for masters who should direct their operations was silently being transferred to the...new class of millowners...." While the coalescing capitalist mode of production suppressed the "loose and idle life" that the poor laws had sought to extirpate in previous centuries, "any attempted revolt against the dictatorship of the capitalist...was met by a ruthless application of the criminal law and the gaol, the penitentiary and transportation, supported...by...the troops." The poor laws, in contrast, to the Malthusians' chagrin, were reoriented toward providing bare subsistence to employed and infirm wage-laborers.[3]

In analyzing the relationship between poor laws and the size of the population or labor force, it is crucial to bear in mind that British authors and politicians in the late eighteenth and nineteenth centuries gave to the terms *the poor* and *poverty* meanings they no longer connote. The Poor Law Commissioners in 1834, for example, asserted that only in England had social policy deemed it fit to relieve more than mere "*indigence*, the state of a person unable to labour, or unable to obtain, in return for his labour, the means of subsistence." There, relief also applied to "*poverty*; that is, the state of one who, in order to obtain a mere subsistence, is forced to have recourse to labour."[4] The poor were, then, identical with the working class.

An earlier influential characterization of poverty was more precise in focusing on that "condition in society where the individual has no surplus labour in store, and, consequently, no property but what is derived from the constant exercise of industry...; or in other words, it is the state of every one who must labour for subsistence. *Poverty* is therefore a most necessary and indispensable ingredient in society...the source of *wealth*, since...without a large proportion of poverty surplus labour could never be rendered productive...." Here Patrick Colquhoun, an economist, statistician, London magistrate, and acquaintance of Adam Smith, came close to defining the poor as the Marxist proletariat—that class of free but nevertheless compulsory working nonowners of the means of production that capital creates and that in turn creates capital. Indigence, in contrast, was for Colquhoun an evil—the "*want, misery*, and *distress*" associated with being "destitute of the means of subsistence" and unable to work to acquire them.[5]

Ironically, Malthusian poor-law policy makers also gave back to this class its original Roman meaning. Thus the Poor Law Commissioners, describing the laborer's position within the rates-in-aid-of-wages-cum-children's-allowance system that they were in the process of abolishing, observed that:

As a single man...his income does not exceed a bare subsistence; but he has only to marry and it increases. Even then it is unequal to the support of a family; but it rises on the birth of every child. If his family is numerous, the parish becomes his principal paymaster; for, as small as the usual allowance of 2s. a head may be, yet when there are more than three children it generally exceeds the average wages...in a pauperized district. A man with a wife and six children, entitled...to have his wages made up to 16s. a week in a parish where the wages...do not exceed 10s. or 12s., is almost an irresponsible being. All the other classes of society are exposed to the vicissitudes of hope and fear; he alone has nothing to lose or to gain.[6]

This proletariat appears closely related to the poorest class of Roman citizens, whom the sixth-century Roman king, Servius Tullius, called *proletarios*, or offspring-givers, in analogy to the richest classes, whom he called *assiduos*, or tribute-givers. Servius, traditionally credited with having created a constitution that classified patricians' and plebeians' duties and rights according to their property, gave this name to those with the least or no property to indicate that from them offspring or "progeny of the state" were to be expected.[7] This Roman proletariat bore a certain resemblance to what Marx called "a merely pullulating proletariat," which arose in England under the old poor laws in the latter part of the eighteenth century.[8] As William Forster Lloyd, looking back as the New Poor Law was enacted, described the mentality that underwrote the old system: since population constituted the wealth of the state, those who staffed manufactories and armies with their superfluous progeny should be supported; to provide that support through the wage system, however, would indifferently raise the income of the single, granting them "unparalleled extravagance"; in order to avoid such waste, wages were reduced to the subsistence level of an unmarried man, and procreational subsidies were granted in the form of poor-rate allowances.[9] Thus the great functional difference between the Roman and Malthusian English proletariats lay in the fact that the Roman state wanted this human output whereas the British ruling classes and their state were seeking under the aegis of the New Poor Law to terminate proletarian fertility rights that were allegedly financed by a drag on capital accumulation. Children constituted the poor-law proletariat's capital—a private financial benefit that the advocates of the New Poor Law regarded as a public demographic vice.

Malthus's most pregnant demographic policy claim culminated in the assertion that England's poor laws, by animating the poor, who would otherwise have been unable to support a family based on their market-given wages, to marry and procreate, "create the poor which they maintain...." He saw the same consequence as resulting from private efforts by farmers to keep wages down during periods of high corn prices by paying their laborers children's allowances: once workers were reconciled to a system in which the connection between wages and means of family support was severed, population might increase rapidly.[10] The chief relief provided by the allowance system may in fact have been to the employing farmers themselves, who succeeded in securing significant wage subsidies by shifting the tax burden to "the wrong people"—those parish inhabitants who employed fewer or no laborers at all and therefore did not directly benefit from the payments. Malthus implicitly accepted an argument, later articulated by demographers, that dismantling the poor-law family-allowance system and forcing couples to reinternalize the costs of their procreativity powerfully promoted the application of economic rationality to reproductive behavior. This linkage also prompted Polanyi to characterize the New Poor Law as "the starting point of modern capitalism." To the extent, however, that for some time after the introduction of the New Poor Law in 1834 child labor remained a mainstay—if no longer the foundation—of British industry, adult workers may have been engaged in economically rational behavior par excellence in regarding procreation as the most "profitable investment" with the fastest payback period available to them.[11]

In describing the genesis of the parish rates in aid of wages during the period of scarcity in the latter half of the 1790s, when prices rose much faster than wages and continued to outpace them for 20 years,[12] one of the commissioners who fashioned the New Poor Law of 1834 pointed to three related material and legitimational advantages accruing to the ruling classes. First, such payments enabled employers to avoid a higher wage level during the postscarcity period; second, the possibility of working-class unrest would be diminished; and third, the recipients would become ideologically accepting of the entire political-economic regime:

> It was apprehended...that either...wages...would rise to a height from which it would be difficult to reduce them when the cause for it had ceased, or that during the high prices the labourers might have to undergo privations to which it would be unsafe to expose them. To meet the emergency of the time, various schemes are said to have been adopted, such as weekly distributions of flour...until at length the practice became general, and a right distinctly admitted by the magistrates was claimed by the labourer to parish relief, on the ground of inadequate wages and number in family. [T]he consequences of the system were not wholly unforeseen at the time, as affording a probable inducement to early marriages and large families; but at this period there was but little apprehension on that ground. A prevalent opinion, supported by high authority, that population was in itself a source of wealth, precluded all alarm. [I]t was deemed wise by many persons...to present the Poor Laws to the lower classes, as an institution for their advantage, peculiar to this country; and to encourage an opinion among them, that by this means their own share in the property of the kingdom was recognized.[13]

Despite these manifest benefits, the propertied classes in the opening quarter of the nineteenth century rebelled against what they deemed the stupendous cost of the poor law. The fall of agricultural prices after the French wars and the ensuing bankruptcies and decline in landlords' rents made the tax burden much more painful to the rural propertied classes. Although Malthus was correct in observing that employers "would gain much more by the cheapness of labour, than they would lose by the payment of their rates," such a redistributive effect was not speculatively conditioned on a new statutory expansion of the rate-payer base, but had always obtained in the rural parishes. At their high point in 1818, these local rates amounted to £8 million and rivaled the total civil expenditures of the national government. Because this tax burden fell not only or even chiefly on the subsidized agricultural employers but on all people with holdings in rural parishes, those bearing this unequal tax burden viewed it as crushing. But even these sums, representing the totality of public services available to wage earners, who accounted for the vast majority of the British population, constituted only 2 percent of the vastly expanded national income—"but a modest premium against a social revolution."[14]

The toleration of relief expenditures was powerfully bolstered by a transformation toward the end of the eighteenth century in the ruling classes' attitude toward the functionality of a large impoverished population. As accumulated capital in new industries insatiably absorbed increasing numbers of proletarians and permanent war demanded a huge volume and never-ending streams of soldiers and sailors, "the poverty of the poor, and even the prevalence of destitution...[was] no longer...regarded as dangerous to the State, or even objectionable as a common nuisance, but actually as a condition, if not a direct cause, of the vast increase in national wealth...." But after the conclusion of the Napoleonic wars in 1815 and the evaporation of the "fabulous profits" in agriculture, when the ensuing depression brought on large-scale unemployment, agitation in opposition to the poor-law system intensified.[15]

Mark Blaug, a leading debunker of the Poor Law Commissioners' 1834 account of the previous system, characterizes the Old Poor Law as a miniature welfare state that sought to maintain a living wage for agricultural workers by means of cost-of-living adjustments, unemployment compensation, a private employment scheme, and family allowances. He takes to task critics of the Old Poor Law such as the Hammonds and Webbs for having failed to realize that their attacks would apply as well to modern welfare legislation because the statutory minimum wage and children's allowances that they proposed as an alternative are the functional equivalent of the Old Poor Law. Blaug argues that family allowances, which antedated the Speenhamland system perhaps by as much as a century, did not inspire the same intense contemporary controversy as Speenhamland's innovation of publicly subsidizing real wages at a minimum-existence level (based on the price of bread and family size); he also charges the Poor Law Commissioners with intentional obfuscation of the difference, especially since the minimum wage subsidies had largely disappeared by 1834. Blaug is also skeptical of the demographic prejudices of "a generation drunk on Malthusian wine," which divined an inexorable pronatalist impact of children's allowances despite the fact that they were modest, rose less than proportionately with each additional child, were continually scaled back, and in many parishes did not kick in until after the family already had one, two, three, or even seven children. The reason that Parliament rejected a minimum wage as the alternative to the Speenhamland system in 1795, according to Blaug, was the same one that has plagued minimum-wage debates ever since: to the extent that agricultural wage levels fell short of the Speenhamland real-wage minimum during the Napoleonic wars when famine prices were high, if a statutory minimum wage had been differentiated according to family size, it would have generated a wage considerably in excess of the market level.[16]

Blaug's claim that the Hammonds and Webbs did not understand that twentieth-century minimum wages and family allowances performed the same function as the Speenhamland system fails to do justice to the Hammonds as authors of a epoch-making context-sensitive social history that took great pains to explain the enormous consequences in terms of legitimation and consciousness even in the early 1800s between the proposed mandatory minimum wage and Speenhamland:

> The labourers, stripped of their ancient rights and their ancient possessions, refused a minimum wage and allotments, were given instead a universal system of pauperism.... The richer classes...were naturally anxious to...pacify the poor before discontent spread...and the Speenhamland system turned out...a very admirable means...for it provided a maintenance for the poor by a method which sapped their spirit and disarmed their independence.... The Speenhamland system after 1812 was not applied so as to maintain an equilibrium between the income and expenditure of the labourer: it was applied to maintain an equilibrium between social forces. The scale fell not with the fall of prices to the labourer, but with the fall of profits to the possessing classes. The minimum was not the minimum on which the labourer could live, but the minimum below which rebellion was certain. This was the way in which wages found their own level. They gravitated lower and lower with the growing weakness of the wage-earner.... There is another respect in which the minimum wage policy would have profoundly altered the character of village society. It would have given the village labourers a bond of union before they had lost the memories and the habits of their more independent life; it would have made them an organised force, something like the organised forces that have built up a standard of life for industrial workmen.[17]

The rational kernel in Blaug's charge is that market-incentive fanatics of both centuries have opposed both systems' goal of maintaining a fixed standard of living despite the economic vicissitudes as "contrary to the ruling of providence."[18] The existence of such a security system was emblematic of the contradictory demands of the masters of the transition from precapitalist to capitalist society in rural England. Nobles, squires, and farmers wanted to combine some of the elements of capitalist labor market determination of wages by reference to supply and demand with traditional paternalistic sustenance of the poor, who were granted a right to live as a means of warding off mass unrest during famines. Because the agrarian ruling classes, in an effort to retain their old powers, sought to modify capitalism by reconciling it with an inherently antagonistic social policy, workers wound up with the worst of both systems—especially by the end of the Old Poor Law period, when, in terms of the Speenhamland system's scale of loaves of bread, a family of four would have found its standard of living one-third lower than at the outset in 1795[19]:

> Agrarian capitalism degenerated into a general lunacy, in which farmers were encouraged to pay as little as they could...and used the mass of pauper labour as an excuse for not raising their productivity; while their most rational calculations would be, how to get the maximum subsidy for their wage-bill from the rest of the ratepayers. Labourers, conversely, were encouraged to do as little work as they possibly could, since nothing would get them more than the official minimum of subsistence.... It is difficult to find words for the degradation which the coming of industrial society brought to...English country labourer[s].... They lost what little traditional right and security they had, and gained not even the the theoretical hope which capitalism held out to the urban labourer, the legal equality of rights in the liberal society.... They and they alone paid for the failure of British rural society to combine tradition and capitalism, for they got the benefits of neither. Stretched on the rack between the pauperisation of a caricatured market economy and the social oppression of those who grew rich from it, they lacked even the only real resource of the British labouring poor, the capacity to organise themselves a class and to fight collectively as such.[20]

That children's allowances, despite their association with repressive poor-law relief, still found favor with potential recipients was suggested by the fact that several years before the Speenhamland system was inaugurated, Tom Paine proposed in his *Rights of Man* that the British state provide a quarter-million families with £4 annually for each child under 14 years of age.[21]

The intensified impoverishment of the mid-1790s also catapulted onto the social policy agenda plans and parliamentary bills for minimum wage regulation. One of the chief arguments summoned against it was that its egalitarianism undermined the incentives that inequality promoted. A more specific subargument has survived two centuries of debate: by disregarding the unequal needs of workers with and without dependents, a fixed minimum high enough to support a family would lead a single man to indolence. Thus in 1795 the Whig Samuel Whitbread presented a bill in the House of Commons empowering justices of the peace to regulate the wages of laborers in husbandry "Respect being had to the Value of Money, and the Plenty or Scarcity of the Time...." During the bill's second reading in 1796, Whitbread, making his obeisances to the shibboleths of upsurging laissez-faire political economy, made a point of announcing that he was second to no man in desiring legislative noninterference so "that the price of labour, like every other commodity, should be left to find its own level." Unfortunately, however, "the deductions of reason were confuted by experience," which revealed that laborers' wages fell below subsistence level not only during periods of scarcity.[22]

Pitt, the Tory Prime Minister, led the debate against the bill by charging that Whitbread's proposal suffered from over- and underbreadth, which rendered it unequal to the task of remedying the hardships of the "class of the labouring poor":

> As there was a difference in the numbers which compose the families of the labouring poor, it must necessarily require more to support a small family. Now by the regulations proposed, either the man with a small family would have too much wages, or the man with a large family, who had done most service to his country, would have too little. So that were the minimum fixed upon the standard of a large family, it might operate as an encouragement to idleness on one part of the community; and if it were fixed on the standard of a small family, those would not enjoy the benefit of it for whose relief it was intended.[23]

Sidetracking Whitbread's initiative by trumping it, Pitt placed "before the House the ideas floating in his mind, though not digested with sufficient accuracy, nor arranged with a proper degree of clearness":

> Let us...make relief in cases where there are a number of children, a matter of right and an honour, instead of a ground for opprobrium and contempt. This will make a large family a blessing, and not a curse; and this will draw a proper line of distinction between those are able to provide for themselves by their labour, and those who, after having enriched their country with a number of children, have a claim upon its assistance for their support.[24]

To be sure, Pitt's proposal seemed to afford such families employment—especially for the children, whose early engagement in manufacturing had contributed so heavily to the country's "opulence." Unable to deny the potential merits of Pitt's counterproposal, Whitbread, who urged immediate institution of "a liberal premium for the encouragement of large families," contented himself with arguing that until any such regime was implemented, his bill remained an effective temporary expedient. Another member of Commons, General Smith, went even beyond Whitbread in criticizing Pitt's claim that the price of labor, like any other commodity's, had to be left to find its own level; Smith observed that "labour does not resemble any other commodity; it is frequently attached to a particular situation, and cannot be exported to foreign ports." The House of Commons, however, disagreed, and the bill died.[25]

Later the same year, Pitt brought in his bill, but the Commons never even discussed it. As promised, Pitt would have conferred a right to children's allowances on poor parents—fathers with more than two children under the age of five years and widows with more than one such child. The entitlement was, to be sure, subject to a major condition—that the parents send their children five years of age and older to "schools of industry...to be instructed and employed in such business as shall be suited to the[ir] age and strength" unless the poor law authorities directed them to be employed in the parents' house. Although Pitt's bill received little support, its child labor provisions, adopted from John Locke's proposal of exactly a century earlier, found even more radical parliamentary imitators two decades later.[26]

In 1800, Whitbread tried to revive his minimum wage bill. In order to allay potential opponents' fears, he emphasized that he did not wish the poor to be "overpaid" and that the magistrates would be merely empowered, not required, to "do justice to the poor": during hard times the law would lie dormant. Pitt adhered to the grounds of opposition that he had staked out in 1796: on the one hand, laissez-faire should be permitted to confer its benefits; on the other hand, a minimum wage was inefficacious because it set one standard without taking into account whether a man was married or had a large family to support. Unlike Pitt's previous criticisms, this rejoinder was unaccompanied by his own family allowance plan because too many people he respected had objected to it. Whitbread's restrained rebuttal was cogent—only unions enabled the price of labor to find its own level but the Combination Laws thwarted such efforts—but his bill died again.[27]

Emblematic of the ideological sea change that had taken place during the intervening decade, the influence of the complex of demographic phenomena associated with Malthus had assumed such stature that, by the time Whitbread presented a bill to reform the Poor Law in 1807, he felt obligated to make his obeisances to them as he had to Smithian laissez-faire. Bestowing on Malthus the title of "philosopher," Whitbread accepted Malthus's principles as "incontrovertible," but as with Smith, found reality irreconcilable with his conclusions.[28]

The next wave of opposition to the Poor Laws was generated at the end of the Napoleonic wars, when England faced an economic crisis that the manufacturer-socialist Robert Owen in 1817 conceptualized as capitalist overproduction and class maldistribution of income that flatly refuted Malthusianism. Before those hostilities, according to Owen, the United Kingdom had carried on its production with 5.5 million workers and comparatively little machinery. The mechanization resulting from the new scope and types of wartime demand meant that at the conclusion of hostilities 6 million workers produced what earlier would have required 150 million. But because the power of consumption failed to keep pace with this extraordinary increase in production and mechanical power proved to be cheaper than human labor, lower wages, unemployment, and misery ensued.[29]

In response to landowners' complaints that they bore a disproportonate share of the poor rates whereas large manufacturers, who were exempt from the tax, contributed to that burden by discharging many of their employees and thus throwing them on to the parish rolls, Parliament created a committee to investigate the possibilities for poor-law reform. In addition to proposing legislation (that was enacted) to strengthen landowners' control over the administration of the local relief apparatus, the committee urged reinvigoration of the rigors of the Elizabethan poor law excluding the able-bodied who were not involuntarily unemployed. Starting from the Malthusian proposition that "when the public undertakes to maintain all who may be born, without charge to the parents, the number born will probably be greater than in the natural state," the committee drew its inspiration from the scheme that John Locke had submitted to the Board of Trade as a commissioner in 1697 in response to the King's request for proposals to promote employment of the poor and to spare taxpayers the expense of supporting them.[30]

In "this appalling document," which was rejected, Locke, asserting that the "multiplying of the Poor" was not the result of a lack of employment, concluded that the first step had to be restraint of the poor's "debauchery." Among these debauchees, Locke focused on the majority, who were neither absolutely unable nor wholly unwilling to support themselves, but either lacked the appropriate work or skills to gain a livelihood. This group, in turn, consisted of adults "decayed from their full strength" and "the wives of day labourers, when they come to have two or three or more children: the looking after their children gives them not liberty to...seek for work; and so having no work at home, in the broken intervals of their time they earn nothing."[31]

In a shrewd move to kill two pauper-debauchees with one poor-law reform, Locke proposed catapulting mothers into profit-generating employment by relieving them of some of their maternal chores. Here Locke was able to accommodate his plan to the century-old Elizabethan antivagabondage poor law, which had instructed the overseers of the poor to "take order from tyme to tyme...for settinge to worke of the children of all suche whose parentes shall not...be thoughte able to keepe and maintaine their children...." For in addition to the adults who "have numerous families of children, whom they cannot, or pretend they cannot, support by their labour," their children, too, represented a burden to the parish because they were "maintained in idleness; so that their labour...is generally lost to the publick till they are...fourteen years old." Locke therefore proposed mandatory employment in "working schools" for woollen manufacture of all children between the ages of three and fourteen of relief-seeking parents. For this arrangement Locke held out the prospect of the fulfillment of two social desiderata that continue to excite capitalist welfare ideologues three centuries later: "the mother will...be at more liberty to work; the children will...from their infancy be inured to work, which is of no small consequence to the making of them sober and industrious all their lives after...."[32] Because Locke calculated that such children would in effect finance their own support, he foresaw an enormous cumulative saving for the rate payers:

> [A] man and his wife...may be able by their ordinary labour to maintain themselves and two children. More than two children at one time, under the age of three years, will seldom happen in one family: if, therefore, all the children above three years old be taken off from their hands, those who have never so many...will not need any allowance for them.[33]

In 1817 the Poor Law Committee dared tread where even Locke had feared to go: it recommended that the children of those poor who could not maintain them be taken away from their parents and be lodged at their place of employment. This forcible separation would not only eliminate relief payments for parents on account of such children, but would also constitute "the only remedy for that practice which has prevailed in the south of England particularly, of defraying what should be part of the wages of labour out of the poor rates, according to an uniform scale...without reference to any other consideration than the numbers of the family..., and the amount of their...earnings, and the price of bread." The committee chairman, Sturges Bourne, urged the House of Commons to use the opportunity to eliminate the "abominable...practice" of forcing rate-payers such as shopkeepers to subsidize other employers' wage bill.[34]

In the course of the parliamentary debates, opposition to the child removal clause derived from two different considerations. In the House of Commons, members focused on the perverse incentives. In his first year as a Member of Parliament, the political economist David Ricardo, a Malthusian convert, expressed the belief that the reform would exacerbate the evil of a redundant poor population when this generation of children grew up by assuring parents of the labouring classes "that an asylum would be provided for their children, in which they would be treated with humanity and tenderness." Despite confusing a juvenile workhouse with an emotional oasis, Ricardo was concerned that the measure would fail to have the effect of raising the wage level sufficiently to enable a man to support a family. Another Malthusian MP, John Curwen, a Whig spokesman on social policy, developed this line of thought by asserting that the "cruel and impolitic system of making wages that will barely support the single man the standard of labour," by making it impossible for him to save toward a family, merely served to remove any incentive to delay the inevitable acts of procreation and insured that they would result in pauperization. The House of Lords, which rejected the clause, was more apprehensive lest consigning paupers' children to the workhouse "weaken those social feelings on which the very strength and consistency of society depended."[35]

At the time of this public debate over the Poor Laws, Ricardo conducted a private one with Hutches Trower, who had retired from the stock exchange to become a country gentleman.[36] Trower initiated the discussion by dividing the poor into two classes—those who were single and those who were married (the assumption being that they coincided with the childless and parents respectively). For the latter, he conceded (as did Malthus), the wage rate

> no doubt is inadequate, and ought to be encreased. But for the 1st it is *more than sufficient.* This surplus, if prudently preserved, could form a *fund* for the supply of future extra demands, but it is all idly spent—as long, therefore, as this want of foresight exists any further encrease of wages to the *single man* would be productive of *mischief* instead of *good.* But you cannot encrease the wages of the *married,* without also encreasing those of the *single,* it is not practicable to make any distinction between them.

Trower therefore concluded that single workers had to learn "prudence and economy" because: "It is obvious, that it would be impossible to establish the rate of wages at such a sum as will be adequate to the support of a man and his family. Nor would it be expedient if it were—for it it would be tantamount to giving a Bonus to the extravagance and profligacy of the single." In Trower's part of the country, the single workers, if given wages adequate to support a family of four, would receive twice what they required—a situation "productive of most mischievous results."[37]

Ricardo's pointed response stressed the primacy of establishing the background conditions for the commodification of labor as a prerequisite to avoiding production of an unemployable supply of laborers inconsistent with the fiscal capacities of the British state and the continued profitability of the employing class:

> Is it not desirable that the poor laws should be done away, and the labouring classes should receive the recompense for their labour in the shape of wages than in that of bounty? If you answer in the affirmative then there is no way of preventing the single man from receiving more than is sufficient for his support, and I can see no reason to regret it. When the wages of a married man with a family are barely adequate to his own and his family's maintenance, the wages of the single man may be ample. All this I admit, but if it is a necessary consequence of the abolition of the poor laws it must be acquiesced in under the circumstances of an abolition. Even if it were an evil, which I think it is not, it must be endured for the sake of the good which would accompany it.... The population can only be repressed by diminishing the encouragement to its *excessive* increase,—by leaving contracts between the poor and their employers perfectly free, which would limit the quantity of labour in the market to the effective demand for it. By engaging to feed all who may require food you in some measure create an unlimited demand for human beings, and if it were not for the bad administration of the poor laws...the population and the rates would go on increasing in a regular progression till the rich were reduced to poverty, and till there would no longer be any distinction of ranks.[38]

A year later Ricardo reiterated to Trower that "the labouring classes" had to be taught to "provide for those casualties to which they are exposed from occasional variations in the demand for particular manufactured goods" rather than relying on the state to do it for them in the form of poor laws. In light of Ricardo's dismal view of wages, his assertion as to how workers should be able to tide themselves over during periods of redundancy is both touching and fantastic: "A man's wage should, and would on a really good system, be sufficient not only to maintain himself and family when he is in full work, but also to enable him to lay up a provision in a Savings Bank for those extraordinary calls...."[39]

As an MP, Ricardo sharpened his position in openly Malthusian fashion in a speech in 1823 on the occasion of a petition by superannuated manual weavers.

He urged the need

> to inculcate this truth in the minds of the working classes—that the
> value of labour, like the value of other things, depended on the relative
> proportion of supply and demand. If the supply of labour were greater
> than could be employed, then the people must be miserable. But the
> people had the remedy in their own hands. A little forethought, a little
> prudence (which probably they would exert, if they were not made such
> machines of by the poor-laws), a little of that caution which the better
> educated felt it necessary to use, would enable them to improve their
> situation.[40]

Given Ricardo's squeamishness with regard to public discussion of
sex—he had chastised James Mill for using the word "procreation" in his *Elements
of Political Economy*—it seems implausible that his claim that workers had a
remedy to the problem of overpopulation "in their own hands" was intended as a
scriptural reference to the method of contraception associated with Onan. The
trope, however, was contagious among political economists, who continued to
assert that workers' economically irrational procreational behavior was to blame
for their low wages. As Johann Heinrich von Thünen observed in midcentury,
whereas the middle and upper classes postponed marriage until their position was
secure enough to give their children a good education, for the worker marriage was
more attractive than the prospect of misery: "To him it is enough to raise his
children merely physically."[41]

The year following enactment of the New Poor Law, the commissioners
were quick to praise the effects of the abolition of allowances in aid of wages. The
pauperized worker found it "to his interest to make it worth the while of the
employer to retain him in employment, not by offering his labour for reduced
wages, but usually by offering to earn, by increased diligence, an increase of wages
proportionate to the discontinued allowance." The employer, in turn, was gratified
that his worker now regarded him rather than the parish as his master. And perhaps
the most pertinent "moral result" in the present demographic context was that "in
the dispauperized districts...the venal and improvident marriages, which were
consequent upon the allowance system, have immediately been diminished."[42]

The economist Nassau Senior, one of the authors of the Poor Law Report,
asserted the next year that in advanced civilizations such as Britain fertility was not
impeded by a fear of a lack of necessaries because the danger of actually perishing
from indigence was too remote: "When an Englishman stands hesitating between
love and prudence, a family actually starving is not among his terrors; against
actual want he knows that he has the fence of the poor-laws." After Senior had
made his contribution to reinstating *in terrorem* antinatalism among the proletariat
by abolishing outdoor relief for the able-bodied, he could turn his attention to the
petty bourgeois, whom he transformed into Everyman. Sounding a theme that
continues to resonate among social scientists, Senior correctly counted on such
men's self-restraint when faced with the recognition that their income was

insufficient to finance the reproduction of their own educational attainment for all their (male) children. Thus what deterred these men from procreating was the fear of losing "caste" or the hope of acquiring "decencies which give a higher rank."[43]

The triumphant incorporation of Malthusianism into the New Poor Law may have been superfluous. For contrary to the belief of many—including Friedrich Engels, who argued in the 1840s that the English workers' "errors" could all be traced back to the dissoluteness and inability to defer gratification that flowed from the animal-like existence to which the bourgeoisie had reduced them—that the old poor laws had promoted an increase in the "superfluous" population, that causality has long been challenged.[44] Even the 1821 British census, which asserted that the poor laws encouraged marriage in order to obtain tax-paid allowances in England, conceded that the rate of population increase was almost as great in Scotland, which lacked a poor-law regime—and was even greater in Ireland, which lacked a poor law altogether.[45]

More recent scholarly reconstructions of the impact of the allowance system under the Old Poor Law, which seek to go behind the cavalier assertions of the poor law officers and reformers, have found that the virtually axiomatically held Malthusian belief should be inverted: instead of having triggered a demographic explosion, allowances merely represented a reaction to the surplus labor phenomena associated with rising population at the turn of the century and the depressed agriculture in the post-Napoleonic era.[46] And earlier scholarly studies, in part inspired by the desire to galvanize support for the introduction of a family endowment in Britain by showing that it would not prompt an avalanche of births among low-income recipients, had compared parishes with and without the allowance system, and concluded that Malthus and his anti-poor law allies had incorrectly gauged the impact of the allowance system on fertility. Rather than having promoted procreation, the payments either had no effect whatever or at best created the impression of having increased population by virtue of having depressed mortality.[47]

NOTES

1. G. Bernard Shaw, "The Basis of Socialism," in *Fabian Essays in Socialism* 15-45 at 36 (G. Bernard Shaw ed., n.d. [1889]).

2. Elie Halévy, 1 *A History of the English People: England in 1815*, at 573, 379 (tr. E. Watkin & D. Barker, 1961 [1913]).

3. Sidney Webb & Beatrice Webb, 7 *English Local Government: English Poor Law History*, Pt. I: *The Old Poor Law* 420-23 (1927).

4. *The Poor Law Report of 1834*, at 334 (S. G. Checkland & E. O. A. Checkland ed., 1974 [1834]).

5. Patrick Colquhoun, *A Treatise on Indigence* 7-8 (1806).

6. *The Poor Law Report of 1834* at 132-33.

7. Cicero, *De re publica*, 2, 22, 40. Engels said that regardless of whether the bourgeoisie practiced birth control, he remained of the opinion that "our proletarians...will honor their name by means of numerous proles." Letter of Feb. 10, 1883 to Karl Kautsky, in Karl Marx [&] Friedrich Engels, *Werke* 35:431, 432 (1967). For another view of the origins, see Arthur Rosenberg, *Untersuchungen zur römischen Zenturienverfassung* 40-43 (1911).

8. Karl Marx, *Zur Kritik der politischen Ökonomie (Manuskript 1861-1863)*, in Karl Marx [&] Friedrich Engels, *Gesamtausgabe (MEGA)* II/3.3:1198 (1978). Hardin erroneously states that Marx ignored the etymologically suggested "ancient hypothesis about the source of poverty." Garrett Hardin, *Exploring New Ethics for Survival: The Voyage of the Spaceship Beagle* 55 (1972).

9. W.F. Lloyd, *Four Lectures on Poor-Laws*, in William Forster Lloyd, *Lectures on Population, Value, Poor-Laws and Rent* 2-4 (1968 [1835]).

10. Thomas Robert Malthus, *An Essay on the Principle of Population* (7th ed.), in *idem, On Population* 366 (Gertrude Himmelfarb ed., 1960 [1872]) (quote); *idem, Principles of Political Economy* 259 (1820).

11. G. Talbot Griffith, *Population Problems of the Age of Malthus* 145-46 (1926) (quote); R. M. Smith, "Transfer Incomes, Risk and Security: The Roles of the Family and the Collectivity in Recent Theories of Fertility Change," in *The State of Population Theory: Forward from Malthus* 188-211 at 205 (David Coleman & Roger Schofield eds., 1986); Karl Polanyi, *The Great Transformation* 80 (1971 [1944]); J. L. Hammond & Barbara Hammond, *The Town Labourer 1760-1832: The New Civilisation* 144 (1919 [1917]); Griffith, *Population Problems* at 101-106 (quote).

12. J. D. Chambers & G. E. Mingay, *The Agricultural Revolution 1750-1880*, at 114-19 (1984 [1966]).

13. *Report from His Majesty's Commissioners for Inquiring into the Administration and Practical Operation of the Poor Laws: Appendix (A.): Reports of the Assistant Commissioners*, Part II, at 14a (1834) (C. P. Villiers).

14. Chambers & Mingay, *Agricultural Revolution* at 121; T. R. Malthus, *A Letter to Samuel Whitbread, Esq. M.P. on His Proposed Bill for the Amendment of the Poor Laws*, in *The Works of Thomas Robert Malthus* 4:1, 11-12 (1986 [1807]) (quote); Sidney Webb & Beatrice Webb, *English Poor Law History: Part II: The Last Hundred Years* 1-3, 7 (1963 [1929]) (quote at 7).

15. Webb & Webb, *English Poor Law History*, Part II: *The Last Hundred Years* at 8 (quote); J. L. Hammond & Barbara Hammond, *The Village Labourer 1760-1832: A Study in the Government of England before the Reform Bill* 166 (1919 [1911]) (quote).

16. Mark Blaug, "The Poor Law Report Reexamined," *J. Econ. Hist.* 24 (2):229-45 at 229, 231-32 (June 1964); *idem*, "The Myth of the Old Poor Law and the Making of the New," *J. Econ. Hist.* 23 (2):151-84 at 152, 153, 160-61 (June 1963); Raymond Cowherd, *Political Economists and the English Poor Laws: A Historical Study of the Influence of Classical Economics on the Formation of Social Welfare Policy* 138-39, 187 (1977).

17. Hammond & Hammond, *The Village Labourer* at 165, 169, 236-37.

18. George Nicholls, *A History of the English Poor Law* 2:132 (2d ed. 1898 [1854]).

19. Hammond & Hammond, *The Village Labourer* at 184-85.

20. Eric Hobsbawm & George Rudé, *Captain Swing* 51-52 (1975 [1968]). Hobsbawm and Rudé overdraw their point concerning the free labor market inasmuch as the residential conditions attached to poor-law relief riveted workers to their locality and made it "madness...to venture anywhere else." *Ibid.* at 50.

21. Tom Paine, *The Rights of Man*, in *The Selected Work of Tom Paine* 263-64 (Howard Fast ed., 1946 [1792]).

22. J. R. Poynter, *Society and Pauperism: English Ideas on Poor Relief, 1795-1834*, at 48-52 (1969); Bill No. 4573, House of Commons, *Parliamentary Papers, 1795-96* (Dec. 9, 1795); *The Parliamentary History of England 1795-1797*, 32:703 (1818) (Feb. 12, 1796). See generally Dean Rapp, *Samuel Whitbread (1764-1815): A Social and Political Study* 210-31 (1987).

23. *Parliamentary History of England* 32:705, 709. David McNally, *Against the Market: Political Economy, Market Socialism and the Marxist Critique* 73 (1993), skews the texture of the debate by emphasizing that Pitt used the language of political economy against Whitbread: the latter used the same language, whereas Pitt also proposed state intervention. McNally may have been misled by the secondary sources he cites in lieu of the parliamentary debates. Because no reporters took notes in Parliament during this period, in the absence of an official version, published accounts varied.

24. *Parliamentary History of England* 32:709-10.

25. *Ibid.* at 32:710 (quote); *The Parliamentary Register* 44:33 (1796) (quote); *Parliamentary History of England* 32:714-15.

26. § XXXVII, *reprinted in* Frederic Eden, *The State of the Poor* 3:cccxiii, cccxix (1965 [1797]) (quote); Webb & Webb, *English Poor Law History* at 34-39. The section on children's allowances of Bentham's privately circulated critique of the bill was jejune. Jeremy Bentham, "Observations on the Poor Bill," in *The Works of Jeremy Bentham* 440-61 at 444-46 (John Bowring ed., 1843 1797]).

27. *The Parliamentary History of England: 1798-1800*, 34:1426-30 (Feb. 11, 1800).

28. Cowherd, *Political Economists and the English Poor Laws* at 28-29; *Cobbett's Parliamentary Debates* 8:869 (1807) (quote).

29. Robert Owen, *Address delivered at the City of London Tavern*, in *idem, A New View of Society and Other Writings* 208-20 at 210-11 (1949 [1817]); *idem, Report to the Committee for the Relief of the Manufacturing Poor*, in *ibid.*, 156-69 at 157-58 (1817). For estimates showing an even greater advance in productivity, see *idem*, "Two Memorials on behalf of the Working Classes," in *A Supplementary Appendix to the First Volume of the Life of Robert Owen* 205-22 at 213-15 (1967 [1818).

30. Elie Halévy, 2 *A History of the English People in the Nineteenth Century: The Liberal Awakening 1815-1830*, at 40-46 (tr. E. Watkin, 1961 [1923]); *Report from the Select Committee of the House of Commons appointed to consider of the Poor Laws, reprinted in Annual Register for the Year 1817*, at 263-302 at 272 (1818 [1817]) (quote).

31. Maurice Cranston, *John Locke: A Biography* 425 (1957) (quote); H.R. Fox Bourne, *The Life of John Locke* 2:392-93 (1876); John Locke, *Report of the Board of Trade to the Lords Justices in the Year 1697, respecting the Relief and Employment of the Poor*, in *An Account of the Origin, Proceedings, and Intentions of the Society for the Promotion of Industry in the Southern District of the Parts of Lindsey, in the County of Lincoln* 99-126 at 101-102, 110 (3d ed., 1789) (quote). Locke's report is also reprinted in Bourne, *Life of John Locke* at 2:377-91. Locke's scheme was apparently never published or included in any edition of his collected works.

32. An Acte for the Releife of the Poore, 43 Eliz., ch. 2 (1601) (quote); Locke, *Report of the Board of Trade* at 103, 112-13 (quote).

33. Locke, *Report of the Board of Trade* at 113.

34. *Report from the Select Committee...to consider of the Poor Laws* at 282 (quote); *Parliamentary Debates* (Hansard) 37:1056 (Mar. 12, 1818) (quote).

35. *Parliamentary Debates* (Hansard) 40:470 (May 17, 1819); *The Works and Correspondence of David Ricardo* 5:1 (Pierro Sraffa ed., 1952 [Mar. 25, 1819]) (quote); *Parliamentary Debates* (Hansard) 38:575-78 (May 8, 1818); *Parliamentary Debates* (Hansard) 40:465-69 at 467-68 (May 17, 1819) (Curwen); *Parliamentary Debates* (Hansard) 38:916 (1818) (Lords).

36. See David Weatherall, *David Ricardo: A Biography* 72 n.2 (1976). Murray Milgate & Shannon Stimson, *Ricardian Politics* 13-14 (1991), discuss the importance of this correspondence for the development of Ricardo's political thought.

37. Letter from Trower to Ricardo, Jan. 17, 1817, in *The Works and Correspondence of David Ricardo* 7:117, 118 (P. Sraffa ed., 1962); Letter fom Malthus to Nassau Senior, Mar. 23, 1829, *reprinted in* Nassau Senior, *Two Lectures on Population*, in *idem, Selected Writings on Economics* 61, 65 (1966 [1829]): "In no old country that I have yet heard of, have the wages of labour...been for any length of time such as to maintain with ease the largest families."

38. Letter from Ricardo to Trower, Jan 27, 1817, in *Works and Correspondence of David Ricardo* at 7:124-25. See also David Ricardo, *On the Principles of Political Economy and Taxation*, in *The Works and Correspondence of David Ricardo* 1:105-107 (P. Sraffa ed. 1975 [1817]).

39. Letter from Ricardo to Trower, Jan 26, 1818, in *Works and Correspondence of David Ricardo* at 7:248.

40. *Works and Correspondence of David Ricardo* 5:303 (P. Sraffa ed., 1952 [May 30, 1823]).

41. Letter from Ricardo to Mill, Dec. 10, 1821, in *The Works and Correspondence of David Ricardo* 9:118 (P. Sraffa ed., 1962); Genesis 38.9; Johann von Thünen, *Der isolierte Staat in Beziehung auf Landwirtschaft und Nationalökonomie* 441-42 (3rd ed. 1930 [1850]).

42. *First Annual Report of the Poor Law Commissioners for England and Wales* 47-49 (1835).

43. Nassau Senior, *An Outline of the Science of Political Economy* 38 (1965 [1836]).

44. Friedrich Engels, *Die Lage der arbeitenden Klasse in England*, in Karl Marx [&] Friedrich Engels, *Werke* 2:225, 355 (1957 [1845]). Engels, however, merely concluded from this fact that "the present societal relations are worthless." *Ibid.* at 495.

45. *Population: viz., Enumeration and Parish Registers; According to the Census of M.D.CCC.XXI*, at xxx (1822). J. Clapham, *An Economic History of Modern Britain: The Early Railway Age 1820-1850*, at 54 (1926).

46. James Huzel, "Malthus, the Poor Law, and Population in Early Nineteenth-Century England," *Econ. Hist. Rev.* 22 (3): 430-51 (Dec. 1969); *idem*, "The Demographic Impact of the Old Poor Law: More Reflextions on Malthus," *Econ. Hist. Rev.*, 33 (3):367-81 (Aug. 1980).

47. J. Blackmore & F. Mellonie, "Family Endowment and the Birth-Rate in the Early Nineteenth Century," *Econ. Hist.* 1 (2):205-13 (May 1927); *idem*, "Family Endowment and the Birth-Rate in the Early Nineteenth Century: A Second Analysis," *Econ. Hist.* 1 (3):412-18 (Jan. 1928).

PART III

THE SOCIALIST RESPONSE

Proletarian horniness therefore, not capital, produces social misery.

Ernst Bloch, *Das Prinzip Hoffnung* 2:542 (1967 [1959])

5

Working-Class Neo-Malthusianism

> What remains of neo-Malthusianism? There is still to consider the
> sufferings of maternity for the woman, but constipation too is a great
> suffering and prevents some people from listening to reason, why not
> create a league of human regeneration by laxatives![1]

Neo-Malthusian currents have coursed through working-class movements since
Francis Place's efforts to promote birth control in England in the 1820s. Sharing
Malthus's view of poverty as rooted in overpopulation caused by excessive
individual procreativity, neo-Malthusians broke with Malthus over the issue of
contraception. Just as uncontrolled copulation brought about poverty, so too
individually implemented population limitation could eliminate it. This chapter
provides an historical outline of the literary and, to some extent, practical
expressions of belief in the efficacy of birth control as a means of ameliorating the
proletarian condition.

One crucial difference marked off some neo-Malthusians from their
movement's eponymous fountainhead: whereas they viewed family limitation
merely as an individualist strategy that households could successfully pursue to
ward off poverty, Malthus himself had regarded overpopulation as the overriding
cause of macroeconomic poverty. James Mill, Malthus's contemporary and
follower, stated this position expressly: "The precise problem...is, to find the means
of limiting births to that number which is necessary to keep up the population,
without increasing it.... The limitation of the number of births, by raising wages,
will accomplish every thing which we desire...[and] may be carried so far as...to
raise the condition of the labourer to any state of comfort...." John Stuart Mill
straddled both camps inasmuch as he took up Malthus's doctrine in the 1820s not
as an argument against perfectibility, but "in the contrary sense, as indicating the
sole means of realizing that improvability by securing full employment at high

wages to the whole labouring population through a voluntary restriction of the increase of their numbers."[2]

This difference between Malthusians and neo-Malthusians received its sharpest profile at the time of the so-called birth-strike debate shortly before World War I, when some German Social Democrats urged birth control as a method of alleviating individual sources of superadded misery while emphasizing that capitalist exploitation was the primary cause of poverty, which could not be eliminated by the advent of small families. They did not attempt to quantify the relative proportions although several nonsocialist investigators, especially in England, did purport to identify the share of the poor whose poverty derived primarily from excessive family size.[3] This controversy, shorn of its socialist or even party-political trappings, has reemerged in contemporary welfare debates: while some argue that individuals can just say no to poverty by just saying no to sex or at least to "unprotected" sex, others believe that poverty at large is a result of macrodemographic overpopulation.

A self-taught artisan and businessman-employer who fathered 15 children, Place was instrumental in the repeal of the anti-labor-union Combination Acts in 1825, although he himself believed that neither the law nor unions themselves were significant determinants of wage levels. Despite his Malthusian belief in the crucial importance of population for establishing equilibrium between supply and demand in the labor market, Place led the struggle against the Combination Laws because he saw them as creating an unnecessary antagonism between employees and their employers. As a utilitarian, he also converted Malthus's theory of population to the cause of Benthamite birth control among artisans.[4]

In his *Illustrations and Proofs of the Principle of Population*, Place sought to "teach these truths" to "the commonest mechanics and labourers"—that "inevitable poverty and misery would result from marrying and having a family" while wages were depressed by the overstocking of the labor market; abstinence from marriage for a few years or the use of "precautionary means" would, however, by reducing the supply of labor below the demand, raise wages "so high as to enable them to maintain themselves respectably, and give many of them a fair chance of rising in the world."[5]

Place, who adhered to a fundamentalist Malthusianism, which projected population backward and forward in history in inexorable lockstep with food production, propagated this program of Malthusian embourgeoisement in contraceptive handbills distributed in 1823 by 17-year-old John Stuart Mill and others.[6] In them Place addressed the specific impoverishing effects of large families on the "genteel" and the working class:

> In the present state of society, a great number of persons are compelled to make an appearance, and to live in a stile, which consumes all their incomes, leaving nothing...as a provision for their children. To such persons a great number of children, is a never failing source of discomfort and apprehension.... This state of things pervades...that respectable class of society called genteel.... To those

who constitute the great mass of the community, whose daily bread is alone procured by daily labour, a large family is almost always the cause of ruin, both of parents and children; reducing the parents to cheerless, hopeless and irremediable poverty.[7]

Place infused the wage-fund doctrine in a handbill designed especially for this latter group of workers in such a way as to lay the groundwork for working-class neo-Malthusianism into the twentieth century:

> It is a great truth...that when there are too many working people in any trade or manufacture, they are worse paid than they ought to be paid, and are compelled to work more hours than they ought to work....
>
> When wages have thus been reduced to a very small sum, working people can no longer maintain their children as all good and respectable people wish...but are compelled to...send them to different employments;—to Mills and Manufactories, at a very early age....
>
> By limiting the number of children, the wages both of children and of grown up persons will rise; the hours of working will be no more than they ought to be....[8]

This neo-Malthusian strategy was, however, comforting to class conciliators because it purportedly operated to reestablish a profitable equilibrium by making use of workers' own biologically innate reproductive drives. Consequently, capitalists who were grievously distressed by "the probability of the labourers reducing their numbers so low, as to oblige the capitalists to give them a large share of the produce instead of a small one," did not need to be alarmed: "the universal propensity and desire to possess offspring, forms a perfectly efficient security that the numbers of the working classes would never decline beyond that point at which a fair remuneration was obtained for their labour."[9]

Place's contraceptive campaign set off a lively debate in the newly founded working-class press, prompting a spate of anti-neo-Malthusian diatribes.[10] The attack was particularly pointed in *The Trades' Newspaper, and Mechanics' Weekly Journal*—Britain's first trade-union newspaper—which was established by unions that had been strengthened by the repeal of the Combination Acts and sought to prevent their reenactment. The newspaper, which Place had helped found, marked the breach between Place's middle-class utilitarianism and trades-unionism emancipating itself from a naturalistic acceptance of capitalism.[11]

The front pages of the first issues were dominated by the alleged connection between wages and procreation. The ostensible occasion was Place's distribution among workers of notes of a lecture on the wages of labor delivered by John McCulloch, an orthodox political economist with whom Place was associated. Discussion of McCulloch's views occupied the front page of the inaugural issue. In keeping with the Malthusian variant of the wage-fund theory, McCulloch had counseled the working classes not to "combin[e] to exact what you may think fair rate of wages," but that they could keep their real wages high by restricting their numbers "'so as not to overstock the demand for labourers.'" *The Trades' Newspaper* then imagined a series of absurd examples of how workers might implement McCulloch's imperative to thin their ranks. The most efficient, it suggested, was abstention from or delay of marriage and propagation, but in adddition to believing that marriage was a duty and the "attempt to limit the consequences of marriage...ridiculous," the newspaper asked a practical question: "How can any man possibly tell when, by adding one or two more to the mass of the population, he will help to overstock, at some future day, the market for labour?" It consequently denied that workers practically had the power to comply with McCulloch's injunction:

> Whatever influence you could possibly exercise...must be *prospective*; and that in so remote a degree, that no rational being would ever think of taking it into his consideration. [Y]ou can at best only resolve that you will not introduce into the world one, two, or more beings who may add to the number of labourers...*some twelve or fifteen years hence.* But how can you tell so long beforehand that one, two, or more hands may not be wanted? Although at one time the market of labour may be overstocked, how many are the casualties—war, pestilence, famine,—which may occur to thin the population in the course of another fifteen years. Again, each man can at best only act for himself; he cannot make sure that any considerable number of other persons will do as he does; he cannot make sure that new inventions in machinery will not, by supplying the place of men, in our arts and manufacture have the same effect as if millions and tens of millions of men were added to the number of labourers in the country; nor can he make sure that some neighboring country—Ireland for example—will not pour in its swarms to assist in baffling all the efforts of individual patriotism to keep down the numbers of our working population.[12]

The Trades' Newspaper thus astutely and acutely combined analysis of the impediments to the realization of the rationality of collective action under a dynamic-spontaneous political-economic system of constant and unforeseeable long-run change with a special focus on the labor-market havoc wreaked by labor-saving capital accumulation and capital-friendly state-aided immigration from lower-wage areas. This prescient anticipation of socialist critiques of neo-Malthusianism made the most of the particularly pressing problems inherent in the interaction structure involving an activity as committed to private, decentralized, individualistic decision-making (or inability to control) as sex and procreation. In this direction *The Trades' Newspaper* went beyond even Sismondi, the anti-Ricardian economist, whose underconsumptionist critique of the classical assumption of equilibrium permitted him as early as 1815 to question the ability of the urban worker to "calculat[e] the lot of the succeeding generation.... How can he judge...the general demand for labor in his country, whilst his master who employs him is incessantly mistaken on these points?"[13]

The Trades' Newspaper quickly shifted from a questioning and ironic posture to aggressive vituperation as it spoke out "in the name of British manhood" against "these eunuch philosophers" who deserved "universal execration...for their conspiracy against nature...."[14] Linking "Messrs. Malthus, M'Culloch, Place and Co." to the "revolting and inhuman...efforts without a name...to introduce into practice, certain abominable means," the newspaper chided them for overlooking the taxation of working-class consumption commodities:

> But what has restriction of population to do with all these evils? It may lessen the pressure on them certainly, because it would lessen both the number of sufferers and the share of suffering to each, but it could by no possibility ever remove them. All the self-denial which it is in the power of the working classes to exercise, could never prevent an aristocracy, possessed of all the powers of the state—the power of capital—the power of making what laws they please, and the power of interpreting and administering them as they please—from interposing these and a thousand other obstacles and restrictions, to prevent the poor and generally *unrepresented* man from obtaining a fair remuneration for his labour. The number of the working classes might to-morrow be reduced one half; and yet the corn tax, the beer tax, the light tax, and all the other taxes which now press British industry to the earth, remain in as much force as ever.[15]

This political deconstruction of Malthusianism "as a self-serving doctrine produced by the upper classes for the purpose of controlling the lower classes" faintly echoed the hyperbolic argument published two years earlier in the radical working-class paper, *The Black Dwarf*, which had been conducting its own debate on the subject: "Why, if the race of labourers were to refuse to propagate the species, Parliament is so omnipotent that it would make it highly penal for any journeyman who should neglect to have a christening every year!"[16]

In response to a letter arguing that, if a laborer were given "a taste for comforts," he would reason and conduct himself like the classes above him, who restrain themselves lest they or their children "should lose their rank in society," the editor of *The Trades' Newspaper* replied in effect that unlike those classes, even the birth-controlling laborer was in control of too few of the variables affecting his wages to be able to rely on such a procreational strategy: "With Malthus and Co. he [the letter writer] would reduce the whole matter to a question between Mechanics and their sweethearts and wives; but...the whole matters rather resolves itself into a question between the employed and their employers—between the Mechanic and the corn-grower and monopolist—between tax-payer and the tax-inflictor."[17] Indeed, just how committed the newspaper was to the logical consequences of Ricardo's admission two years earlier that the use of machinery may "render the population redundant" was evident in its rhetorical question to McCulloch: "how a mere diminution in the number of improvident marriages, even to one in a million, could *possibly*...prevent the competition of machinery with human labour?"[18]

The Trades' Newspaper also excoriated Place for aligning himself with the "supply and demand gentry," who urged the labourers to reduce their numbers "for we have already enough of you," and for devising a system the practical effect of which "would be precisely the same as if our capitalists were, after the example of Pharaoh, to order every fifth or tenth son that is born of a labourer to be cast into the river." Why capitalists would have wanted to adopt Malthusianism or neo-Malthusianism, thus reducing the oversupply of labor that allegedly redounded to their profit and made it unnecessary for them to "'reduce...the unduly large share which [they] have hitherto been pleased to take to [them]selves of the national product," the newspaper failed to explain. Instead, it advocated the "Live and Let Live System," which expressed the theological belief "that there can be no more mouths in the land, than Providence has, for some good purpose, sent there...."[19]

Neo-Malthusian adherents have struggled ever since with socialists over the question of whether working-class misery stems from excessive numbers or a "bad organization of society." The surface plausibility of the Malthusian explanatory framework to the working-class experience, Henry George observed in 1879, was hardly mysterious: "To the mechanic or operative the cause of low wages and of the inability to get employment is obviously the competition caused by the pressure of numbers, and in the squalid abodes of poverty what seems clearer than that there are too many people?"[20]

As early as 1870, the prominent American economist Francis Bowen stated that in a densely populated country, "children are a hindrance, from the difficulty of establishing them in an equal position of life with their parents." Commentators have observed that by the 1870s English middle-class parents began limiting the size of their families in an effort to close the gap between their aspirations and levels of living caused by the increasing cost of children and the decreasing supply of servants. In particular the transformation of secondary and university education from attributes of social status into means of achieving and maintaining status and the advent of free state-provided mass education impelled middle-class parents to focus on costly education for their sons. Hence the origins of the middle-class "strike against parentage."[21]

According to the received stylized accounts of the phases of the demographic transition to modernity, a variant of this middle-class construction of the good life eventually trickled down to the working class, which with a time lag modified its procreational behavior to reduce its fertility. By the last quarter of the nineteenth century, when industrialization and child labor laws meant that children had to be maintained by their parents at least for 10 years—twice as long as in an earlier period—they ceased to be an "economic asset.... When depression followed the problem arose as to which of the least necessary things should be dispensed with." The choice was made easy: as "an unrelieved expense, [i]n the individualistic competitive struggle, children became increasingly a handicap...and the greater the number of children the smaller the chances of each child (and of the parents) of advancing in the competitive struggle...." Therefore, the British Royal Commission on Population later concluded, "it paid to travel light."[22]

By the turn of the century, neo-Malthusianism had become a political movement in Britain, France, and other advanced capitalist countries. More than the nuances of each national movement were governed by its attitude toward the struggle between socialism and capitalism. In Germany, where some socialist-feminists propagated smaller families, the aim was not to supplant socialism, but to provide individual parents (and especially mothers) with the economic and social-psychological wherewithal to participate in the socialist movement. In contrast, British neo-Malthusians, for example, did not limit themselves to advocating birth control merely on the basis of the benefits accruing to the individual (small) family. Rather, by adoption of a policy of working-class-wide restriction of fertility based on the wage-fund theory and the notion—later known as optimum population (growth)—that a diminution in the growth of the labor supply would bring about an increase in per capita production, they expressly offered an ideological alternative to the socialists' answer to the social question.[23]

Ironically, neo-Malthusians shared both the socialists' goal of eliminating poverty on the macrosocial rather than merely on the individual level and their rejection of reliance on personal natality policies. However, because British neo-Malthusians also rejected collectivist social policies, they, unlike the socialists, were compelled to found their future on the invisible hand's governance of procreativity. Indeed, just as bourgeois neo-Malthusians alleged that British socialists opposed them because smaller and economically more secure working-class families would be less receptive to revolutionary appeals, there is also evidence that the Malthusian League saw itself as contributing precisely to that antirevolutionary evolution.[24]

In France, too, socialists saw neo-Malthusians as quacks promising illusory instantaneous and painless happiness to those unwilling to be part of a struggle that might last ten years or a century. Without adopting a unified position or, like their counterparts in Germany, even conducting a formal debate, French socialists launched even more vitriolic and less reasoned attacks on the neo-Malthusians. Some spewed contempt for a movement that merely sought to ameliorate the condition of the proletariat which it was the goal of socialism to eliminate. Segments of the French trade union movement, in contrast, adopted a much more sympathetic attitude toward neo-Malthusian goals. Reducing proletarian misery, the supply in the labor market, and the reproductive travails of women all appealed to a number of labor unions. The main journal of the unified Socialist Party published a laudatory review of Robert Hertz's socialist attack on neo-Malthusianism, a brochure that emphasized the consequences of French depopulation for the country's military rivalry with Germany.[25]

The more militant critical neo-Malthusians allied to socialism even charged that the "proletarians, the makers of children, are the accomplices of capital" in the sense that the reserve army of the unemployed, which rendered strikes unsuccessful, "is not of capitalist origin, but rather of a sexual and proletarian origin. It is the workers who aliment it by their procreational incontinence and who thus furnish the capitalists with the means of perpetuating their serfdom." This position was, to be sure, associated with a eugenic approach, which castigated these counterrevolutionary incontinents for procreating "in their misery beings dedicated to downfall, resigned and brutish, alcoholic, degenerate, tainted in all ways, incapable of thought and action, ineducable."[26] Anti-Malthusian socialists who did not oppose individual proletarians' personal decisions to improve their situation by remaining childless reminded them, however, that they were no more contributing to the emancipation of their class than a worker who became a wine merchant. But even socialists such as Hertz identified sufficiently with the existing state and society to worry that declining population might enhance the relative importance of the most fertile but also most "backward" European peoples who were still "refractory to the ideas of emancipation...."[27]

As was the case in Germany, the most influential French leftists rejected neo-Malthusianism. Because the decline in fertility had begun much earlier and assumed a much sharper demographic and political profile in France, the neo-Malthusian movement there was older and more diverse. The Left's reaction to it was therefore also more diverse. Although the primary argument of anti-neo-Malthusian socialists in both countries was the ruling classes' use of the population question to deflect attention from the social question, the French Left also stressed two points that were alien to German Social Democrats: first, that "nature or providence" would insure that the uncontrollable demographic process would not eventuate in overpopulation; and second, that by relieving women of their natural duties, birth control would undermine the family. This French socialist peculiarity of supporting bourgeois family and gender norms, it has been suggested, derived from the Left's self-perceived need to demonstrate that socialist economics would not bring about social disintegration.[28] The German Social Democratic Party (SPD), in contrast, was preoccupied with the purely demographic-economic dimension of neo-Malthusianism because it was concerned to project itself as worthy of being entrusted with the legacy of Europe's most powerful economy.

While a similar division between working-class pronatalists and anti-natalists also manifested itself in Sweden and Norway before World War I, the struggle over the socioeconomic and political content of neo-Malthusian birth control was nowhere sharper than in the United States.[29] There it was exemplified in the career of Margaret Sanger, who converted from the belief that birth control was a weapon in the class war to deprive capitalists of military and industrial fodder to its aggressive "biological and racial" use to spare society from "spending...billions, keeping alive thousands who never, in all human compassion, should have been brought into this world. We are spending more in maintaining morons than in developing the inherent talents of gifted children. We are coddling the incurably defective and neglecting potential geniuses." In the course of this transition to Malthusian eugenics Sanger concluded that "[u]ncontrolled sex has rendered the proletariat prostrate, the capitalist powerful." Overpopulation was the ultimate cause of low wages, unemployment, peonage, sweatshops, and child labor, and all labor problems, which workers could get rid of if they would just "stop breeding." Indeed, Sanger declared that the "most serious evil of our times is that of encouraging the bringing into the world of large families. The most immoral practice of the day is breeding too many children." Thus she wound up blaming the victims and especially women. Labor's enemy in general was "the reproductive ability of the working class which gluts the channels of progress with the helpless and weak," and therefore "the workers who produce large families have themselves to blame for the hundreds of thousands of unemployed grasping for jobs, for the strike breakers...." More particularly the culprit was "woman...unknowingly creating slums, filling asylums with insane, and institutions with other defectives.... Had she planned deliberately to achieve this tragic...human waste and misery, she could hardly have done it more effectively.... By failing to withhold the multitudes of children who have made inevitable the most flagrant of our social evils, she incurred a debt to society."[30]

For some socialists the ideological filtration that shapes neo-Malthusian procreative decision-making has always stood in need of deconstruction. J. C. Kincaid, a British academic Trotskyist, for example, applauds the rationality of the proletariat's rejection of the "bourgeois" norm of producing fewer children but providing them with a certain standard of living.[31] He considers it "a sensible response" to low and unstable earnings, exclusion from educational opportunity, and the struggle for housing

> to build up a large family which will provide resources of social and psychological support to its members.... For the poor to convert themselves to middle-class values and strategies would be disastrous, given the insecurities they face. They are thoroughly sensible in relying on their own kin rather than on the uncertain benevolence of bureaucratic agencies of support and control. Besides, the enthusiasts for eugenic or Malthusian solutions to poverty take too little account of the possibility that the very poor *like* to have a lot of children, given that to be poor is to be excluded from many other kinds of social opportunities.[32]

Kincaid's reference to the proletariat's noneconomically motivated lust for big-family life not only takes Engels' Hungry Forties' culture-of-poverty view of the proletariat's reduction to primitive sensual pleasures one step further, but reproduces John Stuart Mill's assertion that the working class, rarely wanting improvement, had as many children as were consistent with the condition of life to which they had been born.[33] Kincaid tries to evade the charge that poor adults would, by and large, not need patronizing state subsidies if they did not have large families to support in the first place by pointing to a limited association between large families and poverty: poor families with a breadwinner had on average only 3.3 children in 1966 in Britain—a figure only marginally higher than the national average. He finds it "important to stress that quite large numbers of workers earn low wages, because in public discussions it has been assumed that the real explanation for poverty among wage-earning families lies not in the lowness of wages, but in the largeness of families. [T]he implication would then be that the fault lies not in the wage system, but in the unwillingness of certain sections of the population to limit their family size to reasonable proportions." Though constrained to admit that "it would seem that many children cause poverty" for the one-fifth of the wage-earning poor with five or more children, Kincaid takes refuge in the venerable argument that if any causality can be identified, it runs in the opposite direction—from poverty to large families.[34]

But as British large-scale studies from the turn of the century to the present have repeatedly shown, regardless of the causal mechanisms at work, it is the combination of low wages and large families that constitutes the basis of poverty for those below retirement age in Britain. Peter Townsend's monumental study of poverty in the United Kingdom, for example, revealed that the probability of poverty increased steeply and monotonically with family size. In 1968-69, the share of man-and-woman-headed families in or on the margin of poverty was 21 percent among those with one child and 69 percent among those with four or more children; whereas only 5 percent of such families with one child received gross disposable income below the deprivation standard, the corresponding figure for those with four or more children was 61 per cent. These large families were the modal group, accounting for one-sixth of all poor persons.[35]

Here the extremes touch as workerism finds a strange anti-neo-Malthusian bedfellow in Catholic moral theology. John Ryan, one of the spiritual authors of the early twentieth-century living-wage movement, conceded that in theory neo-Malthusianism would, through supply-and-demand forces, raise wages. But even apart from the "disgusting...criminal...and degrading" practices involved, Ryan argued that justice nevertheless did not obligate the laborer to limit his procreativity:

> The man who marries and brings into the world children whom he cannot maintain in the minimum conditions of decency, will sometimes sin against prudence, but he violates no rights, either of his wife, his offspring, or his fellow laborers.... His wife freely consents to the union; his unborn children have no rights sufficiently potent to annul his right of fatherhood; and the right of his fellow working men to the larger advantages that they would obtain if fewer children were born to the group, is inferior to his right to become the head of a family. Indeed, it is doubtful whether even charity toward his children or his fellows obliges the laborer to forego the advantages and consolations of family life in order that the hand of social injustice may fall less heavily upon them. It would seem that charity does not bind at the cost of such great personal inconvenience.[36]

Apart from such moral compunctions, the prisoner's dilemma or free-rider obstacles to a neo-Malthusian strategy are said to be considerable. Theoretically, if workers accepted the correctness of Malthus's analysis, a decision to trade off a larger number of children for a generally higher wage level would improve the condition of all working-class families. But critics find such an approach flawed even as an individualistic strategy because no small family would benefit from higher wages unless many or all limited their size.[37] Modern demography voices a similar objection:

> as soon as individual families expect others to change to lower fertility, their private satisfactions will be maximized by not going along with the scheme. Since their individual actions concerning childbearing will have only an infinitesimally small impact on [the labor market], rationally they will attempt both to maintain full parental satisfaction (by having [more] children) and enjoy [the higher wages] inherent in the [smaller-family] system. Identical calculations on the part of other families will result in the stability of the initial fertility behavior.[38]

However, unlike the canonical free rider, proletarian procreators may have no incentive to defect from the collectivity; for by limiting the number of children it must support, each set of parents can achieve an increase in its family's standard of living equivalent to a real wage increase regardless of its class-mates' reproductive behavior and whether the Malthusian macroeconomic wage-fund mechanism ever functions.[39] In other words, since private, individualistic action prior to, independent of, and even in the absence of collective decision-making or action would motivate them to reduce family size, free riders would not be a problem—unless the general wage increase expected from a smaller supply of labor and tighter labor markets were so much larger than the increase in per capita family income to be derived from the smaller number of children to be supported that a family would have the best of both worlds by defecting. Moreover, so long as children begin to earn more than they cost at an early age, once child labor is prohibited and children become long-term financial drains, family limitation benefits any individual family regardless of what other families do.[40]

But the certainty and immediacy of the effects of the personal decision to limit fertility vis-à-vis the speculative and long-term impact of the collective decision make this latter imagined scenario implausible. It is precisely the palpable and significant benefits accruing to individual sets of parents (and their already existing children) that presumably reinforced that segment of the so-called demographic transition that was manifested in the shift to smaller families.[41] Thus whereas 63 percent of marriages entered into in 1860 in England and Wales produced five or more children and 16 percent ten or more, the corresponding figures for those entered into in 1925 were 12 percent and 0.7 percent. Similarly in Germany, in 47 percent of all marriages taking place between 1900 and 1904, four or more children were born compared to only one in twenty marriages entered into between 1968 and 1972; by 1990, a single child lived in 51 percent of all households whereas three or more children lived in only 13 percent of households. The U.S. data exhibit, from a slightly different perspective, the same trend. The proportion of the cohort of ever-married white women born in the mid-nineteenth century and surviving until the 1910 census that gave birth to seven or more children was about one-third; in contrast, fewer than one-twentieth of their counterparts born between 1915 and 1924 reported seven or more births at the 1970 census.[42]

The most plausible conclusion is therefore that when the requisite changes in economic conditions, the proliferation of cheap contraceptive techniques, and the transformation of the position and consciousness of women all coincide, working-class (and other) procreators, prompted by the new societal conditions of collective rationality, make individual decisions to produce fewer children. In the 1820s and even later, only some preconditions were in place. In particular, widespread child labor continued to give parents an incentive to defect from any neo-Malthusian birth-limitation schemes. In pre-World War I France, fertility declined more dramatically than in Germany or Britain, but differentially as the bourgeois family preceded the working-class family in lucratively shedding its share of procreational "duties." Socialist opponents of neo-Malthusianism resented the "injustice and especially the absurdity" of the manner in which an anarchic society allocated these costs, which were wearing out proletarian parents.[43]

It was precisely because all the conditions had been met by the time of World War I that the so-called birth-strike movement was so threatening to the ruling classes in Germany, who had nevertheless not fully grasped the reasons why fertility had spontaneously been in decline for decades. The threat was, to be sure, considerably undercut by the ease with which the employing class could import cheaper labor. Once the labor market was internationalized, a working-class population control movement would have had to respond in kind or lose even its hypothetical force.[44] The failure of the socialist parties to achieve even the far more basic solidarity of refraining from slaughtering one another's national proletariats during World War I revealed how unrealistic an international working-class neo-Malthusian movement was.

NOTES

1. Dr. Oguse, "Socialisme et Néo-Malthusianisme," *Revue socialiste* 46:97-124 at 123 (Aug. 1907).

2. James Mill, *An Essay on the Impolicy of a Bounty on the Exportation of Grain*, in *idem*, *Selected Economic Writings* 41, 55-56 (Donald Winch ed., 1966 [1804]); James Mill, *Elements of Political Economy*, in *ibid*. 203-366 at 242-44 (3rd ed. 1826) (quote); John Stuart Mill, *Autobiography*, in *Essential Works of John Stuart Mill* 68 (Max Lerner ed., 1965 [1873]) (quote).

3. See below ch. 7-8.

4. Graham Wallas, *The Life of Francis Place [1771-1854]* (1919 [1898]); I.J. Prothero, *Artisans and Politics in Early Nineteenth-Century London: John Gast and His Times* 172-82 (1979); Angus McLaren, "Contraception and the Working Classes: The Social Ideology of the English Birth Control Movement in its Early Years," *Comp. Studies in Society & Hist.* 18 (2):236-51 at 238 (Apr. 1976).

5. Francis Place, *Illustrations and Proofs of the Principle of Population* 164-65 (Norman Himes ed., 1930 [1822]).

6. F.P., "Machinery—Employment—Population," *The Republican* 14 (6):162-70 at 169 (Aug. 18, 1826); William Petersen, *Malthus* 124 (1979).

7. Francis Place, "To the Married of Both Sexes," *reprinted in* Norman Himes, *Medical History of Contraception* 214 (1936 [1823]).

8. Francis Place, "To the Married of Both Sexes of the Working People," *reprinted in* Himes, *Medical History of Contraception* at 216-17.

9. A. Z., "Depression of the Bulk of the People: Causes and Remedies," *Black Dwarf* 11(20): 664, 676 (Nov. 12, 1823).

10. "Practical Endeavours to Apply the System of Mr. Malthus in Checking Population," *Black Dwarf* 11 (12):404, 405 (Sept. 17, 1823): "we do not see how the exact quantity of children should be born, to keep up, what some of our political economists would call, the exact ratio between mouths, and the means of keeping them employed."

11. Sidney Webb & Beatrice Webb, *The History of Trade Unionism* 76 n.2, 85-100 (new ed. 1902 [1894]); E.P. Thompson, *The Making of the English Working Class* 769-78 (1963); Prothero, *Artisans and Politics* at 183-91.

12. "Wages of Labour," *The Trades' Newspaper, and Mechanics' Weekly Journal*, No. I at 1-2, July 17, 1825. For the background of the lecture and its repercussions, see N.E. Himes, "McCulloch's Relation to the Neo-Malthusian Propaganda of His Times: An Episode in the History of English Neo-Malthusianism," *J. Pol. Econ.* 37:73-86 (Feb. 1929); Prothero, *Artisans and Politics* at 205-206.

13. Gary Langer, *The Coming of Age of Political Economy, 1815-1825*, at 175 (1987); J. C. L. Simonde de Sismondi, *Political Economy* 124-25 (1966 [1815]).

14. "The Population Restricting System," *The Trades' Newspaper, and Mechanics' Weekly Journal*, No. II, July 24, 1825 at 7.

15. "Population and Wages," *The Trades' Newspaper, and Mechanics' Weekly Journal*, No. III, July 31, 1825, at 33-34.

16. Angus McLaren, *Birth Control in Nineteenth-Century England* 61 (1978); "Inquiry into the Principles of Population: No. 2," *Black Dwarf* 11 (21):695, 703 (Nov. 19, 1823).

17. T.R.L., "To the Editor," *The Trades' Newspaper, and Mechanics' Weekly Journal*, July 31, 1825 at 34; "Population and Wages" at 34.

18. David Ricardo, *On the Principles of Political Economy and Taxation*, in *idem, The Works and Correspondence of David Ricardo* 1:388 (Piero Sraffa ed., 1952) (chapter added to 3rd ed. in 1823); "Population Restricting System," *The Trades' Newspaper, and Mechanics' Weekly Journal*, No. VI, Aug. 21, 1825, at 82.

19. "The Economy of Nature Defended Against the Population Restricting System," *The Trades' Newspaper, and Mechanics' Weekly Journal*, No. IX, Sept. 11, 1825, at 129-30.

20. André Armengaud, "Mouvement ouvrier et néo-malthusianisme au début du xxᵉ siècle," 1966 *Annales de Démographie Historique* 7-19 at 7 (quote); Henry George, *Progress and Poverty* 98 (n.d. [1879]) (quote).

21. Francis Bowen, *American Political Economy* 145 (1969 [1870]); J. Banks, *Prosperity and Parenthood: A Study of Family Planning Among the Victorian Middle Classes* 139-207 (1954); D. Glass & E. Grebenik, "World Population, 1800-1950," in 6 *The Cambridge Economic History of Europe: The Industrial Revolution and After: Incomes, Population and Technolgical Change (I)* 56, 117 (H. Habbakuk & M. Postan eds., 1965); J. Banks & Olive Banks, *Feminism and Family Planning in Victorian England* (1964); J. Banks, *Victorian Values: Secularism and the Size of Families* (1981); H.G. Wells, *Socialism and the Family* 37 (1908 [1906]) (quote).

22. John Innes, *Class Fertility Trends in England and Wales 1876-1934*, at 37-55 (1938); Ethel Elderton, *Report on the English Birthrate*, Part I: *England, North of the Humber* 233-34 (1914) (quote); [U.K.] Royal Commission on Population, *Report* 39-40, 42 (Cmd. 7695, 1949) (quote).

23. F. Micklewright, "The Rise and Decline of English Malthusianism," *Population Studies* 15 (1):32-51 (1961-62); G. Searle, "Socialism and Malthusianism in Late Victorian and Edwardian Britain," in *Malthus Past and Present* 341-56 (J. Dupâquier et al. eds., 1983); L. Devance, "Malthus and Socialist Thought in France Before 1870," in *ibid.* at 275-86; Madeleine Rebérioux, "The Attitudes of French Socialists to Malthus During the Third Republic," in *ibid.* at 287-98; [National Birth-Rate Commission], *The Declining Birth-Rate: Its Causes and Effects* 284-89 (1916) (testimony of John Hobson).

24. Richard Soloway, *Birth Control and the Population Question in England, 1877-1930*, at 70 (1982); Rosanna Ledbetter, *A History of the Malthusian League: 1877-1927*, at 94-99, 110-11 (1976).

25. Oguste, "Socialisme et néo-malthusianisme" at 97; Francis Ronsin, "La Classe ouvrière et néo-malthusianisme: l'exemple français avant 1914," *Le Mouvement social*, No. 100, at 85-117 at 95-107 (Jan.-Mar. 1979); Henri Guernut, "Review of Robert Hertz, Socialisme et dépopulation," *La Revue socialiste* 53 (317):475-76 (May 1911).

26. Gabriel Giroud, "Le Nèo-malthusianisme prépare le socialisme," *reprinted in* Francis Ronsin, *La Grève des ventres: Propagande néo-malthusienne et baisse de la natalité française (XIXe-XXe siècles)* 187-88 (1980) (without source). Giroud was one of the founders of the French neo-Malthusian movement. *Ibid.* at 71 n.13.

27. Robert Hertz, "Socialisme et Dépopulation," in *Les Cahiers du socialiste*, No. 10, at 16, 9, 11 (1910).

28. Angus McLaren, "Sex and Socialism: The Opposition of the French Left to Birth Control in the Nineteenth Century," *J. Hist. Ideas* 37(3):475-92 at 477, 492 (July-Sept. 1976).

29. Allan Carlson, *The Swedish Experiment in Family Politics: The Myrdals and the Interwar Population Crisis* 7-16 (1990); Ida Blom, *Barnebegrensning—synd eller sunn fornunft* 178-81 (n.d. [ca. 1980]).

30. Margaret Sanger, "Is Race Suicide Probable?" *Collier's*, Aug. 15, 1925, at 25 (quote); Margaret Sanger, *The Pivot of Civilization* 165 (1969 [1922]) (quote); Margaret Sanger, *Woman and the New Race* 3, 146, 57, 150, 143, 4, 6 (1923 [1920]) (quote). See also David Kennedy, *Birth Control in America: The Career of Margaret Sanger* 109-13 (1970)

31. Rosalind Petchesky, *Abortion and Women's Choice: The State, Sexuality, and Reproductive Freedom* 377 (rev. ed. 1990 [1984]).

32. J.C. Kincaid, *Poverty and Equality in Britain: A Study of Social Security and Taxation* 184-85 (1973).

33. John Stuart Mill, *Principles of Political Economy* 159 (new ed. W. Ashley ed., 1926 [1848]). In contrast, Ricardo adopted a sociopsychologically more optimistic perspective: If a worker's wages rise, his amended condition "does not necessarily oblige him to marry and take upon himself the charge of a family.... But although this might be the consequence of high wages, yet so great are the delights of domestic society, that in practice it is invariably found that an increase of population follows the amended condition of the labourer...." Ricardo, *On the Principles of Political Economy* at 406-407.

34. Kincaid, *Poverty and Equality in Britain* at 183-84. Kincaid is not the first to try to have it both ways. Francis Bowen asserted both that it "is not the excess of Population which causes the misery, but the misery which causes the excess of Population," and that "a man's condition as married or single, and the size of his family, are decisive of his

worldly fortune." Bowen, *American Political Economy* at 143.

35. Peter Townsend, *Poverty in the United Kingdom: A Survey of Household Resources and Standards of Living* 288-89, tab. 7.12 at 290 (1979). The income standard here refers to that below the state supplementary benefit scales plus housing cost or up to 40 percent higher; for a description of the standard, see *ibid.* at 267-71.

36. John Ryan, *A Living Wage* 152, 151 (rev. ed. 1920 [1906]).

37. Linda Gordon, *Woman's Body, Woman's Right: A Social History of Birth Control in America* 81 (1981 [1976]).

38. Paul Demeny, "Welfare Considerations in U.S. Population Policy," in U.S. Commission on Population Growth and the American Future, 6 *Research Reports: Aspects of Population Growth Policy* 153-72 at 163 (1972).

39. For a contrary suggestion from an early-20th-century Canadian neo-Malthusian, see Angus McLaren & Arlene McLaren, *The Bedroom and the State: The Changing Practices and Politics of Contraception and Abortion in Canada, 1880-1980*, at 74 (1986).

40. For a distinct but related argument, see Ann Ferguson & Nancy Folbre, "The Unhappy Marriage of Patriarchy and Capitalism," in *Women and Revolution: A Discussion of the Unhappy Marriage of Marxism and Feminism* 313-38 at 323 (Lydia Sargent ed., 1981).

41. Blaug's assertion that by the 1830s "saving the cost of bearing children...was probably thought to be too slight an incentive for family limitation," is unsubstantiated. Mark Blaug, *Ricardian Economics: A Historical Study* 115 n.47 (1958).

42. Royal Commission on Population, *Report*, tab. XVII at 26; *Verhandlungen des Deutschen Bundestages*, 8. Wahlperiode 1976, Anlagen-Band 256, Drucksache 8/3299: "Antwort der Bundesregierung: Grundprobleme der Bevölkerungsentwicklung in der Bundesrepublik Deutschland," tab. 2 at 4 (Oct. 26, 1979); Marlene Lohkamp-Himmighofen, "Deutschland," in *Zwölf Wege der Familienpolitik in der Europäischen Gemeinschaft: Eigenständige Systeme und vergleichbare Qualitäten?—Länderberichte* 81-148 at 92 (Erika Neubauer et al. eds., 1993); U.S. Bureau of the Census, *Historical Statistics of the United States, Colonial Times to 1970*, Part 1, ser. B 42-48 at 53 (bicentennial ed., 1975).

43. Louis Blanc, *Organisation du travail* 68-71 (5th ed. 1848 [1839]); Hertz, "Socialisme et Dépopulation" at 22 (quote).

44. L. Brentano, "The Doctrine of Malthus and the Increase of Population During the Last Decades," *Economic J.* 20 (79):371-93 (Sept. 1910).

6

Was Marx a Crypto-Malthusian?

> Marx...taught that...if a man had to fight for the hungers and necessities of ten or twelve children, he made a better revolutionary. "Let 'em have as many as they can," was the cry.[1]

> Marx, the most powerful critic of Malthus, may also be dismissed as being largely irrelevant to the mainstream of modern empirical demography.... Marx's theory of the process by which "population pressure" develops was not based on research.[2]

If the working-class movement was ever to articulate a demographic program of its own, Marx of all social theorists should have been most vitally interested in providing the requisite foundations. Yet even David Harvey, an orthodox Marxist social theorist, plausibly speaks of "Marx's rather surprising failure to undertake any systematic study of the process governing the production and reproduction of labour power itself." Although he regards the omission as one of the most serious gaps in Marx's theory and a very difficult one to plug, Harvey suggests that Marx's short-circuited approach can be defended by reference to the limited purpose to which Marx sought to put the discussion of the labor supply—namely, that within the framework of the general law of accumulation, capitalist production inexorably generates the industrial reserve army it needs regardless of the absolute size of the population. Other Marxist critics maintain that Marx and Engels failed to take a step beyond bourgeois economics not only in the general sense of treating population as an exogenous factor, but also more specifically in taking the existence of a laboring population as a self-explanatory and natural prerequisite of societal reproduction. By taking the proletarian family for granted, Marx is said to have mystified the production of children and hence of working-class reproduction.[3]

This chapter explains how the stereotyped charges that political and academic critics have leveled against Marx fail to do justice to his surprisingly subtle theorization of the interaction between the mechanisms of capital accumulation and proletarian population development. By the same token, the fruitfulness of Marx's contribution to the debate over the need for direct societal regulation of population is shaped by his peculiar synthesis of the theory and practice of transformative historical change. Because Marx concluded that population, by and large, was not a significant impediment to the profitability of individual capitals or capital in general, he saw little systemic motivation for demographic intervention by the state. Thus, unlike the situation, for example, with regard to the length of the working day, which generated a tension between the short-term interests of individual firms and the long-term viability of British capitalism, ultimately resulting in compulsory state norms, demographic change failed to set in motion any capital-oriented state intervention. Marx's analysis of what he regarded as a surplus population specific to the capitalist mode of production does not simply presuppose that some economic mechanism would always insure a quantitatively adequate supply of labor, but actually constructs a detailed theoretical model. By the same token, Marx does not make the functionalist assumption that economic mechanisms automatically and agentlessly ward off all demographic threats to capitalism's long-term viability.

As for the other historically critical social formation, socialism, Marx denied in principle the possibility or even desirability of analyzing—and thus preempting active construction of—this future mode of production.[4] Since Marx also believed that the subjective roots of the revolutionary working-class consciousness that would eventually impel the proletariat to overthrow capital would not, at least, given Marx's sense of the potential propinquity of a socialist society, within any politically relevant period, tap into workers' reproductive desires, habits, or patterns, he also refrained from proffering a transitional demographic program.

Despite these self-imposed methodological constraints, Marx has persistently been taken to task for having failed to develop a theory of population. Some critics appear to believe that *Das Kapital* was designed as a kind of *Encyclopædia Capitalistica* or *Pauly-Wissowas Real-Encyclopädie der classischen Kapitalismuswissenschaft*. Just as Marx has been faulted for ignoring "the implications of man's mortality" for human nature, for more than a century economists and demographers have identified his neglect of natality as a near fatal missing link in his analysis of capitalism.[5]

Even during Marx's lifetime, commentators began insisting that family and fertility were black boxes for him. One of the earliest discussions of *Das Kapital* in a scholarly economics journal mocked Marx for blithely assuming that early proletarian marriages were somehow forced upon workers by a capitalist law of nature which they were powerless to resist. In fact, wrote Julius Platter in the prestigious *Jahrbücher für Nationalökonomie und Statistik* in 1877, since marriage was a free act subject to human will, any number of motives would have supported late marriages and sparing procreation in order to thwart the interests of the class enemy. Platter, ignoring that in preindustrial traditional Europe the positive correlation between household size and wealth or social status was a "moral law," asserted that the highly positive correlation between poverty and procreativity was "a much more absolute, more abstract law of population" than Malthus's and "a pure law of nature, equally in effect at all times and in all places..., a law that makes the poor poorer and poorer and the rich richer and richer," and immune from knowledge and education. Platter completed his attack by charging that whereas Marx found a "purely physical relation between poverty and human fertility," identifying poverty with overfertility, Malthus operated with a moral or psychic relation, identifying the poor with those who gave little thought to the future.[6] Ironically, this interpretation, which resembles twentieth-century culture-of-poverty explanations, was also embodied in Marx's and especially Engels' understanding of proletarian fertility patterns.

Other nineteenth-century German critics labelled Marx's account of the early age at which workers married under capitalism at best circular. Like much of neoclassical economics, Marxism stands accused of having failed to forge the mediating links between the theoretical or systemic demand for labor and the social-psychological microfoundations of human procreation.[7]

An even harsher, albeit less theoretically grounded, attack on Marx stemmed from Margaret Sanger, one of the founders of the birth control movement in the United States. After having passed through a more socialist-oriented phase, Sanger concluded, soon following World War I, that because Marx "failed to recognize the interplay of human instincts in the world of industry," he neglected "the dangers of irresponsible parenthood and reckless breeding" and overlooked that the "greatest asset of the capitalism of that age was...the uncontrolled breeding among the laboring classes."[8]

More recently, feminists have charged that "since Marx did not see women as an integral part of the proletariat, as both producers and reproducers, he had no basis for theorizing a 'law of population' whose dynamics included women's need for fertility control, apart from shifts in the capitalist demand for labor; he did not see fertility control as part of the class struggle, much less the gender struggle."[9] Some Marxist feminists assert that because Marx's labor theory of value assumes that the value of labor power, unlike that of other commodities, is not determined by the societally necessary labor time to produce it, Marxists fail to discuss the labor time that mothers devote to their children, that is, future workers.[10]   Alternatively, Harvey, a very friendly interpreter, is constrained to admit that Marx failed to rise above the dismal scientists of his era: "When it comes to features promoting a high rate of birth (early age of marriage, rising birth rates, etc.), Marx does not read very differently from Malthus.... Marx seems to be trapped in the same general swamp of ignorance with respect to the process of reproduction of labor power as were his contemporaries." And even where Marxists understandingly condone Marx's politically justified denunciations of Malthus, they charge him with having inadvertently misled his followers into abandoning demography to "our enemies."[11]

Critics have attacked Marx for mutually incompatible failings. Some take Marx to task for having been completely blind to the existence of population problems. Because he is said to have regarded the growth of the labor force as a necessary and automatic consequence of capital accumulation, some social scientists consider him a demographic optimist, who could not imagine that depopulation could ever be capitalism's undoing.[12] Yet Marx's failure to have problematized absolute population decline is, in light of capitalism's development during the twentieth century, largely academic. Thus, the demographic historian William Petersen chides Marx for having ahistorically constructed his system around the unusually strong population growth of the nineteenth century; consequently, demographic forecasts of population decline during the 1930s could not even have been a "hypothetical contingency."[13] Marxist economics is, however, hardly an appropriate object of criticism for inadequate understanding of the Great Depression. Similarly, the actual population decline in several Western European countries since the 1970s has scarcely posed insoluble puzzles for Marxist analysis of economic development. It is William Stanley Jevons, one of the initiators of the marginalist revolution, against whom the charge of demographic obtuseness should be raised. Because he believed that the problem of economics was to find the mode of employing a given population and powers of production so as to maximize the utility of the output, for him the doctrine of population "forms no part of the direct problem of economics."[14]

Others have charged that Marx was committed to an "implicit Malthusian theory of population," which blinded him to "the fact of mass progress... [which] made men rethink the calculus of having children" by means of a non-Malthusian check on the birth-rate...."[15] In a variant on this theme, other economists, echoing Sanger's judgment that Marx "fail[ed] to realize that it is to the capitalists' advantage that the working classes are unceasingly prolific," make the counterintuitional assertion that Marx and Marxists have actually understated the extent of capitalist exploitation by deemphasizing the reproductive surplus that the proletariat creates at home for capital, thus adding to the live stock of golden egg-laying geese. Marxists, so goes this argument, have deprived themselves of this additional agitational tool because it would only lend credence to neo-Malthusian propaganda.[16]

Unlike Malthus, however, Marx was not attempting to develop a general theory of population (change). Indeed, contrary to the claims of many of his critics and supporters, Marx did not even purport to have uncovered The Law of Population of the Capitalist Mode of Production. What Marx did theorize in *Das Kapital* was the "Progressive Production of a Relative Overpopulation or Industrial Reserve Army" as an indispensable element of the "General Law of Capitalist Accumulation."[17] This self-sustaining mechanism of cyclical labor-saving capital investment booms that disemploy more workers than they hire is a perennial source of mystery to amnesic economic analysts, although sociodemographers confirm that the labor force participation rate of such "marginal" groups as women, the young, and the old fluctuates during the course of the business cycle in accordance with endogenous socioeconomic rather than exogenous demographic forces.[18]

The statement in the first volume of *Das Kapital* that has misled critics to characterize Marx as a demographer manqué, even of capitalism, is his insight that the laboring population, by producing the accumulation of capital, produces its own relative redundancy or overpopulation: "This is a law of population peculiar to the capitalist mode of production, as indeed every special historical mode of production has its special historically valid laws of population. An abstract law of population exists only for plants and animals, insofar as human beings do not intervene historically." Marx is not saying here that he has laid bare the totality of the laws of population for capitalism. Rather, he has merely singled out one of the set of population laws that no mode of production prior to capitalism had fashioned for regulating the growth of its working population. Because the "population fanatics" applied the term *surplus population* exclusively to labor power and expressly exempted from it the leisure consuming class, Marx studied a class-based subset of capitalist laws of population.[19]

A decade before he published *Das Kapital*, Marx began exploring the concept of overpopulation in the context of the free laborer qua virtual pauper in the so-called *Grundrisse*. He observed that various societal modes of production were characterized by "various laws of the increase of population and over-population" (pauperism). These laws were "simply to be reduced to the various modes of relating to the conditions of production or with regard to the living individual conditions of reproduction of him as member of society.... It is only in the mode of production grounded on capital that pauperism appears as the result of labor itself, of the development of the productive power of labor." Consequently, what appeared as overpopulation in one stage of societal production might not be in another. Marx criticized Malthus precisely for his inability to grasp these historical differences and thus for reducing the complicated and changing relationships of overpopulation in various historical phases "stupidly to one relationship...an abstract numerical relationship." Malthus's ahistorical approach caused him therefore to transmogrify the immanent, historically changing limits of human procreation into external limitations and the external checks of natural reproduction into internal limits or natural laws of procreation. Instead, Marx noted, surplus population had to be grasped generally with regard to "the social mediation through which the individual relates to the means of his reproduction and creates them.... The invention of surplus workers, i.e., of propertyless people, who work, belongs to the epoch of capital."[20]

Marx had formed this view of Malthusianism a decade earlier in the course of preparing a series of lectures for workers on wages. Based on the less sophisticated understanding of capital accumulation that he had developed by 1847, Marx charged that Malthus's claim that it was a law of nature that population grew faster than the means of employment or subsistence enabled the bourgeoisie to transform a societal law into a law of nature. This naturalization process was an ideological benefit to the bourgeoisie by portraying the proletariat's misery as its own fault.[21]

In contrast, Malthus, because he forged a mechanical linkage between wages and population guaranteeing a perpetual equilibrium, was, counter-intuitively, a demographic optimist.[22] Thus given stationary national resources and population, wages could not fall below what is necessary to maintain stationary population "because...the principle of demand and supply would always interfere to prevent such wages as would either occasion an increase or diminution of population." Ironically, Malthus's impressively long-lived population theory has been characterized by a leading developmental economist as a nonstarter "for the capitalist epoch."[23] As Wrigley and Schofield explain in their monumental English population history, before 1800, faster population growth was associated with a declining standard of living; after about 1811, however, the Industrial Revolution broke that historic link:

> And by an ironic coincidence Malthus had given pungent expression to an issue that haunted most pre-industrial societies at almost the last moment when it could still plausibly be represented as relevant to the country in which he was born.... After 1800 poverty was, so to speak, no longer inevitable and the stage was set for the high indignation about poverty so characteristic of many nineteenth-century reformers.... Perhaps now it can be seen that both Malthus and his successors were right in their generations, for the world viewed by a man of Marx's generation had changed fundamentally.... The tension between population growth and living standards...gave way before a change in productivity so profound that an increase in poverty was no longer the price of an increase in numbers.[24]

Marx's estimation of the futility of population control as a means of counteracting the expansion of the reserve army and thus mitigating its wage-depressing effect was driven by his theory of capital accumulation, which explained the individual worker's poverty not as a consequence of his personal superfertility, but, rather, of his displacement by constant capital—a fate to which even the childless were vulnerable. Marx's insight was hardened by his observation of contemporary demographic ruptures in Ireland. The depopulation following in the wake of the famine of 1846 fashioned the best possible experiment for testing the Malthusian dogma that overpopulation causes misery and "equilibrium is restored through depopulation." Yet the consequence for those who remained behind, liberated from overpopulation, was wages as low as ever because relative overpopulation more than kept pace with depopulation.[25] English agriculture in the 1850s furnished Marx with additional evidence. A rise in wages brought about by the confluence of factors such as the decline in labor supply caused by emigration and absorption by factories and heightened demand for soldiers had prompted tenant farmers to introduce new labor-saving machinery. The resulting "artificial overpopulation" and renewed decline in wages occurred despite the relative and absolute decrease in the agricultural population.[26] As generalized by Gunnar Myrdal: "If we could 'wish away'...all the unemployed, this change would bring about secondary changes in the various supply and demand curves, with the result that in...a short time a new unemployment would develop...if this...change is not assumed to improve the social organization of the economic process."[27]

Even before presenting his theory of accumulation, Marx made clear in that part of his model that assumed merely simple (that is, nonexpanding or nonaccumulating) reproduction that the continuous transformation of money into capital presupposed that the possessor of labor power had to be continuously present in the market. Since the seller of labor power was mortal, he had to immortalize himself through procreation. Marx's starting point is therefore that "at the very least" the workers who are withdrawn from the labor market as a result of having been used up or died must constantly be replaced by an equal number of substitutes. Marx operates with the classical political economic assumption of a proletarian family wage, that is, that the means of subsistence required for the production of labor power include those for the departing worker's replacements, which, conventionally enough, Marx assumed to be his children. Thus "this race of peculiar commodity owners immortalizes itself in the commodity market."[28]

Marx's view thus far bears a superficial resemblance to Ricardo's, which posited that the "natural price of labour" sufficed to enable labourers "to subsist and to perpetuate their race, without either increase or diminution." But in spite of Ricardo's insistence that the natural price of labor included a historical, moral, political, cultural, and place-based component, he also maintained a naturalistic-biologistic version, according to which labor became dear when it was scarce; when the market price of labor—that is, "the price which is really paid for it, from the natural operation of the proportion of the supply to the demand"—exceeded its natural price, the laborer's enhanced purchasing power enabled him to rear a "numerous family. When, however, by the encouragement which high wages give to the increase of population, the number of labourers is increased, wages again fall to their natural price, and indeed...sometimes fall below it." At this depressed standard of living, the mirror-image process of readjustment of wages and supply of labor was ignited: "It is only after their privations have reduced their number" that the market price moves back up to the natural price of labor.[29]

This naturalistic mechanism was explicated even more explicitly by J.B. Say, a Smithian popularizer for whom Marx had bottomless contempt. After stating that the diminished supply that would result from the inability of workers to raise families on their wages would soon lead to higher wages as demand exceeded supply, Say remarked that the same process would apply if significant numbers of workers did not marry. Since the childless could offer their labor more cheaply than, and would thus displace, worker-parents, they would soon bulk proportionately larger within the working class: "not only would they not contribute to recruiting the class, but they would prevent others from being able to recruit it." But the old equilibrium would promptly reassert itself because the lower wage level of the childless would be followed by an increase resulting from the decline in the number of workers.[30]

Marx criticized this received dogma of political economy as an unrealistic abstraction from the way capitalism functioned and had to function. Malthus had laid out the logic of what became known as the wage-fund doctrine in his critique of Adam Smith in the first edition of the *Essay on the Principle of Population*:

> the comforts of the labouring poor depend upon the increase of the funds destined for the maintenance of labour, and will be very exactly in proportion to the rapidity of this increase. The demand for labour which such increase would occasion, by creating a competition in the market, must necessarily raise the value of labour, and, till the additional number of hands required were reared, the increased funds would be distributed to the same number of persons as before the increase, and therefore every labourer would live comparatively at his ease.[31]

Schematically, then, Ricardian political economy believed in the following cyclical mechanism: ↑ capital accumulation → ↑ wages→ ↑ working-class procreation → over-full labor market → ↓ wages → ↓ working population (or ↑ exploitation) → ↑ capital accumulation. Marx explained why this model was unrealistic:

> For modern industry with its ten-year cycle and its periodic phases...it would indeed be a pretty law that regulated the demand and supply of labor not by the expansion and contraction of capital, that is, according to its valorization needs at any particular time, so that the labor market now appears relatively under-full because capital is expanding, and now again relatively over-full because it is contracting, but, instead, made the movement of capital dependent on the absolute movement of the absolute amount of population.... A pretty method of motion this for developed capitalist production! Before any positive growth of the really able-bodied population could take place as a result of the increase in wages, the deadline would have run again and again during which the industrial campaign must have been conducted, the battle fought and decided.[32]

A more realistic account of capitalist development showed that a surplus-worker population or, as political economy characterized it, overpopulation, both was a necessary product of capital accumulation and in turn became a lever of the latter and "a condition of existence of the capitalist mode of production. By having this industrial reserve army at its disposal, capital has, for its changing valorization needs, ready access to the "exploitable human material, independent of the limits of the real increase in population." Real or mere biological population growth would be much too inflexible to meet accumulating capital's sudden and explosive expansive force as its frenetic invasions of branch after branch require the capacity to throw large masses of workers into these operations without interrupting the scale of production in other industries. This enormous volatility of capitalist production not only was unprecedented, but was also impossible even in early capitalism, when accumulation progressed in step with the relative growth of demand for labor and finally ran up against "natural limits of the exploitable worker population" that historically were cleared away through enforced proletarianization of noncapitalist producers. The expansion-contraction cycles of developed capitalism, in contrast, hinge on the availability of an increased supply of workers that is both "independent of the absolute growth of population" and largely generated within the capitalist sector of the economy. Specifically, this reserve army is recruited by "constantly setting free a part of the workers through methods that reduce the number of employed workers in proportion to the increased production" and thus make some of them unemployed or underemployed.[33]

Marx's repeated insistence that capitalist production cannot be satisfied with the quantity of labor power supplied by the natural increase of population and "needs for its free play an industrial reserve army independent of this natural limit" manifestly presupposes that this violently fluctuating labor reservoir was superior to a (theoretically conceivable) system of a vast perpetually inexhaustible surplus population that would so far exceed the needs of capital even at the height of the investment cycle that capital would be additionally freed of the limits of the disemployment mechanism inherent in an increasing organic composition of capital. This reinstatement of what amounts to Malthus's "narrow-minded" naturalistic conceptualization of overpopulation was presumably not practicable because it would have required an enormous program of alimentation of this enlarged pool of quasipermanently unemployed; since the British propertied classes had already forced an end to the Old Poor Law regime, which had fed the unemployed victims of the Industrial Revolution, because the taxes were unacceptably high, there was no political, economic, or ideological leeway in mid-Victorian England for restoring such a system on an even larger scale. Moreover, to the extent that some subset of the reserve army was unemployed for such extended periods that it lost its industrial skills, discipline, and morale, it became dysfunctional for capital although it was a necessary product of the accumulation process. As such, this pauperized dead weight already constituted *faux frais* that capital strove to avoid or shift to others.[34] At the same time, however, Marx acknowledged that the history of modern industry demonstrated that constant overpopulation was possible "although it formed its stream from quickly-lived, swiftly succeeding generations of humans picked unripe so to speak."[35]

Although the relative diminution of variable capital vis-à-vis constant capital seems to bring forth a more rapid absolute growth of the worker population than of the variable capital, the accumulation process constantly produces an addition to the worker population that is, relative to capital's average valorization needs, an excessive and redundant population. Capital's ability to create such a flexible labor force is, however, even greater if the assumption is dropped that the increase or decrease of the number of workers employed corresponds exactly to the increase or decrease in variable capital. Capital can extract more labor from the same number of workers through greater extensive or intensive exploitation of individual workers. Capital can thus increase its supply of labor faster than its demand for workers, and by overworking part of the working class, capital further inflates the reserve army, which in turn exerts yet greater competitive pressure on the overworked sector to submit to its deteriorating conditions. So convinced was Marx of the crucial importance of this segmentation of the labor force as a substitute for biological demographic growth that he believed that, if the working day were reduced to a "rational" level in England, the existing working population would be insufficient to carry on the existing volume of production, which could be achieved only by converting "'unproductive'" workers into "'productive'" ones.[36] The extraction of more labor from the same absolute number of workers is also secured, for example in the United States, by means of multiple jobholding by 8 million workers. This method, which—unlike one employer's increasing the length of its employees' workday—benefits capital in general and circumvents the financial deterrence embodied in overtime statutes, substitutes for biological accretions to the labor force inasmuch as multiple jobholding parents and especially mothers have correspondingly less time to devote to childbearing and -raising.[37]

The system-immanent relative overpopulation, fluctuations in which regulate the general movements in wages, not only depresses wages during the stagnation and average prosperity phases of the business cycle, but also moderates wage demands during the phase of highest production sufficiently so that, even when the law of supply and demand should be operating for the benefit of the active worker army, capital's rule is not threatened. Capital can succeed in this manner because, just as the demand for labor has become distinct from the growth of capital, the supply of labor is not identical with the growth of the working class: "Les dés sont pipés. Capital acts on both sides simultaneously." By setting free some workers, whose consignment to the reserve army puts additional pressure on the workers newly absorbed into production, the process of accumulation "to a certain degree makes the supply of labor independent of the supply of labor."[38]

A contentious theoretical question arises here as to whether Marx's alleged proclivity to take population growth for granted as an implicit precondition of capitalist production fatally undermines his claim that the processes sustaining the reserve army of the unemployed operate independently of absolute increases in population.[39] In an alternative formulation, critics argue that by presupposing that variable capital increases absolutely even if it declines in relation to constant capital, Marx could not demonstrate the inevitability of the formation of the reserve army without implying that population grows more rapidly than variable capital.[40] A half-century ago, Paul Sweezy, a Marxist economist, conceded that Marx, writing in the middle of the nineteenth century, not implausibly assumed that, with a growing population, a mechanization-induced rise in the organic composition of capital would bring about a relative decline in demand for labor together with an expansion of the reserve army as a more or less stable share of the total labor force. But regardless of the particular historical circumstances underlying Marx's theory, "the principle of the reserve army is independent of any particular population assumption; it works equally well with a stationary or even a declining population...." In other words, capitalism is sufficiently dynamic that, with time, it can adapt to and remold the demographic supply of labor through restructuring, which enables it to increase and differentiate the supply of and reduce the demand for labor.[41]

To be sure, Marx did not contend that capital had at its disposal magical powers that enabled it to maintain profitability in the face of any demographic disaster. Thus after recounting that Ireland's population had fallen by almost one-third in less than two decades following the famine year of 1846, Marx explained that agricultural rents and profits had nevertheless risen. But if a similar loss of population had taken place in England, a predominantly industrial country of developed capitalist production, it would have "bled to death." And even less catastrophically, Marx argued that where the rate of exploitation—in part as a result of workers' resistance—temporarily cannot be raised, the size of the working population would become the limiting factor on the mass of extractable surplus.[42]

This reasoning, however, has been contested. Samuel Hollander, a historian of political economy, argues that, vis-à-vis declining population, the aforementioned mechanism of labor-saving accumulation "could only limit the resultant wage increase; there is no reason to expect the creation of an excess labor supply with downward pressure on the wage."[43] Hollander, for his part, overlooks the fact that although reduced population may shrink the reserve army as compared to a scenario in which population continues to grow, a one-time loss of population "may provoke offsetting technological changes which raise the *level* of the reserve army back to where it was before the population change [or trigger] a resumption of the original *growth rate* of that reserve.... Even if the counteracting effects do not provide a complete offset, they may still be substantial, rendering population control a very limited means of improving the workers' condition."[44]

Although Marx did not expressly adopt a position on the issue in *Das Kapital*, in the course of criticizing Ricardo's theory of accumulation in a preliminary draft, he discussed the question of how the surplus value from the previous period of production is transformed into capital. Assuming that the "mode of production" and hence the organic composition of capital were un-changed—that is to say, that the increase of capital cost the same amount of labor as the previous year's production of capital of the same amount—Marx traced through the possibilities for transforming part of the surplus value into variable capital in order to buy "new labor." After disposing of a longer working day because it was not a constant means of accumulation, and bracketing the incorpora-tion of previously nonworking women, children, and paupers, he focused on the absolute growth of the working population together with the absolute growth of the general population: "If accumulation is to be a constant, continuous process, then this absolute growth of population (although it decreases relatively as against the applied capital) [is a] condition. *Augmentation of population* appears as the foundation of accumulation as a constant process.... Capitalist production takes care of sudden cases by overworking one part of the working population and holding the other in readiness as reserve army half[-] or pauperized."[45]

Here, then, Marx explicitly assumed biological growth as a prerequisite of accumulation, but only under the further assumption that constant capital was not increasing faster than variable capital. As Marx observed later in the same manuscript, however, if population increases at the same rate as capital, a mechanism inherent in capitalist development—the faster growth of constant at the expense of variable capital—insures that a part of the population becomes redundant.[46] Implicit in this argument is the possibility that where absolute population growth lags behind the increase in capital, stronger increases in the organic composition of capital could compensate for the absence of newly produced recruits by making even larger masses of workers superfluous.

Precisely because these mechanisms inherent in capitalism constantly accommodate the number of workers to capital's valorization needs, Marx was contemptuous of Ricardian-Malthusian preaching to the working class of the necessity to regulate its procreativity in accordance with these same profitability considerations. The bourgeoisie's counsel to the proletariat to reduce its rate of reproduction was permeated with "stupidity, vileness, and hypocrisy" since the bourgeoisie knew that the advice was impossible for the class as a whole to follow and capital benefited from overpopulation.[47] As early as 1853, Marx mocked the *Economist* for reprimanding the working classes for having thrown away the "golden opportunities" "of not marrying and not multiplying,...of living less luxuriously, of not asking for higher wages, of becoming capitalists at 15 shillings a week, and of learning how to keep the body together with coarser food, and how to degrade the soul with the pestiferous doctrines of Malthus."[48]

Although Marx rejected such bourgeois reproductive sermons as both superfluous from capital's perspective and harmful to workers, he has been criticized for following in the footsteps of the bourgeois economists he despised by virtue of viewing procreation naturalistically—for taking for granted that the working class would deliver sufficient absolute-biological increases to the capitalist class to satisfy the specific requirements of large-scale machine industry. Yet Marx was under no illusion that the laws of capital accumulation executed themselves agentlessly: he was, for example, acutely aware of the energetic and complicated recruitment campaigns throughout Britain and Ireland that firms had to undertake periodically to overcome temporary and cyclical shortages of labor in certain industries.[49]

By the same token, however, the capital-functional impact of the reserve army is insulated from demographic constraints in the sense that proletarian producers and sellers of labor power cannot act as minifirms, which would withdraw supply from the labor market as demand declines because supply is driven by the need to secure subsistence rather than investment opportunities. Moreover, nineteenth-century working-class families were trapped by their own response to capital's growing absorption of child labor and devaluation of adult labor: by accommodating that demand, individual families may have survived but only at the expense of the whole class, whose conditions deteriorated as a result of the very effort at improvement by means of increasing the supply of working children.[50]

The rapid consumption of the labor power of young men in mechanized factories characterized by a detailed division of labor meant that capital developed a differentiated age- and gender-specific demand for workers as a contradictory result of which "the natural accretion of the mass of workers does not sate the needs of capital accumulation and nevertheless at the same time exceeds them...."[51] Since these industries required fresh labor power and could not rely on partially consumed recruits from the reserve army, a demographic question arose as to where young men come from. Thus whereas in other settings Marx could neglect the issue of the real, absolute, or natural growth of the working class in favor of its social reconstruction and redistribution within the reserve army, here he had to face the Malthusian question. The brevity of Marx's published answer suggests its self-explanatory character for him—as if the underlying phenomenon had become second (or remained first) nature:

> Under these circumstances the absolute growth of this fraction of the proletariat requires a form which swells its numbers although its elements are used up quickly. Hence rapid replacement of the genera-tions of laborers. (The same law does not apply to the other classes of the population.) This societal need is satisfied by early marriages, necessary consequence of the relations in which the workers of large-scale industry live, and by the premium that the exploitation of working-class children sets on their production.[52]

The question raised here is how this objective requirement of capitalist production, this societal need, came to functionalize for its own ends the contem-poraneous form of proletarian familial reproduction. Was this functional corre-spondence serendipitous? And if the new industrial proletariat had not been in a position to begin procreating at an early age, where would capital have recruited its requisite fresh troops? Marx may have been right to point out that unlike previous and other fractions of the proletariat, these new industrial workers, whose earnings at the outset of their careers were as high as they would ever become, were economically able to found families at a younger age; in any event, they had no reason to postpone marriage in the expectation that their income would rise later. The question, however, is why for Marx these early marriages were a "nec-essary consequence" of, rather than merely a possibility created by, large-scale industry. The choice of words suggests that working-class procreation, if not a natural phenomenon, was at least a social phenomenon that stood in no particular need of critical theoretical explanation.

If the industrial proletariat, unlike independent producers, who had to rely on their children to carry on their businesses, had no such self-interested repro-ductive motivation, Marx apparently saw the matter of producing children for capital as a sufficiently analogous lucrative side business to furnish a proletarian self-interested motivation to reproduce. As early as 1847, Marx had argued that one reason that bourgeois Malthusianism's advice to the working class that it exercise moral restraint could not be taken seriously was precisely the premium that modern industry distributed for procreation by replacing adults with children. A dozen years later, Marx reiterated in the *New York Daily Tribune* that many working-class parents conspired with factory owners to violate factory laws so that their young children could be paid full-time wages.[53] As one of Marx's bourgeois-economist contemporaries put it: "A population in which child labor has taken root must necessarily produce many children." Widespread nineteenth-century European reports of parents' resistance to compulsory education as an interference with their optimal utilization of their children as economic resources and the very high rates of labor force participation still prevalent among young children in the latter part of the century formed the basis for and thus lend force to Marx's view.[54]

Marx's literally mechanical view of the mechanics of working-class reproduction also appears in his popular-propagandistic 1865 address to the General Council of the First International, posthumously published as *Value, Price and Profit*. In explaining the value of labor power, Marx observed that "the man, like the machine, will wear out, and must be replaced by another man. Besides the mass of necessaries required for his own maintenance, he wants another amount of necessaries to bring up a certain quota of children that are to replace him on the labour market and to perpetuate the race of labourers." One Marxist has characterized this approach as a "teleological absurdity" because it attributes the existence of a reproductive component within labor power to capital's desire for workers two decades later rather than to workers' struggle for such provision.[55]

Marx, however, also sketched a richer account of the specific social background to proletarian reproduction. In an unpublished draft of *Das Kapital* he observed that capital increased the relative number of workers even with a stationary total population by increasing productivity, and extensivity and intensivity of working time, subjecting artisans to capitalist wage labor, and incorporating women and children into the labor force. Additionally, however, capital produced an absolute rise in the working population since it could be achieved not only through an increase in births, but also as a result of the fact that more children grew up and could be fed until they were old enough to work. "The development of the forces of production under the regime of capital increases the mass of annually produced means of subsistence and cheapens them so far that the average wage can be calculated on the larger scale of reproduction of the workers although its value sinks...."[56] At a time when he had not yet accorded a central place to the theory of the reserve army of the unemployed, Marx devoted more attention to the reasons for proletarian procreation:

> [T]he life situation in which capital places the working class, the conglomeration and the separation from all other enjoyments of life, the total hopelessness of reaching a higher social standpoint and of maintaining a certain decorum, the lack of substance of his whole life, the mixing of the sexes in the workshop, the isolation of the worker himself, all drives to precocious marriages. The shortening and almost abolition of the learning period, the early age at which children themselves can appear as producers, the shortening of the time during which they have to be fed, increases the stimulus towards accelerated human production. If the average age of the worker generations

declines, then an always superfluous and constantly rising mass of shortlived generations is found in the market and that is all that capitalist production needs.[57]

Significantly, although Marx did not anticipate the modern feminist claim that mass child production was "extorted by capitalist-patriarchal compulsions," both the prosperity and depression phases of capital accumulation conspire, in Marx's view, to increase proletarian procreation: a temporary excess of surplus capital beyond its potential labor force would bring about a higher wage level, which would in turn alleviate the influences decimating working-class progeny and stimulate marriages; but faster than it would increase population absolutely, this excess capital would, by prompting the introduction of labor-saving and relative surplus value-extracting mechanization, create an "artificial, redundancy of population, which in turn again—as misery creates population within capitalistic production—is the hotbed of real increase of population."[58]

When Marx observes that if production has the capitalist form, reproduction does too, the interpretation that suggests itself initially is that he is referring to overall societal reproduction rather than to its procreative variety. Yet, closer examination reveals that Marx viewed human reproduction under capitalism as subsumed under the reproduction of capitalist relations. Because the worker's labor was, even before he entered into the process of production, alienated from him and incorporated into capital, during that process it constantly objectifies itself in an alien product—capital. Just as the worker constantly produces objective wealth as capital, as a power that dominates and exploits him, so too the capitalist reproduces and perpetuates the worker as wage laborer. In the course of this process the worker engages in two types of consumption, which appear to be "totally different." In the first or productive consumption, the worker consumes the means of production while the capitalist consumes his labor power. In the other, individual, consumption, the worker uses the money he received for selling his labor power to buy his means of subsistence. In the former he "belongs to the capitalist; in the second he belongs to himself and performs vital functions outside the process of production. The result of the one is the life of the capitalist, that of the other is the life of the worker himself."[59]

When this microperspective is abandoned in favor of a class-wide view of the whole capitalist process of production, however, it is revealed that the capital that the capitalist exchanges for labor power "is transformed into means of subsistence the consumption of which serves to reproduce the muscles, nerves, bones, brain of existing workers and to beget new workers." In this sense, then,

> the individual consumption of the working class is reconversion of the means of subsistence...into labor power that can be newly exploited by capital. The worker's individual consumption thus remains a moment of the production and reproduction of capital, whether it proceeds inside or outside the workshop, factory, etc....just like the cleaning of the machine, whether it happens during the labor process or certain pauses.

> It is immaterial that the worker carries out his individual consumption
> for his own sake and not the capitalist's. A beast of burden's consump-
> tion does not remain a less necessary moment of the process of produc-
> tion because the beast itself enjoys what it eats. The constant mainte-
> nance and reproduction of the working class remains the constant con-
> dition of the reproduction of capital. The capitalist can confidently
> leave its fulfillment to the workers' instinct of self-preservation and
> propagation.... From the societal point of view the working class is
> therefore, even outside the immediate labor process, just as much
> appendage of capital as the dead instrument of labor. Even its
> individual consumption is within certain limits only a moment of the
> reproduction process of capital.[60]

To be sure, Marx emphasized that despite the fact that the conditions of
the worker's existence and the narrow scope of monetary value of his labor power
forced him to spend his wages in a circumscribed circle of goods, some variation
was possible which enabled, for example, the English urban worker to buy
newspapers or to save something. By the same token, he was as a free agent also
able to waste it on schnapps. Unlike the serf or slave, the free wage laborer learned
to be his own master, taking the responsibility and bearing the consequences of his
consumption decisions. Marx was quick to recognize the enormous cultural leap
that this emancipation process represented, but also stressed that when independent
peasants or artisans underwent proletarianization, their lives were subjected to
capital's one-dimensional abstractification.[61] This new class of proletarians thus
enjoyed a long-term potential for self-liberation, but in the near term was
materially, psychologically, and culturally subordinated to a new structure of needs
that capital was imposing on societal life.

It is not, however, the mere fact that workers exercise some control over
discretionary spending within the sphere of individual consumption that prompted
Marx to conclude that capital could rely on them to reproduce at a level appropriate
for capital.[62] Marx must have also held the opinion that it was implausible that any
contemporaneous national proletariat would undergo, within a politically relevant
time period, a social-psychological upheaval so radical as to depress its childbearing habits or desires to such an unprecedently low threshold that it could
render inoperative the built-in mechanisms of capital accumulation to generate a
range of labor supplies adequate to the self-valorization of capital in general.

In 1847, Marx characterized the Malthusian advice that the working class
resolve not to have children as nonsensical because such a classwide decision was
an impossibility; moreover, he accepted as a social fact of capitalism that the
proletarian condition made the sex drive that class's principal pleasure. Because he
adhered to such a view, economic logic and political strategy dictated that Marx
reject any tactic that recommended to the working class a fertility pattern that
would have succeeded only in improving the living conditions of a small subset of
exceptionally self-disciplined proletarian families. Moreover, Marx suggested that
even if the class as a whole succeeded in restricting its growth below the standard

of the accumulation of capital, paradoxically the ensuing rise in wages "would only accelerate the application of machinery...and, hence, make the population redundant." In particular, Marx argued that the chapter on the effect of machinery on the condition of the working class that Ricardo had added to the third edition of his *Principles* refuted the Malthusian population theory and especially the vulgar economists' advice to workers "to keep their multiplication below the standard of accumulation of capital." For such "keeping down of the labouring population, diminishing the supply of labour, and, consequently, raising its price, would only *accelerate* the application of machinery...and, hence, make the population artifically 'redundant'...."[63]

Marx's characterization of the parallel growth of societal wealth, capital, and the proletariat on the one hand and the industrial reserve army on the other as the noncontradictory presence of overproduction of capital and relative overpopulation—the "absolute general law of capitalist accumulation"—must be analyzed in connection with his gloss that the law's realization was modified by manifold circumstances that he alluded to as inappropriate for discussion at the level of abstraction at which he had written the chapter on accumulation.[64] Perhaps the most significant of these modifications is the development of labor unions, which seek to "break or weaken the ruinous consequences of that natural law of capitalist production" for the working class by organizing cooperation between the employed and unemployed.[65]

Outside of Marx's magnum opus, neither he nor Engels devoted much attention to demographic questions. Some demographers argue, however, that late in life Marx acknowledged the power of Malthus's proposition even for socialism. This claim is based on Marx's statement in his comments on the Gotha Program that: "If this [Malthus's population theory] is correct, then I can not abolish the law [Lassalle's Iron Law of Wages], even if I abolish wage labor a hundred times, because the law then rules not only the system of wage labor, but every societal system."[66] But this claim overlooks the fact that Marx was not at all conceding the correctness of Malthus's theory of population. Rather, in the context of a polemic against what he viewed as the generally worthless programmatic principles of the newly united German workers' party, he was merely explaining to Lassalle's acolytes that their proposed "abolition of the wage system with the iron law of wages" was rhetorical nonsense since the abolition of wage labor of necessity entailed the abolition of its laws "whether they be iron or spongy."[67]

Marx was merely trying to make clear that acceptance of Lassalle's iron law of wages—which Marx contested sharply—entailed acceptance of Malthus's population theory on which it was based. Far from being resigned to the correctness of that theory, Marx stressed that it undermined the socialist movement because if Malthus were right, socialism could not abolish misery, which was allegedly grounded in nature. By the same token, it is undeniable that Marx, like many other socialists and scholars before and after him, was deeply suspicious of Malthus because he had, as the British economist Edwin Cannan observed, been "inspired...by the desire...to produce acquiescence, if not contentment, with the existing order of things."[68]

The potential problem that population might pose for an ideal socialist society was not, as a German Social Democratic revisionist later asserted, the misery associated with Malthusian overpopulation. Rather, it was the fact that, contrary to Engels' flippant and sibylline assertion that if communist society were ever forced to "regulate the production of people just as it has already regulated the production of things," it and only it would be able to do so "without difficulties," no society can plan and regulate the production of human beings as easily as that of steel. Even if there were societal consensus that members should and would strive for (say) replacement-rate fertility, it would be impossible to predict whether and when all members making good-faith efforts would succeed biologically or how many members were biologically incapable of reproducing. These inescapable uncertainties would necessarily introduce some disproportionalities in economic planning of consumption and accumulation funds especially with regard to age-specific types of investment goods such as education as well as possible over- or underproduction of certain products such as children's clothing.[69]

Contrary to the impression left by some scholars, Marx's position on Malthusianism was not opportunistic. Thus James Bonar, an economist who wrote an intellectual biography of Malthus immediately after Marx's death, asserted that: "Marx is seeking to demonstrate the hopelessness of the labourer's position; and he is too acute not to know that his demonstration would be seriously weakened if he admitted the truth of the Malthusian doctrine and the bare possibility of the adoption of prudential habits by the labourers." It was not the case that Marx believed that small proletarian families would eliminate capitalist poverty or the proletariat for that matter; nor was he of the opinion that the correctness of Malthus's population theory and the availability of contraceptive methods had to be withheld from the working class lest its class consciousness be jeopardized.[70] On the contrary: the whole thrust of Marx's theory of the industrial reserve army was that the process of capital accumulation was relatively immune to the problem of "natural" underpopulation because it had its own methods for creating surplus labor, which reinstated the proletarian condition regardless of the size of working-class families.

This implied charge of opportunism later became express when feminist scholars claimed that SPD leaders had rejected so-called birth-strike propaganda because they feared that smaller families might reconcile workers to existing society.[71] By the same token, in light of the intense barrage of ad hominem (but largely accurate) invective against Malthus strewn throughout *Das Kapital*,[72] it appears bizarre to charge that Marx was "reticent to launch an all-out attack on the law of population" because the population question was "touchy" among German socialists as a result of Lassalle's incorporation of Malthusianism into his iron law of wages.[73]

Arguably the most pertinent shards of a theory of population that Marx and Engels left for their followers were contained in Engels' correspondence with third persons. At the time Marx was writing *Das Kapital*, Engels commented to the German social economist and working class advocate, Friedrich Lange, that the rational kernel of Malthusianism consisted in the fact that "humanity could multiply more rapidly than modern bourgeois society can endure." For Marx and Engels, however, this finding constituted yet further proof that bourgeois society was a barrier to development, which had to fall. Not until science was applied to agriculture as it had been to industry, and production in such areas as southeastern Europe and western America nevertheless failed to increase faster than world population, would Engels be willing to reconsider Malthus's theory. Until then, he remained convinced that scarcity was a function of underproduction caused by "moneyless stomachs, the labor that cannot be employed *profitably*...."[74]

Of greater policy interest to socialist parties was a letter from Engels to Karl Kautsky, the future chief theoretician of the SPD, but who in 1881 was a neo-Malthusian and not yet a Marxist. Commenting on the latter's book on population, Engels dismissed the challenge posed by academic socialists as to how a socialist society would ward off overpopulation and collapse as a waste of time, particularly since the rise of American mass agricultural production threatened to suffocate Europe and would necessarily bring about an increase of population. To be sure, Engels conceded the "abstract possibility" that population growth might become so great that limits would have to be set on its further increase. A principal reason for Engels' lack of concern, however, was his belief that if France and Austria were able to achieve this result spontaneously (*naturwüchsig*), so, a fortiori, could a planned society. Here the socialist Engels appeared to come close to sharing the belief of many, especially British, neo-Malthusians, that population problems could be avoided individually by procreating couples who accommodated their reproduction to the economic realities facing them.[75]

Two years later, a few weeks before Marx's death, Engels returned to the subject. In another letter to Kautsky, he made light of the fact that within a few years Kautsky had shifted from being a "Neonato-Malthusian" to underpopulation-ism. Despite the fact that under the latter circumstance (Francis Place's) famous sponge or some other contraceptive procedure would not be in much demand, Engels noted that it could nevertheless remain

> very practical in bourgeois families, in order to keep the the number of children in proportion to income, in order not to ruin the woman's health through too many pregnancies, etc. The only thing is that I remain of the view that that is a private matter between husband and wife, and at most the family doctor...and that our proletarians also in the future as in the past will do honor to its name by numerous proles.[76]

These fragments of a theory, then, constituted the whole of the demo-graphic legacy that Marx and Engels left to the European proletariat for its use in analyzing and shaping public discourse and struggle over micro- and macrolevel population issues. The quasi-inexorability of Marx's capital-accumulation-oriented mechanisms of surplus labor production can create the impression that Marx himself believed in the existence of a demographic invisible hand. Although Marx's theory posits that capital in general can, over a broad range of possible historical-empirical circumstances, liberate itself from the limitations of biological population growth, the periodic overproduction of workers was functional for capital but only within a self-contradictory regime that progressed by means of disruptive and cleansing crises. By the same token, although the constant replenishment of an industrial reserve army was dysfunctional for the working class, Marx did not view proletarian procreational proclivities as causative because capital accumulation could wring surplus labor out of virtually any empirically relevant absolute level of population. Consequently, because Marx's narrowly conceived demographic theory was not geared toward formulating practical policy recommendations, it tended to leave Marxist parliamentary political parties without an independent purchase that might have enabled them to overcome the appearance of indifference to the here-and-now problems of working-class existence insofar as they were exacerbated by individual superfertile families' inability to secure subsistence incomes.

NOTES

1. Margaret Sanger, *An Autobiography* 275 (1938).

2. Donald Bogue, *Principles of Demography* 15, 17 (1968).

3. David Harvey, *The Limits to Capital* 163 (1989 [1982]); Gunnar Heinsohn, Rolf Knieper, & Otto Steiger, *Menschenproduktion: Allgemeine Bevölkerungstheorie der Neuzeit* 116-27 (1979).

4. Marc Linder, *Reification and the Consciousness of the Critics of Political Economy: Studies in the Development of Marx' Theory of Value* 52-53 (1975).

5. Jon Elster, *Making Sense of Marx* 61 n.3 (1985). For a sympathetic account and partial vindication of Marx's theory, see Charles Tilly, "Demographic Origins of the European Proletariat," in *Proletarianization and Family History* 1-85 (David Levine ed., 1984).

6. J. Platter, "Carl Marx und Malthus," *Jahrbücher für Nationalökonomie und Statistik* 29:321-41 at 331, 332-33 (1877); Peter Laslett, *The World We Have Lost* 48, 67 (1973 [1965]) ("moral law").

7. Heinrich Soetbeer, *Die Stellung der Sozialisten zur Malthus'schen Bevölkerungslehre* (1886); D.E.C. Eversley, *Social Theories of Fertility and the Malthusian Debate* 268 (1959).

8. Margaret Sanger, *The Pivot of Civilization* 148, 139 (1969 [1922]).

9. Rosalind Petchesky, *Abortion and Women's Choice: The State, Sexuality, and Reproductive Freedom* 40 (rev. ed. 1990 [1984]). Despite her thesis that "[f]ertility control is not...simply a private strategy of individuals or families to help them cope with economic...pressures [but] occurs within definite social contexts and sexual power relations," Petchesky herself lacks a theory as to why women want children. *Ibid.* at 25.

10. Ann Ferguson & Nancy Folbre, "The Unhappy Marriage of Patriarchy and Capitalism," in *Women and Revolution: A Discussion of the Unhappy Marriage of Marxism and Feminism* 313-38, at 317, 335 n.1 (Lydia Sargent ed., 1981). For an example of party-Marxist admission that these so-called invisible costs correspond to the opportunity costs

or wage income that mothers forgo and should be added to the visible costs, see Harry Maier, "Die Reduktion der komplizierten auf einfache Arbeit im Lichte der Marxschen Werttheorie," in *Probleme der politischen Ökonomie* 10: 147-207 at 197-98 n.128 (1967). See generally Ludmilla Müller, "Kinderaufzucht im Kapitalismus—wertlose Arbeit; über die Folgen der Nichtbewertung der Arbeit der Mütter für das Bewußtsein der Frauen als Lohnarbeiter," *Probleme des Klassenkampfs*, No. 22, at 13-65 (1976).

11. Harvey, *The Limits to Capital* at 164-65 (quote); Wally Seccombe, "Marxism and Demography," *New Left Rev.* No. 137 at 22-47 at 22 (Jan.-Feb. 1983) (quote).

12. Lewis Lipsitz, "Political Philosophy and Population Policy: Insights and Blindspots of a Tradition," in *Political Science in Population Studies* 129-39 at 131-32 (Richard Clinton et al. eds., 1972); Richard Lewinsohn, "Die Stellung der deutschen Sozialdemokratie zur Bevölkerungsfrage," *Schmollers Jahrbuch für Gesetzgebung, Verwaltung und Volkswirtschaft im Deutschen Reiche* 46:813, 816-25 (1922); Werner Sombart, *Der moderne Kapitalismus: Das Wirtschaftsleben im Zeitalter des Hochkapitalismus* 3/1:312-15 (1927). Some have even charged that Marx never read Malthus carefully or at all. Warren Thompson, *Population Problems* 40 (1953); Michelle Perot, "Malthusianism and Socialism," in *Malthus Past and Present* 257-74 at 261 (J. Dupâquier at al. eds., 1983).

13. Michael Teitelbaum & Jay Winter, *The Fear of Population Decline* (1985); Jay Winter, "Socialism, Social Democracy, and Population Questions in Western Europe: 1870-1950," in *Population Resources in Western Intellectual Traditions* 122-46 (Michael Teitelbaum & Jay Winter eds., 1989); William Petersen, *The Politics of Population* 84 (1964).

14. W. Stanley Jevons, *The Theory of Political Economy* 254 (1970 [1871]).

15. W.W. Rostow, *The Stages of Economic Growth: A Non-Communist Manifesto* 153, 154 (1960). For a competent exegesis of Marx's critique of Malthus, see Samuel Levin, "Marx vs. Malthus," *Papers of the Michigan Academy of Science, Arts, and Letters* 22:243-58 (1936).

16. Sanger, *The Pivot of Civilization* at 150; Herman Daly, "A Marxian-Malthusian View of Poverty and Development," *Population Studies* 25 (1):25-37 at 29-30 (Mar. 1971).

17. Paul Mombert, *Bevölkerungslehre* 420 (1929); Karl Marx, 1 *Das Kapital*, in Karl Marx [&] Friedrich Engels, *Werke* 23:657-70 (1962 [1867]). Although Erich Unshelm, *Geburtenbeschränkung und Sozialismus: Versuch einer Dogmengeschichte der sozialistischen Bevölkerungslehre* 10 (1924), correctly noted that Marx did not attempt a theory of population, he incorrectly reduced what Marx was attempting to a theory of unemployment.

18. Louis Uchitelle, "Corporate Spending Booms, But Jobs Stagnate," *N.Y. Times*, June 16, 1994, at C1, col. 3 (nat. ed.); Philip Hauser, "The Labor Force As a Field of Interest for the Sociologist," *Am. Sociological Rev.* 16: 530-38 (1951); S. Wolfbein & A. Jaffe, "Demographic Factors in Labor Force Growth," *Am. Sociological Rev.* 11: 392-96 (1946).

19. Marx, 1 *Kapital* at 660 (quote); Karl Marx, *Ökonomische Manuskripte 1857/58*, in Karl Marx [&] Friedrich Engels, *Gesamtausgabe (MEGA)* II/1.2:496-97 (1981) (quote). G.S.L. Tucker, "Ricardo and Marx," *Economica* 28 (No. 111):252-69 at 264-65 (Aug. 1961), asserts that Marx's revolutionary political objectives required him to devise the theory of the reserve army because otherwise exploitation would be compatible with supra-subsistence wages buoyed by increases in productivity translated into a higher standard of living. See also Mark Blaug, "The Empirical Content of Ricardian Economics," *J. Pol. Econ.* 64 (1):41-58 at 57 (Feb. 1956); *idem, Ricardian Economics: A Historical Study* 120-27 (1958).

20. Marx, *Ökonomische Manuskripte 1857/58* at 493-96. Marx's critique of Malthus was adumbrated in Friedrich Engels, "Umrisse zu einer Kritik der National-ökonomie," in Karl Marx [&] Friedrich Engels, *Werke* 2:499, 518-21 (1964 [1844]).

21. Karl Marx, "Arbeitslohn," in Karl Marx [&] Friedrich Engels, *Werke* 6:535-56 at 551, 553 (1959 [1847]).

22. Sombart, *Der moderne Kapitalismus* at 310. But see T.H. Marshall, "The Population Problem During the Industrial Revolution," *Econ. J.* (Econ. Hist. Ser. No. 4), Jan. 1929, at 429-56 at 435: "Nature does not, as a rule, imitate the ballet dancer, who springs accurately through the air and lands in perfect equilibrium. She is more likely, under the influence of a severe shock, to oscillate like a drunkard steering for a lamp-post."

23. Thomas Robert Malthus, *Principles of Political Economy*, in *The Works of Thomas Robert Malthus* 5:246 (E.A. Wrigley & David Souden ed., 1986 [1820]); Angus Maddison, *Phases of Capitalist Development* 8 (1982). Malthus was scarcely blind to the wage-depressing capacity of a machine-created reserve army of the unemployed. In his testimony before the Select Committee on Emigration from the United Kingdom of the House of Commons in 1827, Malthus agreed with his questioner that in the English manufacturing districts whose population was in "the greatest redundance," capitalists could prevent any detriment in the form of higher wages resulting from the emigration of some workers by introducing machinery: "[M]achinery may sometimes increase with such rapidity as to deteriorate the condition of the labourers for a certain time, as it appears to do at present." When asked whether "the tendency of a redundant supply of labour ready at all times to fill up the decrease of the labouring population by want and disease, [is] beneficial to the manufacturing and commercial interest, inasmuch as it lowers wages and raises profits," Malthus lamely responded that he could not imagine people who "could possibly bring themselves to encourage such a system...." *Third Report from the Select Committee on Emigration from the United Kingdom: 1827*, at 316-17 (1827).

24. E.A. Wrigley & R.S. Schofield, *The Population History of England 1541-1871: A Reconstruction* 404, 412 (1981). This realistic historically oriented demography should be compared with Hayek's, which concedes that an increase in population may lead to a decline in average incomes, but insists that this outcome results simply from the fact that the incremental population is poorer: "The proletariat are an additional population that, without new opportunities of employment, would never have grown up." F. Hayek, *The Fatal Conceit: The Errors of Socialism* 123 (1991 [1988]).

25. Heinsohn, Knieper, & Steiger, *Menschenproduktion* at 119; Marx, *Das Kapital* 1:730-32 (quote).

26. Karl Marx, 3 *Das Kapital*, in Karl Marx [&] Friedrich Engels, *Werke* 25:641-42 (1964 [1894]). For contemporaneous acceptance of the argument that a decrease in labor supply would merely trigger further mechanization and recreation of relative over-population, see H. M. Hyndman, *The Historical Basis of Socialism in England* 254 (1883).

27. Gunnar Myrdal, *Population: A Problem for Democracy* 138 (1940). In structure, this anti-wage-fund argument is reminiscent of the refutation that a British socialist offered of a similar ecological fallacy to the effect that poverty would disappear if the poor were all "industrious, sober, and thrifty": "It is quite true that a sober man will succeed better than a drunken man; but it is not true that if all the people were sober their wages would increase." Robert Blatchford, *Merrie England* 162 (1895).

28. Marx, *Kapital* 1:185-86.

29. David Ricardo, *On the Principles of Political Economy and Taxation*, in *The Works and Correspondence of David Ricardo* 1:93, 96-97, 94 (Piero Sraffa ed., 1975 [1817]). Ricardo and Malthus engaged in what may merely have been a terminological

dispute over wage determination. Malthus argued that what Ricardo termed the "natural price of labour" was "really...a most unnatural price [which] could not generally occur for hundreds of years." It was, consequently, erroneous to regard the market price as only a temporary deviation from the natural price. Malthus's point, apparently, was that Ricardo's assumption of zero population growth among the working class was improbable; to the extent that the rate of growth was instead either positive or negative, the market price would usually deviate from the natural price. Malthus's alternative definition of the natural or necessary price of labor was "'that price which, in the actual circumstances of the society, is necessary to occasion an average supply of labourers, sufficient to meet the average demand.'" T.R. Malthus, *Principles of Political Economy* 247 (1820), *reprinted in The Works and Correspondence of David Ricardo* 2:227-28 (Piero Sraffa ed., 1966 [1820]). In his notes on Malthus's book, Ricardo remarked that "natural price" meant that "necessary to supply constantly a given demand" just as the natural price of corn was that "at which it can be supplied affording the usual profits." Only if maintaining the usual rate of profit performs the same function for pricing other commodities as perpetuating the race of laborers does for labor (power), would Ricardo's concession that Malthus's definition "will do nearly as well for my purpose" mean that the new terminology did not implicate a change in meaning. David Ricardo, *Notes on Malthus's Principles of Political Economy*, in *Works and Correspondence of David Ricardo* 2:227-28.

30. Jean-Baptiste Say, *Traité d'économie politique* 2:278-79 (5th ed. 1826 [1803]).

31. Thomas Robert Malthus, *An Essay on the Principle of Population* (1st ed.), in *idem, On Population* 109-10 (Gertrude Himmelfarb ed., 1960 [1798]).

32. Marx, *Kapital* 1:666-67.

33. *Ibid.* at 661-62.

34. *Ibid.* at 664, 663, 673. See also Francesco Nitti, *Population and the Social System* 45 (1894): "it is not presumable that the capitalist class should always induce the development of a systematic over-population...; the loss which capital experiences when one part of the population becomes excessive, is much graver than the advantage which Marx presumes to be derived from it."

35. Karl Marx, *Zur Kritik der politischen Ökonomie (Manuskript 1861-1863)*, in Karl Marx [&] Friedrich Engels, *Gesamtausgabe (MEGA)*, II/3.1:162 (1976).

36. Marx, *Kapital* 1:658, 664-66.

37. *Employment and Earnings* 43 (3):tab. A-35 at 50 (Mar. 1996); Louis Uchitelle, "Moonlighting Plus: 3-Job Families on the Rise," *N.Y. Times*, Aug. 16, 1994, at A1, col. 1 (nat. ed.); John Stinson, Jr., "Multiple Jobholding Up Sharply in the 1980's," *Monthly Labor Rev.* 113 (7):3-10 (July 1990); ch. 2 above.

38. Marx, *Kapital* 1:668-69.

39. Petersen has repeated these claims for several decades. William Petersen, "Marx versus Malthus: The Men and the Symbols," *Population Rev.* 1 (2):21-32 (July 1957); *idem, Politics of Population* 82-83; *idem, Malthus* 76-77 (1979).

40. Mombert, *Bevölkerungstheorie* at 226, 422-23.

41. Paul Sweezy, *The Theory of Capitalist Development: Principles of Marxian Political Economy* 89 (1968 [1942]); Bob Rowthorn, *Capitalism, Conflict and Inflation: Essays in Political Economy* 204-205 (1980).

42. Marx, *Kapital* 1:730 (quote); Marx, *Kapital* 3:253; Henryk Grossmann, *Das Akkumulations-und Zusammenbruchssystem des kapitalistischen Systems (Zugleich eine Krisentheorie)* 373-88 (1929); Paul Mattick, *Arbeitslosigkeit und Arbeitslosenbewegung in den USA 1929-1935*, at 34-41 (1969 [1936]).

43. Samuel Hollander, "Marx and Malthusianism: Marx's Secular Path of Wages," *Am. Econ. Rev.* 74 (1):139-51 at 150 (Mar. 1984).

44. Allin Cottrell & William Darity, Jr., "Marx, Malthus, and Wages," *Hist. Pol. Econ.* 20 (2):173-90 at 184-85 (Summer 1988).

45. Karl Marx, *Zur Kritik der politischen Ökonomie (Manuskript 1861-1863)*, in Karl Marx [&] Friedrich Engels, *Gesamtausgabe (MEGA)*, II/3.3:1101-1102 (1978).

46. *Ibid.* at II/3.4:1440 (1979).

47. Marx, *Kapital* 1:674; Marx, "Arbeitslohn" at 547, 552 (quote).

48. Karl Marx, "The Labor Question," in Karl Marx [&] Frederick Engels, *Collected Works*, 12:460-63 at 460, 462 (1979 [1853]) (quote); "Golden Opportunities and the Use Made of Them," *Economist* 11 (532):1238-39 (Nov. 5, 1853).

49. Heinsohn, Knieper, & Steiger, *Menschenproduktion* at 119; Wally Seccombe, "Domestic Labour and the Working-Class Household," in *Hidden in the Household: Women's Domestic Labour Under Capitalism* 25-99 at 90 n.11 (Bonnie Fox ed., 1980); Karl Marx, "The State of British Manufacturing Industry," in Karl Marx [&] Friederich Engels, *Gesamtausgabe (MEGA)* I/18:454-60 at 455-56 (1984 [1860]).

50. Wally Seccombe, *Weathering the Storm: Working-Class Families from the Industrial Revolution to the Fertility Decline* 17, 74 (1993).

51. Marx, *Kapital* 1:670.

52. *Ibid.* at 671.

53. Marx, "Arbeitslohn" at 552; Karl Marx, "The State of British Manufactures," in Karl Marx & Frederick Engels, *Collected Works* 16:206 (1980 [1859]). In this sense it is incorrect that "[n]o wife and mother...could...be described as a self-interested 'producer of labour power'...." Diemut Bubeck, *Care, Gender, and Justice* 59 (1995).

54. Carl Roesler, *Zur Kritik der Lehre vom Arbeitslohn: Ein volkswirthschaftlicher Versuch* 245 (1861) (quote); Louise Tilly & Joan Scott, *Women, Work, and Family* 82, 107, 113, 133-34 (1989 [1978]) (39 percent of girls aged 10 to 14 worked in Roubaix, France, in 1872).

55. Karl Marx, *Value, Price and Profit*, in Karl Marx [&] Friedrich Engels, *Gesamtausgabe (MEGA)* I/20:143-86 at 168 (1992 [1865]); Michael Lebowitz, *Beyond Capital: Marx's Political Economy of the Working Class* 90 (1992).

56. Karl Marx, *Zur Kritik der politischen Ökonomie (Manuskript 1861-1863)*, in Marx [&] Engels, *Gesamtausgabe (MEGA)*, II/3.1:275-76 (1976).

57. *Ibid.* at 276.

58. Anneliese Bergmann, "Geburtenrückgang—Gebärstreik: Zur Gebärstreik-debatte 1913 in Berlin," *Archiv für die Geschichte des Widerstandes und der Arbeit* 4:7-55 at 14 (1981); Marx, Kapital 3:228; Karl Marx, *Ökonomische Manuskripte 1863-1867*, in Karl Marx [&] Friedrich Engels, *Gesamtausgabe (MEGA)* II/4:293 (1992) (the quoted sentence is partially in English in the manuscript).

59. Marx, *Kapital* 1:591, 596-97.

60. *Ibid.* at 597-99.

61. Karl Marx, *Resultate des unmittelbaren Produktionsprozesses* 59 (1969 [1863-1865]).

62. For an example of this short-circuited logic, see James Dickinson & Bob Russell, "Introduction: The Structure of Reproduction in Capitalist Society," in *Family, Economy and State: The Social Reproduction Process Under Capitalism* 1-20 at 8 (James Dickinson & Bob Russell eds., 1986).

63. Marx, "Arbeitslohn" at 552; Karl Marx, *Zur Kritik der politischen Ökonomie (Manuskript 1861-1863)* at 1193 (quote).

64. Marx, *Kapital* 3:266; Marx, *Kapital* 1:673-74. Marx did not argue that the overproduced means of production were excessive in relation to the task of employing the able-bodied population, but merely qua means of exploitation designed to yield a certain rate of profit; in fact, capitalism failed to produce enough means of production for the entire able-bodied population to work under the most productive circumstances, which would permit a shortening of the workday. *Kapital* 3:268.

65. Marx, *Kapital* 1:669.

66. Daly, "A Marxian-Malthusian View of Poverty and Development" at 27; Nathan Keyfitz, *Population Change and Social Policy* 18 (1982); William Petersen, "Malthus: The Reactionary Reformer," *Am. Scholar* 59 (2):275-82 at 279 (Spr. 1990); Karl Marx, "Randglossen zum Programm der deutschen Arbeiterpartei," in Karl Marx [&] Friedrich Engels, *Werke* 19:25 (1962 [1875]).

67. Letter from Marx to Wilhelm Bracke, May 5, 1875, in Marx [&] Engels, *Werke* 19:13, 14; Marx, "Randglossen" at 25 (quote).

68. Marx, "Randglossen" at 25; Edwin Cannan, *A History of the Theories of Production and Distribution in English Political Economy from 1776 to 1848*, at 384 (2d ed. 1903). According to Franz Mehring, *Geschichte der deutschen Sozialdemokratie* 45-46 (1960 [1897-98]), Marx exaggerated Lassalle's reliance on Malthus.

69. Albert Südekum, "Über das Malthus'sche Gesetz und das Bevölkerungsproblem der kommunistischen Gesellschaft" 30 (Ph.D. diss., Christian-Albrechts University Kiel, 1894); Letter from Friedrich Engels to Karl Kautsky, Feb. 1, 1881, in Karl Marx [&] Friedrich Engels, *Werke* 35:150-51 (1967) (quote); Günter Manz, "Lebensstandard und Wirtschaftswachstum," in *Zu Grundfragen der sozialistischen Wachstumstheorie* 254-69 (Harry Maier et al. eds., 1968).

70. James Bonar, *Malthus and His Work* 391 (1885); Perot, "Malthusianism" at 262, claims that Marx stated that "[t]o advocate birth control is...a dangerous illusion."

71. See, e.g., Jean Quataert, "Unequal Partners in an Uneasy Alliance: Women and the Working Class in Imperial Germany," in *Socialist Women: European Socialist Feminism in the Nineteenth and Early Twentieth Centuries* 112, 127 (Marilyn Boxer & Jean Quataert eds., 1978). On the birth-strike debate, see below ch. 7.

72. Marx stated that the first edition of Malthus's *Essay* was "nothing but a schoolboy-like superficial and priest-like declaimed plagiarism from Defoe, Sir James Steuart, Townsend, Franklin, Wallace etc. and contains not a single self-thought sentence." Marx, *Kapital* 1:644 n.75. For non-Marxist confirmation of Malthus's lack of originality, see Kenneth Smith, *The Malthusian Controversy* 3-33 (1951).

73. Michael Perelman, *Marx's Crises Theory: Scarcity, Labor and Finance* 28-29 (1987).

74. Letter of Friedrich Engels to Friedrich Lange, Mar. 29, 1865, in Karl Marx [&] Friedrich Engels, *Werke* 31:465-68 at 466-67 (1965).

75. Letter from Engels to Kautsky, Feb. 1, 1881, in Marx [&] Engels, *Werke* 35:150-51; Richard Soloway, *Birth Control and the Population Question in England, 1877-1930*, at 83 (1982). Karl Pearson, a British eugenicist socialist, expected that "[u]nder Socialism alone will it be possible to reap the advantages of any limit of population, because one class will not be interested in the over-production of another." Karl Pearson, "The Moral Basis of Socialism," in *idem, The Ethic of Freethought* 301-29 at 322, 323 (2d ed. 1901 [1887]).

76. Letter from Engels to Kautsky, Feb. 10, 1883, in Marx [&] Engels *Werke* 35:431-32.

7

The Birth-Strike Debate:
Can Lysistrata Conquer Capital?

Every unborn proletarian child is...to be compared to a worker, who does and can strike throughout his whole life without enduring the suffering and afflictions of such a way of acting.[1]

But the proletariat has learned a still more dangerous piece of wisdom than emigrating—not being born![2]

The European socialist movement in the late nineteenth century not only had no comprehensive theory of population, but, beyond Marx's capital-accumulation-centered analysis of surplus population, lacked even coherent fragments from Marx or Engels to guide its public policy choices in countries in which it participated in legislative bodies. In the absence of theoretical direction, however, socialists were reduced to jabs at the remnants of Malthusianism in the economics of "timid governmental and clerical hemorrhoidists," and to dry assurances that the abolition of mass poverty through the elimination of the underlying antagonistic capital-labor relationship was the only effective remedy for modern overpopulation.[3] At the same time, some revisionist members of the SPD adhered to Malthus's doctrine. Given the intimate linkage between population and copulation, the SPD's ambiguous and ambivalent relation to Imperial Germany's official cramped view of sex made it impossible for the party to develop its own unique position with regard to population matters.[4]

Socialist sexual political and intraproletarian controversy over the micro- and macrosocietal consequences of child-rich families reached it high point in the so-called birth-strike debate on the eve of World War I. This German debate focused on the question of whether the working class could improve its condition and simultaneously hasten the demise of capitalism by creating small families and, correlatively, limiting the size of the next generation of labor market competitors. Some advocated smaller families regardless of the macroeconomic impact in order to relieve the poverty associated with large families for all members and the crushing physical and pyschological burdens borne by mothers, thus enabling them to participate more fully in societal movements. Others envisioned such a radical drying up of recruits for the reserve army of the unemployed and of the real army of soldiers that capital's coercive economic and military power would be significantly curbed. Centrist SPD birth-strike opponents did not so much contest the legitimacy of birth control as challenge the notion that families' private ameliorist plans could ever add up to a revolutionary working-class strategy—in part because party leaders supported demographic growth for the socialist society of the future and in part because orthodox Marxists believed that a smaller supply of labor could not overcome the accommodating forces of capital accumulation to generate a higher overall wage level.

Early twentieth-century conflicts over agitation within the working class to limit its reproduction in Germany, as elsewhere in Europe, must be understood against the background of the ruling classes' fears of the impact of declining fertility on the military and industrial reserve armies and their efforts to suppress various means of contraception. Their representatives expressed these concerns repeatedly in the Reichstag in 1913. Baron Knigge, for example, stated that births, which had declined in almost all capitalist countries since the mid-1870s, had declined from 40.1 per 1,000 inhabitants in 1870 to 31.9 in 1909 in Germany. Nevertheless, Germany's population had advanced so far beyond France's during that period that Count von Kanitz added that the population problem had attained such proportions in France that Germany's rival was having difficulty maintaining the size of its army.[5]

The conflict over the adequacy of German population growth, the causes of diminished fertility, and the measures proposed to increase the birth rate were sharpened by the publication in 1912 of a semi-official polemic by Dr. Jean Bornträger, a government and medical councillor in Düsseldorf. Following its publication in an official series, the Prussian Minister of the Interior authorized its republication the next year in book form. After presenting a number of demographic indicators of the declining birth rate and raising the specter that Germans would be unable to assert themselves "in the concert of peoples" and especially against Russia, whose growth was unencumbered by organized opposition, Bornträger launched into an attack against the SPD for its association with and promotion of fertility limitation. Two-fifths of the book were devoted to methods designed to combat birth control, and five pages to measures "to stem the emancipation of women." Although he could accept women as doctors, nurses, messengers, salespeople, and in certain other occupations, Bornträger found female clergy, police, lawyers, and chimney sweep masters a caricature: "As the men can never even come close to reaching the women e.g. in patient care, so too the women the men in all male occupations. The difference must remain." Among the repressive measures he proposed were the prohibition as pornography of popular publications recommending or even discussing birth control and the prevention of public lectures and meetings on the same subject by neo-Malthusian organizations, feminists, the society against the alleged overpopulation of Germany, and others. He was willing to exempt "strictly scientific, not popular papers and treatises in technical journals," but would have withheld discretion from the daily press to print excerpts from such articles.[6]

Without any supporting evidence, Bornträger charged that it was easier to assert than to prove that the working class suffered under the financial burdens of supporting large families, for although it might seem at first sight that people with little income might be in a better position to raise one or two than five or six children, the older children in fact soon helped take care of the younger ones and to earn money for the parents; they were, after all, "walking nest eggs." Moreover, if small working-class families succeeded in sending their children to universities, they would create a danger that occupations requiring such an education would become overfilled with "inferior elements." In spite of his proclivity for flight into folk adages instead of empirically tested reasoning, Bornträger did recognize that economic assistance for financially limited families was one of the main tasks in the struggle against birth control—especially because it was the focal point where economists, hygienists, Social Democrats, and neo-Malthusians converged. He therefore proposed a wide-ranging catalog of aids for (low-income) large families including tax exemptions, housing subsidies, exemptions from military and jury service, educational subsidies, preferential poor-relief and hiring in state employment, reduced railway fares, children's premiums, and food subsidies; at the same time, bachelors would receive an incentive to marry and to procreate by means of special taxes and increased military and jury obligations.[7]

Given its extraordinary personal character, obvious "hysterical" party-political prejudices, and lack of scientific-medical learning, Bornträger's book became easy prey for the SPD. Procapitalist economists struck themes similar to Bornträger's. Julius Wolf, for example, noting the negative correlation between birth rates and the share of SPD votes in the 1907 parliamentary elections, pointed to a common cause: "The representative of a Weltanschauung that is atheistic and/or founded on egoistic motivations and emancipated in every direction will not and cannot give life to a large family...." Wolf also stressed that the fact that Germany's fertility had far exceeded that of France and Britain during the previous several decades, had exerted a great impact on world politics, prompting France to seek an alliance with Russia, and had channeled so many millions of workers into German industry that it had recourse to industrial and colonial expansion in competition with Britain.[8]

Of greater political brisance were the German antisocialist parliamentarians' charges that the SPD was consciously propagating fertility limitation as a tool in the class struggle. Knigge pointed to the high positive correlation between low birth rates and high proportions of SPD votes in Berlin and elsewhere. Several months after the birth-strike debates, the Reichstag returned to the subject in connection with its deliberations on a bill to amend the Industrial Code to prohibit pedlars from selling contraceptives; the bill was motivated by stories of pedlars who had obtained from the civil marriage registry newlyweds' addresses, to which they proceeded directly with their wares. Count von Carmer, a conservative representative, accused the SPD of propagating the restraints on fertility that were undermining Germany's military strength.[9]

The Social Democratic Reichstag members tried to parry these allegations largely by means of sarcastic countercharges. Among these were the fact that aristocrats had smaller families than proletarians and the claim that one of the reasons the propertied classes limited their families was the (mothers') fear of ruining their figures.[10] While arguing that capitalists opposed birth control because they saw the threat that in the future "the working hands will furnish a more valuable object," the SPD also expressed its own regret concerning the decline in population growth because in the future social-democratic society an increase in the labor force would bring in its wake a smaller quantum of labor per capita. Later the party attacked the proposed legislative suppression of contraceptives as "state birth compulsion."[11]

The SPD leadership saw both left-wing birth-strikers and right-wing birth-compellers as methodological individualists who, in their zeal to generalize from individual motives for reduced fertility, overlooked the societal causes that guided the will of many individuals.[12] Thus the party was hardly blind to the specific ways in which capitalism shaped poverty for proletarian parents or to the latter's efforts to ward off the worst consequences; the leadership merely sought to combat illusions that intentionally diminished fertility constituted a revolutionary act or strategy. Although the SPD stood between the bourgeois neo-Malthusians on the one side and the representatives of the state and capital on the other, which demanded more military and industrial recruits, the party was unable to adopt a fully independent position because it too regretted the decline in fertility as an unfavorable trend for the future socialist society. The party was also caught between its traditional principled macrosocietal anti-Malthusianism and the fact that a large and increasing proportion of its membership "privately acted Malthusianly."[13]

The concept of the "general birth strike" was introduced in Germany in the first decade of the twentieth century by a Social Democratic doctor in Zurich, Fritz Brupbacher. Without propagating it or even proposing family limitation as a party program, and recognizing that such conduct was "not a means of doing away with capitalist society," he supported proletarian women's efforts to limit their procreativity for "private-economic reasons" and to foster the development of the personality of the living generations. Such motivations were especially relevant for the working-class woman, whose total preoccupation with pregnancies and how to avoid them had made her "a walking uterus, who thinks with the uterus. Without interest in her class interest...she...becomes...unreceptive...for everything that does not relate to her uterus."[14]

At the time of the birth-strike campaign in Germany, neo-Malthusian Social Democrats adapted a quasi-bourgeoisification approach to explain the trend toward smaller families in large cities:

> During his bachelor period, the worker becomes accustomed to

attending the theater, concerts, and other public events, which he does not want completely to forgo in marriage. That of course is possible only if he limits the number of children.... A worker who takes part in cultural goods easily decides to tolerate a reduction of pleasurable sensations in marital intercourse through the use of preventive means rather than to destroy his higher standard of living through too large a number of children.[15]

The leading theoretician of Social-Democratic revisionism, Eduard Bernstein, expressed this same thought jocularly when he observed that: "Having many children doesn't go with modern furniture." The explosion of the wage-fund doctrine—which saw wage rates as determined by the labor supply since the amount of capital earmarked for wages was fixed at any given time—undermined in Bernstein's view whatever macroeconomic logic had ever inhered in Malthusianism. Family limitation might aid individual households economically, but monster meetings were not needed to enlighten workers as to these private benefits. The decline of large working-class families, was, instead, in large part a result of the labor movement's agitation to extend the scope of compulsory education and to prohibit child labor. Moreover, the movement, anticipating the culture-of-poverty thesis (and taking up Engels' view), educated the worker "not to seek the enjoyments of life in grossly sensual intoxication"; instead, it "induces him to think beyond the day, prevails upon him to have the best possible care bestowed upon his children," and consequently to limit family size. Since a universal tendency toward intentional reduction of fertility set in at a certain cultural stage, Bernstein concluded that it could not represent a "socialist *solution of the social question*."[16]

That supporters and opponents of the birth strike split along many intersecting and overlapping axes was illustrated most prominently by Ludwig Quessel. A revisionist SPD member of the Reichstag and Malthusian, Quessel nevertheless rejected the neo-Malthusian birth strike on racial grounds: if the German proletariat declined appreciably, a massive influx from the "Slavic East" would fill the gap, bringing about a lower standard of living and dooming the nation to decline and fall. Only from the standpoint of some "misunderstood internationality" would it be "a matter of indifference whether German or Slavic workers supply German capital with the next generation of proletarians." And even if it were possible to close the German borders to "the importation of the Slavic human commodity," Quessel would still have rejected the birth strike because it would so dangerously reduce the military fitness of the German people that it would threaten the latter's national existence. Although he was constrained to concede to Eduard Bernstein that the racial differences among nations belonging to "the white cultural circle" were theoretically not great enough to preclude the cultural assimilation of Slavs, the clinching argument for Quessel was that it remained "incomprehensible how a person who does not know the language of Kant and Goethe can be drawn into the culture of the German people."[17]

Kautsky, German Social Democracy's leading centrist theoretician, offered a somewhat different perspective on the birth-strike controversy. Until the recent decline in fertility, proletarian wives, "the most patient pack animals," had never had the leisure to think through their excessively burdensome procreational role—unlike the "ladies" of the propertied class, who limited their conceptions because it was impossible to delegate the travails of pregnancy and birth to their "service slaves." Since small families had become synonymous with affluence and large families with poverty, some economists had come to regard the recent decline in fertility as a sign of mass prosperity. For Kautsky, however, this development merely meant that poverty had, in the wake of the increasing incorporation of married women into the wage-labor force and their increasing independence, begun to change phenomenologically. In combination with advances in medical science and the proliferation of safer forms of birth control, the new objective position and consciousness of women made the decline in fertility inevitable. Where the advocates of a birth strike erred, according to Kautsky, was in believing that the "private matter" of how individual proletarian women acquiesced in this inevitable turn had anything to do with "politics and party," let alone qualified as a weapon of class struggle. The birth-strikers had committed the ecological fallacy of assuming that the beneficial effects on the microlevel would replicate themselves in society at large; but if the individual proletarian's correct conclusion that he could fight more easily without a family were adopted by the working class as a whole, the class would be doomed to extinction. Finally, Kautsky cautioned that any untoward effect that fertility limitation might exert on the size of the military or industrial reserve army would take place so far in the future that it would become meaningless as a political weapon.[18]

Several weeks before the birth-strike meeting, the SPD press began a campaign attacking the movement. In the party's chief women's periodical, *Die Gleichheit*, Mathilde Wurm published a very hard-line piece. Although low fertility among the wealthy had never been of concern to the ruling classes, she argued, a decline in the potential supply of soldiers, workers, and strikebreakers caused them alarm. Whether a smaller number of pregnancies reduced the exhaustion of the individual woman and mother was of importance for the public only if it also improved the socioeconomic condition of women and the working class in general. The proliferation of the two-child system in France unaccompanied by improvement, however, undermined any such conclusion. Thus even if the individual couple could feed and raise two children better than six, both the parents and the children remained "subject to the very same capitalist regime of exploitation." Claiming that the working class had never achieved any successes through abstention, Wurm reminded her readers that limiting the number of their children would mean a significant renunciation of "present joys and future hopes." Finally, Wurm rejected as "bourgeois" any notion that the road to proletarian progress ran through material improvement for individual families or that women could secure equality by producing smaller families rather than more energetic struggle.[19]

Two weeks later, *Gleichheit* published a similarly dogmatic piece by Heinrich Vogel, who traced the movement for smaller families to the recent inflation and the German Reich's antipopular (*volksfeindlich*), proagrarian and large-capitalist economic policies of increasing tariffs and indirect taxes on mass consumption commodities. Vogel also focused on another cause of the decline in births—capitalistic exploitation of women, especially those employed sewing clothes on pedal-driven machines, which subjected the female organism to dangers and damage that reduced their ability to give birth to healthy children. His position culminated in the aggressive slogan that: "The working people should not allow the whip of exploiting capitalism to dictate to them how many progeny they may have. If today they must maintain countless loafers in luxury and debauchery, then they can also demand for themselves and their flesh and blood a decent existence."[20]

The party's main newspaper, *Vorwärts*, published a two-part article attacking the birth strike as calculated to mislead workers as to how to bring about socialism. The article sought to refute the efficacy of the birth strike empirically by asserting that in countries, such as France, where proletarian fertility had declined significantly, the condition of the working class had not improved. On the programmatic level, the article chided advocates for confusing a sign of capitalist degeneration with a weapon of class struggle.[21]

The high point of the German birth-strike controversy was the two debates that took place on two successive Friday evenings, August 22 and 29, 1913, in Berlin under the auspices of the Union of Social-Democratic Election Associations of Greater Berlin and chaired by the leader of the Berlin party organization, Eugen Ernst.[22] The party convened the meeting ostensibly to deal with the movement headed by two Berlin family physicians and Social Democrats, Alfred Bernstein and Julius Moses, who were reacting to the consequences of large numbers of births for working-class women whom they had treated in their practices.[23] As another Social Democratic physician speculated, it was understandable that doctors, who are professionally concerned with individual patients, would project this perspective onto social policy and adopt a neo-Malthusian "symptomatic doctoring about...."[24] The SPD advertised extensively what it with manifest bias called a large public meeting in which Comrade Clara Zetkin would speak on the subject, "Against the Birth Strike." The party announced that women were especially invited and in fact a large majority of those attending were women—the first time in the history of the German labor movement that the SPD was confronted with a large mass crowd of women. The crowds were so large at the large New World hall in Hasenheide, that even after all the tables were removed, every seat was taken and the police had to close off the overfilled arena. The meetings were widely reported on in the bourgeois press.[25]

Zetkin, a leftist and the party's leading spokesperson on women's issues, unleashed a wave of invective against the birth strike, calling it both "bourgeois quackery" and "bourgeois-anarchistic" in its individualist orientation, and nothing but a "very reactionary utopia." Against the macroeconomic extrapolations of the birth-strikers, who claimed that a smaller supply of labor would bring about an increase in the wage level, Zetkin brought to bear Marx's theory of capital accumulation and its quasiautomatic accommodation of capital's need for surplus-value producers.[26]

For Zetkin there was no doubt that the main cause of misery was "capitalist exploitation" and not the number of children. The fact that the proletarian woman was overburdened by the number of children was not caused by the number of children per se, but by the circumstance that "capitalism does not give her enough of that which (including house servants) the loafing women of the bourgeoisie had prodigally." She also lamely denied that caring for a large number of children necessarily interfered with working women's participation in the labor movement; individual character, mental alertness, and health also played a role, although she conceded that a woman's participation would increase if her husband abandoned the philistine habit of having her wait hand and foot on him. These claims were continuous with the uncharitable view that Zetkin had nourished for more than a decade that neo-Malthusianism was merely an expedient for egotists, in particular among the SPD's educated members, who wanted to enjoy the comforts of life. Zetkin also came close to imputing a culture-of-poverty mentality to the proletariat in general. She noted that the "more intelligent strata" had fewer children and a lesser incidence of alcoholism than "the mentally backward" strata because schnapps and sexual intercourse were all that bourgeois society had left to the workers. Her conclusion, however, was not that preventive measures were called for, but that it was necessary "to lead workers to a higher mental stage. If greater demands are made of the brain, then the lower drives will be repressed."[27]

In response to Zetkin's keynote speech, Dr. Moses criticized the party leadership for failing to title the evening's discussion, "For or Against the Birth Strike?" He credited himself with the spiritual authorship of the protest meeting, although for a decade the audience had been practicing the birth strike, which he denied having tried to elevate to the status of "the revolutionary weapon"; rather, it was merely one of the possible remedies for the proletariat's physical recovery.[28]

Luise Zietz, one-time radical and now centrist member of the party directorate with responsibility for political agitation among women, after expressing her distress that Malthus could still find resonance among Social Democrats, also criticized Zetkin's refusal to tolerate propagation of birth control, which was not *the*, but *a* means to increase women's participation. Zietz also pointed to one factor that deterred women from controlling their fertility, at least to the extent that they had moved beyond fatalism—that in certain areas in which homework flourished children began work by the age of three. By the same token, Zietz rejected the notion that individually justifiable fertility limitation was a Social Democratic weapon.[29]

Perhaps the debate's most pungent remarks came from Rosa Luxemburg, the left-wing's most prominent theoretician and, together with Rudolf Hilferding, the party's most important political economist. Contrary to the claims of the parliamentary antisocialists, "Frau Rosa Lübeck alias Luxemburg" strenuously criticized the birth strike.[30] Unconcerned with women's issues as separate from class struggle, Luxemburg, obviously disgusted even by the need for a debate, found it a humiliating sign of the backwardness of Social Democratic enlightenment in Berlin that a slogan such as the birth strike could find such resonance: "That slogan appeals to the superficiality, stupidity, and mental indolence among the masses" which diverted attention from the struggle for economic and political liberation: "With humiliation one has to ask where then the great masses, who are there today, were when it was a matter of protesting against militarism." Luxemburg also reminded her audience shortly before midnight that socialists "fight for the living and not for those who are not born thanks to the advice of Dr. Moses."[31]

When the debate resumed the next week, Dr. Bernstein announced that the decline in births was sapping capitalism's vital strength: "If we do not recruit the objects of exploitation, if we do not increase the army, then capitalism is at an end." Wurm, recapitulating her article in *Die Gleichheit*, urged that the whole matter be confined to its proper place—the physician's office and the married couple's bedroom. Zetkin agreed, including birth control along with love, religion, and literary taste as private questions.[32]

The chairman was compelled to withdraw the resolution before the house because it had failed to obtain a binding vote; he therefore suggested that the question be resumed in the election associations. One such discussion took place the next month in Berlin at which Zietz was the main speaker. She emphasized that fertility limitation, which retarded economic development and thus the advent of socialism as well, instead of undermining capitalism and militarism, thwarted socialist efforts to raise and educate "in our sense" the next generation of fighters. The main speaker for the birth-strikers, Dr. Bernstein, argued that the small families that fertility limitation made possible enabled Social Democrats to produce "better and more noble" people. Dr. Moses denied ever having viewed birth control as a solution of the social question; rather it was a means of diminishing a source of need, misery, and indifferentism among working-class women. Confirming every suspicion ever raised that the movement was Malthus-inspired, Moses virtually quoted Malthus and Mill: "There is nothing more ethical than preaching to the workers: Do not place any more children into the world than you believe you are able to feed." In the same vein, he recommended birth control as a tool against unemployment. After conceding that a large number of children multiplied the privation caused by capitalism, Zietz in her concluding salvo declared that the party had never objected to the birth control advice that Bernstein, Moses, and other physicians had dispensed on an individual basis; only when they sought to stylize it as a revolutionary weapon, did the party intervene in order to insure that working women's attention was not diverted from the fundamental class economic facts.[33]

The debate also continued in party journals. Therese Schlesinger, though no adherent of the birth strike, attacked Wurm for characterizing fertility limitation and class struggle as mutually exclusive. One way of attaining an accommodation she saw in a deepening division of labor and development of technology that would relieve mothers of much of their overburden by placing children during the day "under expert supervision." Wurm's sharply worded reply merely repeated her position that it diverted attention from class struggle to preach egotistical personal life arrangements. Apodictically she also claimed that a reduction in the number of able-bodied "always" expressed itself in general societal decline. *Die Gleichheit* also published a contribution by a midwife, Luise Eichhoff, for whom the ideal of womanhood was the happiness of the high woman's occupation of motherhood. Her practice instructed her that working-class women did not limit their fertility in order to join the proletarian women's movement, but to avoid economic privation. She reported that working-class women were animated to improve their economic position by comparing their own wretchedness with the luxury and idleness of the women of the propertied classes who practiced birth control. But the working woman who acted from such motives would be found at afternoon coffee-circles and cheap entertainments—not at a union or party meeting. Such women disqualified themselves in Eichhoff's eyes because they lacked the self-sacrifice to serve the interests of the working class; she contrasted them sharply with the women with large families whom she did see at such meetings and who were motivated by a mother's love, although she did concede that that same love deterred some women from giving birth to still more children when their already living ones existed in a vale of tears.[34]

In the wake of the debate, Oda Olberg, writing in the beginning of 1914 in the SPD's chief theoretical—and arguably the world's premier Marxist—journal, *Die Neue Zeit*, supported the party's leadership with atypical arguments while conceding some points to the opposition. Unlike her comrades, Olberg evaluated as untoward that, in light of the proletariat's growing importance as mass consumer and of children's status as pure consumers for 12 years, a decline in births would bring about massive shifts, especially among mass-consumption food items, in demand precipitating long-term economic crises. Noting that the party agreed that it was barbaric to expect women to bear 10 or 15 children, Olberg admitted that birth control was desirable, but argued that three to five children were more appropriate than one or two. A principal reason for this party preference was rooted in the claim that people grew with their tasks; by the same token, because parents' sense of responsibility for one child was as great as for five and parents never risked their economic existence lightheartedly the way childless people did, she saw no greater potential for participation in class struggle by parents with one than with five children. But, once again, unlike the party leaders, Olberg asserted that fertility decisions were not merely private matters or ones to be resolved by physicians. Rather, considering the pervasive societal consequences, a societal standard was required. Olberg's conclusion therefore read that the party should openly declare that it valued that party comrade higher who raised five children to become fit workers like himself [*sic*] than the member who has his one pitiful delicate child study at the university.[35]

The response from outside the SPD to the debate was lively. That extreme reactionaries joined Rosa Luxemburg in attacking the birth strikers gave the controversy, as Franz Pfemfert, the editor of *Die Aktion*, Germany's leading oppositional literary journal, noted, a comic aspect. Other political observers pointed out that the birth-strike debate was the first occasion on which the masses of radical Social Democrats in Berlin had rebelled against such popular leaders as Luxemburg and Zetkin. The birth-strike debate was also followed closely in socialist circles outside Germany. In the United States, William Walling reported on it critically in the

Masses. An American physician active in the birth control movement who had attended the second, three-and-one-half-hour, meeting, and who was decidedly in favor of the birth strikers, reported in the *International Socialist Review* that the sense of the crowd was that "though Clara Zetkins and Rosa Luxemburgs and all other literal and figurative old maids" might have correctly disparaged the efficacy of limiting fertility in eliminating militarism and capitalism, it remained "a wonderful measure" for individual families and women's health.[36]

Perhaps substantively even more interesting because more pointed than the German debate was the exchange conducted in 1913 and 1914 in the main journal of Austrian Social Democracy, *Der Kampf*. The most sustained contribution stemmed from Otto Bauer, one of the leading Austro-Marxist theoreticians, who, like Kautksy in Germany, represented the orthodox rejection of the birth strike. Convinced that only a rapid increase in population would lead to proletarian victory, Bauer argued that a limitation of births was compatible with the promotion of socialism only if it accelerated population growth. Bauer then outlined what has since come to be known as the stages of the demographic transition: (1) high fertility matched with high mortality leads to slow population growth; (2) a decline in the number of births is exceeded by the decline in mortality, leading to quickened population growth; and (3) fertility declines while mortality falls more slowly, resulting in a slower increase in population. Whereas the transition from the first to the second stage, characterized by a proliferation of birth control, a fall in infant mortality, and a reduction in the burdens of frequent pregnancies, constituted enormous progress, Bauer asked whether the transition from the second to the third stage was also progressive. For the individual worker, Bauer conceded, there was no doubt that a smaller family alleviated the struggle for existence. "However we are not individualists, but *socialists*." And as socialists, whose goal was to smash the capitalist world, it was insufficient to make the worker's lot "a little friendlier" in it.[37]

Unlike most Marxist contributors to the birth-strike debate, Bauer was theoretically *parti pris*: in connection with a larger debate between Bauer and Luxemburg on the limits to capital accumulation and the nature of crises, Bauer had taken the position that population growth was the independent variable to which capital accumulation must and did accommodate itself.[38] Indeed, Bauer found this relationship to be societally invariant: in any society with positive population growth the production apparatus would have to be expanded; the only difference between socialist and capitalist societies lay in the fact that planning agencies in the former would insure that that expansion kept pace with population growth, whereas capital accumulation depended on individual capitalists' arbitrary will.[39]

Taking a view that bourgeois economists would also later ascribe to Marx, Bauer started from the assumption that the accumulation of capital presupposes the growth of the working class in order to staff the new factories and the expansion of existing ones. Where the growth of the population seeking work exceeds that of capital accumulation, the resulting emigration of labor is a consequence of the underaccumulation of capital. Where capital accumulates faster than the growth of the working population, as in France, domestic capitalists must invest their capital for which there are no available domestic workers in other countries; this emigration of capital was a consequence of its overaccumulation. With the transition from the second to the third demographic stages, economic development is not impeded in countries characterized by underaccumulation because the primary reaction is merely a decline in emigration. In countries, such as Germany, however, where an approximate equilibrium between accumulation and population growth had obtained, the advent of the third demographic transition stage would result in the same phenomena of overaccumulation-driven outflow of capital. Consequently, Bauer concluded, slower population growth does not improve the working class's position in the labor market because the demand for labor declines in proportion with the decline in supply.[40]

Bauer illustrated his point on the national level:

> To be sure, the French worker, who has two children, lives better with the same wage than the German workers with his four or five children. But the nation, industry, socialism grow much faster where population growth is great enough to carry out the accumulation of capital in its own country than there where capital, since it does not find enough workers in its own country, must flow off to foreign economies.

Bauer's syllogistic thinking proceeded along these lines: "The whole hope of socialism is based on economic development. But economic development comes to a standstill where the population does not grow." Moreover, the working class can neither conquer nor retain power as long as it is not the majority of the population: "The working class becomes the majority, however, only through the growth of population; it becomes the majority so much the faster the faster the population grows! The slowing of population growth therefore has a counterrevolutionary effect: it lengthens the duration of the capitalist mode of production!"[41] Bauer then built toward an astounding demographic determinism:

> The working class feels that very precisely. In France, where the population does not grow, the working class sees no hope of becoming the majority. It therefore vacillates between weak-hearted reformism, which seeks the alliance of the bourgeois parties, and violent syndicalism, which fancies it is able to defeat the bourgeois majority through the terror of a proletarian minority. In the German Empire with its so enormous population growth the working class goes its way certain of victory, calm; it knows that the course of social development itself, which augments the number of workers every year by hundreds of thousands, must finally lead it to victory.[42]

Here Bauer, one of the best Marxist political economists of the first half of the twentieth century, fell victim to the mechanistic, quantitative-progress thinking that was to prove the downfall of Social Democracy in Europe in 1914 and 1933.[43] Bauer then imparted a strange twist to his argument by admitting that:

"Of course, in Great Britain, in the German Empire, in Belgium, the proletariat is already today the majority of the population. There it can be victorious without a growth in its numbers." Bauer, however, immediately trumped his own argument by adding that no proletariat could "maintain its victory if the rule of capital endures in overpowering neighboring countries." The specific demographically centered process then ran as follows: Because of its falling fertility, France, which feared Germany's numerical superiority, had become a pillar of reaction in Europe by seeking an alliance with tsarism. The same demographically driven process was at work on the economic level: because excess labor was lacking in France, French capitalists were compelled to make their billions available to tsarism. Thus if the Central European proletariat was eventually successful, it might be crushed by Eastern European barbarism: if only the Russian peasant continued to increase his numbers, "then Europe would not become republican, but cossack...."[44]

Bauer seemed to wax even more pessimistic when he also admitted that—but failed to explain why—no ideology (including, implicitly, socialism) could motivate people to increase their birth rate and no law could successfully prohibit all contraceptives. With this path blocked, the only remaining strategy from the orthodox social-democratic perspective was yet a further reduction of mortality, and particularly of infant mortality; and here, given the much higher rate in Austria than in Germany, for example, there was ample possibility. Ironically, however, to achieve this reduction, Bauer had recourse to the same catalog of measures that the mere "bourgeois social policy maker, who wishes that the worker could live somewhat cosier within the capitalist world," would have proposed—combating alcoholism, venereal disease, and tuberculosis, raising the workers' standard of living, expanding public health care, instruction of mothers, and assisting mothers through public welfare institutions.[45]

More forcefully and straightforwardly than the Germans, Social Democrats in Austria argued that workers with large families forfeited much of the freedom that was required to remain "ready for battle" against employers. This position was advanced with the greatest poignancy by a laborer with only four years of school, who dared challenge the rejection of the birth strike that had been offered by Bauer. Karl Kirschleder of Rainfeld explained how difficult it was to rouse from their "lethargy" those workers with large numbers of children who had neither the energy to participate in meetings nor money to buy a newspaper or to pay membership dues let alone to endure a strike. Employers knew well how to terrorize such workers who, in their anxiety to feed their families, frequently wound up lowering their co-workers' wages. In his brief reply, Bauer was forced to concede that quality was as important as quantity and that workers who had to feed eight to twelve people were generally incapable of participating in the class struggle. Bauer therefore proposed a procreational golden mean—a fertility rate not so great as to immiserate the working class but nevertheless sufficient to guarantee a rapid increase of the working class. Bauer's conclusion was similarly ambiguous, poised halfway between patronizing and appreciative. Although for "Rainfeld on the Gölsen the artificial limitation of the number of births may be a new art, the spread of which is desirable," the workers in large cities and in Europe's industrial areas were delaying their victory by refraining from increasing their numbers.[46]

In yet another Austrian contribution to the debate, Otto Jenssen stressed that although the utopian political illusions of the birth-strikers that imperialism and militarism could be overcome without any personal sacrifices by workers needed to be combated, the neo-Malthusian decline in fertility was apparently a universal phenomenon of high capitalism that also permitted the individual worker to increase his ability to take part in labor resistance and to better prepare the next generation for the "struggle for life." Jenssen therefore called for "limitation of births and class struggle."[47]

Once the world war began, the SPD leadership squelched the birth-strike debate and threatened reprisals against members who continued to agitate on the issue.[48] (Bourgeois opponents of the very short-lived Munich Soviet Republic in 1919 charged that " neomalthusian...communist propaganda for the birth strike" in support of world revolution had resurfaced there.)[49] The claim, however, that "[p]arty leaders—male and female—had decided that individual or family needs in this case were immaterial for the working class as a whole" is overdrawn insofar as the SPD did not oppose individual acts of procreational self-restraint. A decade later, the SPD's theoretical journal characterized the birth strike as having played a not very gratifying role in the party press before the war. And the philosopher Max Scheler, speaking at a population policy congress in 1921, contended that only a "mass-hysterical atmosphere of obstinacy" could have prompted the birth-strike movement, which was a transfer of the French syndicalist theory of direct action to the social-sexual sphere. It was a "haughty phrase which passes over God, nature, and the will of the husband and contradicted all reality." Scheler therefore found it a good sign of the SPD leadership's "circumspection and sobriety" that it had rejected this slogan, which had been introduced by "little hysterical French men and women."[50]

In summary, the claim that the SPD's identification of the substance of the birth-strike movement with Malthus's population theorem was demagogic and absurd would be difficult to maintain. Equally untenable, however, is the assertion that the birth-strike's goal of combining improvement of working women's condition with "an upward movement in wages" represented the "most extreme logical conclusion of the wage-fund theory."[51] The birth strikers emphasized both the economic advantages accruing to individual families and the political power accruing to the working class as a whole from smaller families and a smaller proletariat, but they did not use a macroeconomic wage-fund argument.

The birth-strike debate grew, on the one hand, out of the ruling classes' dissatisfaction with the reduced rate of population increase and, on the other, out of proletarian women's dissatisfaction with the unequal and physically and psychologically destructive burdens associated with giving birth to and raising large numbers of children. In Germany, as elsewhere, larger socioeconomic forces were leading to the production of smaller families independently of such sharply ideological discussions. What is of interest here is the contribution that the birth-strike debate may have made to resolving the question as to whether a visible hand was a more reliable guide to optimal macrodemographic trends than millions of uncoordinated microdecisions.

Significantly, neither side in this intrasocialist debate proposed a visible-hand solution. Most supporters of the birth strike focused on the benefits accruing individually to families from reducing their own procreativity. Ironically, despite the grandiloquent strike rhetoric, even those who dwelt on such class-wide benefits as the higher wages associated with a smaller labor supply and the more intensive political involvement resulting from less demanding child-care obligations did not advocate collective action, but left the decision to have fewer children up to the individual parents. Since supporters envisioned individual families as benefiting from their reduced fertility regardless of other potential procreators' decisions, the birth "strike" was metaphorical in the sense that self-regarding motives could be relied on to impel parents to limit family size without direct political coordination of such decisions.

Party centrists such as Kautsky believed that even if a coordinated birth strike were organized, small families' advantages would not be translated into macrodemographic benefits because the strength of the working class would be undermined while the impacts on the military and industrial reserve armies were too long-term to be politically effective. By the same token, despite the party leadership's pronounced anti-Malthusianism, it implicitly trusted in overarching macrosocietal processes to guide population in the direction most favorable to the advent of socialism.

NOTES

1. Anton Menger, *Volkspolitik* 49-50 (1906).

2. Otto Ehinger, "Der Gebärstreik," *Der Zeitgeist, Beiblatt zum Berliner Tageblatt*, Oct. 6, 1913 (unpaginated [at 2, col. 1]).

3. H[einrich]. C[unow]., "Review of Fritz Brupbacher, Kindersegen und kein Ende?," in *Neue Zeit*, 22/II: 572-74 at 572 (1903-04) (quote); Max Schippel, *Das moderne Elend und die moderne Uebervölkerung: Zur Erkenntnis unserer sozialen Entwicklung* 242 (1888). For an admission that "socialists have given no satisfactory refutation of" Malthus's theory, see P. Maßloff, "Droht der Menschheit eine Übervölkerung?" *Neue Zeit*, 29/I: 583-87 at 583 (1911).

4. Ludwig Quessel, "Karl Kautsky als Bevölkerungstheoretiker," *Neue Zeit*, 29/I:559-65 (1911); R. P. Neuman, "The Sexual Question and Social Democracy in Imperial Germany," *J. Social Hist.* 7 (3):271-86 (Spring 1974); Christiane Dienel, *Kinderzahl und Staatsräson: Empfängnisverhütung und Bevölkerungspolitik in Deutschland und Frankreich bis 1918*, at 170, 183-84 (1995).

5. James Woycke, *Birth Control in Germany 1871-1933* (1988); Peter Marschalck, *Bevölkerungsgeschichte Deutschlands im 19. und 20. Jahrhundert* 41-67, tab. 3.1, 3.2, & 3.4 at 156-58, fig. 4 at 186 (1984); *Verhandlungen des Reichstags*, XIII. Legislaturperiode, I. Session, vol. 287: Stenographische Berichte, 3299 (Jan. 28, 1913); *Verhandlungen des*

Reichstags, XIII. Legislaturperiode, I. Session, vol. 289: Stenographische Berichte, 4548 (Apr. 8, 1913)

6. J. Bornträger, "Der Geburtenrückgang in Deutschland: Seine Bewertung und Bekämpfung," *Veröffentlichungen aus dem Gebiet der Medizinalverwaltung,* 1: No. 13 at 631-794 (1912); J. Bornträger, *Der Geburtenrückgang in Deutschland: Seine Bewertung und Bekämpfung* 22-23, 43, 82, 154, 119-20 (1913).

7. Bornträger, *Geburtenrückgang* at 91-92, 105-19.

8. Julius Wolf, *Die Volkswirtschaft der Gegenwart und Zukunft: Die wichtigsten Wahrheiten der allgemeinen Nationalökonomie* 290-96, 203-205 (quote at 293-94) (1912).

9. *Verhandlungen des Reichstags* 287:3298-3300 (Knigge); Entwurf eines Gesetzes betreffend Änderung der §§ 56, 56c der Gewerbeordnung, Aktenstück No. 1179, *Anlagen zu den Stenographischen Berichten der Verhandlungen des Reichstags,* 303:2373-75 (1914); *Stenographische Berichte der Verhandlungen des Reichstags* 291:6035-36 (Nov. 27, 1913) (Carmer).

10. *Stenographische Berichte der Verhandlungen des Reichstags* 291:6078 (Nov. 29, 1913) (Stolle); *ibid.* at 6028 (Nov. 27, 1913) (Brey). For a Social Democratic concession that even among the propertied classes in the vast majority of cases limitation of fertility was not the product of egotism but of the increasing difficulty of meeting the economic and psychological demands of raising a large family, see Oda Olberg, "Über den Neo-Malthusianismus," *Neue Zeit,* 24/I:846-54 at 847 (1905-06).

11. *Stenographische Berichte der Verhandlungen des Reichstags* 291:6090 (Nov. 29, 1913) (Fischer); for a broader-based critique, see Luise Zietz, "Gegen den staatlichen Gebärzwang," *Die Gleichheit* 24 (15):227-28 (Apr. 15, 1914); *ibid.* 24 (16):242-43 (Apr. 29, 1914).

12. "Gebärzwang und Gebärstreik," *Die Gleichheit* 24 (14):209-10 (Apr. 1, 1914); *ibid.* 24 (17):257-59 (May 13, 1914); *ibid.* 24 (19):289-91 (June 10, 1914). At the very same time, Lenin was taking a position similar to that of the SPD leadership, denouncing neo-Malthusianism while defending freedom of medical propaganda. V.I. Lenin, "Rabochii klass i neomal'tuzianstvo," in *idem, Polnoe sobranie sochinenii* 23: 225-57 (1961 [June 16, 1913]).

13. Ulrich Linse, "Arbeiterschaft und Geburtenentwicklung im Deutschen Kaiserreich von 1871," *Archiv für Sozialgeschichte* 12:205-71 at 238 (1972); Dienel, *Kinderzahl und Staatsräson* at 176 (quote). The fact that R. P. Neuman, "Working Class Birth Control in Wilhelmine Germany," *Comp. Studies in Society & Hist.* 20 (3):408-28 at 427 (July 1978), relies heavily on secondary sources in discussing the birth-strike debate may explain the author's overinterpretation of the claim that the SPD leadership mistook the fall in fertility as an expression of bourgeoisification.

14. Fritz Brupbacher, *Kindersegen—und kein Ende? Ein Wort an denkende Arbeiter* 17, 38, 50, 30 (enlarged ed., 1909 [1903]). See generally Karl Lang, *Kritiker, Ketzer, Kämpfer: Das Leben des Arbeiterartzes Fritz Brupbacher* 59-69 (n.d. [1975?]).

15. Ludwig Quessel, "Das Zweikindersystem in Berlin," *Sozialistische Monatshefte* 17:253-60 at 259 (1911).

16. Eduard Bernstein, "Geburtenrückgang, Nationalität und Kultur," *Sozialistische Monatshefte* 19:1492-99 at 1493-94, 1499 (1913). Although Bernstein characterized this method as without old or neo-Malthusian elements, it clearly includes the moral restraint that Malthus urged in later editions of his *Essay.* See, e.g., Thomas Robert Malthus, *An Essay on the Principle of Population* (7th ed.), in *idem, On Population* 588-89 (Gertrude Himmelfarb ed., 1960 [1872]). On Engels' view, see letter from Engels to Kautsky, Feb. 1, 1881, Karl Marx [&] Friedrich Engels, *Werke* 35:151 (1967).

17. Ludwig Quessel, "Die Ökonomie des Gebärstreiks," *Sozialistische Monatshefte* 19:1319-25 at 1324-25 (1913); *idem*, "Die Philosophie des Gebärstreiks," *Sozialistische Monatshefte* 19:1609-16 at 1615 (1913).

18. K. Kautsky, "Der Gebärstreik," *Neue Zeit* 31/II:904, 905-909 (1913). Kautsky's argument that a birth strike can exert only a long-term impact was later echoed by a bourgeois critic; Fritz Burgdörfer, "Die Bevölkerungsentwicklung während des Krieges und die kommunistische Propaganda für den Gebärstreik," *Münchener medizinische Wochenschrift* 66:433-35 (1919). Three decades earlier, before he had become a Marxist, Kautsky had argued that remaining free of family obligations would benefit an individual only so long as the practice was not generalized—at which point everyone would be in the same position as at the outset except the population would be smaller. Karl Kautsky, *Der Einfluss der Volksvermehrung auf den Fortschritt der Gesellschaft* 193 (1880).

19. Mathilde Wurm, "Der Geburtenrückgang in Berlin," *Die Gleichheit*, 23 (22):338-40 (July 23, 1913).

20. Heinrich Vogel, "Eine Ursache des Geburtenrückgangs," *Die Gleichheit*, 23 (24):374-75 (Aug. 20, 1913); *idem*, "Eine Ursache des Geburtenrückgangs," *Die Gleichheit* 24 (4):50-52 at 52 (Nov. 12, 1913) (quote).

21. "Gebärstreik," 1. *Beilage des "Vorwärts" Berliner Volksblatt*, July 31, 1913 (unpaginated [at 3]); *ibid.*, Aug. 7, 1913, 3. *Beilage des "Vorwärts" Berliner Volksblatt* (unpaginated [at 1]). Linse, "Arbeiterschaft und Geburtenentwicklung" at 245, speculates that Clara Zetkin was the author.

22. Demographers have repeatedly referred to these debates as the Party's 1913 Congress. They in fact had nothing to do with the latter, which took place in Jena in September. Alfred Sauvy, "Les Marxistes et le malthusianisme," in *Cahiers internationaux de sociologie* 30 (n.s.):1-14 at 7 (July-Dec. 1966); *idem*, "Marx et les problèmes contemporains de la population," *Information sur les sciences sociales* 7(4): 27-38 at 31 (Aug. 1988); William Petersen, "Marxism and the Population Question: Theory and Practice," in *Population and Resources in Western Intellectual Traditions* 77-101 at 84 (Michael Teitelbaum & Jay Winter eds., 1989).

23. Alfred is not to be confused with the aforementioned Eduard Bernstein as is done by Gerhard Mackenroth, *Bevölkerungslehre: Theorie, Soziologie und Statistik der Bevölkerung* 317, 355, 505 (1953). On Moser, see Kurt Nemitz, "Julius Moses und die Gebärstreik-Debatte 1913," *Jahrbuch des Instituts für Deutsche Geschichte* 2:321-35 (1973); Daniel Nadav, *Julius Moses (1868-1942) und die Politik der Sozialhygiene in Deutschland* (1985).

24. Georg Wagner, "Ist der Neomalthusianismus vom ärtzlichen Standpunkt aus zu empfehlen?" *Die Gleichheit* 24 (6):81-84 at 83 (Dec. 10, 1913). As the birth-strike movements in Germany and France show, Michael Katz & Mark Stern, "History and the Limits of Population Policy," *Politics & Society* 10 (2):225-45 at 243 (1980), apodictically but incorrectly assert that "at no time in history has a general reduction in the birthrate emerged as a working-class demand."

25. 2. *Beilage des "Vorwärts" Berliner Volksblatt*, Aug. 21, 1913 (no pagination) (quote); *Vorwärts*, Aug. 29, 1913, 2. Beilage (no pagination [at 4]) (advertisement); Anneliese Bergmann, "Frauen, Männer, Sexualität und Geburtenkontrolle: Die Gebärstreik-debatte der SPD im Jahre 1913," in *Frauen suchen ihre Geschichte: Historische Studien zum 19. und 20. Jahrhundert* 81-108 at 94 (Karin Hausen ed., 1983); "Gegen den Gebärstreik!" 1. *Beilage des "Vorwärts" Berliner Volksblatt*, Aug. 24, 1913 (no pagination [at 2]); "Ein Gebärstreik?" *Frankfurter Zeitung* (Abendblatt), Aug. 23, 1913, at 2, col.2; "Die Debatte über den Gebärstreik," *Frankfurter Zeitung* (Abendblatt), Aug. 30, 1913, at 1, col. 4.

26. "Gegen den Gebärstreik!" (no pagination [at 2]). The speakers are quoted here according to various contemporary newspaper accounts, which differ from one another. As Zetkin's argument and other contributions—e.g., Otto Jenssen, "Geburtenbeschränkung und Klassenkampf," *Der Kampf* 7:212-14 (1913-14)—show, the assertion that the birth strike debate was remarkable for the fact that neither side based its position on Marx's analysis of the relationship between population and surplus labor or wages is erroneous. Jean Quataert, "Unequal Partners in an Uneasy Alliance: Women and the Working Class in Imperial Germany," in *Socialist Women:European Socialist Feminism in the Nineteenth and Early Twentieth Centuries* 112-45 at 144 n.43 (Marilyn Boxer & Jean Quataert eds., 1978).

27. "Gegen den Gebärstreik!" (no pagination [at 2]) (quote);"Gebärstreik?" *Leipziger Volkszeitung*, 3. Beilage, Aug. 26, 1913, *reprinted in* Karl Heinz Roth, "Kontroversen um Geburtenkontrolle am Vorabend des Ersten Weltkriegs: Eine Dokumentation zur Berliner 'Gebärstreikdebatte' von 1913," *Autonomie* 9 (12):78-103 at 90 (1978); Heinz Niggemann, *Emanzipation zwischen Sozialismus und Feminismus: Die sozialdemokratische Frauenbewegung im Kaiserreich* 267 (1981) (citing unpublished correspondence from Zetkin to Kautsky from 1902); "Die Debatte über den Gebärstreik," *Frankfurter Zeitung*, Aug. 30, 1913 at 2, col. 1 (quote).

28. "Gegen den Gebärstreik!" (no pagination [at 2-3]). In a text that dates from later in 1913, Moses in fact did call the birth strike a "weapon with a revolutionizing effect vis-à-vis the ruling circles...." Julius Moses, "Der Gebärstreik," *published in* Roth, "Kontroversen" at 87-89 at 88.

29. "Gegen den Gebärstreik!" (no pagination [at 3]). On Zietz, see Dieter Fricke, *Die deutsche Arbeiterbewgung 1869-1914: Ein Handbuch über ihre Organisation und Tätigkeit im Klassenkampf* 284-45, 291, 329-30 (1976).

30. *Stenographische Berichte der Verhandlungen des Reichstags* 291:6086 (Nov. 29, 1913) (Dr. Werner). David Kennedy, *Birth Control in America: The Career of Margaret Sanger* 21, 110 (1970), also attributes to Luxemburg the position she vigorously opposed. Stalinists, too, distorted the record. See, e.g., V. Smulevich, *Burzhuaznye teorii narodonaseleniia v svete marksistko-leninskoi kritiki* 172 (1936), who undifferentiedly asserted that "Social-Democrats, depicting neo-Malthusianism as a means of class struggle of the proletariat, recommend limiting the number of children as a means of reducing the number of unemployed and thus of improving the economic position of the masses, and also as a means of depriving the imperialist state's army (!)."

31. "Gegen den Gebärstreik!" *Vorwärts*, Aug. 24, 1913 (no pagination [at 3]) (quote); "Gebärstreik?" *Leipziger Volkszeitung* at 91 (quote).

32. "Gegen den Gebärstreik!" *Vorwärts*, 3. Beilage, Aug. 31, 1913 [no pagination [at 1]). Richard Evans, *Sozialdemokratie und Frauenemanzipation im deutschen Kaiserreich* 248 (W. Sebald tr. 1979), incorrectly states that Zetkin spoke out against any kind of family planning.

33. "Die Debatte über den Gebärstreik," *Frankfurter Zeitung*, Aug. 30, 1913, at 2, col. 1; "Die Geburteneinschränkung," *Vorwärts*, 1. Beilage, Sept. 25, 1913 (no pagination [at 1-2]) (quotes).

34. Therese Schlesinger, "Der Geburtenrückgang in Berlin. I," *Die Gleichheit* 24 (1):6-7 (Oct. 1, 1913); Mathilde Wurm, "Der Geburtenrückgang in Berlin," *Die Gleichheit* 24 (1):7-8 (Oct. 1, 1913); Luise Eichhoff, "Zur Frage des Geburtenrückgangs," *Die Gleichheit* 24 (3):36-37 (Oct. 29, 1913).

35. Oda Olberg, "Zur Stellung der Partei zum Gebärstreik," *Neue Zeit*, 32/I:47-55 (1914). On the party leaders' view regarding fertility decisions, see Wally Zepter, "Frauenbewegung," *Sozialistische Monatshefte* 19:644-46 (1913).

36. Franz Pfemfert, "Der Zeugungsstreik," *Die Aktion*, 3, Nr. 46, at 1063 (Nov. 15, 1913); "Gebärstreik und Sozialdemokratie," *Berliner Volks-Zeitung*, Oct. 16, 1913, *reprinted in* Roth, "Kontroversen" at 93; William Walling, "The World-Wide Battle Line," *Masses* 5 (1):20 (Oct. 1913); *idem*, "The World-Wide Battle Line," *Masses* 5 (2):20 (Nov. 1913); William Robinson, "The Prevention of Conception," *New Rev.* 3 (4):196-99 (Apr. 1915) (on birth control); William Robinson, "The Birth Strike," *International Socialist Rev.* 14(7):404-406 (Jan. 1914).

37. Otto Bauer, "Volksvermehrung und soziale Entwicklung," *Der Kampf* 7:322-29 at 324, 328 (1913-14). See Otto Leichter, *Otto Bauer: Tragödie oder Triumph* (1970).

38. Otto Bauer, "Die Akkumulation des Kapitals," *Neue Zeit*, 31/I:831-38, 862-74 at 869-73 (1912-13); Rosa Luxemburg, *Die Akkumulation des Kapitals oder was die Epigonen aus der Marxschen Theorie gemacht haben: Eine Antikritik* 71-101 (1921). E. Varga, "Wanderungen der Arbeiter und des Kapitals," *Der Kampf* 7:408-11 (1913-14), who did not touch on the birth-strike debate, argued that comparative location costs as determined by natural-geographic endowments, rather than demographic movements, explained labor and capital migration. For the reply see Otto Bauer, "Kapitalsvermehrung und Bevölkerungswachstum," *Der Kampf* 7:411-12 (1913-14).

39. Bauer, "Die Akkumulation des Kapitals" at 835.

40. Samuel Hollander, "Marx and Malthusianism: Marx's Secular Path of Wages," *Am. Econ. Rev.* 74 (1):139-51 at 150 (Mar. 1984); Bauer, "Volksvermehrung und soziale Entwicklung" at 324-25 (quotes).

41. Bauer, "Volksvermehrung und soziale Entwicklung" at 326, 327.

42. *Ibid.* at 327-28.

43. Walter Benjamin, "Geschichtsphilosophische Thesen," in *idem*, *Illuminationen: Ausgewählte Schriften* 268-79 at 273-74 (1961 [1950]): "There is nothing that has corrupted the German working class like the opinion that it is swimming with the current."

44. Bauer, "Volksvermehrung und soziale Entwicklung" at 328.

45. *Ibid.* at 328-29.

46. I. Gründorfer, "Die Stellung der Partei zum Gebärstreik," *Der Kampf* 7: 116-23 at 119, 123 (1913-14) (quote); Karl Kirschleder, "Volksvermehrung und soziales Elend," *Der Kampf* 7:468-70 (1913-14) (quote); Otto Bauer, [untitled reply], *Der Kampf* 7:470-71 (1913-14) (quote).

47. Jenssen, "Geburtenbeschränkung und Klassenkampf" at 212-14.

48. Quataert, "Unequal Partners" at 128; *idem*, *Reluctant Feminists in German Social Democracy, 1885-1917*, at 98-99 (1979). On the fading of the debate, see Linse, "Arbeiterschaft und Geburtenentwicklung" at 250-56.

49. Burgdörfer, "Die Bevölkerungsentwicklung während des Krieges und die kommunistische Propaganda für den Gebärstreik" at 433; Max Nassauer, "Zum Gebärstreik," *Münchener medizinische Wochenschrift* 66: 544-45 (1919).

50. Quataert, "Unequal Partners" at 128 (quote); Alfred Grotjahn, "Proletariat und Geburtenrückgang," *Neue Zeit*, 41/II:164, 168 (1923); Max Scheler, "Bevölkerungsprobleme als Weltanschauungsfragen," in *idem*, *Schriften zur Soziologie und Weltanschauungslehre* 290-324 at 318 (1963 [1921]). On Scheler's contribution to the consolidation of bourgeois society in Germany following the post-World War revolutionary turmoil, see Georg Lukács, *Die Zerstörung der Vernunft* 416 (1962).

51. Roth, "Kontroversen" at 85; D. Eversley, *Social Theories of Fertility and the Malthusian Debate* 159 (1959) (quote).

Part IV

Procreation, Poverty, and Solidarity

There is something out of place...in equalizing possessions and not establishing the number of citizens....

Aristotle, *Politica* 1265[a]38-39

8

Do Children Cause Poverty or Vice Versa?

[T]his much is certain: A nation in which the average family has two children will have a higher per-capita income than one in which the average family has three. It's a matter of simple arithmetic: If the family has an income of $10,000 a year, three children will mean a per-capita income of $2,000; two children, $2,500.[1]

How prevalent is poverty among large families and how large does their poverty bulk among aggregate poverty in advanced capitalist societies? Do modern statistics corroborate the observation of Jacksonian-era businessman Matthew Carey that a laborer with a wife and one child or neither fares well, while five children would create a deplorable case? And do the expenses of supporting children thrust adults into poverty or does preexisting poverty foster a culture that encourages large families? This chapter focuses on two-parent families to avoid the special issues associated with the feminization of poverty. For despite the fact that the majority of poor children have since the 1970s lived in female-headed families, the more pertinent economic-demographic question still remains why many two-parent families are unable to afford replacement-level procreation. Nevertheless, for comparative purposes, pertinent data on single-parent families are also pre-sented.[2]

The chapter begins with an exploration of the way in which the relationship between poverty and procreation was conceptualized before the advent of the War on Poverty in the United States in the 1960s and the kinds of empirical information that underlay and flowed from such discussions. Following an examination of the statistical methodology that underlay the creation and collection of poverty data in the United States during the 1960s, a broad variety of contemporary U.S. poverty data are presented and analyzed, leading to the conclusion that those who make individually supra-replacement-level procreative contributions—which are macrodemographically required to make up for the millions who do not reproduce at all—are exposed to a considerably heightened economic vulnerability.

The data marshalled here can be viewed as evidence brought to bear on what in Aristotelian logic is the following simple constructive dilemma:

> *Major Premise*: If people have children they do not want, they become poor; and if people have children they do want, they become poor.
> *Minor Premise*: Either people have children they want or have children they do not want.
> *Conclusion*: People are either poor or poor.

Escape between the horns of this dilemma is made possible by showing that the alternatives of the minor premise are not exhaustive. For example, some people do not have children (and relatively fewer of them are poor). The dilemma can also be taken by the horns by challenging the truth of the major premise. Showing that one or the other of its antecedents leads to a different consequent is one such method. The dilemma is taken by the alternatives offered if some people have children and are not poor.

CONCEPTUALIZATION AND PREHISTORY OF THE PROBLEM OF CAUSATION

> All our problems are the result of overbreeding among the working class....[3]

> [P]eople are not poor because they have large families. Quite the contrary: they have large families because they are poor.[4]

A persistent theme of social policy, particularly in the United States, has been the pervasive poverty among children. Children's advocacy organizations in the United States regularly highlight the proportion of children living in poverty. Thus the National Commission on Children recently announced that: "Today, children are the poorest Americans. One in five lives in a family with an income below the federal poverty level." One-way causality was put most starkly by the U.S. Government Accounting Office (GAO); stating that children had become the age group at greatest risk of poverty in the 1980s, it added: "The poverty of these children, of course, derives from that of their parents." The GAO and many child poverty analysts overlook the possibility that the parents of these poor children might not have become impoverished had they not been faced with the additional expenses of reproduction. Or as Michael Harrington described one of the slopes into impoverishment: "young girls...in a loveless world,...willingly courting pregnancy as a way of finding love...can sentence themselves to a life of poverty."[5]

Economists, too, in seeking to explain the finding that the poverty rate among children is double that among adults in the United States, first ask "Why Are Children Poor?" instead of focusing on the causes of the poverty of those children's parents. Victor Fuchs, for example, observing in the mid-1980s that this poverty gap was almost as wide even when female-headed households were excluded, discovered a key element in the unequal distribution of children across households. Only 9 percent of all adults but 40 percent of all children lived in households with three or more children in 1984. The average income of such child-rich households was considerably below the national average and per capita incomes were far below those of households without any children, in which 57 percent of adults lived. The proportion of children in poverty rose monotonically with the number of children in the household—from one-eighth among only children to one-half among those with four or more siblings. Although Fuchs concluded that an improvement in the economic position of children depends in part on reducing the "large families that account for a disproportionate share of children's poverty," he ignored the potential for improvement in the living standards of the adults who refrain from creating large families.[6]

This bias in analysis has its analog in policy. Even at the height of the war on poverty in the United States, for example, two family sociologists, who urgently advocated income maintenance programs to prevent parents from passing their legacy of poverty on to their children, expressly refused to extend such programs to aged parents whose childraising may have impoverished them on the ground that the connection "has only indirect bearing on the intergenerational continuity of poverty." The equalization of family burdens which is, at least outside the United States, the central objective of family policy, is designed to make it possible for parents to reproduce without suffering a significant reduction in their standard of living, although this policy does not adequately protect those adults whose standard of living was unacceptably low even before they procreated. But even if social policy succeeds in securing a minimum existence or subsistence for adults, such a floor may not be adequate let alone optimal for a growing child. The specific purpose of a family policy is precisely to offer the children of needy parents the same opportunities that are available to other children; in contrast, general public assistance programs do not purport to offer their beneficiaries, who are not supposed to become habituated to such benefits, the same standard of living that the nonneedy enjoy.[7] This differential solicitude shown children thus may explain in part the dilemma of (especially U.S.) public policy: how to protect children without 'spoiling' their parents or, alternatively, how to punish their parents without harming them.

To be sure, advocates and analysts may mention the statistical association of family size and child poverty, especially in connection with proposals for state-funded children's allowances. Thus long-time social security advocate Eveline Burns noted that the "size of family is a major determinant of whether children live in poverty or comfort."[8] But only rarely or sporadically have iconoclastic observers ventured to invert the causality by arguing that it is rather children who cause the poverty of their parents, "introduce insecurity into the home," or, less provocatively, parents who bring on their own poverty through procreation. Contrary, however, to the claim of Senator Joseph Tydings, who supported the Nixon administration's initiative in 1970 to promote public health and welfare by inducing poor people to restrict their procreativity, it was not "only in the past few years that family size has been perceived as a cause of poverty...."[9]

The etiological trope linking children and poverty was not new at all. As early as 1829, a French work on charity stated that "[n]o cause of indigence [is] more general and more powerful than the support of a number of children which exceeds the resources of the parents. The political sciences do not contain any truth susceptible of a more rigorous demonstration." And the following year it was estimated that a "superabundance" of children accounted for a majority of the indigent population in France.[10] On the eve of World War I, the British eugenicist Karl Pearson and his collaborators at the Francis Galton Laboratory for National Eugenics massively deployed his newly developed statistical analysis to correlate the number of children per family with "bad home conditions" such as the father's low wages. That a "dirty home" exhibited the highest positive correlation with the number of children born did not, however, prompt the investigators to consider the ambiguities of causality. More serious was Seebohm Rowntree's private survey of poverty in York at the turn of the century. Rowntree found that 22 percent of those living under what he designated the primary poverty line were so situated because of "largeness of family, i.e., cases in which the family is in poverty because there are more than four children, though it would not have been in poverty had the number of children not exceeded four." Arthur Bowley identified even higher shares in studies he conducted in five English towns in 1912-14 and 1923-24; poverty resulting from wages insufficient for three or more children ranged from 18 percent to 87 percent of all cases of poverty. When Rowntree resurveyed York in 1936, he discovered important shifts in the causes of poverty. Largeness of family accounted for only 8 percent of the families in poverty—a result he found unsurprising in light of the halving of the birth rate during the intervening period.[11]

Rowntree was nevertheless still so impressed by the presence of children as a contributory cause of poverty in families of all sizes that he advocated state-organized family allowances on the ground that "no...social reform...would accomplish more in relation to its cost...."[12] He calculated that a weekly family allowance of 5 shillings (s.) per child would raise almost three-fourths of all dependent children out of poverty resulting from inadequate wages. Because poverty resulting from unemployment was largely a problem of families with two or more children, Rowntree also recommended an increase in the already existing 3s. per week allowance for the children of unemployed families, who bulked much larger during the depression of the 1930s than they had at the turn of the century, as a further means of alleviating poverty. The reasons for Rowntree's continued focus on child-rich families despite the relative decline of family-size-related poverty were easily identifiable. First, even within the working class, there was a highly negative correlation between wage level and number of children. Whereas 21 percent of families with weekly wages below the level (53s.) that just maintained a level of physical efficiency for a three-child family had four children, the proportion among the highest-income wage-earners (70s. and over) was only 5 percent; the corresponding shares accounted for by childless families were 15 percent and 35 percent respectively. And second, whereas the aggregate rate of poverty among all families was 31 percent, that among families with three, four, and five or more children was 46, 59, and 68 percent respectively.[13]

Studies of modest working-class budgets in Britain shortly before World War II provided further support for the view that as family size increases, both parents and children suffer declines in their standard of living vis-à-vis smaller or childless families because "the effect of the accession of a child to a family is to make the family poorer, i.e., the...same effect as if a certain amount of income were taken away." These studies showed that the budgetary margin of economic safety disappeared with the advent of children: whereas 41 percent of childless couples had no savings, 75 percent of three-child families had none.[14] Unsurprisingly, a survey correlating nutritional adequacy and size of family during World War II revealed that, on average, British schoolchildren from large families were shorter and lighter and showed lower hemoglobin levels and a weaker strength of grip than classmates from small families.[15]

William Beveridge, one of the architects of the British welfare state, motivated the adoption of family allowances during World War II by arguing that "the greatest single cause of poverty in this country is young children." When Parliament debated family allowances in 1942, supporters repeated this argument.[16] Beveridge's claim provoked a member of the opposition to launch into a pronatalist theological refutation:

> Each new child is a blessing...in the human community.... There is God's economy—the creation of human beings with the physical power to produce the things they require from the earth.
>
> Is there anything in that arrangement which should bring about a state of affairs where some children create poverty?... Good God. Have we sunk to this depth that children are the cause of poverty...![17]

The theme of procreation-linked poverty became as internationalized as the phenomenon. Arguably the most successful public policy shapers advancing this analysis have been the Swedish Social Democrats, Alva and Gunnar Myrdal, who in the 1930s reignited worldwide debate on state policy toward population and poverty. Alva Myrdal not only stated unequivocally that "the chief cause of poverty in modern society is children," but accused nations of "allow[ing] parents, young, normal people, to become poor on account of children." Three decades later, Gunnar Myrdal continued to argue that "America is far behind the majority of other rich countries in taking measures to prevent children from becoming a cause of poverty to their families...."[18] The thought is pure Malthus: "the common people...are themselves the cause of their own poverty"—except that the Myrdals believed, at least for advanced capitalist societies, that unemployment resulted not from overpopulation, but from a societal organization of production and of distribution that had failed to keep pace with technical development. The Myrdals were chiefly concerned about the effects on the children and, through them, on the "quality of the coming generation.... The more children...in a family the more decidedly will poverty become their atmosphere. It will change the very volume of air they breathe...."[19]

Other social policy shapers and analysts have displayed more ambivalence on the issue of causality. Charles Booth, the turn-of-the-century private investigator of social conditions in London, while conceding that numerous children were "to some extent a cause" of poverty, opined that they "appear more definitely as consequences" without offering any stringent explanation. His reasoning, however, seemed chiefly teleological: because he regarded the prospects of limiting the fertility of the poor as dim, smaller families fell by the wayside as practical policy.

> Marriage is early for social or industrial reasons, and not, as a rule, on account of recklessness, while the number of births follows almost inevitably from physical causes, partly the vigour of youth and partly the influence on physique...of bodily labour and spare diet. [N]o reasonably possible exercise can be expected to stand against the stream. Not in this direction can we look for a solution of the problem of poverty.[20]

George Bernard Shaw at least offered a reason: "The introduction of the capitalistic system...produces a delusive promise of endless employment which blinds the proletariat to those disastrous consequences of rapid multiplication which are obvious to the small cultivator and peasant proprietor."[21]

At the end of the nineteenth century, one of France's most prominent demographers, Arsène Dumont, coined the expression *capillarité sociale* to account for why each "social molecule" does its utmost to "rise ceaselessly toward a luminous ideal that seduces and attracts it." For those on the rise toward luxury, elegance, and pleasure, children were therefore intolerable encumbrances. Where social capillarity could not flourish, fertility would. Thus among miners and factory workers, who had no opportunity to penetrate to the top of the industrial feudality, self-multiplication was inevitable: "Just as zero is the only number which, divided by four or six, gives equally zero as the quotient, the proletarian who has nothing will always bequeath to his sons an inheritance equal to his, namely a pair of arms...."[22]

All of these negative valuations of the impact of above-average procreativity on families' economic welfare stand in sharp contrast to some other prominent contemporaneous sources. In analyzing the results of the survey that he conducted among working-class families in Massachusetts in 1875, Carroll Wright was so impressed by children's contributions to aggregate family income—in six-child families they accounted for half of the earnings—that he concluded: "It would seem..., seriously speaking, that, if the number of children was doubled, there would be no need of adult labor at all." Although Wright originally intended to furnish data showing "the extra expense caused by the addition of each child to the family," table 1 failed to convey that information because "child labor...adds to the earnings more than the support of the child adds to the expenses."[23]

Table 1: **Earnings, Expenses, and Savings of Massachusetts Two-Adult Working-Class Families by Number of Children, 1875**[24]

No. of Children	No. of Families	No. of Working Children	Average Annual Earnings ($)	Average Annual Expenses ($)	Average Annual Surplus ($)
0	4	0	872	667	205
1	27	0	711	686	25
2	92	13	738	711	27
3	121	96	714	699	15
4	102	129	781	766	15
5	42	67	859	823	36
6	9	20	1,116	1,014	102
Total	397	325	763	738	25

Among the families with children, income and expenditures increased almost monotonically with family size (the exception being families with three children). With the exception of the atypical six-child families, which were the only ones with an average of more than two working children, the incremental progressions were modest; consequently, per capita income declined as family size rose. Thus the per capita income of two-child families was $185 compared with $123 for five-child families. Wright's claim that child labor compensated for the expenses associated with an additional child must, therefore, be taken to mean that it was traditionally understood that fewer per capita resources were available to larger families, which, however, were spared impoverishment by virtue of the older children's earnings. The earnings profile would perhaps have been more prominent had Wright published separate data on those families with and without working children.

As U.S. Commissioner of Labor, Wright conducted several larger national and international comparative surveys of working-class families. In 1890, he published the results of his study of more than 3,000 U.S. and European families of iron, steel, and coal workers, including more than 1,200 so-called normal families without boarders and with five or fewer children none of whom was older than 14. Although the progression among U.S. working-class families was not strictly monotonic, the average income of the five-child families was only 18 percent higher than that of the one-child families. In Wright's 1903 survey of 25,440 U.S. families, 11,156 of which were "normal" families, total annual family income varied relatively little by number of children, rising from $633 for those with no children to $683 for four-child families, and declining slightly to $665 for five-child families. The only significant difference emerged with regard to the proportion of family income expended, which rose from 90 percent among childless families to 101 percent among five-child families.[25]

That Wright's assumptions were not idiosyncratic was underscored by studies of wage-earning families in New York City three decades later. Robert Chapin, for example, who excluded families of more than four children, rejected the notion that an excessive number of mouths to feed could create a subnormal standard of living "unless we are willing to set a standard so high that the population at large must be diminished in order to reach it." Louise More too stressed not that children caused impoverishment, but that: "The larger the family, the larger is the income in most instances, as a large family usually implies more persons contributing to the income." This difference in valuation of procreativity and welfare was manifestly associated with a regime under which child labor was still representative. More characterized the parents she studied as so eagerly anticipating the time when their children could legally work that they frequently overstated their ages to secure working-papers. Poles apart was the position of Samuel Patterson, an economist at the Wharton School, who in 1929 appended to the not unprecedented argument that large families' inability to educate their children "perpetuate the problem of low wages" the much more extreme claim that: "The tendency of population to grow from the bottom more rapidly than from the top is the chief explanation of the social pyramid of non-competing economic groups."[26]

The more systematically collected data from the Great Depression of the 1930s forward began to shed additional light on the relationship between procreativity and income. The 1935-36 census in Sweden, for example, revealed a monotonically declining median "unbroken" family income ranging from 2,148 crowns in marriages with no children to 1,612 crowns for four-child families, and 1,191 crowns among those with nine or more children. A special study of 34 provincial cities conducted on behalf of the Swedish Population Commission showed an even sharper monotonic drop in per capita family incomes: in 1932, childless married couples reported median annual income of 1,322 crowns compared with only 697 crowns for a couple with four children. Thus on a per capita basis, the four-child family had only 53 percent as much income at its disposal; the corresponding figure on a family basis was 75 percent in 1935-36.[27]

The post-World War II U.K. Royal Commission on Population analyzed social surveys and family budget inquiries to quantify "the important part that children play as a cause of poverty...." In Bristol (1937) and Birmingham (1939) 51 percent and 55 percent respectively of families with four or more children fell below the poverty line compared to only 11 percent and 14 percent respectively of all families. In Birmingham, a "relentless gradation" marked the financial incapacity of families of different sizes to provide an adequate level of nutrition, rising from 13 percent among one-child families to 96 percent in those with six or more children.[28] In London (1929) 18 percent of four-child families were poor compared to 8 percent of two-child families; in York (1936) the corresponding shares were 59 percent and 37 percent respectively. These relationships prompted the Royal Commission's economists to conclude that: "Having a large family was in the 1930's, in the working class at any rate, almost enough to guarantee poverty."[29]

The U.S. National Health Survey conducted among urban families with children under 16 years of age in 1935-36 revealed that whereas only two-fifths of families with one or two children had income below $1,000 or were receiving relief, two-thirds to almost three-quarters of families with five or more children fell into this group. Conversely, whereas 1 in 17 of the smallest families had incomes above $3,000, the corresponding figure for the largest families ranged from 1 in 50 to 1 in 166. Overall the survey revealed that the "economic status of the families with children...is distinctly less favorable than that of families without children." The proportion of families on relief rose monotonically from those without children (13.3 percent) to those with nine children (58.4 percent).[30] Contemporary demographers offered no explanation other than that wives' ability to engage in gainful employment was reduced by the presence of large numbers of children.[31]

Another mid-1930s study of the incomes and expenditures of families of wage earners and clerical workers by the U.S. Bureau of Labor Statistics (BLS) revealed striking differences between the situations of the childless and parents. The modal adult-equivalent expenditure among the white families, whose size averaged 3.6 members, was $400-$500 annually. The childless married couples, who accounted for only 21 percent of the sample, constituted the overwhelming majority of all families in the highest expenditure groups, ranging from 49 percent in the $700-$800 group to 82 percent in the $1,200 and over group. The married couples with two to four children, who accounted for almost the same proportion (20 percent) of all families, were barely represented at all in any of these highest groups. They did, however, account for 21, 36, and 34 percent of all families in the less than $200, $200-$300, and $300-$400 groups respectively, which accounted for one-third of all families, whereas the childless couples accounted for 0, 1, and 4 percent respectively.[32]

The Depression years also marked the beginning of the U.S. Bureau of the Census's systematic collection of data on low-income families. The Sixteenth Census in 1940 published data (from 1939) on the wage and salary income of families according to number of children (under eighteen years old); because, unfortunately, the largest family-size category was that of three or more children, the full impact of the economic burden of raising an above-average number of children was submerged. The classification of families by age of family head was a particularly useful tool of disaggregation: in breaking out elderly couples with no children in an era when Social Security old-age pensions were not yet making a significant contribution to the diminution of poverty, the Census Bureau made it possible to compare age-specific couples with and without children. Among the half of U.S. families with only wage and salary income (and having at least $1 in income), the median income was approximately $1,300. Among husband-wife families, who constituted four-fifths of this group, the lowest (positive) income group with $1-$499 showed the characteristics in table 2.

Among the families with the youngest husbands, only one-fifth of those with no children earned less than $500 compared to one-third of those with two children and two-fifths with three or more children. Even among the wage-earning men between the ages of 35 and 54 who were at the height of their earning capacity and therefore underrepresented in this income group, the proportion of those with three or more children was twice as great as among those with fewer or no children.

Table 2: **Percentage of Husband-Wife Families with (Only) Wage-Salary Income of $1 to $499, 1939**[33]

	Age of Male Head					
	<25	25-29	30-34	35-44	45-54	55-64
No. of Children						
0	21.7	10.8	9.1	9.2	8.8	11.9
1	28.2	13.7	8.5	7.3	8.4	13.5
2	34.8	18.5	10.9	7.6	9.3	16.3
3 or >	41.4	29.1	21.1	15.1	15.7	21.8

These results prompted the Bureau of the Census to comment that: "The economic handicap of a large family is recognized as a major reason for the long-term decline of the birth rate in the United States and in many other parts of the world." The Bureau calculated per capita incomes showing monotonic declines as family size increased. Thus if the median wage or salary income of a husband (35 to 44 years old) and wife without children was $759 in 1939, by the time the family reached seven members, the per capita income declined to a mere $123.[34]

In spite of this impressive array of data linking poverty to children, prominent analyses of poverty during the pronatalist postwar baby boom era failed to single out large families as a location let alone a cause of poverty in the United States.[35] In this respect they resembled naive late-nineteenth-century studies of the causes of poverty, which insisted that "large families is [sic] a relatively unimportant cause of destitution," and focused instead on such factors as shiftlessness, sexual excess, and bad climatic conditions, but also on "undue power of class over class." As Ernest Burgess, one of the founders of urban sociology, observed as late as the time of World War I: "Largeness of family as a cause of dependency has never been satisfactorily treated by the students of the problem of poverty." Methodologically family size was commonly obscured by its submersion under the rubric "insufficient earnings," an ambiguous "omnibus well-meaning but unmeaning phrase" that failed to distinguish between subnormal industrial wage rates and normal wage rates inadequate to cover a large family's subsistence needs.[36]

A congressional investigation of low-income families carried out in the wake of the largely aspirational Employment Act of 1946 mentioned family size merely as a "circumstance," along with food consumption, rent, and condition of dwelling unit, rather than as a "factor contributing" to low income such as age, sex, color, occupation, education, disability, and broken family. When, on the eve of the Korean War, Robert Heilbroner asked "Who Are the American Poor?" he, too, pointed, on the one hand, to the "economic and social problem children," the rural population, the aged, blacks, "broken families," and the disabled, and, on the other, to the scarcity of productive capital that kept 10 million workers in low-productivity jobs. Large families, however, received no mention. As the lead witness in congressional hearings in 1955 devoted to *Low-Income Families*, the Secretary of Health, Education, and Welfare, Marion Folsom, presented a litany of causes—unemployment, old age, disability, death of a breadwinner, broken homes, and lack of education—from which family size was conspicuously lacking. Another witness, Howard Bowen, an economist, testifying about a report that he had prepared for the big-business association, the Committee for Economic Development, did mention large families, together with alcoholism, extravagance, and the costs of illness, floods, and legal disputes, but merely as a factor contributing to the largeness of need in contradistinction to factors contributing to the smallness of family resources such as low wages, unemployment, unemployability, and unavailability for employment arising from family responsibilities.[37]

The *New Republic*'s contribution to the subject in 1958 virtually duplicated Heilbroner's categories. When *Fortune* published an article in the midst of the Kennedy-Johnson upswing in 1964 with exactly the same title as Heilbroner's, the focus was also similar: those with little education, who lived in the South or in rural areas, who were nonwhite, old, or unemployed. Although "broken homes" and early marriages were also mentioned, the magazine added that many of the latter had no children. The popular book published the same year by Herman Miller of the U.S. Bureau of the Census on income distribution, apart from a brief account of "broken families," also failed to identify large families as a source of poverty. Indeed, in a contemporaneous scholarly study based on the 1960 census, Miller even speculated that in a large proportion of higher-income families grown children still living at home actually contributed to that above-average income. The influential study published by James Morgan and his associates in 1962, despite defining poverty in part by reference to family size, failed to mention that factor in its classification of causes. And even Michael Harrington, whose popular study of poverty is widely believed to have galvanized federal social programs in the 1960s, elided the whole issue of family size: "The family structure of the poor...is different from that of the rest of the society. There are more homes without a father, there are less marriage, more early pregnancy and...materially different attitudes toward sex." To be sure, the omission is also interpretable as the realization that large numbers of children were not the only cause of family poverty during the Keynesian boom.[38]

One celebrated work of the late 1950s, *The Affluent Society*, did mention "excessive procreation" as a cause of poverty, but Galbraith's naively naturalistic taxonomy ascribed "modern poverty" either to "intrinsically deficient" individuals or a "homing instinct" that self-condemned them to "insular poverty." The Pax Americana of the 1950s meant that "[n]early everyone else has mastered his environment; this proves that it is not intractable." The times were not propitious even for an irreverent economist to imagine the possibility that the elimination of alcoholism, mental deficiency, and other "handicaps" might not usher in povertyless capitalism.[39]

Ignored by all these authors was a convenient official series revealing the association between family size and low income. Gabriel Kolko made some use of it in 1962 in his dissenting view of *Wealth and Power in America*, which made a few brief references to the higher rates of below-maintenance-level incomes of larger families. James Vadakin, a vigorous and isolated academic advocate of family allowances, had made much more extensive use of the data already in the late 1950s, stressing the negative correlation between both total family income and per capita income and the average number of children.[40] As early as the end of World War II, the Bureau of the Census, through its Current Population Survey (CPS), began collecting annual data comparing median family income and distributions by number of children. In 1945, when the median income of families with zero or two children was $2,553 and $2,784 respectively, those with four or more children recorded a median of only $2,140. Similarly, almost one-third of the largest families reported incomes below $1,500 compared to about one-sixth of the two-child families. In 1948, median income in childless families was $3,152, peaked in two-child families at $3,334, and then monotonically declined 25 percent to a low of $2,488 for those with six or more children; whereas 29 percent of these largest families had incomes below $1,500—approximately half of the aggregate median family income—only 12.5 percent of the two-child families did. As impressive as these size-related income gaps are, they drastically understate the real impact on living standards since they were not calculated on a per capita basis.[41]

In 1961, families with only one child had a median income of $6,000 while those with six or more children reported a median income of $4,855. With incomes almost one-fifth lower and at least six times as many children, the larger families obviously plunged far below the smaller families in per capita income. The same pattern obtained among husband-and-wife families the heads of which worked year-round full-time: the median money income for such families with 1, 2, 3, 4, 5, and 6 or more children was $7,115, $6,925, $6,985, $6,785, $6,035, and $5,620 respectively. The corresponding per capita incomes were $2,372, $1,731, $1,397, $1,131, $862, and < $702.[42] Thus per capita incomes in families with four or more children, which accounted for almost one-fifth of all husband-and-wife families, amounted to considerably less than half of those with only one child.

At such levels of deprivation the argument loses its plausibility that it "is not obvious...that having children makes adults worse off in any meaningful sense, even if it reduces their consumption of 'luxury' goods...and increases the fraction of their income that they allocate to 'necessities.'" What these huge absolute gaps in income between child-rich and child-poor families clearly do cast doubt on is Simon Kuznets's assertion, which ultimately derives from Malthus, that: "Inasmuch as children provide an incentive to work and save, it is not certain that the savings per child...generated in a family unit with a large number of children would not be at least as high as in the same family if it had fewer or no children."[43]

From 1948 to the transition between the Kennedy and Johnson administrations, when poverty became a subject of intense public debate and policy, these patterns held steady. Median incomes of two-child families were approximately

27 percent to 34 percent higher than those of the largest families; the proportion of six-or-more-child families with median incomes below one-half the aggregate median family income remained about 2.5 times larger than that of two-child families.[44] (The ratio between median incomes of two- and six-child families remained in the same range until the late 1970s; by 1986, the ratio exceeded 2 to 1 for the first time. By that year, too, childless families' median income had almost drawn even with that of two-child families.) The most striking change took place in the proportions of the size-classes: in 1949, two-child families were 11.4 times as numerous as those with six or more children; by 1964 the figure had fallen to 6.3 times. These U.S. data resembled the aforementioned Swedish data from 1935-36, which had revealed a perfectly monotonic decline in median family income from childless couples to those with nine or more children, the latter amounting to 55 percent of the former. The social burden of this mismatch between family size and income can be measured by the fact that in 1954, four-or-more-child families, accounting for 30 percent of all children in the United States, reported annual incomes one-fifth less than that of the national median.[45]

During the remainder of the 1960s and into the early 1970s, as various antipoverty programs were debated and implemented, this income pattern persisted although the gap between small and large families narrowed somewhat. Thus in 1970, the median income of families with two children ($10,601), which were 8.3 times as numerous as those with six or more children, was 22 percent greater than that of the latter ($8,686); the proportion of six-child families with incomes below half of the aggregate median (24.4 percent) was now only 1.9 times that of two-child families (12.9 percent). By this time, however, the Bureau of the Census was publishing disaggregated data that permitted a more nuanced understanding of the dynamics of poverty associated with large families. Although white families were 9.4 as numerous as black families in 1970, white families with six or more children (745,000) were only 2.1 times as numerous as black ones (352,000). If the income gap between small and large families is broken down by race, the 22 percent gap in total median incomes between two- and six-child families is revealed as masking significant racial differences. The median income among two-child white families ($10,922), which were 11.2 times as numerous as the largest ones, was only 6.5 percent greater than among the latter ($10,253). Among the "Negro" population, two-child families, which were only 2.3 times more numerous than six-or-more-child families, reported a median income ($6,701) 17 percent greater than that of the largest families ($5,740). (In 1969 the corresponding gaps between small and large families for whites and blacks was 2 percent and 22 percent respectively.) If attention is focused exclusively on husband-wife families, the median income of the largest white families ($10,942) actually exceeded that of two-child families ($10,832); among blacks, the small family-large family gap still amounted to 11 percent.[46]

By the mid-1960s, the abundance of annually collected data revealing an invariant negative correlation between family income and the number of children per family in the United States made it clear that parents with many children faced not only higher costs of living but also a competitive disadvantage in earning and increasing their income.[47] Alvin Schorr, a leading researcher on the subject, rather than trying to identify the direction of causality, suggested that: "Poverty and large families may both result from the same unfortunate circumstances—premature family and occupational choices, limited education and competence in general, limited resources. Poverty, family breakdown, and family size interact; year by year they contribute to one another." Since, however, as Schorr also noted, "most people who die poor were born poor," the personal composition of this generation's poor appears largely predetermined by their family's income. Consequently, fertility-related poverty "tends to subject the next generation to poverty conditions in greater degree than is called for by the existing distribution of income."[48]

Daniel Moynihan, who has perhaps been the most forceful advocate in the United States of family-centered welfare policies during the last third of the twentieth century, both asserted that U.S. experience corroborated Alva Myrdal's dictum that children were the main cause of poverty in modern society and plumped for two-way mutually reinforcing causality: "Poverty is both the cause and the result" of large families. Although he diagnosed low-income families "who simply had more children than their income would support" as the chief beneficiaries of such maintenance programs as the negative income tax, the Family Assistance Plan that he urged during the Nixon administration was not even intended to eliminate poverty among very large families: "concern about possible criticism for providing a 'baby bonus' imposed a cut-off point of seven-person families."[49]

Nor were such concerns confined to the United States. In the mid-1960s, Richard Titmuss, the English-speaking world's leading socialist welfare theoretician, confirmed that "next to old age still the commonest cause of relative poverty in Britain today is the large family." Ten years later and after three decades of family allowances, the Royal Commission on the Distribution of Income and Wealth confirmed that dependent children remained "a factor causing low income" both as costs and because they prevented mothers from working. Of families with four or more children, for example, one-half fell into the lowest income quartile. Whereas only 6 percent of childless two-adult families (below retirement age) were in that lowest quartile in 1976, the corresponding share for one-, two-, and three-child two-parent families was 15, 24, and 37 percent respectively. And by the 1990s, it was the case in Britain that "families with children make up nearly all of the *working* low income group."[50]

In West Germany, too, despite the postwar "economic miracle," the same correlation between child-riches and monetary impoverishment identified in the United States manifested itself. A study of wage earners in 1955 explicitly compared the income per family member in families of various sizes with the aforementioned U.S. data. Setting the per-capita income of childless families at 100, the study, the results of which are synthesized in table 3, disclosed a striking similarity between the two countries.

Table 3: **Relative Per-Capita Family Incomes in West Germany (1955) and the United States (1952)**[51]

No. of Children	West Germany	Bavaria	United States
0	100	100	100
1	69	69	74
2	56	55	58
3	47	47	47
4	n.a.	39	36
5	n.a.	36	28
6	n.a.	28	16

Another study, from 1956-57, found a monotonically rising proportion of West German worker-families with net incomes below the level of public assistance rates with an ascending number of children: whereas only 1 percent of families with one child fell within this group of income-weak familes, almost one-fifth of families with five or more children was so classified. Similarly, whereas fewer than 3 percent of children in families with one or two children lived in income-weak families, in the larger families the rate was more than three times higher. Later, the oppositional Christian Democrats, berating the Social Democrats for having failed to stem the precipitous decline in the birth-rate, charged that an employee with an average income could not afford a third child without sliding down into the welfare system. Such complaints become comprehensible against the background of estimates for the United States that the total cost of raising three children amounts to almost three-fifths of a lower-income family's income.[52]

Other analysts have been ambivalent about the direction of causality between children and poverty. Herman Daly has offered the most avowedly syncretistic approach to the issue, devising four social classes or logical categories based on Marxist property classes and (neo-)Malthusian differential fertility. By distinguishing between those who control their fertility and those who do not, Daly labels one subset of property owners the upper class or stable bourgeoisie and the other the middle class or bourgeoisie in transition downward; within the working class, he identifies the classical Malthusian proletariat as precluding the possibility to accumulate its way into capital by procreating uncontrollably, while the neo-Malthusian laborers hold open this possibility by limiting fertility. Despite his combinatory framework, Daly is ultimately not agnostic on the issue of causation since his abstract model appears to make remaining in or moving to a richer or poorer class hinge on individual procreative tastes or volition.[53]

Skeptics or opponents of state intervention, in contrast, see procreationally induced poverty as volitional. Charles Murray, a Reagan- and Gingrich-era policy guru, argues that people who fall below the poverty line by virtue of expanding their families "chose to be poor—or more accurately, they chose to have a child, and unbeknownst to them became poor." In any event, their situation was the

product of the choices they made.[54] Stanley Lebergott, an irreverent labor economist and economic historian, takes an even more cavalier attitude:

> If parents objected to poverty as much as some publicists do, they would never
> have more than two children per family.... Our moral and religious princi-
> ples...all declare that a man and his wife may have any number of children.
> Hence anyone is free to move his family into the "poverty" group: by adding
> children. Our value system declares it desirable for the poor to have as many
> children as they please, however distraught some people may be by the resultant
> impact on the national poverty totals. Hence, if every worker were paid
> $10,000 a year, we would still have poverty—among the families with five, six,
> or ten children.[55]

THE METHODOLOGY OF POVERTY STATISTICS

> Some recent statistical enquiries bring out clearly how important a factor in
> well-being is the size of the family in relation to earnings. This fact is, of
> course, well known in daily life, but it has often been ignored in theoretical
> discussions.[56]

By the time of the Johnson administration's War on Poverty, Mollie Orshansky, a Social Security Administration researcher, had helped create what has
ultimately become a large joint government-academic policy industry by fashion-
ing the U.S. federal government's official definition of poverty, which still dominates the field. The definition of poverty that Orshansky first outlined in 1963 was,
by her own admission, "crude." The sole criterion was whether a person or family
had to devote more than one-third of its income to purchase the items entering into
a low-cost or economy diet priced by the U.S. Department of Agriculture. This
diet worked out to 22 cents per meal per person—the expenditure of which did not
guarantee an adequate diet although any lesser amount made it likely that recommended allowances for certain nutrients could not be met. Orshansky did, to be
sure, soon make the definition considerably more flexible by devising differentia-
tions according to 124 family size, age-sex, and farm-nonfarm classifications, yet
the basic unidimensional criterion kept the definition "relatively crude" and "admittedly arbitrary."[57]

The definition, which the federal government adopted in 1969 as the basis of
its official statistical poverty thresholds, has been subject to repeated and to some
extent devastating methodological criticism, especially for its invariant set of die-
tary customs, underestimated food expenditure-income multiplier, and outdated and
quirky family-size equivalences (designed to make possible comparisons among
families with varying numbers of members of different ages).[58] Many of the
proposed alternative definitions, however, not only are flawed in some way but also
generate results not significantly different from Orshansky's.[59] For this reason and
also because the Bureau of the Census has generated decades worth of series based

solely on the official definition, it is used here, where the chief issue is not the absolute level of poverty but the extent to which the presence of children affects the standard of living.

The make-believe character of the official poverty thresholds should, however, be emphasized, as was done by the President's Commission on Income Maintenance Programs in 1969. It noted, for example, that in 1967, when the poverty threshold for a four-member nonfarm family was $3,553, the moderate family budget developed by the BLS was $7,836 (neither of which allowed for costs of employment or taxes paid) and the national median income was $9,120. A family living just at the threshold and thus definitionally nonpoor was not even budgeted for medical care, insurance, or a bed for each family member let alone school supplies or an occasional movie. Because the food plan presupposes meal-planning and buying skills rare at any income level, only one-fourth of those who actually spent the allotted $1.00 per day per person could achieve the goal of a nutritionally adequate diet. The U.S. poverty threshold thus fails to incorporate a component of sociocultural subsistence, which would permit the poor, as some European welfare programs are designed to do, to continue to participate in the social and cultural life of their environment.[60]

The federal government's certification of extraordinarily low standards of living as nonpoor must therefore be regarded as Pickwickian. Because the per capita incomes of child-rich families are vastly lower than those of smaller or childless families by any measure, the choice of an indicator is not crucial—unless the radical universal commoditization thesis is adopted according to which, "if children themselves are a consumption good, it is not even clear that larger families need more income to maintain the same level of utility."[61] Even if children were their parents' monetized consumption goods, siblings are not one another's; there is no evidence that children themselves adopt their parents' alleged propensity to accept deprivation for the sake of a larger reproductive contribution—at least not until they themselves replicate that behavior as adults.

The final methodological issue that must be considered relates to the possibility that the average family standard of living or average income per family member may be as misleading as economy-wide averages in societies with skewed income distribution. Although the following data presuppose that income is distributed equally among family members, some, especially British historical, qualititative, and empirical survey data suggest that some father-husbands regarded their discretionary expenditures as a first charge on the family income so that: "The financial burden of having an extra child was not...shared equally by all members of the family, but fell with especial severity upon the mother and upon previous children. Some husbands behaved like employers. They did not increase their wives' 'wages' as the size of the family increased."[62] To the extent that unequal power relations permit father-husbands (or parents generally) to engage in such self-regarding economic behavior, their procreativity at the margin might well impoverish their children or wives more than themselves.

CONTEMPORARY DATA FROM THE UNITED STATES

[T]he difficulty is not being born, it is subsisting.[63]

At the outset in 1963, Orshansky provided a comparison of the extent of poverty as measured by her diet-multiplier method and the Council of Economic Adviser's (CEA) flat $3,000 threshold for all families regardless of size (table 4).

Table 4: **Poverty Levels of Families and Unrelated Individuals, 1963**[64]

	Income Below $3,000 (%)	Income Below Economy Diet (%)	Median Income of Male-Headed Husband-Wife Families ($)
Families by Number of Children			
0	25	13	5,415
1	16	12	6,450
2	11	11	7,000
3	14	17	6,900
4	15	23	6,865
5	18	36	6,590
6 or >	30	49	5,765

Poverty as measured by Orshansky's economy diet encompassed at its lowest point one-ninth of all two-child families and then spread continuously until at its high point almost one-half of all families with six or more children fell below the threshold. Although the rank order is identical according to the CEA's method, the absolute shares are considerably lower for the child-richest families because it does not take family size into account but only total income. The rank-ordering is nevertheless preserved because, as the next column reveals, median income peaked at two children and then fell continuously, presumably reflecting the fact that relatively fewer mothers work in the largest families. Despite the fact that all (including single-parent) families with 6 or more children constituted only 2.5 percent of all families, they accounted for 11.0 percent of the entire national poverty gap (the total gap between actual income and the economy-diet income for all individuals and families): "those families with the highest poverty rate—the families with several children—tended also to include the poorest poor."[65]

The foregoing data understate the actual burden of poverty borne by child-rich families insofar as the relatively high poverty share and low median income of the childless families reflected the still very low incomes of older (and presumably largely retired) persons in the period before social security reforms reduced poverty levels among old-age pension recipients to the national average.[66] The impact of the lack of age-differentiation on the poverty shares can be gauged by the fact that the poverty rate in 1963 among families whose head was 65 years of age or older was 24 percent compared to 13 percent among families headed by someone between the ages of 25 and 54 years according to Orshansky's method; the gap was even greater as measured by the CEA data: 45 percent and 12 percent respectively. The incidence of poverty in child-rich families was also significantly higher among black families and female-headed families, between which there was considerable overlap.[67]

Although the incidence of poverty declined generally from the 1950s to the 1970s, the ratio between the poverty rates for the child-richest and child-poorest families was only slightly compressed. An almost perfect monotonically increasing rate of poverty according to family size for whites and blacks was preserved. Table 5 shows the proportion of male-headed families below the poverty level:

Table 5: **Percentage of Male-Headed Families Below Poverty Level, 1959, 1968, and 1974**[68]

	White			Negro		
	1959	1968	1974	1959	1968	1974
No. of Children						
Total	13.3	6.3	4.9	44.2	18.9	14.2
0	14.0	6.8	4.3	34.7	15.4	10.5
1	8.0	4.0	3.9	31.5	11.1	9.5
2	9.5	4.1	3.8	32.8	15.9	14.6
3	13.9	6.0	6.7	58.1	21.0	17.8
4	20.5	8.0	9.8	67.4	23.7	22.6
5	36.3	18.3	15.9	N.A.	34.1	21.2
6 or >	45.0	19.0	21.0	82.4	46.2	44.1

Among male-headed white families, the critical family size was the advent of a fourth child in 1959 and of a fifth child in the later years: the proportion of poor families more than doubled when it supported five children in 1959 and almost doubled in 1968. Among blacks and other groups, whose rate of poverty was catastrophic regardless of family size in 1959, the addition of a third child jolted the poverty rate from one-third to almost three-fifths in 1959; by 1968, the poverty rates among the larger (except the largest) black families had begun to approximate those for white families. The difference here lay in the specific weight of these male-headed families with five or more children: whereas they represented only 12 percent of poor white families in 1959 and 1968, they accounted for almost double that proportion (23 percent to 25 percent respectively) among the other races. By 1974, the shares had declined for both whites and nonwhites (9 percent and 17 percent respectively), but their ratio remained stationary. The degree to which large-family poverty is race-associated is shown by the fact that by 1962, the absolute number of nonwhite families with six or more children permanently surpassed that of white families: if in 1959 the former were 93 percent of the latter, by 1968, nonwhites exceeded whites by 18 percent. This shift was chiefly caused by the increase in large nonwhite female-headed poor families: as the total number of six-child poor families fell by 37 percent from 1959 to 1968, poor nonwhite female-headed families rose absolutely by 53 percent. Their share of all poor six-child families thus increased from 11 percent to 26 percent, whereas that of male-headed white and nonwhite families fell from 44 percent to 34 percent and 37 percent to 28 percent respectively. By the end of the Nixon administration, this trend had become further accentuated: by 1974, female-headed six-or-more-child families had declined absolutely, but now, almost as numerous as their male-headed white families, accounted for 30 percent of all such families.[69]

The largest families constitute, to be sure, only a small segment of the total adult poverty population—albeit a large share of the total number of poor; by the same token, however, they are, by a wide margin, the most profoundly impoverished. In 1965, for example, only 7 percent of nonpoor families (with children) included five or more children compared to 23 percent of poor families.[70]

Table 6 shows the gap between total income and the poverty threshold by the number of children:

Table 6: **Median Gap Between Total Income and Poverty Threshold Among Families and Unrelated Individuals Below Poverty Level, 1965**[71]

	White		Nonwhite	
	Number (000)	Gap ($)	Number (000)	Gap ($)
Unrelated Individuals	3,935	621	831	679
No. of Children				
0	1,844	616	359	736
1	680	1,016	276	910
2	579	1,108	241	1,095
3	566	1,202	270	1,211
4	424	1,333	206	1,518
5	248	1,250	202	1,955
6 or >	249	1,586	307	1,919

Again, the almost perfect monotonically widening poverty gap as the number of children increases is conspicuous. The systematic persistence of such structures seemed to lead some scholars to abandon the problematization of the phenomenon. One student of family planning argued that: "The statement that the poor have high fertility is, in part, redundant. Because the definition of poverty is based upon both income and number of people in the household, the families designated as 'poor'...tend to have more children than other families."[72]

Although Moynihan's controversial 1965 report on black families focused on their alleged fatherlessness, he and others at the time also linked their poverty and size. "Because...Negro families have the largest number of children and the lowest incomes, many Negro fathers literally cannot support their families." That between 1950 and 1960 average nonwhite family size rose from 4.07 to 4.30 while white family size was stable at 3.54 and 3.58 respectively, and the black fertility rate was 40 percent higher, Moynihan concluded Malthusianistically, "must inevitably lead to an unconcealable crisis in Negro unemployment." (From 1959 to 1974, the mean number of children in poor white families declined from 2.99 to 2.51; among poor black families, the decline from 1969 to 1974 was from 3.36 to 2.87. By 1992, the gap had narrowed even further, the mean number of children having fallen to 2.15 and 2.31 respectively.)[73]

At the same time, the American Academy of Arts and Sciences arranged a symposium, *The American Negro*, in which the same issue was taken up. Philip Hauser, one of the most eminent American students of population, found that blacks in the United States, 350 years after their introduction into North America, remained quasi-foreign bodies; they were going through the throes of the historic demographic transition that European peoples had long ago completed:

> The Negro, like the inhabitant of the developing regions in Asia, Latin America, and Africa, in his new exposure to amenities of twentieth-century living, is experiencing rapidly declining mortality while fertility rates either remain high or...actually increase.... The high birth rate also operates...to contribute to the misery of the Negro population.... High fertility with its consequent large family size handicaps the Negro by limiting the investments the family can make in human resources—that is, in the education and training of the child.... Poverty and high fertility are at present linked in the United States, as in the world as a whole. Largely unrestrained birth rates are found primarily among the poor and uneducated. [M]uch more remains to be done to help the relatively uneducated and impoverished Negro family to restrict its size.[74]

Harold Sheppard tried to remove any racist taint from the mission of breaking the "vicious circle of poverty, large family size...and high unemployment rates": "If all Negroes were in the upper 5 percent of the income distribution, concern about family size would...be irrelevant.... Millionaires—Negro or white—can afford to have families of six or more children.... Low-income persons—Negro or white—cannot afford large families, at least in the current stage of human history."[75]

Developments during the next two decades shed interesting light on this claim. From 1968 to 1986, the proportion of black children in husband-wife families with four or more children fell sharply, from 38 percent to 9 percent, while the poverty rate among such children declined from 38 percent to 25 percent. Among white children, on the other hand, while the proportion of children in two-parent four-or-more child families fell almost as much, from 33 percent to 10 percent, their poverty rate almost doubled—from 13 percent to 24 percent.[76] Thus, whereas in the late 1960s, the poverty rate among black children in the largest two-parent families had been almost triple that among whites, two decades later the rates virtually coincided. By the latter half of the 1980s, even among the most privileged and stable families with the greatest access to dual incomes, white husband-wife families, one-quarter could not raise four children without sinking into official poverty.

Later more detailed income data underscore the disadvantaged position of families with children. Table 7 shows the share in the total number of family units (including unrelated individuals) of selected groups and the development of the adequacy of their income. The "adjusted family income" is pretax cash family income measured as a percentage of the appropriate official poverty thresholds adjusted for inflation.

Thus whereas the median income of all two-earner married couples with chil-

Table 7: **Adjusted Family Income of Selected Groups, 1970 and 1986** (in %)[77]

	Share of All Families		Adjusted Income		Below Poverty Threshold	
	1970	1986	1970	1986	1970	1986
Family Type						
Nonelderly Childless Families	22	21		491	4	4
1 Worker			393	471		
2 Workers			541	642		
Unrelated Individuals	14	23		289	22	18
1 Worker			354	397		
Married Couples with Children	36	25		336	7	7
1 Worker			271	329		
2 Workers			362	449		
Elderly Childless Families	10	10		323	14	4
0 Workers			175	286		
1 Worker			358	473		
2 Workers			460	614		

dren was 4.5 times the poverty threshold in 1986, that of two-earner nonelderly childless couples was 6.5 times the poverty threshold. A similar gap separates the one-earner couples. These figures still underestimate the burdens of reproduction insofar as the data for married couples with children refer to all such families; if the income adequacy of the child-richest families had been published and were segregated out, it would fall much below that of the average for all such families. Even these undifferentiated data show that 22 percent of married couples with children had adjusted incomes below twice the poverty threshold compared to only 13 percent of nonelderly childless couples.

Not only do nonelderly working unrelated individuals rise farther above the threshold than one-earner married couples with children, but even elderly childless couples had by 1986 reached virtual parity with such married couples; and whereas in 1970, nonworking elderly childless couples' adjusted income was only 65 percent of one-earner married couples with children, by 1986 it had risen to 87 percent—meaning in effect that it was higher than that of the child-richer families

The greater empirical detail that Bureau of the Census collected, processed, and published in recent years (but ceased doing for 1993)[78] makes it possible to give a sharper comparative profile of reproduction-related poverty. Table 8 shows the specific weight of selected groups among the poor in 1992:

Table 8: **Persons in Poverty in the United States, 1992**[79]

Group	Number (000)	Share of All Poor (%)	Poverty Rate (%)	Share of National Population (%)	Index of Severity (%)
Total	36,880	100	14.5		
Unrelated Individuals	7,991	21.7	21.8	14.5	150
Families & Subfamilies	28,890	78.3	13.3	85.5	92
Families	27,947	75.8	13.0	84.9	89
Families w/children	24,008	65.1	17.4	54.4	120
Children	13,876	37.6	21.1	25.9	145
Married couples	12,830	34.8	7.5	67.5	52
Children	5,268	14.3	10.9	19.1	75
Spouseless mothers	13,716	37.2	38.5	14.0	266
Children	8,032	21.8	54.3	3.2	681
Children	14,432	39.1	21.7	26.2	149
Unrelated subfamilies	943	2.6	54.8	0.6	433
Children	556	1.5	59.9	0.4	375
Adults w/ children	10,484	28.4	11.0	28.8	99
Adults wo/children	11,930	32.3	10.7	44.1	73
Married couples	2,306	6.3	4.1	22.1	29
2-person families headed by person 65+	1,384	3.8	7.6	7.2	53
Individuals 65+	2,498	6.8	24.9	4.0	170
Individuals <65	5,493	14.9	20.6	10.5	142

Despite the absence of data differentiated by number of children, the profile is nevertheless unmistakable. The poverty rate among adults in families with children, who accounted for 29 percent of the population, was, at 11 percent, both below the national average of 14.5 percent and barely higher than that of all adults without children (10.7 percent). But a more fine-grained examination reveals much larger gaps. Most important, the poverty rate among married couples without children, who make up 22 percent of the total population, was only 4.1 percent. Although the poverty rate among children, who constituted a little more than one-quarter of the total population, was 21 percent, this figure was elevated by the massive poverty characteristic of households headed by spouseless females. Whereas the poverty rate among married couples was 7.5 percent and among their children 10.9 percent, the corresponding rates among spouseless female-headed families and their children were 38.5 percent and 54.3 percent respectively. The index of severity in the final column adds another dimension to the poverty rate. It expresses the group's share of the poor population as divided by its share of the total population. Ratings below 100 or above 100 show that the group in question has disproportionately escaped or been trapped in poverty. Married couples without children are the most underrepresented group, whereas the children of single mothers are by far the most overrepresented.

Tables 9 and 10 reintroduce the number of children as a reference point. They show the poverty rate and average family income by the number of children in 1987, the last year for which the Bureau of the Census has published data at this level of detail.

Table 9: Poverty Rates (in %) of Families by Number of Children, 1987[80]

	All Families All Races		Spouseless Black Female Head		All White Families Except Spouseless Female Heads	
	Number	Rate	Number	Rate	Number	Rate
No. of Children						
Total	65,133	10.8	3,074	51.8	48,809	5.5
0	31,175	4.9	637	22.4	25,405	3.7
1	14,359	12.0	972	42.3	9,614	5.1
2	12,500	13.8	729	60.3	9,112	6.0
3	4,904	24.4	414	80.1	3,356	11.5
4	1,503	35.3	199	81.1	934	19.6
5	389	44.7	50	NA	239	28.3
6	174	54.2	32	NA	91	38.2
7+	128	54.8	40	NA	59	NA

Table 9 shows the poverty rate for three groups of families: all families and races, those headed by black single mothers, and all white families except those headed by single mothers. Among white two-parent families, raising one or two children placed only 5 or 6 percent in poverty—only 1 or 2 percentage points higher than that of childless families, which, however, included the elderly. Although one additional child almost doubled the poverty rate, it still remained below the national average. Four children, however, almost doubled the rate again, to one-fifth. Thus even this most securely composed group could not reproduce one or two children above the replacement level without running a significant risk of impoverishment. The deterioration of procreative conditions over time is manifest. At the depth of the Reaganomic depression, poverty rates rose to 13.8 and 14.7 percent for three-child, 22.4 and 21.6 percent for four-child, and 29.9 and 31.2 percent for five-child families in 1982 and 1983 respectively.[81] These rates were double those prevailing in 1974 (table 5); comparable rates then were recorded only in families with an additional two children. The poverty rates among families headed by single black mothers were catastrophically high for all birth orders.

As shown in table 10, mean income in 1987 peaked for all married couples at one child and per capita income thus fell off quite steeply in the child-richer families. The mean total income of families with six or more children was only 65 percent of that of families with one child. The configurations 12 years earlier were somewhat different. In 1975, median income among white families peaked in those with three children; the poorest and child-richest families had income 86 percent of that peak. Among black couples, income peaked in two-child families; in the largest families mean income reached 74 percent of that peak.

CPS poverty data for 1992, as indicated in table 11, underscore the vastly dif-

Table 10: **Average Income of Married Couples, 1987 and 1975**[82]

	1987 All		1975 White	Black
	No. of Families (000)	Mean Income ($000)	Mean Income ($000)	Mean Income ($000)
No. of Children				
0	26,273	39,392	15,976	11,537
1	10,260	43,701	17,629	13,683
2	9,853	42,052	18,142	14,379
3	3,809	37,976	18,318	13,076
4	1,133	35,491	17,655	13,461
5	282	32,428	16,495	11,517
6 or more	199	28,259	15,829	10,673

fering poverty rates even according to a compressed range of children and age of family head:

Table 11: **Poverty Rates Among Married Couples, 1992**[83]

Without Children

	White		Black	
	No. of Families (000)	Poverty Rate (%)	No. of Families (000)	Poverty Rate (%)
Age of Head				
<25	621	7.3	26	NA
25-34	2,547	1.6	128	0.9
35-44	2,238	2.2	208	5.7
45-64	11,482	3.3	715	6.2

With 1 Child

	White		Black	
	No. of Families (000)	Poverty Rate (%)	No. of Families (000)	Poverty Rate (%)
Age of Head				
<25	442	16.7	43	NA
25-34	2,424	4.3	222	10.7
35-44	2,785	3.0	252	7.5
45-64	2,768	3.7	290	9.1

With 2 or More Children

	White		Black	
	No. of Families (000)	Poverty Rate (%)	No. of Families (000)	Poverty Rate (%)
Age of Head				
<25	250	39.2	45	NA
25-34	4,468	12.7	444	21.2
35-44	6,936	6.4	537	10.9
45-64	2,083	9.5	257	20.3

Among husband-and-wife families without children—regardless of whether both spouses are employed—the rate of poverty is very small. Its highest level, disregarding the minuscule youngest cohort, is a mere 1 in 16 among black couples aged 45 to 64 years. Intriguingly, the lowest level, less than 1 percent, is also recorded among black couples—those 25 to 34 years old. The problem, in this respect, for black economic welfare is that childless black couples account for a very small share of the total black population. Thus white married childless couples aged 25 to 64 years are 76 percent as numerous as their counterparts with children and more than three times as numerous as households with children headed by spouseless women aged 18 to 64 years; there are, however, only about half as many 25- to 64-year-old black married couples without children as their counterparts with children and little more than a third as many as single mothers.[84]

White married couples with only one child (again bracketing those under 25) also experience very little official poverty; and even among one-child black couples, the highest poverty rate of 10.7 percent (for 25 to 34-year-old heads) is lower than the national average of 11.7 percent for all families.[85] Lumping together all married couples with two or more children, as the published data do, suppresses the characteristically extreme poverty rates among the child-richer whites (which here peak at one-eighth in the 24 to 34-year-old group), but does reveal that among blacks, only the peak-earning 35-44 year-old group escaped the one-in-five chance of poverty.

A more detailed overview of the familial structure of poverty in 1992 emerges from the matrix of table 12, which matches number of children and family size:

Table 12: **Poverty Rates of 1- and 2-Adult Families by Number of Children, 1992**[86]

Number of Persons

No. of Children	1	2	3	4	5	6	7	8	9+	Share of all Poor Persons (%)	Poverty Rate by Persons (%)
0	21.8	5.8								33.2	10.7
1		36.6	7.1							14.4	11.5
2			44.9	8.1						19.7	14.1
3				66.3	15.6					16.2	22.6
4					87.6	23.8				8.4	34.3
5						95.5	33.9			4.0	44.8
6							100.0	43.6		2.1	62.8
7								100.0	60.0	1.2	62.4
8									66.7	0.6	68.9

The matrix sharply contrasts the poverty rates for two-parent and single-parent families as they both rise monotonically with the number of children. Single-parent families (the lower diagonal row) begin with a very high rate of almost 37 percent even for one child and quickly descend to near-universal poverty with five children and universal poverty with six; two-adult households (the upper diagonal row) that refrain from above-replacement-level reproduction by and large manage to stave off poverty, but once they have a third child, almost one in six is poor.[87] Two-person childless families achieved the lowest rate, whereas even among single persons under age 65 one-fifth were poor. This somewhat surprising result derives in part from the very high poverty rate among 15-to-24-year-old unrelated individuals, which reached 32 percent in 1988.[88] The next-to-last column (which adds up to 100 percent) shows the share of all impoverished persons according to the number of children per family. Thus childless families of all sizes accounted for one-third of all families in poverty; the child-richest families, despite their extraordinarily high rates of poverty, accounted for a small proportion of all poor families because their total numbers were so small. By 1992, only 259,000 families were composed of six or more children—only one-fifth as many as in 1965; whereas 2-child families were only 6 times as common as 6-or-more-child families in the mid-1960s, by the early 1990s there were 52 times as many of them. Whereas the median income of the child-richest husband-and-wife families in 1970 was marginally higher than that of two-child families, by 1987 the smaller families' income was 44 percent higher.[89] Similarly, the last column shows that the rate of poverty rises almost perfectly monotonically from one-tenth for childless families to more than two-thirds among families with eight or more children.

Two contrary trends in family structure and size shaped the distribution of poverty. On the one hand, the number of children whom families had to support declined significantly. From 1960 to 1990, the proportion of one- and two-child families rose from 64 percent to 80 percent of families with children, whereas the child-richer families declined from 36 percent to 20 percent. The increasing proportion—from 40 percent to 60 percent between 1970 and 1990—of dual-earner two-parent families brought greater purchasing power to bear in raising children. During the same period, however, child-supporters' economic power also declined. Whereas in 1960 there were ten times as many married couples with children as single parents, by 1990 the ratio had fallen to three to one. The overall result was that the poverty rate for families with children rose from 12.3 percent during the 1970s to 16.5 percent during the 1980s.[90]

The impact of children on the standard of living of women without spouses is portrayed in table 13. White or black, for single mothers the economic burden of supporting children is crushing. For childless single white women between the ages of 25 and 54, poverty is relatively marginal, peaking at about one-sixth for women 45 to 64 years old. Single black women even without children, however, face a much harsher economic environment: in no age group does the poverty rate fall even as low as one-quarter. The gender comparison is instructive: childless single men have lower poverty rates in all age groups but especially among those aged 55 and older. But whereas single white men experience comparatively little poverty, black men in all age groups show rates as much as three times higher. Thus poverty, which is clearly associated with race and gender, is exacerbated by the economic consequences of procreation. This linkage is especially pronounced among young heads of families. Whereas 48 percent of 15-24 year-old family heads with children lived in poverty in 1988, only 7 percent of their childless counterparts did.[91]

Table 13: **Poverty Rates Among Women, 1992**[92]

Female Householder Without Spouse and with Children

	White		Black	
	Number (000)	Rate (%)	Number (000)	Rate (%)
Age				
Total	5,060	39.1	2,898	57.2
< 18	11	NA	1	NA
18-24	510	75.2	355	81.5
25-44	3,492	38.5	1,981	56.7
45-64	873	23.9	451	43.9
65 +	173	18.5	110	42.2

Unrelated Female Individuals

	White			Black		
	Number (000)	Rate (%)	(Men) (%)	Number (000)	Rate (%)	(Men) (%)
Total	16,886	22.8	(15.6)	2,093	41.8	(30.3)
< 18	71	NA		5	NA	
18-24	1,832	36.5	(27.8)	197	43.9	(42.7)
25-44	4,471	14.7	(12.3)	609	26.4	(24.7)
45-64	3,565	22.8	(14.8)	632	39.2	(30.3)
65 +	6,946	23.8	(14.5)	651	57.5	(44.4)

Although race and sex discrimination, by limiting opportunities in manifold dimensions, worsens the precarious economic condition of nonwhites and women, the financial responsibility for children constitutes an independent source of impoverishment, which depresses the living standards of even the most privileged group—white men. This hierarchical relationship can be seen in tables 14 and 15.

Table 14: **Poverty Rates by Family Type, Sex, and Presence of Children, 1992**[93]

	White		Black	
	Without Children	With Children	Without Children	With Children
Type of Family				
Married Couple	3.7	7.6	9.6	15.4
Male Householder	7.4	19.3	15.2	33.3
Female Householder	8.0	39.1	22.5	57.2

Wifeless male householders with children are relatively uncommon—one and a quarter million whites and a quarter-million blacks, representing only one-fourth and one-twelfth respectively of their female counterparts. Yet whereas poverty rates among the childless are quite similar, they are about twice as high among spouseless women with children as spouseless men of both races.

Table 15: **Median Income (in $) by Family Type, Sex, and Presence of Children, 1992**[94]

	White			Black		
	Number of Children					
	0	1	2 +	0	1	2+
Type of Family						
Married Couple	40,372	46,277	44,719	30,860	39,919	34,626
Male Householder	35,568	22,003	26,991	24,942	16,928	19,558
Female Householder	29,323	17,332	14,179	19,548	13,297	8,789

Several structural characteristics are conspicuous in table 15. First, whereas married couples with children have somewhat higher total incomes than their child-less counterparts, spouseless male and female householder-parents have much lower total incomes than their childless counterparts. Perhaps Malthus's imperative is operative: reproduction compels parents to work more—but only where two parents are present can this compulsion routinely be implemented. Second, whereas spouseless fathers with two or more children have higher incomes than those with only one, single mothers, presumably, at least in part, because their child-care duties interfere with employment, experience a further decline in income as their financial responsibilities extend from one to two or more children. Interestingly, one reason that single fathers' earning power may be less impeded by child-care responsibilities than single mothers' is that a much lower proportion of male single parents actually lives alone. In 1988, for example, only 58 percent of them did compared to 78 percent of their female counterparts; the remainder cohabited with a person of the opposite sex or lived with other adults.[95]

The inadequacy of one working parent's income to sustain a family has driven the trend toward the proletarianization of mothers. That the income-distributional basis of family allowances has not disppeared since Ricardo debated the issue 180 years ago emerges from recent wage data. Table 16 shows the proportion of all jobs and hourly jobs compensated at less than the official poverty threshold for various family sizes:

Table 16: **Share of Jobs Paying Wages Below Poverty Threshold, 1985 (in %)**[96]

No. Family Members	All Jobs	Hourly Jobs
2	9.5	11.1
3	19.2	25.9
4	31.6	42.6
5	41.9	54.5

With almost half of all jobs inadequately compensated to sustain a modal-sized family above poverty level (the figures for hourly jobs are underestimates because they do not reflect the fact that many such jobs are less than full-time) and 84 percent of working-poor families having children, double-earner families have unsurprisingly become the norm. Thus in a manner not anticipated by Malthus—namely, through the massive incorporation of mothers into the wage-earning labor force—the ever-looming threat of market-mediated poverty has precluded the slackening of effort the prospect of which so horrified Malthus.

The limitations on the ability of single parents to combine care for children with higher-paid employment are a persistent tendency. In 1974, for example, only 5 percent of female family heads all of whose children were under six years old worked year-round full-time; among them the poverty rate was only 11 percent. Husband-wife couples have also not systematically responded positively to the advent of children by securing additional income. Thus, for example in 1975, the median income of childless couples aged 25 to 44 was more than $1,000 higher than of those with children. This lack of consistency is, however, largely a function of the lumping together of child-poor and child-rich families. Husband-and-wife couples with children do earn more than childless couples but only up to a certain number of children, which varies from one to three. At that point, child-care work presumably becomes so overwhelming that the mother cannot remain in full-time paid employment. Among the 8 percent of single mothers living alone who managed to work in paid employment full-time all-year, the poverty rate in 1988 was 17 percent compared to 63 percent for all single mothers.[97] The association between full-time year-round employment and poverty is strikingly illustrated in table 17.

Table 17: **Poverty Rates (in %) Among Selected Groups of Year-Round Full-Time Workers, 1992**[98]

| | White | | Black | |
	Poverty Rate	Year-Round Full-Timers as Share of Group	Poverty Rate	Year-Round Full-Timers as Share of Group
Household Relationship				
Married couple w/children < 6 years	1.2	26	3.8	38
Spouseless female householder w/ children < 6 years	11.1	31	20.5	27
Unrelated individual				
Male	3.2	59	3.8	50
Female	3.2	55	0.8	46

Although the poverty rates are somewhat higher among blacks than whites—except single black women, who exhibit the lowest rate among all age-race-household relationships combinations—all these categories, which include several of the most vulnerable, displayed extraordinarily low rates. The problem, especially for single mothers with young children, is that only a minority work these full schedules. The Census Bureau's longitudinal Survey of Income and Program Participation (SIPP) corroborates these findings. The poverty rate in the mid-1980s in white and black married-couple families with children in which both parents worked full-time was 1.4 percent and 1.7 percent respectively; where only the husband worked full-time, the so-called family wage failed to keep 7.2 percent of white families and 21.4 percent of black families out of poverty. Full-time wages were also insufficient to furnish 9.3 percent of white and 16.7 percent of black single-mother families with a non-impoverished standard of living.[99]

The diverse composition of the poor is visible from the comparative overview of the development during the 1980s in table 18. On the assumption that neither the elderly nor the disabled became impoverished as a result of having supported children, but rather that previous low income and an underdeveloped social security system are independent sources of their current poverty, these two categories accounted for 35-39 percent of all poor families in the 1980s. This assumption is probably accurate for the disabled, unless widespread disablement is a little-known private and internalized cost of parenting. The other assumption cannot be made so facilely: some nontrivial proportion of the elderly poor would have become less poor had they been in a position to save for their old age what they in fact spent on children, whose own compulsory commitment to the social security system may preclude their financially supporting their aged procreators.[100] Even if reproduction did impoverish some of the elderly, it is unknown what proportion regret or would gladly repeat that course of events.

Table 18: **Composition of Poor Families by Family Type (in %), 1980 and 1988**[101]

	All Families		Poor Families		Poverty Rate	
	1980	1988	1980	1988	1980	1988
Family type						
Elderly-headed	20	20	26	21	19	15
Disabled-headed	5	5	13	14	42	45
Single-parent	7	8	20	22	39	40
Married couple w/children	28	24	13	11	7	6
Families wo/ children	20	20	4	5	3	3
Unrelated individuals	20	23	23	26	16	16
Total	100	100	100	100	14	14

Families with children accounted for only one-third of all poor families although they accounted for a much larger proportion of all poor persons, while the childless constituted the final 30 percent. Childless families and married couples with children exhibited by far the lowest rate of poverty. Since most nonelderly single persons are in transition to a family status, some poverty is itself temporary. Indeed, enhanced old-age pensions especially for single or wid-owed women and improved disability pensions might eliminate most non-reproduction-related official poverty. As of 1988, for example, social insurance and means-tested benefit programs reduced the poverty rate of all disabled-headed families from the 71 percent that would have obtained had they subsisted solely on their private income to 38 percent; the corresponding figures for disabled married couples with and without children were 61 percent and 29 percent, and 42 percent and 16 percent respectively. In 1992, non-means-tested government transfers reduced the poverty rate among whites over 65 living alone from 68 percent to 23 percent; the corresponding rates for blacks were 86 percent and 57 percent respectively.[102]

Because the aforementioned categories in table 18 are mutually exclusive, they submerge and hide overlapping. Thus, for example, of the approximately 2 million impoverished disabled-headed families in 1988, the almost 650,000 with children are not double-counted among the poor families with children. Although it is unknown whether the disability or the economic burden of child-raising was the primary source of impoverishment for these families, it is noteworthy that in 1988 the poverty rate for disabled-headed childless married couples was only 18 percent compared to 31 percent for married couples with children.[103]

The dramatic shifts in composition of the poor population resulting from a focus on persons rather than families are shown in table 19:

Table 19: **Composition of Poor Persons by Family Type (in %), 1980 and 1988**[104]

	All Persons		Poor Persons		Poverty Rate	
	1980	1988	1980	1988	1980	1988
Family type						
Elderly-headed	13	14	16	13	16	12
Disabled-headed	4	4	13	13	40	41
Single-parent	9	10	29	34	42	43
Married couple w/children	46	42	27	23	8	7
Families wo/ children	19	20	5	5	3	3
Unrelated individuals	8	9	10	12	16	16
Total	100	100	100	100	13	13

From this perspective, the elderly- and disabled-headed families accounted for only one-quarter and the childless for one-sixth of all poor persons, whereas families with children constituted 57 percent of the total poverty population.

Overall, the data presented in this chapter underscore the continuing real economic vulnerability of those who make supra-replacement-level procreational contributions. The economic burdens borne by child-rich families can also be illustrated for European countries in spite of the greater equality of market incomes and equalizing redistributional consequences of their social security and children's allowance systems. Table 20 shows the significant gap in average household expenditures between child-rich and other families in the European Economic Community (EEC) in the later 1970s and early 1980s. Table 21 takes into account inequalities within household types by presenting poverty rates for each type as a proportion of the national poverty rate. Unlike U.S. poverty data, which are based on an absolute measure, the European poverty line is defined as 50 percent of the national average equivalent expenditure. Here the influence of children's allowances manifests itself in the fact that in the more advanced countries such as Denmark, Germany, the Netherlands, and the United Kingdom, a significantly above-average poverty rate does not emerge until the third child. In countries with the oldest and most developed allowance systems, Belgium and France, this exacerbated impoverishment either never sets in or only with the fourth child.[105]

Table 20: **Average Equivalent Expenditure per Household Type as a % of the National Average in the EEC, 1978-82**[106]

	BE	DK	GE	GR	FR	IR	IT	NL	PO	UK
Household Type										
1 person <65 yrs	111	130	153	138	129	142	128	126	130	130
1 person >65 yrs	81	93	80	83	73	87	97	62	76	96
Couple, 0 children	103	107	114	101	112	113	112	111	108	112
Couple, 1 child	106	105	106	117	105	115	124	100	124	98
Couple, 2 children	96	91	94	102	93	93	103	88	116	84
Couple, 3 children	90	80	82	84	85	86	80	76	90	80
Couple, 4+children	79				69	71			65	
Single parent	95	87	92	118	93				90	72

Table 21: **Poverty Rates per Household Type as a % of National Poverty Rate in the EEC, 1978-82**[107]

	BE	DK	GE	GR	FR	IR	IT	NL	PO	UK
Household Type										
1 person <65 yrs	85	65	58	59	102	60	42	130	64	104
1 person >65 yrs	213	180	174	208	222	132	98	171	199	89
Couple, 0 children	132	89	100	132	84	102	89	77	97	86
Couple, 1 child	41	49	42	71	52	29	35	55	63	36
Couple, 2 children	59	63	75	66	66	56	74	91	69	84
Couple, 3 children	101	149	135	105	106	77	148	190	115	180
Couple, 4+children	72				179	181			167	
Single parent	177	121	138	42	116				104	182

In half of the countries, relative expenditures of families with even one child are lower than those of childless couples; in all ten countries this relative diminution sets in at the latest with the second child. By the time of the third child, the gap vis-à-vis the childless couple varies between 13 percent and 31 percent. This gap would, as is the case in the United States, be even greater if the predominantly lower-income elderly married couples could be segregated out.

APPENDIX: FINDING CAUSALITY IN THE ABSENCE OF DATA

Mollie Orshansky, the key figure in the creation of the U.S. poverty standard, concluded that the data on per capita income and single-parent female-headed families "suggest...that it is the poor who have more children—not that the family is poor because it has children." Whether or not this claim is empirically correct, it is a non sequitur. In order to sustain it, Orshansky would have had to collect longitudinal data showing that a couple had been poor before the birth of their first child or several children and remained poor after (further) procreation. The kind of frozen-in-time snapshot data that Orshansky used cannot resolve the question of causality: it would be ecologically fallacious to conclude from aggregate data that today's poor large families were yesterday's nonpoor small ones. To be sure, Orshansky later conceded that "most large families that are poor would obviously be somewhat better off if they had fewer children...."[108]

Sheppard, in his report to the congressional subcommittee studying the success of the War on Poverty, formulated the appropriate question more precisely than Orshansky. While conceding—without showing—that a higher proportion of poor adults than nonpoor adults came from poor families, he insisted that combating the fatalistic "poverty breeds poverty" approach presupposes understanding that many nonpoor adults were born into poor families and many poor adults into nonpoor families. The question for him thus became why some people were able to extricate themselves from their childhood poverty orbit and and how they differed from their childhood poverty-mates who were never graduated into some level of nonpoverty. He speculated, again without statistical support, that the key variable was family size. Parents of poor small families had greater per-child economic, educational, and emotional resources to invest in each child, resulting in greater "returns" per capita—including the parents themselves.[109]

To arrive at sound conclusions on causality it would be best to collect comparative data on lifetime income and wealth of those past childbearing age who never procreated and those who did. Such data have, unfortunately, never been collected or tabulated for the United States. Because large-scale government surveys by and large still do not ask the requisite questions to capture the relevant information, several second-best statistical series must serve as surrogates.[110] One caveat is in order in examining data comparing the economic situation of the childless and parents. Economists and demographers often warn of the dangers inherent in basing analyses of life-cycle distributions of assets and burdens on comparisons of households at one point in time: since every adult has been a child and most adults eventually become parents, intertemporal comparisons may be misleading.[111]

One data set that shed some comparative light on the economic consequences of procreation was generated after World War II as government agencies began to collect information relevant to maintaining the high consumption economy that they saw as the antidote to depressive tendencies. The Federal Reserve Board was particularly interested in consumer finances, data on which the Survey Research Center at the University of Michigan proceeded to collect for many years for the federal government. Although the questionnaire for the *Survey of Consumer Finances* secured information on family size, the published data distinguish merely between those with and without children. Because the economic situation of families with one or two children may be closer to that of the childless than to that of families with four or more children, the divide between the childless and parents, though impressive, is less prominent than a more differentiated view would offer. The survey data on liquid assets are the most pertinent. In 1960, for example, 43 percent of childless married couples whose head was 45 or older reported liquid asset holdings in the highest range ($2,000 or more) compared with only 29 percent of their parental counterparts; at the other extreme, only 18 percent of these childless couples had no assets compared with 23 percent of the parents. Eight years later, with the over 45-year-old head defined as in the labor force, 33 percent of the childless held liquid assets of $5,000 or more compared with only 14 percent of the parents; 12 percent of the childless but 18 percent of the parents held no such assets. More particularly, 26 percent of the childless held at least $5,000 in savings accounts whereas only 11 percent of the parents reached that degree of income security. By 1970, 41 percent of the same category of childless reported liquid assets in excess of $5,000 in contrast with only 20 percent of the parents. And, again, in 1971, 41 percent of the older childless but only 18 percent of their parental counterparts had savings of at least $5,000.[112]

A special study carried out for the President's Commission on Income Maintenance Programs based on CPS data and Orshansky's poverty thresholds examined the issue for 1965 and 1966. Specifically, Terence Kelly linked gross flows (escape rates) out of and (entrance rates) into poverty to family size. "Strangely enough," the larger families were disproportionately represented among those who escaped poverty and those did not enter poverty from 1965 to 1966. This counterintuitive result may in part have been a function of the fact that the data on family size did not specify the number of children. Inclusion of a variable for the presence of children under six years of age did, however, alter the picture, indicating that they inhibited escape from and facilitated entrance into poverty. Although this variable did not directly touch on the issue of an addition or departure from the family, Kelly came closer to the point by introducing a variable for changes in family size minus changes in the number of earners. An increase in the number of nonearners (who may not have been children) did decrease the likelihood of escaping and increase that of entering into poverty.[113]

The Bureau of the Census has published data correlating the number of children ever born to married women 45 years and over—that is, women whose childbearing had presumably been completed—with their husbands' annual income. In 1957, a perfect monotonic decline obtained: from 3.8 children in the under-$1,000 income bracket to 2.1 children in the over-$7,000 group. Using total family income as the reference point in 1964 generated the same perfect negative correlation: women in families with income below $2,000 had given birth to 3.5 children as compared to 2.2 children in families with more than $10,000 income. The 1960 Census of Population collected data that come closer to capturing the desired relationship. Among white wives 50 years and older, there was again a perfect mono-tonic decline in children ever born per mother as family income rose: from 4.0 in the under-$2,000 group to 2.7 in the over-$15,000 group.[114]

The 1970 Census of Population provided even more pertinent detail. The focus here is on total family income and on wives in the labor force inasmuch as among those who have remained voluntarily childless or who have voluntarily curtailed their fertility, the wife's income plays an important part in reproductive decisions.[115] A revealing comparison is possible between the fertility of working white wives aged 45 to 49 in the richest group ($25,000 or more in 1969) and those not in the labor force in all income groups at or below the official poverty thresholds adjusted for family size. The impressive result is that only 11 percent of the highest-income wives in the labor force had given birth to five or more children in contrast with 35 percent of all poor wives; whereas 31 percent of the affluent working wives had produced two children, only 17 percent of the poor women had.[116] Such data may reflect the cumulative impact of procreation on lifetime living standards since some appreciable number of these families presumably no longer supported children under 18 years of age. The families less burdened by the necessity of supporting large numbers of children generated higher incomes even after procreation had ceased. Even these data, however, cannot demonstrate that families became poor as a result of above-average reproduction or that others did not become impoverished because they engaged in below-average procreation.

The longitudinal SIPP also sheds some light on this question. It discovered that in the mid-1980s, approximately two-fifths of white married-couple households with children that had existed for one year and were poor at the end of the year had not been poor at the beginning of the year; of white single-mothers only one-sixth made the transition into poverty. Among newly formed white married-couple households with children less than one year old and poor at the end of the year, 60 percent were maintained by people who had not been poor at the beginning of the year; the proportion among single mothers was similar, but that of single-mother households that had emerged from married-couple households was three-fourths. Although the study did not identify the causes of the impoverishment, it found that in 28 percent of the transitions into poverty among newly formed and continuing households the parents experienced no reduction in work; it speculated that in some of these cases the advent of additional persons in the family may have thrust it below the poverty threshold. Since SIPP did not explore the reasons for families' original poverty, it also fails to resolve this alleged chicken-and-egg controversy.[117]

Perhaps the most creative effort at unraveling causality was undertaken by James Smith, who used a file constructed from the 1970 wave of the Institute for Social Research's *Panel Study of Income Dynamics*. Smith in effect simulated a birth strike among this representative sample of the U.S. noninstitutional population by identifying each record for a family below Orshansky's poverty level with a child one year old and then deleting the child and recalculating the family's poverty status. He repeated this simulated birth control for ten years into the past. As a result of this rewriting of reproductive history, the number of poor families declined by 40 percent and that of poor persons by 60 percent. After ten years, the decline in the number of poor persons was proportionally greatest among families that began with four children and smallest among one-child families. The decreases in ascending order from one- to eight-child families were as follows: 37, 63, 81, 94, 88, 76, 82, and 80 percent respectively. Among families headed by white males between the ages of 20 and 50, the number of persons in poverty fell by 79 percent. Because the angel of death passed over all childless households, unrelated individuals and persons in childless families rose as a proportion of all the poor from 18 percent to 45 percent; persons in families with four or more children fell from 30 percent to 8 percent. These illuminating results cannot, however, reveal whether some third factor(s) stand behind and explain both above-average procreativity and poverty.[118]

NOTES

1. "If You're a Businessman, This Chart May Be The Shape of Your Future," *Forbes* 110 (5):37-44 at 38 (Sept. 1, 1972).

2. Matthew Carey, *An Appeal to the Wealthy of the Land* 11 (1833); Mary Jo Bane & David Ellwood, "One Fifth of the Nation's Children: Why Are They Poor?" *Science* 245:1047-53 (Sept. 8, 1989); table 8 below.

3. Margaret Sanger, "Morality and Birth Control," *Birth Control Rev.* 2 (2): 11, 14 (Feb.-Mar. 1918).

4. Mahmood Mamdani, *The Myth of Population Control: Family, Caste, and Class in an Indian Village* 14 (1973 [1972]).

5. *American Families and the Economy: The High Costs of Living* (Richard Nelson & Felicity Skidmore eds., 1983); *Escape from Poverty: What Makes a Difference for Children?* (P. Lindsay Chase-Lansdale & Jeanne Brooks-Gunn, eds., 1995); Susan Chira, "Study Confirms Worst Fears on U.S. Children," *N.Y. Times*, Apr. 12, 1994, at A1, col. 2 (nat. ed.); National Commission on Children, *Beyond Rhetoric: A New American Agenda for Children and Families* 24 (1991); GAO, *Poverty Trends, 1980-88: Changes in Family Composition and Income Sources Among the Poor* 61 (GAO/PEMD-92-34, 1992); Michael Harrington, *The New American Poverty* 196 (1985 [1984]). Far from denying mothers agency, Harrington granted it to both procreators: "it is not their decision, but the man's, that pushes them under the poverty line." *Ibid.* at 194.

232   *Dilemmas of Laissez-Faire Population Policy*

6. Victor Fuchs, "What's Leaving Children Poor?" *Wall Street Journal*, Oct. 2, 1986, at 30, col. 4; *idem*, "Why Are Children Poor?" tab. 3 at 9 (NBER Working Paper No. 1984, July 1986).

7. Joan Aldous & Reuben Hill, "Breaking the Poverty Cycle: Strategic Points for Intervention," *Social Work* 14 (3):3-12 at 12 (July 1969) (quote); Christiane Dienel, "Familien vor Armut bewahren: Politik zur Existenzsicherung von Familien in Europa," in *Zwölf Wege der Familienpolitik in der Europäischen Gemeinschaft: Eigenständige Systeme und vergleichbare Qualitäten* 461-500 at 468-69 (Erika Neubauer at al. eds., 1993).

8. Eveline Burns, "Childhood Poverty and the Children's Allowance," in *Children's Allowances and the Economic Welfare of Children: The Report of a Conference* 3, 5 (Eveline Burns ed., 1968). And even more obliquely: "Along with old-age, disability, or death of the bread winner, the years of child-raising can place special pressure on the economic situation of a family." Mollie Orshansky, "Benefits and Costs of Children," in *ibid.* at 178.

9. Richard Titmuss & Kathleen Titmuss, *Parents Revolt* 96 (1985 [1942]) (quote); *Family Planning and Population Research: Hearings Before the Subcommittee on Health of the Senate Committee on Labor and Public Welfare*, 91st Cong., 1st & 2d Sess. 26 (1970) (quote).

10. C. Duchâtel, *De la Charité, dans ses rapports avec l'état moral et le bien-être des classes inférieures de la société* 314 (1829); Alban de Villeneuve-Bargemont, *Économie politique chrétienne, ou recherches sur la nature et les causes du paupérisme, en France et en Europe, et sur les moyens de le soulager et de le prévenir* 2:28 n.1, 312 (1834).

11. Ethel Elderton et al., *On the Correlation of Fertility of Social Value with Social Value: A Cooperative Study* tab. A at 3 (1913) (Pearson study); B. Seebohm Rowntree, *Poverty: A Study of Town Life* 119-20 (1908 [1901]) (large families were next in importance to low wages [52 percent] as a cause of poverty); A.L. Bowley & Margaret Hogg, *Has Poverty Diminished? A Sequel to "Livelihood and Poverty"* tab. F at 19 (1925); B. Seebohm Rowntree, *Poverty and Progress: A Second Social Survey of York* 109-10, 115 (1941).

12. B. Seebohm Rowntree, "Family Allowances," *Contemporary Rev.* No. 154 at 287-94 at 294 (Sept. 1938).

13. Rowntree, *Poverty and Progress* at 161, 164, 47-48, 112, 168, 294-95, 35-37, 144-49.

14. J. Hajnal & A.M. Henderson, "The Economic Position of the Family," in 5 *Papers of the Royal Commission on Population: Memoranda Presented to the Royal Commission* 1-33 at 10-18 (quote at 11) (1950).

15. John Yudkin, "Nutrition and Size of Family," *Lancet* 247/2: 384-87 (1944). "Large" families were those with three or more children.

16. W.H. Beveridge, "The Standard of Living," *Times*, Jan. 12, 1940, at 7, col. 5 (letter to editor); *Parliamentary Debates*, House of Commons, 5th Series, 380:1857 (June 23, 1942) (Wing-Commander Wight).

17. *Ibid.* at 1878-79 (Mr. MacLaren).

18. Alva Myrdal, *Nation and Family: The Swedish Experiment in Democratic Family and Population Policy* 66, 76 (1941); Gunnar Myrdal, *Challenge to Affluence* 63 (1965 [1962]).

19. Thomas Robert Malthus, *An Essay on the Principle of Population* (7th ed.), in *idem*, *On Population* 498 (Gertrude Himmelfarb ed., 1960 [1872]) (quote); Alva Myrdal & Gunnar Myrdal, *Kris i befolkningsfrågan* 10-11 (1934); Alva Myrdal, *Nation and Family* at 99 (quote).

20. Charles Booth, 17 *Life and Labour of the People in London: Notes on Social Influences and Conclusion* 20 (1903). Nevertheless, Booth's position should not be confused with the super-Malthusian pessimism that abandons any hope of motivating a lower class/lumpenproletariat to control its fertility. Edward Banfield, *The Unheavenly City: The Nature and Future of Our Urban Crisis* 214-15, 220-21 (1970).

21. G. Bernard Shaw, "The Basis of Socialism," in *Fabian Essays in Socialism* 15-45 at 36 (*idem* ed., n.d. [1889]).

22. Arsène Dumont, *Dépopulation et civilisation: Étude démographique* 106, vi, 110, 127-28 (1890).

23. "Condition of Workingmen's Families," in [Mass.] Bureau of Statistics of Labor, *Sixth Annual Report* 189-450 at 371, 373 (Public Document No. 31, Mar. 1875).

24. *Ibid.*, tab. XIII at 373, tab. XV at 377.

25. Calculated according to [U.S.] Commissioner of Labor, *Sixth Annual Report: 1890: Cost of Production: Iron, Steel, Coal, Etc.* tab. 4 at 679 (1891); *idem, Eighteenth Annual Report, 1903: Cost of Living and Retail Prices of Food*, tab. V.E. at 568, V.H. at 573-77 (1904).

26. Robert Chapin, *The Standard of Living Among Workingmen's Families in New York City* 248 (1909); Louise More, *Wage-Earners' Budgets: A Study of Standards and Cost of Living in New York City* 25, 87 (1907); S. Patterson, *Social Aspects of Industry: A Survey of Labor Problems and Causes of Industrial Unrest* 169-70 (1929).

27. Befolkningskommissionen, *Betänkande i sexualfrågan*, tab. 3 at 26 (Statens offentliga utredningar, 1936:59, 1938); Rich. Sterner, "Levnadsstandarden i svenska familjer," in *ibid.* at 207-51, tab. 7 at 225.

28. Royal Commission on Population, *Report* 137-38 (Cmd. 7695, 1949); M. Soutar, E. Wilkins, & P. Sargant Florence, *Nutrition and Size of Family: Report on a New Housing Estate—1939*, at 33-37, 48 (1942) (quote at 36).

29. Hajnal & Henderson, "The Economic Position of the Family" at 7.

30. Frank Lorimer, Ellen Winston, & Louise Kiser, *Foundations of American Population Policy* tab. 13 at 120 (1940); I.S. Falk & Barkev Sanders, "The Economic Status of Urban Families and Children," *Social Security Bull.* 2 (5):25-34 at 31, tab. 7 at 32 (May 1939) (quote). For similar figures for single-family households, see Barkev Sanders, "Children and Income in Urban Single-Family Households," *ibid.* 2 (11):3-10, tab. 2 at 4 (Nov. 1939). This pattern was replicated within family types; in three- and four-person families with three workers, 26.4 percent of those with no children received either relief or less than $1,000 in income, whereas 41.7 percent of those with one child fell into that lowest group. Barkev Sanders & Anne Kantor, "Income, Children, and Gainful Workers in Urban Single-Family Households," *ibid.* 3 (2):21-30, tab. 3 at 24 (Feb. 1940). For the same year, another government study revealed that among two-adult urban families 15 percent of those with one child had insufficient funds to maintain themselves at the emergency standard but failed to benefit from any relief program; the corresponding figure among five-child families was 35 percent. *Security, Work, and Relief: Report of the Committee on Long-Range Work and Relief Policies to the National Resources Planning Board* 155 (1942).

31. Frank Lorimer & Herbert Roback, "Economics of the Family Relative to the Number of Children," *Milbank Memorial Fund Q.* 18 (2):114-36 at 114-15 (Apr. 1940).

32. U.S. BLS, *Money Disbursements of Wage Earners and Clerical Workers 1934-36: Summary Volume*, tab. 2 at 53, tab. 8 at 62 (Bull. No. 638, 1941) (written by Faith Williams & Alice Hanson).

33. U.S. Bureau of the Census, *Sixteenth Census of the United States: 1940, Population: Families: Family Wage or Salary Income in 1939*, tab. 9 at 107-11 (1943). Because the Bureau of the Census collected only wage and salary data for families with income other than wages and salaries and thus gave no accurate account of their total income, they have been disregarded here.

34. U.S. Bureau of the Census, "Per Capita Income in Wage-Earner Families, By Size of Family: 1939," at 1 (Ser. P-44, No. 19, Sept. 8, 1944).

35. The following discussion casts doubt on the assertion that from the end of World War II until 1962 poverty was seldom discussed let alone a constituent part of political discourse. Charles Murray, *Losing Ground: American Social Policy, 1950-1980*, at 4-5, 26 (2d ed. 1994 [1984]).

36. Amos Warner, *American Charities* 60 (1908 [1894]) (rev. by Mary Coolidge) (quote); Amos Warner, "Notes on the Statistical Determination of the Causes of Poverty," *Pubs. Am. Statistical Assoc.* (n.s.) 1 (5):183-201 at 184, 197 (Mar. 1889) (quote); Ernest Burgess, "Special Report I. A Study of Wage-Earning Families in Chicago," *Report of the Health Insurance Commission of the State of Illinois* 179-317 at 280, 281 (1919) (quote). Investigators of charity relief did recognize large family size as an important "disability" of recipients; e.g., Edward Devine, *Misery and Its Causes* 204, 212 (1913).

37. U.S. Congress, Staff of the Subcommittee on Low-Income Families of the Joint Committee on the Economic Report, 81st Cong., 2d Sess., Senate Doc. No. 231: *Low-Income Families and Economic Stability: Materials on the Problems of Low-Income Families* 10-34 (1950); Robert Heilbroner, "Who Are the American Poor?" *Harper's Magazine*, 200 (1201): 27-33 (June 1950); *Low-Income Families: Hearings Before the Subcommittee on Low-Income Families of the Joint Committee on the Economic Report*, 84th Cong., 1st Sess. 9, 39-40 (1955).

38. Helen Miller, "Today's 'One Third of a Nation,'" *New Republic* 139 (20):13-15 at 14 (Nov. 17, 1958); Edmund Faltenmayer, "Who Are the American Poor?" *Fortune* 69(3): 118-19, 218-29 (Mar. 1964); Herman Miller, *Rich Man Poor Man* 71-95 (1965 [1964]); Herman Miller, *Income Distribution in the United States* 40 (1966); James Morgan et al., *Income and Wealth in the United States* 191-95 (1962); Michael Harrington, *The Other America: Poverty in the United States* 16 (1964 [1962]); A.B. Atkinson, *The Economics of Inequality* 216 (1975).

39. John Kenneth Galbraith, *The Affluent Society* 252-53 (1958).

40. Gabriel Kolko, *Wealth and Power in America: An Analysis of Social Class and Income Distribution* 87-88, 97-102 (1968 [1962]); James Vadakin, *Family Allowances: An Analysis of Their Development and Implications* 6-11 (1958); *idem, Children, Poverty, and Family Allowances* 14-21 (1968).

41. U.S. Bureau of the Census, " Family and Individual Money Income in the United States: 1945," Current Population Reports [CPR]: Consumer Income, tab. 5 at 13 (Ser. P-60, No. 2, 1948); *idem*, "Incomes of Families and Persons in the United States: 1948," CPR: Consumer Income, tab. 6 at 19 (Ser. P-60, No. 6, 1950). The structure was similar but less extreme in 1946 and 1947. *Idem*, "Income of the Nonfarm Population: 1946," CPR: Consumer Income, tab. 3 at 14 (Ser. P-60, No. 3, 1948); *idem*, "Incomes of Families and Persons in the United States: 1947," CPR: Consumer Income, tab. 6 at 19 (Ser. P-60, No. 5, 1949). From 1945 to 1947, the highest cut-off point was four or more children; thereafter the largest family-size was six or more.

42. Mollie Orshansky, "Children of the Poor," *Social Security Bull.* 27 (7):3-13, tab. 1 at 4, tab. 2 at 5 (July 1963). These data refer to "own" children under 18 rather than to the more comprehensive category of "related" children. The per capita incomes have

been calculated based on Orshansky's data; since the latter do not differentiate among the families with six or more children, the per capita income for this group cannot be specified.

43. John Palmer, Timothy Smeeding, & Christopher Jencks, "The Uses and Limits of Income Comparisons," in *The Vulnerable* 9, 19 (John Palmer & Isabel Sawhill eds., 1988); Simon Kuznets, "Population Change and Aggregate Output," in *Demographic and Economic Change in Developed Countries* 324-40 at 332 (NBER, 1960).

44. Calculated according to the data published in the CPR, annual series P-60.

45. U.S. Bureau of the Census, *Trends in Income, by Selected Characteristics: 1947 to 1988*, tab. 16 at 22 (CPR, Ser. P-60, No. 167, 1990) (written by Mary Henson); *idem*, "Income of Families and Persons in the United States: 1949," CPR: Consumer Income, tab. 6 at 22 (Ser. P-60, No.7, 1951); *idem*, "Income in 1964 of Families and Persons in the United States," CPR: Consumer Income, tab. 5 at 26 (Ser. P-60, No.47, 1965); U.S. Congress, Staff of the Subcommittee on Low-Income Families of the Joint Committee on the Economic Report, *Characteristics of the Low-Income Population and Related Federal Programs: Selected Materials*, 84th Cong., 1st Sess., tab. 2 & 3 at 54 (1955).

46. U.S. Bureau of the Census, "Income in 1970 of Families and Persons in the United States," tab. 19 at 41-45 (CPR, Ser. P-60, No. 80, 1971); *idem*, "Income in 1969 of Families and Persons in the United States," tab. 19 at 45, 47 (CPR, Ser. P-60, No. 75, 1970). For husband-wife families, the largest reported size was five or more children. Among white and black female-headed families, the largest families (four or more children) reported 21 percent and 40 percent higher incomes than those with only two children. *Idem*, "Income in 1970 of Families and Persons in the United States," tab. 19 at 43-46.

47. Alvin Schorr, *Poor Kids: A Report on Children in Poverty* 147 (1966). In analyzing the relationship between children and poverty, it is necessary to use data identifying the number of children per family rather than family size per se since some large households may include several working adults. For a study that does not make the distinction, see Dean Worcester, Jr. & Robert Lampman, "Income, Ability, and Size of Family in the United States," *J. Pol. Econ.* 53 (5):436-42 (Oct. 1950).

48. Alvin Schorr, "Income Maintenance and the Birth Rate," *Social Security Bull.* 28 (12):22-30 at 28 (Dec. 1965) (quote); *idem*, "The Family Cycle and Income Development," *ibid.* 29 (2):14-25, 47 at 14 (Feb. 1966) (quote); Kingsley Davis, "Some Demographic Aspects of Poverty in the United States," in *Poverty in America* 299-319 at 308 (Margaret Gordon ed., 1975 [1965]) (quote).

49. Daniel Moynihan, "Foreword," in Vadakin, *Children, Poverty, and Family Allowances* at xii; *idem*, "Employment, Income, and the Ordeal of the Negro Family," in *The American Negro* 134, 148 (quote); *idem*, *The Politics of a Guaranteed Income: The Nixon Administration and the Family Assistance Plan* 140, 248 (1973) (quote).

50. Richard Titmuss, *Commitment to Welfare* 169 (1968 [1965]) (quote); Royal Commission on the Distribution of Income and Wealth, Report No. 6: *Lower Incomes* 106, 105, tab. 2.10 at 28 (Cmnd. 7175, 1978) (quote); Alan Marsh & Stephen McKay, *Families, Work and Benefits* 13 (1993) (quote). The continued impoverishment of large families was in part a function of the state's failure to index family allowances as it did other social security benefits; consequently, in 1977, family allowances supplemented poor large families' income proportionately less than at the time of their introduction three decades earlier. In 1977, the children's allowance as a share of average earnings in four-child families was 7.6 percent compared to 12.0 percent in 1946. Although the revised allowance scheme raised the share by 1980, the payments still fell below a child's subsistence-level needs. Lynn Ellingson, "Children's Allowances in the United Kingdom," *Social Security Bull.* 43 (10):21-24, tab. 1 at 22 (Oct. 1980).

51. Helga Schmucker, "Einfluß der Kinderzahl auf das Lebensniveau der Familien: Empirische Untersuchung an Hand der Ergebnisse der Lohnsteuerstatistik 1955," *Allgemeines Statistisches Archiv* 43 (1):35-55 at 47 (1959).

52. Erhard Knechtel, "Die Zahl der einkommensschwachen kinderreichen Familien in der Bundesrepublik," *Soziale Welt* 11 (4) 330-39, tab. 1 at 334, tab. 2 at 336 (Feb. 1961); *Verhandlungen des Deutschen Bundestages*, 8 Wahlperiode: Stenographische Berichte 114:16,462 (Mar. 6, 1980) (Erhard); Thomas Espenshade, *The Cost of Children in Urban United States* 54-55 (1973) (data referring to 1960-61 and covering a 22-year period from the birth of the first child to the third child's 18th year).

53. Herman Daly, "A Marxian-Malthusian View of Poverty and Development," *Pop. Studies* 25 (1):25-37 (Mar. 1971).

54. Charles Murray, "In Search of the Working Poor," *Pub. Interest*, No. 89, at 3, 14 (Fall 1987).

55. Stanley Lebergott, *Wealth and Want* 17-18 (1975). From the opposite perspective, that of the individual motivation underlying or expressed by aggregate reductions in fertility, two leading poverty researchers question whether reducing family needs in relation to income should qualify as an avoidance of measured poverty. They perceive ambiguous normative implications flowing from parents' forgoing additional offspring in order to ward off a decline in living standards; for the prevailing definition of poverty fails to capture these "costs associated with raising the income-to-needs ratio...." Peter Gottschalk & Sheldon Danziger, "Family Structure, Family Size, and Family Income: Accounting for Changes in the Economic Well-Being of Children, 1968-1986," in *Uneven Tides: Rising Inequality in America* 167-93 at 168-69 (Peter Gottschalk & Sheldon Danziger eds., 1993).

56. Mabel Buer, "The Historical Setting of the Malthusian Controversy," in *London Essays in Economics in Honour of Edwin Cannan* 137-53 at 150 (T. Gregory & Hugh Dalton eds., 1927).

57. Orshansky, "Children of the Poor" at 8-9; Mollie Orshansky, "Counting the Poor: Another Look at the Poverty Profile," *Social Security Bull.* 28 (1):3-29 at 6, 3, 4 (Jan. 1965). Orshansky, "How Poverty Is Measured" at 38, stated that only one-tenth of persons spending the poverty threshold amount or less "actually were able to get a nutritionally adequate diet."

58. For an early U.S. attempt to construct adult male maintenance equivalents, see Edgar Sydenstricker & Wilford King, "A Method of Classifying Families According to Incomes in Studies of Disease Prevalence," *Pub. Health Reports* 35 (48):2829-46 (Nov. 25, 1920).

59. See, e.g., Victor Fuchs, "Redefining Poverty and Redistributing Income," *Pub. Interest*, No. 8:88-95 (Summer 1967); Peter Townsend, *Poverty in the United Kingdom: A Survey of Household Resources and Standards of Living* 34-39 (1979); Edward Lazear & Robert Michael, "Family Size and the Distribution of Real Per Capita Income," *Am. Econ. Rev.* 70 (1):91-107 (Mar. 1980); *Census and Designation of Poverty and Income: Joint Hearing Before the Subcommittee on Census and Population and Subcommittee on Oversight of the House Committee on Ways and Means*, 98th Cong., 2d Sess. (1984); Harrington, *The New American Poverty* at 69-88; Isabel Sawhill, "Poverty in the U.S.: Why Is It So Persistent?" *J. Econ. Lit.* 26:1073-1119 at 1075-82 (Sept. 1988); Patricia Ruggles, *Drawing the Line: Alternative Poverty Measures and Their Implications for Public Policy* (1990); Gordon Fisher, "The Development and History of the Poverty Thresholds," *Social Security Bull.* 55 (4):3-14 (Winter 1992); Daniel Slesnick, "Gaining Ground: Poverty in the Postwar United States," *J. Pol. Econ.* 101 (1):1-38 (Feb. 1993).

60. President's Commission on Income Maintenance Programs, *Poverty Amid Plenty* at 14-15; Bundessozialhilfegesetz § 12, in Bundesgesetzblatt, I, 815, 817 (June 30, 1961); Volker Hentschel, *Geschichte der deutschen Sozialpolitik (1880-1980): Soziale Sicherung und kollektives Arbeitsrecht* 197 (1983).

61. Sawhill, "Poverty in the U.S." at 1077.

62. Michael Young, "Distribution of Income Within the Family," *Brit. J. Sociology* 3 (4): 305-21 at 312 (Dec. 1952) (quote); Laura Oren, "The Welfare of Women in Laboring Families: England, 1860-1950," *Feminist Studies* 1 (3-4):107-25 (Win.-Spr. 1973). For survey data, see Charles Madge, *War-Time Pattern of Saving and Spending* 52-62 (1943).

63. Jean-Baptiste Say, *Traité d'économie politique* 2:277 (5th ed. 1826 [1803]).

64. Orshansky, "Counting the Poor," tab. 2, 5, 4 at 12-13. For a description and justification of the CEA method, see *Economic Report of the President* 55-84 (1964). Whereas the data for poverty shares cover all families, those for median income are restricted to nonfarm male-headed husband-and-wife families. Among all husband-wife families, the poverty rate was about twice as high in those in which the wife was not in the paid labor force as in those in which she was. Orshansky, "Counting the Poor," tab. 2 at 12.

65. Orshansky, "Counting the Poor" at 14.

66. For some evidence that in terms of material hardship (specifically with respect to food, housing, and medical care) as distinguished from income, official poverty statistics may underestimate the extent of poverty among families with children, see Susan Mayer & Christopher Jencks, "Poverty and the Distribution of Material Hardship," *J. Human Resources* 24 (1):88-113 (Winter 1989). From 1970 to 1974, the poverty rate among those 65 years and older fell from 24.5 percent to 15.7 percent; during the same period, the share of the same group in the total poor population fell from 18.9 percent to 13.6 percent. U.S. Bureau of the Census, *Characteristics of the Population Below the Poverty Level: 1974*, tab. F at 7, tab. 1 at 13 (CPR, Ser. P-60, No. 102, 1976). In 1981, for the first time, the poverty rates for elderly whites fell below the national average. The rates for blacks and women living alone, however, remained above average. Robert Pear, "How Poor Are the Elderly?" *N.Y. Times*, Dec. 9, 1982, at 4, col. 3.

67. Orshansky, "Counting the Poor," tab. 2 at 12. The economy-diet poverty rate among black families with four, five, and six or more children was 61 percent, 74 percent, and 77 percent respectively; the corresponding share in female-headed families was 74 percent, 91 percent, and 93 percent. Orshansky, "Counting the Poor," tab. 8 at 19, tab. 7 at 15. In 1964, one-third of poor nonwhite families with five or more children were female-headed. Mollie Orshansky, "Recounting the Poor—A Five-Year Review," *Social Security Bull.* 29 (4):20-37 at 26-27 (Apr. 1966).

68. U.S. Bureau of the Census, "Poverty in the United States 1959 to 1968," tab. 3 at 32 (CPR, Ser. P-60, No. 68, Dec. 31, 1969); *idem*, "Characteristics of the Population Below the Poverty Level: 1974," tab. 21 at 87 (CPR, Ser. P-60, No. 102, 1976). "Negro" includes all races other than white; "N.A." means that the population base was too small to warrant reliability.

69. See sources for table 5.

70. Harold Sheppard, "Effects of Family Planning on Poverty in the United States," in U.S. Senate, Subcommittee on Employment, Manpower, and Poverty of the Committee on Labor and Public Welfare, *Examination of the War on Poverty: Staff and Consultant Reports* 3:715-35 at 718 (90th Cong., 1st Sess., Comm. Print, 1967).

71. U.S. Bureau of the Census, "The Extent of Poverty in the United States 1959 to 1966," tab. 15 at 32 (CPR, Ser. P-60, No. 54, 1968).

72. Arthur Campbell, "The Role of Family Planning in the Reduction of Poverty," *J. Marriage & the Family* 30 (2):236-45 at 236 (May 1968). The predominance of unrelated individuals and families without children—whose poverty gap ranges far below that of families with children—was again exaggerated by the overrepresentation of the nonworking elderly.

73. Office of Policy Planning and Research, U.S. Department of Labor, *The Negro Family: The Case for National Action* 25-26 (1965) (quote); U.S. Bureau of the Census, "Characteristics of the Population Below the Poverty Level: 1974," tab. 4 at 25-26; *idem*, "Poverty in the United States: 1992," tab. 18 at 100 (CPR, Ser. P60-185, 1993). Data were not available for 1959 for black families.

74. Philip Hauser, "Demographic Factors in the Integration of the Negro," in *The American Negro* 71-101 at 88-90 (Talcott Parsons & Kenneth Clark eds., 1970 [1965]).

75. Harold Sheppard & Herbert Striner, "Family Structure and Employment Problems," in Lee Rainwater & William Yancey, *The Moynihan Report and the Politics of Controversy* 354-68 at 363 (1969 [1966]).

76. Gottschalk & Danziger, "Family Structure, Family Size, and Family Income," tab. 5.3 at 175, tab. 5.4 at 176.

77. U.S. Congressional Budget Office, *Trends in Family Income: 1970-1986*, tab. A-1 at 66, A-16 at 86, C-1 at 108-109 (1988).

78. U.S. Bureau of the Census, "Income, Poverty, and Valuation of Noncash Benefits: 1993" at vii (CPR, Ser. P60-188, 1995).

79. Calculated according to data in U.S. Bureau of the Census, "Poverty in the United States: 1992," tab. F at xviii, tab. 1 at 1, tab. 5 at 10-11.

80. U.S. Bureau of the Census, "Poverty in the United States: 1987," tab. 14 at 67 (CPR, Ser. P-60, No. 163, 1989).

81. U.S. Bureau of the Census, "Characteristics of the Population Below the Poverty Level: 1982," tab. 18 at 73 (CPR, Ser. P-60, No. 144, 1984); *idem*, "Characteristics of the Population Below the Poverty Level: 1983," tab. 18 at 71 (CP R, Ser. P-60, No. 147, Feb. 1985).

82. U.S. Bureau of the Census, "Money Income of Households, Families, and Persons in the United States: 1987," tab. 20 at 82 (Ser. P-60: No. 162, 1989); *idem*, "Money Incomes in 1975 of Families and Persons in the United States," tab. 24 at 104-105 (Ser. P-60: No. 105, 1977).

83. U.S. Bureau of the Census, "Poverty in the United States: 1992," tab. 18 at 101-102.

84. Calculated according to *ibid.*, tab. 18 at 101-103.

85. *Ibid.*, tab. 18 at 100.

86. Calculated according to *ibid.*, tab. 23 at 147. The limitations of the published data make it necessary to estimate that families with more than nine persons averaged 10 persons. The data for 1993 are similar; *idem*, "Income, Poverty, and Valuation of Noncash Benefits," tab. 7 at 21. The scale of poverty embodied in the official thresholds can be gauged by the absolute dollar amounts, which in 1992 ranged from $7,299 for one person to $28,211 for families with nine or more members including eight children; the thresholds for four-person two-child families and seven-person six-child families were $14,228 and $20,171 respectively. *Idem*, "Poverty in the United States: 1992," tab. A-3 at A-8.

87. The advent of a third child, which is necessary to guarantee macrodemographic replacement and commonly results in the mother's departure from the labor force and the need for a larger apartment or house, also subjects parents in the European Community (EC) to an increased risk of poverty; even in Belgium and France, the two member-

countries with the most intense progression in transfer payments to three-child families, the poverty rate of such families is marginally above the national average although they are the only countries in the EC in which net incomes after taxes and child allowances exceed the additional calculated costs associated with raising three children. Erika Neubauer, "Familienpolitische Ansätze zum Ausgleich der Aufwendungen für Kinder," in *Zwölf Wege der Familienpolitk in der Europäischen Gemeinschaft* at 267-312 at 294-95, 300-303, 305-306; Christiane Dienel, "Familien vor Armut bewahren: Politik zur Existenzsicherung von Familien in Europa," in *ibid.* at 461-500 at 474, 495-96.

88. GAO, *Poverty Trends, 1980-88*, tab. 4.1 at 62.

89. U.S. Bureau of the Census, "Income in 1964 of Families and Persons in the United States," tab. 5 at 26; *idem*, "Poverty in the United States: 1992," tab. 23 at 147; *idem*, "Income in 1970 of Families and Persons in the United States," tab. 19 at 43-46; *idem*, "Money Income of Households, Families, and Persons in the United States: 1987," tab. 20 at 82 (CPR, Ser. P-60, No. 162, 1989).

90. U.S. Bureau of the Census, "Households, Families, and Children: A 30-Year Perspective," fig. 11 at 17, fig. 9 at 15 (CPR, P23-181, 1992); *idem*, "Studies in Household and Family Formation: When Households Continue, Discontinue, and Form" 1 (CPR, Ser. P-23, No. 179, 1992) (written by Donald Hernandez). By 1992, the ratio fell below 2.9 to 1; *idem*, "Household and Family Characteristics: March 1993," tab. A at vii (CPR, P20-477, 1994) (written by Steve Rawlings).

91. GAO, *Poverty Trends, 1980-88*, tab. 4.2 at 63.

92. U.S. Bureau of the Census, "Poverty in the United States: 1992," tab. 5 at 14-15.

93. U.S. Bureau of the Census, "Poverty in the United States: 1992," tab. 4 at 6-9. The poverty rates for families without children were calculated by subtracting the figures for families with children from the aggregate data.

94. U.S. Bureau of the Census, "Money Income of Households, Families, and Persons in the United States: 1992," tab. 18 at 71-74 (CPR, Ser. P60-184, 1993).

95. GAO, *Poverty Trends, 1980-88*, tab. 3.2 at 38. Such families continue to be defined as single-parent in spite of cohabiting because the Bureau of the Census defines families by reference to blood or marriage relations. *Ibid.* at 35-38, 53-58.

96. Robert Reischauer, "Welfare Reform and the Working Poor," in *Work and Welfare: The Case for New Directions in National Policy* 35-46, tab. 2 at 37 (Center for National Policy, 1987), *reprinted in Welfare: Reform or Replacement? (Work and Welfare): Hearing Before the Subcommittee on Social Security and Family Policy of the Senate Committee on Finance*, 100th Cong., 1st Sess. 288-300 at 291 (1987).

97. U.S. Bureau of the Census, "Characteristics of the Population Below the Poverty Level: 1974," tab. 30 at 100; *idem*, "Money Income in 1975 of Families and Persons in the United States," tab. 25 at 109 (CPR, Ser. P-60, No. 105, 1977); GAO, Poverty Trends, 1980-88, tab. 3.10 at 49.

98. U.S. Bureau of the Census, "Poverty in the United States: 1992," tab. 19 at 115, tab 14 at 84-86.

99. U.S. Bureau of the Census, "Studies in Household and Family Formation," tab. M at 27.

100. Caleb Solomon, "Warning: Little Kids Are a Health Hazard to the Older Parent," *Wall Street Journal*, Nov. 7, 1994, at A1, col. 4; James Smith, "Birth Control and Economic Well-Being," in *Human Behavior in Economic Affairs: Essays in Honor of George Katona* 501-22 at 508 (Burkhard Strumpel et al. eds., 1972).

101. GAO, *Poverty Trends, 1980-88*, tab. 2.1 at 29. As a result of rounding, the columns deviate slightly from 100 percent.

102. GAO, *Poverty Trends, 1980-88*, tab. 5.8 at 90; U.S. Bureau of the Census, "Measuring the Effect of Benefits and Taxes on Income and Poverty: 1992," tab. 2 at 26-29 (CPR, Ser. P60-186RD, 1993).

103. GAO, *Poverty Trends, 1980-88*, tab. 5.6 at 88.

104. *Ibid.*, tab. 2.1 at 29. As a result of rounding, the columns deviate slightly from 100 percent.

105. For the absolute values of the relative poverty rates, see *ibid.*, tab. 5.4, 5.6, 5.9, 5.10, C.1, C.2, D.1, D.3, D.6, D.7 at 48, 51, 57, 59, 82, 84, 105, 109, 115, 117.

106. Statistical Office of the European Communities, *Poverty in Figures: Europe in the Early 1980s*, tab. 5.1 at 40 (1990). The data were collected for Belgium, Denmark, (West) Germany, Greece, Spain, France, Ireland, Italy, Netherlands, Portugal, and the United Kingdom between 1978 and 1982.

107. *Ibid.*, tab. 5.2 at 42.

108. Orshansky, "Children of the Poor" at 10 (quote); Mollie Orshansky, "How Poverty Is Measured," *Monthly Labor Rev.* 92 (2):37-41 at 40 (Feb. 1969) (quote). Mary Jo Bane & David Ellwood, "Slipping Into and Out of Poverty: The Dynamics of Spells," *J. Human Resources* 21 (1):1-23, tab. 3 at 14-15 (Winter 1986), present longitudinal data showing that in 57 percent of all cases the primary reason that children in male-headed families began a spell of poverty was that the head's earnings fell, while in 14 percent of the cases the child was born into poverty. Even such data, however, cannot resolve the question of whether small nonpoor families become large poor ones or whether poor childless or small families become even poorer as they procreate. For related data for AFDC spells, see *idem, Welfare Realities: From Rhetoric to Reform* tab. 2.7 at 54 (1994).

109. Sheppard, "Effects of Family Planning on Poverty in the United States" at 724-25. For evidence that large families may also be a burden on the children themselves inasmuch as sibsize and achievement are inversely related, see Judith Blake, *Family Size and Achievement* (1989).

110. Telephone interview with Stephanie Shipp, U.S. BLS (Nov. 21, 1994). When two Census Bureau analysts read a paper to the Population Association of America on childlessness in 1958, they stated that, to their knowledge, no one before had ever devoted a report to census data on the subject. Wilson Grabill & Paul Glick, "Demographic and Social Aspects of Childlessness: Census Data," *Milbank Memorial Fund Q.* 37 (1):60-86 at 61 (Jan. 1959). The study presented virtually no relevant income or poverty data.

111. Eugene Steuerle, "The Tax Treatment of Households of Different Size," in *Taxing the Family* 73-97 at 86 (Rudolph Penner ed., 1984).

112. Survey Research Center, *1960 Survey of Consumer Finances* tab. 4-4 at 80 (1961); George Katona et al., *1968 Survey of Consumer Finances*, tab. 6-6 at 115, tab. 6-8 at 119 (1969); George Katona, Lewis Mandell, & Jay Schmiedeskamp, *1970 Survey of Consumer Finances*, tab. 6-4 at 102 (1971); Lewis Mandell et al., *Surveys of Consumers 1971-72*, tab. 5-4 at 64 (1973).

113. Terence Kelly, "Factors Affecting Poverty: A Gross Flow Analysis," in The President's Commission on Income Maintenance Programs, *Technical Studies* 1-81 at 13, 24-27, 36-37, 39-40, 58-60 (n.d. [1969]) (quotation at 25).

114. U.S. Bureau of the Census, *Statistical Abstract of the United States: 1961*, tab. 51 at 53 (82d ed., 1961); *idem*, "Fertility of the Population: June 1964 and March 1962," tab. 5 at 17; *idem, U.S. Census of Population: 1960: Subject Reports: Women by Number of Children Ever Born* tab. 38 at 188 (Final Report PC(2)-3A, 1964).

115. Dudley Poston, Jr., "Income and Childlessness in the United States: Is the Relationship Always Inverse?" *Social Biology* 21 (3):296-307 at 299-300 (Fall 1974).

116. Calculated according to U.S. Bureau of the Census, *1970 Census of Population: Subject Reports: Women by Number of Children Ever Born*, tab. 53 at 274 (PC(2)-3A, 1973).

117. U.S. Bureau of the Census, *Studies in Household and Family Formation: When Households Continue, Discontinue, and Form*, tab. J at 22, tab. K at 24, 29 (CPR, Ser. P-23, No. 179, 1992) (written by Donald Hernandez).

118. Calculated according to Smith, "Birth Control and Economic Well-Being," tab. 4 & 5 at 510-11. A somewhat differently constructed contemporaneous British study reinforces the negative correlation between assets and number of children. A study conducted by the Ministry of Social Security, which excluded childless and one-child families, revealed a monotonic decline in the proportion of families headed by fathers in full-time work with £300 or more in savings: from 22 percent among two-child families to 6 percent among families with six or more children. The economic insecurity associated with procreation is underscored by the fact that the families encompassed only those which, because their resources exceeded their assessed requirements, were ineligible for national assistance benefits. Ministry of Social Security, *Circumstances of Families*, tab. A.9 at 143 (1967).

9

Is the Road to Communism
Paved with Family Allowances?

> The wages of the poor diminish as their wants and families increase, for the care and labor of attending to the family leaves them fewer hours for profitable work. With negro slaves, their wages invariably increase with their wants. The master increases the provision for the family as the family increases in number and helplessness. It is a beautiful example of communism, where each one receives not according to his labor, but according to his wants.[1]

> [T]he absolute size of the families stands in inverse proportion to the wage level, that is, to the mass of means of subsistence at the disposal of the various categories of workers. This law of capitalist society would sound absurd among savages.... It recalls the mass reproduction of individually weak and much-hunted-down animal species.[2]

> [B]oth the workingmen and their political patrons...firmly maintain the belief that the rate of wages ought to be what a workingman needs to make him "comfortable," let his habits and the size of his family...be what they may.... This, disguise it as we may, is communism, doubtless imperfectly developed and unorganized, but still communism....[3]

The most specialized or targeted policy that states (and employers) have developed for alleviating the impoverishment associated with above-average or even any reproduction is the system of family or children's allowances or endowments.[4] The controversy surrounding these redistributive programs is rooted in their perceived multivalence, ranging from payments for reproductive services rendered to an authoritarian state to a proto to-each-according-to-his-needs regime. The first section of this chapter is devoted to the theoretical and social policy arguments that have traditionally been used to justify or attack such intervention. The second and third sections then survey the history of such programs in Europe and of their exceptional absence in the United States.

THE STRUGGLE FOR AND AGAINST FAMILY ALLOWANCES

> The significant question is not whether they have more dependants than their wages can support, or what level of wage supports a "reasonable" number of dependants, but why...such a high proportion of the national resources available for distribution...is channeled through the individual wage system rather than through the child benefit and social security systems and, say, an income scheme for married women working in the home.[5]

For two centuries, from the time of the classical political economists' debates over the relationship between wages and the poor laws to late-twentieth-century polemics in the United States over capping AFDC payments to mothers who continue to procreate while on the dole, contestants have bemoaned or extolled the fact that wages are paid without reference to individual workers' special needs, in particular to the costs associated with the size of their generational contribution. Malthus, for example, asserted that "nothing would tend so effect-ually to destroy" the purchasing power of the working classes as family allowances. A century later, Beatrice Webb rejected the principle of determining wages based on family obligations because it contravened the trade union principle of a standard rate of remuneration. Wages differentiated according to family size would prompt employers to hire childless workers, whose lower wages would contradict the principles underlying the market, individual differences in efficiency, and collec-tive bargaining. With both employers and workers opposed to wages that made provision for dependents, Webb proposed a state-organized children's endowment in order to maintain the population without recourse to alien immigration.[6]

When European Catholics, feminists, humanitarians, and socialists began, about the time of World War I, advocating state-financed redistributional schemes in the form of family allowances in order to avoid the major cause of poverty associated with large families that employers could not be expected to alleviate by means of individually graduated wages, both critics and supporters promptly recognized the proposal as ushering in a quasi-communist regime of "to each according to his needs." In Australia, a pioneer in state intervention in capital-labor relations, the notion that the costs of producing the supply of labor should be socialized gained ground in the 1920s. A.B. Piddington, an industrial arbitration court judge, conceded that individual employers had no economic or humane obligation to pay their workers according to family size, but insisted that there was "every reason why employers as a whole...should pay for the living needs of their employees as a whole. Indeed, that they should do so is the basis of the whole theory of the living wage."[7]

A typical antisocialist response of the 1920s characterized family allow-ances as "a scheme for the nationalisation of children and married women." And D.H. Macgregor, the editor of Britain's most prestigious economics journal and a professor at Oxford, expressed his contempt by asking whether "there were no such thing as personal responsibility" especially since children, rather than being "a pure tax, an obligation undertaken by parents on behalf of the community...should be regarded as...a usual way of obtaining the real values from money." Paternalist and socialist advocates of the allowance praised it for exactly the same reason antisocialists rejected it. A French deputy, proposing the adoption of family allowances for state employees in 1908, reasoned that whereas the wage was "an act of justice" and consequently did not signify any inequality between the bachelor and married man, the allowance "is a remuneration for a service. The family is a social service." Even in opposition, Harry Holland, the first parliamentary leader of the Labour Party in New Zealand, the first country to enact a state-financed family allowance, justified it on the ground that "every mother of a large family, who renders a supreme service to the country by the fact of her motherhood, is made to suffer because she has rendered that service."[8]

The Swedish social democrats Alva and Gunnar Myrdal, who internationalized and reenergized the debate about family allowances and population in the 1930s, rejected the family wage as a dysfunctional ideological merger between employers' interest in low wage costs and a national interest in children's welfare. Alva Myrdal also detected an unacceptable connection between substandard wages and family allowances: the family wage becomes "a belly-strap...drawn as close to the spine as possible" because employers can use family allowances to reduce the wage level. The solution that the Myrdals offered—driven in part by a eugenicist program—was to "nationalize differential child costs" by socializing segments of consumption through in-kind, non-means-tested free goods and services associated with childbirth and childrearing largely by redistributing income from those with below-average procreative contributions. In-kind programs would moderate the cost because they would make possible economies of cooperation and large-scale enterprise. Although the costs would be colossal, since children had to be supported in any case, they represented transfers rather than additional costs.[9]

Liberal Canadian Prime Minister Mackenzie King, a lifelong bachelor, whose World War II government enacted North America's first and only universal state-financed family allowance program, also paternalistically stressed the service rendered by the one-fifth of the gainfully employed who were raising 84 percent of the children—who "are an asset to the state"—"by ensuring the survival of the nation." But King also advanced an egalitarian motive. Although he denied that he was inveighing against capital in the interests of labor, he observed that "the new order of things" would cease to take for granted "these differences in class and opportunity" and would "shift the emphasis from the sacredness of possession to the sacredness of life." Arguing that only the agency of the state could save the industrial classes from the degradation of their standard of living, King supported family allowances because generally: "Capital...can wait; labour cannot wait. Capital can find other means of investment; labour cannot. Labour...cannot change quickly from one occupation to another; capital is mobile; labour is not...." The egalitarian rhetoric is impressive—especially in light of the legislation's origin in Canadian capital's interest in devising an alternative to the removal of controls on substandard wages to which King was known to be sympathetic.[10]

Family allowances, like many family- and birth control-related policies, are politically multivalent. The European experience of rationing during World War I made family-size as a criterion of distribution both familiar and plausible. After all: "No one would have proposed...that the unmarried worker should have as much sugar or flour as his fellow-employee who was the father of a family. The absurdity of giving uniform allowances of food to men with unequal numbers of mouths to feed was so patent that it led...to the inquiry whether it was any less absurd to give these men equal amounts of money to spend for food." When French socialist unions attacked the system in the early 1920s on the grounds that it both relieved employers of even larger wage payments and aimed at playing off parents and childless workers against each other: "The paradoxical spectacle was then presented of the C.G.T. unionists, who are anti-capitalistic and largely communistic in their beliefs, raising the individualistic shibboleth of 'equal pay, equal work,' while the conservative French capitalists declared that the proper standard of wage payment was that of 'to each according to his needs.'"[11]

In contrast, other early advocates sought to cast economic subsidies for large families as yet another contingency or vicissitude of life against which social insurance could protect workers: "The arrival of a child and the cost of providing for it have the same effect in lowering the standard of living as a stretch of unemployment or the occurrence of illness." Just as a segment of the British labor movement in the 1920s took a socialist view of family allowances as falling within the scope of the principle, "to each according to his needs," by the following decade Conservatives favored them in imperialist, racialist, and pronatalist terms. The British government, in turn, adopted family allowances in order to hold down wages, combat inflation, and enforce labor mobility, work incentives, and the welfare principle of less eligibility. Yet another part of the labor movement opposed family allowances precisely because of their wage-suppressing properties, while the radical left, arguing that allowances transformed the poor into paupers, instead proposed a guaranteed minimum in kind.[12]

British eugenicists on the eve of World War I offered yet another reason for family endowments. Harold Laski, who as a precocious high school student had fallen under the influence of Francis Galton and Karl Pearson, found in his study of Glaswegian families that: "The addition of 9 to 10 children to a family does not on the average involve an increase of the wages by more than a shilling a week, which is absolutely inadequate.... No regard is on the whole paid to size of family when the wages are fixed." Viewing this relationship as "one of the gravest points of our modern civilisation," Laski joined Pearson and the latter's collaborators in positing the proportionality between wages and "social value as measured by physique and mentality" as well as between family size and wages as "for the future of the race far more important than doles to the aged or vails to the sick and unemployable."[13]

Catholic doctrine, animated especially by Pope Leo XIII's 1891 anti-socialist encyclical, *Rerum novarum*, and even more specifically, by Pius XI's

Quadragesimo anno, took the position that "to each according to his needs" as a principle of compensation both embraced family allowances and was consistent with the family living wage in its full patriarchal sense of gender subordination. John Ryan, a Catholic theologian who provided a powerful animus to the movement for the family living wage at the beginning of the twentieth century, personified this dual position. Not only did he vindicate "the right to a family Living Wage...to every adult male laborer, whether he intends to marry or not" and propose four or five children as the average number to be supported by that wage, but he also urged that: "The welfare of the whole family, and that of society likewise, renders it imperative that the wife and mother should not engage in any labor except that of the household." The wife who became a worker was no longer a wife because she would no longer be able to "make her home what it should be for her husband, her children and herself." In the United States, President Samuel Gompers of the still youthful American Federation of Labor, while opposing any state measures to impose such a wage on private employers and employees, supported a minimum living wage as "sufficient to maintain an average-sized family in a manner consistent with whatever the contemporary local civilization recognizes as indispensable to physical and mental health...."[14]

Although the assumption that an adult male worker's wage should be sufficient to support his family may at one point have been "the cornerstone of our social organization with its family unit," it was equally true that his wage was "inadequate to maintain a desirable standard of living" for a family with several children. This pre-World War II finding assumes greater comparative significance in light of recent right-wing antifeminist lamentations over the state's "infinite capacity to harm...the family and very limited ability to help it." Allan Carlson has stood at the scholarly center of these efforts. Without offering a historically detailed account of its chronological rise, Carlson asserts that an informally or culturally constructed family wage emerged in the United States prior to World War I, which was then supplemented by a state-coerced family wage during the New Deal. He finds that this living wage system, which enabled the male of the species to finance its reproduction while the female was linked to motherhood and home, "held together" until the early 1970s. At that point it began to collapse under the weight of "the devastating effects of state-enforced gender equality in the workplace...."[15]

The breakdown of gender-segregation is symbolized above all by the rise of the wage-working wife-mother. Thus if the participation rate in the civilian labor force of married women (spouse present) with offspring under 6 years of age was only 10.8 percent in 1948 and 18.6 percent in 1960, by 1987 the figure had tripled to 56.8 percent; the corresponding figures for those with offspring between the ages of 6 and 17 were 26.0, 39.0, and 70.6 percent respectively. For all married women with children, the participation rates in 1960, 1970, 1980, and 1992 were 27.6, 39.7, 54.1, and 67.8 percent respectively. Looked at from a somewhat different perspective: in 1962, two-thirds of white families with children consisted of two parents of whom the wife-mother was not a wage-worker while one-quarter consisted of two parents including a wage-working wife-mother; by 1983 parity was almost achieved: the corresponding figures were 44.8 percent and 40.9 percent respectively.[16]

The problem with Carlson's idealized account of the halcyon days of the family living wage is that they never existed. The need for and introduction of family allowances in Europe and Australasia beginning in the 1920s demonstrated at the time that going wages for men, even specifically designated by arbitration courts as family living wages, did not suffice to support large families.[17] Worse still for Carlson's thesis, the minimum wage established in the United States by the Fair Labor Standards Act, which he views as the centerpiece of the New Deal's creation of a "family wage for dad" and as "keyed to a 'living standard' for a family of four," was never seriously considered as guaranteeing a family living wage—especially since at the time of its enactment the vast majority of sub-minimum-wage workers were excluded from coverage. Even at 40 cents an hour, which was 15 cents higher than the initial minimum wage in 1938, Congress was clear that this mandatory floor could not, even for those workers "fortunate enough" to work year-round, guarantee "a wage sufficient to maintain...the minimum American standard of living." By 1959, at the height of what Carlson calls the postwar resurgence of family values, and the first year for which the federal government created poverty thresholds, the minimum wage failed to reach that line for families even with one child. By the mid-1980s, it fell below the poverty threshold even for two people.[18] The failure of the family wage was underscored when the Bureau of the Census revealed that, in 1992, 14 percent of men working full-time received wages below the poverty level for a family of four—a share almost double that in 1979. Nevertheless, conservative poverty policy analysts blithely continue to assert that: "It seems clear that wages are generally high enough to avoid poverty by the government's definition."[19]

Precisely the multipurpose and multivalent character of the agitation on behalf of family allowances prompted the dean of pre-New Deal U.S. advocates of social security to complain about the extraneous ideological baggage with which family wage proponents had unnecessarily weighed down the security for the overburdened large family, which was the last of all the contingencies of modern life to be recognized. Abraham Epstein believed that shorn of "exotic theories...to...reform...everything in sight," to redistribute income, create a living and minimum wage, establish the principle of "to each according to his needs," or equal pay for equal work, to improve the race, honor motherhood, promote feminism, or increase or decrease the birth rate, family allowances could escape from their supposed status as a panacea and be reduced to social insurance against yet another form of economic insecurity.[20] Ironically, Epstein advanced this criticism just as family allowances had embarked on their almost universal incorporation into the world's social welfare systems.

Whether, however, the "general case for Family Allowances follows so clearly from the Socialist maxim, 'To each according to his need': that we do not propose to enlarge upon the principle," as the British socialist Independent Labour

Party (ILP) asserted in the mid-1920s, deserves examination. The ILP's advocacy of family allowances was an adjunct to its campaign for a more clear-cut socialist policy ("Socialism in our Time"), which it pressed after the fall of the Labour government in 1924. Although the drive subsided in the wake of the defeat of the general strike of 1926, for several years the ILP achieved some success in impressing upon the Labour Party the overarching importance of a living wage for all workers as a first charge on national income.[21]

One obstacle to the implementation of such a proposal was the frequently voiced empirical complaint—which can be traced back to the Ricardo-Trower debate—that if the principle of equal pay for equal work was to be preserved, childless workers would receive a bonus. Thus in the 1920s, more than half of English adult male workers were bachelors, widowers, or married with no children, whereas only one-fifth had more than three dependent children; in Australia, the corresponding figures were three-fifths and one fifth, whereas only one-fifth of Belgian families had no children and more than two-fifths had three or more. Rowntree's special study of the working class in York in 1936 revealed that of men 21 years of age and older 58 percent had no dependent children, 21 percent only one child, 12 percent two children, and 5 percent three children; among the child-rich fathers, only 2 percent four children, and 2 percent five or more children, although they accounted for 23 percent of all children.[22]

Early twentieth-century budget studies scrutinizing the adequacy of adult males' wages commonly adopted the three-child family as a norm. Researchers may have used this standard because they believed both that it was empirically accurate and represented replacement-level reproduction. By the mid-1920s, however, Paul Douglas demonstrated that the five-person family was far from modal. In England and the United States only 10 percent and 12 percent respectively of adult male workers supported three children; and whereas 50-60 percent of workers had fewer children, 10-15 percent had more. Consequently, a wage sufficient to support a five-person family "would be more than adequate in English speaking countries for between 70 and 80 per cent of all workers while it would be less than needed in from 10 to 15 per cent." In the United States alone such a wage "would mean paying for...47 million fictitious dependents.... Without meeting the basic needs of those with large families, it would pour into the pockets of the unmarried and the married with few or no children a great excess over their wants."[23]

Accepting the statistical demolition of the myth that the three-child family was modal, the ILP conceded that "[n]o living wage which would satisfy a civilised standard of life [wa]s attainable" on that model. In order to avoid bankrupting the fisc, the ILP therefore proposed "to base the Living Wage on the needs of a man and his wife" and to add to it a children's allowance. Disbelieving the ability of grown men to clean up for themselves, the ILP justified wage equality between a married man and a bachelor or widower on the ground that "the latter must pay in some way for the services of a housekeeper...." Equally arresting was the ILP's Malthusian proposal to cap payments. Although it found it implausible that allowances would cause "undesirable multiplication" because it was convinced that "[r]eckless breeding" was a product of "abject poverty" rather than well-being, it nevertheless recommended out of an overabundance of caution that either the weekly sum be reduced as family size increased, or that the allowance, "while providing for all children born before the appointed date, should thereafter cease after the fourth or fifth child...."[24]

The Labour Party leadership, prodded by the trade unions, scorned and buried the ILP's family allowances. One reason for this standoff was the "gender tension" the plan produced: "There were men who deeply resented cash allowances paid to wives whose husbands were earning wages because it threatened the traditional division of responsibility in the working-class household." This perception by male trade unionists that their financial potency was under attack corresponded, in other countries, such as New Zealand, where the allowances were implemented, to a sense of increased financial independence among wives. Eleanor Rathbone, England's most vigorous campaigner for family allowances, explained some men's paternalistic opposition to allowances as based on their "dislike [of] the recognition of their wives and children as separate personalities with claims equivalent to their own."[25] This attitude was congruent with the presuppositions underlying the family or living wage, which

> regard[ed] the family not as it really is—an aggregate of individual human beings, each with an actual or potential value to the community—but as the "dependants" of the wage-earner. The very word suggests something parasitic, accessory, non-essential. A wife and children, and the wherewithal to keep them, are conceded to the wage-earner as though they were part of the "comforts and decencies promotive of better habits" for which he may reasonably ask as necessary to his development as a full human being. But if he prefers to use the margin thus allowed him for breeding pigeons or racing dogs or for some other form of personal gratification...that is assumed to be his affair, not the State's or his employer's.[26]

While the ILP program was under attack from the right, the Communist Party of Great Britain challenged it from the left. R. Palme Dutt criticized the proposal as of a piece with the demand for a living wage: a lever not for socialism but for Fordism, it encouraged the illusion that redistribution rather than class struggle over production was the key to overcoming capitalism. Approving of a "provision for motherhood and for the complete upbringing of children (but certainly not 'family allowances') [a]s a first obligation of Socialism," Dutt did not question the possibility that, like social insurance, family allowances might benefit workers under capitalism. What he did dispute was that a system that capitalists supported as a means of lowering the aggregate wage bill would redistribute income toward the working class, let alone hasten the transition to socialism. Dutt reasoned that once "capitalist statistical hacks" had uncovered the three-child family as a myth, capital discovered that "[i]f only some collective pooling system could be devised to pay for the actual dependent children in the minority of cases where these do exist, then a much lower basic wage could be fixed for...the majority of workers...." Even where family allowances were financed wholly by the capitalist class through income taxes, Dutt insisted, "the more scientific system of only paying for...children in the minority of cases where such...children exist" and thus reducing the aggregate wage bill constituted "under capitalism...the inevitable working out of any system of Family Allowances."[27]

The fact that German socialist trade unions in the 1920s opposed private firm-level family allowances based on a minimum-existence wage standard for unmarried men, which would in turn be used to exert downward pressure on all wages in the same way as piecework, was contemporaneously viewed as ironically revealing the tenuousness of their commitment to socialist principles:

> Their principle of 'equal pay for equal work' has a definitely socialist character only when it is applied to those who receive incomes without working. When it is applied inside the world of labour it appears as pure orthodox liberalism. It acknowledges as just the results of the existing competitive system on a unitary wage basis without reference to human needs. In true liberal style the socialists accept the pursuit of gain as a motive of all conduct; only recognising solidarity in theory, where it is profitable.[28]

Yet in making this criticism, the economist Eduard Heimann failed to integrate the fact that the family wage or social wage or bonuses granted by employers were "merely redistributed as between fathers of families and bachelors." Especially because young workers without children had been able before World War I to save enough from their higher wage to prepare for creating a family, which was no longer possible, and because unionists feared that the reduction of the bachelors' wage was merely a prelude to a future take-back of the parents' bonus as a temporary measure and a reduction of the general wage level, accusing them of having abandoned socialist principles was an impermissible simplification of a complex overlay of motives. In particular, Heimann overlooked the potentially critical problem that in the post-World War I period "single men [we]re...virtually the only members of the working class who ha[d] a surplus of money over and above their needs. To pare this surplus down would...deprive the labor movement of one of its chief sources of funds." Redistributing some or even all of this "surplus" to parents could not provide any relief to the depleted treasuries of working-class organizations because those parents were supposed to spend the allowances on their children.[29]

Family allowances can also be viewed in a capital-logical framework as state intervention to enforce the aggregate interest in the long-term flow of income sources (including the creation of the next generation of the working class) against the economic interests of individual wage workers, which the invisible hand would not transmogrify in a manner necessary to reproduce the proletariat. In this sense state-financed child endowments represent a transition from merely alleviating the poverty of large families to the tendential creation of equal conditions for all who contribute to reproduction.[30]

The need for children's allowances has also been justified by reference to the deep ethical obligation that those who, despite their own nonconsensual existence, owe to the next generation whom they create without prior mutual agreement. As generalized by John Stuart Mill: "Since no one is responsible for having been born, no pecuniary sacrifice is too great to be made by those who have more than enough, for the purpose of securing enough to all persons already in existence." The comparatively extensive Swedish system of children's allowance further specifies the guiding policy as "the ultimate right of every child...to be welcomed, to have an economically and socially secure childhood..., with equal opprtunities for a good start in life...." Underlying this policy is the fundamental redistributive principle "that the costs of raising a family should, to a reasonable extent, be shared by all members of society through measures decided by and carried out through society." The rationale buttressing this principle is threefold: (1) reducing the differences in the standard of living between families with and without children; (2) eliminating poverty; and (3) recognizing the fact that children will eventually work and, through the social security system, support the aging regardless of whether the latter have contributed children to society or not. The salient principle in Sweden then has been that the childless must contribute to the "necessary investment in the future generation."[31]

Morally based redistributional considerations also underlay the Conservative Political Centre's advocacy of the expansion of family allowances in Britain in the 1950s. Emphasizing that poverty had not yet been abolished in large families, it argued that per capita food expenditures were affected more by family composition than by social class: "Those who grumble about contributing to the upbringing of other people's children might ponder" data showing how much more relatively well-off childless couples spent on food than poor families.[32]

Such an approach, however, fails to deal with the following question: If the number of children whom parents create is the independent variable to which they accommodate their standard of living, is it meaningful to say that children bring about a decline in their parents' standard of living since in some utilitarian sense, at least with regard to "planned" or intended children, parents must be obtaining more utility from eating fast food with their creations than eating filet mignon by themselves? Moreover, why should parents be subsidized for augmenting the national wealth when such a contribution is merely the unintended consequence of their acts and intentions? This position has been taken seriously in the United States, where one member of the Reagan administration subcabinet hinted at dismantling richer families' children's allowance, the personal income tax deduction for dependent children, on the ground that the latter are consumption goods. And Reagan ideologue George Gilder underscored the point by asserting that, although the income of a two-child family must after ten years be double that of a childless couple in order to maintain the same standard of living: "No one who has children is likely to accept the idea that one's life is impoverished by their arrival, that one's standard of living declines when money is spent on them rather than on maintaining a childless person's schedule of outside entertainments."[33]

One response to this arch-American view, which would be scarcely imaginable in Europe, suggests that it is in capitalism's own interest to subsidize proletarian procreation lest the golden geese disappear. As Magdalen Reeves pointed out in Britain on the eve of World War I, the "masculine State," which represented an all-male electorate, was dealing crudely and unwisely with "all parents guilty of the crime of poverty" by imposing responsibilities on them without the requisite assistance.[34] Instead, theories were being advanced to "cure...poverty by the dying out of all the poor people":

> [W]ere the children of the poor limited according to wage...the wage-earner would automatically cease to reproduce himself. It seems an heroic way of curing his difficulties. Obviously as a palliative in individual cases the plan of limiting the family according to wage appeals with great force to the well-fed and more fortunate observer, but as a national measure to deal with poverty it fails to convince. That a man with 24s. a week is unwise to have six children is perfectly true. But, then, what sized family would he be wise to have? If he were really prudent and careful of his future he would...neither marry nor have children at all.... But we cannot expect...2,500,000 adult men to act on those lines. The fact is they want to marry and they want to have children. As either of these courses is unwise on 24s. a week, they are in for a life of imprudence anyhow.[35]

Despite their broadly egalitarian redistributional impact, family allowances in their earliest manifestations—especially as private, voluntary employer-initiated plans—failed to find favor with labor unions, which viewed them as insidious plots by employers to control their workforces by penalizing strikes and mobility and to "drive a wedge between [heads of families] and the childless workers who have not so much to lose." In post-World War I Germany, many employers favored firm-level family allowances in order to retain their older workers, who were more "conscious of [their] responsibility" to their employer and who formed "the best breakwater against" younger workers who "often intro-duce[d] revolutionary...elements into the factory...." Unions also acted on the premise that family allowances operated to lower the unmarried workers' wages. In France, unions ultimately abandoned their opposition in the 1920s only because the allowances became too deeply embedded in economic life and workers sought to fight the increasing cost of living. Even Eleanor Rathbone conceded at the time that family allowances would create redistributional losers, but in effect advised those who had benefited from wages calculated by reference to phantom wives and children that they had been free riders on "Society's provision for maternity and childhood as the reserve force of industry and of the State."[36]

Family allowances undeniably have also been put to much less egalitarian uses by fascist states pursuing neomercantilist population policies designed to recapture women as a professional class of labor-power procreators. Sidney Webb, a social Darwinist-eugenicist Fabian socialist, adduced the record-low birth rates in England and Wales at the beginning of the twentieth century as a refutation of the political economy of Ricardo and Senior, which claimed that limiting population would save the lowest grade of laborers from starvation and famine. In fact, however, depopulation did not spare them "the horrors of 'sweating' or the terrors of prolonged lack of employment."[37] Because factory acts and trade union collective bargaining had secured a national minimum, Webb thought it time to shift the focus of demographic policy

> to alter the economic incidence of child-bearing. Under the present social conditions the birth of children in households maintained on less than three pounds a week (and these form four-fifths of the nation) is attended by almost penal consequences.... The parents know that for the next fourteen years they will have to dock themselves and their other children of luxuries and even of some of the necessaries of life, just because there will be another mouth to feed. To four-fifths of all the households...each succeeding baby means...less opportunity for advancement for every member of the family.[38]

Because "the most valuable of the year's crops, as it is the most costly, is not the wheat harvest or the lambing, but the year's quota of adolescent young men and women enlisted in the productive service of the country," Webb favored "the systematic 'endowment of motherhood' [to] place this most indispensable of all professions upon an honorable economic basis." As if anticipating a more ominous *Kinder und Küche* agenda, Webb contended that: "To the vast majority of women...the rearing of children would be the most attractive occupation, if it offered economic advantages equal to those, say, of school teaching or service in the post office." Webb and his wife Beatrice, whose massive scholarly productions substituted for any contribution of their own to the human harvest, knew that: "Child-bearing...is an occupation that the bulk of women would prefer to any other, if any proper provision were made for it."[39]

Their fellow Fabian, H. G. Wells, partial to the same kinds of metaphors, argued that: "The children people bring into the world can be no more their private concern entirely, than the disease germs they disseminate or the noises a man makes in a thin-floored flat." In order to combat the "*Strike against Parentage*" in which the British middle class was engaged at the turn of the century, Wells proposed that the socialist state, which denied parents the right "to beget children carelessly and promiscuously," pay women a wage "for children born legitimately in the marriage it will sanction."[40]

Hitler took important steps toward implementing the Fabians' authoritarian vision. In the 1920s *Mein Kampf* announced that the mission of his future *völkisch* state was "to make sure that the healthy woman's fertility is not limited by the financially debauched economy of a state regime that shapes the blessing of children into a curse for the parents." Once in power, the Nazis undertook an unprecedented array of statutory programs subsidizing large families.[41] Indeed, it was this type of gendered regimentation that purportedly induced a contemporaneous Australian Royal Commission to recommend against adoption of family allowances: "we are opposed to a scheme which would treat a mother as a salaried servant of the State, by virtue of her child-bearing." Yet precisely this commodified view of reproductive services and utilitarian view of children have found favor at times among advocates of family allowances. Thus the commission appointed by President Johnson to study income maintenance programs found both that U.S. "social policy does not reflect any...recognition to children as a resource of the country for whom society has an interest in equalizing the burden of their care" and that "children's allowances can be considered a remuneration for the hard work that child-rearing and housekeeping entail."[42]

FAMILY ALLOWANCES EVERYWHERE EXCEPT THE UNITED STATES?

> Referring to the family-allowance program..., a French government official insisted that..."[i]n France, when you have children, you have solved the poverty problem. The French poverty problem is a problem of childless adults."[43]

The British antipodean states became family allowance pioneers because their industrial arbitration award systems had encountered difficulties in fixing minimum wages based on the cost of maintaining a family of average size. Facing the same dilemma that Ricardo and Trower had debated a century earlier, New Zealand and Australian state officials discovered that calibrating that wage to a two-child, four-person family provided smaller families with more and larger families with less than a "fair living wage." In New Zealand in the early 1920s, for example, almost three-quarters of adult males either were unmarried or married without children, or had only one child.[44]

The first modern general, if not universal, national legislated family allowance scheme was enacted in New Zealand in 1926 by an "ostensibly antisocialist Government." As enacted, the allowance was chiefly restricted by reference to the number of children, size of income, and race. Application for the allowance could be made "by any person being the father of three or more children," although it was actually paid to the mother, for every child in excess of two under the age of 15 years. Only three-child-or-more families with weekly incomes of £4 or less were eligible for the two-shilling per child weekly allowance. At the time, families with more than two children accounted for three-eighths of all families with such incomes, the family-size cut-off point supposedly representing the number of people whom the family wage was thought sufficient to support. Despite these limitations, this first enactment was comprehensive in the sense that it was not limited to the working class and was financed out of general revenues.[45]

Because New Zealand was then, and continues to be, regarded by the bulk of its inhabitants as underpopulated in the sense of falling below some optimum population size permitting the efficient production of certain material and cultural goods, family allowances found favor among pronatalists there although the perfunctory New Zealand parliamentary debate did not deal with the issue. Instead, allowances were designed to raise the living standard of the one-eighth of the country's children in the larger than four-person households whose condition neared destitution. A decade later, in 1936, the legislature inserted a pronatalist element into the Industrial Conciliation and Arbitration Act by requiring the Arbitration Court to fix the basic rate of wages for adult male workers at a level "sufficient to enable a man...to maintain a wife and three children in a fair and reasonable standard of comfort." By the end of World War II, all of the afore-mentioned limitations were abolished in favor of a universal family benefit.[46]

From its inception at the beginning of the twentieth century, the Australian Court of Conciliation and Arbitration articulated the following principle as the foundation of its wage-setting: "Treating marriage as the usual fate of adult men, a wage which does not allow of the matrimonial condition and the maintenance of about five persons...would not be treated as a living wage." That basic wage, the court's president explained, "is the same for the employee with no family as for the family with a large family. [T]he employer need not concern himself with his employee's domestic affairs." In the landmark case, the so-called Harvester Judgment of 1907, the court, applying the statutory terms of reference "fair and reasonable" to the wage, declared the standard as "the normal needs of the average employee, regarded as a human being living in a civilized community." A study of household budgets led the judge to deem a five-person family the average.[47] The five-person standard family was then incorporated into several state statutes. The Queensland Industrial Arbitration Act of 1916 provided that: "The basic wage of an adult male employee shall be not less than is sufficient to maintain a well-conducted employee of average health, strength, and competence and his wife and a family of three children in a fair and average standard of comfort...." The Industrial Arbitration Act, 1912, of the state of Western Australia provided that no minimum wage could be awarded "which is not sufficient to enable the average worker...to live in reasonable comfort, having regard to any domestic obligations to which such average worker would be ordinarily subject."[48]

Yet the suspicion that the industrial arbitration award system was requiring employers to pay a basic wage on behalf of 450,000 nonexistent wives and 2,100,000 nonexistent children also drove the politics of family allowances in Australia in the post-World War I period. In 1927, the Australian state of New South Wales shifted the basis of its industrial arbitration wage awards from a four-person, two-child family to "a man and wife without children." Having removed the number of children from consideration for the purposes of wage settings, the state government was in a position to address the poverty of large families through the Family Endowment Act enacted that same year. It provided five shillings weekly to every mother for each child 14 and under if the family income during the preceding year did not exceed "the living wage based on the requirements of a man and wife without children" plus £13 per child. Unlike the New Zealand scheme, the New South Wales allowances were financed by employers and payable only to employees.[49]   The New South Wales regime became "the centre of violent controversy" when the Industrial Commission, on the ground of vested rights, retained the old basic wage despite employers' contention that the legislature's intention in adopting a smaller family unit as the foundation of the basic wage was to reduce the latter. After the Industrial Commission reversed itself, the legislature intervened, requiring the Commission to use the needs of a man with a wife and one child as the basis.[50] The initial result of the new basic wage and family endowment was a reduction in annual payroll for employers by £60,000, which "was probably gratifying to the employers in New South Wales," and may explain why unions remained skeptical of family allowances. When the Commonwealth of Australia enacted a national child endowment in 1941, the scope was both narrowed and expanded. It covered only families with more than one child, but with state assumption of responsibility for financing, all families, not merely those of employees, became eligible.[51]

As early as 1921, Austria enacted a welfare statute that conferred an entitlement on employees to receive children's subsidies from their employers, but it was a temporary measure during a period of high prices driven by the simultaneous repeal of state subsidies for certain foodstuffs, and was opposed by labor and capital. The first national family allowance to cover even only children was enacted in Belgium in 1930, although it was confined to employees and financed by employers. Six decades later, Belgium's family program came closer to covering the additional costs of child-rich families than any other system in the European Community.[52]

The French state had a long tradition of providing child subsidies to its employees. The Ministry of the Navy initiated this practice in 1860, and the state, under the influence of the inflation brought on by World War I, extended the system to all its functionaries. As early as 1913, the French parliament, wishing both to "discharge a social debt...to the unhappy family, overburdened by the number of children and deprived of the resources necessary to provide for their needs" and to combat the "national peril" of a declining natality, enacted aid to families whose resources were insufficient to raise more than three children. Again in 1923 the French parliament, actuated by the need to encourage large families in order to "expiate[] the blame of those whom a narrow calculation, whom a criminal egotism had persuaded to reduce the number of their children"—thus giving Germany ground for believing that it could successfully attack France—provided for state allowances for each child in families of four or more children.[53]

In France, where the concern that the advent of a third child brought about the financial ruin of the typical working-class household and thus held back pro-creation united pronatalist organizations and the Catholic family movement, the legislature struggled for a dozen years, against the opposition of employers' associations, to generalize and make compulsory membership in a compensation fund for the pooled payment of what until 1932 had been voluntarily paid family allowances. In order to frustrate the temptation to discriminate against child-rich workers, employers had created equalization funds into which they paid on the basis of a criterion unrelated to the number of children in their employees' families such as their total wage bill or total employment. Ironically, French employers that were already paying family allowances to their employees resisted state intervention precisely because they feared that converting a gratuity granted by a benevolent employer into a legal entitlement would create a rights consciousness that might prompt demands by workers for higher allowances and thus spawn a new area of labor-capital conflict. Ultimately, however, the refusal of many smaller and medium-sized firms to join the funds prompted antietatist employers' organizations to accept state intervention.[54]

Unsurprisingly, the left-wing of the labor movement opposed privately organized allowances, which employers were wont to use as a weapon by withdrawing them from employees who participated in strikes or whose children worked in firms outside the fund. These unions did, however, support collectively organized allowances for child-rich families as a social right and completely independent of work and interruptions of work such as sickness and unemployment, although even after enactment of a state-supported program unions continued to criticize the lack of redistributory financing, which required childless workers to finance the allowances of proletarian families. This class policy reached its high point under the Vichy government, which enacted a tax on agricultural products to finance family allowances for the agrarian sector; consequently, the allowances of child-rich urban families spent on such necessities as meat, wheat, and sugar in effect paid for the agrarians' allowances.[55]

The statute enacted in 1932 accommodated the strategy of larger employers, which had been heavily influenced by price rises during World War I, of using allowances "to equalize and restrain their wage costs and to bind workers to the firm"; the new law imposed that strategy on small businesses, which had tended to ignore their obligations especially since allowances were less functional for them. By the 1930s, family allowances had also found favor with French employers, which recognized that the payments had "prevented trade unions from making use of family men for helping in their 'revolutionary' aims, and that the majority of family men...ha[d] remained outside the 'class-struggle.'"[56]

The reasons for the structure assumed by the French system during the 1930s, as shown by Joseph Spengler's contemporary historical-demographic analysis, lay in the merging of the struggle for population with class struggle. Since the effort to increase population tended to depress labor income and raise income from property, and since the pronatalists were largely representatives of the propertied classes, it was hardly surprising that their program bore a "pronounced class bias" and benefited largely the "haute bourgeoisie." This bias embraced the following elements: allowances were in large part self-financed by the working class; the pronatalist economic arguments were motivated by such "anti-worker" considerations as providing an adequate labor supply and stimulating industry; and "the military arguments [we]re essentially 'cannon fodder' arguments...." Spengler was of the opinion that this class contradiction could be solved together with the problem of avoiding depopulation if the state financed the private costs of demographic reproduction out of surplus income, which would simultaneously reduce inequalities in income distribution. This solution, however, turned out merely to exacerbate the contradiction since taxing away the surplus would have caused the upper classes to resist the destruction of the foundation of their economic and political power.[57]

On the eve of World War II, when government officials expressed grave concern over the military impact of the falling birth rate, France, which had amended its Labor Code in 1934 to prohibit employers from using the introduction of obligatory allowances as a pretext to reduce wages, incorporated family allowances into its Family Code. The French legislature viewed the allowances as a "solidary contribution of all the French" designed to reverse the trend toward smaller families. Instead of "encouraging them to increase the number of their children to send them to prospect for new sources of wealth," "solicitude for preserving a situation as fortunate for their descendants" caused parents to reduce their fertility. The new legislation provided both a one-time premium for the birth of the first child and a monthly allocation for each child thereafter amounting to 10 percent of the (notional) average monthly departmental adult salary and higher proportions for higher birth-order children. The allowances did not presuppose an employment relationship and thus *travailleurs indépendants* were also entitled to receive them. The Family Code's pronatalist thrust was amply on display in its penal sanction for abortion and sale of birth control devices. The allowances were financed by means of graduated income taxes on bachelors and divorced men and widows without children as well as on childless husbands who had been married at least two years. The Vichy government in 1941 granted allowances to one-earner families (or persons) already for the first child.[58]

That family allowances failed to eliminate the sharply hierarchical French income pattern, amounting to a "disequilibrium" in family budgets—per capita incomes (including family allowances) in four-child families were less than one-third those in two-earner childless families—was discovered during World War II. Statistical confirmation of the "great social injustice" of condemning those who insured the country's "perenniality" to an insufficient standard of living far inferior to that of childless households triggered more intense debate about the role of family allowances, which nevertheless prevented large families literally from starving to death. A series of studies in the French journal *Population*, which began appearing as soon as the postwar allowance program went into effect, revealed a permanent gap in the standard of living between the childless family in which both spouses worked and the family with children in which only the husband worked. Defined as the result of the confrontation between revenues and needs, the standard of living of a three-child family in 1946 was only about half of that of a childless family, which retained its privileged position despite the expansion of family allowances. Later studies consistently confirmed this gap.[59]

When the allowance rates were increased in 1946, France, impelled for reasons of "social justice" and as "a confirmation of the right to exist" to reduce "the inequality in the standards of living according to family burdens," was well on its way to offering the world's most developed program, which eventually has come to encompass more than a dozen different benefits including prenatal and postnatal grants, housing allowances (which covered almost half of the rent even in two-child families), loans to young couples, paid maternity leaves, and free kindergartens for virtually all children from the age of three.[60]

In a country where large families (three or more children) account for 40 percent and very large families (five or more children) for 8 percent respectively of all children, family allowances have become a vital source of income maintenance. Thus despite the fact that large wage-earning families in France still have, on average, lower incomes than childless couples, in large part because unemployment is much more common among the fathers and more than two-thirds of the mothers of three or more children do not work outside the home, the comprehensive family allowances, which entitle the five-child wage-earning family to the equivalent of a second full wage, have created rough total income parity between childless couples and families with five children. But even France's "world's family-friendliest" system of subsidies, which has provided more than two-thirds of the net income of a childless couple in additional income to a four-child family, is insufficient to compensate for more than a tiny part of the significant gap in per capita living standards between large and small families. They have compressed but nevertheless left intact "an income pyramid, in which the childless double-earners stand on top and the child-rich families with only one earner at the bottom."[61]

That family allowances large enough to hold parents harmless are now regarded as financially "utopian" in France is less surprising than that they have failed to realize Paul Douglas's prediction in the 1920s that they "would largely abolish poverty." French allowances nevertheless still make up a higher proportion of total social security payments and national income than in most advanced capitalist countries.[62]

When William Beveridge floated a family allowance proposal in Britain at the beginning of World War II, he was acutely aware of the same problems that had beset the program in the antipodes. Thus Beveridge and *The Times* agreed that among the luxuries that wartime Britain could not afford was state subsidization of "non-existent children." As the Australian state had charged two decades earlier, "in the case of children inadequate incomes and large families are so strongly correlated that any attempt to remedy the former by measures which treated all households as equal units would be fantastically expensive." The Chancellor of the Exchequer echoed these sentiments, alluding to "the difficulty of putting the parents of large families into a position to meet the increased cost of living by means of increased wages without increasing wages all round, and so setting up an inflationary movement." Shortly before the beginning of the war, Seebohm Rowntree, the private poverty investigator and convert to the cause of family allowances, had urged concentrating the allowance on three-or-more-child families below the income-tax line.[63]

Beveridge included children's allowances in his comprehensive wartime social insurance program in part because large families, together with unemployment, remained the chief cause of want in Britain despite the advance in real wages, which, based on productivity, could never afford a national minimum for families of different sizes. Malthus-like incentives constituted another basis for inclusion. In order to create the "the greater fluidity of labour" that he saw as the prerequisite for maintaining high employment after the war, Beveridge reverted to the lesser eligibility principle of the New Poor Law of 1834: "The first and most essential of all conditions...is that his situation...shall not be made really or apparently so eligible as the situation of the independent labourer of the lowest class.... Every penny bestowed that tends to render the condition of the pauper more eligible than that of the independent labourer, is a bounty on indolence and vice." The modern version of the principle read: "the gap between income during earning and during interruption of earning should be as large as possible for every man." The only acceptable way to keep the gap large for low-paid workers with large families and to prevent them from attaining a higher standard of living out of work than while employed was to provide children's allowances during periods of employment and unemployment. Finally, Beveridge recommended allowances as a means of increasing the rate of reproduction in order to insure the survival of the "British race." Although the allowance was not set at a level that would "lead parents who do not desire children to rear children for gain," it would enable parents to have additional children without harming the interests of their already existing ones—a point that eugenicists had been making for at least two decades.[64]

In the event, the Family Allowances Act, as hived off from the rest of Beveridge's National Insurance Act and enacted in 1945, scarcely contravened the lesser eligibility principle. It provided only five shillings weekly for each child beyond the first. Thus for a British worker with three children, the allowance amounted to only one-tenth of the average adult male wage. Nevertheless, allowances did initially make a moderate contribution to the alleviation of reproduction-related poverty. When Rowntree resurveyed York in 1950, a half-century after his first study there, he found that without family allowances, an additional 19 percent of all families with two or more children would have been in poverty. When, during the following decades, the state permitted the family allowances to lag behind the cost of living, families with many children bulked larger among the total population in poverty.[65]

The much more generous early post-World War II French family allowance provided approximately as much again as the average wage. Because the French allowances were financed by employers' contributions based on their wage bills, they became an alternative to higher wages. The French system implemented intraclass horizontal redistribution by means of which childless workers subsidized their co-workers' human production—as European labor unions had always predicted. Indeed, the French system, within which ultimately a married worker with two children recieved the lowest annual gross income and highest annual net income in Europe, may in large part have owed its earlier implementation and broader scope to the fact that unlike British pronatalists, those in France "were entirely uninterested in income redistribution across classes or sexes and never identified their goals with other 'progressive' causes." Instead, they perceived as "the greatest social injustice...not class inequality but rather inequality between families and single people of the same social class." In contrast, the British Royal Commission on Population rejected horizontal redistribution on the ground that it risked the danger of transfers from those who were over a lifetime relatively poor to the relatively rich because it mistakenly assumed that someone's economic position at any one time accurately reflected his position over his life.[66]

The greater material support that European states provide for families with children may in part account for the relatively subordinate position that respondents there attribute to superabundant children as a cause of poverty. As shown in table 22, when presented with twelve causes and asked to choose three, those questioned in the European Community in 1989 listed too many children in ninth place:

Table 22: **Most Frequently Listed Reasons for Poverty in the EC, 1989**[67]

Reason for Poverty	%
1. Victims of long-term unemployment	53
2. Alcoholism or drug abuse	38
3. Sickness	30
4. Family breakups	27
5. Brought up in deprived conditions	23
6. Social welfare cuts	20
7. Laziness	17
8. Loss of community spirit	14
9. Too many children	13
10. Living in a poor area	12
11. Educational system not catering to them	10
12. Lack of concern among neighbors	5

The only countries in which respondents accorded "too many children" a significantly above-average rank as a cause of poverty were the poorest EC members, Spain, Portugal, Ireland, and Italy.[68]

AMERICAN EXCEPTIONALISM

A voluntary, Bohemian poverty for adults is one thing; an involuntary poverty imposed upon babies is something else. [T]he nuclear family...is based on the egotistic assumption that one's children should have at least as many opportunities as one has had, preferably more. It therefore provides an idealistic self-sacrificing rationale for greed, competitiveness, and the other Adam Smithian virtues.[69]

It is commonly said that: "The United States is the only Western industrialized nation that does not have a child allowance policy or some other universal public benefit for families raising children." Yet the United States has, a popular misconception to the contrary notwithstanding, dispensed family subsidies through the income tax system almost since the inception of the federal individual income tax.[70] This effect is achieved primarily by means of dependent child exemptions, which enable parents to reduce their tax liability. What makes the United States unique is that it has relied almost entirely on this method to the exclusion of a direct family allowance. The only express national family policy in the United States operates through the AFDC poor-law system. Thus whereas European family allowance programs aspirationally pursue a preventive approach to poverty and deprivation, assistance in the United States is triggered only when impoverishment has already beset a family—an arrangement that in countries with non-poor-law programs such as Canada, Britain, and France, would, as Moynihan has observed, "be viewed as a form of social insanity."[71]

This lack of public, universal children's allowances characteristic of virtually the entire rest of the industrialized world has meant that social insurance benefits for families with children is much more extensive and generous in Europe as are child care facilities and parental leave programs.[72] Unsurprisingly, the poverty rate among adults with children is 2.4 times higher in the United States (12.7 percent) than in other wealthy capitalist countries (5.4 percent). Similarly, a much higher proportion of poor families with children is classified as "severely poor" (75 percent of the U.S. poverty line or below) in the United States than in other relatively wealthy advanced capitalist countries—57 percent compared with a low of 30 percent in West Germany and a high of 46 percent in Canada.[73]

A special study comparing non-Hispanic white children in two-parent families in the United States and children in Sweden revealed that in the mid-1980s, 9 percent of the former and 5 percent of the latter were market-poor—that is, lived in families with less than 40 percent of the national median disposable income adjusted for family size. But whereas virtually all such market-poor Swedish families received government transfer payments, only 71 percent of their U.S. counterparts did; consequently, fewer than 2 percent of Swedish children in two-parent families were disposable-income-poor, whereas the meager means-tested U.S. transfer payments left the proportion of poor children barely touched at 9 percent. These very low poverty rates in Sweden are all the more remarkable in light of the fact that children's allowances make up a small proportion of total family income even among the lowest-income families. Thus even in societies with advanced welfare systems, child allowances have sufficed only to eliminate poverty for some families, but have not provided enough support "to solve the child poverty problem in any country...." Nevertheless, the gap in state-redistributed monetary benefits between the United States and Western Europe is so significant that even in Italy, where the median income is much lower than in the

United States, the income of poor households with children (defined as at the 90th percentile) is absolutely greater ($12,552 and $10,923 respectively). More recent data reinforce the finding that U.S. government assistance programs are the most ineffective in reducing child poverty. Whereas state aid in Sweden, Britain, and France, for example, reduced the poverty rate from 14 to 3 percent, 30 to 10 percent, and 25 to 7 percent respectively, U.S. programs managed to lower it merely from 26 to 22 percent—a level more than 50 percent higher than the next highest rate.[74]

One of the earliest important contributions to the discussion of reproductive subsidies in the United States stemmed from the country's leading labor statistics official. In what was perhaps one of the first such proposals anywhere, Carroll Wright, the then chief of the Massachusetts Bureau of Statistics of Labor and later the first U.S. Commissioner of Labor, was animated by his disappointment with the reality of the family wage. His starting point was the belief that "it seems natural and just that a man's labor should be worth, and that his wages should be as much as, with economy and prudence, will comfortably maintain himself and his family, enable him to educate his children, and also to lay by enough for his decent support when his laboring powers have failed." But a study that Wright conducted of 397 working-class families in Massachusetts in 1875 concluded that the wage system enabled only a minority of workingmen to achieve that end by their own earnings; a majority maintained that standard of living by the labor of their wives and especially of their children. The wage system thus "usurps to its benefit the future productive power of the state, by employing children who should be in school or at play...."[75]

Without offering a substitute for the wage system, Wright proposed a twofold reform to ameliorate it. On the one hand, he recommended that all competent adult labor be paid a minimum yearly or daily wage to be enforced, if necessary, by legislation. Wright conceived of the minimum wage as enabling the unmarried workman to save money towards marriage. On the other hand: "An advance would be made for one child, then for the second and third, providing him with the means for their support and education. At the proper age, he could give to the state healthy workers.... And what would the state have done for him? Simply provided that his return for labor should pay for his living, and that of his children,—the latter, in turn, adding to the productive power of the state." This remarkably precocious yet instrumental statism, designed in part to eliminate "baneful...wife-labor" and to restore the mother to the home "for her own physical good," was in part driven by Wright's speculation that the wage system might eventually be superseded by cooperation, industrial partnerships, or even communism.[76]

By the beginning of the twentieth century, procreation-subsidizing state intervention had emerged. The state of Wisconsin, for example, included a $200 exemption for each child under the age of 18 in its income tax statute in 1911. The national income tax also contained such exemptions early on. The Senate version of the first post-16th Amendment federal income tax law provided for a dependent child exemption (of up to $1,000) on equitable grounds in recognition of the additional obligations associated with childrearing and also to "emphasiz[e] the family as the unit in our social structure."[77]

The Senate debate on the issue was instructive. Controversy centered on the limitation of the $500 per child exemption to a maximum of two children. Proponents of an amendment to eliminate this cap motivated it expressly by reference to the need to combat "race suicide." Since the basic exemption level was set high enough to exclude the vast majority of income recipients from the tax, senators were concerned exclusively with the procreational habits of the relatively well-off and not at all with the size of the working class. Senator Lawrence Sherman, for example, who would have put "a bounty on children," in opposing the limitation to "the fashionable number" of two children, adopted the eugenic position that "race suicide...began...among the people who ought to raise children and send them out into the world, because they are able so to nurture and train them as to make them good citizens and better fathers and mothers of future generations. Do not leave all the babies in the country to be raised by those who have not the means so to nurture them as well as have some whom I have in mind." When Progressive Republican George Norris moved to strike the cap on the ground that there "ought to be encouragement...to the men and the women who are raising families and perpetuating the race and continuing the stability of the country," Senator John Williams of Mississippi, speaking on behalf of the committee that reported out the bill, merely stated that its purpose was "to adapt the tax to the ability of the taxpayer, and not...as a means to encourage large families...." Norris tried to meet Williams's argument by denying that he wished to give a "premium for families of any particular size" and emphasizing the reduced ability to pay of the man with many children. Yet when Williams observed that 10 let alone 17 children were too many to subsidize, Norris replied that "we ought to let nature take its course, and not make an arbitrary stop...."[78]

The exemption cap prompted ex-President Theodore Roosevelt, who had led the rhetorical struggle against race suicide while in office, to rebuke "these Solons of the income tax [for] deliberately penalizing this third child, whose absence means speedy racial extinction, speedy racial death." Whereas legislatures in some countries with declining birth rates had "sought to reward an honorable woman who performs her prime duty to the State by bearing and rearing the children without whom the State will have no future whatever," Roosevelt continued, "this is the first time that any legislative body has ever put itself on record as in favor of discouraging the performance of the most sacred and the most vital of all duties." Although the child-exemption provision was absent from the statute in 1913, even it contained a $1,000 personal exemption for a head of family or married person. In 1917 Congress amended the statute, establishing a $200 personal exemption for dependent children under the age of eighteen.[79]

Another early discussion of reproductive subsidies took place in the 1920s at a time of intense debate over family allowances in Europe. U.S. Commissioner of Labor Statistics Ethelbert Stewart started from the assumption that just as firms must set aside amortization funds to replace worn-out machinery, so too "industry must provide for the renewal of the labor supply." But when he had broached the issue of the European family wage with U.S. manufacturers, they objected that whereas children in Europe might work in the same industry as their parents, in the United States there was no assurance "that the children born to the workers engaged by such industry...would be available to that industry as a labor supply when such children were grown." Despite capitalists' self-paralyzing fears of free-riding competitors, Stewart believed that family allowances, even in the form of a wage, could be defended on an industry basis if an industry-wide pool were created to finance it in the manner of workers' compensation. Nevertheless, he regarded the industrial argument as too narrow. From an aggregate-capitalist perspective, he directed attention to the larger question: "The existence of the State, the existence of society, of civilization, the perpetuation of the race, is much more essential than that any particular industry or all industries should have an ample supply of workers." Stewart's core demographic concern, however, was that although firms could substitute machines for men, "[w]e have utterly failed...to invent a machine which will use and pay cash down for the products of other machines."[80]

Segueing to the problem of rich and poor, Stewart sought to unravel cause and effect: "The poor do not have children because they are poor, they are poor because they have children." This hardly novel but nevertheless controversial claim was then linked to an original claim: "The rich are not childless because they are rich, they are rich because they are childless. It is the cost of rearing a family." Coming at the height of the speculative boom of the 1920s, Stewart's fairy-tale account of the ontogeny of capitalist wealth did point out that at whatever standard of living, rearing a child to tne age of 18 amounted to three years of a man's earnings. Concentrating on these "real facts," Stewart believed that unless the discussion moved "away from the replacing labor supply theory as expressed in the term 'family wage,'" the movement to hold harmless those who have been impoverishing themselves while enriching the world would not "be able to carry with it a sufficient increase of compensation to make it of any great value." Stewart rejected industrial wage-rate marriage differentials because "every man should earn enough to enable him to marry and rear a family of five if he wants to and...every married man should receive a wage which will enable him to save up against the day when he will have a family of five or more." He did, however, advocate a "social allowance by which our political and social institutions will pay for the replacement of the race" so that no "man...should be penalized for his loyalty to the race...." This allowance assumed so much the greater importance as the spread of birth control meant that men and women could for the first time "simply refuse to become poor for the public welfare...." Unwilling to trust the invisible hand, Stewart predicted that if the visible hand of the public fisc did not intervene, "the race will...cease to exist."[81]

Despite his key government position, Stewart failed to move the debate in the United States into new channels. Unlike some European governments, which introduced children's allowances early in the twentieth century for their own state employees, U.S. governmental employers did not adopt such differentiated compensation systems. The isolated exceptions failed to coalesce into a movement. Public school teachers in some districts received allowances earlier in the century, while Congress introduced family allowances for dependents of enlisted members of the military during World War II.[82]

As the federal government made plans to avoid a replication of the economic depression that had followed in the wake of demobilization after World War I, the left-leaning National Resources Planning Board as early as 1942 raised the issue of the need for family allowances as part of a basic family-security program for the postwar period. At the same time the Board published a brochure by the leading U.S. Keynesian, Alvin Hansen, who proposed family allowances among the expanded public-welfare expenditures that he regarded as prerequisites of the shift toward a postwar high consumption economy. Wilbur Cohen, one of the key figures in the formulation of the original U.S. Social Security program and technical adviser to the Social Security Board during World War II, also recommended family allowances in 1942 as part of a more comprehensive system. In light of this quasi-official support, it was "distressing" to the Left (and the Catholic Church) that the so-called American Beveridge plan, the wide-ranging security program embodied in the Wagner-Murray-Dingell bill, lacked a system of children's allowances. The *Nation*, for example, found "no other phase of social security...more important." Spurred by stories of poor families who had furnished as many as eight soldiers for the war and of a million boys who failed to meet the simple military educational tests, Senator William Langer introduced a bill in 1945 to pay "gratuities" (of $500 to $1,000) to future parents of two or more children, but it was stillborn.[83]

During World War II, the popular press published a spate of articles praising family allowances in the wake of Beveridge's inclusion of them in his plan. F. Emerson Andrews, who worked at the Russell Sage Foundation, was particularly adept at placing his deftly argued pieces. In the *Atlantic Monthly* he introduced children's allowances—"in effect, salaries for mothers"—as a "democratic, practical" way out of the insolvency into which "we" had plunged families.

> And why not salaries for mothers?... A woman who raises pigs is called
> a producer by the Census Bureau and is paid for her pigs. A few years
> ago she was even paid money for *not* raising pigs. But a woman who
> chooses the vastly more difficult occupation of both producing and
> rearing children—the job that is basically the most important to us as
> a nation—is not even a "gainful worker"...and is not paid, either by the
> government or her husband....[84]

Because the adoption of children's allowances by Germany, Italy, and Japan had enabled conservative opponents to disqualify them "as totalitarian devices for increasing cannon fodder," Andrews tried to remove the alien stigma by alluding to institutions such as public schools, "which the bachelor landowner helps to pay." Pulling out all the propagandistic stops, Andrews somberly depicted a postwar economy that might find the former "soldier father," whose military family allowance had supported his children, beginning civilian life again "at the bottom," perhaps even "selling apples on street corners," cut loose by a society for which he had risked his life. By D-Day, Andrews was explaining to the middle-class readers of *Parents' Magazine* that the $10,000 that each of their children cost them was the equivalent of a 20-year mortgage. But "if America was to survive as a nation," they would have to contract for the equivalent of three concurrent mortgages—except that "[u]nlike houses, children cannot handily be abandoned if the going gets rough, to be repossessed by the bank." Andrews pushed the historical analogy to the democratic-labor-liberal struggle for free public schools as confiscation of bachelors' property to subsidize other people's children's education.[85]

By the end of the war, children's allowances had become a sufficently respectable income maintenance proposal that the Brookings Institution published a large-scale study of the Social Security system that included means-tested allowances as a component of a future comprehensive program. The resurgence of interest in children's allowances in the United States during the 1950s was institutionally manifested by Senator Richard Neuberger's repeated filing of bills modeled on the World War II-era Canadian system. Enacted in 1944, Canadian allowances, which unions initially opposed and then tentatively accepted, were funded by the state and covered all children, providing $5 per month for those under 6 years of age and up to $8 monthly for those 13 to 15 years of age. To be sure, as a "concession to the clash of racial attitudes," the allowances were reduced for the fifth child and all higher birth-order children, who were disproportionately represented among French-Candian families in Quebec.[86]

In 1955, as the U.S. birth rate reached its highest level ever and the proportion of childless married couples under the age of 45 declined significantly vis-à-vis the pre-World War II period, Neuberger, together with seven of the most liberal senators, including Paul Douglas, who had written extensively on allowances three decades earlier, submitted a resolution to create a special committee to study the Canadian program with a view to implementing a similar system in the United States. Why, when "America [wa]s growing its biggest crop of children" ever without direct state subsidies, family allowances had become "unusually pertinent" Neuberger failed to explain. Nor did his proposal to omit any means test and make the payment a universal entitlement, thus reducing administrative costs, make it any more palatable to Congress. The same year, the congressional Subcommittee on Low-Income Families heard testimony from several witnesses who tentatively advocated family allowances. The somewhat iconoclastic economist, Richard Lester, "thr[e]w out what some people may think is a wild idea": if low-income families have proportionately more children, "I am not sure but that we ought to consider seriously...family allowances...." The only interest that it sparked on the committee was a personal pecuniary one in Alabama Senator John

Sparkman, who, upon hearing that it might amount to $6 to $7 per month per child, opined that he would like to have it for his tenant farmer.[87]

The 1950s were not, however, ideologically propitious for such blatant state intervention, and only sparse mainstream support for allowances emerged; emblematic of the subject's marginalization was the inclusion of a proposal for a $3 per week family allowance in the 1952 platform of the radical Progressive Party. The glorification in the popular media and social sciences of the male-headed medium-sized family, taking care of which fully occupied the wife/mother, constructed a norm that left no room for government largesse. Yet that same middle-class family appreciatively became the recipient of government handouts in the form of pro-family tax code revisions such as joint filing, increases in the personal exemption, and homeowner-related tax benefits paid for by lower-income taxpayers, and Veterans Administration and Federal Housing Administration home mortgage insurance programs, which encouraged the proliferation of child-focused suburbs.[88]

Interest in family allowances was sustained propagandistically during this period by Catholic welfare specialists "as an alternative to limiting family size." Thus a leading Catholic magazine stated that: "The answer to the economic problem they [children] create must not be a limiting of family size to fit income. Rather we must find ways to help the larger families obtain the income they need for a decent family life." Based on census data showing that median family income peaked in families with two children, the authors proposed that the allowance be triggered by the advent of the third child: "Our present wage system is geared to the needs of the two-child family, so that in many families with only one or two children the need for supplementing income is slight." The misogynist orientation of some Catholic contributions, however, was scarcely calculated to appeal to women.[89]

Family allowances found a new champion in Representative John Conyers, who introduced the Family Allowances Act in 1967, which would have paid $10 per month per child. Like its predecessors, however, it died. At the same time, Daniel Moynihan, in between high-ranking policy appointments in the Johnson and Nixon administrations, was agitating for a universal non-means-tested family allowance. In the 1960s, too, Mollie Orshansky, creator of the federal government's poverty definition, was showing how monthly child allowances of $50 would push the vast majority of large families above the poverty line. Perhaps the most thoroughly thought-out proposal came from an economist, Harvey Brazer, who had been the Treasury Department's principal economic advisor on tax policy. He coupled a children's allowance and discontinuation of the dependent child exemptions under the federal income tax with a children's allowance tax, which at its maximum would have equaled 95 percent of the allowance received. Peaking at $3,300 for a four-child family and no other income, it would have cost $7.6 billion and efficiently reduced the poverty gap in families with children by 81 percent, removing more than half of all poor children from poverty.[90]

By the end of the Johnson administration, Congress heard several more advocates of family allowances as components of income maintenance programs. New York State and New York City welfare officials, for example, urged adoption of a non-means-tested universal program to close the gap between "a worker's productive capacity and the cycle of his family needs." Family sociologists proposed income maintenance programs specifically keyed to the phases of the family life cycle in which the gap between needs and resources was greatest. The radical potential of the late Johnson administration, thwarted by its Indochina war, was symbolized by an intraliberal debate in which negative income tax supporters such as James Tobin and Henry Aaron could afford the political luxury of criticizing family allowances on the grounds that they not only wasted resources on the nonpoor while offering monetarily mere token gestures to large families, but failed to do anything for the 10 million single adults and childless couples below the poverty line. A children's allowance demonstration project planned by the federal government in 1968 to study its effects on birth rates and labor force participation rates was cancelled the next year when the Nixon administration began pursuing its (abortive) Family Assistance Plan.[91]

When the U.S. Congress in 1993 amended the Internal Revenue Code to introduce a modest increment in the Earned Income Tax Credit for families with two or more children, it institutionally and ideologically opened the way to the ultimate enactment of a family allowance—albeit one that initially would be confined to low-income families. In light of the renewed call by feminists and policy analysts for a full-fledged family endowment especially to help the burgeoning number of single-parent families, the United States may yet introduce a program that the rest of the capitalist world began implementing 70 years ago.[92] Until that time, however, Myrdal's rhetorical admonition that it was "impossible that the majority of good Americans should really think that so many...families who are forced into poverty or destitution because the number of their children is so large...should be left largely unaided" will remain unheeded.[93]

Such a prospect is, however, dimmed by the lingering effects of eugenicist, racist, and antipaternalistic individualist ideologies. During the Great Depression, for example, Paul Popenoe, a eugenicist at the Human Betterment Foundation, was appalled that families on public relief in Los Angeles were "producing children steadily at public expense," necessitating further "charitable aid." By means of this "vicious circle," the "self-supporting part of the population" is so burdened that it reduces its own procreation while "paying for...the reproduction of a class of persons many of whom are eugenically inferior." The multivalence of family allowances was amply on display when eugenicists became anxious because the fertility rate had fallen below the replacement level in the United States. Popenoe, convinced that the wage system was incompatible with the family, demanded equalization of "the economic position of the fertile and the sterile." The particular object of his concern, however, was that "the feeble-minded and the dependent...on relief" were overreproducing while "educated people" were not. He therefore suggested a "selective family wage" for the "white collar class" "not to evaluate the children of the community and say one is worth more than another [but] merely to neutralize the economic pressure for childlessness [and] to ensure that educated people will not have to sacrifice their own standard of living...."[94]

Thirty years later, even the staff of President Johnson's liberal Commission on Income Maintenance Programs warned that:

> The point is made much too frequently that every industrialized nation except the United States has a children's allowance.... What is never mentioned...is that those countries...are demographically much more homogeneous.... To the middle income white suburbanite, black has significant negative externalities. So does illegitimacy. The combination is overwhelming. Although illegitimate black children are a small proportion of children in poverty, the myth of a high proportion is real impediment to adoption of general programs in aid of children.[95]

Moynihan, whose 1965 memorandum was responsible for galvanizing public debate about black families, observed in connection with his account of the Nixon administration's failure to enact its Family Assistance Plan that by the end of the 1960s it had become clear that poor families with children were large, southern (or southern migrant), black, and "living in a state almost of population siege." The likelihood of passage of a family allowance diminished in proportion as it was projected as a "'baby bonus'" for "teeming working-class quarters so disagreeable to social welfare enthusiasts." For Moynihan, the chances of introducing a family wage in the United States were diminished by its association with religion and race: on the one hand, its "pronatalist conservative cast was disastrously confirmed by the zeal that the Roman Catholic Church exhibited for the subject"; and, on the other, at "its most crude, the question of family policy...might be reduced to that of providing stability for the Negro slums." Nor is the continued pull of original Malthusianism to be underestimated. Even as liberal a policy analyst as David Ellwood, who became the guiding intellect in the Clinton administration's project to "end welfare as we know it," rejected children's allowances on the ground that "if...set at a high level, it becomes simply a guaranteed income" and by "offering a reasonable level of security...may discourage work."[96]

If there was a time when it was not outlandish for the early nineteenth-century Ricardian socialist William Thompson to ask: "Why should a father and mother be punished—in diminished comforts—for having large families?," that period lies as far in the past as the belief that large families were caused by "[p]eculiar fecundity," which struck people by "chance [or] causes which they could not...controul...."[97] The widespread availability of birth control means in combination with the Center's adoption of the Right's emphasis on personal responsibility makes such a position politically untenable in the United States.

Ironically, recent trends in family size undermine the racially motivated Malthusian claim that poor law payments promote large families. Thus from 1976 to 1992, the proportion of single women receiving AFDC payments who had one child rose from 29.5 percent to 35.9 percent while that of single-women AFDC-recipients with four or more children dropped from 22.5 percent to 12.8 percent.[98] Moreover, the birthrate among welfare recipients is lower than the national average. In fact, with the possible exception of the ideologically unique case of Nazi Germany, scholars have been unable to conclude that modern family allowances or the nineteenth-century English poor laws have stimulated birth rates.[99]

There may therefore be some validity to Eveline Burns's claim that, for opposite reasons—namely, wealth and hopelessness—financial considerations play little or no part in decisions about family size among high- and low-income families, so that only middle-income groups are fully subject to Malthusian preventive checks of economic rationality.[100] Nevertheless, regardless of whether they are a demographic incentive, children's allowances are one of the most efficacious and egalitarian means of alleviating impoverishment associated with the unequal burdens that people bear in contributing to the production of the next generation.

NOTES

1. George Fitzhugh, *Sociology for the South, or the Failure of Free Society,* reprinted in *Ante-Bellum: Writings of George Fitzhugh and Hinton Rowan Helper on Slavery* 41-95 at 59 (Harvey Wish ed., 1960 [1854]).

2. Karl Marx, 1 *Das Kapital,* in Karl Marx [&] Friedrich Engels, *Werke* 23:672 (1962 [1867]).

3. "Labor and Politics," *Nation* 14: 386-387 (June 13, 1872).

4. The terms will be used interchangeably here although in some countries they may have different meanings. By "family or child benefits" is sometimes meant a more inclusive catgeory embracing cash and in-kind transfers including direct benefits for children with a social security program, tax exemptions, and means-tested public assistance; "family allowances," a narrower category, may include in addition to cash allowances social services and earmarked cash transfers; the narrowest category, "children's allowances," refers only to unrestricted cash transfers for children. T. Marmor & Martin Rein, "Post-War European Experience with Cash Transfers: Pensions, Child Allowances, and Public Assistance," in The President's Commission on Income Maintenance Programs, *Technical Studies* 259-91 at 269 (n.d. [1969]).

5. Peter Townsend, *Poverty in the United Kingdom: A Survey of Household Resources and Standards of Living* 919 (1979).

6. Daniel Moynihan, *The Negro Family: The Case for National Action* 21, 24 (Office of Policy Planning and Research, U.S. Department of Labor, 1965); Thomas Robert Malthus, *An Essay on the Principle of Population* (6th ed.), in *The Works of Thomas Robert Malthus* 3:618 (E.A. Wrigley & David Souden ed., 1986 [1826]); Mrs. Sidney Webb, "Minority Report," in *Women in Industry: Report of the War Cabinet Committee on Women in Industry* 286, 305, 307 (Cmd. 135, 1919). Malthus's position casts doubt on Polanyi's claim that at the outset of the nineteenth century it was not understood that right-to-live public wage subsidies were incompatible with capitalism. Karl Polanyi, *The Great Transformation* 81 (1971 [1944])

7. A.B. Piddington, *The Next Step: A Family Basic Income* 28, 23 (1921).

8. Alexander Gray, *Family Endowment: A Critical Analysis* 78 (1927) (quote); D.H. Macgregor, "Family Allowances," *Economic J.* 36 (141):1-10 at 9, 2-3 (Mar. 1926) (quote); E. Penrose, *Population Theories and Their Application: With Special Reference to Japan* 19-20 (1935 [1934]); *Annales de la Chambre des Députés*, 9ᵐᵉ Législature: Débats parlementaires, Session extraordinaire de 1908 1: pt. at 122-23 (Oct. 20, 1908) (1909) (M. Lemire) (quote); New Zealand, *Parliamentary Debates*, 21st Sess., 22d Parl., 210:629 (1926) (quote).

9. Alva Myrdal, *Nation and Family: The Swedish Experiment in Democratic Family and Population Policy* 138, 135, 98, 126-27, 133, 140-41 (1941); Gunnar Myrdal, *Population: A Problem for Democracy* 209 (1940). On the Myrdals' eugenicism, see Alva Myrdal & Gunnar Myrdal, *Kris i befolkningsfrågan* 223, 224 (1934): "Society is...purely economically interested in a limiting of this reproductive freedom of the slightly imbecilic. Again and again we see for example large flocks of children of imbecilic mothers, where the whole litter has to be supported by the public." The "race-biological" and "race-hygienic" considerations prompting a decision to limit or expand reproduction were in their view, however, not tied to social classes.

10. Dominion of Canada, *Official Report of Debates*, House of Commons, Fifth Session—Nineteenth Parliament, 243:5330-31, 5333-34 (July 25, 1944) (1945) (quotes); Jane Ursel, *Private Lives, Public Policy: 100 Years of State Intervention in the Family* 190-98 (1992). King achieved renown 30 years earlier when, as a highly paid agent of the Rockefellers, he was instrumental in launching the company union movement in the United States as part of that family's effort to whitewash itself in the wake of the Ludlow massacre. Peter Collier & David Horowitz, *The Rockefellers: An American Dynasty* 106-29 (1977 [1976]); David Montgomery, *The Fall of the House of Labor: The Workplace, the State, and American Labor Activism, 1865-1925*, at 347-51 (1989 [1987]).

11. Paul Douglas, *Wages and the Family* 47, 91 (1927 [1925]); the C.G.T. is the Confédération Générale du Travail. Fred Pampel & Paul Adams, "The Effects of Demographic Change and Political Structure on Family Allowance Expenditures," *Social Serv. Rev.* 66 (4):524-46 at 527 (Dec. 1992), vitiate their analysis by one-dimensionally focusing on family allowances as "a direct and overt expression of a nation's institutional commitment to families with children."

12. Joseph Cohen, *Family Income Insurance: A Scheme of Family Endowment by the Method of Insurance* 11 (1926) (quote); John Macniol, *The Movement for Family Allowances, 1918-45: A Study in Social Policy Development* 138, 196 (1980) (quote); Hilary Land, "The Introduction of Family Allowances: An Act of Historic Justice?" in Phoebe Hall et al., *Change, Choice, and Conflict in Social Policy* 157-230 at 177, 193-94 (1975).

13. H.J. Laski, "Data from Glasgow," in Ethel Elderton et al., *On the Correlation of Fertility with Social Value: A Cooperative Study* 6-13 at 8 (1913); Elderton et al., *On the Correlation of Fertility with Social Value* at 45-46. See also Isaac Kramnick & Barry Sheerman, *Harold Laski: A Life on the Left* 34-45 (1993).

14. Pope Leo XIII, *Rerum novarum* ¶ 35 (1891); Pope Pius XI, *Quadragesimo anno* ¶ 71 (1931); Hubert Callaghan, "The Family Allowance Procedure: An Analysis of the Family Allowance Procedure in Selected Countries" ix (Ph.D. diss. Catholic U., 1947); Allan Carlson, *From Cottage to Work Station: The Family's Search for Social Harmony in the Industrial Age* 101-102 (1993); John Ryan, *A Living Wage* 88-90, 101 (rev. ed. 1920 [1906]); Samuel Gompers, "A Minimum Living Wage," *Am. Federationist* 5 (2):25-30 at 25 (Apr. 1898).

15. Barbara Armstrong, *Insuring the Essentials: Minimum Wage Plus Social Insurance—A Living Wage Program* 146 (1932) (quote); Allan Carlson, *Family Questions: Reflections on the American Social Crisis* xvi (quote), 18-19, 139-54 (quote at 149) (1989); *idem, From Cottage to Work Station* at 35-63; *idem,* "What Happened to the 'Family Wage'?" *Pub. Interest* No. 83:3-17 at 9 (1986) (quote).

16. U.S. BLS, *Labor Force Statistics Derived from the Current Population Survey, 1948-87,* tab. C-12 at 801 (Bull. 2307, 1988); U.S. Bureau of the Census, *Statistical Abstract of the United States: 1993,* tab. 633 at 400 (1993); Robert Haveman et al., "Disparities in Well-Being Among U.S. Children over Two Decades: 1962-83," in *The Vulnerable* 149, tab. 7.1 at 155 (John Palmer et al. eds., 1988). These proportions are still considerably lower than in Scandinavia, where, in part as a result of the state provision of child care facilities, almost nine-tenths of mothers are employed. Constance Sorrentino, "The Changing Family in International Perspective," *Monthly Labor Rev.* 113 (3):41-58, tab. 9 at 53, 54 (Mar. 1990); Markus Jäntti & Sheldon Danziger, "Child Poverty in Sweden and the United States: The Effect of Social Transfers and Parental Labor Force Participation," *Industrial & Labor Relations Rev.* 48 (1):48-64, tab. 2 at 53 (Oct. 1994).

17. At the other extreme, the demographer Martha Riche is wrong in claiming that the special conditions generated by U.S. hegemony between the end of World War II and the 1960s marked "'the one and only time in our history [when] an ordinary guy with a high school degree could afford to have a non-working wife.'" Mary Lee, "The American Family Isn't Mom, Dad, and the Kids Anymore," *Atlanta J. and Constitution,* Nov. 13, 1988, at 1A, col. 1, at 16, col. 1 (Lexis).

18. Carlson, *Family Questions* at 148, 149 (quote); Senate Rep. No. 884, 75th Cong., 1st Sess. 4 (1937) (quote); Carlson, *Family Questions* at xvii; Ralph Smith & Bruce Vavrichek, "The Minimum Wage: Its Relation to Incomes and Poverty," *Monthly Labor Rev.,* June 1987, at 24-30, chart 2 at 26.

19. Jason DeParle, "Sharp Increase Along the Borders of Poverty," *N.Y. Times,* Mar. 31, 1994, at A10, col. 1 (nat. ed.); Lawrence Mead, *The New Politics of Poverty: The Nonworking Poor in America* 71 (1992) (quote).

20. Abraham Epstein, *Insecurity: A Challenge to America: A Study of Social Insurance in the United States and Abroad* 637-40 (1933).

21. H.N. Brailsford, John A. Hobson, A. Creech Jones, & E.F. Wise, *The Living Wage: A Report submitted to the National Administrative Council of the Independent Labour Party* 20 (1926) (quote); G.D.H. Cole, *A History of Socialist Thought, IV/I: Communism and Social Democracy: 1914-1931,* at 448 (1958).

22. Ch. 4 above; International Labour Office [ILO], *Family Allowances: The Remuneration of Labour According to Need* 3-4 (Studies and Reports, Ser. D [Wages & Hours] No. 13, 1924); B. Seebohm Rowntree, *Poverty and Progress: A Second Social Survey of York* 171 (1941). Although the data were not available at the time, the 1921 census for England and Wales revealed that three-fifths of all men over 20 years of age were either single or married or widowers with no children; the proportion was as high as 65 percent among agricultural workers and as low as 48 percent among miners. Eleanor Rathbone, *Family Allowances* 258 (1947 [1924]).

23. Paul Douglas, "Is the Family of Five Typical?" *J. Am. Statistical Assoc.,* n.s. 19(147):314-28 at 327 (Sept. 1924).

24. Brailsford et al., *The Living Wage* at 21-23. The ILP was merely following the English-speaking world's foremost advocate of family allowances: "The provision for phantom wives may...be defended on the ground that a man who has not a wife to keep has to pay someone to do his cooking, washing and housekeeping for him, whether it be a

landlady, a mother or some other woman relative." Eleanor Rathbone, *The Disinherited Family: A Plea for the Endowment of the Family* 20 (1924). See also *ibid.* at 296.

25. Pamela Graves, *Labour Women: Women in British Working-Class Politics 1918-1939*, at 106-107 (1994) (quote); oral communication by Geoffrey Palmer, former Prime Minister of New Zealand, of his recollections of the significance of family allowances while he was growing up during the 1940s (Sept. 15, 1994); Rathbone, *The Disinherited Family* at 256-57. As ultimately enacted in Britain, family allowances "shall belong...to the wife...." Family Allowances Act, 1945, 8 & 9 Geo. 6, ch. 41, § 4-(I)(a).

26. Rathbone, *The Disinherited Family* at viii.

27. R. Palme Dutt, *Socialism and the Living Wage* 120-23 (1927).

28. Eduard Heimann, "The Family Wage Controversy in Germany," *Econ. J.* 33 (132):509-15 at 515 (Dec. 1923). On the unions' stance, see U.S. BLS, *Family Allowances in Foreign Countries* 94 (Bull. No. 401, 1926) (by Mary Waggaman).

29. Heimann, "The Family Wage Controversy in Germany" at 513-14 (quote); ILO, *Family Allowances* at 7; Douglas, *Wages and the Family* at 269-70 (quote).

30. Gunnar Heinsohn & Rolf Knieper, *Theorie des Familienrechts: Geschlechts-rollenaufhebung, Kindesvernachlässigung, Geburtenrückgang* 109, 193 (1974).

31. John Stuart Mill, *Principles of Political Economy* 363 (Ashley ed. 1909 [1848]); Inga Thorsson, "Children's Allowances in Sweden," in *Children's Allowances and the Economic Welfare of Children* at 115, 117; Alva Myrdal, "A Program for Family Security in Sweden," *International Labour Rev.* 39(6): 723-63 at 740 (June 1939).

32. Conservative Political Centre, *Family Allowances* 21 (No. 182, 1958).

33. Daniel Moynihan, *Family and Nation* 163 (1986); George Gilder, *Wealth and Poverty* 17-18 (1982 [1981]).

34. Mrs. [Magdalen] Pember Reeves, *Round About a Pound a Week* 215 (1913).

35. *Ibid.* at 219-20.

36. Eveline Burns, "The Economics of Family Endowment," *Economica*, 5 (14):155-64 at 158-59 (June 1925) (quote); Heimann, "The Family Wage Controversy in Germany" at 512 (quote); Marjorie Clark, "Organized Labor and the Family-Allowance System in France," *J. Pol. Econ.* 39(4): 526-37 at 527 (Aug. 1931); Rathbone, *The Disinherited Family* at 265 (quote). On French socialist unions' opposition to private family allowances and their demand for a universal compulsory system in the 1920s, see Hugh Vibart, *Family Allowances in Practice* 122-25 (1926).

37. Sidney Webb, *The Decline in the Birth-Rate* 16 (Fabian Tract No. 131, 1907). On his social Darwinism, see Sidney Webb, "The Economic Theory of Legal Minimum Wage," *J. Pol. Econ.* 20: 973, 992 (1912).

38. Webb, *The Decline in the Birth-Rate* at 17-18.

39. *Ibid.* at 18-19; Sidney Webb & Beatrice Webb, *The Prevention of Destitution* 319 (1911).

40. H. G. Wells, *Socialism and the Family* 37, 61-62 (1908).

41. Adolf Hitler, *Mein Kampf* 447 (1940 [1925/1927]); Horst Hoffmann, *Was jeder Kinderreiche wissen muß* (1938).

42. *Report of the Royal Commission on Child Endowment or Family Allowances*, in Parliament of the Commonwealth of Australia, *Session Papers*, 2:64 (1929); The President's Commission on Income Maintenance Programs, *Background Papers* 413 (1970).

43. Sheila Kamerman & Alfred Kahn, "What Europe Does for Single-Parent Families," *Pub. Interest*, No. 93, at 70-86 at 77 (Fall 1988).

44. "Progress of Family Endowment Movement in Australia and New Zealand," *Monthly Labor Rev.* 28 (3):564-73 at 564-65 (Mar. 1929). After describing these and other "contradictions in the family wage system" in the United States and Britain in the 1920s, a historian writes that: "This swirling discourse revealed dilemmas that were insoluble within the gender order of the time." Linda Gordon, *Pitied But Not Entitled: Single Mothers and the History of Welfare 1890-1935*, at 59 (1994). Yet despite the existence of the same "gender order" in New Zealand, Australia, France, and Belgium enacted family allowances.

45. R. Campbell, "Family Allowances in New Zealand," *Econ. J.* 37 (147):369-83 at 379 (Sept. 1927) (quote); Family Allowances Act, 1926, N.Z. Stat., 1926, No. 30, §§ 2, 3, 6(1.), 8(1.)(a.), 18 (quote); New Zealand, *Parliamentary Debates*, 21st Sess., 22d Parl., 210:590 (1926) (statement of Mr. Anderson, Minister in Charge of Pensions). The family allowance, which was not payable to Asians, was not intended for single mothers.

46. Oral communication from Geoffrey Palmer; H.I. Sinclair, *Population: New Zealand's Problem* (n.d. [1944]); Campbell, "Family Allowances in New Zealand" at 373-74; New Zealand, *Parliamentary Debates*, 21st Sess, 22d Parl., 210:587-633, 667, 762-74, 833-45 (1926); "Progress of Family Endowment Movement in Australia and New Zealand" at 567-68; Industrial Conciliation and Arbitration Amendment Act, 1936, N.Z. Stat., No. 6, § 3(5) (quote); [New Zealand] Royal Commission on Social Security in New Zealand, *Social Security in New Zealand: Report of the Royal Commission of Inquiry* 216-40 (1972).

47. Henry Higgins, "A New Province for Law and Order," *Harv. Law Rev.* 29 (1):13-39 at 16 (Nov. 1915) (quote); Ex parte McKay, 2 Commonwealth Arbitration Reports 1, 3, 6 (1907) (quote). The statute, the Excise Tariff 1906, imposed excise duties on agricultural implements but exempted firms in Australia that provided fair and reasonable remuneration. Rhetorically interesting was the judge's use of analogy in determining the standard: "If A lets B have the use of his horses, on the terms that he give them fair and reasonable treatment...it is B's duty to give them proper food and water, and such shelter and rest as they need; and as wages...." *Ibid.* at 4.

48. Industrial Conciliation and Arbitration Act, 1932, § 9 (3.) (ii), Queensland Acts, 23 Geo. V. No. 36; Industrial Arbitration Act, 1912, § 84(2), W. Austr. Acts No. 57, at 205, 232-33.

49. E. Burns, *Wages and the State: A Comparative Study of the Problems of State Wage Regulation* 326-34 (1926); "Progress of Family Endowment Movement in Australia and New Zealand" at 568-69; Industrial Arbitration (Living Wage Declaration) Act, N.S.W. Stat., No. 38, 1927, § 2(2) (quote); Family Endowment Act, New South Wales Stat., 1927, No. 39, §§ 3, 12, 39 (quote). For a description of the dead end to which efforts to adjust wage-fixings for so-called normal families had led, see Burns, "The Economics of Family Endowment" at 158. According to the 1921 census, one-third of all male employee householders in New South Wales had no children and only one-seventh had more than three. In re Standard of Living Determination and Living Wage Declarations, N.S.W. Industrial Arbitration Reports 165, tab. IV at 207 (1927).

50. "The Family Allowance System: A Survey of Recent Developments," *International Labour Rev.* 21 (3):395 at 414 (Mar. 1930) (quote); In re Standard of Living Determination and Living Wage Declarations, N.S.W. Industrial Arbitration Reports 165 (1927); In re Living Wage Inquiry—General and Rural, N.S.W. Industrial Arbitration Reports 353 (1928); In re Standard of Living and Living Wages for Adult Male Employees, N.S.W. Industrial Arbitration Reports 375 (1929); Family Endowment (Further Amendment) Act, New South Wales Acts, 1929, No. 58, § 3(a)(ii).

51. Armstrong, *Insuring the Essentials* at 137 (quote); Child Endowment Act 1941, Austl. Acts, §§ 4, 13, 23.

52. Bundesgesetz vom 21. Dezember 1921 über den Abbau der Lebensmittel-zuschüsse des Bundes und die damit zusammenhängenden Fürsorgemaßnahmen (Abbau-gesetz), §13, Bundesgesetzblatt für die Republik Österreich 2167, 2169 (1921); U.S. BLS, *Family Allowances in Foreign Countries* at 108-109; Loi portant généralisation des allocations familiales, Recueil des lois et arrêtés royaux, 1930, No. 288, art. 1-3, 18, 43; Marlene Lohkamp-Himmighofen, "Belgien," in *Zwölf Wege der Familienpolitik in der Europäischen Gemeinschaft: Eigenständige Systeme und vergleichbare Quali-täten?—Länderberichte* 1-40 at 10 (Erika Neubauer et al. eds., 1993).

53. Dominique Ceccaldi, *Histoire des prestations familiales en France* 14-16 (1957); Loi relative à l'assistance aux familles nombreuses, Sirey, Législation 614-23 at 615 (July 14, 1913) (1914) (quote from Senate legislative history); Loi concernant l'encouragement national à donner aux familles nombreuses, Sirey, Législation 1770 (1924) (quote from legislative history in Chamber of Deputies); Loi concernant l'encouragement national à donner aux familles nombreuses, Sirey, Législation 1770--74 (July 22, 1923) (1924).

54. Franz Schultheis, *Sozialgeschichte der französischen Familienpolitik* 177-78, 309 (1988); Douglas, *Wages and the State* at 75-88; Cicely Watson, "Population Policy in France: Family Allowances and other Benefits. I," *Pop. Studies* 7 (3):263-86 at 265-67 (Mar. 1954). Forty years later Japanese employers paying family allowances as fringe benefits also opposed enactment of an employer-financed mandatory system on the ground that they would have to pay twice. Elizabeth Kirkpatrick, "Children's Allowances in Japan," *Social Security Bull.* 35 (6):39, 43 (June 1972). On the origins of firm-level allowances in heavy industry during World War II, see Andrew Gordon, *The Evolution of Labor Relations in Japan: Heavy Industry, 1853-1955*, at 290-93, 297 (1988); on a recently enacted state children's allowance, see Kōseihō, *Jidō teate: jukyūsha no shori* (1994).

55. Schultheis, *Sozialgeschichte der französischen Familienpolitik* at 262; Ceccaldi, *Histoire des prestations familiales en France* at 30-31; Loi portant institution d'un fonds national de solidarité agricole, Sirey, Législation 952-53 (Feb. 8, 1942); Watson, "Population Policy in France" at 269, 271, 277-78.

56. Loi modifiant les titres III et V du livre Iᵉʳ du Code du travail, Sirey, Législation 441-47 (Mar. 11, 1932); Susan Pedersen, *Family, Dependence, and the Origins and the Welfare State: Britain and France, 1914-1945*, at 378 (1993) (quote); Douglas, *Wages and the Family* at 88-93; D.V. Glass, *Population: Policies and Movements in Europe* 103-104 (1940) (quoting a 1935 letter to author from the director of an employers' fund).

57. Joseph Spengler, *France Faces Depopulation: Postlude Edition, 1936-1976*, at 297 (quote), 289-90, 299 (1979 [1938]).

58. Watson, "Population Policy in France" at 270; Sirey, Législation 1433-34 (Dec. 9, 1934) (1935); "Décret relatif à la famille et à la natalité françaises: Rapport au Président de la République Française," *Journal officiel de la République Française* 9607-9609 at 9607 (July 30, 1939) (quote); "Décret relatif aux allocations familiales: Rapport au Président de la République Française," *Journal officiel de la République Française* 12,978-79 (Nov. 15, 1938); Code de la famille, Sirey, Législation, art. 1, 10, 13, 34, 82, 91, 160 at 1361, 1362, 1364 , 1367-68, 1376 (July 29, 1939); Loi portant création d'une allocation de salaire unique, Sirey, Législation 395-96 (Mar. 29, 1941).

59. Fernand Boverat, *Niveau d'existence et charges de famille: Étude comparative* 4-5, 51, 42 (1944) (quote); Bernard Quillon, "Comparison des revenus et des besoins familiaux suivant le nombre d'enfants," *Population* 1 (4):683-98 at 696, 698 (Oct.-Dec. 1946); Albert Michot, "Comparaison des revenus et des besoins des familles modestes au 1ᵉʳ octobre 1947 suivant le nombre des enfants," *ibid.* 2 (4):691-703 at 701-703 (Oct.-Dec.

1947); Georges Malignac, "Minimum vital et niveau d'existence suivant le nombre d'enfants," *ibid.* 4 (2):249-68, tab. IX at 266 (Apr.-June 1949); Frédéric Tabah, "Niveau de vie des familles suivant le nombre d'enfants," *ibid.* 6 (2):287-304, tab. IV at 297 (Apr.-June 1951); Yves Martin, "Niveau de vie des familles suivant le nombre d'enfants," *ibid.* 11 (3):407-28, tab. V at 418 (July-Sept. 1956); Paul Paillat, "Influence du nombre d'enfants sur le niveau de vie de la famille," *ibid.* 26:13-36 (June 1971); Gérard Calot, "Niveau de vie et nombre d'enfants: Un bilan de la législation familiale et fiscale française de 1978," *ibid.* 35 (1):9-55 (Jan.-Feb. 1980); Dienel, "Frankreich" at 155-56, 172.

60. Loi fixant le régime des prestations familiales, Sirey, Législation, art. 11 at 477 (Aug. 22, 1946); A[lfred]. S[auvy]., "Les Conditions d'existence des famille," *Population* 1 (4):681-82 at 681 (Oct.-Dec. 1946) (quote); Code de la sécurité sociale, art. 510-43; Claude Ameline & Robert Walker, "France: Poverty and the Family," in *Responses to Poverty: Lessons from Europe* 193-209 at 197-205 (Robert Walker, Roger Lawson, & Peter Townsend eds., 1984); Colin Dyer, *Population and Society in Twentieth Century France* 167-68 (1978); *Zwölf Wege der Familienpolitik in der Europäischen Gemeinschaft: Eigenständige Systeme und vergleichbare Qualitäten?* 84-90 (Erika Neubauer et al. eds., 1993); Christiane Dienel, "Frankreich," in *Zwölf Wege der Familienpolitik in der Europäischen Gemeinschaft—Länderberichte* 149-77 at 163-67.

61. Suzanne Thave, "Are Large Families Mutants?" International Social Security Association, *Social Security and Changing Family Structures* 105-14 at 105-106 (Studies & Research No. 29, 1992) (data for 1982); Gèrard Calot, "Der französische Weg zum Geburtenüberschuß," in *Keine Kinder—Keine Zukunft? Zum Stand der Bevölkerungsforschung in Europa* 67-75 at 73-74 (Lutz Franke & Hans Jürgens eds., 1978); Roger Lawson, "Family Policies and Poverty: Editorial Overview," in *Responses to Poverty* at 185-92, tab. III.1 at 189; Dienel, "Frankreich" at 156 (quote).   On the debate concerning the juridical character of family allowances (in particular as supplementary wages), see Jean-Jacques Dupeyroux, *Sécurité sociale* 394-95 (1967).

62. Calot, "Der französische Weg zum Geburtenüberschuß" at 74 (quote); Douglas, *Wages and the Family* at 272 (quote); Thave, "Are Large Families Mutants?" at 106-108; Nicole Questiaux, "Family Allowances in France," in *Children's Allowances and the Economic Welfare of Children* 76-89 at 79, 83.

63. W. Beveridge, "The Standard of Living," *Times*, Jan. 12, 1940, at 7, col. 5; "Incomes and Needs," *Times*, Jan. 12, 1940, at 7, col. 3 (quote); W. Reddaway, *The Economics of a Declining Population* 251 (1939) (quote); *Family Allowances: Memorandum by the Chancellor of the Exchequer* 2 (Cmd. 6354, 1942) (quote); B. Seebohm Rowntree, "Family Needs," *Times*, Mar. 17, 1941, at 5, col. 5 (letter to the editor).   See also J.M. Keynes, "How to Pay for the War," in *idem, Essays in Persuasion*, in *The Collected Writings of John Maynard Keynes* 9:367, 394-403 (1972 [1940]).

64. William Beveridge, *Social Insurance and Allied Services: Report* ¶¶ 411-12 at 154 (1942); *The Poor Law Report of 1834*, at 335 (S.G. Checkland & E.O.A. Checkland eds., 1974 [1834]) (quote); Beveridge, *Social Insurance and Allied Services* ¶¶ 412-413 at 154 (quotes); *Parliamentary Debates*, 5th Ser., House of Commons, 380:1856 (June 23, 1942); Leonard Darwin, "Family Allowances," *Eugenics Rev.* 24 (4):276-78 (Jan. 1925); R.A. Fisher, "The Birthrate and Family Allowances," *Agenda* 2 (2):124-33 (May 1943).

65. Family Allowances Act, 1945, 8 & 9 Geo. 6, ch. 41, § 1; Royal Commission on Population, Report ¶ 446 at 166 (Cmd. 7695, 1949); B. Seebohm Rowntree & G. R. Lavers, *Poverty and the Welfare State: A Third Social Survey of York Dealing Only with Economic Questions* 42-44 (1951); Brian Abel-Smith & Peter Townsend, *The Poor and the Poorest* 62 (1966 [1965]); Townsend, *Poverty in the United Kingdom* at 151, 162-63, 586.

66. Loi fixant le régime des prestations familiales, Aug. 23, 1946, §§ 11-12, Sirey, Législation at 477; [U.K.] Royal Commission on Population, *Report*, ¶ 447 at 167; Schultheis, *Sozialgeschichte der französischen Familienpolitik* at 384-85; Pedersen, *Family, Dependence, and the Origins of the Welfare State* at 366-67, 390-91 (quote); John Baker, "Comparing National Priorities: Family and Population Policy in Britain and France," *J. Social Policy* 15 (4):421-42 (Oct. 1986); [U.K.] Royal Commission on Population, *Report* ¶¶ 464-70 at 171-74.

67. "The Perception of Poverty in Europe: Poverty 3," *Eurobarometer*, Mar. 1990, at 40.

68. *Ibid.* at 41. The survey conducted by the Commission of the European Communities did not even present low wages as a choice.

69. Michael Harrington, *Fragments of the Century* 182 (1977 [1972]).

70. National Commission on Children, *Beyond Rhetoric: A New American Agenda for Children and Families: Final Report* 94 (1991). *Ibid.* at 85, states erroneously that the personal exemption was established in 1948. Allan Carlson, "A Pro-Family Income," *Pub. Interest*, No. 94:69-76 at 71 (Winter 1989), incorrectly asserts that the 1948 amendments to the tax code were "strongly pro-child" because they "raised the personal exemption from $200 to $600 per family member, in a conscious attempt to relieve the financial burdens of parents with numerous children." In fact, the Revenue Act of 1948 increased the exemption only by $100 (from $500 to $600) expressly to compensate for the postwar inflation. H. Rep. No. 1274, 80th Cong., 2d Sess., *reprinted in* 1948 *U.S. Code Cong. Service* 1258, 1269. For an overview of the history of the exemption levels, see John Witte, *The Politics and Development of the Federal Income Tax*, fig. 6.3 at 127 (1985); for an overview of other elements of the social wage containing a reproductive component, see below ch. 10.

71. University of Iowa, Public Policy Center, *Welfare Reform in Iowa: Options and Opportunities* 73 (1989); Daniel Moynihan, "A Family Plan for the Nation," in *The Moynihan Report and the Politics of Controversy* 385-94 at 392 (Lee Rainwater & William Yancey eds., 1969 [1965]).

72. See, e.g., Sheila Kamerman & Alfred Kahn, *Child Care, Family Benefits, and Working Parents: A Study in Comparative Policy*, tab. 2.6 at 76-81 (1981); *idem*, "Social Policy and Children in the United States and Europe," in *The Vulnerable* at 351, 356-65; Tamar Lewin, "Panel Asks $5 Billion to Improve Child Care," *N.Y. Times*, Mar. 15, 1990, at B1, col. 5 (nat. ed.); *Zwölf Wege der Familienpolitik in der Europäischen Gemeinschaft: Eigenständige Systeme und vergleichbare Qualitäten* at 67-129, 533.

73. Timothy Smeeding, "Why the U.S. Antipoverty System Doesn't Work Very Well," *Challenge* 35 (1):30-35, tab. 1 at 31 (Jan. 1992) (poverty defined as less than 40 percent of the adjusted median family income after taxes and transfer payments; the other countries are Canada, Australia, Sweden, W. Germany, Netherlands, France, and U.K.; data refer to the mid-1980s); Timothy Smeeding, Barbara Torrey, & Martin Rein, "Patterns of Income and Poverty: The Economic Status of Children and the Elderly in Eight Countries," in *The Vulnerable* at 89, tab. 5.4 at 90.

74. Jäntti & Danziger, "Child Poverty in Sweden and the United States," tab. 1 at 51; Lee Rainwater, Martin Rein, & Joseph Schwartz, *Income Packaging in the Welfare State: A Comparative Study of Family Income* tab. 10.2 at 175 (1986) (in 1968 child allowances represented 8.4 percent of family income among families at the 90th income percentile in Sweden); Timothy Smeeding, "The Children of Poverty: The Evidence on Poverty and Comparative Income Support in Eight Countries," in *Children and Families in Poverty: The Struggle to Survive: Hearing Before the House Select Committee on Children, Youth, and Families*, 100th Cong., 2d Sess. 82, 93 (1988); Keith Bradsher, "Low Ranking

for Poor American Children," *N.Y. Times*, Aug. 14, 1995, at A7, col. 1 (nat. ed.) (data for 1991); Robert Pear, "Thousands to Rally in Capital on Children's Behalf," *N.Y. Times*, June 1, 1996, at 8, col. 1 (nat. ed.) (the Luxembourg Income Study defines children as poor if their families' income is less than half the national median).

75. "Condition of Workingmen's Families," in [Mass.] Bureau of Statistics of Labor, *Sixth Annual Report* 189-450 at 445-46 (Pub. Doc. No. 31, Mar. 1875); [Mass.] Bureau of Statistics of Labor, *Sixth Annual Report* at viii.

76. "Condition of Workingmen's Families" at 447-49, 360-61, 450.

77. Ch. 658, § 1087-5(c), 1911 Wis. Laws ch. 658; U.S. Senate Report No. 80, 63d Cong., 1st Sess. 25 (1913).

78. 50 *Cong. Rec.* 3801-3802, 3851-52 (1913).

79. Theodore Roosevelt, "A Premium on Race Suicide," *Outlook* 50:163-64 at 163 (Sept. 27, 1913); Act of Oct. 3, 1913, ch. 16, § II.C, 38 U.S. Statutes 114, 168; Act of Oct. 3, 1917, ch. 63, § 1200(1), 40 U.S. Statutes 300, 331.

80. Ethelbert Stewart, "A Family Wage-Rate vs. a Family Social Endowment Fund," *Social Forces* 6 (1):120-25 at 120-21 (Sept. 1927).

81. Stewart, "A Family Wage Rate" at 121-25. Kenneth Boulding, *The Meaning of the Twentieth Century: The Great Transition* 135-36 (1964), fancifully proposed equalizing income by inducing the rich to become poor by establishing marketable licenses to give birth: each female would be given a certificate entitling her to have the number of children corresponding to the replacement rate; the rich could then purchase the rights, thus spending themselves into poverty.

82. U.S. BLS, *Family Allowances in Various Countries* 49-58 (Bull. 754, 1943) (written by Mary Waggaman); Servicemen's Dependents Allowance Act of 1942, ch. 443, 56 Stat. 381.

83. National Resoruces Planning Board, *National Resources Development: Report for 1942*, at 112 (1942); National Resources Planning Board, *After the War—Full Employment: Post-War Planning* 19 (1942) (Alvin Hansen); *idem, After the War—Full Employment: Post-War Planning* 21 (revised ed. 1943) (Alvin Hansen); Wilbur Cohen, "Next Steps and Future Goals," in Arthur Altmeyer et al., *War and Post-War Social Security: The Outlines of an Expanded Program* 31-42 at 40-41 (1942); "The New Wagner Bill," *The Nation* 156 (24):824-25 (June 12, 1943); *Cong. Rec.* 91:3146, 79th Cong., 1st Sess. (1945).

84. F. Emerson Andrews, "What Price Children?" *Atlantic Monthly* 172 (5):94-99 at 95 (Nov. 1943).

85. *Ibid.*, at 95, 96, 99; F. Emerson Andrews, "How About Family Allowances?" *Parents' Magazine* 19 (6):26-27, 46-47, 50 at 26, 47, 50 (June 1944). For a contemporaneous proposal to provide subsidies in kind of goods and services required for child development, see Frank Lorimer, Ellen Winston, & Louise Kiser, *Foundations of American Population Policy* 155-57 (1940).

86. Lewis Meriam, *Relief and Social Security* 669-72, 843-44, 874-77 (1946); Edward Schwartz, "Some Observations on the Canadian Family Allowances Program," *Social Serv. Rev.* 20:451-73 at 469-70 (Dec. 1946); The Family Allowances Act, 1944, Can. Stat., 1944, No. 40, § 3; Charlotte Whitton, "The Family Allowances Controversy in Canada," *Social Serv. Rev.* 18:413-32 at 416-17 (Dec. 1944) (quote).

87. Paul Glick, "The Family Cycle," *Am. Sociological Rev.* 12 (2):164-74, tab. 2 at 169 (Apr. 1947); Paul Glick, "The Life Cycle of the Family," *Marriage & Family Living* 17 (1):3-9, tab. 2 at 7 (Feb. 1955) (on birth rates); S. Res. 109, Cong. Rec. 101:8139-43, 84th Cong., 1st Sess. (1955) (quote); Cong. Rec. 102:1124, 84th Cong., 2d Sess. (1956);

Low-Income Families: Hearings Before the Subcommittee on Low-Income Families of the Joint Committee on the Economic Report, 84th Cong., 1st Sess. 143 (1955) (quote). On the favorable impression that the Canadian program made on U.S. welfare and family scholars, see Bernice Madison, "Canadian Family Allowances and Their Major Social Implications," *J. Marriage & the Family* 26 (2):134-41 (May 1964).

88. *National Party Platforms: 1840-1956*, 1:492 (Donald Johnson ed., 5th ed. 1978 [1956]); Carlson, "What Happened to the 'Family Wage'?" at 7-8; *idem, From Cottage to Work Station* at 65-77.

89. Gilbert Steiner, *The State of Welfare* 7 (1971) (quote); Robert Cissell & Helen Cissell, "Case for Family Allowances," *America* 92(3):65-67 (Oct. 16, 1954) (quote; in 1952, the median income of two-children familes was $4,268 and that of families with six or more children was $3,045); John Cort, "Wages and Big-Family Men," *Commonweal* 53 (25):614, 616 at 614 (Mar. 30, 1951): "Men should be superior in the economic marketplace. Any system under which it is easier for women to get jobs than for men is headed for the dogs."

90. H.R. 14496, 90th Cong., 1st Sess. (1967); "The Case for a Family Allowance," *N.Y. Times Magazine*, Feb. 5, 1967, § 6 at 13, 68-72 (Moynihan); Mollie Orshansky, "Who Was Poor in 1966?" in *Children's Allowances and the Economic Welfare of Children: The Report of a Conference* 19, tab. 21 at 57 (Eveline Burns ed., 1968); Harvey Brazer, "The Federal Income Tax and the Poor: Where Do We Go from Here?" *Cal. Law Rev.* 57 (2):422-49 at 440-49 (Apr. 1969).

91. *Income Maintenance Programs: Hearings Before the Subcommittee on Fiscal Policy of the Joint Economic Committee*, 90th Cong., 2d Sess., I: Proceedings at 6 (1968) (testimony of Lisle Carter, Jr.) (quote), at 12-13, 20 (Mitchell Ginsberg) and 347-51 (Eveline Burns); Joan Aldous & Reuben Hill, "Breaking the Poverty Cycle: Strategic Points for Intervention," *Social Work* 14 (3):3-12 (July 1969); James Tobin, "Do We Want Children's Allowances?" *New Republic* 157 (2):16-18 (Nov. 25, 1967); James Vadakin, "Helping the Children," *New Republic* 157 (26):15-18 (Dec. 23, 1967) (including Tobin's comment at 17); Henry Aaron, "Income Transfer Programs," *Monthly Labor Rev.* 92 (2):50-54 at 53 (Feb. 1969); Charles Valentine, *Culture and Poverty: Critique and Counter-Proposals* 38-40 (1968); Irwin Garfinkel, "Negative Income Tax and Children's Allowance Programs: A Comparison," *Social Work* 13 (4):33-39 (Oct. 1968); Scott Briar, "Why Children's Allowances?" *Social Work* 14 (1):5-12 (Jan. 1969); David Gil, *Unravelling Social Policy: Theory, Analysis, and Political Action Towards Social Equality* 98, 200-201 n.32 (rev. ed. 1976 [1971]).

92. Omnibus Budget Reconciliation Act of 1993, Pub. L. No. 103-66, 107 Stat. 312, 433-35, § 13131 (1993) (to be codified at 26 U.S.C. § 32); *Welfare: Reform or Replacement? (Work and Welfare): Hearing Before the Subcomm. on Social Security and Family Policy of the Senate Finance Comm.*, 100th Cong., 1st Sess. 238-39 (1987) (testimony of Robert Reischauer); Theresa Funiciello, *Tyranny of Kindness: Dismantling the Welfare System to End Poverty in America* 297-320 (1993); Sara McLanahan, "The Consequences of Single Motherhood," *Am. Prospect*, No. 18, at 48-58 (Summer 1994), skirts the issue of family allowances, although Sara McLanahan & Irwin Garfinkel, "Welfare Is No Incentive," *N.Y. Times*, July 29, 1994, at A13, col. 5 (nat. ed.), do advocate redistributing more of the costs of child raising from parents to society. Prefeminist advocates include Maxwell Stewart, *A Chance for Every Child: The Case for Children's Allowances* (Public Affairs Pamphlet No. 440, 1970). On the radically different treatment of single mothers in Europe, see Kamerman & Kahn, "What Europe Does for Single-Parent Families." For an overview of the European programs, see Commission of the European Communities, *Com-*

parative Tables of the Social Security Schemes of the Member States of the European Communities 100-107 (13th ed. 1985); Margaret Gordon, *Social Security Policies in Industrial Countries: A Comparative Analysis* 282-305 (1988); ILO, *From Pyramid to Pillar: Population Change and Social Security in Europe* 41-75 (1989); Bundesministerium für Arbeit und Sozialordnung, *Euroatlas: Soziale Sicherheit im Vergleich* 18-27 (1995).

93. Gunnar Myrdal, *Challenge to Affluence* 63 (1965 [1962]).

94. Paul Popenoe & Ellen Williams, "Fecundity of Families Dependent on Public Charity," *Am. J. Sociology* 40 (2):214-20 at 214, 219-20 (Sept. 1934); Paul Popenoe "Can We Afford Children?" *Forum* 98 (6):315-318 (Dec. 1937).

95. The President's Commission on Income Maintenance Programs, *Background Papers* 15 (1970).

96. *The Moynihan Report and the Politics of Controversy*; Daniel Moynihan, *The Politics of a Guaranteed Income: The Nixon Administration and the Family Assistance Plan* 32, 49-50 (1973) (quote); Daniel Moynihan, "Foreword," in Alva Myrdal, *National and Family: The Swedish Experiment in Democratic Family and Population Policy* xi, xv (1968) (quote); David Ellwood, *Poor Support: Poverty in the American Family* 118 (1988) (quote).

97. William Thompson, *An Inquiry into the Principles of the Distribution of Wealth* 553 (1968 [1824]).

98. GAO, *Families on Welfare: Sharp Rise in Never-Married Women Reflects Societal Trend*, fig. 1.7 at 29 (GAO/HEHS-94-92, 1994). The trend paralleled that among single women not receiving AFDC payments: 41.2, 51.7, 12.4, and 6.0 percent respectively. If a broader category of public assistance (SSI, food stamps, Medicaid, and housing subsidies) is used, recipient families in 1992-93 on average included 1.3 children compared to 0.6 among nonrecipients. U.S. BLS, "Spending Patterns and Other Characteristics of Families Receiving Public Assistance," *Issues in Labor Statistics* (Summary 96-2, Jan. 1996).

99. Mark Rank, *Living on the Edge: The Realities of Welfare in America* 71-76 (1994); Vincent Whitney, "Fertility Trends and Children's Allowance Programs," in *Children's Allowances and the Economic Welfare of Children* at 123-39; C. Alison McIntosh, *Population Policy in Western Europe: Responses to Low Fertility in France, Sweden, and West Germany* (1983).

100. Burns, "Childhood Poverty and the Children's Allowance" at 13. T. J. Woofter, Jr., "Size of Family in Relation to Family Income and Age of Family Head," *Am. Sociological Rev.* 9 (6):678-84 at 684 (Dec. 1944), argued at a time when there was interest in using allowances to increase family size that direct assistance to the lowest-income families was problematical since "the higher birth rate in this group is controlled by disregard rather than regard for family financial competence."

10

Is Reproductive Solidarity Possible Under Laissez Faire?

> Modern children...appear to be valued for similar reasons that modern
> pets appear to be valued.... A household pet...rarely disappoints its
> owner-investor; and if it does, it can be given up without paying high
> penalties in the form of guilt or social disapproval.[1]

This final chapter explores contemporary family policies and policy debates from
the perspective of their impact on overall social solidarity. The analysis focuses on
attitudes and practices that foster or hinder the development of fissures between the
material conditions and perceived interests of those with current parental responsibilities on the one hand and those who have definitively discharged such obligations, those who intend to or at least will become parents, and those who reject
parenthood, on the other.

As the example of several European countries demonstrates, even capitalist societies can, through family allowances, parental leave payments, and other
horizontally and vertically redistributive programs, make a significant contribution
to mitigating the economically impoverishing impact of, if not physically and psychologically equalizing, the burdens of producing the next generation. None, however, has proved capable of moving beyond indirect financial incentives to the creation of mechanisms for direct macrosocietal guidance of demographic development.

To the extent that capital has colonized formerly seemingly independent
socioeconomic domains so that "[w]e have become a nation of employees," the
narrower question of the size of the proletariat has tendentially merged with that
of the overall population. In that sense, the political-economic tradition, to which
both Smith and Marx belonged, that could abstract from the laws governing the
demographic development of non-working-class strata might appear antiquated at
a time when the U.S. Department of Labor makes occupational employment pro-

jections of the number of physicians, fashion models, judges, rabbis, and stock-brokers.[2] This universal quasi-proletarianization explains why even procapital policy-formulating entities like the Rockefeller commission can speak of population in general without needing to identify class-specific subgroups.

Capital-specific population policy today embraces two areas recognizably continuous with classic nineteenth-century cyclical demographic interests of employers (although stylized accounts of multigenerational AFDC paupers have created the trope of a secular problem): the first joins the public costs of alimenting the surplus population generated by AFDC families, calibrating the size of the surplus population to discipline the labor market, and the appropriate cost-benefit analysis to gauge the point at which growth of pauperdom becomes dysfunctional; the second involves regulating immigration to act as the more controllable aspect of the exogenously given supply of labor. In contrast, the perceived demographic problems of age-specific underpopulation and disproportionalities conjuring up an old-age pension crisis and environmentally catastrophic overpopulation are not commonly analyzed as specifically capitalist phenomena. Fortunately, for capitalism, pauperage is still constructed, albeit contestedly, as rooted in personal rather than systemic defects, while the labor supply dimensions of immigration policy can be conveniently submerged beneath the humanitarian concerns of reuniting families and admitting selected Third World people to the First World lifeboat.

CHILDREN'S IMPACT ON PARENTS' CLASS CONSCIOUSNESS

> He that hath wife and children hath given hostages to fortune; for they are impediments to great enterprises.... Certainly the best works, and of greatest merit for the public, have proceeded from the unmarried or childless men; which both in affection and means, have married and endowed the public. Yet it were great reason that those that have children should have greatest care of future times, unto which they know they must transmit their dearest pledges. Some there are, who, though they lead a single life, yet their thoughts do end with themselves, and account future times impertinences; nay, there are some other that account wife and children but as bills of charges.... Certainly wife and children are a kind of discipline of humanity....[3]

The birth-strike controversy raised, with great intensity, the issue of the effect of raising large families on the class consciousness and political activity of mothers. Advocates of small families argued that proletarian women with many children to care for were simply too overburdened and fatigued to devote themselves to the class struggle.[4] Others have maintained that having children to care for gave workers an even greater stake in the struggle against capitalism. One of the chief architects of the Australian family wage and family allowance after World War I, for example, articulated a structure of differential political consciousness based on relative deprivation:

> [A]ll the propagandist material either for strikes or for evolutionary change comes invariably from the privations of the family. It is the wives and the children, who as they suffer most, so they furnish the readiest and most poignant illustrations of industrial injustice in the matter of the living wage awarded. Workers without family obligations may feel resentment at the unequalness of fortune; they do not know the year-long bitterness of the underpaid family man.[5]

Considerable empirical evidence corroborates the existence of relative deprivation rooted in the so-called family-cycle squeeze, which is shaped by the financial pressures of supporting a large number of children. Regardless of the ultimate impact on parents' consciousness, the crucial initial effect is the compulsion toward multiple jobholding.[6] Preoccupation with making ends meet plausibly preempts mental and physical energy that could be directed toward political or social activities or movements organized to deal with the underlying causes of poverty.

The more modern argument, deemphasizing individual economic hardship, runs to the effect that children give parents more of a stake in the (future of the) world so that they are more concerned, for example, about pollution than are childless adults, who may take an *après moi le déluge* egotistical stance. The childless (and especially the potential mothers among them) may be inspired by popular writers who urge them to choose either "Housework and children—or the glamor, involvement and excitement of a free life."[7] This view is hardly new. Three centuries earlier the complaint was also voiced that a "Free and Generous Way of Living" was "maimed" by children. The emergence of a post-baby boom protoantinatalism was perhaps presaged by the appearance in 1965 in that arch-pro-family magazine, *The Saturday Evening Post*, of a piece entitled, "Children Are a Waste of Time." Five years later, both *Redbook* and *Look* unleashed unprecedented torrents of letters to the editor by publishing articles that irreverently pooh-poohed the notion of motherhood as biological destiny and promoted childlessness as a sensible way of life.[8]

A very different view of the political ramifications of large families goes back to the early nineteenth century and continues to inform public debate. John Bray, for example, a Ricardian socialist in the 1830s, pondered the consequences of parents' anxiety for their offspring's well-being: "how long and patiently does the workman toil—how many of the insolences of upstart authority does he silently receive—how enduringly does he bear the galling of every chain which the present accursed system fastens upon him?" The remedy that Bray proposed for such parental diversion was the socialization of childrearing. At the time of the German birth-strike debate, Fritz Brupbacher, the Social Democratic physician, charged that a father, whose fears for his family made him a tractable employee, "must become a bad soldier in the proletarians' army...." He therefore easily concluded that "the less baggage we have to carry in the social war, the more strength we will have left to fight campaigns in forced marches against our traditional enemy capitalism." Similar sentiments were common on the left in the United States too. The *International Socialist Review*, for example, published a neo-Malthusian manifesto on the eve of World War I asserting that: "It does not take a philosopher to see that having many children renders working class parents almost helpless in the hands of their masters. When they go on strike the children's cry for bread drives them back."[9]

Unlike these socialists, employers have appreciated and at times sought to encourage multiplication of the family obligations that bind workers to the paternalistic firm. In proposing that the French legislature introduce family allowances for the low-paid civil servants, "un prolétariat de fonctionnaires," a member of the Chamber of Deputies observed that even for private employers such benefit payments were

> a good deal, for the workers burdened with families are generally very conscientious, very faithful to their agreements; they are steadfast...; they remain attached to the entreprise because they must be stable in order to receive their wages regularly, in the interest of their wife and their children; they cannot follow the law, sometimes capricious, deceptive, and shimmering, of supply and demand; these workers burdened with families cannot move so easily as the others, they remain attached to the industry, bound...by their heart; they are the best reserve of an industry.[10]

Jacques Bertillon, one of the leaders of the pre-World War I French repopulationist movement, synthesized its rhetorical charge by asserting that both strike agitators and the families most prone to follow them generally had few children. At the time of the birth-strike controversy, the Alliance nationale pour l'Accroissement de la Population française, a repopulationist organization supported by French firms and the state, distributed a circular, *Un grand péril industriel—la dépopulation*, to employer circles warning of the close connection between birth strikes and industrial strikes and including a fulsomely invidious comparison of parent-workers and childless workers. How, it asked, could the workers' spirit not become worse and worse when more and more, not having "young mouths to feed...spend more at the tavern, [and] having no fear of being rapidly plunged into misery if their employer dismisses them, are always disposed to lend an ear to the labor union leaders' incitements"? It was, therefore, in order to avoid strikes, in employers' interest to "urge their workers to have children...."[11]

A century and a half after Bray wrote, many, especially child-rich, parents continue to put up with degrading substandard conditions in order to feed their children. The blunt postmodern sociological version reads: "He who has a wife and two children to feed does what he is told."[12] Standing for many parents, a truck driver exposed to a high daily risk of being murdered by teenage robbers observed: "'I have two kids, bills. I can't say, "Forget this job." You keep working.'" Others are reluctant to participate in strikes or engage in other kinds of workplace resistance for fear that a sharp fall or cessation of income or loss of a job would adversely affect their children's welfare. As a 45-year-old formerly unemployed worker remarked on his decision to take a job as a strike-breaker: "'I turned the corner and saw there was a strike in progress,' he said. Taking a striker's job gave him pause. 'But my family is more important...so I went to work.'"[13]

Dispensation from meeting children's urgent nondeferrable daily needs enables the traditional breadwinner to refrain from taking the highest-paying steadiest job: "Not having a family to support almost certainly reduces a man's willingness to take a job he does not want." Occupational risk-taking becomes a more plausible life choice. Thus whereas childlessness permits women to devote themselves singlemindedly to their professional careers in a manner that was once possible only for men whose wives devoted themselves to the reproductive mission, men can regard elimination of the economic costs of parenting as a partial liberation from rigid adherence to customarily prescribed career paths. Such subjective willingness may, however, become impotent as parents find that they cannot underbid those with only a single mouth to feed. Indeed, in the mid-nineteenth century, the socialist Louis Blanc viewed this displacement as the representative case: a competitive compulsion inherent in the labor market prompted employers to prefer the childless, who could afford to work for less, thus supplanting proletarian parents, who, together with their children, could then starve or steal.[14]

The extent to which familial financial obligations serve to press men into employment is presumably reflected in table 23, which compares the labor force participation rates of single and married men of various ages in 1960 and 1993:

Table 23: **Labor Force Participation Rates (in %) of Single and Married Men, 1960 and 1993**[15]

	Age				
	16-19	20-24	25-34	35-44	45-64
Status			1960		
Single	42.6	80.3	91.5	88.6	80.1
Married	91.5	97.1	98.8	98.6	93.7
			1993		
Single	52.5	80.5	89.2	84.5	68.2
Married	91.2	95.0	96.6	96.1	82.5

The considerable gaps in labor force participation rates between single and married men in all age groups strongly suggests that the assumption of financial responsibility for a family significantly reduces the freedom to abstain from employment. Data on married fathers would presumably show an even greater spread of participation rates. Conversely, some self-selection appears to take place as only 43 percent of men in their 30s earning less than $10,000 annually were married in 1990 compared to 83 percent of their counterparts with income in excess of

$50,000.[16] The fact that married women's and mothers' participation rates, which were formerly much lower than single women's, have begun to converge with them, underscores the labor-compulsive impact of parenthood.

Unlike the birth-strikers, however, adherents of the hostages-to-fortune position do not imply that childless adults are more likely to be activists. On the contrary: whereas as late as the 1950s and 1960s few married couples in the United States wanted to be childless, a spate of press reports beginning in the late 1970s, when the two-earner childless couple had replaced the employed husband, house-wife, and two children as the typical American family, suggests that a new wave of relatively well-paid double-earner (including working-class) spouses, believing that even *Three's A Crowd*, choose not to procreate precisely in order to dedicate themselves to expensive adult consumerism.[17]

Malthus himself provided the strongest imaginable evidence in support of the claim that an ideology promoting procreation may be a prerequisite of capitalism by arguing that contraception or any other procedure that would enable people to control their fertility to the point of volitional childlessness would be highly undesirable because it would remove or at least dull the incentive that compels them to work. In the late twentieth century this admonition might be framed more plausibly in terms of consumerism than work-shyness. As a soon-to-be Secretary of Labor noted in the mid-1970s, the "higher" standard budget for a family of four that the U.S. Bureau of Labor Statistics (BLS) compiled, which was "more in line with the popular conception of American affluence, carried a price tag" that exceeded husbands' median income by 69 percent; filling that gap motivated millions of wives to enter the paid labor force.[18]

The extent to which parents have succeeded in achieving an idealized standard of living by virtue of mothers' paid labor is striking. The Consumer Expenditure Survey compiled by the BLS shows that in 1991, the average husband-and-wife couple whose oldest child was 6 to 17 years old and who had a total of 2.2 children reported a before-tax income of almost $48,000—18 percent higher than that of the average childless husband-and-wife consumer unit. Although the detailed breakdown of expenditure items does not include any exclusively adult luxury commodities that would make possible a comparison of the higher reaches of per capita conspicuous consumption between the two groups, in absolute terms, the two-child family outspends the childless parents in virtually every category.[19] For 1993, data reveal that even with regard to luxury goods, the childless spend less in the aggregate if not on a per capita basis. In that year, the same average 2.2-child family reported both before- and after-tax income 20 percent higher than that of the childless couple, while its annual expenditures were 26 percent greater. The only consumption items on which the childless outspent parents were coffee (11 percent), alcoholic beverages (8 percent), owned vacation homes (33 percent), lodging on out-of-town trips (12 percent), mattresses and springs (14 percent), refrigerators/freezers in owned homes (26 percent), cooking stoves and ovens in owned homes (33 percent), lawn and garden equipment (10 percent), men's coats and jackets (118 percent), men's sweaters and vests (14 percent), all women's apparel (1 percent), new cars (30 percent), airplane tickets (9 percent), pets (41 percent), boats (without motor) (420 percent), motorized recreational vehicles (219 percent), gifts to persons outside the consumption unit (655 percent), charitable contributions (50 percent), church contributions (11 percent), contributions to educational organizations (22 percent), newspapers (23 percent), magazines (16 percent), and gifts of goods and services (17 percent).[20]

Regardless of the original motive for childlessness, once couples become accustomed to the standard of living that the nonreproductive state makes possible, the decline in material wealth that sharing their income with progeny may entail can convert opportunistic nonparenting into a permanent way of life. In West Germany, where despite very marked differences in per capita private consumption levels between childless couples and families with children—in 1973, for example, the gap ranged from 17 percent in one-child families to 44 percent in three-child families—the proportion of households with various major appliances varies very little according to the number of children, an official family commission nevertheless took the position that if parents raised a claim to achieve the same material consumption chances as the childless, then either child care would have to be socialized so as not to interfere with the parents' labor force participation or a much more decisive distribution of income in favor of families with children would have to be instituted.[21]

CONFLICT AND SOLIDARITY BETWEEN PARENTS AND THE CHILDLESS

> There would be two classes, not of exploiters and exploited, but of makers of children and of makers of sterile love! For the celebrated formula: "Workers of the world, unite!" it would be necessary to substitute this other motto: "Workers of the world, buy Dr. Mascaux's contraceptives at 3 francs 50 a bottle."[22]

Beginning several decades before Malthus published his *Essay on the Principle of Population* and extending well into the Victorian age, the "chaotic period of large-scale industry" swallowed up enormous numbers of very young children. Looking back a century later, Paul Leroy-Beaulieu, a laissez-faire advocate, asserted that: "The man of the people would not, in general, run any risk in setting up house and having children without calculating...." Workers could "[d]uring their rare hours of leisure indulge in what one has sometimes called the pleasure of the poor without fearing the consequences." From Leroy-Beaulieu's perspective, the poor man could combine pleasure with business because children already by the age of six or seven years were paying their own way and by eleven or twelve were receiving wages in excess of the very modest costs of maintaining them. Malthus and others may have conflated natural fertility with an enhanced fertility brought about by the transitory "indirect bounty on the production of children" associated with the social customs of the industrial revolution. After all, proletarian parents in Britain and elsewhere during the latter part of the eighteenth century and the first three-quarters of the nineteenth century made a major contribution toward the achievement of a capitalistically optimum population.[23]

While bourgeois parents contradicted the allegedly rational principle of individualism by preserving irrational or altruistic motives, workers were, according to the founding father of the Frankfurt School, subject to a new set of forces:

> That something was wrong in the society of free and just exchange was not coincidentally revealed first in the working-class family, whose children at the time of the industrial revolution were pressed into the production process as labor slaves. Bourgeois society could perpetuate itself only by strengthening the compulsion of the principle of exchange through immediate forms of dependence, and the family was its agent also in the sense that the autocratic father took care of this business so much more thoroughly the more he himself was under economic pressure.[24]

Once the movement to reduce the scale and scope of child labor had removed the economic advantages accruing to working-class parents of large families, their incentive to overreproduce faded. Indeed, as early as the 1830s, British economist Robert Torrens recognized that except in areas of new settlement, such as North America, where insufficiently dense population and the concomitant flagging division of labor made the large family a lever of wealth, "a family deprives the working man of the ease, and comfort, and independence which he enjoys in the single state." Since the demise of the kind of child labor that made procreation a quickly paying proposition, economists and demographers have recognized that those with few or no children enjoy great advantages on the labor market vis-à-vis those carrying the burden of supporting a large family. This differential has, in the wake of the feminization of poverty, become particularly prominent among single (including divorced custodial) mothers.[25]

The fact that an owner of the income source "labor" who has children must withdraw time that could be used to earn additional income to raise children disadvantages her or him vis-à-vis childless competitors. Even a lawyer surmised that one reason the fathers of dual-professional families may earn less than male professionals with children whose wives do not work outside the house is that child-care activity makes them less alert, rested, flexible, and concentrated. The uneven distribution of the burden is manifest. A social fact supporting the enactment of Canadian family allowances during World War II was that 84 percent of that nation's children under 16 years of age were dependent on only 19 percent of the gainfully employed adults. In Britain, one-quarter of the families were raising three-quarters of the children in 1944. A decade later, one-third of the civilian labor force in the United States carried the burden of supporting more than nine-tenths of those under 18 years of age. To be sure, these disproportions in part reflect life cycles: adults not supporting children today may be past or future reproducers. By the same token, the assertion that a working man's earnings tend to rise and decline in synchronization with the life cycle of family responsibilities underscores how hopeless it is to depend on market forces to eliminate poverty associated with above-average reproduction.[26]

Depending on which end of the spectrum of demographic policy they occupy, policy analysts call for state intervention to accentuate or diminish such handicaps. As early as 1952, the U. N. Department of Social Affairs stated that the movement in most countries to equalize the standard of living of the "family group" with that of persons without dependants had not only become the driving force of postwar social thinking and planning, but had implemented "the principles proclaimed in the Universal Declaration of Human Rights that 'the family is the natural and fundamental unit of society [and] that everyone has a right to a standard of living adequate for the health and well-being of himself and his family....'" In contrast, Paul Ehrlich, the discoverer of the population bomb, has urged a reversal of the tax advantages for richer parents on the ground that "the plush life would be difficult to attain for those with large families—which is as it should be, since they are getting their pleasure from their children, who are being supported in part by more responsible members of society." Instead, Ehrlich proposed prizes for the childless.[27]

In contrast to the tradition that has bemoaned the labor-market disadvantages attaching to parenthood, in recent years organized groups of the childless have formed to attack what they see as the discrimination to which they are subjected at work (such as requests to give their accumulated vacation time to co-workers who are facing childbirth or being refused time off to see an accountant when parents are permitted absences to care for sick children). Unless these militants are end-of-the-worldists, they fail to see the main point—namely, how large the next generation should be and how the burden of creating that population should be shared. Perhaps fortunately, but surely inadvertently, such antiprocreationists are complying with Hannah Arendt's admonition that "[a]nyone who refuses to assume joint responsibility for the world should not have children...." Yet even some of those who understand that adults were once children aspire to a balkanized society bereft of cross-linked ties of solidarity. The founder of ChildFree Network urges that parents should shoulder the cost of workplace day care whereas she, as a single person, does not expect families to subsidize her long-term disability insurance.[28]

This movement must be seen in the context of an increasingly childless society. The proportions of adults and children living in three-child-or-more families in the United States have declined significantly since 1959, when they amounted to 20 and 60 percent respectively, and only 46 percent of adults lived in childless families. By 1992, only 8 percent of adult and 38 percent of children lived in households with three or more children; in contrast, 60 percent of adults lived in childless households. If in 1960 married couples with children and single parents accounted for 48 percent of all households while childless couples and one-person units accounted for 43 percent, by 1988 the two childless groups surpassed those with children, accounting for 54 percent of all households compared with only 35 percent for those with children. The growing preponderance of childless adults in the United States cannot, however, by itself explain the emergence of aggressive organizations dedicated to the maximum privatization and internalization

of the costs of childrearing by parents while accepting externalization of the benefits in the form of fresh contingents, inter alia, of Social Security taxpayers. After
all, other advanced capitalist societies have experienced the same quantitative inversion between parents and the childless during the same period (or, as in the case
of Sweden and the United Kingdom, even earlier) without giving rise to similar
movements. The 1981-82 European Community (EC) censuses, for example,
revealed that 62 percent of all households in the 12 countries were childless—West
Germany reaching the highest level at 72 percent. Three or more children lived in
only 6.5 percent of EC households—West Germany, again, reaching the lowest
level at 2.9 percent. It therefore seems more plausible that the recent increase in
the childless in the United States merely created the opportunity for giving vent to
yet another expression of the peculiarly American lack of social solidarity. In this
particular setting, the individualists fail to appreciate that the gap between the
macro- and microsocietal consequences of procreation for living standards can be
closed by subsidizing the costs either of raising children or of old age (or both).[29]

States have been using positive and negative financial incentives for at least
2,500 years in an effort to guide population change. Until the impoverishing
effects of the Industrial Revolution made themselves felt in Britain at the end of the
eighteenth century, state power had largely been used to promote population
growth. Eighteenth-century English mercantilists believed that the population was,
in spite of massive poverty, too small; based on the ideology of the utility of
poverty and the disciplinary consequences of dense population, they placed a
premium on "a numerous population of unskilled laborers, driven by the very
competition of numbers to a life of constant industry at minimum wages...." In
parts of pre-capitalist Europe, however, including Austria-Hungary and Germany,
the state into the nineteenth century denied men permission to marry unless they
could prove that they could maintain a family.[30]

As early as 403 B.C., Roman censors allegedly fined old bachelors for having
failed to perform their duty to the state. Actions against bachelors were known in
ancient Greece, especially in Sparta but also in Athens. Spartan legislation
encouraged citizens to have as many children as possible: fathers of three sons were
exempt from military service and fathers of four from all state burdens. Plato
would have subjected men who were still unmarried at age 35 to an annual fine
graduated according to their wealth. Caesar prohibited women who by the age of
44 had neither husband nor children from wearing jewels or being carried in a
litter—a measure that Montesquieu called a "méthode excellent d'attaquer le
célibat par la vanité." Caesar also partitioned farm land among fathers of three or
more children. The Lex Papia Poppaea of A.D. 9 required men and women to
produce a certain number of children by a certain age. Throughout the Middle
Ages, European states imposed taxes on bachelors and conferred awards on those
with many children. In France in 1666, Louis XIV ordered pensions for those with
ten or more children to support the propagation of the species; as late as the 1920s,
employees with 10 or more children were exempted from rent and income taxes
and had the privilege of free matriculation at all official educational institutions.[31]

Bachelor taxes, which are a counterpart to the construction of child raising itself "as a form of tax," have abounded in modern states as well. Britain introduced an abatement of income taxes for parents in 1799. It amounted to 5 percent for each child for persons with incomes between £60 and £400, and tapered off to 2 percent for children over six years of age and 1 percent for those under six for persons with incomes in excess of £5,000. Both the French Revolution and Napoleon made extensive pronatalist use of bachelor taxes and political fines (such as greater vulnerability to military service) in addition to providing tax exemptions and financial assistance to economically needy worker-parents. Fascist Italy in 1927 imposed a tax on bachelors between the ages of 25 and 65, exempting priests and war invalids. When the United States finally enacted a national income tax in 1913, the $1,000 exemption for married couples was debated as "amount[ing] to the taxation of bachelors."[32]

Even before the Nazi regime introduced the system, an SPD social policy expert in the Weimar Republic proposed a tax on bachelors and on parents with a below-average number of children in order to finance social insurance to compensate for the burdens of childrearing. The Nazis, impelled by alleged biological dangers to the race—the introduction of children's allowances in the form of subsidies to families with five or more children under the age of 16 and with a monthly income of no more than 185 marks was announced the same day that the Nuremberg Laws were promulgated—undertook great efforts to eliminate financial impediments to large families by equalizing economic burdens between child-rich and childless families (*Familienlastenausgleich*). In order to finance marriage loans, which were granted to couples who married after the statute went into effect if the wife had been employed between June 1, 1931 and May 31, 1933, and obligated herself not to be employed again so long as her husband's income remained below 125 marks, marriage aid was raised by taxing the unmarried. The latter were defined to include widowed or divorced persons whose marriages produced no children, but exempted those over 55.[33]

In seeking to eliminate the economic privilege of the childless or child-poor, the Nazi regime was painfully aware that reducing basic wages to finance family supplements could not act as a work incentive for the childless. But the supreme principle read: "There is no such thing as equal right for all. Right protects only him who is of some value to his people." Not even the involuntarily childless had ground for complaint: they had to be weaned from the "liberalistic" attitude that they were being punished when in fact they should have been "proud of being able...to contribute to Germany's again becoming a country of laughing children and laughing parents."[34] Beneath the mendacious Nazi bombast lay an insight into one of the bases of a solidary society which liberal-capitalist formations have indeed found it difficult to foster.

A half-century later, Germany again debated bachelor taxes. The economic-demographic occasion is unmistakable. Complaints are voiced by the governing conservative Christian Democratic Union (CDU) and the oppositional SPD that "children in Germany have become the number one poverty risk"—specifically, that even a second child places a family with an average income in Germany at risk of falling into poverty. The virulence of the debate is not coincidental since Germany has experienced long-term below-replacement-rate fertility.[35]

This economic-demographic complex must be analyzed in connection with the history of comparatively small state-redistributed children's allowances in West Germany. When first introduced in 1954, the family allowance, which was financed by employers' contributions, was 25 marks and applied only to families with at least three children. The dominant political figure of the period, the CDU chancellor Konrad Adenauer, himself the father of seven children, regarded the subsidies as superfluous: "One needn't pay the people for having kids. They'll have them anyway." In 1965 an allowance, which was now financed by the federal government, was introduced for the second child. Although since 1975 the German Social Code has expressly conferred on every person who supports children the right to a reduction of the associated economic burdens, the amount set for the first child was only 50 marks per month, for the second 70 marks, and for every higher birth-order child 120 marks; at that time the subsidy was thought to amount to 25 percent of the cost of one child, rising to 50 percent for six children. When the amounts were raised to 100, 220, and 240 marks for the second, third, and fourth and all additional children respectively in 1986, they were subject to graduated reduction in higher-income families. By the time the children's allowance was raised to 70 marks for the first child in 1992, it amounted to only 8 percent of the 830 marks viewed as the minimum monthly cost of a child.[36]

Rather than being financed by the rich or even the childless, children's allowances have, according to one jaundiced view of the German tax system ("transfer exploitation"), in fact been financed by parents themselves. As a result, parents' per capita income is only 40 percent of that of the childless. A CDU member of parliament therefore called child-rich families "'the idiots of the tax system.'" Despite the fact that the German constitution places the family under the special protection of the state, the Federal Constitutional Court has acknowledged and held constitutional the systemic disadvantaging of child-rich families for the benefit of the childless in the tax and social security systems.[37]

As the parliamentary parties began floating proposals to provide existing and potential parents with an economic incentive to stave off perceived ethnic suicide, federal Family Minister Hannelore Roensch urged imposition of a 7.5 percent wage and income "solidarity surtax" on the childless, which would be used to raise children's allowances to 200 marks for the first child, 300 for the second, and 400 for each higher birth-order child from the current 70 marks for the first, 130 for the second child, 220 for the third child, and 240 for the fourth and higher birth-order children. Her plan would have limited payments to low-income and child-rich families, higher-income families being taken care of by increasing the dependent child exemption for income tax purposes to the level of the so-called existence minimum. Its most sensational provision would have defined parents whose children have been financially independent for five years as taxably childless.[38]

The proposal gained some public support from those outraged by the fact that children heftily cofinance the old-age pensions of that half of the adult population that is childless or has only one child. After all, as reproduction faltered, German public debate has included plans to reduce procreators' old-age pension contributions to reflect their in-kind contributions or to reduce pensions of the childless. Nevertheless, the bachelor tax met with almost universal denunciation from the major political parties, including Roensch's own ruling CDU, one of whose leading parliamentary members remarked that Germany needed a tax on the childless as much as one on beards or bald heads. Rejecting the tax, the SPD instead proposed abolishing the tax exemptions for dependent children altogether as disproportionately benefiting those with higher incomes and introducing a uniform monthly children's allowance of 250 marks. In a surprising preelection move, the CDU, which for years had complained that its demands for additional support for child-rich families had inspired the SPD to attack the CDU for seeking to shift the question of distributional justice between rich and poor to that between child-poor and child-rich, essentially adopted the SPD's proposal.[39]

In the end, the CDU and the SPD enacted compromise legislation. The 1995 amendments to the Bundeskindergeldgesetz both eliminated the graduated reductions for richer parents and increased the allowance to 200 marks per month (and to 220 marks beginning in 1997) for the first and second child, 300 for the third, and 350 for the fourth and higher birth-order children. To be sure, the necessity of choosing between income-tax dependent exemptions and children's allowances under the new amendments means that the economic situation of two-child families with average income may remain unchanged.[40]

Arguably the most interesting insight to be gleaned from this German debate for the question of how to mobilize broad-based support for the collectivization of reproductive costs refers to public perceptions of redistributional fairness. The SPD had also proposed a children's or family fund to be financed by a 5 percent tax on all income recipients; parents would then be entitled to 600 marks monthly for each child. A public opinion survey revealed that 40 percent of the childless supported the plan and only 30 percent opposed it. More than half of the childless, however, opposed a tax to be imposed only on them.[41]

Macrosocietally self-destructive solipsistic parental behavior has, according to James Coleman, become critical as parents' liberation from dependence on their own progeny for an economically secure old age has made them lose sight of the fact that collectivized pay-as-you-go pensions merely shift their dependence onto other people's children. Being trapped in a race to the bottom of the socialization process deprives parents of any motivation "to bring up their child to maximize the child's value to society." Not coincidentally, then, the United States has witnessed a resurgence of interest in the functional equivalent of bachelor taxes after a crisis atmosphere developed over a potential gap in financing the pay-as-you-go social security old-age pension system as the ratio of younger contributing workers to older retired former workers has declined. Ben Wattenberg, who did much to popularize the notion of a "birth dearth," depicted the childless as "'free riders'" who receive "full pensions paid for by children who were raised and reared—at a large expense—by children of other people. That's not fair. Couples without children have extra discretionary income while they are young, which they can invest for their retirement." He therefore proposed that more Social Security taxes be withheld from the childless or, to make it politically less unpalatable, that parents be exempted from already enacted future Social Security tax raises.[42]

At the same time, however, legislators have become solicitous of the 62 percent of the labor force without any children living at home. In connection with the abortive health care bill of 1994, for example, the Subcommittee on Health of the House Ways and Means Committee expressly considered and rejected the notion that the childless should subsidize the cost of providing health care coverage for other people's children. Such arithmetically popular political decisions overlook the possibility that the increasing workplace labor-intensity to which more and more parents are subjected as mothers' rate of employment reaches ever newer highs in an attempt to maintain family living standards may be undermining their physical, mental, and emotional substance while interfering with their capacity for socializing their progeny. At some point parents but especially mothers may begin to be used up, like the natural environment, by those who are not required to pay for the costs of restoration.[43] This analogy is, to be sure, complicated by one subjective difference: unlike humanity as a whole, which is never heard to complain that it can do without the air, water, and soil it has destroyed, many childless protest that some (quantitatively or qualitatively indeterminate) proportion of procreativity is not a social benefit on which they are free-riding, but rather an externalized cost, which should be internalized or, better yet, never created in the first place.

Proposals for redistributing the costs of producing the next generation of social security old-age pension pay-as-you-go payors have not been the exclusive preserve of pronatalist men. Feminist economists have also used the specter of a twenty-first-century Social Security crisis to urge an alleviation now of the collective burdens one-sidedly borne by parents. Shirley Burggraf, for example, takes as her point of departure two assumptions that seek to assimilate to the market phenomena that economists have heretofore failed to incorporate into their models. On the one hand, "Femina Economica" has at last emerged who "understands the concept of opportunity cost" and must "balance gains and costs at the margin." On the other hand, now that women, liberated by neoclassical economics, have rationally made their cost-benefit analysis and collectively depressed the fertility rate below replacement level, society has grasped that "starting a family involves as much effort, investment, and risk as starting a business...." The question has therefore become how to "reverse the current disinvestment in family" that has resulted from the heavy financial penalties imposed on parents.[44]

At stake is no trivial issue for Burggraf: "The essential question for our culture in the twenty-first century is whether...to socialize or privatize the roles and functions of family." These two modes correspond to tax-financed redistribution to families and strengthening incentives for parents to invest in families. Burggraf criticizes the new home economists for their preoccupation with children as private consumption goods and their failure to see that, although children as private investment goods may belong to the past, "[c]ollectively, we are just as dependent on our children for old-age security as families used to be." The obvious question is therefore: Who will produce the producers and how will they be induced to do so? Putting "economic rationality at the center of the family decision process," Burggraf cautions that before embarking upon a socialization of the costs of parentage, feminists and economists should give privatization of benefits a chance. As Adam Smith and the male chauvinist classical school would have put it had women's reproductive labor not been invisible to them: Give parents a contractual claim to whatever wealth they individually succeed in generating. Specifically, Burggraf targets the enormous wealth transfer system ($16 trillion) embodied in Social Security, which requires each current recipient of earned income to support everyone else's parents who are retired former recipients of such income rather than reimbursing her own personal procreators, who contributed most in labor and commodity and service expenditures to the creation of the labor power that is the foundation of her current earning power. Burggraf instead proposes "using the market system to promote family values" by creating a "parents' dividend" to be earmarked and collected, like the Federal Insurance Contributions Act (FICA) tax, from their own children's earnings.[45]

Burggraf wants it understood that her system solipsistically privatizes both costs and benefits: it appears to do away with the safety net. Because "economic rationality means consistency between the costs and benefits of individual choices, according to their social productivity," if, for example, the human output of a "single, career-tracked parent...turns out badly," "her choice" would become her problem. Like the former Soviet-bloc countries, the parent must understand that a choice must be made "between two major economic systems...." Burggraf fails to sketch what the fate of the voluntarily or involuntarily childless would be in the wake of this atavistic secular reprivatization. But since she wants to subject parents to the rigors of the market, it would only be fair to place the childless in the same regime. Thus if the existing Social Security system were terminated and nonprocreators were free to dispose of what they were formerly required to pass on to retirees, they would finally regain their Friedmanesque "freedom to make their own mistakes."[46] Opting for this type of dissolution of the compulsory, paternalistic, solidary, somewhat redistributionist Social Security system might, ironically, undermine Burggraf's refeudalization of the family, which in effect garnishes procreatees' earned income in perpetuity. For if parents observed that the emancipated childless invested their former FICA taxes in private annuities that yielded more than the fixed share of their own children's wages, parenting would remain a substandard investment and socialization of the costs of procreation would once again advance on the agenda.

Irrationality, contradiction, and dysfunctionality must abound in societies that continue to commit childbearing and childrearing to unfettered private inititative while collectivizing the social security system. To the extent that parents withdraw from the market in order to carry on reproduction, they lower not only their standard of living contemporaneously, but, through reduced earnings, also their old-age pensions; at the same time, the fact that their children are legally obligated to transfer part of their income to finance the old-age pensions of the members of their parents' generation, including many who made no procreative contribution, may render them financially impotent to subsidize their own progenitors' retirement. This hybrid system partially reproduces a striking phenomenon of the turn-of-the-century U.S. poorhouse, a very high proportion of whose elderly male inmates spent their last years there precisely because they had no children.[47] While European societies have been struggling for decades toward a system that harmonizes reproduction and social security by moving toward greater socialization of reproduction, both U.S. state policy and even many of its critics insist on maintaining a rigidly outdated private-public divide.

Nancy Folbre, a Marxist-feminist economist, is also concerned about childless Social Security recipients' "free-riding on parental labor"—especially mothers' unpaid labor—because children are fiscally positive externalities. Folbre is nevertheless torn by Burggraf's proposal. She welcomes its rewarding of parental labor, but presumes that it would reduce the level of income security. Folbre recognizes that eliminating pay-as-you-go social security would put an end to free-riding by nonparents, but the worst consequence she mentions is that dissolution "would impose stringent and inefficient limits on macroeconomic and social policy." What Folbre finds most unsatisfactory, however, is the Burggraf plan's potential for "encourag[ing] parents to treat their children in instrumental terms," which would be "inconsistent with liberal principles of individual autonomy...." Against the history of hundreds of millions of parents who have created children for nonpecuniary, psychologically instrumental reasons, this fear, however, comes somewhat late in the day. For Folbre, then, the "best alternative" is to compensate parents "through a greater tax exemption or credit...."[48]

This preference for the tax system unites strange bedfellows since it has also become a favorite of the religious Right, which promotes atavistic patriarchy and gender roles while rejecting state-redistributed cash allowances as propelled by an "egalitarian impulse": as soon as recipients come to embrace them as entitlements, "the positive incentive effect is lost." Consequently, such authors call the "[p]ro-family tax...that distinctively American form of crafting social policy...." Contrary to a widespread misperception that family allowances and tax deductions or allowances are different because one is a cash transaction and the other merely an accounting procedure, their impact on family purchasing power is the same. Indeed, in Britain the introduction in 1909 of income deductions for tax purposes based on number of children is viewed as "even more revolutionary" than that of family allowances after World War II. Although the reduction in tax liability may not be observed as an income flow, "the State is sharing in the responsibility of caring for each taxpayer's family just as certainly as if it were paying cash allowances...."[49]

The problem with dependent child exemptions as a welfare measure is that they benefit parents in higher income tax brackets more than those whose incomes are taxed at lower marginal rates (and whose incomes may be so low that part or all of the exemption is wasted). In Britain, for example, socialist critics complained in the 1950s that dependent child exemptions were costing the state three times as much as child allowances; consequently, this segment of the welfare state, like others, benefited the middle class more than the working class. A man with £20,000 of annual income and two children received 13 times as much from exemptions and allowances as one earning only £500. For reasons of fairness, Sweden had already eliminated the exemptions in 1948; for budgetary reasons, other countries with family allowance programs, such as Denmark, Britain, and Canada, have also reduced, phased out, or eliminated the exemptions, which the SPD has opposed since 1950 and still characterizes as a "bitter social injustice."[50]

In the United States, the money value of dependent child exemptions exceeds the cost of the entire AFDC system and is double that of the federal share of AFDC. In 1991, almost 73 million exemptions for dependent children were granted on almost 41 million returns. The exemption, which amounted to $2,150, was worth $322 to taxpayers in the lowest (15 percent) bracket, $602 to those in the middle (28 percent) bracket, and $667 to those in the highest (31 percent) bracket. For joint returns of married persons, these brackets encompassed adjusted gross income from $0 to $34,000, $34,000 to $82,000, and above $82,000 respectively. The total value of these exemptions was almost $34 billion. The richest taxpayers, who accounted for about 10 percent of the exemptions, obtained about 15 percent of the value of the exemptions. The poorest taxpayers with 55 percent of the exemptions obtained only 38 percent of their value.[51]

The exemption reduced the tax liability of a jointly-filing working-class married couple with two children, vis-à-vis a childless couple, by $644 or $1,204 depending on whether they were in the 15 percent or 28 percent bracket. These sums amount to 2 to 3 percent of the annual income of families earning $20,000 to $50,000. In contrast, children's allowances for a similar family in such welfare states as Australia, Germany, Denmark, the United Kingdom, the Netherlands, and Sweden represented 4 to 9 percent of the average production worker's annual wage in 1990. This quantitative comparison significantly understates the gap in state support between the United States and European countries inasmuch as the latter is embedded in a complex of family policies including housing allowances, prenatal and postnatal allowances, birth grants, paid maternity leave, and day care centers. The Swedish reproductive subsidies were significant enough that the prospect of an austerity-driven 15 percent reduction in child allowances (from $114 to $97 per child per month) and the complete elimination of additional benefits for child-rich families in 1996 purportedly prompted the sharpest decline in births in 70 years.[52]

A number of children's advocates in the United States have begun to press for the establishment of a refundable child tax credit as a means of creating income security for families with children without having to embark upon the politically more difficult task of proposing that the United States join Western Europe in enacting a universalist communitarian welfare state. Instead, the National Commission on Children, for example, suggests that new initiatives "build upon the momentum of pro-family tax reform begun in the 1980s." Specifically, it proposed replacing dependent child exemptions with a $1,000 inflation-adjusted refundable tax credit, which would entitle a low-income family to a cash payment from the Internal Revenue Service if its tax liability were less than $1,000. Although this credit would, unlike the exemption system, operate progressively by creating the equivalent of a $6,666 exemption for families in the lowest income tax bracket and only $3,225 in the 31 percent bracket, it would still not restore the inflation-adjusted value of the $600 exemption from 1948.[53]

The political direction in which such proposals appear to drift is revealed by the Democratic Party's and Clinton administration's initiative to compete with a right-wing Republican Congress by offering additional regressive nonrefundable tax credits to all but the wealthiest taxpayers. The $500 tax credit embodied in the American Dream Restoration title of the Republicans' proposed Contract with America Tax Relief Act of 1995, in Newt Gingrich's words, "categorically rejects...class warfare" by creating a supraclass tax code which recognizes that "the cost of raising children...is consistent across all economic boundaries." By treating "every child equally" and excluding only 1 percent of all taxpayers, the bill purports to view tax issues "through the prism of family" rather than that of class. One-third of all children who live in families too poor to pay federal income tax would not benefit at all from the nonrefundable credit; an additional 10 percent live in families that would receive only a fractional benefit since their total tax liability is less than $500.[54]

In addition to providing dependent exemption subsidies, the United States has been operating a refundable tax credit system for low-income parents for two decades. The Earned Income Tax Credit (EITC), dating from 1975, was originally designed to compensate for the regressive impact of the employment taxes on low-income families. As the FICA taxes became increasingly burdensome in the wake of the increase in old-age pension benefits during the 1970s, pressure grew to provide relief to low-paid workers from a tax that was not only flat regardless of income level, but did not apply at all to wage or salary income beyond a middle-class level (which was raised from $7,800 in 1971, to $14,100 in 1975, and $60,600 in 1994). As a result of recent increases and differentiation for families with more than one child, a multichild family with earned income between $8,425 (the equivalent of full-time year-round work at the minimum wage) and $11,000 in 1994 is entitled to the maximum credit of $2,528. This program cost the federal government in 1991 about the same amount as AFDC ($10.5 billion), but subsidized about three times as many families (13 million); three-fourths of the credit is refunded. Some on the Left, however, object to the EITC on the ground that it functions as a Speenhamland-type wage depressant and subsidy to low-productivity and/or low-wage firms, since wage offers and acceptances are made with background knowledge of the supplement.[55]

In light of this recent interest in the tax system, it is intriguing that as mainstream an economist as Victor Fuchs finds family allowances financed by the childless to be efficient and equitable. He points out that between 1960 and 1988, childless households increased as a proportion of all households from 49 percent to 62 percent; in the prime age group for parentage, 25 to 44 years old, the shares rose even more markedly, from 20 percent to 37 percent. Because childless households have considerably higher average incomes than those with children, redistribution from the former to the latter would promote equality; similarly, children's allowances financed out of general revenue would also have a progressive redistributional impact because children are overrepresented in low-income households.[56]

The primary tension inherent in a system of family income security exists between universality and progressivity: How can the stigma of means- or income-testing be avoided without wasting too much of the redistributed income on richer families that arguably do not need subsidies? Is a blunting of the drive toward equalization of conditions by means of the distribution of equal amounts of benefits to the poor and the nonpoor the price that must be paid to secure abiding political support for an income security plan that does not degenerate into a poorly financed and staffed poor law? If even at the moment that the solidaristic welfare state triumphed, the "social utility of targeting benefits was a virtue against which the dilemma of squandering scarce resources on the well-off in the name of national solidarity had to be weighed," the resurgence of market-knows-best ideology and policy in the last two decades of the twentieth century has reinforced the dilemma. That even European societies permitted the value of family allowances to be significantly eroded during much of the post-World War II period casts doubt on the strategic assumption that universalism offers the kind of political protection that programs targeted on the poor lack.[57]

Nevertheless, if the origins of welfare universalism had more to do with the self-interest of the middle classes desirous of the benefits already afforded the working class than with incorporating the working class into full social citizenship rights, then arguably a frank reorientation of children's allowances toward overall systemic egalitarianism to the exclusion of the rich from whose income and wealth the redistributive wherewithal would derive might be a sound political program. It is noteworthy, for example, that in the Netherlands, a society with a well-developed social wage and a long tradition of family allowances, the left-wing parliamentary opposition and the trade unions have advocated the introduction of income-related benefits in order to generate some vertical income redistribution. By the same token, framing the debate in terms of a policy choice between universalism and target efficiency may itself be misguided if it is in fact the overall societal context that is decisive. Thus in a society such as Sweden where almost as many people are recipients of state aid as are taxpayers, income testing may engender so little stigmatization that the alleged functional division between those two groups does not become an axial line of cleavage grounding fundamental political conflict. Although it might prove possible to destigmatize income-dependent family benefits in the United States by conceptualizing them as equalization of family burdens rather than as welfare, the by-product of such a step would be the creation of a new hierarchy of public assistance recipients, depressing the status of the childless.[58]

That even the United States, which has developed a Social Security system remote from if not hostile to universalism, can create a targeted benefit to families with children that does not stigmatize is shown by the National School Lunch Act. Passed by Congress in 1946, it was designed "as a measure of national security, to safeguard the health and well-being of the Nation's children...." It provides free lunches to children from families with incomes below 130 percent of the federal poverty guidelines and reduced-price lunches to those from families with incomes between 130 percent and 185 percent of the guidelines. For the school year 1994-95, these guidelines meant that children from four-member families with incomes below $14,800 were entitled to free lunches, while those from such families with as incomes as high as $27,380 received lunch at reduced prices. What is particularly interesting about the school lunch program is that, in response to the "humiliating discrimination" to which many poor children had been subjected, in 1970 Congress wrote an antistigmatization clause directly into the statute: "No physical segregation or other discrimination against any child eligible for a free lunch or a reduced price lunch...shall be made by the school nor shall there b[e] any overt identification of any child by special tokens or tickets, announced or published lists of names, or by other means." U.S. Department of Agriculture regulations further specify that "children shall not be required to use a separate dining area, go through a separate serving line, enter the dining area through a separate entrance, or consume their meals or milk at a different time." As the major judicial vindication of the right to nonstigmatizing receipt of benefits glossed the statute: "many youngsters are ashamed to have it [poverty] seen, and federal lawmakers...have decreed respect for their feelings." Almost 25 million students, more than half of total U.S. school enrollment, participate in the program, of whom 11 million receive free, 2 million reduced-price, and 12 million full-price lunches (which receive a small subsidy). Even if there is no such thing as a free school lunch, at $4 billion for 4 billion meals, nonstigmatizing and perhaps even invisible support for poorer families with children need not be expensive. Unsurprisingly, the profamily market-knows-besters of the 104th Congress bent on undermining the rudiments of the U.S. welfare state targeted this program for extinction.[59]

One way of resolving the tension between selectivity and substantive equality on the one hand and universalism and formal equality on the other is to abolish general children's allowances and to replace them with income-dependent programs. Italy instituted this change in 1988, eliminating payments altogether to families above a certain ceiling and providing allowances to lower-income families (depending on the number of children), in part as an austerity measure but also to anchor redistribution for the purpose of reducing social inequality as the basis of Italian family policy. For somewhat different reasons, a similar program was implemented in 1992 by the Conservative government in Canada—where the demise of family allowances through neglect had been predicted two decades earlier—when it eliminated universality and increased payments to the poorest families. The center-right coalition government in Germany at one time announced legislative plans for a similar transformation. The communitarian spirit underlying social security systems could be better preserved by a progressive subsidy, as in

Italy and Australia, that tapers off or is phased out at higher income levels, or clawbacks, as in Britain and Canada, which recoup payments to the rich families through a progressive income tax system. The Reaganomic flattening of marginal tax rates would, to be sure, make the latter plan infeasible in the United States. By the same token, however, as President Johnson's Commission on Income Maintenance Programs observed, clawback financing, "[h]owever cleverly disguised," as based on a postpayment means test will erode the supposed benefits of universalism. The Commission ultimately rejected child allowances in favor of a minimum supplementary income for the poor regardless of whether they had children; it foresaw a role for children's allowances only as a French-style horizontally redistributive program between families with and without children with similar incomes once the United States had created a higher statutory income floor.[60]

MALTHUS REDUX, OR THE END OF THE POOR LAW AS WE KNOW IT?

> Nothing symbolizes the vacuity of serious political thinking more than the resurgence of popularity of theorists as irrelevant to the modern world as Smith, Locke, Malthus.... Malthus, like an ancient talisman, is brought out whenever liberal society is in trouble.[61]

The Reagan-Bush administrations brought to bear on the formulation of public policy a recrudescence of political Malthusianism that would have been inconceivable just a few years earlier. Its most prominent social welfare analyst was Charles Murray, who offered a quick solution to the problems of hard-core unemployment among the young, procreation among single teenage girls, and the breakup and immobilization of poor families. To this end, his "most ambitious thought experiment...consists of scrapping the entire federal welfare and income-support structure for working-aged persons, including AFDC, Medicaid, Food Stamps, Unemployment Insurance, Worker's Compensation, subsidized housing, disability insurance, and the rest. It would leave the working-aged person with no recourse whatsoever except the job market, family members, friends, and public or private locally funded services."[62]

Once his patrons were out of office, Murray sharpened the focus of his Malthusian misogyny, and discovered to his surprise that right-wing politicians espoused it. First in the *Wall Street Journal* and then before Congress, he announced that rising (white) illegitimacy, "the single most important social problem of our time...because it drives everything else," signaled that "the sky really is falling." Although "the constants are that boys like to sleep with girls and that girls think babies are endearing," Murray trained the penalties for procreating without the financial wherewithal on single mothers. Their growing numbers, a persistent Ricardian-Malthusian echo resounds, "must destroy the community's capacity to sustain itself." Murray's only innovation is that "the government should spend lavishly on orphanages" where a "warm, nurturing environment" will be provided for the children whose single mothers abandon them. This "stern, self-selection process...increases the chances that the child will survive." Without offering all that Murray demanded, the proposed Real Welfare Act of 1994, a right-wing Republican congressional bill that would have eliminated AFDC benefits for the children of single mothers under the age of 21, pointed in his direction. The Right's gender-specific attack on teenage procreators is illuminating in view of the finding that the impregnators of high school girls are 2.5 times as likely to be men over the age of 20 as high school boys and four times as likely to have impregnated junior high school girls as the boys in those schools.[63]

The Clinton administration, despite having at its disposal several of the most liberal social policy analysts ever to have advised a president on poor-law reform, itself began the march down the Malthusian road. Its most visible step was to authorize states to impose a so-called family cap on AFDC recipients that eliminates additional payments for any children born after the mother becomes a recipient. Although the $67 average monthly increment is so far below the incremental cost of another child that it can scarcely qualify as an economic incentive to have more children, President Clinton apparently shares the conviction of the governor of Mississippi "that mothers on welfare became pregnant precisely so that they could collect the $24 a month in extra benefits offered by the state." Ironically, however, when officials of a state that had implemented the cap were later forced to concede that the restriction turned out to be less efficacious than originally claimed, they promptly denied that lower birth rates were the goal; instead, its purpose had always been to make poor-law beneficiaries take responsibility for their procreative decisions and nondecisions.[64]

The Republican capture of the 104th Congress brought about the legislative embodiment of neo-Malthusianism as the Personal Responsibility Act of 1995 featured the prohibition of AFDC payments with respect to a child born to a woman already receiving such aid. The current fascination with AFDC caps represents another turn of the Malthusian wheel, which has attracted conservatives and liberals alike over the years. At the height of agitation over population and the poor law during the Nixon administration, the American Bar Association's Committee on Law and Family Planning opined that "a salient reason for indifference to birth control...on the part of the many-offspring welfare mothers is that...since they are supported by public assistance, which is of course increased for each offspring, they do not fear the need to divide the same loaf of bread among more mouths—a fear which may motivate birth control among self-supporting parents." It therefore proposed that the new Work Incentive Program for AFDC mothers "be programmed to provide a specific economic incentive to birth control. The amount the welfare mother keeps from her wages without deduction from her public assistance grant, should decrease a small amount with each additional child. That is, she should contribute more from her wages to the family budget as her number of children increases. Such a policy would bring her economic situation into some conformity with that of self-supporting parents for whom more children mean increased economic stringency."[65]

Politicians who have promoted the cap and rushed to implement it have resurrected the same arguments that Malthus introduced against miscegenation of wages and poor-law payments. In announcing that the Clinton administration's Department of Health and Human Services had granted a waiver to Wisconsin—New Jersey, Arkansas, and Georgia had already received waivers—to cap cash benefits to women who have additional children while receiving AFDC payments, Governor Tommy Thompson justified the change on the ground that across "society, wages are not increased when families have additional children. They shouldn't be in the AFDC program either." Yet this right-wing politician with an unparalleled record of ejecting recipients from the AFDC and food stamp rolls was merely repeating what James Florio, then the liberal governor of New Jersey, which imposed the cap in 1992, had told Congress earlier: "If...a working poor woman...chooses to make that decision to have a child, she does not go to her boss and demand that she get a pay increase." This response soon assumed the status of a mantra in other state campaigns to eliminate additional benefits for additional children born to AFDC recipients as government officials hastened to personalized the issue: "'If my wife and I have another baby, my salary does not go up.'" In upholding the constitutionality of the New Jersey provision against claims that it denies due process and equal protection of the laws to needy children based on their parents' behavior, a federal judge joined the chorus by agreeing that the cap merely "puts the welfare household in the same situation as that of a working family, which does not automatically receive a wage increase every time it produces a child."[66]

Senate Finance Committee Chairman Moynihan joined the issue by first conceding that indeed "in a working-class family, when another child comes along, they put more water in the soup," and then observing that nevertheless the United States is the world's only industrial democracy to fail to provide child allowances to avoid that predicament. The debate was broadened when a New Jersey legislator, a descendant of slaves, argued to Moynihan that people had to bear the consequences of their personal decisions to use condoms, or to have a child or an abortion: "I am trying to prepare my people for America. And, therefore, American values; not some other country, because this is where they have to survive. In America, we do not automatically add income as you add family members." Governor Pete Wilson of California gave the debate a divisive intraclass point by charging that it is "'unfair'" to make a hard-working young couple, who must save to afford a child, "'pay taxes to provide a greater stipend to a woman on welfare who continues to have one child after another out of wedlock'"—an issue that his rival for the Republican presidential nomination, Senator Phil Gramm, reiterated in a losing effort to mobilize Senate support for retaining the family cap in the Family Self-Sufficiency Act.[67]

Despite the politicians' generally correct characterization of the U.S. wage system's lack of an express reproductive component, they have overlooked a venerable tradition of paying variable sums to families with unequal numbers of mouths to feed. As long ago as the 1920s Paul Douglas catalogued the precedents for the family wage. During World War I, for example, the United States Government provided family allowances graduated according to family size to enlisted men. The so-called mothers' pensions that most states afforded mothers who had lost their husbands' financial support were also largely graduated according to the number of children. The death benefits provided by numerous state workers compensation programs also varied according to the number of dependents.[68]

One important area in which the United States has followed the European model of family allowances is unemployment insurance. Fourteen state unemployment compensation systems do provide for additional benefits in the form of dependents' allowances. Congress itself was the first legislature to enact such a program when it created the District of Columbia Unemployment Compensation Act immediately after passage of the Social Security Act in 1935. The statute set the insurance payment at 40 percent of the worker's wage plus 10 percent of the wage for a spouse and 5 percent for each dependent relative up to a maximum of 65 percent. In Florio's own New Jersey, the unemployment insurance statute provides for an additional 7 percent of the worker's weekly benefit amount for the first dependent and 4 percent for each of the next two. In other states the number of dependents is not capped. In Massachusetts, for example, the unemployed worker receives an additional $25 per week for each dependent up to a maximum of 50 percent of his or her weekly benefit rate.[69]

The introduction of procreative allowances in the unemployment insurance programs has, to be sure, not taken place without controversy. Significantly, the debate mirrors that surrounding wages and family allowances. Congress, which regarded the whole benefit system as a compromise between providing subsistence and preserving workers' former standard of living, noted that: "Benefits are based on normal earnings but at a very low rate for the single man, which may be supplemented if an employee is married or has dependents." The chief argument against dependents' benefits has always focused on their injection of the element of need into a non-needs-tested program. Advocates, accepting the framework set out by their protagonists, argue that the need in question is merely presumptive: the state agency does not conduct an individualized inquiry into the worker's particular circumstances to determine whether he or she in fact needs the additional amount to support the dependent. This conclusion derives from sample studies showing that weekly benefits for single persons equaled or exceeded nondeferrable expenditures for food, shelter, utilities, and health care, whereas benefits for even four-person families fell far short of the cost of necessaries.[70]

The clinching argument in favor of dependent-adjusted unemployment compensation benefits, however, is the same one that has historically attracted employers to family allowances:

> Dependents' benefits can also be a means of providing total benefits for the family head without raising the basic benefit to a level that would weaken the incentive of workers without dependents to find jobs. [I]f basic benefits were

increased to 80 percent of gross weekly wages in order to provide adequate benefits for heads of families, a working wife who is laid off while her husband is working might be strongly tempted to "take it easy" in looking for work. Also, a single man who averages almost as much as male heads of families might lack incentive to work, particularly since a benefit of 80 percent of gross wages would provide an income more closely approximating his former net wages.[71]

Like many European employers during the period before the enactment of mandatory family allowances who saw private allowances as a way of fending off general wage increases, some states introduced dependents' allowances into their unemployment compensation systems as a lower-cost method of enhancing benefits than an across-the-board increase. And although there is no evidence that allowances have depressed basic unemployment benefit levels, states with dependents' allowances tend to provide low basic maximum benefit levels in relation to average wage levels.[72]

Dependents' allowances have also been adopted in supplementary unemployment benefits that some unions have negotiated with large firms. Then, too, some states have included dependents' allowances in workers' compensation awards for total and partial incapacitation. The chief benefit that some employees receive from some employers that is differentiated according to the number of children is probably health care, although many workers must share the cost of the premiums for dependents. Other major elements of the social wage in the United States also contain a reproductive component. The Social Security Disability Insurance program includes a child's insurance benefit. And the death benefits provision of many state workers compensation programs pay amounts to children.[73]

Thus although politicians have understated the extent to which the principle of reproductive need has penetrated the social wage even in the United States, the positions that they have staked out have come to mold the politically and rhetorically plausible field of discussion in a society characterized by ever thinner public opinion. Stripped of its Malthusian ornamentation, the argument that what is good enough for the working class should also apply to poor-law beneficiaries must, therefore, be addressed. It may be sufficient to reply simply that it is unacceptable to permit the latter's children to suffer irreparable harm, but it is evasive to argue that an AFDC recipient, like middle-class women, may reproduce to satisfy "the desire to give a grandchild to one's own mother" (to whom she has by definition already given at least one).[74]

It is inaccurate and politically perilous to insist that the assumption underlying child-cap programs "is that middle-class people are intelligent enough to refrain from having children when they cannot support them and that poor women should do likewise." Rather, such programs are predicated on the empirical reality that anarcholiberal ideology and policy condemn working-class procreators and their children, by and large, to suffer the untoward consequences of the parents' lack of self-discipline, poor judgment, or bad luck. The appropriate response to the argument that AFDC recipients should not be exempted from this fate cannot lie in reciting the altruistic and selfish reasons that motivate rich and poor alike to have

children, but in criticizing the atavistic foundations of the overall pseudoindividual-
istic, antisolidaristic reproductive and demographic policies of the existing poor-
law state.[75]

How difficult it might be to muster outraged majoritarian opposition to implementation of a reproductive cap on AFDC payments can be gauged by the
extent to which the U.S. Supreme Court cut off such discourse a quarter-century
earlier. In *Dandridge v. Williams* it rejected an equal protection challenge to a
Maryland regulation that imposed a cap on the total AFDC grant that any one
family could receive regardless of the number of its dependent children. Because
the case involved merely "the most basic economic needs of impoverished human
beings" rather than commercial free speech or some other right deemed protected
by the U.S. Constitution, the Supreme Court subjected the cap not to a standard of
strict scrutiny, but only a reasonable basis standard. And here it found such a basis
in "the State's legitimate interest in...avoiding discrimination between welfare
families and the families of the working poor." If Justices Marshall and Brennan
were unable to persuade a majority that it was unconstitutional for a state to inflict
a deprivation on the children of a large family in order to "wield its economic
whip" in the form of a work incentive for the parents, it is improbable that the
current Supreme Court would come to any conclusion other than that of a liberal
legal commentator two decades earlier, who argued that "a sound birth planning
rationale" would also support *Dandridge*: "such a regulation creates an incentive
to limit births in welfare families closely analogous to that which exists in non-
welfare families, and thus is neither discriminatory nor unduly harsh." And indeed,
the federal judge who upheld New Jersey's cap found it analogous to the maximum
family payment that passed statutory and constitutional muster in *Dandridge*.[76]

The sea change in political discourse on poverty and reproduction that has
taken place during the last quarter of the twentieth century can be measured by an
argument that plaintiffs' legal services attorneys made in their brief in *Dandridge*,
deployment of which in the post-Reagan era seems inconceivable. They attacked
the cap on the ground that "by penalizing families of seven or more for the birth of
additional children the regulation's harshness falls heaviest upon those who do not
believe in artificial means of controlling birth." The Attorney General of Maryland, who had turned the tables on the underdogs by submitting a remarkable
sociologically oriented Brandeis brief replete with quotations from Alva Myrdal,
Daniel Moynihan, and E.H. Carr, directly joined the issue by replying that: "What
plaintiffs seek in this litigation is essentially a judicially conferred family allowance
system limited to welfare recipients." Asserting that European family allowance
systems had originated in response to concerns about inadequate population,
Maryland argued that at "a time of rising concern with population increase it
would...seem unwise to...require the state to eliminate the normal checks on
population increase on behalf of" large AFDC families but not with regard to "the
'working poor' or the public at large." Although the Supreme Court chose not to
rule on this dispute, even the dissenters obliquely acknowledged the socioeconomic
and legal constraints circumscribing their arguments: "It is true that government in

the United States, unlike certain other countries, has not chosen to make public aid available to assist families generally in raising their children."[77]

An earlier libertarian proposal to install a pure laissez-faire regime of pro-creation by eliminating as many externalities as possible underscores the *aporia* of the child-cap for AFDC recipients. Singling out welfare payments (together with public education) as the main subsidies to childbearing, David Friedman proposed making procreation a "losing proposition" for the Banfieldian lower-class parents with short time horizons rather than for the family as a whole. "It can be made so by making the welfare payments received by a family independent of the number of children. In terms of calculations of 'need' this procedure would oversubsidize small families, undersubsidize large ones, or do both. But it would also impose the cost of an additional child entirely on the parents." Apparently oblivious of the 200-year-old debate over family wages, all Friedman succeeded in doing was reproducing within the poor-law sector the dilemma of the so-called productivity-oriented wage system that abstracts from individualized needs such as family size. As Friedman ultimately acknowledges of his own proposal: "The disadvantage of this imposition is that the... [parents] may transfer the costs to the child, thus thwarting the purpose of the program."[78]

No capitalist society has yet discovered how to penalize guilty overpro-creators without visiting their sins on their innocent overprocreatees. To be sure, a resurgent Republican Party inspired by Charles Murray and led by Newt Gingrich purports to have found the holy grail in the form of the abolition of the poor laws altogether for miscreant reproducers and the consignment of millions of their now lucky offspring to lavish neo-Lockean and neo-Malthusian orphanages. Somewhat less preposterous and mean-spirited alternatives are also imaginable. The state could, for example, wait to impose special penalty taxes on its overreproductive citizens until all of their children had reached the age of 18, thus making their older age as miserable as possible. Such a system would be unlikely to act as a deterrent to the rich unless it were steeply progressive; and how many poor people have at age 18 the requisite quarter-century time horizon to engage in the necessary procre-atively evasive action to avoid the taking? The implausibility of these scenarios is rooted in the lack of a consensus that any advanced capitalist society is suffering from general overpopulation.

Nevertheless, to assert, in spite of this renewed Malthusian onslaught, that perceived "irresponsible reproduction...in the face of overpopulation" among the poor is not a source of such proposals as requiring welfare mothers to use Norplant is naive. After all, even the black U.S. Surgeon General at the time asserted that: "'Medicaid...must have been developed by a white male slave owner. It pays for you to be pregnant and have a baby, but it won't pay for much family planning. White male slave owners wanted a lot of healthy slaves, people to work. We don't need slaves any more. We need healthy, educated, motivated children with hope.'" The labor-recruitment metaphor is disorienting since the illegitimate births that Dr. Joycelyn Elders wanted to reduce reputedly contribute relatively little even to the reserve army of the unemployed. Eighty percent of the children of unwed, teenage high school dropouts will themselves be poor, and single teenage- mother-headed families in the United States are said to cost taxpayers $34 billion dollars to support. Indeed, the Republican Party expressly motivated its Malthusian Personal Responsibility Act of 1995 by reference to the $120 billion in AFDC payments, food stamps, and Medicaid that births to teenage mothers cost between 1985 and 1990.[79] A capitalistically dysfunctional lumpenproletariat is a pure cost, which confers no benefits on whomever the Surgeon General views as the structural successors of the slave owners.

To be sure, the initial impetus for the population control movement in the United States as the post-World War II baby boom came to an end was not the perception of a general overpopulation crisis—although the Nixon-Rockefeller Commission on Population Growth declared that a larger population would confer no benefits—but rather overpopulation among a distinct subpopulation. "The importance of high fertility among the underprivileged," according to the National Academy of Sciences, "lies not so much in its contribution to the national birth rate as in the difficulties that excessive fertility imposes on the impoverished themselves." If, for example, in the mid-1960s families with incomes less than $4,000 had produced the same average number of children as those with more than $4,000, the total number of children ever born to women 40 to 44 years of age would have been reduced by only 4 percent.[80]

Indeed, the connection between Norplant and Malthusian overpopulation-cum-poverty has been made clear by proponents and opponents of state-provided contraception targeted at the poor imagined to be largely black ghetto residents. The *Philadelphia Inquirer*, for example, noting in 1990 the happenstantial appearance of two news reports the previous day that the Food and Drug Administration had approved Norplant and that half of black children lived in poverty, wondered editorially whether "foolproof contraception" could "reduce the underclass." It made the link the cornerstone of a trial-balloon proposal that "welfare mothers" be offered a larger benefit in exchange for using Norplant or that it be made available free to poor women. Bombarded with accusations of racism by its own reporters and editors, the *Inquirer* apologized profusely for having "hastily and foolishly juxtaposed" contraception, poverty, and race. In resuming the 200-year-old debate over the direction of causality between procreation and poverty, or, seen from the perspective of the birth-strike controversy, over whether poverty can be avoided or eliminated by individual action or only by macrosocietal changes, the editorial board moved toward what had once been an orthodox Marxist position but has now become the adoptive shared rhetorical patrimony of an otherwise politically heterogeneous front of anti-Malthusians and anti-blame-the-victim-ologists: "It's true that many single young women lessen their chances of escaping poverty by having children too early in life. But it's also true that the very hopelessness of their circumstances often underlies the decision not to postpone childbearing. Creating hope...must be the main tenet of any effective war on poverty." The newspaper even accepted its antiracist critics' charge that "to dangle cash...in front of a desperately poor woman is tantamount to coercion," although the offer does not deny her any otherwise existing entitlement.[81]

The link between contraception and demographically caused poverty is so prominent among some on the Left that they view proposals such as state payments to AFDC recipients to undergo Norplant implants as "gas-chamber economics...." According to Alexander Cockburn, racist "child disincentive" programs such as the caps on benefits to women who have additional children while receiving AFDC payments will permit "Nazis" to impose Norplant as a condition for conferral of any social benefit on poor black teenagers. Nevertheless, a refurbished version of the birth strike in the form of state-aided technological contraceptive solutions to proletarian poverty has not met with monolithic resistance even among blacks. Former Surgeon General Elders, for example, enthusiastically welcomed Norplant as a means of preventing teenage pregnancies, bemoaning only its high price.[82]

LAISSEZ FAIRE OR SOLIDARITY FOREVER?

> In a life where the only thing that counts anymore is money, young people are beginning to see children as a handicap.[83]

The laissez-faire underpinnings of the state's and capital's implicit policy that population is unimportant for capitalism are, ironically, supported by leftist historical research arguing not only that "working-class men and women accurately gauged the relation of family size to their own interests," but that such conscious and deliberate fertility behavior is "simply not susceptible to very much direct control." Michael Katz and Mark Stern, for example, believe that workers' procreational "choice makes sense in terms of their class situation...even if its consequences in the aggregate seem to contribute to problems such as the imbalance between people and resources." The pull of microprocreational and macrodemographic individualism even on the Left can be gauged by the indignation with which Katz and Stern reject the possibility or propriety of public policy's or education's influencing fertility: "Rather, people will determine for themselves the family size that seems most appropriate to their lives."[84]

How individual proletarian couples could be acting in conformity with their class interests and yet uncoordinatedly unleash macrosocial consequences that may weaken their class, strengthen the capitalist class, or perhaps even undermine the ecological vitality of any society remains unclear. After all, if the working-class standard of living is controlled by the typical family with the average number of wage earners, incorporation of additional family earners into the labor force does not in the long run necessarily raise the average family's aggregate real wages, although it may immediately increase the individual family's income; "instead, the intensified competition in the labor market and the lowering of...wages simply spread the family wage over more workers [and] the degree of exploitation would be increased." At the very least, even if members of advanced capitalist societies have voluntarily reduced their fertility in response to overall economic pressures, a question still remains as to how close they have come to exhausting the potential for a societally optimal adjustment.[85]

The logic of left-wing demographic laissez faire is reminiscent of Harvey Leibenstein's rejection of the claim that fertility behavior in underdeveloped countries was irrational because it is based on conventions uninformed by capitalist rationality or technology. Yet the advantages that might accrue to the economy as a whole from a smaller population do not necessarily create the requisite microincentives to induce macroeconomically sound decisions: "For what may be appropriate when viewed from the standpoint of the economy as a whole may be most inappropriate when viewed from the position of an individual.... This error involves something...akin to the fallacy of composition." Specifically, Leibenstein means that subsistence-level families may be acting rationally in maximizing births despite their detrimental impact on the larger economy. What is most striking here is Leibenstein's inversion of the vantage point: he appears almost to be saying that rationality is the result of spontaneous aggregation of individual decisions. Missing is any sense of the independent existence of a macrosocietal plan with which individual procreators could democratically interact in order to mediate among and inform people in their collective and individual roles. But whatever the exigencies of Third World impoverishment, hunger, and starvation, they afford no basis for upholding laissez faire in societies possessing the manifold resources to eliminate poverty. Procreational individualism should be even less unquestioned where the behavior is not rational even from the individual economic perspective and parents instrumentally create offspring as a "valued asset," "investments in parental status," or "a hedge against loneliness."[86]

By the same token, however, the fear expressed by the British Royal Commission on Population in 1949—that "a community...in which birth control is generally accepted can only...survive, if its members think it worthwhile to have families large enough to replace themselves"—underscores the heavier burden that ideological conformity has been made to bear in modern capitalist societies. The question of whether "the cult of childlessness and the vogue of the one-child family" were symptoms of "decadence" during the interwar period and whether the widespread failure to reproduce in capitalist societies in the last quarter of the twentieth century reflects a similar phenomenon is, here at least, subsidiary to the fact that it has become politically more difficult for capital and the state to correct demographic course if such a change were necessary.[87]

By promoting moral and cultural understandings that elevate individual over collective rationality, capitalist societies foster attitudes and behavior—adequately captured or at least reproduced by the market-beholden "new household economics"—that treat children, that is, humanity's future, as fungible consumer commodities, between which and nonhuman commodities individuals or couples are free to allocate their scarce time and monetary and emotional resources. This conception contrasts sharply with the frameworks of traditional societies in which reproductive behavior was "guided by norms embedded in a cultural-institutional superstructure that overwhelmed rational choice at the...household level and substituted a time-tested, survival oriented group rationality [that] left the individual couple (particularly the wife) with little or no discretionary control over completed family size."[88] The obviously progressive enlargement of freedom associated with modernity's vindication of women's liberation from collectivist prescription of reproductive fate has less obviously annihilated and superseded the collective rationality that regarded children (perhaps instrumentally) as unique, since they guaranteed survival of the community in a way that transcended whatever individual interests procreators may have managed to nurture in such societies.

Against the background of the need to consolidate that liberation from premodern forms of gender oppression, even the most reflective women's organizations have difficulty transcending the bounds of liberal individualism in vindicating reproductive rights. Thus the "Women's Declaration on Population Policies," which was drafted by an international network of women's health advocates in preparation for the 1994 International Conference on Population and Development, stated that: "Women have the individual right and the social responsibility to decide whether, how, and when to have children and how many to have...." How women qua atomized individuals would ever have the knowledge to exercise that responsibility the authors of the Declaration failed to explain. That a feministically gendered invisible hand, like any other Smithian system, must generate collective irrationality is itself an invisible problem to those who reject "the idea that individuals in the present generation will not, left to their own free desires, make sound decisions...for the good of future generations...."[89]

Only the theoretically most sophisticated feminist population discourse problematizes the "mystical 'harmony of interests' between individual women and public authorities [or] conflicts between 'private' and 'public' interests...." Sônia Correa and Rosalind Petchesky, for example, while conceding that the existence of a biologically based fundamental right to procreate "is clearly more complicated than whether one has a right, as a matter of bodily integrity, to prevent or terminate a pregnancy," nevertheless insist that the recognition that childbearing has third-person and collective consequences does not necessitate the conclusion that women have a societal duty to refrain from reproducing. Their reasoning, tailored to the situation of women in underdeveloped countries, carries pregnant implications for the advanced capitalist world and beyond: "Such a duty could begin to exist only when all women are provided sufficient resources for their well-being, viable work alternatives, and a cultural climate of affirmation outside of childbearing so that they no longer depend on children for survival and dignity." To the extent that such societies do provide the material resources and degendered social structure and values that deprive single- or absent-minded devotion to the creation of large families of any collectively or even individually rational basis, feminists may then come to accept the need for the formulation of joint collective-individual demographic and hence fertility goals. The 1994 United Nations Conference on Population and Development took a step in that direction by declaring that couples and individuals, in exercising "the basic right...to decide freely and responsibly the number...of their children...should take into account the needs of their living and future children and their responsibilities towards the community."[90]

To the extent that the invisible hand proves to be as inept at guiding billions of self-regarding decision-makers toward a collectively rational demographic outcome as it has been in so many other areas marked by "market failure"—that is, if procreators fail to identify, measure, and balance the collective costs and benefits of additional children now and 20 years hence and to refrain from producing them when the former exceed the latter—the state's visible hand may have to intervene to steady it. The sanctity shrouding procreative choices, which ironically has reached its apotheosis in social formations that reify children, has, at least in the United States, added its ideological weight to the inevitable rearguard struggles against decommodification—in this case in the form of family or children's allowances. But regardless of how warranted such subsidies are as a matter of social welfare and social justice, bribing people to multiply or to limit their fertility cannot substitute for the creation of an objective and felt community: "We cannot, in a democracy, appeal to parents to bear children as part of their democratic responsibilities whilst at the same time they are forced to serve their own economic interests at the expense of the rest of the community."[91]

A profound demographic dilemma, which is presumptively inescapable in any society riven by class, racial, ethnic, gender, generational, or religious cleavages, lies in developing within the individual procreators a sustained psychological identification through the current and adjoining generations with the larger community as a living and life-giving collectivity that has a past as well as a future—a project that can hardly be fulfilled merely by establishing, as France has done, a ministry for "solidarity between the generations." Creation of a quasiuniversally perceived identity between personal and collective interests so that individual and societal reproductive needs can mesh and be harmonized is a task that is difficult enough in a tabula rasa microcommunity such as a kibbutz, where the generational existential context is palpable, but becomes almost impossibly heroic even in a relatively homogeneous nation, and barely imaginable on an international level. The social-psychological and moral delicacy of the dilemma is captured in the need to nurture both an abstract analytical and a felt emotional commitment to solidarity with the collectivity and the other people, past, present, and future, who compose it—a commitment that never collapses into a merely repressive and ultimately feckless procreational duty to the state.[92]

If these desiderata of an intergenerational demographic solidarity appear not to extend beyond vague generalities, the reason lies in their purely aspirational character in a society grounded in individualism, competition, privacy, exploitation, greed, indifference and, at best, mutual toleration. Where virtually no one reproduces for the sake of the preservation of the human community but only for various self-regarding reasons, it is perilous to impute changing macrosocietal goals to changes in overall fertility rates. Nevertheless it is plausible that a kind of demographic Zeitgeist speaks, for example, through a massive shift toward childless or one- or two-child families. Whether, however, the fact that millions simultaneously decide, for personal economic, psychological, or cultural reasons, to limit their procreativity means that they have been guided by a vision of the long-term collective outcomes of those decisions is doubtful.

Articulating a collective judgment as to the appropriate future size of the population presupposes a structure of democratic planning that no capitalist society has ever undertaken. Although the Nixon administration and the Rockefeller-led Commission on Population Growth and the American Future spoke vaguely about the need for foresight in this area, the state shrank back from taking any concrete initiatives. How, after all, should a society that is quasireligiously opposed to planning something as mundane as how many automobiles or pairs of socks it will produce next year suddenly be able to lay down a framework as to how large the population should be and how many new members of the human race should be born. To be sure, Congress is deemed to possess the organizational capacity and administrative expertise to determine how many B-1 bombers should be produced and how many already existing human beings from other countries should be admitted as immigrants annually, but, given the intensely personal character of procreative decisions, governmental intervention would, without more, be perceived merely as intolerable fiat. Societies are imaginable in which even such decisions could be integrated into an interactive process between the democratically formulated needs of the community at large and those of each potential individual procreator, but a militantly competitive capitalism in which a Spencerian wall divides the family that "exists to protect...the weak" from the society that "exists to reward the strong," is not one of them.[93]

NOTES

1. S. Ryan Johansson, "Status Anxiety and Demographic Contraction of Privileged Populations," *Pop. & Dev. Rev.* 13 (3):439-70 at 443-44 (Sept. 1987).

2. K Mart Corp. v. Ponsock, 732 P.2d 1364, 1372 (Nev. 1987) (quote); U.S. BLS, *Occupational Outlook Handbook: 1994-95 Edition* (Bull. 2350, 1994).

3. Francis Bacon, *The Essays or Counsels, Civil and Moral*, in *The Works of Francis Bacon* 1: 23-24 (1825 [1612]).

4. See above ch. 7.

5. A.B. Piddington, *The Next Step: A Family Basic Income* 15 (1921).

6. See above ch. 1; Alvin Schorr, "The Family Cycle and Income Development," *Social Security Bull.* 29 (2):14-25, 47 at 20-22 (Feb. 1966).

7. Ellen Peck, *The Baby Trap* 9 (1971). See also Peck's statement in The Commission on Population Growth and the American Future, 7 *Statements at Public Hearings of the Commission on Population Growth and the American Future* 162-65 (1972); *Pronatalism: The Myth of Mom and Apple Pie* (Ellen Peck & Judith Sanderowitz eds., 1974). Judith Blake & Jorge del Pinal, "The Childlessness Option: Recent American Views of Nonparenthood," in *Predicting Fertility: Demographic Studies of Birth Expectations* 235-64, tab. 13-3 at 244, 259 (Gerry Hendershot & Paul Placek eds., 1978), argue that although two-thirds of survey respondents saw the costs of children as primarily the direct ones of burdensome demands and inability to organize time, the fact that three-fifths rejected the notion that childless couples led more intimate or varied lives showed that they did not

believe that nonparenthood permits them to lead more "glamorous" lives.

8. [Samuel Dugard], *Peri Polupaidias or, A Discourse Concerning Having Many Children* 7 (1695); Nigel Balchin, "Children Are a Waste of Time," *Sat. Evening Post* 238 (20):10, 12 (Oct. 9, 1965); Lynnell Michels, "Why We Don't Want Children," *Redbook* 134 (3):10, 14 (Jan. 1970); Betty Rollin, "Motherhood: Who Needs It?" *Look* 34 (19):15-17 (Sept. 22, 1970); J. Mayone Stycos, "Some Minority Opinions on Birth Control," in *Population Policy and Ethics: The American Experience* 169-96 at 185 (Robert Veatch ed., 1977). See also Rollin's statement in The Commission on Population Growth and the American Future, 7 *Public Hearings* at 207-209. Rollin was a senior editor at *Look*.

9. John Bray, *Labour's Wrongs and Labour's Remedy* 166 (1968 [1839]); Fritz Brupbacher, *Kindersegen—und kein Ende? Ein Wort an denkende Arbeiter* 38, 50 (enlarged ed., 1909 [1903]); Caroline Nelson, "Neo-Malthusianism: The Control of Child-Bearing," *International Socialist Rev.*, 14 (4):228-30 at 230 (Oct. 1913). See also William Robinson, "The Prevention of Conception," *New Rev.* 3 (4):196-99 at 197 (Apr. 1915) ("it is a well known fact that the fathers of big families...make very poor strikers").

10. *Annales de la Chambre des Députés*, 9ᵐᵉ Législature, *Débats parlementaires*, Session extraordinaire de 1908, 1: pt 1, at 122, 123 (1909) (M. Lemire).

11. Jacques Bertillon, *La Dépopulation de la France: Ses conséquences, ses causes, mesures à prendre pour la combattre* 25 (1911); Francis Ronsin, *La Grève des ventres: Propagande néo-malthusienne et baisse de la natalité française (XIXᵉ-XXᵉ siècles)* 128-29, 133-34 (1980) (cited without source).

12. Tony Horwitz, "Getting Nowhere: Boomtowns Lure Poor with Plenty of Work—But Not Much Else," *Wall Street Journal*, June 16, 1994, at A1; Ulrich Beck, *Risikogesellschaft: Auf dem Weg in eine andere Moderne* 173 (1986) (quote).

13. Joe Sexton, "Delivery Drivers in Brooklyn Work in Fear of Young Guns," *N.Y. Times*, Dec. 3, 1994, at 1, col. 1, 10, col. 6 (nat. ed.) (quote); Dirk Johnson, "Family Struggles to Make Do After Fall from Middle Class," *N.Y. Times*, Mar. 11, 1994, A1, col. 4 (nat. ed.); Peter Kilborn, "California Strike Becomes a Battle Over Permanent Job Replacements," *N.Y. Times*, Apr. 17, 1994, § 1 at 8, col. 1 (nat. ed.) (quote).

14. Christopher Jencks, *Rethinking Social Policy: Race, Poverty and the Underclass* 162 (1993 [1992]) (quote); J. Veevers, *Childless by Choice* 82-83 (1980); Louis Blanc, *Organisation du travail* 30 (5th ed. 1848 [1839]).

15. U.S. Bureau of the Census, *Statistical Abstract of the United States: 1994*, tab. 624 at 401 (114th ed., 1994).

16. Steven Holmes, "Low-Wage Fathers and the Welfare Debate," *N.Y. Times*, Apr. 25, 1995, at A7, col. 4 (nat. ed.).

17. Ronald Freedman, "Social Values about Family Size in the United States," in Union international pour l'étude scientifique de la population, *Internationaler Bevölkerungskongress* 173-83 (1959); Judith Blake, "Reproductive Motivation and Population Policy," *BioScience* 21 (5):215-20 at 216 (Mar. 1971); Alfred Malabre, Jr., "More and More People Seek—and Find—Jobs Even Though Unemployment Rate Stays High," *Wall Street Journal*, Jan. 18, 1978, at 34, col. 1; "Three's A Crowd," *Newsweek*, Sept. 1, 1986, at 68-76; "The Upward Mobility Two Incomes Can Buy," *Business Week*, Feb. 20, 1978, at 80-86; also Peter Kilborn, "Job Security Hinges on Skills, Not on an Employer for Life," *N.Y. Times*, Mar. 12, 1994, at A1, col. 1 (nat. ed.).

18. Thomas Robert Malthus, *An Essay on the Principle of Population*, in *The Works of Thomas Robert Malthus* 3:607 (6th ed.; E. Wrigley & David Souden eds., 1986 [1826]); Sar Levitan, Garth Mangum, & Ray Marshall, *Human Resources and Labor Markets: Labor and Manpower in the American Economy* 34 (2d ed., 1976 [1972]).

19. U.S. BLS, *Consumer Expenditure Survey, 1990-91*, tab. 5, 47, 56 at 30-33, 194-96, 221-23 (Bull. 2425, 1993). Since heads ("reference person") of the childless couples were on average 55 years old, most of them presumably had already discharged their reproductive duties. On the inconsistencies of this survey resulting from the fact that expenditures may be financed from sources not reflected in income data, see Nicholas Eberstadt, "A Poor Measurement," *Wall Street Journal*, Apr. 22, 1996, at A22 (Westlaw).

20. U.S. BLS, "Consumer Expenditure Survey, 1993" (Nov. 2, 1994) (unpublished tables). The average age of the reference person of the childless couple was 57.

21. Veevers, *Childless by Choice* at 86-90; *Die Lage der Familien in der Bundesrepublik Deutschland—Dritter Familienbericht*, tab. 16 at 37, tab. 10 at 191 (appendix), 57 (Deutscher Bundestag, 8. Wahlperiode, Drucksache 8/3121, 1979).

22. Dr. Oguste, "Socialisme et néo-Malthusianisme," *Revue socialiste* 46:97-124 at 112-13 (Aug. 1907).

23. Paul Leroy-Beaulieu, *La Question de la population* 45-47, 52, 258 (1913); Arno Herzig, "Kinderarbeit in Deutschland in Manufaktur und Protofabrik (1750-1850)," *Archiv für Sozialgeschichte* 311-75 (1983); Jürgen Kuczynski, *Studien zur Lage des arbeitenden Kindes in Deutschland von 1700 bis zur Gegenwart* (1968).

24. Institut für Sozialforschung, *Soziologische Exkurse* 122 (1968 [1956]) (Max Horkheimer).

25. Robert Torrens, *On Wages and Combinations* 29-30 (1969 [1834]); Rudolf Goldscheid, *Höherentwicklung und Menschenökonomie: Grundlegung der Sozialbiologie* 417 (1911); Diana Pearce, "Welfare Is Not for Women: Why the War on Poverty Cannot Conquer the Feminization of Poverty," in *Women, the State, and Welfare* 265-79 at 267-69 (Linda Gordon ed., 1990). An extreme example of child labor among white working-class and professional families suggests that parents benefit by having their children finance their own discretionary consumption. In Aroostook County, Maine, the entire school system, which has to be "'empathetic to the farmers' needs,'" shuts down for three weeks so that all students 12 and older can pick potatoes in lieu of their mothers, who now work part-time outside of agriculture. Sara Rimer, "School Can Wait, but Potatoes Can't," *N.Y. Times*, Oct. 7, 1994, at A9, col. 1 (nat. ed.).

26. "Ask a Tired Father Why He Earns Less," *N.Y. Times*, Oct. 17, 1994, at A14, col. 4 (nat. ed.) (letter to editor); House of Commons, *Official Report of Debates*, Fifth Session—Nineteenth Parliament, 5:5330 (July 25, 1944); J. Hajnal & A.M. Henderson, "The Economic Position of the Family," in *Papers of the Royal Commission on Population: Memoranda Presented to the Royal Commission* 5:1-33 at 1 (1950); *Cong. Rec.* 101:8141, 84th Cong., 1st Sess. (1955); U.S. BLS, *Workers' Budgets in the United States: City Families and Single Persons, 1946 and 1947*, at v (Bull. No. 927, 1948).

27. U.N. Department of Social Affairs, *Economic Measures in Favour of the Family* iv (1952); Paul Ehrlich, *The Population Bomb* 123, 124 (1968).

28. Lena Williams, "Childless Workers Demanding Equity in Corporate World," *N.Y. Times*, May 29, 1994, at 1, col. 1 (nat. ed.); "All Things Considered," Sunday, Aug. 14, 1994, 6:45-7:00 p.m., WSUI, Iowa City, Iowa; Hannah Arendt, *Between Past and Present* 189 (1961); Leslie Lafayette, "Fair Play for the Childless Worker," *N.Y. Times*, Oct. 16, 1994, § 3, at 11, col. 3. Although the author may be referring to private firm-level insurance, long-term disability insurance benefits under the social security system are, like old-age pensions, financed by other people's children.

29. Victor Fuchs, "Why Are Children Poor?" NBER Working Paper Series, tab. 2 at 7 (Working Paper No. 1984, July 1986); U.S. Bureau of the Census, *Poverty in the United States: 1992*, tab. 23 at 147 (CPR, Ser. P60-185, 1993); Constance Sorrentino, "The

Changing Family in International Perspective," *Monthly Labor Rev.* 113 (3):41-58, tab. 6 at 47 (Mar. 1990); Statistical Office of the European Communities, *A Social Portrait of Europe* 28 (1991); Gunnar Myrdal & Sven Wicksell, "Utsikterna i fråga om den framtida befolkningsutvecklingen i Sverige och de ekonomiska verkningarna av olika alternativt möjliga befolkningsutvecklingar," in Befolkningskommissionen, *Betänkande i sexualfråga 252-95 at 286 (Statens Offentliga Utredningar* 1936:59, 1938).

30. Louis Boucoiran, *La Famille nombreuse dans l'histoire et de nos jours* 17-35 (1921); E. Johnson, *Predecessors of Adam Smith: The Growth of British Economic Thought* 250-52 (1937); Edgar Furniss, *The Position of the Laborer in a System of Nationalism: A Study in the Labor Theory of the Later English Mercantilists* 150 (1920) (quote); H.C. Carey, *Principles of Political Economy* 3:55-56 (1840).

31. Susan Treggiari, *Roman Marriage: Iusti coniuges from the Time of Cicero to the Time of Ulpian* 58 (1991); Theodore Mommsen, *The History of Rome* 2:65-66 (William Dickson tr. 1895) (mentioning the *aes uxorium* of the censor Camillus in 351 B.C); Valeri Maximi, *Factorum et dictorum memorabilium*, II, 9, 1; John McCullough, *The Principles of Political Economy* 165 n.1 (5th ed. 1965 [1864]); Theodor Mommsen, *Römisches Staatsrecht* 2/1:395-96 and 395 n.6 (3rd ed. 1969 [1887]) (although the censors had the right to increase the self-declared estimation of the wealth subject to taxation in part by reference to personal reasons such as unmarried status, there was no separate bachelor tax as was once assumed); Pollux, *Onomasticon* VIII, 40; Aristotle, *Politica* 1270^{b}1-4; Plato, *Leges* 774a; Montesquieu, *De l'Ésprit des lois*, liv. 23, ch. 21 (quote); Suetonius, *De Vita Caesarum*, Bk. I, ch. xx; Ludwig Elster, "Bevölkerungslehre und Bevölkerungspolitik," in *Handwörterbuch der Staatswissenschaften* 2:703, 705-706 (1899); Wilhelm Roscher, *Grundlagen der Nationalökonomie* 823 (Robert Pöhlmann ed., 1906 [1854]); Montesquieu, *De l'Ésprit de lois,* liv. 23, ch. 27; U.S. BLS, *Handbook of Labor Statistcs 1924-1926*, at 167 (Bull. No. 439, 1927).

32. Bertillon, *La Dépopulation de la France* at 265 (quote); 39 Geo. 3, ć. 13, § III, 55, 57-58 (1799) (quote); Boucoiran, *La Famille nombreuse* at 46-49; D.V. Glass, *Population: Policies and Movements in Europe* 145-46 (1940); Applicazione dell'imposta sui celibi, Feb. 13, 1927, No. 124, in Raccolta Ufficiale delle Legge e dei Decreti del Regno d'Italia, 2:1447 (1927); "Taxing Bachelors and Bananas," *Literary Digest* 47 (1):5 (July 5, 1913) (quote).

33. Alfred Grotjahn, "Proletariat und Geburtenrückgang," *Neue Zeit* 41/II:205-209 (1923); Verordnung über die Gewährung von Kinderbeihilfen an kinderreiche Familien, Reichsgesetzblatt, I:1160 (1935); Dritte Durchführungsbestimmungen zur Verordnung über die Gewährung von Kinderbeihilfen an kinderreiche Familien, Reichsgesetzblatt, I:252-53 (1936); Helmut Schubert, "Bevölkerungspolitische Maßnahmen und der Familienlastenausgleich," *Deutsches Recht* 7 (11/12):231-34 (June 15, 1937); Gesetz zur Verminderung der Arbeitslosigkeit, June 1, 1933, Abschnitt V, §§ 1, 4-5, Reichsgesetzblatt, I, 323, 326-27; Gesetz über die Einkommensbesteuerung für 1933, Dec. 21, 1933, § 1(2), Reichsgesetzblatt, I, 1 (1934).

34. M. Staemmler, "Der Ausgleich der Familienlasten," *Deutsches Recht* 7 (11/12):228-30 (1937). The inimitable original read: "Es gibt kein gleiches Recht für alle. Recht hat nur, wer für sein Volk etwas wert ist."

35. "Familie und Senioren SPD: Kinder sind Armutsrisiko," *Süddeutsche Zeitung*, Sept. 10, 1993 (Lexis) (citing an SPD legislator); "Arm durch Kinder," *Der Spiegel* No. 42 (Oct. 17, 1994) at 140-43.

36. Gesetz über die Gewährung von Kindergeld und die Errichtung von Familien-ausgleichskassen, Nov. 13, 1954, § 4, Bundesgesetzblatt I, 333, 334; "Gesellschaftskrieg: Singles Contra Familien," *Focus*, Aug. 14, 1995, at 68-74 (Lexis) (quote); Bundeskinder-geldgesetz, Apr. 14, 1965, § 10, Bundesgesetzblatt I, 265, 269; Sozialgesetzbuch § 6, Bundesgesetzblatt I, 3015, 3016 (Dec. 11, 1975); Gunnar Heinsohn & Rolf Knieper, *Theorie des Familienrechts: Geschlechtsrollenaufhebung, Kindervernachlässigung, Geburtenrück-gang* 193 (1974); Bundeskindergeldgesetz, § 10, Jan. 21, 1986, Bundesgesetzblatt I, 222, 225; Alexander Jung, "Kein Kinderspiel," *Die Woche*, Mar. 3, 1994, § Wirtschaft at 12 (Lexis).

37. Bundesverfassungsgericht, Entscheidungen 87: No. 1, July 7, 1992, 1-48 at 28-29 (1993) (brief of die Arbeitsgemeinschaft der Deutschen Familienorganisationen) (quote); Kostas Petropulos, "Bonn schröpft die Familien," *Die Woche*, Feb. 3, 1994, § Politik at 6 (Lexis); Kostas Petropulos, "1000 Mark für jedes Kind," *Die Woche*, Oct. 14, 1994, at 38 (Lexis); Ines Zoettl, "SPD sieht sich mit Geissler einig," Reuter German News Service, Sept. 14, 1994 (Lexis) (quoting Heinrich Lummer); Grundgesetz, Art. 6 para. 1; Bundesverfassungsgericht, Entscheidungen 87:37-38.

38. "Roensch-Aufmacher: Familien mit Kindern fördern Kinderlose steuerlich belasten," *Süddeutsche Zeitung*, Feb. 19, 1994 (Lexis). The Federal Constitutional Court had ruled in 1990 that exemptions below that level were unconstitutional.

39. "Frau Roensch, die Familie und das alte Lied," *Süddeutsche Zeitung*, Feb. 14, 1994 at 4 (Lexis); Lutz Spenneberg, "Zwischenruf: Bravo, Hannelore Roensch!" *Die Woche*, Feb. 24, 1994, § Politik at 5 (Lexis); Petropulos, "Bonn schröpft die Familien"; Theodor Schmidt-Kaler, "Kinder statt Beiträge: Anregungen zu einer Rentenversicherung mit Selbstbeteiligung," *Die politische Meinung* 25:66-76 at 74 (Jan.-Feb. 1980); Alexander Jung, "Rentenlücke Kinder," *Die Woche*, July 12, 1996, at 10 (Lexis); "Ministerin Vorschlag," *Süddeutsche Zeitung*, Feb. 21, 1994 (Lexis); *Verhandlungen des Deutschen Bundestages*, 8. Wahlperiode: Stenographische Berichte 114:16,462 (Mar. 6, 1980) (Erhard); Zoettl, "SPD sieht sich mit Geissler einig." On the similar impact of dependent tax allowances in Britain, see Peter Townsend, *Poverty in the United Kingdom: A Survey of Household Resources and Standards of Living* 150-51 (1979).

40. Jahressteuergesetz 1996, Oct. 11, 1995, Art. 2: Bundeskindergeldgesetz, §§ 6(1), 20(1), Bundesgesetzblatt, I, 1249, 1380, 1382; "Vierköpfige Durchschnittsfamilie bekommt keinen Pfennig extra," *Süddeutsche Zeitung*, Aug. 11, 1995 (Lexis). In connection with its drive to curtail welfare-state programs, the CDU subsequently pressed to delay the 1997 increase. *Süddeutsche Zeitung*, Apr. 20, 1996 (Lexis)

41. Petropulos, "Bonn schröpft die Familien"; Petropulos, "1000 Mark für jedes Kind."

42. James Coleman, "The Rational Reconstruction of Society," *Am. Sociological Rev.* 58 (1):1-15 at 12 (Feb. 1993); Ben Wattenberg, *The Birth Dearth* 154-55 (1987).

43. Robert Pear, "Panel Backs Family Size as Health Cost Factor," *N.Y. Times*, Mar. 18, 1994, at A12, col. 1 (nat. ed.); Petropulos, "1000 Mark für jedes Kind" (discussing a proposal by Christian Leipert).

44. Shirley Burggraf, "How Should the Costs of Child Rearing Be Distributed?" *Challenge* 36 (5):48-55 at 49, 52 (Sept.-Oct. 1993).

45. *Ibid.* at 50, 52, 54-55.

46. *Ibid.* at 55, 52; Milton Friedman, *Capitalism and Freedom* 188 (1964 [1962]).

47. Bundesverfassungsgericht, Entscheidungen 87:38; Michael Katz, *In the Shadow of the Poorhouse: A Social History of Welfare in America* 88 (1986).

48. Nancy Folbre, "Children as Public Goods," *Am. Econ. Rev.* 84 (2):86-90 (May 1994). The argument concerning positive externalities maybe difficult to reconcile with Folbre's belief that the current system of parental impoverishment is inherited by their children in the form of below-average educational investments and social capital; perceiving a small chance of success, such children "have less incentive to try hard and greater incentive to subvert the rules." Regardless of this claim's empirical validity, it creates an inconsistency : if such children exist in sufficient numbers to constitute a social problem, they are not good candidates for FICA taxpayers and may represent negative externalities.

49. Allan Carlson, "What Happened to the 'Family Wage'?" *Pub. Interest* No. 83 at 3-17 at 15 (1986) (quote); Sheila Kamerman & Alfred Kahn, "Family Policy: Has the United States Learned from Europe?" *Policy Studies Rev.* 8 (3):581-98 at 590 (Spring 1989); Richard Titmuss, "The Social Division of Welfare: Some Reflections on the Search for Equity," in *idem, Essays on 'The Welfare State'* 34-55 at 44-45 (1969 [1955]); Allan Cartter, "Income-Tax Allowances and the Family in Great Britain," *Pop. Studies* 6 (3):218-32 at 219 (Mar. 1953) (quote).

50. Brian Abel-Smith, "Whose Welfare State?" in *Conviction* 55-73 at 62-63, 72 (Norman Mackenzie ed., 1958); Richard Titmuss, "Goals of Today's Welfare State," in *Comparative Perspectives on Stratification: Mexico, Great Britain, Japan* 89-98 at 92 (Joseph Kahl ed., 1968 [1965]); Kenneth Messere & Jeffrey Owens, "The Treatment of Dependent Children Under Income and Social Welfare Systems," *Int. Social Security Rev.* 32 (1):50-59 (1979); "Children's Allowances in the United Kingdom," *Social Security Bull.* 43 (10):21-24 (Oct. 1980); Leif Haanes-Olsen, "Children's Allowances: Their Size and Structure in Five Countries," *Social Security Bull.* 35 (5):17-28 at 26 (May 1972); Volker Hentschel, *Geschichte der deutschen Sozialpolitik (1880-1980): Soziale Sicherung und kollektives Arbeitsrecht* 203 (1983); "Die Antwort von SPD-Oppositionsführer Rudolf Scharping," *Süddeutsche Zeitung,* Nov. 24, 1994 (Lexis) (quote).

51. Calculated according to Internal Revenue Service, *Individual Income Tax Returns 1991,* tab. 2.3 at 48 (Pub. 1304, 1994). The figures in the text are subject to error because the published adjusted gross income size classes do not coincide exactly with the maximum bracket amounts. For more detailed estimates, see Steven Pressman, "Child Exemptions or Child Allowances: What Sort of Antipoverty Program for the United States?" *Am. J. Econ. & Sociology* 51 (3):257-72 (July 1992); *idem,* "Tax Expenditures for Child Exemptions: A Poor Policy to Aid America's Children," *J. Econ. Issues* 27 (3):699-719 (Sept. 1993). The total value of the exemptions as well as that accruing to the lowest-income group are overestimates because about 28 percent of the exemptions appeared on nontaxable returns, which constituted about 28 percent of all returns with these exemptions. The brackets for unmarried heads of household were somewhat lower, but the published data on dependent child exemptions by size of adjusted gross income do not distinguish between married people and heads of household. Married persons accounted for 72 percent of all such exemptions. IRS, *Individual Income Tax Returns 1991,* tab. 2.4 at 49. The bulk of these returns were presumably in the lowest-income group, whose income fell below the tax threshold. The cost in lower tax revenues to the Treasury was estimated at $21 billion. National Commission on Children, *Beyond Rhetoric: A New American agenda for children and Families* 84-85 (1991). Total AFDC benefit expenditures in 1991 were $20 billion, of which the federal share was $11 billion. U.S. House of Representatives, Committee on Ways and Means, *Overview of Entitlement Programs: 1994 Green Book: Background Material and Data on Programs Within the Jurisdiction of the Committee on Ways and Means,* 103d Cong., 2d Sess., tab. 10-1 at 325 (Comm. Print, WMCP 103-27, 1994).

52. Calculated according to OECD, *The Tax/Benefit Position of Production Workers, 1987-1990*, at 117, 121, 144-45, 159, 161, 205-206, 233-34, 250-51 (1991); *Family Policy, Government and Families in Fourteen Countries* (Sheila Kamerman & Alfred Kahn eds., 1978); Sheila Kamerman & Alfred Kahn, *Child Care, Family Benefits, and Working Parents: A Study in Comparative Policy* (1981); Pia Ohlin, "Cuts in Welfare System Force Swedes to Save in 1996," Agence France Presse, Jan. 2, 1996 (Lexis); Georg Ring, "Für Schweden begann ein rauhes Jahr: Einschnitte ins soziale Netz," *Süddeutsche Zeitung*, Jan. 3, 1996 (Lexis).

53. National Commission on Children, *Beyond Rhetoric* at 94-95; C. Eugene Steuerle & Jason Juffras, "A $1,000 Tax Credit for Every Child: A Base of Reform for the Nation's Tax, Welfare, and Health Systems" (Urban Institute, 1991).

54. David Rosenbaum, "Modest Cuts at High Cost," *N.Y. Times*, Dec. 14, 1994, at A1, col. 1; "Text of Clinton Speech Proposing Tax Breaks," *ibid*, Dec. 16, 1994, at A1, col. 1; H.R. 1215, 104th Cong., 1st Sess. § 101 (1995); Newt Gingrich, "The Contract's Crown Jewel," *Wall Street Journal*, Mar. 21, 1995, at A20 (Westlaw) (quote); Statement of Leslie Samuels before the House Committee on Ways and Means, Jan. 10, 1995 (Asst. Secretary of Treasury) (Lexis); Statement of Gary Bauer before House Committee on Ways and Means, Jan. 10, 1995 (Lexis) (quote); David Rosenbaum, "With Skepticism and Tax Cuts for All," *N.Y. Times*, July 2, 1995, § 1, at 10, col. 4-6 (nat. ed.).

55. Internal Revenue Code, § 32; John Brittain, *The Payroll Tax for Social Security* (1972); Joseph Pechman, *Federal Tax Policy* 112 (5th ed., 1987); Jonathan Forman, "Improving the Earned Income Credit: Transition to a Wage Subsidy Credit for the Working Poor," *Florida State U. Law Rev.* 16 (1):43-101 (Spring 1988); 42 U.S. Code § 430 (1994 Supp.); U.S. House of Representatives, *Overview of Entitlement Programs*, tab. 16-11 at 700, tab. 16-13 at 704; Steven Pressman, "The $1000 Question: A Tax Credit to End Child Poverty?" *Challenge* 35 (1):49-52 at 50 (Jan. 1992); John McDermott, "And the Poor Get Poorer," *Nation*, 259 (16):576-80 (Nov. 14, 1994); but see Brad De Long, "Beating the Wrong Horse," *ibid.*, 259 (22):782 (Dec. 26, 1994) (letter to editor).

56. Victor Fuchs & Diane Reklis, "America's Children: Economic Perspectives and Policy Options," *Science* 255:41-46 at 44-45 (Jan. 3, 1992).

57. *Income-Tested Transfer Programs: The Case For and Against* (Irwin Garfinkel ed., 1982); Gene Steuerle, "Why I Favor Tax Credits or Allowances," *Tax Notes* 65 (6):775-6 (Nov. 7, 1994) (arguing that family-size adjustments should operate at all income levels because even the rich family's ability to pay taxes is reduced by child costs); Neil Gilbert, *Capitalism and the Welfare State: Dilemmas of Social Benevolence* 47-88 (1983); Peter Baldwin, *The Politics of Social Solidarity: Class Bases of the European Welfare State 1875-1975*, at 115 (1990) (quote); T. Marmor, Martin Rein, & Sally Van Til, "Post-War European Experience with Cash Transfers: Pensions, Child Allowances, and Public Assistance," in President's Commission on Income Maintenance Programs, *Technical Studies* 259-91 at 278 (n.d. [1969]).

58. Abel-Smith, "Whose Welfare State?"; Baldwin, *The Politics of Social Solidarity*; Robert Goodin & Julian Le Grand, *Not Only the Poor: The Middle Classes and the Welfare State* (1987); Wim Huizing, "The Netherlands: Family Benefits," in *Responses to Poverty: Lessons from Europe* 210-26 at 216 (Robert Walker, Roger Lawson, & Peter Townsend eds., 1984); Lee Rainwater, "Stigma in Income-Tested Programs," in *Income-Tested Transfer Programs* at 19-46 at 41-42; James Coleman, "Income Testing and Social Cohesion," in *Income-Tested Transfer Programs* at 67-88 at 68-69; Christiane Dienel, "Familien vor Armut bewahren: Politik zur Existenzsicherung von Familien in Europa," in *Zwölf Wege der Familienpolitik in der Europäischen Gemeinschaft: Eigenständige Systeme*

und vergleichbare Qualitäten? 461-500 at 485, 494-95 (Erika Neubauer et al. eds., 1993).

59. 42 U.S.C. § 1751 (1992) (quote); 42 U.S.C. § 1758(b)(1)(A); 59 Fed. Reg. 9182, 9183 (1994); Nick Kotz, *Let Them Eat Promises: The Politics of Hunger in the United States* 56-58 (1971 [1969]) (quote); 42 U.S.C. § 1758(b)(4) (quote); 7 C.F.R. § 245.8(d) (1994) (quote); Justice v. Board of Education, 351 F. Supp. 1252, 1263 (S.D.N.Y. 1974) (quote); U.S. House of Representatives, Committee on Ways and Means, *Overview of Entitlement Programs: 1993 Green Book*, 103d Cong., 1st Sess. 1677-80 (1993); Sara Rimer, "Where a School Lunch Is Food, Not a Policy Issue," *N.Y. Times*, Mar. 7, 1995, at A1, col. 2 (nat. ed.).

60. *Zwölf Wege der Familienpolitik in der Europäischen Gemeinschaft* at 102-104; Christiane Dienel, "Italien," in *Zwölf Wege der Familienpolitik in der Europäischen Gemeinschaft: Eigenständige Systeme und vergleichbare Qualitäten?—Länderberichte* 243-68 at 255-60 (Erika Neubauer et al. eds., 1993); Robert Kudrle & Theodore Marmor, "The Development of Welfare States in North America," in *The Development of Welfare States in Europe and America* 81-121 at 98-99 (Peter Flora & Arnold Heidenheimer eds., 1984 [1981]); Statutes of Canada 1992, ch. 48, § 31 (repealing Family Allowances Act); Carl Mollins, "The Baby Bonus: R.I.P.," *Maclean's* 105 (9):34 (Mar. 9, 1992); Peter Newman, "Time to Kiss Off the Universality Myth," *ibid.* at 37; "Übereinkunft bei den Koalitionsverhandlungen: Mehr Kindergeld für Familien mit geringem Einkommen," *Süddeutsche Zeitung*, Oct. 31, 1994 (Lexis); OECD, *The Tax/Benefit Position of Production Workers* at 118, 183; The President's Commission on Income Maintenance Programs, *Poverty Amid Plenty: The American Paradox* 147-48 (1969) (quote).

61. Alan Wolfe, *The Limits of Legitimacy: Political Contradictions of Contemporary Capitalism* 253 (1980 [1977]).

62. Charles Murray, *Losing Ground: American Social Policy, 1950-1980*, at 227-28 (1984).

63. Jason DeParle, "Scrap Welfare? Surprisingly, The Notion Is Now a Cause," *N.Y. Times*, Apr. 22, 1994, A1, at 1 (nat. ed.); Charles Murray, "The Coming White Underclass," *Wall Street Journal*, Oct. 29, 1993 at A14 (quote) (also submitted as testimony at the House Committee on Ways and Means, Hearing on Welfare Reform, July 29, 1994, in Federal Document Clearing House Congressional Testimony (Lexis); *Changes in State Welfare Reform Programs: Hearing Before the Subcommittee on Social Security and Family Policy of the Senate Committee on Finance*, 102d Cong., 2d Sess. 45 (1992) (testimony of Charles Murray) (quote); H.R. 4473, 103d Cong., 2d Sess. (1994); S. 2134, 103d Cong., 2d Sess. (1994); Mike Males, "Why Blame Young Girls?" *N.Y. Times*, July 29, 1994, A13, at col. 2 (nat. ed.); Jennifer Steinhauer, "Study Cites Adult Males for Most Teen-Age Births," *ibid*, Aug. 2, 1995, at A10, col. 4 (nat. ed.). For further right-wing condemnation of the female half of procreators, see Lisa Schiffren, "Penalize the Unwed Dad? Fat Chance," *ibid*, Aug. 10, 1995, at A11, at col. 4 (nat. ed.); on the Swiftian annual ejaculation tax on all men who have not undergone a vasectomy as a means of supporting children with unknown paternity as an antidote to this demonization of procreatrixes, see Heidi Hartmann, letter to the editor, *Nation* 260 (10):330 (Mar. 13, 1995).

64. Nancy Gibbs, "The Vicious Cycle," *Time* 143 (25):24-33 at 29 (June 20, 1994); House Committee on Ways and Means, Hearings on Welfare Reform, July 29, 1994 (testimony of Robert Greenstein); Mireya Navarro, "Threat of a Benefits Cutoff: Will It Deter Pregnancies?" *N.Y. Times*, Apr. 17, 1995, at A1, col. 1 (nat. ed.); Kevin Sack, "In Mississippi, Will Poor Grow Poorer with State Welfare Plan?" *ibid.*, Oct. 23, 1995, at A1, col. 1, A13, at col. 1 (nat. ed.) (quote); Melinda Hennenberger, "State Aid Is Capped, But to What Effect?" *ibid.*, Apr. 11, 1995, at A1, col. 2 (nat. ed.).

65. H.R. 4, 104th Cong., 1st Sess. § 106 (1995); Nanette Dembitz, "Should Public Policy Give Incentives to Welfare Mothers to Limit the Number of Their Children?" *Family Law Q.* 4 (2):130-45 at 135, 144-45 (June 1970).

66. Karen Cohen, "Administration Gives OK to Wisconsin Welfare Cap," States News Service, June 24, 1994 (Lexis) (quote); Amy Rinard, "Prosser Says Thompson Welfare Cuts Record Stands Alone in U.S.," *Milwaukee Sentinel*, July 4, 1994, at 7A, col. 1; Norman Atkins, "Tommy Thompson, Governor Get-a-Job," *N.Y. Times Magazine*, Jan. 15, 1995, at 22-25; Act of Jan. 21, 1992, ch. 526, 1991 N. J. Laws 2782; *Changes in State Welfare Reform Programs: Hearing Before the Subcommittee on Social Security and Family Policy of the Senate Committee on Finance* at 6 (quote); Michael Cooper, "Tighter Welfare in Massachusetts," *N.Y. Times*, Feb. 4, 1995, at 1, col. 5, at 6, col. 3 (nat. ed.) (quoting Thomas Finneran, Mass. legislator); Michael Cooper, "Massachusetts Governor Signs Bill Overhauling Welfare," *ibid.*, Feb. 11, 1995 at 6, col. 3 (nat. ed.); Hennenberger, "State Aid Is Capped, But to What Effect?" at A9, col. 2 (New Jersey poverty official making same claim); Re C.K. v. Shalala, 883 F. Supp. 991, 1014 (D.N.J. 1995) (quote).

67. *Changes in State Welfare Reform Programs* at 10 (Moynihan and Wayne Bryant); John Cushman, Jr., "Dole Rivals Say Welfare Plan Is Weak on Curbs," *N.Y. Times*, Aug. 7, 1995, at A1, col. 5, at A8, col. 1-2 (nat. ed.) (Wilson); 141 *Cong. Rec.* S 13481 (Sept. 13, 1995) (Lexis).

68. Paul Douglas, "Some Precedents for the Family Wage System," *Int. Labour Rev.* 11 (3):353-65 (Mar. 1925); Act of Oct. 6, 1917, ch. 105, § 204, 40 Stat. 398, 403.

69. U.S. Department of Labor, *Comparison of State Unemployment Insurance Laws* tab. 307 and 308 at 3-43 and 3-44 (rev. no. 2, 1992); Olga Halsey, "Dependents' Allowances Under State Unemployment Insurance Laws," *Social Security Bull.* 14 (2):3-9 (Feb. 1951); Chapter 794, § 8(a), 49 U.S. Statutes 946, 949 (1935); New Jersey Revised Statutes § 43:21-3 (c)(2)(A) (1991); Massachusetts General Laws, Employment and Training Law, § 151 A:29(c) (1992).

70. U.S. House of Representatives, Report No. 858: *Unemployment Compensation for the District of Columbia*, 74th Cong., 1st Sess. 10 (1935) (quote); Joseph Becker, *Unemployment Benefits: Should There be a Compulsory Federal Standard?* 62-63 (1980); Richard Lester, *The Economics of Unemployment Compensation* 32-33 (1962).

71. William Haber & Merrill Murray, *Unemployment Insurance in the American Economy: An Historical Review and Analysis* 194 (1966).

72. Margaret Dahm & Phyllis Fineshriber, "Examining Dependents' Allowances," in National Commission on Unemployment Compensation, *Unemployment Compensation: Studies and Research* 1:77-93 at 78, 80-81 (1980).

73. Joseph Becker, *Guaranteed Income for the Unemployed: The Story of the SUB* 106-15 (1968); Massachusetts General Laws, § 152:35A (1992) ($6 per week under workers' compensation for each dependent subject to limitations); William Wiatrowski, "Family-Related Benefits in the Workplace," *Monthly Labor Rev.* 113 (3):28-33 (Mar. 1990); 42 U.S.C. § 402(d) (1988) (disability); e.g., Iowa Code, § 85.31(b) (1995) (death benefit). AFDC recipients' children also have medicaid coverage.

74. Lucy Williams, "The Ideology of Division: Behavior Modification Welfare Reform Proposals," *Yale Law J.* 102 (3):719-46 at 739 (Dec. 1992).

75. *Ibid.* at 739, 737. Yvette Barksdale, "And the Poor Have Children: A Harm-Based Analysis of Family Caps and the Hollow Procreative Rights of Welfare Beneficiaries," *Law & Inequality* 14 (1):1-71 at 68 (Dec. 1995), merely reproduces those obsolete foundations by asserting that: "Although the birth of an additional child increases a working family's need, the increased need should not affect the individual's salary, because that

salary is not determined by...need."

76. Dandridge v. Williams, 397 U.S. 471, 477, 485, 486, 525 (1970) (quotes); Edward Rabin, "Population Control Through Financial Incentives," *Hastings Law J.* 23 (5):1353-99 at 1398 (May 1972) (quote); In re C.K. v. Shalala. Even Barksdale, "And the Poor Have Children" at 15, an opponent of family caps, concedes that they are "probably constitutional under current Supreme Court doctrine."

77. Brief for Appellees at 33 n.41, Dandridge v. Williams, 371 U.S. 497 (1970), in *Landmark Briefs and Arguments of the Supreme Court of the United States: Constitutional Law* 69:97, 140 n.41 (Philip Kurland & Gerhard Casper eds., 1975) (quote); Brief for Appellants at 32-41, Dandridge v. Williams, in *Landmark Briefs* 69:85-94; Reply Brief for the Appellants at 13-14, Dandridge v. Williams, in *Landmark Briefs* 69:192-93 (quote); Dandridge v. Williams, 371 U.S. at 525 (quote).

78. David Friedman, *Laissez-Faire in Population: The Least Bad Solution* 25 (1972).

79. John Robertson, *Children of Choice: Freedom and the New Reproductive Technologies* 78 (1994) (quote); Robert Pear, "Surgeon General Says Medicaid Enslaves Poor Pregnant Women," *N.Y. Times*, Feb. 26, 1994, at A7, col. 5 (nat. ed.) (quote); Jason DeParle, "Clinton Target: Teen-Age Pregnancy," *ibid.*, Mar. 22, 1994, at A10, col. 4 (nat. ed.); Jason DeParle, "Clinton to Propose a Strategy to Curb Youth Pregnancies," *ibid.*, June 10, 1994, at A1, col. 6 (nat. ed.); "Poor Mother, Poor Child," *ibid.*, June 17, 1994, at A12, col. 1 (nat. ed.) (editorial); Steven Holmes, "'96 Cost of Teen Pregnancy Is Put at $7 Billion," *ibid.*, June 13, 1996, at A11, col. 4 (nat. ed.); H.R. 4, § 100(3)(M).

80. U.S. Commission on Population Growth and the American Future, *Population and the American Future* 12 (1972); Committee on Population, *The Growth of U.S. Population: Analysis of the Problems and Recommendations for Research, Training, and Service* 6 (quote), 11 (Nat. Acad. Sciences-Nat. Research Council Pub. No. 1279, 1965).

81. "Poverty and Norplant: Can Contraception Reduce the Underclass?" *Philadelphia Inquirer*, Dec. 12, 1990, at A18 (Lexis); "An Apology: The Editorial on 'Norplant and Poverty' Was Misguided and Wrongheaded," *ibid.*, Dec. 23, 1990, at C4 (Lexis).

82. Alexander Cockburn, "Welfare, Norplant, and the Nazis," *Nation*, 259 (3):79-80 (July 18, 1994); testimony before the House Subcommittee on Regulation, Business Opportunities, and Technology, Mar. 18, 1994 (Federal Document Clearing House Congressional Testimony, Lexis).

83. Howard French, "Does Sharing Wealth Only Promote Poverty?" *N.Y. Times*, Jan. 14, 1995, at 4, col. 5 at 6 (nat. ed.) (quoting tailor in Ivory Coast).

84. Michael Katz & Mark Stern, "History and the Limits of Population Policy," *Politics & Society* 10 (2):225-45 at 240, 242, 243, 245 (1980). See also Norman Ryder, "The Future of American Fertility," *Social Problems* 26 (3):359-69 at 369 (Feb. 1979): "I doubt that governments are able to modify the trend of fertility more than marginally.... And I doubt that they should even if they could—because the people know what they are doing."

85. Jane Humphries, "The Working-Class Family: A Marxist Perspective," in *The Family in Political Thought* 197-222 at 211 (Jean Elshtain ed., 1982) (quote); Richard Easterlin, "Does Human Fertility Adjust to the Environment?" *Am. Econ. Rev.* 61 (2):399-407 at 406-407 (May 1971). The individual-class dynamic triggered by proletarianization of an above-average number of family members is the mirror image of that created by individual family decisions to have smaller families so that the same nominal wage can be converted into a higher standard of living for a smaller number of family members regardless of its impact on the working class.

86. Harvey Leibenstein, *Economic Backwardness and Economic Growth: Studies in the Theory of Economic Development* 160 (1957) (quote); Irwin Garfinkel & Sara McLanahan, *Single Mothers and Their Children: A New American Dilemma* 85 (1986) (quote); Judith Blake, "Is Zero Preferred? American Attitudes Toward Childlessness in the 1970s," *J. Marriage and the Family* 41:245-57 at 247, 251 (May 1979) (quote). The trend toward absolute privileging of a woman's decision to reproduce extends to those with AIDS because in "poor black and Hispanic communities...women often depend entirely on men and their babies for both pleasure and their self-esteem." According to the director of obstetrics at a state medical institution, "'Reproductive and sexual relations are a very important part of their lives. It's not like they can say, 'I'm depressed so I'll go to Bloomingdale's.'"" Jane Gross, "The Bleak and Lonely Lives of Women Who Carry Aids," *N.Y. Times*, Aug. 27, 1987, at 1, col. 2, 14 col. 3-4 (nat. ed.). See also Gina Kolata, "Debate on Infant AIDS vs. Mother's Rights," *ibid.*, Nov. 3, 1994, at A13, col. 1 (nat. ed.). Among the mothers with AIDS who believe that "the decision to have a child is so personal that no one has a right to pass judgment" is a pregnant doctoral candidate who believes that her decision to have a baby who might live only five years is "'selfish'" but no more so than that of healthy mothers whom she sees "'screaming and...hitting their kids....'" Felicia Lee, "For Women with AIDS, Anguish of Having Babies," *ibid.*, May 9, 1995, at A1, col. 1 (nat. ed.).

87. Royal Commission on Population, *Report* 232, 136 (Cmd. 7695, 1949). On Italy's shrinking population, see Alan Cowell, "In an Affluent Europe, the Problem Is Graying," *N.Y. Times*, Sept. 8, 1994, at A4, col. 5 (nat. ed.). Overall in Europe "couples average only 1.5 children." "Report Expects AIDS to Depress Africa's Fast Population Growth," *ibid.*, July 3, 1996, at A4, col. 1 at col. 2 (nat. ed.).

88. Johansson, "Status Anxiety and Demographic Contraction of Privileged Populations" at 442.

89. "Women's Declaration on Population Policies," in *Population Policies Reconsidered: Health, Empowerment, and Rights* 31, 32 (Gita Sen et al. eds., 1994) (quote); Reed Boland, Sudhakar Rao, & George Zeidenstein, "Honoring Human Rights in Population Policies: From Declaration to Action," in *ibid.*, at 89-105 at 97 (quote).

90. Sônia Correa & Rosalind Petchesky, "Reproductive and Sexual Rights: A Feminist Perspective," in *Population Policies Reconsidered* at 107-23 at 112, 114; *Programme of Action of the United Nations International Conference on Population and Development* 34 (n.d. [1994]) (unedited version to be published as official U.N. document).

91. Victor Fuchs, *Women's Quest for Economic Equality* 97-98 (1988); Paul Demeny, "The Economics of Population Control," in *Rapid Population Growth: Consequences and Policy Implications* 199-221 at 214-15 (Nat. Acad. of Sciences, 1971); Richard Titmuss & Kathleen Titmuss, *Parents Revolt* 122 (1985 [1942]) (quote). The visible hand, however, may be shaky too: "Since there are no very convincing models of long-run economic development, economists are not in a position to decide these issues, and I doubt whether anyone else is." James Mirrlees, "Population Policy and the Taxation of Family Size," *J. Pub. Econ.* 1:169-98 at 197-98 (1972).

92. "Courtoisies et amabilités républicaines," *Le Monde*, May 22, 1995 (Lexis); Gunnar Myrdal, *Population: A Problem for Democracy* 84, 209, 222-23 (1940); Gunnar Heinsohn, Rolf Knieper, & Otto Steiger, *Menschenproduktion: Allgemeine Bevölkerungstheorie der Neuzeit* 11, 243-44 (1979).

93. Crane Brinton, *English Political Thought in the 19th Century* 234 (1962 [1933]). The United States is so far from being a solidary society that its leading paper sees family allowances as a "legacy of Israel's socialist past." Douglas Jehl, "Netanyahu Infuriates Unions by Assault on Welfare State," *N.Y. Times*, July 31, 1996, at A1, col. 4 (nat. ed.).

Bibliography

Omitted are all newspaper and magazine articles, unsigned or brief articles or comments, government publications, as well as books and articles only peripherally related to the central themes of the book. The first reference to each source in each chapter contains a full citation.

Abel-Smith, Brian. "Whose Welfare State?" In *Conviction* 55-73 (Norman Mackenzie ed., 1958)
_____. & Peter Townsend. *The Poor and the Poorest* (1966 [1965])
Abernethy, Virginia. *Population Politics: The Choices that Shape Our Future* (1993)
Adams, Paul. "Children as Contributions in Kind: Social Security and Family Policy." *Social Work* 35 (6):492-98 (Nov. 1990)
Aldous Joan, & Reuben Hill. "Breaking the Poverty Cycle: Strategic Points for Intervention." *Social Work* 14 (3):3-12 (July 1969)
Alter, George. "Theories of Fertility Decline: A Nonspecialist's Guide to the Current Debate." In *The European Experience of Declining Fertility, 1859-1970: The Quiet Revolution* 13-27 (John Gillis et al. eds., 1992)
Ameline, Calude, & Robert Walker. "France: Poverty and the Family." In *Responses to Poverty: Lessons from Europe* 193-209 (Robert Walker et al. eds., 1984)
Aries, Philippe. "Two Successive Motivations for the Declining Birth Rate in the West." *Pop. & Dev. Rev.* 6 (4):645-50 (Dec. 1980)
Armengaud, André. *Les Français et Malthus* (1975)
_____. "Mouvement ouvrier et néo-malthusianisme au début du xxᵉ siècle." *Annales de Démographie historique* 7-19 (1966)
Armstrong, Barbara. *Insuring the Essentials: Minimum Wage Plus Social Insurance—A Living Wage Program* (1932)
Atkinson, A. *The Economics of Inequality* (1975)
Baker, John. "Comparing National Priorities: Family and Population in Britain and France." *J. Social Policy* 15 (4):421-42 (Oct. 1986)
Baldwin, Peter. *The Politics of Social Solidarity: Class Bases of the European Welfare State 1875-1975* (1990)

Bane, Mary Jo, & David Ellwood. "Slipping into and out of Poverty: The Dynamics of Spells." *J. Human Resources* 21 (1):1-23 (Winter 1986)
_____. *Welfare and Realities: From Rhetoric to Reform* (1994)
Banks, J. *Prosperity and Parenthood: A Study of Family Planning Among the Victorian Middle Classes* (1954)
_____. *Victorian Values: Secularism and the Size of Families* (1981)
_____, and Olive Banks. *Feminism and Family Planning in Victorian England* (1964)
Barksdale, Yvette. "And the Poor Have Children: A Harm-Based Analysis of Family Caps and the Hollow Procreative Rights of Welfare Beneficiaries." *Law & Inequality* 14 (1):1-71 (Dec. 1995)
Barnett, Larry. *Population Policy and the U.S. Constitution* (1982)
Bauer, Otto. "Die Akkumulation des Kapitals." *Neue Zeit* 31/I:831-38, 862-74 (1912-13)
_____. "Kapitalsvermehrung und Bevölkerungswachstum." *Der Kampf* 7:411-12 (1913-14)
_____. "Volksvermehrung und soziale Entwicklung." *Der Kampf* 7:322-29 (1913-14)
Becker, Gary. "An Economic Analysis of Fertility." In *Demographic and Economic Change in Developed Countries* 209-31 (NBER, 1960)
_____. *A Treatise on the Family* (1981)
Berelson, Bernard. "Beyond Family Planning." *Science* 163:533-43 (1969)
Bergmann, Anneliese. "Frauen, Männer, Sexualität und Geburtenkontrolle: Die Gebärstreik-debatte der SPD im Jahre 1913." In *Frauen suchen ihre Geschichte: Historische Studien zum 19. und 20. Jahrhundert* 81-108 (Karin Hausen ed., 1983)
_____. "Geburtenrückgang—Gebärstreik: Zur Gebärstreikdebatte 1913 in Berlin." *Archiv für die Geschichte des Widerstandes und der Arbeit* 4:7-55 (1981)
Bernstein, Eduard. "Geburtenrückgang, Nationalität und Kultur." *Sozialistische Monatshefte* 19:1492-99 (1913)
Bertillon, Jacques. *La Dépopulation de la France: Ses conséquences, ses causes, mesures à prendre pour la combattre* (1911)
Beveridge, W. "Population and Unemployment." *Econ. J.* 33:447-75 (1923)
_____. *Unemployment: A Problem of Industry* (1909 and 1930) (new ed. 1930 [1909])
Bigelow, Howard. *Family Finance: A Study in the Economics of Consumption* (rev. ed., 1953 [1936])
Blackmore, J., & F. Mellonie. "Family Endowment and the Birth-Rate in the Early Nineteenth Century." *Econ. Hist.* 1 (2):205-13 (May 1927)
_____. "Family Endowment and the Birth-Rate in the Early Nineteenth Century: A Second Analysis." *Econ. Hist.* 1 (3):412-18 (Jan. 1928)
Blake, Judith. "Are Babies Consumer Durables? A Critique of the Economic Theory of Reproductive Motivation." *Pop. Studies* 22 (1):5-25 (Mar. 1968)
_____. "Coercive Pronatalism and American Population Policy." In Commission on Population Growth and the American Future. 6 *Research Reports: Aspects of Population Growth Policy* 81-109 (1972)
_____. "Demographic Science and the Redirection of Population Policy." In *Public Health and Population Change: Current Research Issues* 41-69 (Mindel Sheps & Jeanne Ridley eds., 1965)
_____. *Family Size and Achievement* (1989)
_____. "Ideal Family Size Among White Americans: A Quarter of a Century's Evidence." *Demography* 3 (1):154-73 (1966)
_____. "Income and Reproductive Motivation." *Pop. Studies* 21 (3):185-206 (Nov. 1967)
_____. "Is Zero Preferred? American Attitudes Toward Childlessness in the 1970s." *J.*

Marriage & the Family 41:245-57 (May 1979)

_____. "Population Policy for Americans: Is the Government Being Misled?" *Science* 164:522-29 (1969)

_____. "Reproductive Motivation and Population Policy." *BioScience* 21 (5):215-20 (Mar. 1971)

_____, & Jorge del Pinal. "The Childlessness Option: Recent American Views of Nonparenthood." In *Predicting Fertility: Demographic Studies of Birth Expectations* 235-64 (Gerry Hendershot & Paul Placek eds., 1978)

Blanc, Louis. *Organisation du travail* (5th ed. 1848 [1839])

Blaug, Mark. "The Myth of the Old Poor Law and the Making of the New," *J. Econ. Hist.* 23 (2):151-84 (June 1963)

_____. "The Poor Law Report Reexamined," *J. Econ. Hist.* 24 (2):229-45 (June 1964)

Blom, Ida. *Barnebegrensing—synd eller sunn fornunft* (n.d. [ca. 1980])

Blumenfeld, Emily, & Susan Mann. "Domestic Labour and the Reproduction of Labour Power: Towards an Analysis of Women, the Family and Class," in *Hidden in the Household: Women's Domestic Labour Under Capitalism* 267-307 (Bonnie Fox ed., 1980)

Bogue, Donald. *Principles of Demography* (1968)

Boland, Reed, Sudhakar Rao, & George Zeidenstein. "Honoring Human Rights in Population Policies: From Declaration to Action." In *Population Policies Reconsidered: Health, Empowerment, and Rights* 89-105 (Gita Sen et al. eds., 1994)

Bonar, James. *Malthus and His Work* (1885)

Boner, Harold. *Hungry Generations: The Nineteenth-Century Case Against Malthus* (1955)

Booth, Charles. 17 *Life and Labour of the People in London: Notes on Social Influences and Conclusion* (1903)

Bornträger, J. *Der Geburtenrückgang in Deutschland: Seine Bewertung und Bekämpfung* (1913)

Bossard, James. *The Large Family System: An Original Study in the Sociology of Family Behavior* (1956)

Boucoiran, Louis. *La Famille nombreuse dans l'histoire et de nos jours* (1921)

Boverat, Fernand. *Niveau d'existence et charges de famille: Étude comparative* (1944)

Bowen, Francis. *American Political Economy* (1969 [1870])

Bowley, A., & Margaret Hogg. *Has Poverty Diminished? A Sequel to "Livelihood and Poverty"* (1925)

Braden, John. "Population, Ethnicity, and Public Goods: The Logic of Interest-Group Strategy." In *Managing the Commons* 252-60 (Garrett Hardin & John Braden eds., 1977)

Brailsford, H., et al. *The Living Wage* (1926)

Brazer, Harvey. "The Federal Income Tax and the Poor: Where Do We Go from Here?" *Cal. Law Rev.* 57 (2):422-49 (Apr. 1969)

Brentano, L. "The Doctrine of Malthus and the Increase of Population During the Last Decades." *Econ. J.* 20 (79):371-93 (Sept. 1910)

Brupbacher, *Fritz. Kindersegen—und kein Ende? Ein Wort an denkende Arbeiter* (enlarged ed. 1909 [1903])

Buer, Mabel. "The Historical Setting of the Malthusian." In *London Essays in Honor of Edwin Cannan* 137-53 (T. Gregory & Hugh Dalton eds., 1927)

Bumpass, Larry, & Charles Westoff. "The 'Perfect Contraceptive' Population." *Science* 169 (3951):1177-82 (1970)

_____ "Unwanted Births and U.S. Population Growth." In *The American Population*

Debate 267-73 (Daniel Callahan ed., 1971)

Burgdörfer, Fritz. "Die Bevölkerungsentwicklung während des Krieges und die kommunistische Propaganda für den Gebärstreik." *Münchener medizinische Wochenschrift* 66:433-35 (1919)

Burggraf, Shirley. "How Should the Costs of Childrearing Be Distributed?" *Challenge* 36 (5):48-55 (Sept.-Oct. 1993)

Burns, E. *Wages and the State: A Comparative Study of the Problems of State Wage Regulation* (1926)

Burns, Eveline. "The Economics of Family Endowment." *Economica* 5 (14):155-64 (June 1925)

Busfield, Joan, & Michael Paddon. *Thinking About Children: Sociology and Fertility in Post-War England* (1977)

Cain, Glen. "Issues in the Economics of a Population Policy for the United States." *Am. Econ. Rev.* 61 (2):408-17 (May 1971)

Caldwell, John. "Mass Education as a Determinant of the Timing of Fertility Decline." *Pop. & Dev. Rev.* 6 (2):225-55 (June 1980)

_____. *Theory of Fertility Decline* (1982)

Callaghan, Hubert. "The Family Allowance Procedure: An Analysis of the Family Allowance Procedure in Selected Countries" (Ph.D. diss. Catholic U., 1947)

Campbell, Arthur. "The Role of Family Planning in the Reduction of Poverty." *J. Marriage & the Family* 30 (2):236-45 (May 1968)

Campbell, Frederick, et al. "Motivational Bases of Childbearing Decisions." In *The Childbearing Decision: Fertility Attitudes and Behavior* 145-59 (Greer Fox ed., 1982)

Campbell, R. "Family Allowances in New Zealand." *Econ. J.* 37 (147):369-83 (Sept. 1927)

Cannan, Edwin. "The Malthusian Anti-Socialist Argument." *Econ. Rev.* 2 (1):71-87 (Jan. 1892)

Carlson, Allan. *Family Questions: Reflections on the American Social Crisis* (1989)

_____. *From Cottage to Work Station: The Family's Search for Social Harmony in the Industrial Age* (1993)

_____. "A Pro-Family Income." *Pub. Interest* No. 94:69-76 (Winter 1989)

_____. *The Swedish Experiment in Family Politics: The Myrdals and the Interwar Population Crisis* (1990)

_____. "What Happened to the 'Family Wage'?" *Pub. Interest* No. 83:3-17 (1986)

Carr-Saunders, A. *World Population: Past Growth and Present Trends* (1937 [1936])

Cartter, Allan. "Income-Tax Allowances and the Family in Great Britain." *Pop. Studies* 6 (3):218-32 (Mar. 1953)

Ceccaldi, Dominique. *Histoire des prestations familiales en France* (1957)

Chapin, Robert. *The Standard of Living Among Workingmen's Families in New York City* (1909)

Children's Allowances and the Economic Welfare of Children: The Report of a Conference (Eveline Burns ed., 1968)

Clark, Marjorie. "Organized Labor and the Family-Allowance System in France." *J. Pol. Econ.* 39 (4):526-37 (Aug. 1931)

Coale, Ansley. "Population and Economic Development." In *The Population Dilemma* 46-69 (Philip Hauser ed., 1965 [1963])

_____, & Melvin Zelnik. *New Estimates of Fertility and Population in the United States: A Study of Annual White Births from 1855 to 1960 and of Completeness of Enumeration in the Censuses from 1880 to 1960* (1963)

Coats, A. "The Classical Economists and the Labourer." In *The Classical Economists and Economic Policy* 144-79 (A. Coats ed., 1971 [1967])

Cochrane, Susan. "Children as By-Products, Investment Goods and Consumer Goods: A Review of Some Micro-Economic Models of Fertility." *Pop. Studies* 29 (3):373-90 (Nov. 1975)

Cohen, Joseph. *Family Income Insurance: A Scheme of Family Endowment by the Method of Insurance* (1926)

Coleman, James. "The Rational Reconstruction of Society." *Am. Sociological Rev.* 58 (1):1-15 (Feb. 1993)

Committee on Population. *The Growth of U.S. Population: Analysis of the Problems and Recommendations for Research, Training, and Service* (Nat. Acad. Sciences-Nat. Research Council Pub. No. 1279, 1965)

Condorcet, Marie Jean. *Esquisse d'un tableau historique des progrès de l'esprit humain* (1966 [1795])

Conservative Political Centre. *Family Allowances* (No. 182, 1958)

Consumer Behavior: 2 *The Life Cycle and Consumer Behavior* (Lincoln Clark ed., 1955)

Coontz, Sidney. *Population Theories and the Economic Interpretation* (1961)

Coontz, Stephanie. *The Way We Never Were: American Families and the Nostalgia Trap* (1992)

Correa, Sônia, & Rosalind Petchesky. "Reproductive and Sexual Rights: A Feminist Perspective," In *Population Policies Reconsidered: Health, Empowerment, and Rights* 107-23 (Gita Sen et al. eds., 1994)

Cottrell, Allin, & William Darity, Jr. "Marx, Malthus, and Wages." *Hist. Pol. Econ.* 20 (2):173-90 (Summer 1988)

Cowherd, Raymond. *Political Economists and the English Poor Laws: A Historical Study of the Influence of Classical Economics on the Formation of Social Welfare Policy* (1977)

Cramer, James. "Births, Expected Family Size, and Poverty." In *Five Thousand American Families—Patterns of Economic Progress: Special Studies of the First Five Years of the Panel Study of Income Dynamics* 2:279-305 (James Morgan ed., 1974)

Curtis, Bruce. "Capital, the State and the Origins of the Working-Class Household." In *Hidden in the Household: Women's Domestic Labour Under Capitalism* 101-34 (Bonnie Fox ed., 1980)

Dalton, Hugh. "The Theory of Population." *Economica* 8 (22):28-50 (Mar. 1928)

Daly, Herman. "A Marxian-Malthusian View of Poverty and Development." *Pop. Studies* 25 (1):25-37 (Mar. 1971)

Dasgupta, Partha. "The Population Problem." In *Population—The Complex Reality: A Report of the Population Summit of the World's Scientific Academies* 151-80 (Francis Graham-Smith ed., 1994)

Davis, Kingsley. "Malthus and the Theory of Population." In *The Language of Research: A Reader in the Methodology of Social Research* 540-53 (Morris Rosenberg ed., 1965 [1955])

_____. "Population Policies: Will Current Programs Succeed?" *Science* 158:730-39 (1967)

_____. "Reproductive Institutions and the Pressure for Population." *Sociological Rev.* 29:289-306 (1937)

_____. "Some Demographic Aspects of Poverty in the United States." In *Poverty in America* 299-319 (Margaret Gordon ed., 1975 [1965])

_____. "The Theory of Change and Response in Modern Demographic History." *Pop. Index* 29 (3):345-66 (Oct. 1963)

Day, Lincoln, & Alice Day. "Family Size in Industrialized Countries: An Inquiry into the Social-Cultural Determinants of Levels of Childbearing." *J. Marriage & the Family* 31 (2):242-51 (May 1969)

Dembitz, Nanette. "Should Public Policy Give Incentives to Welfare Mothers to Limit the Number of Their Children?" *Family Law Q.* 4 (2):130-45 (June 1970)

Demeny, Paul. "The Economics of Population Control." In *Rapid Population Growth: Consequences and Policy Implications* 199-221 (Nat. Acad. Sci., 1971)

_____. "Population and the Invisible Hand." *Demography* 23 (4):473-87 (Nov. 1987)

_____. "Pronatalist Policies in Low-Fertility Countries: Patterns, Performance, and Prospects." In *Below-Replacement Fertility in Industrial Societies: Causes, Consequences, Policies* 335-58 (Kingsley Davis et al. eds., 1986)

_____. "Welfare Considerations in U.S. Population Policy." In Commission on Population Growth and the American Future. 6 *Research Reports: Aspects of Population Growth Policy* 153-72 (Robert Parke, Jr. & Charles Westoff eds., 1972)

Dennett, Mary. *Birth Control Laws: Shall We KeepThem, Change Them or Abolish Them* (1926)

De Quincey, Thomas. *The Logic of Political Economy*. In *idem. Political Economy and Politics* 118-294 (David Masson ed., 1970 [1844])

Devine, Edward. *Misery and Its Causes* (1913)

Dickinson, James. "From Poor Law to Social Insurance: The Periodization of State Intervention in the Reproduction Process." In *Family, Economy and State: The Social Reproduction Process Under Capitalism* 113-49 (James Dickinson & Bob Russell eds., 1986)

_____, & Bob Russell. "Introduction: The Structure of Reproduction in Capitalist Society." In *ibid.* 1-20

Dienel, Christiane. *Kinderzahl und Staatsräson: Empfängnisverhütung und Bevölkerungs-politik in Deutschland und Frankreich bis 1918* (1995)

Dienes, C. Law, *Politics, and Birth Control* (1972)

Dixon-Mueller, Ruth. *Population Policy and Women's Rights: Transforming Reproductive Choice* (1993)

Douglas, Paul. "Some Objections to the Family Wage System Considered." *J. Pol. Econ.* 32 (6):690-706 (Dec. 1924)

_____. "Some Precedents for the Family Wage System." *International Labour Rev.* 11 (3):353-65 (Mar. 1925)

_____. *Wages and the Family* (1927 [1925])

Dublin, Louis, & Alfred Lotka. *The Money Value of a Man* (1930; rev. ed. 1946)

Duchâtel, C. *De la Charité, dans ses rapports avec l'état moral et le bien-être des classes inférieures de la société* (1829)

[Dugard, Samuel]. *Peri Polupaidias or, A Discourse Concenring Having Many Children* (1695)

Dumont, Arsène. *Dépopulation et civilisation: Étude démographique* (1890)

Dutt, R. Palme. *Socialism and the Living Wage* (1927)

Dyck, Arthur. "Population Policies and Ethical Acceptability." In *The American Population Debate* 351-77 (Daniel Callahan ed., 1971)

Dyer, Colin. *Population and Society in Twentieth Century France* (1978)

Easterlin, Richard. "Does Human Fertility Adjust to the Environment?" *Am. Econ. Rev.* 61 (2):399-407 (May 1971)

Ehrlich, Paul. *The Population Bomb* (1969 [1968])

Elder, Jr., Glen. "Family History and the Life Course," in *Transitions: The Family and the*

Life Course in Historical Perspective 17-64 (Tamara Hareven ed., 1978)

Elderton, Ethel. *Report on the English Birthrate*. Part I: *England, North of the Humber* (1914)

_____, et al. *On the Correlation of Fertility with Social Value: A Cooperative Study* (1913)

Ellwood, David. *Poor Support: Poverty in the American Family* (1988)

Engels, Friedrich. *Die Lage der arbeitenden Klasse in England*. In Karl Marx [&] Friedrich Engels. *Werke* 2:225-506 (1957 [1845])

_____. "Umrisse zu einer Kritik der Nationalökonomie." In *ibid*. 1:499-524 (1964 [1844])

Enke, Stephen. "Population Growth and Economic Growth." *Pub. Interest*. No. 32:86-96 (Summer 1973)

Epstein, Abraham. *Insecurity: A Challenge to America* (1933)

Espenshade, Thomas. *The Cost of Children in Urban United States* (1973)

_____. "The Value and Cost of Children." *Pop. Bull.* 32 (1) (Apr. 1977)

Eversley, D. *Social Theories of Fertility and the Malthusian Debate* (1959)

Family Policy, Government and Families in Fourteen Countries (Sheila Kamerman & Alfred Kahn eds., 1978)

Ferguson, Ann, & Nancy Folbre. "The Unhappy Marriage of Patriarchy and Capitalism." In *Women and Revolution: A Discussion of the Unhappy Marriage of Marxism and Feminism* 313-38 (Lydia Sargent ed., 1981)

Field, James. *Essays on Population* (1931)

Fisher, R.A. "The Birthrate and Family Allowances." *Agenda* 2 (2):124-33 (May 1943)

Fitzhugh, George. *Sociology for the South, or the Failure of Free Society, reprinted in Ante-Bellum: Writings of George Fitzhugh and Hinton Rowan Helper on Slavery* 41-95 (Harvey Wish ed., 1960 [1854])

Flew, Anthony. "The Structure of Malthus' Population Theory." *Australian J. Phil.* 35 (1):1-20 (May 1957)

Folbre, Nancy. "Children as Public Goods." *Am. Econ. Rev.* 84 (2):86-90 (May 1994)

_____. "Of Patriarchy Born: The Political Economy of Fertility Decisions." *Feminist Studies* 9 (2):261-84 (Summer 1983)

Franklin, Benjamin. "Observations Concerning the Increase of Mankind, Peopling of Countries." In *The Papers of Benjamin Franklin* 4:225-34 (Leonard Labaree ed., 1961 [1751])

Freedman, Ronald. "Social Values about Family Size in the United States." In Union international pour l'étude scientifique de la population. *Internationaler Bevölkerungskongress* 173-83 (1959)

_____, & Lolagene Coombs. "Childspacing and Family Economic Position," *Am. Sociological Rev.* 31 (5):631-48 at 632 (Oct. 1966)

_____. "Economic Considerations in Family Growth Decisions." *Pop. Studies* 20 (2):197-222 (Nov. 1966)

Freville, Jean. 1 *La Misère et le nombre: L'Epouvantail malthusien* (1956)

Friedman, David. *Laissez-Faire in Population: The Least Bad Solution* (1972)

Fryer, Peter. *The Birth-Controllers* (1965)

Fuchs, Victor. "Redefining Poverty and Redistributing Income." *Pub. Interest* No. 8:88-95 (Summer 1967)

_____. "Why Are Children Poor?" (NBER Working Paper No. 1984, 1986)

_____. *Women's Quest for Economic Equality* (1988)

Galbraith, John Kenneth. *The Affluent Society* (1958)

Garfinkel, Irwin. "Negative Income Tax and Children's Allowance Programs: A Comparison." *Social Work* 13 (4):33-39 (Oct. 1968)

_____, & Sara McLanahan. *Single Mothers and Their Children: A New American Dilemma* (1986)

Gérando, [Marie Joseph] de. *De la Bienfaisance publique* (1839)

Gilbert, Neil. *Capitalism and the Welfare State: Dilemmas of Social Benevolence* (1983)

Gilder, George. *Wealth and Poverty* (1982 [1981])

Glass, D. *Population: Policies and Movement in Europe* (1940)

Glick, Paul. *American Families* (1957)

_____. "The Family Cycle." *Am. Sociological Rev.* 12 (2):164-74 (Apr. 1947)

_____. "The Life Cycle of the Family." *Marriage & Family Living* 17 (1):3-9 (Feb. 1955)

Goodin, Robert, & Julian Le Grand. *Not Only the Poor: The Middle Classes and the Welfare State* (1987)

Gordon, Linda. *Pitied But Not Entitled: Single Mothers and the History of Welfare 1890-1935* (1994)

_____. *Woman's Body, Woman's Right: A Social History of Birth Control in America* (1981 [1974])

Gordon, Margaret. *Social Security Policies in Industrial Countries: A Comparative Analysis* (1988)

Gottlieb, Manuel. "The Theory of Optimum Population for a Closed Economy." *J. Pol. Econ.* 53(4):289-316 (Dec. 1945)

Gottschalk, Peter, & Sheldon Danziger. "Family Structure, Family Size, and Family Income: Accounting for Changes in the Economic Well-Being of Children, 1968-1986." In *Uneven Tides: Rising Inequality in America* 167-93 (*idem* eds., 1993)

Gove, Walter, et al. "The Family Life Cycle: Internal Dynamics and Social Consequences." *Sociology and Social Research* 57 (2):182-95 (Jan. 1973)

Grabill, Wilson, & Paul Glick. "Demographic and Social Aspects of Childlessness: Census Data." *Milbank Memorial Fund Q.* 37 (1):60-86 (Jan. 1959)

Gray, Alexander. *Family Endowment: A Critical Analysis* (1927)

Griffith, G. *Population Problems in the Age of Malthus* (1926)

Grotjahn, Alfred. "Proletariat und Geburtenrückgang." *Neue Zeit* 41/II:205-209 (1923)

Gründorfer, I. "Die Stellung der Partei zum Gebärstreik." *Der Kampf* 7:116-23 (1913-14)

Haines, Michael. "Industrial Work and the Family Life Cycle, 1889-1890." *Research in Econ. Hist.* 4:289-356 (1979)

Hardin, Garrett. *Living Within Limits: Ecology, Economics, and Population Taboos* (1993)

_____. "Multiple Paths to Population Control." In *The American Population Debate* 259-66 (Daniel Callahan ed., 1971 [1970])

_____. "An Operational Analysis of 'Responsibility.'" In *Managing the Commons* 66-75 (idem & John Braden eds., 1977)

_____. "The Tragedy of the Commons." *Science* 162:1243-48 (1968)

Hareven, Tamara. "Introduction: The Historical Study of the Life Course." In *Transitions: The Family and the Life Course in Historical Perspective* 1-16 (Tamara Hareven ed., 1978)

Harper, John. "Be Fruitful and Multiply: Origins of Legal Restrictions on Planned Parenthood in Nineteenth-Century America." In *Women of America: A History* 245-69 (Carol Berkin & Mary Norton eds., 1979)

Harrington, Michael. *The New American Poverty* (1985 [1984])

_____. *The Other America: Poverty in the United States* (1964 [1962])

Harvey, David. *The Limits to Capital* (1989 [1982])

Hauser, Philip. "Demographic Factors in the Integration of the Negro." In *The Negro American* 71-101 (Talcott Parsons & Kenneth Clark eds., 1970 [1967])

_____. "The Labor Force as a Field of Interest for the Sociologist." *Am. Sociological. Rev.* 16:530-38 (1951)

Heather-Bigg, Ada. "The Wife's Contribution to Family Income." *Econ. J.* 4:51-58 (1894)

Heberle, Rudolf. "Social Factors in Birth Control." *Am. Sociological Rev.* 6 (6):794-805 (Dec. 1941)

Heeren, Henk. "Pronatalist Population Policies in Some Western European Countries." *Pop. Research & Policy Rev.* 1:137-52 (1980)

Heimann, Eduard. "The Family Wage Controversy in Germany." *Econ. J.* 33 (132):509-15 (Dec. 1923)

Heinsohn, Gunnar, & Rolf Knieper. *Theorie des Familienrechts: Geschlechtsrollen-aufhebung, Kindesvernachlässigung, Geburtenrückgang* (1974)

_____, & Otto Steiger. *Menschenproduktion: Allgemeine Bevölkerungstheorie der Neuzeit* (1979)

Henderson, A. "The Costs of Children. Parts I & II." *Pop. Studies* 4 (3):267-98 (Dec. 1950)

Hertz, Robert. "Socialisme et Dépopulation." *Les Cahiers du socialiste* 10 (1910)

Higgins, Henry. "A New Province for Law and Order." *Harv. Law Rev.* 29 (1):13-39 (Nov. 1915)

Hill, Adelaide, & Frederick Jaffe. "Negro Fertility and Family Size Preferences: Implications for Programming of Health and Social Services." In *The Negro American* 205-24 (Talcott Parsons & Kenneth Clark eds., 1970 [1967])

Himes, Norman. "John Stuart Mill's Attitude Toward Neo-Malthusianism." *Econ. J.* (Econ. Hist, Ser. No. 4), Jan. 1929, at 457-84

_____. "McCulloch's Relation to the Neo-Malthusian Propaganda of His Times: An Episode in the History of English Neo-Malthusianism." *J. Pol. Econ.* 37:73-86 (Feb. 1929)

_____. *Medical History of Contraception* (1936)

Himmelfarb, Gertrude. *The Idea of Poverty: England in the Early Industrial Age* (1985 [1983])

_____. *Poverty and Compassion: The Moral Imagination of the Late Victorians* (1992 [1991])

Hoffmann, Horst. *Was jeder Kinderreiche wissen muss* (1938)

Hollander, Samuel. "Marx and Malthusianism: Marx's Secular Path of Wages." *Am. Econ. Rev.* 74 (1):139-51 (Mar. 1984)

_____. "On Malthus's Population Principle and Social Reform." *Hist. Pol. Econ.* 18 (2):187-236 (1986)

Hollingsworth, Leta. "Social Devices for Impelling Women to Bear and Rear Children." *Am. J. Sociology* 22 (1):19-29 (July 1916)

Horkheimer, Max. "Allgemeiner Teil." In *Studien über Autorität und Familie: Forschungs-berichte aus dem Institut für Soziaforschung* 3-76 (1936)

Huber, Joan. "Will U.S. Fertility Decline Toward Zero?" *Sociological Q.* 21:481-92 (Aut. 1980)

Hughes, Gwendolyn. *Mothers in Industry: Wage-Earning by Mothers in Philadelphia* (1925)

Humphries, Jane. "The Working-Class Family: A Marxist Perspective." In *The Family in Political Thought* 197-222 (Jean Elshtain ed., 1982)

Hutchinson, E. *The Population Debate: The Development of Conflicting Theories up to 1900* (1967)

Huzel, James. "The Demographic Impact of the Old Poor Law: More Reflexions on Malthus." *Econ. Hist. Rev.* 33 (3):367-81 (Aug. 1980)

_____. "Malthus, the Poor Law, and Population in Early Nineteenth-Century England." *Econ. Hist. Rev.* 22 (3): 430-51 (Dec. 1969)

Income-Tested Transfer Programs: The Case For and Against (Irwin Garfinkel ed., 1982)

Innes, John. *Class Fertility Trends in England and Wales 1876-1934* (1938)

Is There an Optimum Level of Population? (S. Singer ed., 1971)

Jackson, J. "Wages, Social Income, and the Family." *Manchester School of Econ. & Social Studies* 29 (1):95-106 (Jan. 1961)

Jäntti, Markus, & Sheldon Danziger. "Child Poverty in Sweden and the United States: The Effect of Social Transfers and Parental Labor Force Participation." *Industrial & Labor Relations Rev.* 48 (1):48-64 (Oct. 1994)

Jencks, Christopher. *Rethinking Social Policy: Race, Poverty and the Underclass* (1993 [1992])

Jenssen, Otto. "Geburtenbeschränkung und Klassenkampf." *Der Kampf* 7:212-14 (1913-14)

Johansson, S. Ryan. "Status Anxiety and Demographic Contraction of Privileged Populations." *Pop. & Dev. Rev.* 13 (3):439-70 (Sept. 1987)

Kälvemark, Ann-Sofie. *More Children of Better Quality? Aspects of Swedish Population Policy in the 1930s* (1980)

Kamerman, Sheila, & Alfred Kahn. *Child Care, Family Benefits, and Working Parents: A Study in Comparative Policy* (1981)

_____. "Family Policy: Has the United States Learned from Europe?" *Policy Studies Rev.* 8 (3):591-98 (Spr. 1989)

_____. "What Europe Does for Single-Parent Families." *Pub. Interest* No. 93:70-86 (Fall 1988)

Katona, George, et al. *1968 Survey of Consumer Finances* (1969)

_____, Lewis Mandell, & Jay Schmiedeskamp. *1970 Survey of Consumer Finances* (1971)

Katz, Michael, & Mark Stern. "History and the Limits of Population Policy." *Politics & Society* 10 (2):225-45 (1980)

Kautsky, Karl. *Der Einfluss der Volksvermehrung auf den Fortschritt der Gesellschaft* (1880)

_____. "Der Gebärstreik." *Neue Zeit* 31/II:904-909 (1913)

_____. "Malthusianismus und Sozialismus." *Neue Zeit* 29/I:652-62 (1911)

_____. *Vermehrung und Entwicklung in Natur und Gesellschaft* (1910)

Keine Kinder—Keine Zukunft? Zum Stand der Bevölkerungsforschung in Europa (Lutz Franke & Hans Jürgens eds., 1978)

Kennedy, David. *Birth Control in America: The Career of Margaret Sanger* (1970)

Keyfitz, Nathan. *Population Change and Social Policy* (1982)

Keynes, John Maynard. "The End of Laissez-Faire." In *idem. Essays in Persuasion* 312-22 (1963 [1926])

_____. "Some Economic Consequences of a Declining Population." *Eugenics Rev.* 29 (1):13-17 (Apr. 1937)

Kincaid, J. *Poverty and Equality in Britain: A Study of Social Security and Taxation* (1973)

Kingsbury, Susan. "Relation of Women to Industry." In *Papers and Proceedings of the Fifteenth Annual Meeting of the Am. Sociological Society* 141-58 (1920)

Kirschleder, Karl. "Volksvermehrung und soziales Elend." *Der Kampf* 7:468-70 (1913-14)

Knechtel, Erhard. "Die Zahl der einkommensschwachen kinderreichen Familien in der Bundesrepublik." *Soziale Welt* 11 (4) 330-39 (Feb. 1961)

Kolko, Gabriel. *Wealth and Power in America: An Analysis of Social Class and Income Distribution* (1968 [1962])

Kuczynski, Robert. *Population Movements* (1936)

Kudrle, Robert, & Theodore Marmor. "The Development of Welfare States in North America." In *The Development of Welfare States in Europe and America* 81-121 (Peter Flora & Arnold Heidenheimer eds., 1984 [1981])

Kuznets, Simon. "Population Change and Aggregate Output." In *Demographic and Economic Change in Developed Countries* 324-40 (NBER, 1960)

Lader, Lawrence. *Abortion* (1966)

_____. *Breeding Ourselves to Death* (1971)

Land, Hilary. "The Introduction of Family Allowances: An Act of Historic Justice?" In Phoebe Hall et al. *Change, Choice, and Conflict in Social Policy* 157-230 (1975)

Langer, William. "The Origins of the Birth Control Movement in the Early Nineteenth Century." *J. Interdisciplinary Hist.* 5 (4):669-86 (Spr. 1975)

Lansing, John, & James Morgan. "Consumer Finances over the Life Cycle." In *Consumer Behavior: The Life Cycle and Consumer Behavior* 2:36-51 (Lincoln Clark ed., 1955)

Lazear, Edward, & Robert Michael. "Family Size and the Distribution of Real Per Capita Income." *Am. Econ. Rev.* 70 (1):91-107 (Mar. 1980)

Lebergott, Stanley. "Population Change and the Supply of Labor." In *Demographic and Economic Change in Developed Countries* 377-414 (NBER, 1960)

Lebowitz, Michael. *Beyond Capital: Marx's Political Economy of the Working Class* (1992)

Ledbetter, Rosanna. *A History of the Malthusian League, 1877-1927* (1976)

Leibenstein, Harvey. *Economic Backwardness and Economic Growth: Studies in the Theory of Economic Development* (1957)

_____. "The Impact of Population Growth on the American Economy." In Commission on Population Growth and the American Future. *Research Reports: Economic Aspects of Population Change* 2:49-65 (Elliott Morss & Ritchie Reed eds., 1972)

_____. "An Interpretation of the Economic Theory of Fertility: Promising Path or Blind Alley?" *J. Econ. Lit.* 12:457-79 (1974)

_____. *A Theory of Economic-Demographic Development* (1954)

Lenin, V. "Rabochii klass I neomal'tuzianstvo." In *idem. Polnoe sobranie sochinenii* 23:225-57 (1961 [1913])

Leroux, Pierre. "De la Recherche des biens matériels, ou de l'individualisme et du socialisme: l'économie politique et l'évangile." *Revue sociale* 1 (3):66-79 (Feb. 1846)

Leroy-Beaulieu, Paul. *La Question de la population* (1913)

_____. *Traité théorique et pratique d'économie politique* (6th ed., 1914)

Lesthaeghe, Ron. "On the Social Control of Human Reproduction." *Pop. & Dev. Rev.* 6 (4):527-48 (Dec. 1980)

Levin, Samuel. "Malthus and the Idea of Progress." *J. Hist. Ideas* 27 (1):92-108 (Jan.-Mar. 1966)

_____. "Marx vs. Malthus." *Papers of the Michigan Acad. Sci., Arts, & Letters* 22:243-58 (1936)

Lewinsohn, Richard. "Die Stellung der deutschen Sozialdemokratie zur Bevölkerungsfrage." *Schmollers Jahrbuch für Gesetzgebung, Verwaltung und Volkswirtschaft im Deutschen Reiche* 46:191-203 (1922)

Lindert, Peter. *Fertility and Scarcity in America* (1978)

Linse, Ulrich. "Arbeiterschaft und Geburtenentwicklung im Deutschen Kaiserreich von 1871." *Archiv für Sozialgeschichte* 12:205-71 (1972)

Lipsitz, Lewis. "Political Philosophy and Population Policy: Insights and Blindspots of a Tradition." In *Political Science in Population Studies* 129-39 (Richard Clinton et al. eds., 1972)

336 *Bibliography*

Lloyd, W.F. *Four Lectures on Poor-Laws.* In *idem. Lectures on Population, Value, Poor-Laws and Rent* (1968 [1835])

———. *Two Lectures on Poor-Laws.* In *ibid.* (1836)

———. *Two Lectures on the Checks to Population.* In *ibid.* (1833)

Locke, John. *Report of the Board of Trade to the Lords Justices in the Year 1697, respecting the Relief and Employment of the Poor.* In *An Account of the Origin, Proceedings, and Intentions of the Society for the Promotion of Industry in the Southern District of the Parts of Lindsey, in the County of Lincoln* (3d ed., 1789)

Loomis, Charles. "The Study of the Life Cycle of Families." *Rural Sociology* 1 (2):180-99 (June 1936)

Lorimer, Frank. "Issues of Population Policy." In *The Population Dilemma* 143-78 (Philip Hauser ed., 1965)

———, & Herbert Roback. "Economics of the Family Relative to the Number of Children." *Milbank Memorial Fund Q.* 18 (2):114-36 (Apr. 1940)

———, Ellen Winston, & Louise Kiser. *Foundations of American Population Policy* (1940)

Macgregor, D. "Family Allowances." *Econ. J.* 36 (141):1-10 (Mar. 1926)

Mackenroth, Gerhard. *Bevölkerungslehre: Theorie, Soziologie und Statistik der Bevölkerung* (1953)

———. "Die Reform der Sozialpolitik durch einen deutschen Sozialplan." *Schriften des Vereins für Sozialpolitik* (n.s.) 4:39-76 (1952)

Macniol, John. *The Movement for Family Allowances, 1918-1945: A Study in Policy Development* (1980)

Madge, Charles. *War-Time Pattern of Saving and Spending* (1943)

Madison, Bernice. "Canadian Family Allowances and Their Major Social Implications." *J. Marriage & the Family* 26 (2):134-41 (May 1964)

Malthus, Thomas. *An Essay on the Principle of Population* (1st ed. & 7th ed.). In *idem. On Population* (Gertrude Himmelfarb ed., 1960 [1798 & 1872])

———. *An Essay on the Principle of Population* (6th ed.). In 3 *The Works of Thomas Robert Malthus* (E. Wrigley & David Souden eds., 1986 [1826])

Malthus, T.R. *An Essay on the Principle of Population* (4th ed. 1807)

———, *A Letter to Samuel Whitbread, Esq. M.P. on His Proposed Bill for the Amendment of the Poor Laws.* In 4 *The Works of Thomas Robert Malthus* (1986 [1807])

———. *Principles of Political Economy* (1820)

Malthus Past and Present (J. Dupâquier et al. eds., 1983)

Mandell, Lewis, et al. *Surveys of Consumers 1971-72* (1973)

Marschalck, Peter. *Bevölkerungsgeschichte Deutschlands im 19. und 20. Jahrhundert* (1984)

Marsh, Alan, & Stephen McKay. *Families, Work and Benefits* (1993)

Marshall, T.H. "The Population Problem During the Industrial Revolution." *Econ. J.* (Econ. Hist Ser. No. 4), Jan. 1929, at 429-56

———. "What the Public Thinks." In *idem* et al., *The Population Problem: The Experts and the Public* 1-63 (1938)

Marx, Karl. "Arbeitslohn." In *idem* [&] Friedrich Engels. *Werke* 6:535-56 (1959 [1847])

———. *Grundrisse der Kritik der politischen Ökonomie* (1953 [1857-58])

———. 1-3 *Das Kapital.* In Karl Marx [&] Friedrich Engels. *Werke* 23-25 (1962-64 [1867, 1885, 1894])

———. "The Labor Question." In Karl Marx [&] Frederick Engels. *Collected Works* 12:460-63 (1979 [1853])

———. "Lohnarbeit und Kapital." In Karl Marx [&] Frederick Engels. *Werke* 6:397-423

(1959 [1849])

_____. *Ökonomische Manuskripte 1857/58.* In Karl Marx [&] Friedrich Engels. *Gesamtausgabe (MEGA)* II/1.2 (1981)

_____. *Ökonomische Manuskripte 1863-1867.* In *ibid.* II/4 (1992)

_____. "Randglossen zum Programm der deutschen Arbeiterpartei." In *ibid.* I/25:9-25 (1985 [1875])

_____. *Value, Price and Profit.* In *ibid.* I/20:143-86 (1992 [1865])

_____. *Zur Kritik der politischen Ökonomie (Manuskript 1861-1863).* In *ibid.* II/3 (1978-82)

Mason, Karen, Maris Vinovskis, & Tamara Hareven. "Women's Work and the Life Course in Essex County, Massachusetts, 1880." In *Transitions: The Family and the Life Course in Historical Perspective* 187-216 (Tamara Hareven ed., 1978)

May, Elaine. *Barren in the Promised Land: Childless Americans and the Pursuit of Happiness* (1995)

May, Martha. "Bread Before Roses: American Workingmen, Labor Unions and the Family Wage." In *Women, Work and Protest: A Century of US Women's Labor History* 1-21 (Ruth Milkman ed., 1985)

Mayer, Susan, & Christopher Jencks. "Poverty and the Distribution of Material Hardship." *J. Human Resources* 24 (1):88-113 (Winter 1989)

McClymer, John. "Late Nineteenth-Century American Working-Class Living Standards. " *J. Interdisciplinary Hist.* 17 (2):379-98 (Aut. 1986)

McCulloch, John. *The Principles of Political Economy* (5th ed. 1864)

McIntosh, C. Allison. *Population Policy in Western Europe: Responses to Low Fertility in France, Sweden, and West Germany* (1983)

McLanahan, Sara, & Julia Adams. "The Effects of Children on Adults' Psychological Well-Being: 1957-1976." *Social Forces* 68 (1):124-46 (Sept. 1989)

McLaren, Angus. *Birth Control in Nineteenth-Century England* (1978)

_____. "Contraception and the Working Classes: The Social Ideology of the English Birth Control Movement in Its Early Years." *Comp. Studies in Society & Hist.* 18 (2):236-51 (Apr. 1976)

_____. *Reproductive Rituals: The Perception of Fertility in England from the Sixteenth Century to the Nineteenth Century* (1984)

_____. "Sex and Socialism: The Opposition of the French Left to Birth Control in the Nineteenth Century." *J. Hist. Ideas* 37 (3):475-92 (July-Sept. 1976)

_____. *Sexuality and Social Order: The Debate over the Fertility of Women and Workers in France, 1770-1920* (1983)

_____, & Arlene McLaren. *The Bedroom and the State: The Changing Practices and Politics of Contraception and Abortion in Canada, 1880-1980* (1986)

McNicoll, Geoffrey. "Economic Growth with Below-Replacement Fertility." In *Below-Replacement Fertility in Industrial Societies: Causes, Consequences, Policies* 217-37 (Kingsley Davis et al. eds., 1986)

Mead, Lawrence. *The New Politics of Poverty: The Nonworking Poor in America* (1992)

Meriam, Lewis. *Relief and Social Security* (1946)

Messere, Kenneth, & Jeffrey Owens. "The Treatment of Dependent Children Under Income and Social Welfare Systems." *International Social Security Rev.* 32 (1):50-59 (1979)

Michaelson, Karen. "Introduction: Population Theory and the Political Economy of Population Processes." In *And the Poor Get Children: Radical Perspectives on Population Dynamics* 11-35 (*idem* ed., 1981)

Micklewright, F. "The Rise and Decline of English Malthusianism." *Pop. Studies* 15 (1):32-51 (1961-62)

Miles, Rufus Jr. "Whose Baby Is the Population Problem?" *Pop. Bull.* 36 (1):1-36 (Apr. 1970).

Mill, James. *Elements of Political Economy* (3d ed.). In *idem. Selected Economic Writings* 203-366 (Donald Winch ed., 1966)

Mill, John Stuart. *On Liberty.* In *The Philosophy of John Stuart Mill* 185-319 (Marshall Cohen ed., 1961 [1859])

_____. *Principles of Political Economy* (W. Ashley ed., 1926 [1848])

Miller, Herman. *Rich Man Poor Man* (1965 [1964])

Mirrlees, James. "Population Policy and the Taxation of Family Size." *J. Pub. Econ.* 1:169-98 (1972)

Modell, John. "Patterns of Consumption, Acculturation, and Family Income Strategies in Late Nineteenth-Century America." In *Family and Population in Nineteenth-Century America* 206-40 (Tamara Hareven & Maris Vinovskis eds., 1978)

Mohr, James. *Abortion in America: The Origins and Evolution of National Policy, 1800-1900* (1978)

Mombert, Paul. *Bevölkerungslehre* (1929)

More, Louise. *Wage-Earners' Budgets: A Study of Standards and Cost of Living in New York City* (1907)

Moynihan, Daniel. "Employment, Income, and the Ordeal of the Negro Family." In *The American Negro* 134-59 (Talcott Parsons & Kenneth Clark eds., 1970)

_____. *Family and Nation* (1986)

_____. *The Politics of a Guaranteed Income: The Nixon Administration and the Family Assistance Plan* (1973)

Murray, Charles. *Losing Ground: American Social Policy, 1950-1980* (2d ed. 1994 [1984])

Myles, John. "States, Labor Markets, and Life Cycles." In *Beyond the Marketplace: Rethinking Economy and Society* 271-98 (Roger Friedland & A. Robertson eds., 1990)

Myrdal, Alva. *Nation and Family: The Swedish Experiment in Democratic Family and Population Policy* (1941)

_____. "A Program for Family Security in Sweden." *International Labour Rev.* 39 (6):723-63 (June 1939)

_____, & Gunnar Myrdal. *Kris i befolkningsfrågan* (1934)

Myrdal, Gunnar. *Challenge to Affluence* (1965 [1962])

_____. *Population: A Problem for Democracy* (1940)

[National Birth-Rate Commission]. *The Declining Birth-Rate: Its Causes and Effects* (1916)

National Research Council. *Population Growth and Economic Development: Policy Questions* (1986)

Nearing, Scott. *Financing the Wage-Earner's Family: A Survey of the Facts Bearing on Income and Expenditures of American Wage-Earners* (1914)

Nemitz, Kurt. "Julius Moses und die Gebärstreik-Debatte 1913." *Jahrbuch des Instituts für Deutsche Geschichte* 2:321-35 (1973)

Neuman, R. "The Sexual Question and Social Democracy in Imperial Germany." *J. Social Hist.* 7 (3):271-86 (Spring 1974)

_____. "Working Class Birth Control in Wilhelmine Germany." *Comp. Studies in Society & Hist.* 20 (3):408-28 (July 1978)

Nicholls, George. *A History of the English Poor Law* (2d ed. 1898 [1854])

Nitti, Francesco. *Population and the Social System* (1894)

Oguse, Dr. "Socialisme et Néo-Malthusianisme." *Revue socialiste* 46:97-124 (Aug. 1907)

Okun, Bernard. *Trends in Birth Rates in the United States Since 1870* (1958)

Olberg, Oda. "Über den Neo-Malthusianismus." *Neue Zeit* 24/I:846-54 (1905-06)

_____. "Zur Stellung der Partei zum Gebärstreik." *Neue Zeit* 32/I:47-55 (1914)

Olson, Lawrence. *Costs of Children* (1983)

Oppenheimer, Valerie. "The Life-Cycle Squeeze: The Interaction of Men's Occupational and Family Life Cycles." *Demography* 11 (2):227-45 (May 1974)

Oren, Laura. "The Welfare of Women in Laboring Families: England, 1860-1950." *Feminist Studies* 1 (3-4):107-25 (Winter-Spr. 1973)

Pampel, Fred, & Paul Adams. "The Effects of Demographic Change and Political Structure on Family Allowance Expenditures." *Social Serv. Rev.* 66 (4):524-46 (Dec. 1992)

Pearce, Diana. "Welfare Is Not for Women: Why the War on Poverty Cannot Conquer the Feminization of Poverty." In *Women, the State, and Welfare* 265-79 (Linda Gordon ed., 1990)

Pearson, Karl. "The Moral Basis of Socialism." In *idem, The Ethic of Freethought* 301-29 (2d ed. 1901 [1887])

Peck, Ellen. *The Baby Trap* (1971)

Pedersen, Susan. *Family, Dependence, and the Origins of the Welfare State: Britain and France, 1914-1945* (1993)

Penrose, E. *Population Theories and Their Application: With Special Reference to Japan* (1935 [1934])

Petchesky, Rosalind. *Abortion and Woman's Choice: The State, Sexuality, and Reproductive Freedom* (rev. ed. 1990 [1984])

Petersen, William. *Malthus* (1979)

_____. "Marx versus Malthus: The Men and the Symbols." *Pop. Rev.* 1 (2):21-32 (July 1957)

_____. "Marxism and the Population Question: Theory and Practice." In *Population and Resources in Western Intellectual Traditions* 77-101 (Michael Teitelbaum & Jay Winter eds., 1989).

_____. *The Politics of Population* (1964)

Piddington, A. *The Next Step: A Basic Family Income* (1921)

Piotrow, Phyllis. *The World Population Crisis: The United States Response* (1974 [1973])

Place, Francis. *Illustrations and Proofs of the Principle of Population* (Norman Himes ed., 1930 [1822])

Platter, J. "Carl Marx and Malthus." *Jahrbücher für Nationalökonomie und Statistik* 29:321-41 (1977)

Polanyi, Karl. *The Great Transformation* (1971 [1944])

Pope Leo XIII. *Rerum novarum* (1891)

Pope Pius XI. *Quadragesimo anno* (1931)

Popenoe, Paul. "Can We Afford Children?" *Forum* 98 (6):315-318 (Dec. 1937)

_____, & Ellen Williams. "Fecundity of Families Dependent on Public Charity." *Am. J. Sociology* 40 (2):214-20 (Sept. 1934)

Poston, Dudley Jr. "Income and Childlessness in the United States: Is the Relationship Always Inverse?" *Social Biology* 21 (3):296-307 (Fall 1974)

Poynter, J. *Society and Pauperism: English Ideas on Poor Relief, 1795-1834* (1969)

Pressman, Steven. "Child Exemptions or Child Allowances: What Sort of Antipoverty Program for the United States?" *Am. J. Econ. & Sociology* 51 (3):257-72 (July 1992)

_____. "Tax Expenditures for Child Exemptions: A Poor Policy to Aid America's Children." *J. Econ. Issues* 27 (3):699-719 (Sept. 1993)

Preston, Samuel. "Changing Values and Falling Birth Rates." In *Below-Replacement Fertility in Industrial Societies: Causes, Consequences, Policies* 176-95 (Kingsley Davis et al. eds., 1986)

Pronatalism: The Myth of Mom and Apple Pie (Ellen Peck & Judith Sanderowitz eds., 1974)

Quataert, Jean. *Reluctant Feminists in German Social Democracy, 1885-1917* (1979)

_____. "Unequal Partners in an Uneasy Alliance: Women and the Working Class in Imperial Germany." In *Socialist Women: European Socialist Feminism in the Nineteenth and Early Twentieth Centuries* 112-45 (Marilyn Boxer & Jean Quataert eds., 1978)

Quessel, Ludwig. "Karl Kautsky als Bevölkerungstheoretiker." *Neue Zeit* 29/I:559-65 (1911)

_____. "Die Ökonomie des Gebärstreiks." *Sozialistische Monatshefte* 19:1319-25 (1913)

_____. "Die Philosophie des Gebärstreiks." *Ibid.* 19:1609-16 (1913)

_____. "Das Zweikindersystem in Berlin." *Ibid.* 17:253-60 (1911)

Rabin, Edward. "Population Control Through Financial Incentives." *Hastings Law J.* 23 (5):1353-99 (May 1972)

Rainwater, Lee. *And the Poor Have Children: Sex, Contraception, and Family Planning in the Working Class* (1960)

_____, Martin Rein, & Joseph Schwartz. *Income Packaging in the Welfare State: A Comparative Study of Family Income* (1986)

Rainwater, Lee, & William Yancey. *The Moynihan Report and the Politics of Contorversy* (1969 [1967])

Rank, Mark. *Living on the Edge: The Realities of Welfare in America* (1994)

Rathbone, Eleanor. *The Disinherited Family: A Plea for the Endowment of the Family* (1924)

_____. *Family Allowances* (1947)

Reddaway, W. *The Economics of a Declining Population* (1939)

Reed, James. *From Private Vice to Public Virtue: The Birth Control Movement and American Society Since 1830* (1978)

Reeves, Mrs. [Magdalen] Pember. *Round About a Pound a Week* (1913)

Reybaud, Louis. *Le Coton: Son régime—ses problèmes, son influence en Europe* (1982 [1863])

Ricardo, David. *Notes on Malthus's Principles of Political Economy.* In 2 *Works and Correspondence of David Ricardo* (P. Sraffa ed., 1966 [1820])

_____. *On the Principles of Political Economy and Taxation.* In 1 *ibid.* (P. Sraffa ed., 1975 [1817])

Rice, Ann Smith. "An Economic Life Cycle of Childless Families" (Ph.D. diss., Florida State U., 1964)

Robbins, Lionel. "The Optimum Theory of Population." In *London Essays in Economics: In Honour of Edwin Cannan* 103-34 (T. Gregory & Hugh Dalton eds., 1927)

Roberts, Robert. *The Classic Slum: Salford Life in the First Quarter of the Century* (1983 [1971])

Robertson, John. *Children of Choice: Freedom and the New Reproductive Technologies* (1994)

Robinson, William. "The Birth Strike." *International Socialist Rev.* 14 (7):404-406 (Jan. 1914)

_____. "The Prevention of Conception." *New Rev.* 3 (4):196-99 (Apr. 1915)

Rockefeller, John D. III. "The Citizen's View of Public Programs for Family Limitation." In *Fertility and Family Planning: A World View* 493-98 (S. Behrman et al. eds.,

1967)

Rodgers, Roy. "The Family Life Cycle Concept: Past, Present, and Future." In *The Family Life Cycle in European Societies* 39-57 (Jean Cuisenier ed., 1977)

Ronsin, Francis. "La Classe ouvrière et le néo-malthusianisme: l'exemple français avant 1914." *Le Mouvement social*, No. 100:85-117 (Jan.-Mar. 1979)

_____. *La Grève des ventres: Propagande néo-malthusienne et baisse de la natalité française (XIXᵉ-XXᵉ siècles)* (1980)

Roth, Karl Heinz. "Kontroversen um Geburtenkontrolle am Vorabend des Ersten Weltkriegs: Eine Dokumentation zur Berliner 'Gebärstreikdebatte' von 1913." *Autonomie* 9 (12):78-103 (1978)

Rowntree, B. Seebohm. "Family Allowances." *Contemporary Rev.* No. 154 at 287-94 (Sept. 1938)

_____. *The Human Needs of Labour* (n.d. [1918])

_____. *The Human Needs of Labour* (1937)

_____. *Poverty: A Study of Town Life* (new ed. 1908 [1901])

_____. *Poverty and Progress: A Second Social Survey of York* (1941)

_____, & G. Lavers, *Poverty and the Welfare State: A Third Social Survey of York Dealing Only with Economic Questions* (1951)

Ruggles, Patricia. *Drawing the Line: Alternative Poverty Measures and Their Implications for Public Policy* (1990)

Ryder, Norman. "The Future of American Fertility." *Social Problems* 26 (3):359-69 (Feb. 1979)

Ryan, John. *A Living Wage* (rev. ed. 1920 [1906])

Sanger, Margaret. *Autobiography* (1938)

_____. *The Pivot of Civilization* (1969 [1922])

_____. *Woman and the New Race* (1923 [1920])

Santurri, E. "Theodicy and Social Policy in Malthus' Thought." *J. Hist. Ideas* 63 (2):315-30 (Apr.-June 1982)

Sauvy, Alfred. "Le Malthusianisme anglo-saxon." *Population* 2 (2):221-42 (Apr.-June 1947)

_____ "Marx et les problèmes contemporains de la population." *Information sur les sciences sociales* 7(4): 27-38 (Aug. 1988)

_____. "Les Marxistes et le malthusianisme." *Cahiers internationaux de sociologie* 30 (n.s.):1-14 (July-Dec. 1966)

Sawhill, Isabel. "Poverty in the U.S.: Why Is It So Persistent?" *J. Econ. Lit.* 26:1073-1119 (Sept. 1988)

Say, Jean-Baptiste. *Traité d'économie politique* (5th ed. 1826 [1803])

Scheler, Max. "Bevölkerungsprobleme als Weltanschauungsfragen." In *idem. Schriften zur Soziologie und Weltanschauungslehre* 290-324 (1963 [1921])

Schippel, Max. *Das moderne Elend und die moderne Uebervölkerung: Zur Erkenntnis unserer sozialen Entwicklung* (1888)

Schmucker, Helga. "Einfluß der Kinderzahl auf das Lebensniveau der Familien: Empirische Untersuchung an Hand der Ergebnisse der Lohnsteuerstatistik 1955." *Allgemeines Statistisches Archiv* 43 (1):35-55 (1959)

Schorr, Alvin. *Poor Kids: A Report on Children in Poverty* (1966)

Schultheis, Franz. *Sozialgeschichte der französischen Familienpolitik* (1988)

Schultz, T. Paul. "An Economic Perspective on Population Growth." In *Rapid Population Growth: Consequences and Policy Implications* 148-74 (Nat. Acad. Sci. 1971)

Schultz, Theodore. "The Value of Children: An Economic Perspective." *J. Pol. Econ.* 81 (2) pt. II:S2-13 (Mar.-Apr. 1973)

Schumpeter, Joseph. *History of Economic Analysis* (Elizabeth Schumpeter ed., 1972 [1954])

Schwartz, Edward. "Some Observations on the Canadian Family Allowances Program." *Social Serv. Rev.* 20:451-73 (Dec. 1946)

Seccombe, Wally. "Domestic Labour and the Working-Class Household." In *Hidden in the Household: Women's Domestic Labour Under Capitalism* 25-99 (Bonnie Fox ed., 1980)

_____. "The Expanded Reproduction Cycle of Labour Power in Twentieth-Century Capitalism." In *ibid* at 217-66

_____. "Marxism and Demography." *New Left Rev.* No. 137: 22-47 (Jan.-Feb. 1983)

_____. *A Millennium of Family Change: Feudalism to Capitalism in Northwestern Europe* (1992)

_____. *Weathering the Storm: Working-Class Families from the Industrial Revolution to the Fertility Decline* (1993)

Senior, Nassau. *An Outline of the Science of Political Economy* (1965 [1836])

_____. *Two Lectures on Population.* In *idem. Selected Writings on Economics* (1966 [1829])

Shapiro, Thomas. *Population Control Politics: Women, Sterilization, and Reproductive Choice* (1985)

Shaw, G. Bernard. "The Basis of Socialism." In *Fabian Essays in Socialism* 15-83 (*idem* ed., n.d. [1889])

Sheppard, Harold, & Herbert Striner. "Family Structure and Employment Problems." In Lee Rainwater & William Yancey. *The Moynihan Report and the Politics of Controversy* 354-68 (1969 [1966]).

Silverman, Anna, & Arnold Silverman. *The Case Against Having Children* (1971)

Simon, Julian. *The Economics of Population Growth* (1977)

_____. *Population Matters: People, Resources, Environment, and Immigration* (1990 [1988])

_____. *The Ultimate Resource* (1981)

Simons, John. "Culture, Economy and Reproduction in Contemporary Europe." In *The State of Population Theory: Forward from Malthus* 256-78 (David Coleman & Roger Schofield eds., 1986)

Sismondi, J. C. L. Simonde de. *Political Economy* (1966 [1815])

Slesnick, Daniel. "Gaining Ground: Poverty in the Postwar United States." *J. Pol. Econ.* 101 (1):1-38 (Feb. 1993)

Smith, Adam. *An Inquiry into the Nature and Causes of the Wealth of Nations* (Edwin Cannan ed., 1937 [1776])

Smith, James. "Birth Control and Economic Well-Being" In *Human Behavior in Economic Affairs: Essays in Honor of George Katona* 501-22 (Burkhard Strumpel et al. eds., 1972)

Smith, Kenneth. *The Malthusian Controversy* (1951)

Smith, R. "Transfer Incomes, Risk and Security: The Roles of the Family and the Collectivity in Recent Theories of Fertility Change." In *The State of Population Theory: Forward from Malthus* 188-211 (David Coleman & Roger Schofield eds., 1986)

Smulevich, V. *Burzhuaznye teorii narodonaseleniia v svete marksistko-leninskoi kritiki* (1936)

Soetbeer, Heinrich. *Die Stellung der Sozialisten zur Malthus'schen Bevölkerungslehre* (1886)

Soloway, Richard. *Birth Control and the Population Question in England, 1877-1930*

(1982)

Soutar, M, E. Wilkins, & P. Sargant Florence. *Nutrition and Size of Family: Report on a New Housing Estate—1939* (1942)

Sowell, Thomas. "Malthus and the Utilitarians." *Canadian J. Econ. & Pol. Sci.* 28 (2):268-74 (May 1962)

Spengler, Joseph. "The Birth Rate—Potential Dynamite." *Pop. & Dev. Rev.* 17 (1):159-69 (Mar. 1991 [1932])

_____. "Declining Population Growth: Economic Effects." In Commission on Population Growth and the American Future. *Research Reports: Economic Aspects of Population Change* 2:91-133 (Elliott Morss & Ritchie Reed ed., 1972).

_____. *France Faces Depopulation: Postlude Edition, 1936-1976* (1979 [1938])

_____. *Population and America's Future* (1975)

_____. "Population Problem: In Search of a Solution." *Science* 166:1234-38 (Dec. 5, 1969)

_____. "Population Threatens Prosperity." *Harv. Bus. Rev.* 34 91):85-94 (Jan.-Feb. 1956)

_____. "Some Economic Aspects of Immigration into the United States." *Law & Contemporary Problems* 21:236-55 (1956)

Stern, Mark. "Poverty and the Life-Cycle, 1940-1960." *J. Social Hist.* 24 (3):521-40 (Spr. 1991)

Steuerle, Eugene. "The Tax Treatment of Households of Different Size." In *Taxing the Family* 73-97 (Rudolph Penner ed., 1984)

_____, & Jason Juffras. "A $1,000 Tax Credit for Every Child: A Base of Reform for the Nation's Tax, Welfare, and Health Systems" (Urban Institute, 1991).

Stewart, Ethelbert. "A Family Wage-Rate vs. A Family Social Endowment Fund." *Social Forces*: 6 (1):120-25 (Sept. 1927)

Stewart, Maxwell. *A Chance for Every Child: The Case for Children's Allowances* (Pub. Affairs Pamphlet No. 440, 1970)

Storer, Horatio. "On the Decrease of the Rate of Increase of Population Now Obtaining in Europe and America." *Am. J. Sci.* 2d ser., 43 (128):141-55 (May 1867 [1858])

Stycos, J. "Some Minority Opinions on Birth Control." In *Population Policy and Ethics: The American Experience* 169-96 (Robert Veatch ed., 1977)

Südekum, Albert. "Über das Malthus'sche Gesetz und das Bevölkerungsproblem der kommunistischen Gesellschaft" (Ph.D. diss., Christian-Albrechts Univ. Kiel, 1894)

Sundquist, James. *Dispersing Population: What America Can Learn from Europe* (1975)

Survey Research Center. *1960 Survey of Consumer Finances* (1961)

Sweezy, Paul. *The Theory of Capitalist Development: Principles of Marxian Political Economy* (1968 [1942])

Teitelbaum, Michael, & Jay Winter. *The Fear of Population Decline* (1985)

Thave, Suzanne. "Are Large Families Mutants?" In International Social Security Association. *Social Security and Changing Family Structures* 105-14 (Studies & Research No. 29, 1992)

Thompson, William. *An Inquiry into the Principles of the Distribution of Wealth* (1968 [1824])

Thornton, William. *Overpopulation and Its Remedy* (1971 [1846])

Thünen, Johann von. *Der isolierte Staat in Beziehung auf Landwirtschaft und National-ökonomie* 3rd ed. 1930 [1850])

Tilly, Charles. "Demographic Origins of the European Proletariat." In *Proletarianization and Family History* 1-85 (David Levine ed., 1984)

Tilly, Louise & Joan Scott. *Women, Work, and Family* (1989 [1978])

Titmuss, Richard. *Commitment to Welfare* (1968 [1965])

_____. *Essays on 'The Welfare State'* (1969 [1955])

_____, & Brian Abel-Smith. *Social Policies and Population Growth in Mauritius: Report to the Governor of Mauritius* (1961)

_____, & Kathleen Titmuss. *Parents Revolt* (1985 [1942])

Tomlinson, Richard. "The French Population Debate." *Pub. Interest* No. 76:111-20 (Sum. 1984)

Townsend, Joseph. *A Dissertation on the Poor Laws by a Well-Wisher to Mankind* (1971 [1786])

Townsend, Peter. *Poverty in the United Kingdom: A Survey of Household Resources and Standards of Living* (1979)

Unshelm, Erich. *Geburtenbeschränkung und Sozialismus: Versuch einer Dogmengeschichte der sozialistischen Bevölkerungslehre* (1924)

Ursel, Jane. *Private Lives, Public Policy: 100 Years of State Intervention in the Family* (1992)

Vadakin, James. *Children, Poverty, and Family Allowances* (1968)

_____. *Family Allowances: An Analysis of Their Development and Implications* (1958)

Valentine, Charles. *Culture and Poverty: Critique and Counter-Proposals* (1968)

van de Kaa, Dirk. "Europe's Second Demographic Transition." *Population Bull.* 42 (1):1-57 (Mar. 1987)

Veevers, J. *Childless by Choice* (1980)

_____. "Voluntary Childlessness: A Review of Issues and Evaluations." *Marriage & Family Rev.* 2 (2):1-26 (1979)

Vibart, Hugh. *Family Allowances in Practice* (1926)

Viederman, Stephen, & Sharmon Sollitto. "Economic Groups: Business, Labor, Welfare." In *Population Policy and Ethics: The American Experience* 325-46 (Robert Veatch ed., 1977)

Villeneuve-Bargemont, Alban de. *Économie politique chrétienne, ou recherches sur la nature et les causes du paupérisme, en France et en Europe, et sur les moyens de le soulager et de le prévenir* (1834)

Vincent, Paul. "La Famille normale." *Population* 5 (2):251-69 (Apr.-June 1950)

Vulnerable, The (John Palmer & Isabel Sawhill eds., 1988)

Ward, Martha. *Poor Women, Powerful Men: America's Great Experiment in Family Planning* (1986)

Warner, Amos. *American Charities* (1908 [1894]) (rev. by Mary Coolidge)

_____. "Notes on the Statistical Determination of the Causes of Poverty." *Pubs. Am. Statistical Assoc.* (n.s.) 1 (5):183-201(Mar. 1889)

Watson, Cicely. "Population Policy in France: Family Allowances and Other Benefits, I." *Pop. Studies* 7 (3):263-86 (Mar. 1954)

Wattenberg, Ben. *The Birth Dearth* (1987)

Wayne, Jack. "The Function of Social Welfare in a Capitalist Economy." In *Family, Economy and State: The Social Reproduction Process Under Capitalism* 56-84 (James Dickinson & Bob Russell eds., 1986)

Webb, Sidney. *The Decline in the Birth Rate* (Fabian Tract No. 131, 1907)

_____, & Beatrice Webb. 7 *English Local Government: English Poor Law History*, Pt. I: *The Old Poor Law* (1927)

_____. *English Poor Law History*, Pt. II: *The Last Hundred Years* (1963 [1929])

_____. *The Prevention of Destitution* (1911)

Weicher, John. "Changes in the Distribution of Wealth: Increasing Inequality?" *Fed. Reserve Bank of St. Louis Rev.* 77 (1):5-23 (Jan.-Feb.. 1995)

Weiner, Lynn. *From Working Girl to Working Mother: The Female Labor Force in the United States, 1820-1980* (1985)

Weinhold, C. *Von der überwiegenden Reproduktion des Menschenkapitals gegen das Betriebskapital* (1828)

Wells, H. G. *Socialism and the Family* (1908 [1906])

Westoff, Leslie, & Charles Westoff. *From Now to Zero: Fertility, Contraception and Abortion in America* (1971)

Whitney, Vincent. "Fertility Trends and Children's Allowances Programs." In *Children's Allowances and the Economic Welfare of Children: The Report of a Conference* 123-39 (Eveline Burns ed., 1968)

Whitton, Charlotte. "The Family Allowances Controversy in Canada." *Social Serv. Rev.* 18:413-32 (Dec. 1944)

Wicksell, Knut. *Vorlesungen über Nationalökonomie auf Grundlage des Marginalprinzips: Theoretischer Teil* 1 (Margarethe Landfeldt tr., 1969 [1913])

Williams, Gertrude. "The Myth of 'Fair' Wages." *Econ. J.* 66 (264):621-34 (Dec. 1956)

Williams, Lucy. "The Ideology of Division: Behavior Modification Welfare Reform Proposals." *Yale Law J.* 102 (3):719-46 (Dec. 1992)

Winter, Jay. "Socialism, Social Democracy, and Population Questions in Western Europe: 1870-1950." In *Population Resources in Western Intellectual Traditions* 122-46 (Michael Teitelbaum & Jay Winter eds., 1989)

Witte, James, & Gert Wagner. "Declining Fertility in East Germany After Reunification: A Demographic Response to Socioeconomic Change." *Pop. & Dev. Rev.* 21 (2):387-97 (June 1995)

Wolf, Julius. *Die Volkswirtschaft der Gegenwart und Zukunft: Die wichtigsten Wahrheiten der allgemeinen Nationalökonomie* (1912)

Wolfe, A. "On the Criterion of Optimum Population." *Am. J. Sociology* 39 (5):585-99 (Mar. 1934)

Wolfenbein, S., & A. Jaffe. "Demographic Factors in Labor Force Growth." *Am. Sociological Rev.* 11:392-96 (1946)

Woofter, T.J. Jr. "Size of Family in Relation to Family Income and Age of Family Head." *Am. Sociological Rev.* 9 (6):678-84 (Dec. 1944)

Works and Correspondence of David Ricardo. Vol. 5, 7, 9 (P. Sraffa ed., 1952, 1962)

Woycke, James. *Birth Control in Germany 1871-1933* (1988)

Wrigley, E. "Fertility Strategy for the Individual and the Group." In *Historical Studies of Changing Fertility* 135-54 (Charles Tilly ed., 1978)

_____. *Population and History* (1969)

_____, & R. Schofield. *The Population History of England 1541-1871: A Reconstruction* (1981)

Wyatt, Frederick. "Clinical Notes on the Motives of Reproduction." *J. Social Issues* 23 (4):29-56 (1967)

Young, Michael. "Distribution of Income Within the Family." *Brit. J. Sociology* 3 (4): 305-21 (Dec. 1952)

Zelizer, Viviana. *Pricing the Priceless Child: The Changing Social Value of Children* (1985)

Zwölf Wege der Familienpolitik in der Europäischen Gemeinschaft: Eigenständige Systeme und vergleichbare Qualitäten (Erika Neubauer at al. eds., 1993).

Zwölf Wege der Familienpolitik in der Europäischen Gemeinschaft: Eigenständige Systeme und vergleichbare Qualitäten?—Länderberichte (Erika Neubauer et al. eds., 1993)

Index

About the Author

MARC LINDER is Professor at the University of Iowa, specializing in labor law. Dr. Linder has taught at universities in Germany, Denmark, and Mexico, and was an attorney in the Farmworker Division of Texas Rural Legal Aid. He is author of a dozen books, including three published by Greenwood Press: *The Employment Relationship in Anglo-American Law: A Historical Perspective* (1987), *Farewell to the Self-Employed: Deconstructing a Socioeconomic and Legal Solipsism* (1992), and *Projecting Capitalism: A History of the Internationalization of the Construction Industry* (1994).